VIRGINIA

Tax Records

VIRGINIA

Tax Records

From The Virginia Magazine of History and Biography, the William and Mary College Quarterly, and Tyler's Quarterly

With an Index by Gary Parks

CLEARFIELD

Reprinted for
Clearfield Company, Inc. by
Genealogical Publishing Co., Inc.
Baltimore, Maryland
2000

Excerpted and reprinted from *The Virginia Magazine of History and Biography*, the *William and Mary College Quarterly Historical Magazine*, and *Tyler's Quarterly Historical and Genealogical Magazine*, with added Publisher's Note, Contents, and Index, by Genealogical Publishing Co., Inc., Baltimore, 1983.

Library of Congress Catalogue Card Number 83-81465
International Standard Book Number 0-8063-1043-X
Made in the United States of America

Note

VIRGINIA TAX RECORDS is composed of articles which have been excerpted from *The Virginia Magazine of History and Biography,* the *William and Mary College Quarterly,* and *Tyler's Quarterly Historical and Genealogical Magazine.* It is primarily a compilation of articles pertaining to tax records—a term used here rather freely to permit inclusion of such records as personal property tax lists, tithables, poll lists, land tax lists, and rent rolls. Like census records, tax records have the distinction of placing people in a particular location at a definite time and identifying them in relation to their households and property, thus providing irrefutable evidence of their existence and places of habitation.

As these lists date, for the most part, from an early period in Virginia's history, their survival has been more a matter of chance than calculated policy. Those printed here, no doubt, represent only a fraction of the early tax records of Virginia, but as they constitute a large proportion of the surviving records, they claim an increased measure of importance. Their consolidation in this volume will not only assure their continued survival but will facilitate research in an otherwise hopelessly scattered body of source materials.

Genealogical Publishing Company

Contents

VIRGINIA

Tax Records

POLL OF AMELIA COUNTY, VA., 1768*

Capt. John Winn's Poll

Roger Thompson
Thos. Vaughan
Francis Whitlow
Nathaniel Page
William Craddock
James Ray
James Meadow
John Craddock
William Quinn
Edmund Hawes
Thomas Liggon
Catlet Mann
Zachariah Hooper
Thomas Chambers
William Cryer
Benjamin Jones
Moses Hunt Jr
John Foster
John Shelton
Isaac Webb
Major Waller
Albery Ford
Thomas Reynolds
John Thorp
William Jackson
John Drinkwater
Thomas Foster
Joshua Rucker

Mr. John Scott's Poll

William Archer
Lodwick Tanner
Peter Farrar
Hodge Dunnivant
William Dunnivant
Henry Worsham
Philip Dunnivant
Francis Roberts
John Royall
Daniel Walthall
William Marshall
Jacob Williamson
Daniel Wilson
Christopher Walthall
Christopher Walthall Jr
Ashley Johnson
Edmund Booker
Daniel Willson Jr
William Farley
Francis Anderson
Richard Jones
John Johnson
Wm Neal
Abel Burton
Wm Worsham
Thomas Atkinson
Miles Bolt
George Ragsdale

---

*Amelia C. H., Va.,
June 26, 1943.

Dear Mrs. Tyler:
I have the Poll List of Amelia Co. for the year 1768. That was only a few years after the county was formed. I think these items of early history should be salvaged before they are lost forever, and I think this Poll List should be printed.
Do you wish it for your Quarterly? It is yours if you wish it.

Yours sincerely,

S. O. Southall.

Capt. John Winn's Poll

Peter Lamkin
William Cannon
John Webb
Charles Irby
Daniel Hutt
Thomas Westbrook
James Beauford
John Foster
Edward Jordan
William Crenshaw Sr
Jordan Yarboro
Archer Yarboro
William Crawley
Raleigh Carter
Peter Jones (shf)
Peter Jones (S H)
Aron Teague
Joseph Williamson
John Scannet
Geo Lewis
Benj Bridgeforth
Charles Connely
James Chappel
Wm Wood
Nelson Jones
Wm Butler
John Pace
Wm Pace
Joseph White
Benjamin Shelton
Thomas Hightower
Edward Manyard
Samuel Vaughan
Moses Estice
Wm Hawes
John Beazley ?
Adam Jones
Thomas Sowell
Gidian Rucker
Jacob Morgan
Thomas Tinsley
John Wingo
William Foster

Mr. John Scott's Poll

Joshua Durham
George Hendrick
Thomas Walke
Wm Hatchett
Wm Kennon
Wm Howlet
Edward Furguson
Henry Harper
James Seay
John Hughes
George C. White
Hugh Havener (or Cavener)
John Hudson
George Booker
Thomas Lorton
Robert Jones
John Hunt
Thomas James
Richard Phillips
Joseph Tanner
Abraham Hurt
George Wilson
William Townes
William Southall
William Hutcherson
John Compton Sr
Gidian Rucker
Richard Borum Jr
Thomas Tinsley
John Wingo
Edward Booker W. H
Gower Parham
John Hord
Matthew Tucker
Henry Tucker
Henry Cox
John Brooks
John Chapman
Wm Hunt
John Clements
Isham Clements
Wm Walthall
Wm Ware

CAPT. JOHN WINN'S POLL

Richard Craddock
Thomas Williams
William Booth Jr
Benjamin Edmundson
William Mauire
Sammie Thomas
Thomas Ball
Wood Jones
WM Hughes
Giles Nance
Oliver Jeter
WM Ford
John Harper
Francis Anderson
Richard Evans
Robert Davis
James Rucker
WM Evans
Frederick Ford
William Ford
Nicholas Vaughan
Major Brumfield
Abner Bates
James Townes
Arthur Moody
WM Jennings Jr
Upton Edmundson
WM Lovell
John Bullington
John Oglesby
John Powell
Richard Hightower
Edwd Robertson
John Anderson
Peter Clarke
Thomas Mitchell
Thos Holt
Henry Nelson
Poley Farguson
John Morgan
WM Morgan
Barthonew Vaughan
WM Verser

MR. JOHN SCOTT'S POLL

James Rucker
Moses Morris
Joseph Jackson
David Neal
Thomas Green
Stephen Neal
Joel Jackson
William Walthall Jr
Roger Neal
William Marshall Jr
John Oglesby
Alexander Walker
Culvira Ford
Abraham Burton
Thomas Walthall
Charles Featherston
Richard Johnson
Francis Hopkins
Jeremiah Meadows
John Bagby
Jeremiah Lester
Mathew Jackson
George Rowlet
William Vasser
John Holt
WM Pardue
Richard Jones
Mathew Hilsman
James Wingo
Robt Echols
John Pride Sr
Bernard Hendrick
Joseph Farley
John Brunskill
Joseph Pollard
WM Hall
William Bibb
George Foster
Elkanah Crenshaw
WM Hamen
John C. Cobbs
Ralph Perkinson
WM Gibbs

Capt. John Winn's Poll

Wm Rucker
Benj Hubbard
Covington Smith
Alexander Marshall
Thomas Jeffrise
Richard Jones
Lewis Vaughan
George Webster
Charles Lovell
John Mauire
James Shelton
Leonard Cheatham
Richard Ellis
John Pride Sr
Peter Claybrook
George Moore
Samuel Bentley
John Wilks
John Knight
Jernald Johnson
John Mann
William Eggleston
William Bibb
John Ford
Richard Burks
William Loving
Jeremiah Ellington
Thomas Hall
John Harris
William Mauire
David Thompson
George Long
John Moore
John Parrot
William Thomas
Hezekiah Coleman
David Zachary
John Morgan
John F Smith
James Harris
Thomas Ellis
John Ford
Richard Burks

Mr. John Scott's Poll

Henry Walthall
Peter Thompson
Daniel Worsham
Isaac Blanchet
Henry Worsham
Richard Verser
Thomas Booth
Philip Major
Alexander Brown
James Borum
Edward Tanner
Francis Tucker
Silvanus Morris
Moses Seay
Joseph Hubbard
John Tucker
Thomas Whitworth
Thomas Davis
Matthew Perkinson
Johns Bentley
John Pride Jr
Essex Bevill
William Foster
Zachariah Compton
Joseph Crowder
Benjamin Hendrick
Tucker Tally
Obediah Hendricks
Matthew Tucker
Christopher Haskins
Simon Clement
Richard Borrum Sr
Stephen Howell
Joseph Noble
Thomas Webster
James Echols
James Barding
George Hamna
Thomas Green
Thos. Whitworth
Richard Dennis Sr
Joseph Motley Jr
Henry Dennis

Capt. John Winn's Poll

William Loving
Jeremiah Ellington
Thomas Hall
John Harris
William Mauire
David Thompson
George Long
John Moore
John Parrot
William Thomas
Hezekiah Coleman
David Zachary
John Morgan
John F. Smith
James Harris
Thomas Ellis
John Patterson
Thomas Osborne
John Lewis
George Worsham
John May
Thomas Jones (Glof)
John Forcey
Wm Grige Featherston
Wm Estis
Thomas Echols
James Sea
Wm Jones
William Wood
Moses Lovell
John Pride Jr
Thomas Reams
Richard Quarles
Matthew Gibbs
Thomas Walker
Joseph Holland
Richard Jones
Lewelling Jones
Edward Dudley
Thomas Jones
Wm Hamlin
Travis McKinnie
Wm Crowder

Mr. John Scott's Poll

Henry Jones
Anderson Radford
John Booker
William Jackson Jr
James Jenkins
Thomas Munford
Thomas Hanner
Richard Dennis Jr
Joshua Standley
Christopher Hudson
Joseph Tucker
Thomas Janckson
Christopher Ford

Capt. John Winn's Poll

Christopher Haskin
Tom Branch Wilson
John Pryor
James Lamkin
Stephen Howell
Charles Sallard
James Gunn
Thomas Walker Jr
Charles Lewis
Francis Jackson
Henry Anderson
Charles Clay
John Gooch
George Hightower
John Winn
James Hawks
Jno. Avary
Peter Webster
Natt Robertson
Abraham Ford
Jn° Vaughan
Richard Dearing
David Lovell
George Cabiness
John Jones
Thomas Short
John Bailey
Benjamin Locket
John Hamlin
Henry Lewis
William Crenshaw
James Crenshaw
William Covington
William Hudson
Rich Smith

Col. Thos. Tabb's Poll

Hodge Dunnevant
William Archer
Lodwick Tanner
Peter Farrer
Benjamin Bennet
Roger Thompson
Thomas Vaughan
William Mullins
Abraham Forrist
William Dunnivant
Henry Worsham
Philip Dunnivant
Francis Whitlow
Anthony Hundley
John Royall
John Norris
Daniel Walthall
Nathaniel Page
William Pulliam
William Marshall
Jacob Williamson
Charles Hundley
Daniel Wilson
Christopher Walthall Jr
Christopher Walthall Sr
Robert Flemming
Ashley Johnson
Wm Cross Craddock
Edmund Booker
Joseph Royall
Daniel Willson, Jr
James Ray
James Meadors
David Ellington Jr.
James Leage
John Craddock
William Farley
Nathaie Hendrick
Francis Anderson
Richard Jones
Robert Bolling
Jesse Johnson
Thomas Liggan

Capt. Robert Munford's Poll

Benjamin Bennet
William Mullins
Abraham Forrest
Francis Roberts
Anthony Hundley
John Norris
William Pulliam
Charles Hundley
Robert Flemming
Joseph Royall
David Ellington Jr
James League
Nathaniel Hendrick
Robert Bolling
Edmund Homes
Thomas Jackson
Mark Jackson
John Tucker
David Greenhill
Laurence Wills
Jeremiah White
Robert Tucker Jr
Francis Starre
William Cousin
William Cryer
Benjamin Jones
Richard Royall
Moses Hurt Jr
William Spain
Abraham Beadle
Charles Stuart
William Cousins Jr
John Dawson
Joshua Durham
Thomas Westbrook
William Craddock Jr
James Beauford
James Westbrook
Henry Dennis
Lewis Tucker
John Tucker Jr
Richard Dennis Sr
William Hood

Col. Thos. Tabb's Poll

Thomas Jackson
Mark Jackson
John Tucker
David Greenhill
Lawrence Wells
Jeremiah White
Catlett Mann
Robert Tucker Jr
Francis Starre
Zacariah Hooper
Wm Cousins
Thomas Chambers
Wm Neal
Abel Burton
William Worsham
Richard Royall
Thomas Atkinson
John Foster
Niles Bott
Abraham Beadle
Isaac Webb
George Ragsdale
John Shelton
Charles Steanart
Wm Cousins Jr
Major Waller
John Dawson
Thomas Reynolds
John Thorp
John Hudson
William Jackson
John Drinkwater
Thomas Foster
Josuah Rucker
George Hancock
Thomas Walke
Wm Hatchett
Peter Lamkin
Charles Irby
John Webb
Wm Craddock Sr
John Foster
Wm Howlett

Capt. Robert Munford's Poll

George Farley
William Crenshaw Sr
Jordan Yarboro
Archer Yarboro
Thomas Bonner
William Tucker
Peter Jones Shf
Peter Jones S. H
Bartholemew Dupee
Isham Clay
Peter Dupee Jr
Arther Jackson
James Bagley
John Scarrat
Wm Wilson
Joseph Williamson
John Wilson Sr
John Pace
William Pace
Joseph White
John Jackson
Hesikiah Bevill
George Bagley Jr
Daniel Coleman
Thomas Hightower
Edward Manyard
Joseph Waldrop
Richard Forrist
Jno. Bartholeman Dupee
Steaurt Farley
Richard Liggon
Samuel Vaughan Sr
William Hawes
Adam Jones
Abraham Smith
Jacob Morgan
John Aplin
Bartholemew Zachary
Gower Parham
Lawrence Browne
Thomas Berry
Abraham Hood
Thos Tucker

Col. Thos. Tabb's Poll

Edward Farguson
Edward Jordan
Wm Hood ?
George Farley
Wm Crawley
Henry Harper
James Seay
Thos Bonner
William Tucker
John Huges
Raw Carter
George White
Ball Dupuy
Isham Clay
Aron Leigue
Peter Dupuy Jr
Arthur Jackson
James Bagby
William Watson
John Willson
Hugh Cavener
Wm Butler
John Jackson Sr
Benjamin Shelton
Tucker Tally
George Booker
Thomas Lorton
Robert Jones
Hesekiah Bevill
John Hurt
Thomas James
Richard Phillips
Joseph Tanner
George Bagby
Daniel Coleman
Joseph Waldrop
Richard Forrest
Abram Hurt
John P Dupuy
Stewart Farley
Richard Liggon
George Willson
Moses Estes Sr

Capt. Robert Munford's Poll

Thomas Williams Gen.
Samuel Thomas
Robert Taylor
Charles Barker
Joseph Grammer
John Hood
Henry Tucker
Henry Green
Wm Farley
Nathan Tucker
Ambrose Lipscome
George Bagby Sr
William Jackson Sr
William Boothe Jr
Benj: Edmundson
William Mauirce
Peter Hudson
Lewis Hammond
Thomas Jackson
John Jackson
Wood Jones
Lawton Fanning
Peter Jones Sr
Frederick Spain
Henry Green
William Hughes
George Lewis
John Ellington
John Hatchett
William Thompson
Robert Hall
Wm Hasting
Benj: Bridgeforth
William Tucker Sr
Charles Connally
Wm Homain
Nelson Jones
Joseph Tucker
Robert Bevill
William Wilson
Isaac Jackson
John Baldwin
John Anderson

Col. Thos. Tabb's Poll

John Beasley
William Southall
William Hutcherson
John Compton Jr
Thomas Sowell
Abraham Smith
Richard Borum
William Foster
Bartholomew Zachary
William Cradock
Edward Booker
Lawrence Brown
Thomas Berry
Abraham Hood
Robert Taylor
Charles Barker
Joseph Grammer
Wm Farley
Ambrose Lipscomb
George Bagley Sr
Wm Jackson
Daniel Jackson
Thomas Ball
Henry Cox
Peter Jones Sr
Frederick Spain
John Ellington
John Hatchet
John Aplin
William Thompson
Robert Hall
William Hastins
John Brooks
John Chapman
William Hurt
John Clement
Isham Clement
William Tucker
William Hamer
William Walthall Sr
James Chappell
Giles Nance
Oliver Jeter

Capt. Robert Munford's Poll

Richard Evans
William Evans
Frederick Ford
William Ford
John Steauart
Thomas Beauford
John Mitchell
James Farley
William Baldwin
Upton Edmundson
Thomas Huggins
Thomas Olley ?
John Booth
Wm Marshall
Richard Hightower
Joshua Standley
Edward Robertson
Daniel Jones
Peter Clarke
Thomas Osslin
Ruler Richardson
James Standley
David Addams
Joseph Hawks
Peleg Ferguson
John Homain ?
Abraham Coleman
Robert Ragsdale
Nathan Booth
John Hall
William Pardue
Thomas Jeffries
Emanuel Weeks
David Ellington Sr
Daniel Tucker
Samuel Pincham
George Hill
John Mauire
John Beadles
Robt Echols
James Shelton
Joseph Harper
Richard Ellis

Col. Thos. Tabb's Poll

Wm Ford
Thomas Tucker
Johns Harper
Lewis Hammond
William Wilson Sr
Frances Anderson Jr
William Ware
John Baldwin Sr
Moses Morris
John Steaurt Sr
Joseph Jackson
Thomas Beauford
Nicholas Vaughan
Major Brumfield
Abner Bates
James Townes
John Mitchell
David Tucker
Arthur Moody
Wm Jennings Jr
James Farley
David Neal
Wm Baldwin
Roger Neal
Wm Lovill
Thomas Huggins
Thomas Oakley
Thomas Green
Stephen Neale
Joel Jackson
Wm Walthall Jr
John Booth
John Bullington
Daniel Jones
Alexander Walker
Thos Mitchell
Ruland Richardson
Thos Holt
James Standley
Henry Nelson
David Adams
Peter Webster Jr
Geo L. Webster

Capt. Robert Munford's Poll

Dibdale Holt
Robert Stoker
Frances Hathaway
Joseph Farley
George Moore
Francis Epps
John Haines
Samuel Bentley
Hall Hudson Sr
John Night
Benjamin Clardy
John Clardy
William Mauire
Peter Beasley
Wm Sale
Thomas Hudson
Thomas Hudson
Wm Sale ?
Gabriel Fowlkes
Reuben Palmore
William Parham
James Parham
James Cates
George Long
John Moore
John Parrot
Wm Thomas
Joell Tanner
Wm Farguson
Jas. Sturdivant
Jno. Wilson Jr.
Wm Jennings Sr.
Jno. Jennings
Jno. Fowlkes
Robert Kennan
Thos. Wilkinson
Jo. Fowlkes
Drury Thompson
Rich. Dennis Jr.
Charles Caviness
Thomas Ellis
John Jennings
George Smith

Col. Thos. Tabb's Poll

Culone Ford
Abraham Burton
Thos Walthall
Charles Featherston
Richard Johnson
Joseph Hawks
John Morgan
William Morgan
John Howsin
Francis Hopkins
Jeremiah Meadows
John Bagby
Jere Lester
Matt Jackson
George Rowlett
Bolt Vaughan
Robert Bevill
Abraham Coleman
Robert Ragsdale
Nath Booth
Wm Rucker Jr
Benjamin Hubbard
Covington Smith
Abam Marshall
Emanuel Wilkes
James Anderson
Wm Stoce ?
David Ellington Sr
Daniel Tucker
Matt Hilsman
Lewis Vaughan
Charles Lovell
Saml Picherson
James Wingo
Joseph Harper
Leonard Cheatham ?
Robert Stoker senr
Peter Claybrook
Francis Hathaway
Francis Epps
John Hawes
John Brumskill
Hall Hudson

Capt. Robert Munford's Poll

Samuel Thompson
Wm Crenshaw
John Marshall
John Lewis
Thomas Clay
Wm Booth
Joseph Coleman
Jn. May
Wm Turner
James Draper
Tho. Jones (Gt)
Robert Vaughan Jr.
Vivian Brooking
Michal Clardy
Matthew Tucker
Thos. Echols
Edward Jackson
James Echols
Wm Grigg Featherstone
Wm Jackson
William Harper
James Oliver
Josiah Hundley
Ambrose Beasley
John Hundley
Wm Hurt
Thos Payne
John Singleton
Philip Williams
Danl Farley
Tho Clarke
Jno Forrist
Henry Anderson
Richd Quarles
Wm Eggleston
Wm Gibbs
Saml Young
Hugh Chambers
Thos Walker
Wm Tucker (H. C)
Stephen Cocke
Joseph Gray
Matt Stokes

Col. Thos. Tabb's Poll	Capt. Robert Munford's Poll
Joseph Pollard	Geo. Davenport
John Wilks	Isham Vaughan
Wm Hall	Richd Jones
Thos Bottom	Edward Dudley
Jerrald Johnson	Thos. Jones
John Clardy	Lewelling Jones
Richard Burks	Charles Jackson
Wm Loving	William Hamlin
George Foster (S C)	William Jones
Jeremiah Ellington	Jno. Gray
Thos Hall	Francis Wallis
John Harris	John Cocke
George Hill	Frances McKinne
John Beadles	John Crain
Thomas Hudson	Richard Hayes
Elkana Crenshaw	Thos Booth
Wm Hamner	Wm Roach
Peter Beasley	John Pryor
Gabriel Fowlkes	Richard Holt
John C Cobbs	James Lampkin
Reuben Palmore	Billington Williams
Wm Parham	Wm Clements
James Parham	Charles Sallard
Jno. Cates	James Gunn
David Thompson	John Clay
Ralph Perkinson	Thos Walker
Wm Gibbs	James Bevill
Henry Walthall	Wm Davis
Peter Thompson	Wm Talley
Daniel Worsham	Henry Clarke
Hezekiah Coleman	George Avory
Joel Tanner	Danl Allen
Wm Farguson	George Hightower
James Sturdivant	Jno Wynne
John Willson	Wm Holoway
David Zachary	Nathan Fletcher
John Morgan	George Ford
Wm Jennings Jr	Richd Lovsie
Joseph Jennings	Wm Munford
John Fowlkes	Tho Jones (note)
Isaac Blanchet	Wm Moore
Robt. Kannon	Jno. Avory
Thomas Wilkinson	Wm Wood

Col. Thos. Tabb's Poll

Joseph Fowlks
John F. Smith
Henry Worsham (G)
Drury Thompson
Richard Vasser
Thos Brooks
Philip Major
Aba^{m} Brown
James Harris
Charles Cabiness
John Jennings
George Smith
Samuel Thompson
Wm Crenshaw
John Marshal
John Patterson
James Borrum
Edw Tanner
Francis Tucker
Sy^{l} Morris
Thos Osborn
Thos Clay
George Worsham
Wm Booth
Joseph Coleman
Wm Turner
Robert Vaughan Jr
Michal Clardy
John Forsey
William Jackson
William Eastice
Moses Seay
Wm Harper
Joseph Hubbard
James Seay Jr
Lewis Tucker
Thomas Whitworth
James T Oliver
Josiah Hendley
Ambrose Beasley
John Hendley
Wm Hurt, Sr.
Thomas Pain

Capt. Robert Munford's Poll

Jno Powell
George Martin
Jno Anderson
Natt Robertson
Abra^{m} Ford
Jno Chappell
Jno Crowder
Robt Vaughan
Henry Jones
Andrew Radford
John Jones
Thomas Shool
William George
John Bailey
Thomas Dobson
Philemon Crain
Wm Jackson
Thomas B Munford
John Smith L
Peter Bland
Thomas Bottom
John Hamlin
Robt Bevil
Henry Lewis
Matthew Cabiness
David Hawkins
Claiborne Anderson
William Crenshaw Jr
James Crenshaw
William Covington
John Clarke

Col. Thos. Tabb's Poll

John Singleton
Phillips Williams
Thomas Davis
Matthew Perkinson
William Jones
Daniel Farley
John Bently
William Wood Carp
Moses Lovall
Thomas Reams
Essex Bevil
William Foster
Zachariah Compton
Henry Anderson
Joseph Crowder
Benj[a] Hendrake Jr
Obadiah Hendrake
Wm Gibbs
Sam[l] Young
Matthew Gibbs
Joseph Holland
Mathew Stoker
George Davenport
John Gray
Francis Wallace
John Crain
Wm Crowder
Rich[d] Hays
Thos B Wilson
Thomas Booth
Wm Roaph
Simon Clement
Rich[d] Borrum
Richard Hall
Wm Clement
James Bevil
Charles Lewis
Francis Jackson F. C
William Davis
Henry Anderson
Charles Clay
John Gooth
Joseph Noble
William Tally
George Avery
Daniel Allen
Thos Webster
Wm Holloway
Nathan Fletcher
George Ford
Rich[d] Louise
Thos Jones
James Hanks
William Wood Sr
John Powell
George Martin
John Anderson
James Barding
George Ham
Joseph Motley Jr
John Vaughan
John Chappel
Thomas Green
Thomas Whitworth
Rich[d] Deaning
Daniel Coleman
David Lovel
John Crowder
George Cabbiness
Rob[t] Vaughan Sr
John Booker
William George
Thos Dodson Jr
Philemon Crain
Benj Lockett
James Jenkins
Thos B. Munford
John Smith
Peter Bland
Thos Munford
Thos Man
Robt Powell
Matt Cabbiness Jr
David Hawkins
Claiborne Anderson
Wm Hudson

Col. Thos. Tabb's Poll

Christ[t] Hudson	John Clark
Richard Smith	Christ[t] Ford

Copy Test—

Richard Jones, Shf.

Dec. 24, 1768.

Amelia

This day the Sheriff of Amelia County made oath before me that the polls contained within these sheets are true and perfect copies of the names of the persons polled at an Election of Burgesses for the said County the 6th day of December, 1768.

Stephen Cocke.

This is an exact copy of the above.

S. O. Southall.

BRUNSWICK COUNTY, VIRGINIA, POLL LIST 1748

Brunswick Co. was created by Act of Assembly in 1720 from Prince George County (see Robinson, *Virginia Counties*, p. 76) with additions from Isle of Wight and Surry in 1732. The first court for Brunswick was held May 2, 1732, from which the records of this county date.

The following poll list for 1748 gives the names of the residents of Brunswick voting for representatives in the House of Burgesses for the sessions of October, 1748, and April, 1749, and which resulted in the election of Sterling Clack and Drury Stith.

Burge of H.—A pole of their votes:

Col. John Wall

George Brewer
Joseph Wright
Moses Vincient
John Ogburn
Ninian Mitchels
William Davis
Joseph Massie
Nathan Harris
Richd. Ledbetter
Francis Deloach
Lozivel Sexton
Joseph Carter
Thomas Corvell
William Jordan
William Ezell
John Peebles
William Wise
Joshua Clark
Charles Stuart
James Judkins
William Adams
Abraham Burton
Nathaniel Clark
William Betty
John Jackson
William McKnight
George Wyche
Thomas Tomerlin
David Lucas
John Dunn
Foster Rives
Thomas Jeffris
Thomas Jacobs
James Douglas
John Massie
Henry Ledbetter
James Upchurch
John Tooke
Henry Cooke
John Vincient
William Moseley
John Betty
William Wawmock
John Irby
William Wyche
Thomas Denton
Amos Horton
William Smith
Thomas Wise
George Moseley
Richd. Lebetter
Edward Denton
Peter Wyche
Matthias Davis
John Misheaux
William Collier
Michael Wall, Junr.
John Carrie (Sworn)
John Wall, Junr.
John Robinson
Absolem Atkinson
Edward Goodrich
Richard Lanier
John Fennal
Jeremiah Brown
Adam Simms
John Butts
Benjamin Sewel
Hugh Daniel
Thomas Lawrence
Thomas Carrie
John Smith
William Brewer
William Barlon
Thomas Rives
John Walton
Richd. Burnett
Robert Lunday

Nicholas Edmunds	Nathaniel Perry	Nathaniel Mitchel
George Walton	Benjamin Ivey	James Hicks
Eades Smith	Thomas Clanton	Daniel Carrie
Richard Hide	Aaron Parks	James Parham
James Jordan	John Jeffres	Joseph Parks
Samuel Harwell	William Huff	Thomas Williams
James Sexton	Valintine White	Charles Collier
William House	Lawrence House	Thomas Morris
John Cooker	Charles Williams	William Fox
Thomas Vincient	William Corvell	Thomas Austin
William White	Daniel Cato	John Cato
John Morgan	William Bishop	John Daniel
William Johnson	Thomas Collier	Thomas Jackson
Joseph Hathcock	William Ren	Isaac Collier
Thomas .Scizon	George Harper	Richard Ransom
George Rives	Timothy Rives	William Whittington
William Lovsey	John Ray	Samuel Clark
Thomas Tatum	John Harwell,	Walter Campbell
John Steed	James Lanier	Burwell Brown

MICHAEL WALL, *Sheriff.*

COL. EDWARDS

George Brewer	John Jackson	Thomas Moseley
Joseph Wright	Geo. Wallton	Aaron Parks
Moses Vincient	Eades Smith	John Jefferis
John Ogburn	Richd. Hide	Jeremiah Brown
Ninian Mitchels	Edward Adams	Ben. Sewells
William Davis	James Jordan	Hugh Daniel
Joseph Massie	Samuel Harwell	Thomas Lawrence
Nathan Harris	James Sexton	John Smith
Richd. Ledbetter	William House	William Brewer
Sizwell Sexton	John Cocker	William Barlow
Joseph Carter	Thomas Vincient	Thomas Reeves
Thomas Powell	John Morgan	John Walton
William Jordan	William Johnson	Robert Lunday
William Ezell	Joseph Hathcock	Joseph Burnett
John Peebles	George Reeves	William Smith
William Wise	William Lovsey	James Parham Mills
Joshua Clark	Sam Cocke	Joseph Parks
Charles Stuart	Thomas Tatum	Thomas Williams
James Judkins	George Wyche	Williams Robinson
William Adams	William Huff	Thomas Morris
John Johnson	Valintine White	Nathaniel Hicks
Nathl. Clark	Lawrence House	James Dupree
Thomas Tomlinson	Charles Williams	John Dupree

David Lucas
John Dunn
Foster Rives
Thomas Jefferis
Thomas Jacobs
James Douglas
John Massie
Henry Ledbetter
James Upchurch
John Tooke
Henry Cooke
John Vinson
James Lanier
William Pettaway
John Betty
William Wawmack
John Irby
William Wyche
William Betty

William Powel
Daniel Cato
William Bishop
Thomas Collier
William Renn
Timothy Rives
Peter Wyche
Matt Davis
William Ledbetter
William Collier
Thos. Denton
Amos Horton
William Smith (Little)
Thomas Wise
William Smith (again)
Richard Ledbetter
Edward Denton
Nathaniel Perry
Benjamin Ivey

John Cato
Lewis Dupree
Thomas Austin
Hubbard Farril
Richard Ransom
Batt Peterson
Charles Lucas
John Yarburough
Benja. Donaldson
John Willis
Thomas Cooke
Thomas Avant
John Hunt
Samuel Clark
Burwell Brown•
John Carril (Sworn)
Absolem Atkinson

MICHAEL WALL, *Sheriff.*

CAPT. EDMUNDS Pole

Walter Campbell

John Wall Junr.

Michael Wall Junr.

MICHAEL WALL, *Sheriff.*

COL. WILLIS

Samuel Lucas
John Sulivant
William Pettaway

James Dupree
John Dupree
Lewis Dupree

Hinchy Mayberry
Drury Stith
Sterling Clack

MICHAEL WALL, *Sheriff.*

POLE FOR DRURY STITH

William Wall
James Denman
Henry Embry
John Moutrey
Giles Kelly
William McKinney
William Maclin
James Speed
Hazekiah Massie
Thomas Loyd (Sworn)
Lewelling Jones
Robert Christy
Thomas Bull
Richd. Hagood
Randal Brasie
William Jones

John Steed
William Petty
William Randle
William Wray
Benjamin Lanier
John Moore
Robert Hicks
John Hicks
Thomas Dean
John Randle
Charles Goulfter
John Maclin
William Read
Peter Simmons
Isaac House
Geo. Clayton

Baxter Davis
Chris. Tatum
George Sims
John Wall
Robt. Rynolds
John Davis
Edward Robinson
Joseph Burnett
James Clack
Abraham Phenix
Chas. Matthis (Sworn)
William Short
John Hagood
James Hicks
James Taply
John Johnson

Augustine Hightower
Geo. Tilman
Stephen Caudle
Mason Bishop
Hubard Quarles
John Johnson
John Avery
William Brewer
William Smith
Roger Reese (Sworn)
Thomas Lanoir
William Lindsey
William Scoggin
William Green
George Deardan
Robert Dunkley
Robert Cunnell
Francis Lett
Hix Jones
Henry Bailey
Hugh Williams
William Averice
William Moseley
Hezekiah Massie
Owen Strange
Thomas Twitty
William Smith
Josias Floyd
Thomas Procter
Drury Malone (Sworn)
Geo. Tilman, Junr.
Francis Hagood
Geo. Hagood
Thomas Brooks
Richard Birch
John Lambert
Nicholas Proctor
Sampson Caudle
William Gorden
John Birch
Robt. Gee
James Rigbie
Francis Stainback
Shep'd Lanier
Curthbert Smith
John Marshall
John Ward
Stephen Scizon
Hinchy Mabry
Richard Pepper
Samuel Lanier
John Mishaux
Charles King
James Cooke
William Ledbetter
George Wilson
Nathl. Harrison
Thomas Lloyd, Senr.
John Ingram
Jesse Tatum
John Pettaway
Jo. Mabry (Sworn)
William Tilman
Sampson Lanier
Theo. Bland
Richd. Swanson
William House
William Smith
Geo. Moseley
Thomas Clanton
Thomas Moseley
Isaac Matthis
John Fennel
James Maclin
John Ezell
Edward Hueland
John Geo. Pennington
William Nance
William Barley
Drury Robinson
Daniel Taylor
James Johnson
Samuel Russell
John Johnson
Peter Tatum
John Butts
Michael Young
Richard Russell
Thomas Jones
John Evans
William Williams
James Love
James Parham
John Edwards
Thomas Hardway
Geo. Scogging
Richard Yarburough
James Bennitt
William Edwards
Nicholas Lanier
Rob. Briggs
Henry Simmons
James McDaniel
John Burrow
William Burrow
William Duggar
John Rose
John Robinson
Thomas Jackson
Charles Collier
George Stainback
William Robinson
John Parker
William Eaton
John Douglas
John Thornton
Henry Jackson
Nathaniel Hicks
Henry Morris
William Morris
John Jackson
David Walker
Hubbard Harvie
Jebrue Peebles
John Collier
Lewis Parham
James Moseley
Samuel Harwell
Isaac Collier
William Pennington
Samuel Cental
Batt Peterson
John Jones
Thomas Johns
Thomas Sadler

William Stroud
William White
Samuel Crafts
Geo. Cain
Ath. Robinson
John Duke
Henry Jones
David Sinclair
Griffin Humphris
George Clark
Richard Scogging
John Moorson
James Parrish
William Scoggin
Richd. Burnett
Edward Davis
Charles Lucas
Benja. C. Donaldson
John Willis
Nicholas Lanier
Thomas Person
William Samford
Sterling Clack

MICHAEL WALL, *Sheriff.*

POLE FOR STERLING CLACK

William Wall
Francis Deloach
James Denman
Henry Embry
John Moutry
Giles Kelley
William McKinney
William Maclin
James Speed
Hezekiah Massie
Thomas Lloyd
Lewelling Jones
Robert Christy
Thomas Bull
Richard Hagood
Randall Brasie
William Jones
Augustine Hightower
Geo. Tilman
Stephen Caudle
Major Bishop
Hubbard Quarles
John Averie
William Brewer
William Smith
Roger Reece
Abraham Burton
Thomas Lanoir
William Lyndsey
William Scogging
William Green
George Deardon
Robt. Dunkley
Robt. Cunnel
Francis Lett
Henry Jones
David Sinclair
Samuel Cocke
William Petty
William Randle
William Wray
Benjamin Lanier
John Moore
Robt. Hicks
John Hicks
Geo. Harper
John Ray
John Harwell
Thomas Dean
John Randle
Charles Goulster
James Lanier
John Maclin
William Read
Peter Simmons
Isaac House
Geo. Clayton
John Marshall
John Ward
Stephen Scizon
Hinchy Mabry
Richard Pepper
Samuel Lanier
Charles King
James Cooke
Geo. Wilson
Nathl. Harrison
Thomas Lloyd Senr.
John Ingram
Geo. Stainback
Chris Tatum
Geo. Simms
John Wall
Robt. Reynolds
John Davis
Edward Robinson
James Clack
Abraham Phenix
Charles Matthis
William Short
John Hagood
James Tapley
John Jackson
Daniel Carrie
William Smith
William Williams
James Love
James Parham
John Edwards
Thomas Hardaway
Geo. Scogging
Richd. Yarburough
James Bennitt
William Edwards
Nicholas Lanier
Robt. Briggs
Henry Simmons
James Macdaniel
John Burrow
William Burrow
William Duggar
John Rose
John Robinson
Thomas Jackson
Jesse Tatum

Hix Jones
Henry Bailey
Hugh Williams
William Averice
Hezekiah Massie
Owen Strange
Thomas Twitty
William Smith
John Sulivant
Jos. Floyd
Thomas Proctor
Drury Malone
Geo. Tilman
Francis Hagood
Geo. Hagood
Thomas Brooks
Richard Birch
Nicholas Edmunds
William McKnight
John Lambert
Nicholas Proctor
Sampson Caudle
William Gorver
John Birch
Robert Gee
James Rigbie
Francis Stainback
Edward Adams
Shep. Lanier
Curthbert Smith
William Stroud
Samuel Crafts
Thomas Scizon
Geo. Cain
Athanatious Robinson
John Duke

John Pettaway
Jo. Mabry
William Tilman
Sap Lanier
Theod'k. Bland
Richard Swanson
William House
William Smith Junr.
William Smith Junr.
Isaac Matthis
James Maclin
John Ezell
Edward Hueland
John Geo. Pennington
William Nance
William Bailey
Drury Robinson
Daniel Taylor
James Johnson
Samuel Russell
John Johnson
Peter Tatum
Adam Sims
Michael Young
Richard Russell
Thomas Jones
Thomas Carrie
John Evans
Griffin Humphris
Geo. Clark
Richard Scogging
John Moreton
James Parrish
William Scoging
Edward Davis
Baxter Davis

John Parker
William Eaton
John Duglas
John Thornton
Henry Jackson
Henry Morris
William Morris
John Jackson
David Walker
John Daniel
Jebrue Peebles
John Collier
Thomas Jackson
Lewis Parham
James Moseley
Hinchy Mabry
Samuel Harwel
William Pennington
Samuel Cental
Batt Peterson
John Jones
Thomas Jones
Thomas Sadler
William Whittington
John Yarburough
Thomas Cock
Thomas Avant
Nicho's. Lanier
John Hunt
Thomas Parson
William Samford
Drury Stith
John Robinson
Edward Goodrich
Richd. Lanier

MICHAEL WALL, *Sheriff.*

This 13th Day of June 1748

Michael Wall Sheriff made oath before me that this is true Copy taken for this County. Given under my hand this day above written.

JOHN WILLIS.

A Copy Teste:

W. T. SLEDGE, Clerk.

	White Tythes 21	do over 16 under 21	Neg^r over 16	do under 16	Horses	Cattle	Wheels	Ordinary Licenses
Anderson, John	1	...	1	5	3	6	...	...
Anderson, James	0?	...	1	1	2	6	...	...
Anderson, Phebe	..	...	1	...	2	4	...	...
Buckner, George	1	...	13	15	12?	41	2	...
Buckner, Mordecia	1	...	1	1	3	9	...	...
Buckner, George, Jr.	1	...	6	11	...	...	...	...
Bailey, William	1	...	...	...	2	...	...	...
Coleman, Daniel	2	...	10	11	8	19	...	...
Conner, James	1	...	5	4	2	10	...	...
Conner, William	2	...	7	16	4	27	...	...
Coleman, Thomas	1	...	5	6	5	11	...	...
Coleman, Julius	1	...	7	8	7	16	...	...
Carter, George	1	...	...	2	1	...	...	...
Coghill, Thos.	4	...	12	12	8	26	...	...
Carter, John	1	...	...	...	1	...	...	...
Coghill, Frederick	1	0	3	5	6	12	...	...
Carter, Joseph	1	...	2	2	6	13	...	...
Chapman, George	1	...	3	1	5	19	...	...
Chapman, William	1	...	2	2	4	13	...	...
Cooper, Mary	..	...	1	1	1	6	...	...
Conner, Frances	1	...	11	9	6	10	...	...
Carter, Benj^a	1	...	1	3	1	7	...	...
Durrett, Richard	1	...	4	9	5	12	...	...
Davey, William	1	...	...	...	3	3	...	...
Donner, John	1	...	5	11	6	15	...	...
Estes, John	1	...	5	5	7	27	...	...
Estes, Elisha	1	...	8	5	4	12	...	...

Goodloe, Henry	..	...	4	4	3	13	...	...
Goodwin, Coleman	..	...	4	3	2	1	...	...
Hawes, Thomas	1	...	6	4	3	13	...	...
Hawes, Isaac	1	...	...	1	1	...	...	...
Hawes, Samuel	1	...	24	30	14	91	...	...
Johnston, Richard	1	...	13	7	14	33	...	...
Jones, Moses	1	...	...	...	1	4	...	...
Jones, William	1	...	...	...	2	4	...	...
Lewis, Richard	1	...	0	0	2	5	...	...
Lewis, Henry	1	...	...	1	1	4	...	...
Long, John	1	...	1	...	1	4	...	...
Marshall, Margarett	...	...	4	7	6	19	...	...
McKinney, James	1	...	1	2	4	12	...	...
Mitchell, Richard	1	...	1	...	3	6	...	...
Mitchell, John	1	...	2	5	1	13	...	...
Madison, George	1	...	9	9	4	28	...	...
Oliver, John	2	...	...	1	3	8	...	...
Oliver, William	1	...	1	1	3	12	...	...
Phlippo, Sarah	...	...	...	...	...	...	...	...
Phlippo, Joseph	1	...	...	1	2	4	...	...
Pollett, John	1	...	1	...	1	...	...	...
Rogers, George	1	...	7	14	9	16	...	...
Ross, Edwd	..	...	...	2	3	8	...	...
Ross, Coleman	1	...	...	...	2	4	...	...
Rennolds, Eliza	..	...	4	2	3	11	...	...
Robinson, George	1	...	...	...	2	18	...	...
Robinson, Charles	1	...	...	1	...	...	...	...
Stevens, Richard	1	...	13	7	6	25	...	...
Samuel, James	1	...	2	4	3	6	...	...
Summers, John	1	...	...	...	2	2	...	...
Samuel, William	1	...	9	19	6	23	...	...
Scott, William	1	...	2	4	3	...	...	...
Standley, John	1	...	1	...	3	13	...	...
Smythes, William	1	...	...	...	2	6	...	...
Scott, Thomas	1	...	10	8	5	28	2	...
Tiller, Thomas	1	...	...	...	1	5	...	...
Tiller, Daniel	1	...	...	...	4	11	...	...

Vevion [Vivion], Charles	2	...	10	9	5	14	..	...
Washington, John	2	...	8	13	7	27	...	...
Wilson, Abraham	1	...	6	8	8	28	...	...
Yates, Charles	1	...	2	3	3	5	...	...
Yates, James	...	...	1	3	2	5	...	...
Yates, Marshal	1	...	2	2	1	2	...	...
Yates, Michael	2	...	13	7	13	28	...	...
Stud horse 20/								
Emmerson, Reuben	1	...	...	0	1	...	...	...
Emmerson, William	1	...	...	2	4	13	...	...
Edge, Benj[n]	1	...	...	1	4	10	...	...
Partlow, John	1	...	3	3	6	14	...	...
Cassell, John	1	...	2	3	4	16	...	...
Branan, Thomas	1	...	...	1	1	4	...	...
Wilson, Richard	1	...	4?	5	4	11	...	...
Armistead, John	2	...	22	27	12	48	4	...
Baylor, Walker	1	...	14	10	9	24	6	...
Bousn [Boush?], William	1	...	1	3	2	...	...	...
Bunus [Burus?], Diana	1	...	4	3	3	10	...	...
Bunus [Burus?], William	1	...	4	6	4	21	...	...
Bullard, Ambrose	1	...	1	3	3	9	...	...
Chiles, John	1	...	5	7	4	22	...	...
Coleman, John	1	...	5	6	5	16	...	...
Coleman, Farish	1	...	3	5	3	12	...	...
Casnall, Moses	1	...	...	...	2	1	...	...
Casnall, William	1	...	2	4	3	10	...	...
Casnall, Patrick	1	...	...	...	2	6	...	...
Collins, Thos. Estate	..	...	3	3	3	17	...	...
Campbell, Joseph	1	...	6	8	8	16	...	...
Collins, John	2	...	5	9	11	19	...	...
Coleman, Samuel	1	...	8	6	5	26	...	...
Collins, James	1	...	2	3	2	8	...	...
Chandler, Rob	1	...	9	4	7	19	...	...
Coleman, Tho[s]	1	...	9	11	6	48	...	...
Cleer, George	1	...	1	1	2	10	...	...
Dismukes, W[m]	1	...	3	2	4	7	...	...
Dismukes, Reuben	1	...	5	1	3	9	...	...

Evans, Robert	2	...	1	1	1	2	...	...
Farish, Robert	1	...	11	17	5	20	...	...
Farish, Stevens	1	...	3	5	4	6	...	...
Goodwin, Peter	1	...	5	10	5	30	...	...
Grady, William	2	...	...	...	3	14	...	...
Hudson, Benj[n]	1	...	1	5	3	4	...	...
Haley, John, Estate	..	...	6	8	7	14	...	...
Hacket, Martin	1	...	2	2	2	6	...	...
Hampton, John	1	...	10	16	13	55	...	...
Herndon, David	1	...	4	4	3	19	...	...
Hampton, George	1	...	2	6	2	10	...	...
Hewlett, Richard	2	...	...	1	3	6	...	...
Johnston, John	2	...	8	6	5	13	...	...
Jones, Joseph	2	...	4	6	6	16	...	...
Jones, Ann	..	...	12	17	7	20	...	...
Jones, Thomas (D Clk)	1	...	4	7	4	10	2	...
Jones, James	1	...	3	5	4	10	...	...
Jones, Thomas (D. T.)	1	...	6	6	6	34	...	...
Lightfoot, Philip	2	...	27	10	12	5	...	...
Lankford, Sarah		...	1	...	2	9	...	...
Lankford, William	1	...	...	...	1	6	...	...
Master, John	1	...	3	4	2	8	...	...
Oliver, Nich[s]	1	...	1	1	3	8	...	...
Rennolds, William	1	...	...	...	...	...	...	...
Riddle, Rebecca	..	...	3	5	4	12	...	...
Smith, [Jury?]	1	...	...	1	2	2	...	...
Smelt, Anna	..	...	2	9	2	...	...	...
Samuel, Anthony	..	...	7	8	6	11	...	...
Taliaferro, Sally	1	...	27	38	14	29	4	...
Taliaferro, Robert (Horse £3.)	4	...	25	34	18	70	6	...
Tyler, Richard	1	...	8	13	3	19	...	...
Terrell, James	1	...	...	...	3	8	...	...
Vaughan, Cern[s]	2	...	5	7	4	18	...	...

Wright, Elizabeth	..	...	7	8?	7	14	...	...
Winston, Nathaniel	2	...	5	9	6	13	...	...
Winston, Anthony	1	...	...	1	3	...	...	...
Harris, Thomas	1	...	1	1	2	5	...	...
Daves, Spilsby	1	...	2	2	2	2	...	...
Anderson, Garland	1	...	12	10	7	25	...	...
Arnold, James	1	...	...	1	3	4	...	...
Brown, Rachel	..	...	...	...	1	3	...	...
Chewning, Samuel	1	...	1	5	2	6	...	...
Clark, John	1	...	9	12	10	38	2	...
Coats, Thomas	2	...	3	10	4	20	...	...
Durrett, John	2	...	6	1	5	14	...	...
Durrett, Joel	1	...	2	4	3	10	...	...
Durrett, William	1	...	2	2	4	11	...	...
Durrett, George	1	...	5	4	4	20	...	...
Durrett, Henry	1	...	2	5	2	6	...	...
Fortion [Fortune?] Frederick	1	...	...	...	1	...	...	...
Oliver, Steven	1	...	1	3	3	8	...	...
Oliver, Richard	1	1	1	1	3	7	...	...
Harris, John	1	...	...	3	2	4	...	...
Hackney, John	1	...	4	5	4	10	...	...
Hudson, William	1	...	...	...	...	2	...	...
Hodges, Francis	1	1	2	4	5	13	...	...
Heggen, James	1	...	1	1	2	7	...	...
Heggen, Joel	1	...	4	2	4	12	...	...
Heggen, Wm Junr	1	...	2	2	2	7	...	...
Heggen, Wm	2	...	5	5	5	21	...	...
Johnston, Jedediah	2	...	1	4?	3	4	...	...
Jones, John	1	...	...	...	3	5	...	...
Johnston, Eliza	..	...	1	3	1	6	...	...
Johnston, Daniel	1	...	1	...	1	...	...	...
Mason, George	1	...	1	...	3	10	...	...
Stud horse £1(?) 12)								
Mooreman, Achiles	1	...	2	2	5	8	...	...
Marshall, William	1	...	11	17	6	16	4	...

Marshall, Elizabeth	...	...	4	8	...	18	...	...
Mason, Elizabeth	..	2	2	...	2	8	...	...
Newton, Mary	1	...	3	6	3	14	...	...
Phillips, George	1	...	3	4	4	12	...	...
Quarles, Roger	1	...	13	18	6	34	...	...
Stanfield, Ephraim	1	...	3	1	5	5	...	...
Sharp, George	1	...	...	...	1	6	...	...
Shields, Cris?	1	...	...	...	2	4	...	...
Tompkins, James	1	...	6	7	3	19	...	...
Tyler, William	3	...	15	9	10	73	...	...
Tompkins, Francis	1	...	6	4	5	17	...	...
Thackfield, Thacker	1	...	...	...	2	2	...	...
Tompkins, Benjamin	3	...	13	16	5	24	...	...
Winn, Benj[a] (Stud 3 s)	1	...	5	4	6	15	...	...
Wiglesworth, William	1	...	3	2	6	18	...	...
Wright, William	3	1	9	5	6	11	...	...
Winn, Jesse	1	...	4	1	3	10	...	...
Winn, Taverner	1	...	4	5	5	12	...	...
White, Francis	1	...	3	6	3	10	...	...
Harris, Judah	..	...	2	...	2	9	...	...
Harris, William	1	...	...	...	1	2	...	...
Yarbrough, Henry	1	...	3	7	3	13	...	...
Hackney, John Junr	1	...	3	1	3	8	...	...
Swily, David	1	...	...	1	1	2	...	...
Durrett, Françis	1	...	4	...	3	11	...	...
Almond, William	1	...	6	13	5	8	...	...
Parker, Alex[r]	1	...	6?	7	3	16	...	...
Martin, John	1	...	...	...	2	...	...	...
Wright, Tho.	1	...	...	2	1	6	...	...
Durrett, William	1	...	7	5	7	20	...	...
Ale, William	1	...	...	...	3	11	...	...
Allen, Erasmus	1	...	...	...	3	7	...	...
Allen, Thomas	1	...	...	...	2	6	...	...
Baylor, George	1	...	38	41	22	32	4	...
Burch, Benj[a]	1	1	4	12	9	39	...	...
Burton, Ann	1	...	3	2	7	10	...	...
Brown, William	1	...	1	1	3	7	...	...

Brown, John	1	...	4	5	4	6	...	...
Burrus, John	1	...	...	...	2	2	...	...
Chewning, William	1	...	3	3	3	7	...	...
Cannon, Joseph	1	...	...	...	1	4	...	...
Cannon, Mary	..	...	...	...	2	7	...	...
Cannon, John	1	...	...	...	...	...	...	...
Carpenter, Nathl	1	...	...	...	1	3	...	...
Chewning, Janett	..	...	6	7	2	9	...	...
Chewning, William	1	...	...	...	2	7	...	...
Chewing, John	1	...	0?	1	1?	4	...	...
Chiles, Henry Junr	..	1	...	...	1	4	...	...
Chiles, Thomas	1	...	3	4	3	11	...	...
Chiles, William	1	...	2	2	4	19	...	...
Chiles, Esther	..	...	2	4	1	6	...	...
Chiles, Jemima	..	1	3	3	4	19	...	...
Chiles, Henry	1	...	3	4	4	16	...	...
Chiles, Manoah	1	1	1	...	3	7	...	...
Clocy, Cato	1	...	...	...	1	...	...	...
Carter, Peter	1	...	...	...	1	...	...	...
Cobb, Robert	1	1	4	7	6	21	...	...
Chivers, John	1	...	...	...	2	5	...	...
Cheadle, Judith	..	1	7	7	5	24	...	...
Cullen, Charles	1	1	1	...	2	4	...	...
Cobb, David	1	...	1	5	3	4	...	...
Chandler, Timothy	1	...	...	...	1	...	...	...
Coleman, Thos	1	...	2	4	4	24	...	...
Duke, James	..	1	...	...	1	...	...	...
Dick, Archibald	..	1	8	13	9	26	2	...
Dickenson, David	1	...	4	6	5	15	...	...
Dickenson, Thos, Junr	1	...	3	5	4	11	...	...
Dickenson, Nathl. Wm	2	...	3	2	5	12	...	...
Dickenson, Thos. Senr	1	...	5	2	4	24	...	...
Daniel, Edmd.	1	...	...	...	3	4	...	...
Dickenson, Benja	1	...	1	...	1	3	...	...
Dickenson, William	2	...	10	5	6	22	...	...
Dickenson, James	1	...	2	1	2	18	...	...
Davis, Philip	1	...	2	2	4	3	...	...
Estis, Philip (stud horse 20/)	1	...	5	3	6	28	...	...
Eubank, Royal	1	...	...	...	1	1	...	...
Fortson[?], Stephen	1	1	1	2	1	10	...	...
Floyd, James	1	...	1	...	2	2	...	...

Faulkner, Johnston	1	1	6	11	5	17	...	...
Fulcher, Sarah	..	...	...	...	2	8	...	...
Fitzhugh, John	1	...	11	12	9	20	2	...
Garlick, John	2	...	10	9	7	29	2	...
George, Lucy	..	...	5	4	3	13	...	...
George, John, Sen[r]	1	...	8	9	5	12	...	...
Godbey, John	1	...	...	1	2	2	...	...
Gatewood, James	1	1	7	11	8	16	...	...
Haley, Humphy	1	2	4	9	4	14	...	...
Hargrove, Jesse	1	...	5	7	2	11	...	...
Hewlett, William	1	1	5	7	6	25	...	...
Hargrove, Samuel	1	0?	1	2	3	9	...	...
Hackett, Thomas	1	...	4	1	4	15	...	...
Hatton, John	1	...	...	...	1	2	...	...
Harper, William	1	...	...	...	1	4	...	...
Harris, James	1	...	2	5	7	26	...	...
Hollaway, Nathan	1	...	2	...	5	5	...	...
Hicks, William	1	...	...	...	1	...	...	...
Johnston, Benj[a]	1	...	2	1	5	18	...	...
Jones, John	1	...	...	...	4	4	...	...
Lenry, John	1	1	...	...	5	12	...	...
Lenry, Micajah	1	...	...	...	1	3	...	...
Luck, Nathan	1	1	1	...	5	8	...	...
Lucas, Edmund	..	...	...	...	2?	3	...	...
Minor, Thomas	..	...	9	...	3	...	...	...
Munah, Mark	1	...	...	1	2	2	...	...
Minor, John	1	...	15	22	8	24	...	...
Minor, Vivion	1	...	7	13	5	20	...	...
Muklebury(?), Robert	1	...	8	7	13?	15	...	...
Mills, Thompson	1	...	2	...	1	6	...	...
McGee, Ann	..	...	7	10	4	21	...	...
McGee, Joseph	1	...	2	4	2	10	...	...
New, Anthony	1	...	10	8	4	16	6	...
Parish, Timothy	1	...	4	5	3	10	...	...
Phlippo, William	..	1	...	...	2	3	...	...
Phlippo, John	1	...	...	...	1	...	...	...
Phlippo, Joseph	1	...	...	...	1	2	...	...

Quarles, William	2	...	7	8	7	21	...	...
Rennolds, Elizabeth	..	...	2	5	3	7	...	...
Rennolds, Rob	1	...	...	...	1	...	...	...
Rennolds, Jacob	1	...	...	5	...	...	...	...
Russell, John	1	...	3	2	3	10	...	...
Redd, Samuel	2	...	7	9	9	20	2	...
Redd, William	1	...	5	9	9	32	2	...
Stears, Achilles	1	...	...	...	1	4	...	...
Southworth, William	1	...	...	...	2	5	...	...
Southworth, William, S. W.	1	...	...	2	1	...	...	...
Sutton, John Junr	1	...	5	8	3	8	...	1
Seaser, John	1	...	2	1	2	8	...	...
Scott, John	..	1	6	13	3	6	...	...
Spearman, John	2	...	...	...	4	15?	...	...
Tenell [Terrell?] Christopher	1	...	3	1	3	20	...	...
Tenell [Terrell?], Thomas	1	1	4	8	6	25	...	...
Tennell [Terrell], George	1	...	4	6	5	13	...	...
Tenell [Terrell], Charles	1	...	4	6	3	26	...	...
Trivillian, Thomas	..	...	3	1	2	16	...	...
Trivillian, Thomas Junr	1	...	3	...	1	...	...	...
Tribble, George	1	...	1	...	1	4	...	...
Tribble, Joseph	1	...	...	...	1	3	...	...
Thompson, John Senr	1	...	8	9	3	31	...	...
Thompson, John Junr	1	...	1	2	2	...	...	...
Tiller, Ann	..	1	...	1	2	8	...	...
Tampler, John	1	...	...	1	4	10	...	...
Tayler, Richard Sq	..	...	2	4	...	6	...	...
Tinsley, William	1	...	3	2	3	17	...	...
Tompkins, Ann	0?	1	8	9	4	19	...	...
Tompkins, Robert	1	0?	16	17	7	37	...	...
Taylor, William	1	...	...	1	1	2	...	...
Temple, Samuel	1	...	12	13	8	40	...	...
Tyter [Tyler], George	2	...	8	12	6	32	...	...
Tribble, George Jno	1	...	...	...	1	2	...	...
Thilman, John	1	1	12	20	11	40	...	...
Thilman, Paul	1	...	4	1	5	6	...	...
Wright, David	1	...	1	1	2	4	...	...
Wyatt, Richard Senr	1	2	13	8	10	63	2	...
Wyatt, Richard Junr	1	...	3	7	5	26	...	...
Wortham, Charles	1	...	2	5	2	3	...	...

Wortham, Margt	..	...	6	1	2	8	...	...
Woolfolk, Elizabeth	1	...	5	4	3	20	...	...
Winston, Samuel	1	...	2	6	3	2	...	...
Young, Joseph	1	...	...	...	2	5	...	...
Young, John	1	...	...	...	...	...	...	...
Young, Nathl	..	...	...	...	4	8	...	...
Turner, Daniel	1	7	9	6	12	...	...	...
Berkley, Edmd, Esq.	1	...	14	24	5	22	...	...
Bullard, Lewis	1	...	4	3	4	8	...	...
Baynham, Gregory	1	...	3	3	6	8	...	...
Barlon, William	1	...	2	6	3	11	...	...
Brame, Milckzk	1	...	7	5	6	34	...	...
Brame, William	1	...	3	5	3	15	...	...
Baber, James	1	...	2	9	4	16	...	...
Baughan, Benja	1	...	1	3	4	8	...	...
Burrus[?], Samuel	1	1	7	6	7	26	...	...
Butler, John	1	...	4	1	3	16	...	...
Burk, John	2	...	12	17	8	31	...	...

CUMBERLAND COUNTY POLL LIST

Contributed by W. S. Morton

Election held in Cumberland County, Nov. 9th. 1804, for the Election of Electors for a President and Vice President of the United States. We, James Deane and John Hatcher, Commissioners, for holding the Election of Electors for a President and Vice President of the United States, for the County of Cumberland, do hereby certify that an Election was held for the said County pursuant to law, and the number of votes herein specified opposite the names of the several persons following, was given for each person as elector for the State of Virginia—of a President and Vice President of the United States, Namely—

Candidates:—

Richard Eve'd. Lee,	of Norfolk Burrough,
John Goodrich,	of Isle of Wight,
Edward Pegram,	of Dinwiddie,
Dr. Richard Field,	of Brunswick,
Thomas Read,	of Charlotte,
Creed Taylor,	of Cumberland,
William H. Cabell,	of Amherst,
George Penn,	of Patrick,
George Wythe,	of City of Richmond,
John Minor,	of Spotsylvania,
John Taylor,	of Caroline,
Larkin Smith,	of King and Queen,
William Ellzey,	of Loudon,
William Dudley,	of Warwick,
Mann Page,	of Gloucester,
John Taliaferro,	of King George
Richard Brent,	of Prince William,
Hugh Holms,	of Frederick,
James Daily,	of Hampshire,
James Allen,	of Shenandoah,
Archibald Stewart,	of Augusta,
James McFarlane,	of Russel,
Gen'l. John Preston,	of Montgomery,
William McKenly,	of Ohio.

Voters Names—

Joel Meggs
Field Roberson
Ben. Allen, Sr.
Robert Smith
Thomas Addams
John Orange
Edward Booker
Samuel Anderson
Henry Lipscomb
Littleberry Scruggs
John Price
William Bond
John Newton
John Warren
Hugh Junior
Samuel Addams
John Holeman, Jr.
William Maxey
Holloway Hudgens
James Anderson, B. S.
George Anserson
Blake B. Woodson
Jerman Baker
John M. Hobson
Jacob Bransford
John A. Trent

John Daniel
William England
Edmond Eggleston
John J. Renalds
Jesse Merryman
Zach Talley
Randolph Harrison
Tucker Baughan
John Hobson, Jr.
Charles Newton
Robert Nouel
John Baughan
Joseph McLauren
Joseph Meadow
Archibald Morrison
William Glen
Capt. Jeffery Roberson, Jr.
Capt. James Blanton
Peter T. Phillips
William B. Taley
Stephen Woodson
William Brown
Jesse Boatright
William Orrange
Walter Kibble, Jr.
Josiah Cox
John Holeman, Sr.
Rice D. (Mountigue ?)
Alexander Guthrey
David Burton
Moses Hubbard
John Glover
Lewis Isball
William Tally, Sr.
John Anderson, Sr.
James Bryant
Capt. William Hobson (son of Jno.)
Henry Guthrey
Lamuel Wheeler
Thomas Hobson Adcock
John Chrisp, Sr.

Elish Woodfin
Henry Martin
Elliott Coleman
Charles Lee
Newton Ford
Dr. Humphry Belt.
Col. Nelson Patteson
William Frazer
William Hobson (Adcock)
Nathaniel Pinnick
Capt. Bernard Sims
Caleb Hobson
James White
Capt. William Palmore
Samuel Oslin
Mose Arnold
Francis Flippin
David Tirey (Tyree)
John Woodson P. Sr.
Harrison Jones
William Daniel
Christopher Roberson
William Guthrey
John Jefferson, Sr.
(John) Jefferson
James Deane
Maj. John Hatcher
Joseph Johns
Richard Booker
Edward Roberson
William Starkly
William Russell
Jessey Davis
John Colquitt
Willis Swann
Thomas Johns
Lawrence Carlile
Jesse Michaux
Miller Woodson
William Russell, Clk.
Thos. Hobson, (son of John)

Attest: James Deane
John Hatcher,

Teste,
Blake B. Woodson
William Daniel.

In all 109 votes for the candidates aforementioned.

Given under our hands and seals at Cumberland Court House, this 9th. day of Nov. 1804.

Teste, John F. Redd,
Sam Hobson.

James Deane — (Seal)
John Hatcher — (Seal)

PERSONAL PROPERTY LIST DINWIDDIE COUNTY, 1782

Dinwiddie County was formed from the westernmost part of Prince George County, by an act of the Virginia Assembly convened February 1752, which act was to become effective May 1, 1752 (6 Hening, p. 254).

The only record book in Dinwiddie Court prior to the year 1800 is an Order Book covering the period 1789-1791. There remain, however, will and deed books from about 1833 on. Therefore, for the Colonial Period the only records that remain are the land patents (in the Office of the Register of the Land Office, Richmond), the Vestry Book and Parish Register of Bristol Parish (edited and published by C. G. Chamberlayne, Richmond, 1898) which covered the northern part of the county lying along Appomattox River and extending some distance inward. For the later period fortunately we have the Personal Property Lists (in the Virginia State Library, Richmond) and the Land Tax Lists (in the Office of the Auditor of Virginia, Richmond), both series dating from 1782 and coming down to 1863 (with, of course, same gaps). These tax lists are of inestimable value to the student of economic conditions and, if, advisedly used are also productive of valuable material for the genealogist.

One who is familiar with colonial legislation knows that various provisions were made (under the tax laws) for listing of tithables and other taxable property from almost the "beginning." There remain of record in volumes in several of the county courts (e. g., Henrico, Surry, Lancaster, etc.) specimens of these early tithe lists, though there seems to have been no systematic method of recording them; while among that heterogenous mass of invaluable material roughly classified "original papers" (stacks of which may be found in almost every court in Virginia) there have been discovered from time to time (and careful search would no doubt discover others) many colonial tithe and land lists. There is a remarkable set of these lists (not, however, complete) for Amelia County, dating from about 1735 among the original papers of that court.

The Assembly of October 1782 passed *An Act to amend and reduce the several acts of Assembly for ascertaining certain taxes and duties, and for establishing a permanent revenue, into one act* (11 Hening, p. 112). This law provided for a poll tax, and tax on slaves, cattle, horses, carriages, billiard tables and ordinary licenses; directed the justices of the county court to take the lists of taxable property and how to compile the lists. The provision was made that *three copies* of the lists should be made by the clerk (from the individual returns made); *one copy to be delivered to the Auditor of Public Accounts,* one copy to be set up at the Court House, and the other to be delivered to the sheriff, or collector of public taxes of the county. Thus we have what are now familiarly known as the Personal Property Lists; the copy directed to be delivered to the Auditor having been so delivered and filed by him. These lists were several years ago turned over by the Auditor's Office to the Virginia State Library.

Under an Act of this same Assembly (October 1782). *An Act for equalizing the land tax* (11 Hening, p. 140) the provision for lists was made under which we have the Land Tax Lists.

The following Dinwiddie County enumerations were copied from the lists in the Virginia State Library, Richmond. In the original lists the names of the negroes are given, but it was impracticable to reproduce here these names, numbering nearly 6,000.

A List of Tithes and taxable property taken by John Jones Junr gent the 9th day of April 1782 for the County of Dinwiddie for district No. ——

	Free Male Tithes	Negro Tithes	Negroes under age	No. Horses	No. Cattle	Bill^d Tables	Ord^y Licenses	Wheels
Roger Atkinson	1	4	1	4	16	...	...	...
John Kingston								
Geo Adams	1	2	3	2	10	...	...	...
Thomas Anderson	1	4	4	10	23	...	...	...
Thomas Andus	1	...	...	2	7	...	...	...
Edward Archer	0	3	0	2	24	...	...	...
Jordan Anderson	0	0	0	1	0	...	...	...
John Bristoe	1	0	1	1	0	...	...	...
Isaac Bradwell	1	2	0	3	2	...	1 Chair	
Jacob Bradwell	1	0	0	1	...	...	...	...
Ja^s Branton	1	0	0	1	2	...	...	...
William Browder	1	0	0	1	5	...	...	...
Edward Birchett	2	0	0	1	3	...	...	...
William Birchett								
Thomas Butler	1	3	3	3	21	...	...	...
George Booth	1	4	9	4	23	...	...	...
George Butler	1	1	0	1	4	...	...	...
Richard Burnett	1	2	4	4	23	...	...	...
James Birchett	1	0	0	3	0	...	...	...

Joseph Burnett	1	5	5	6	15	...	...	...
Littleberry Browder	1	2	1	1	2	...	...	...
Gilliam Booth	1	13	13	6	22	...		1 Chair
Jeremiah Bailey	1	3	2	5	24	...	...	...
George Beville	1	3	1	2	7	...	...	...
John Birchett	1	0	0	1	0	...	...	...
William Birchett	1	2	4	2	11	...	...	...
Robert Bolling Jessie Clay	1	9	14	11	44	...	...	...
David Browder	1	2	2	2	7	...	...	...
Robert Brown	1	...	...	1	4	...	...	...
Wm. E. Broadnax	1	...	1	8	...	...	...	...
Richard Burch	1	2	1	2	...	...	...	...
William Cousins	1	9	10	11	30	...	...	...
William Cassels	..	1	...	2	3	...	...	...
Mrs. Sarah Coleman	..	1	1	...	2	...	...	...
William Cross	1	1	1	2	8	...	...	...
William Carnell	1	...	...	2	8	...	...	...
John Coleman	1	3	2	2	8	...	...	...
Robert Cryer	1	...	...	1	...	...	...	...
Mrs. Temperance Clark	..	4	4	6	16	...	...	...
Cuthbert Coleman	1	4	6	3	7	...	...	...
Estate James Cocke	..	8	16	5	37	...	...	...
Thomas Cheely	1	2	2	6	19	...	...	...
Wmson Coleman	1	6	11	7	20	...	...	...
John Cryer	1	18	18	7	46	...	...	...
William Clark	1	4	3	5	16	...	...	...
John Chandler	1	...	...	3	10	...	...	...
Bolling Clark	1	3	2	5	21	...	...	...
William Clay	1	4	8	8	29	...	...	...
Thomas Chandler	1	2	2	3	16	...	...	...
William Chandler	1	...	...	1	5	...	...	...
William Claiborne	1	3	4	1	10	...	...	...
Matthew Coleman	1	5	11	4	...	...	...	...
Wyatt Collins	1	...	...	3	6	...	...	...
Richard Coleman	1	3	8	2	9	...	...	...
Mrs Cassells	..	4	4	4	11	...	...	...
Frances Christian	..	...	1	4	1	...	...	...
Thomas Clay	1	4	3	5	17	...	...	...
Rebecca Cassels	..	...	1	...	...	...	...	...
John Compton	1	2	1	3	14	...	...	...
Richard Cross	1	...	2	2	6	...	...	...
Isham Coleman	1	...	...	1	2	...	...	...
John Coleman	1	...	...	1	...	...	...	...

Obedience Cardwell	..	2	3	2	22	...	...	...
Sarah Cassells	..	...	1	...	...	...	...	...
Brittain Chandler	1	1	...	...	...	...	...	...
Francis Coleman	1	1	1	2	11	...	...	...
Daniel Claiborne	1	11	17	6	20	...		1 Chair
Daniel Call	3	8	9	6	4	...	...	...
Danl Call Jr								
James Wilkie								
Thos S Coleman	1	2	1	3	5	...	...	...
Mrs C. Darville	..	4	6	3	14	...	...	...
James Dyson	1	...	...	1	4	...	...	...
William Downman	..	6	4	8	24	...	...	...
Rauleigh Portius Downman	..	8	9	7	22	...	...	...
Giles Davis	1	...	2	1	7	...	...	...
John Davis	1	...	1	1	2	...	...	...
Matthew Dance	1	4	7	5	16	...	...	...
Barzilla Dance	1	2	3	4	5	...	...	...
Thomas Dance	2	14	18	14	36	...	...	...
Thomas Dance Junr								
Cary Wells Daniel	1	4	4	3	8	...	...	...
Francis Drew	1	...	...	1	5	...	...	...
John Drew	1	...	...	1	2	...	...	...
Mrs Martha Drew	..	2	1	2	5	...	...	...
Judith Draper	..	1	2	1	...	...		1 Chair
John Edmondson	2	6	13	6	20	...		1 Chair
Ambrose Gresham								
Peter Epes (P. Geo)								
John Chambers	1	13	15	9	67	...	...	...
Peterson Eppes	1	2	1	2	10	...	...	...
Joshua Eppes	1	4	4	3	14	...	...	...
Peter Eppes (P. Geo)								
Thomas Burnett	1	8	12	8	47	...	...	...
Edmund Elder	1	4	4	6	8	...	...	...
Claiborne Elder	1	...	...	...	...	...	...	...
Mary Elder	..	...	...	1	10	...	...	...
John Eppes	1	4	3	5	26	...	...	...
Edward Eanes	1	2	1	5	15	...	...	...
Francis Eppes	1	...	...	1	...	...	...	...
Robert Eckles	1	3	2	4	22	...	...	...
John Elder	1	...	...	1	12	...	...	...
Nathaniel Epes	1	1	1	3	7	...	...	...
Amey Epes	1	3	4	4	23	...	...	...
Randall Lee								

Thomas Elder	1	1	3	1	13	...	...	...
William Elder Senr	1	...	...	1	6	...	...	...
Richard Eppes	1	1	1	3	6	...	...	...
Joseph Fowler	1	5	7	6	23	...		
2 Wheels								
1 Chair								
Gideon Freeman	1	4	3	4	13	...	...	...
James French	1	16	6	22	83	...	...	...
Alex^{r} Frazier	1	1	...	...	...	...	...	...
Winny Ford	..	...	...	...	3	...	...	...
John Frazier	1	3	2	3	14	...	...	...
Daniel Furguson	1	...	...	...	...	...	...	...
Ben Fowler	1	1	...	...	3	...	...	...
Richard Furguson	1	2	3	4	10	...	...	...
James Geddy	3	10	6	6	24	...		1 Chair
William Waddle								
Peter Jones								
John Grant	2	2	5	5	19	...	...	...
Stephen Grant								
Harwood Goodwyn	1	7	4	5	21	...	...	...
Abner Grigg	1	1	...	1	6	...	...	...
Jesse Grigg	1	1	...	2	5	...	...	...
Ruth Grigg	..	1	1	2	4	...	...	...
William Gohlson	1	...	...	1	...	...	...	...
Fred^{k} Eppes	1	1	1	3	5	...	...	...
Peter Grammer	1	...	...	2	7	...	...	...
Thomas Goode	1	...	...	6	15	...	...	...
Abram Grant	1	2	4	5	11	...	...	...
Samuel Greenhill	1	8	...	8	...	...	...	...
Micajah Harriss	1	...	...	2	5	...	...	...
Samuel Hinton	1	5	6	8	16	...	...	...
Charles Hutchings	1	...	...	1	9	...	...	...
John Holycross	1	...	...	1	7	...	...	...
Ishum Hogan	1	2	6	5	9	...	...	...
Turner Hamblett	1	...	1	2	5	...	...	...
William Hudson	2	9	2	9	10	...	...	...
William Harper Jun.	1	2	3	5	15	...	...	...
Irby Hudson	1	3	6	2	6	...	...	...
Robert G Hardaway	1	5	5	5	3	...	...	...
Jno P Harper	1	4	4	3	18	...	...	...
David Hood	1	...	1	1	8	...	...	...
John Howell	1	2	4	5	12	...	...	...
William Harriss	1	4	8	2	18	...	...	...
Jno Clay								
Bozwell Hutchings	1	...	...	2	7	...	...	...

Nathaniel Harper	1	9	14	7	40	...	...	...
Nathaniel Hobbs	1	5	11	10	24	...	...	...
Parrott Hardy	1	...	...	2	3	...	...	...
William Harper Sen[r].......	1	7	12	8	34	...	...	...
Joseph Harper	1	10	8	7	24	...	...	...
George Harper	1	7	10	7	34	...	...	...
Jessee Hobbs	1	...	...	1	...	...	...	...
William Hardaway	1	7	8	5	15	...	...	...
William Hardaway Jun[r]....	1	3	3	2	5	...	...	...
Vincent Inge	1	...	...	2	6	...	...	...
Betty Inge	..	...	...	1	4	...	...	...
Rev[d] Devereux Jarrett......	1	9	15	11	26	...		1 Chair
Lewis Jones	1	1	3	2	10	...	...	...
Frederick Jones	1	15	14	14	29	...	...	...
Philip Jones	1	10	10	6	20	...		1 Chair
Col[o] John Jones	1	6	6	5	22	...		1 Chair
James Johnson	1	4	6	13	8	...	...	...
Edward Jackson	1	...	...	2	...	...	...	...
Kennon Jones	1	14	16	10	35	...		1 Chair
Matthew Jones	1	2	2	3	3	...	...	...
Mary Jones	..	1	...	1	9	...	...	...
Samuel Jones	1	...	...	2	2	...	...	...
John Jackson	1	1	...	2	...	...	...	...
Thomas Johnson	1	1	1	1	2	...	...	...
Col[o] Joseph Jones..........	1	7	3	16	25	...	...	...
Joseph Baugh								
David Jones	1	1	4	4	11	...	...	...
Ralph Jackson	1	3	4	4	15	...	...	...
Ralph Jackson Jun[r]........	1	2	1	4	9	...	...	...
John Jones Jun[r]...........	3	26	43	13	41	...		1 Chair
John Poythress								
Joseph Hazlewood								
Richard Jumper	1	...	...	7	3	...	...	...
Abner Jackson	1	2	2	7	14	...	...	...
John Kington	..	...	...	1	...	...	...	...
Fisher Lenoir	1	3	6	4	8	...	...	..
John Loyd	1	...	1	...	...	...	...	...
John Leach	1	1	...	3	12	...	...	...
Nicholas Lamb	1	2	1	1	2	...	...	...
William Lamb	1	2	...	2	8	...	...	...
Nathan Ledbetter	1	...	3	3	7	...	...	...
Edward Lewis	1	...	...	1	9	...	...	...

James Leach	1	3	5	5	16	...	...	...
Thomas Lewis	1	...	...	1	5	...	...	...
Matthew Liggon	1	1	...	3	5	...	...	...
James Look	1	...	...	1	1	...	...	...
John Lamb	..	1	1	...	3	...	...	...
Drury Ledbetter	1	2	...	2	6	...	...	...
Peter Manson	1	8	11	11	17	...	...	...
John Manson	1	4	6	3	34	...	...	...
Starkey Moore	1	2	9	3	13	...	...	...
Francis Muir	1	23	24	4	36	...	...	...
William Meredith	1	3	1	2	6	...	...	...
Edward Mitchell	1	10	6	7	28	...	...	...
Benjamin Moore	2	1	2	3	13	...	...	...
Jno Moore								
William Mayes	1	...	1	1	...	...	...	...
Daniel Mayes	1	...	...	1	1	...	...	...
Gardiner Murrell	1	1	...	3	10	...	...	...
Francis Merrymoon	1	1	5	1	5	...	...	...
John Murrell	1	1	...	2	2	...	...	...
Robert Moreland	1	...	3	1	2	...	...	...
Richard Malone	1	2	...	3	5	...	...	...
Nancy Malone	1	3	3	5	15	...	...	...
Ben Moore	1	3	...	2	15	...	...	...
James Moore								
David Merrymoon	1	...	...	1	10	...	...	...
John Meredith	1	2	1	2	4	...	...	...
Richard Mason	1	3	...	6	4	...	...	...
John Marshall	1	2	3	3	2	...	...	...
John North Junr	1	2	2	2	6	...	...	...
John North Sen	1	4	6	8	33	...	...	...
John Nunnelly, Jun	1	...	...	1	...	...	4	...
John Nunnelly Senr	1	1	...	2	4	...	...	...
Thomas Nunnelly	1	...	...	...	...	...	...	...
Thomas Nunnelly	1	...	...	1	12	...	...	...
Caleb Overton	1	...	...	...	...	...	...	...
James Old	1	7	7	5	24	...	...	...
John Old	1	1	1	3	2	...	...	...
Edward Old	1	3	5	2	10	...	...	...
Richard Overby	1	6	5	2	12	...	...	...
John Pritchett	1	5	6	6	19	...		1 Chair
Esta Anthony Penniston	1	4	2	4	11	...	...	...
——— Cross								
Jere Pritchett	1	2	2	3	6	...	...	...

Frances Pritchett	..	2	...	2	6	...	...	...
Thomas Piercey	1	1	2	1	3	...	...	...
Aaron Pritchett	2	...	...	...	5	...	...	...
Jesse Pritchett								
Jere Potts	2	1	0	2	8	...	...	...
Jesse Stegall								
Wm Penticost	1	1	...	2	4	...	...	...
Elizabeth Pegram	1	3	1	4	8	...	...	...
Daniel Pegram								
Stith Parham (Parson)	1	7	8	4	15	...	...	...
James Pritchett	1	7	16	5	28	...	...	...
Joshua Pritchett	1	5	2	6	17	...	...	...
Francis Pritchett	1	...	...	2	3	...	...	...
Edward Pegram	1	4	5	5	21	...	...	...
Esta Wm Pegram	..	...	1	...	...	...	...	...
Do Anthony Penniston	..	5	1	3	21	...	...	...
Peter Poythress	1	6	11	3	23	...	...	...
John Lamb								
Peter Pritchett	1	...	...	2	...	...	...	...
Peter Pride	1	3	...	3	8	...	...	...
Joseph Parsons	1	2	1	2	8	...	...	...
Ephraim Potts	1	...	...	1	...	...	...	...
Francis Poythress	2	1	...	...	...	...	...	...
D. G. Meanly								
Peter Poythress	..	12	14	8	47	...	...	...
Joanna Parham	..	1	2	...	...	...	...	...
Martha Piercey	..	...	...	1	6	...	...	...
Edward Puckett	1	...	...	1	10	...	...	...
John Pegram	1	3	7	6	25	...	...	...
Capt Edward Pegram	1	8	13	11	32	...	...	...
George Pegram	1	1	2	5	8	...	...	...
Baker Pegram	2	4	1	4	12	...	...	...
John Manson								
Hugh Rees	1	5	2	6	21	...	...	...
Hugh Rees	1	7	10	4	19	...	...	...
William Rieves	2	5	6	8	33	...	...	...
Thomas Parham								
William Rather	1	2	1	6	20	...	...	...
Jordan Rees	1	4	5	5	14	...	...	...
Josiah Rees	1	...	3	4	...	...	...	...
Francis Rees	1	1	...	2	13	...	...	...
William Rees	1	4	2	6	38	...	...	...
William Rees	1	...	1	1	...	...	...	...
James Rees	1	1	...	4	10	...	...	...
Amey Rees	..	2	5	4	13	...	...	...
Isham Rees	1	4	5	6	13	...	...	...

Edward Rees	1	4	5	7	18	...	...	...
Wm Rees	1	...	1	...	2	...	...	...
Frederick Rees	1	...	2	3	5	...	...	...
John Reames	1	...	...	3	8	...	...	...
Wm Robertson (Pr Geo)	1	10	17	9	43	...	...	...
Wm Stone								
Charles Roper Jr	1	...	...	2	10	...	...	...
Charles Roper Senr	2	2	1	4	17	...	...	...
Daniel Fergusson								
Thomas Rogers	1	2	2	5	13	...	...	...
Thomas Ross	1	2	4	4	27	...	...	...
Esta Patrick Ramsey	..	9	15	3	24	...	...	...
Buckner Raney	1	3	3	6	16	...	...	...
Robert Rees	1	...	...	2	3	...	...	...
John Sturdivant	1	1	2	2	...	...	...	...
Henry Spain	1	6	4	4	16	...	...	...
Eppes Spain	1	3	2	3	19	...	...	...
Wm Scott	1	6	3	11	33	...	...	...
John Stow	1	...	...	3	6	...	...	...
Dicey Shackleford	..	1	1	1	3	...	...	...
Bridget Smith	..	6	9	6	24	...	...	...
John Spain	1	5	7	3	13	...	...	...
Major Thomas Scott	3	32	25	12	60	...	...	...
Burwell Carter								
Charles Adson								
Dennis Still	1	1	4	3	11	...	...	...
Shadrach Stell	1	...	1	3	9	...	...	...
George Stell	1	3	3	1	15	...	...	...
John Slorter	1	...	...	2	10	...	...	...
Thomas Scott Junr	2	7	4	4	12	...	...	...
Jonathan Cook								
John Epes Scott	1	1	...	5	...	...	...	...
John Smith	2	3	3	5	6	...	...	...
Wood Burge								
Francis Scott	1	1	...	3	3	...	...	...
William Stembridge Sen	1	...	...	1	12	...	...	...
William Stembridge Jun	1	...	...	1	...	...	...	...
John Stow	1	2	7	4	17	...	...	...
William Stow	1	1	4	2	7	...	...	...
Samuel Sandifer	1	1	2	3	7	...	...	...
Daniel Spain Senr	2	2	2	5	20	...	...	...
Thomas Spain								
John P Spain	1	2	2	3	8	...	...	...
Daniel Spain Junr	1	1	...	2	8	...	...	...

John Smith	1	...	1	...	...	...	...	...
Francis Smart	1	2	4	5	18	...	...	...
Mrs Frances Sturdivant	..	3	5	5	9	...	...	...
Batt Spain	1	3	...	7	12	...	...	...
William Sallard	1	3	4	5	13	...	...	...
Thomas Stewart	1	8	9	12	29	...	...	...
John Stell	1	3	2	4	13	...	...	...
Joseph Sydnor	1	3	...	3	10	...	...	...
James Stewart	1	...	...	2	10	...	...	...
Mary Stell	..	...	1	2	8	...	...	...
Matthew Spain	1	...	1	1	4	...	...	...
John Scott (Car)	1	6	6	6	16	...	...	...
John Spain Junr	1	...	1	1	4	...	...	...
William Sydnor	1	3	6	4	8	...		1 Chair
Charles Stell	1	1	3	3	16	...	...	...
Richard Stewart	1	3	5	5	19	...	...	...
Ambrose Vaughan								
James Stewart	1	...	...	1	3	...	...	...
William Spain	1	2	1	3	5	...	...	...
William Thompson	1	9	13	4	26	...	...	...
John Tucker	1	1	...	1	8	...	...	...
John Tucker Senr	1	8	16	10	39	...	...	...
Daniel Tucker	1	3	9	5	10	...	...	...
Robert Tucker	1	...	...	2	4	...	...	...
William Thompson Junr	1	...	...	1	...	...	...	...
Benjamin Tucker	1	7	5	6	7	...	...	...
Isaac Tucker	1	4	5	3	18	...	...	...
Robert Tucker	1	1	...	1	11	...	...	...
Joseph Tucker	2	4	5	8	9	...	...	...
John Tucker								
Joseph Thweatt	1	1	1	2	12	...	...	...
Burwell Thweatt	1	2	4	4	15	...	...	...
William Thweatt	1	8	3	4	18	...	...	...
John Traylor	1	...	...	4	10	...	...	...
George Thweatt	1	3	9	4	27	...	...	...
Charles Thweatt	1	...	...	2	...	...	...	...
William Thweatt	1	2	...	2	9	...	...	...
Richard Taliaferro	1	18	25	6	81	...	...	...
Robert Morris								
John Tally	1	...	...	1	7	...	...	...
John Tucker Junr	1	3	10	5	9	...	...	..
Drury Thweatt	1	3	2	2	2	...	...	...
John Thompson	1	1	...	4	13	...	...	...
Alex^{r} Thweatt	1	2	2	3	11	...	...	...
David Taylor	1	...	...	1	5	...	...	...

David Thweatt	1	1	2	1	...	...	...	...
Joseph Traylor	1	...	...	2	3	...	...	...
George Thweatt Junr	1	...	...	3	6	...	...	...
David Tucker	1	...	...	2	4	...	...	...
Henry Thweatt	1	3	2	6	23	...	...	...
Amey Turnbull	..	2	2	4	...	...	...	...
Peter Thweatt	1	...	...	3	...	...		1 Chair
John Verrell	1	18	22	7	35	...	...	...
William Vaughan	1	...	...	2	5	...	...	...
Zachariah Vaughan	1	...	...	1	2	...	...	...
Richard Vaughan	1	...	...	3	7	...	...	...
Jacob Wray	1	5	6	3	19	...	...	...
William Wells	1	1	4	5	14	...	...	...
Benjamin Whyley	1	...	...	4	9	...	...	...
John Wood	1	1	...	2	5	...	...	...
Ethelred Wood	1	1	...	2	...	...	...	...
John Wmson	2	7	4	8	21	...	...	...
Charles Wmson								
Benjamin Woodward	1	12	11	6	18	...	...	...
Stephen Williamson	1	4	3	6	24	...	...	...
John Woodward	1	4	3	5	12	...	...	...
Robt West Senr	1	7	2	4	34	...	...	...
Thomas Woodward	1	7	3	10	37	...	...	...
Cornelius Wainwright	1	2	6	4	13	...	...	...
Samuel Wainwright	1	1	5	6	13	...	...	...
Thomas Wyne	1	3	3	2	14	...	...	...
John Wilkerson	1	3	6	5	8	...	...	...
Eliza Whitmore	..	4	3	2	9	...	...	...
William Whitmore	1	2	...	3	4	...	...	...
John West	1	4	5	7	18	...	...	...
John Watts	1	...	...	1	7	...	...	...
Charles Whitmore	1	2	1	3	9	...	...	...
Thomas Morgan								
Richard Wells	1	...	1	2	10	...	...	...
Charles Watson	1	...	...	1	...	...	...	...
Isham Walding	1	...	...	1	...	...	...	...
Charles Wyne	1	1	2	1	8	...	...	...
Lodwick Wilson	1	...	...	...	6	...	...	...
Wm Yates	1	26	29	8	38	...	...	...
Tinsley Young	1	2	5	4	9	...	...	...
Francis Young	1	1	2	5	19	...	...	...
Jno Young	1	1	...	1	2	...	...	...
James Yeargain	1	5	...	8	18	...	...	...

(To be concluded)

PERSONAL PROPERTY LIST DINWIDDIE COUNTY, 1782

A List of Tithes & Taxable Property taken by Dun [Duncan] Rose Gent the 10th day of April 1782 for Dinwiddie County.

	Free Male Tithes	Negro Tithes	Negroes under age	No. Horses	No. Cattle	Bill^{d} Tables	Ord^{y} Licenses	Wheels
John Archer	1	...	...	2	5	...	...	...
William Archer	1	1	1	4	13	...	...	...
George Archer	1	4	5	12	14	...		1 Chair
John Butler	1	1	...	4	6	...		1 Chair
Wallace Butter	1	1	5	3	1	...	...	...
John Baird	1	2	3	...	...	...	...	...
James Butler	2	4	...	4	16	...	...	...
Thomas Browder	1	2	...	2	5	...	...	...
Frederick Bonner	1	3	2	4	5	...	...	...
Ambrose Byrd	1	...	...	...	...	...	...	...
Joseph Butler	1	1	...	4	14	...	...	...
Joel Burge	1	...	...	1	1	...	...	...
Alice Brown	..	2	...	2	2	...	...	...
William Browder	1	6	14	6	9	...	...	...
Thomas Bonner	1	7	8	5	21	...	...	...
Nicholas Butterworth	1	...	...	1	...	...	...	...
Col° John Banister	3	46	42	28	126	...		1 Charriott
Francis Ford								
Abram Ford (overseer)								
John Browder	1	1	4	4	8	...	...	...
Edward Butler	1	...	1	...	1	...	...	...
Isaac Butler	1	...	...	2	9	...	...	...
Elizabeth Brown	..	...	...	1	5	...	...	...
Rebecca Brown	..	...	...	1	4	...	...	...
George Blick	1	1	2	3	6	...	...	...
Samuel Brassington	1	1	...	4	7	...	...	...

John Baugh	1	...	...	1	...	...	...	...
Martha Baugh	..	2	...	3	12	...	...	...
Hezekiah Brown	1	...	...	2	3	...	...	...
William Bradley	2	4	1	5	3	...		
1 Pheton								
1 Chair								
Samuel White								
John Boisseau	1	4	6	5	12	...	...	...
John Bell	1	2	1	1	5	...	...	...
Noah Brown	1	2	2	1	...	...	...	...
Joseph Butler	1	...	2	3	4	...	...	...
James Butler Jun[r]	1	1	1	2	5	...	...	...
John Butler	1	1	3	2	7	...	...	...
Henry Butler	1	1	...	1	...	...	...	...
Ann Butler	..	1	6	3	5	...	...	...
Stephen Butler	1	...	1	2	7	...	...	...
Jesse Bonner	1	3	4	3	14	...	...	...
Daniel Boisseau	1	4	5	3	8	...	...	...
John Blick	1	...	...	3	10	...	...	...
William Colvin	2	1	2	2	4	...	...	...
William Colvin Jun								
Joseph Cornwell	1	1	...	2	5	...	...	...
John Clements	1	...	...	2	3	...	...	...
William Clements	1	...	...	4	6	...	...	...
John Conway	1	1	4	5	6	...	...	...
William Conway	1	1	...	3	7	...	...	...
John Crews	1	...	1	3	...	...	...	...
John Coles	1	5	5	4	15	...		1 Chair
John Carpenter	1	1	...	3	9	...	...	...
William Cole	1	18	16	8	24	...		
1 Chariott								
1 Phaeton								
John Dalton	1	...	1	2	...	...	...	...
Benjamin Dabney	1	4	7	6	17	...	...	...
Edward Dillard	1	...	...	1	...	...	...	...
Thomas Dillard	1	3	6	3	8	...	...	...
John Dillard	1	...	...	...	...	...	...	...
William Durell	1	4	2	3	3	...	...	...
Samuel Davies	1	5	4	3	2	...	...	...
Daniel Dodson	1	5	4	2	5	...	...	...
Thomas Daniel	1	2	...	1	5	...	...	...
Christopher Daniel	1	...	1	11	...	...	...	...
Thomas Dillard	3	2	7	4	9	...	...	...
John Dillard								
Edward Dillard								

John Day	1	...	...	2	2	...	...	...
Col^{o} William Diggs	1	27	45	16	6	...		
1 chariott								
1 chair								
Morriss Davis	1	1	2	2	9	...	...	...
William Epps	1	7	8	7	7	...	...	...
Ruth Epps	..	...	...	...	3	...	...	...
Peter Epps	1	1	1	2	3	...	...	...
Francis Epps	1	5	6	6	6	...	...	...
George Elliott	1	10	11	7	6	...		
1 Phaeton								
1 chair								
John Flanders	1	...	...	1	2	...	...	...
David Fisher	1	3	2	4	9	...	...	...
Joseph Gray	1	2	...	3	10	...	...	...
John Gray	1	2	2	3	6	...	...	...
David Gray	1	2	3	...	...	...	...	...
Bozwell Goodwin	3	3	6	6	10	...	...	...
Stephen Goodwin								
Armistead Goodwin								
Nathaniel Harrison	1	8	15	6	21	...	...	...
Richmund Rawlings								
Dennis Holladay	1	...	...	...	...	...	...	...
Fred^{k} Hawks	1	...	...	...	...	...	...	...
William Hill	2	13	10	3	18	...	...	...
Robert Williams								
John Hitchcock	1	3	...	4	14	...	...	...
Robert Hall	1	5	9	5	13	...	...	...
Revd William Harrison	1	5	10	6	10	...		1 Chair
Joseph Harding	1	3	2	2	4	...	...	...
Thomas Harmon Senr	1	6	4	4	26	...	...	...
John Harmon	1	...	3	3	9	...	...	...
William Harmon	1	...	...	2	...	...	...	...
Thomas Harmon	1	...	...	1	...	...	...	...
James Hardaway	1	5	5	4	15	...	...	...
Henry Hardaway	1	5	4	4	20	...	...	...
John Hawks	..	...	...	2	5	...	...	...
(Exempted by Court)								
Andrew Hardy	1	...	...	1	5	...	...	...
Ainsworth Hardaway	1	5	6	4	34	...	...	...
Stith Hardaway	1	8	5	5	35	...	...	...
Goodrich Haddin	1	3	4	3	7	...	...	...
Instance Hall	1	2	5	3	6	1		1 1 chair

William Hunnitcut	1	1	...	4	13	...	...	...
John Innis	1	3	4	2	16	...	...	...
William Jones	2	...	...	4	9	...	...	...
James Jones								
John Jones	1	...	...	2	...	...	...	...
William Kirby (Kerby)	1	5	2	5	7	...	...	...
John Kirby	1	3	6	6	19	...	...	...
Bennett Kirby	1	4	4	5	13	...	...	...
Thomas Kirby	..	1	1	1	...	...	...	...
Miss Fanny Kirby	..	...	5	...	...	...	...	...
John Lewis	1	...	...	2	...	...	...	...
George Loyd	1	1	1	2	3	...	...	...
Robert Langley	1	12	14	4	26	...	...	...
Isaac Lunsford	1	...	...	5	6	...	...	...
Jesse Lee	1	3	13	5	18	...	...	...
Thomas Lamb	1	4	7	5	9	...	...	...
Lewis Lanier	1	1	3	3	3	...	...	...
Richard Lunsford	1	3	...	2	6	...	...	...
Thomas Loyd	1	1	...	3	2	...	...	...
William Loyd	1	4	2	3	6	...	...	...
Phillip Moore	1	...	...	2	5	...	...	...
Thomas Moore	1	...	...	...	...	...	...	...
Peter Minor	2	1	...	1	...	...	...	...
Benja Lewis								
William Meanley	1	3	8	4	11	...	...	...
Richard Meanley	1	6	6	3	11	...	...	...
Matthew Mayes	1	5	4	4	19	...		1 Chair
John McCullock								
John McCullock Junr								
D. McCullock	3	...	...	4	7	...	...	...
David McCullock	1	1	...	6	10	...	...	...
Christianna Major	.	4	10	4	10	...	...	...
Barnett Major	1	...	...	...	...	...	...	...
Henry Morriss	1	2	...	...	...	...	...	...
Thomas Norton Senr	1	...	...	1	2	...	...	...
Thomas Norton Junr	1	...	...	2	...	...	...	...
William Noble	1	1	2	3	6	...	...	...
Edward Perkins	1	3	3	5	18	...	...	...
Lewis Perkins	1	...	...	1	8	...	...	...

William Perkins	1	3	6	3	11	...	...	...
Joshua Perkin[s]	1	...	...	1	...	...	...	...
John Perkins	1	3	4	2	2	...	...	...
Mrs Ann Portlock..........	..	1	2	1	1	...	...	...
James Pultrey	1	3	7	5	15	...	...	...
Honorias Powell	1	3	...	8	5	...	...	...
Agnes Perry	..	3	7	2	11	...	...	...
James Perkins	1	8	...	4	12	...	...	...
William Perkins	1	2	6	3	7	...	...	...
John Perkins	1	2	2	1	2	...	...	...
Anne Perkins	..	5	4	1	7	...	...	...
Francis Pace	1	1	2	2	5	...	...	...
John Quarles	1	1	...	1	2	...	...	...
Thomas Reid...............	1	...	...	1	8	...	...	...
Samuel Rouse	1	...	...	...	...	...	...	...
Dun[can] Rose	1	8	6	6	6	...	...	...
John Randolph	1	6	8	4	2	1 Billiard Table		
David Ross & Co..........	4	2	...	3	...	...	...	...
Hector McNeil								
Wm Barksdale								
John Calder								
William Cassells								
Michael Rosser	1	1	...	3	2	...	...	...
Stephen Scott	1	2	9	2	...	...	...	...
Stegar & Co...............	..	1	...	1	...	...	...	...
William Stegar	1	1	...	0	2	...	...	...
David Smith	1	1	...	1	3	...	...	...
Archibald Smith	1	...	...	1	...	...	...	...
Clement Smith	1	3	7	1	4	...	...	...
Richard Smith	1	1	2	3	2	...	...	...
Messrs Shore & McConnico (at Mill)...	7	11	3	1	...	...	...	...
Hugh Galt								
John McConnico								
Fredk Nance								
At Store								
John Lany								
Peter Davis								
Marshall Booker								
George Craighead								
Esta Robert Skipwith......	1	18	26	8	28	...	...	...
John Phillups								

Joshua Smith	1	3	8	6	18	...	...	...
George Smith	1	6	8	6	3	...	...	...
Esta John Tabb	..	15	19	27	52	...	...	...
James Turnbull	1	3	3	2	5	...	...	...
John Thompson	1	3	3	6	9	...	...	...
Daniel Teasdale	1	...	1	3	...	...	...	...
Joseph Turner for Abram	..	1	...	...	...	...	...	...
Elizabeth Todd	..	...	...	1	4	...	...	...
John Todd	1	...	...	3	4	...	...	...
Henry Todd	1	...	...	1	3	...	...	...
Capt Joseph Tucker	1	10	10	5	18	...	...	...
Wood Tucker	1	5	6	5	20	...	...	...
William Vaughan	1	2	3	2	5	...	...	...
Drury Vaughan	1	...	...	1	6	...	...	...
Peter Vaughan	1	4	6	6	6	...	...	...
Henry Vaughan	1	3	...	6	20	...	...	...
Morris Vaughan	1	...	...	1	12	...	...	...
Susanna Wane	..	1	...	2	4	...	...	...
Miles Williams	1	3	2	3	16	...	...	...
James Williams	2	4	1	3	...	...	...	...
Clement Williams								
Livy Ward	1	...	...	1	...	...	...	...
Joseph Whitehead	1	3	3	6	8	...	...	...
Richard Williams	1	...	2	2	4	...	...	...
John Watlington	1	...	...	1	...	...	...	...
Joshua Williams	1	...	...	1	...	...	...	...
Charles Williams	..	4	6	4	27	...	...	...
(Exempted by Court)								
Daniel Wood	1	...	...	1	...	...	...	...

(To be concluded in next issue)

PERSONAL PROPERTY LIST DINWIDDIE COUNTY, 1782

A List of Tithes & Taxable Property taken by Joseph Jones Gent, 10 April 1782.

Roger Atkinson	2	23	28	10	23	...	1 charriott	
John Atkinson								
William Allen	1	...	...	3	11	...	...	...
David Andrews	1	...	...	...	...	...	...	...
Edward Archer	..	3	...	...	20	...	...	...
Peter Bedlock	1	...	1	9	...	...	...	...
Elizabeth Bedlock	..	...	...	...	2	...	...	...
Thomas Barrett	1	12	13	9	43	...	...	...
Arthur Browder	1	...	...	2	7	...	...	...
Benjamin Boisseau	1	8	6	9	24	...		1 chair
Mrs Mary Bolling	..	32	19	11	9	...		
(B[olling] Brook)								
1 charriott								
1 chair								
(Hardwick)								
Robert Bolling junr	1	3	2	4	...	...	1 phaeton	
Jesse Browder	1	1	...	2	...	...	...	...
Richard Browder	1	2	4	3	8	...	...	...
Thompson Browder	1	...	...	1	...	...	...	...
Mrs Margaret Bissett	..	1	1	3	1	...	...	...
Joseph Butler	1	1	1	3	10	...		1 chair
Peter Boiser [Boisseau?]	1	...	2	...	1	...	...	...
Gray Briggs	1	20	23	16	41	...	1 charriott	
George Chandler	1	...	...	...	2	...	...	...
Phebe Crowder	..	1	4	6	26	...	...	...
Richard Crowder	1	4	6	2	20	...	...	...
Augustine Claiborne junr	2	13	12	4	28	...	1 charriott	
Henry Crowder								
Joseph Crowder	1	...	...	1	...	...	...	...
Colo Augustine Claiborne	..	7	18	3	25	...	...	...
Buller Claiborne	..	9	19	9	3	...	...	...
James Crowder	1	2	1	2	12	...	...	...
William Crowder	2	2	...	5	21	...	...	...
Joshua Spain								

Zachr Crowder	1	...	...	1	8	...	...	...
Drury Crowder	1	2	...	5	15	...	...	...
John Wagnon Crowder	1	...	...	...	2	...	...	...
Drury Crowder junr	1	...	...	2	4	...	...	...
Drury Cross	..	...	...	3	9	...	...	...
Edm[d] Cooper	1	1	1	1	2	...	...	...
Daniel Crowder	1	5	3	4	20	...	...	...
Sackiveritte Criswell	1	1	3	1	...	...	...	...
Henry Crowder Sen[r]	1	...	...	2	13	...	...	...
Drury Dance	1	2	...	2	3	...	...	...
Solomon Davis	1	4	3	3	3	...	...	...
John Durand	..	1	3	...	...	...	...	...
Stephen Dance	1	2	2	2	7	...		1 chair
John Dorlon	2	5	7	3	3	...	...	...
Lewis Holmes								
James Durell	1	...	1	1	1	...	...	...
John Dabney	1	1	4	1	6	...	...	...
Grissett Davis	1	3	2	5	4	...		1 Phaeton
Daniel Dodson	1	5	4	2	5	...	...	...
Maj[r] William Eppes	1	14	14	10	36	...		1 chair
Martha Elliott	..	...	...	3	...	...	...	...
William Ford, Sen[r]	1	3	1	3	21	...	...	...
Jarrell Ford	1	2	3	7	6	...	...	...
Matthew Ford Sen[r]	1	1	...	4	11	...	...	...
Francis Ford	1	...	2	1	...	...	...	...
Henry Ford	1	1	1	2	13	...	...	...
Martin Farrell	1	3	2	4	7	...		1 chair
Elizabeth Fitzhugh	..	13	17	2	8	...	...	...
George Farrell	1	3	...	...	4	...	...	...
Alexander Gordon	1	1	2	2	3	...	...	...
Thomas Gresham	1	..	...	2	4	...	...	...
William Grant	1	1	3	1	...	...	...	...
Younger Hardwick	1	2	...	3	...	...	...	...
Erasmus Hardin	1	3	4	4	15	...	...	...
Col[o] William Heth	..	...	4	2	...	...		1 Phaeton
Frederick Hanky	1	...	...	...	...	...	...	...
Frank Hollaway	1	1	2	3	5	...	...	...
Bazwell Hackney	1	...	...	...	...	...	...	...
Stephen Hamlin	1	20	19	10	30	...		1 Phaeton
James Haldane	1	1	2	3	4	...	...	...

Daniel Jackson	1	1	2	3	10	...	...	...
Joseph Jackson	1	4	...	5	20	...	...	...
Joseph Jones	1	10	5	11	17	...		1 chair
Martha King	..	1	...	2	2	...	...	...
Mary King	..	1	2	2	7	...	...	...
James King	1	...	...	3	...	...	...	...
Capt William Lewis	1	7	8	4	22	...		1 chair
Francis Lewis	1	3	...	4	16	...	...	...
Joseph Lewis	2	...	...	2	16	...	...	...
Wm Lewis								
John Lewis	1	3	6	8	22	...	...	...
William Murrell	1	3	5	3	18	...	...	...
Archibald Minitree	2	1	4	4	18	...	...	...
Bolling Bottom								
Robert Murrell	1	...	...	...	...	...	...	...
Thomas Moon	1	1	1	2	9	...	...	...
Philip Moody	1	...	...	4	8	...	...	...
John Moody	1	2	...	1	6	...	...	...
Mary Murrell	..	2	1	3	9	...	...	...
William Malone	1	3	5	8	7	...	...	...
Archibald Middlemast	1	3	1	3	3	...	...	...
James Murray	1	...	2	...	2	...	...	...
William Minitree	1	1	1	1	...	...	...	...
John Maclin	1	...	...	...	...	...	...	...
John Morriss	1	1	2	...	...	...	...	...
Docr Robt Macky	1	...	...	3	...	...		1 chair
John Nicholas	1	8	7	3	5	...	...	...
Robert Overby	1	...	...	1	4	...	...	...
John Overby		...	...	1	5	...	...	...
Jeremiah Overby	1	2	5	4	14	...	...	...
William Phillips	1	...	...	1	3	...	...	...
George Pegram junr	1	3	...	3	15	...	1	...
Lucy Peterson	..	8	9	4	11	...		1 chair
John Roberts	1	...	...	1	2	...	...	...
Edward Reams	2	1	...	5	13	...	...	...
Robert Reams								
Simon Reams	1	...	1	2	7	...	...	...
Jesse Reams	1	...	...	1	3	...	...	...
Wood Reams	1	1	1	2	7	...	...	...
Henry Randolph	2	7	7	4	...	...	...	...
(and overseer)								

John Roberts	1	...	...	...	...	...	...	...
Capt William Stainback	1	5	5	1	...	...	...	...
Edward Stabler	2	1	...	2	1	...	...	...
Herbert Smith	1	...	...	...	2	...	...	...
Alexander G. Strachan	1	12	12	6	21	...	...	...
George Taylor, overseer								
Alexander G. Strachan	1	6	11	4	2	...		1 charott
At Petersburg								
William Spain Sr.	1	3	10	6	32	...	...	...
Abram Spain	1	...	...	4	13	...	...	...
Robert Spain	1	1	1	4	2	...	...	...
Thomas Spain Junr	1	...	1	3	6	...	...	...
Thomas Spain Senr	1	...	...	5	14	...	...	...
Jno Stewart	1	...	...	...	...	...	...	...
Elizabeth Spencer	..	2	2	4	2	...		1 chair
George Simmons	1	1	2	3	6	...	...	...
James Thweat	1	1	1	4	5	...	...	...
Solomon Tye	1	2	1	3	9	...	...	...
Henry Thweat jun^{r}	1	5	6	5	20	...	...	...
Abram Tally	1	...	...	...	...	...	...	...
David Vaughan	1	1	4	4	9	...		1 chair
John Vaughan	1	2	2	2	2	...	...	...
Samuel Vaughan	1	4	6	5	9	...	...	...
William Williams	1	3	2	4	22	...	...	...
Joshua Wright	1	...	...	2	3	...	...	...
Thomas Woodlife	..	...	1	...	11	...	...	...
John Warren	1	...	...	...	...	...	...	...
Thomas Worsham	1	5	6	4	22	...	...	...
Margarett Wheehouse	..	...	...	1	6	...	...	...
William Watkins	1	15	23	12	112	...	...	...
Abram Wills	1	...	...	3	5	...	...	...
Thomas Walke	1	3	1	1	1	...	...	...
Herbert Wills	1	...	1	1	...	...	...	...
William Wills Senr	1	...	1	3	7	...	...	...
Edward Watlington	1	5	12	4	7	...	...	...
Edmund Williams	1	1	4	2	6	...	...	...
Rachel Williams	...	1	...	3	9	...	...	...
Charles Williams	...	...	...	1	5	...	...	...
(Expd by C^{t}.)								
Noel Waddle	1	1	...	1	...	...	...	...
Robert Watkins	1	...	2	3	...	...	...	...
Frederick Williams	1	3	2	3	2	...		1 chair
James Young	2	7	...	4	...	...	...	...
(Petersburg)								
David Pagan								
Richard Yarbrough	1	11	11	4	24	...	...	...

A List of Tithes & Taxable Property taken by Phillip Jones, Gent 10th April 1782.

Liles Abernathy	1	1	3	4	18	...	...	...
Mary Abernathy	..	...	1	1	...	...	...	...
Signal Abernathy	1	1	1	2	...	...	...	...
Henry Broadnax	1	12	11	11	35	...		1 chair
Robert Bolling (Amelia)	..	6	6	6	20	...	...	...
Estate Ellexr Bolling	..	3	7	4	6	...	...	...
Ambras Brown	1	...	1	1	...	...	...	...
John Burwell	1	19	23	14	17	...		1 chariott
Martha Burrow	..	4	2	2	7	...	...	...
Philip Burrow	1	1	1	3	2	...	...	...
John Burrow	1	7	5	5	15	...	...	...
Henry Burrow	1	4	7	7	18	...	...	...
John Bland (P. George)	..	4	...	2	11	...	...	...
Dudley Brown	1	1	1	2	4	...	...	...
Jeremiah Bishop	1	...	...	2	4	...	...	...
James Bishop	1	...	...	2	2	...	...	...
James Bane	1	...	...	...	...	...	...	...
John Carter	1	2	12	6	17	...	...	...
William Carter	1	6	2	5	20	...	...	...
Harris Carter	1	...	...	2	2	...	...	...
William Carter junr	1	2	1	2	2	...	...	...
Foster Cook	1	3	2	5	6	...	...	...
William Crittington	1	2	...	4	6	...	...	...
William Crawley	1	4	3	2	5	...	...	...
Wm Dunavant								
William Chapple	1	2	...	6	7	...	...	...
John Childs	1	...	...	1	...	...	...	...
William Davis, junr	1	4	7	5	22	...	...	...
Hardaway Davis	..	4	...	5	22	...	...	...
Esta Fredk Dixon	..	3	2	1	5	...	...	...
Randall Daniel	1	4	5	8	7	...	...	...
William Davis, Senr	1	4	3	4	18	...	...	...
William Dwyer	1	...	...	3	10	...	...	...
Patty Darby	..	3	4	1	4	...	...	...
John Dwyer	1	...	...	...	...	...	...	..
Thomas Evans	1	7	14	8	6	...	...	...
Wilmyrth Evans	1	3	4	1	...	...	...	...
William Evans	1	1	...	...	...	...	...	...
William Evans	1	1	...	2	...	...	...	...

Hannah Farley	..	9	12	8	21	...	...	...
Nancy Tailer	..	1	7	...	4	...	...	...
(Failer or Farley?)								
James Floyd	1	1	...	1	...	...	...	...
William Fowler	1	...	...	1	...	...	...	...
Joseph Goodwyn	1	6	8	3	30	...		1 chair
Peterson Goodwyn	1	5	5	5	23	...	...	...
Braddock Goodwyn	1	2	5	5	5	...	...	...
Richard Gregory	1	11	10	5	10	...		1 chariott
John Gibbs	1	1	...	2	8	...	...	...
Richard Graves	1	4	2	7	6	...	...	...
Hannah Goodwyn	..	3	3	5	12	...	...	...
Mark Goodwin	1	...	...	3	3	...	...	...
Richard Garrott	1	...	...	...	...	...	...	...
Doct^{r} James Greenway	1	11	18	10	9	(Vehicles not named)		6
Richard Hill	1	15	19	9	32	...	...	...
Thomas Hardaway	1	7	9	6	21	...	...	...
Thomas Hardaway	1	9	10	11	19	...	...	...
Samuel Harwell Senr	1	6	11	4	23	...	...	...
Samuel Harwell jun^{r}	1	5	3	7	22	...	...	...
John Hardiway	1	2	7	1	2	...	...	...
Samuel Hardaway	1	6	8	5	35	...	...	...
James Harwell	1	3	7	2	10	...	...	...
Jane Harrison	..	4	4	4	11	...	...	...
Edwd Harrison	1	...	...	2	3	...	...	...
Josiah Heath	1	3	1	4	20	...	...	...
Ann Harrison	..	1	3	2	9	...	...	...
Thomas Heath	1	3	3	4	10	...	...	...
Phillamon Hawkins	1	...	...	2	9	...	...	...
Richd Harwell	..	...	...	2	3	...	...	...
Martha High	..	1	...	1	5	...	...	...
John Hood	1	...	...	1	5	...	...	...
Isham Hawkins	1	...	...	2	9	...	...	...
Jane Hawkins	...	...	...	...	4	...	...	...
Hamilton Hawkins	...	...	...	1	6	...	...	...
Joseph Hull	1	...	...	...	...	...	...	...
John Hawkins	1	...	...	2	3	...	...	...
William Harrison	1	1	...	3	4	...	...	...
John Holloway	1	1	4	...	...	...	...	...
Carter Hamlett	1	...	...	1	...	...	...	...
Ishmael Harwell	1	3	3	10	7	...	...	...
Betty Jones	..	7	16	2	8	...		1 chair
Mary Jackson	..	2	...	2	6	...	...	...

Robert Jackson	1	2	1	3	...	...	...	...
William Jackson	1	3	1	4	10	...	...	...
James Jackson	1	...	1	2	4	...	...	...
John Jackson	1	1	2	5	8	...	...	...
James Jennings	1	6	4	11	13	...	...	...
Joel Jackson	1	3	...	4	7	...	...	...
John Jolly	1	...	...	4	2	...	...	...
Phillip Jones (Stony Creek Pltn)	..	6	6	3	15	...	...	...
Edward Jolly	1	...	...	2	...	...	...	...
Lewis Loyd	1	3	5	4	4	...	...	...
Kemmon Loyd	1	...	...	2	3	...	...	...
Miles Lewis	1	...	...	3	3	...	...	...
James Lewis	1	...	...	2	6	...	...	...
Charles Lock	1	1	3	3	5	...	...	...
Lewis Lanier	1	7	...	5	5	...	...	...
Peter Leith	1	...	...	1	...	...	...	...
Winfield Mason	1	17	23	24	65	...	...	...
Daniel Mason	1	11	11	9	20	...	...	...
John Mitchell	1	9	9	7	23	...	...	...
Robert Mitchell	1	5	6	5	14	...	...	...
Francis Moreland	1	6	6	3	5	...	...	...
Hercules Morriss	1	4	5	8	15	...	...	...
William Mitchell	1	1	...	2	4	...	...	...
Henry Mitchell	1	1	...	1	...	...	...	...
James Miles	1	...	...	1	9	...	...	...
Joseph Moreland	1	2	7	4	7	...	...	...
John Moreland	1	1	1	2	...	...	...	...
Michael Malone	1	2	...	4	11	...	...	...
Michael Maidlin	1	...	...	1	4	...	...	...
Richard Maidlin	1	...	...	1	...	...	...	...
Frederick Maidlin	1	...	...	1	...	...	...	...
Jonadab Miles	1	...	...	2	6	...	...	...
Elizabeh Mangram	..	...	1	2	6	...	...	...
Doctr C. Manlove	1	7	7	8	28	(Vehicles not named)		4
Jeremiah Overby	1	...	...	4	8	...	...	...
Antony Overby	1	1	1	2	7	...	...	...
William Osmore	1	...	...	1	3	...	...	...
Seth Pettipool	1	5	6	9	17	...	...	...
John Pettipool	1	...	...	3	6	...	...	...

Joel Pennington	1	2	5	5	17	...	...	...
Nathan Pepper	1	2	...	2	9	...	...	...
William Pettipool	1	...	...	2	...	...	...	...
Benjamin Perkins	1	4	...	5	12	...	...	...
William Pail	1	...	...	2	...	...	...	...
Mary Parish		...	...	3	1	...	...	...
Robert Rivers	1	3	2	4	27	...	...	...
Thomas Roney	1	4	10	5	10	...	...	...
William Rivers	1	3	6	6	12	...	...	...
Susanna Rachell		3	7	3	7	...	...	...
Joel Rivers	1	3	2	5	9	...	...	...
Daniel Raney	1	3	...	4	9	...	...	...
David Robertson	1	3	...	4	2	...	...	...
Thomas Roberts	1	...	...	2	7	...	...	...
John Roberts	1	...	...	1	...	...	...	...
Thomas Roberts junr	1	...	...	...	...	...	...	...
Elizabeth Stark		5	4	5	...	...	...	...
Mary Seward		3	2	5	6	...	...	...
Robert Sturdivant	1	2	1	3	16	...	...	...
Millington Smith	1	3	...	4	15	...	...	...
Winifred Simmons		1	3	2	9	...	...	...
Joseph Simmons	1	2	2	3	10	...	...	...
Richard Smith	1	2	...	3	4	...	...	...
Batt Smith	1	6	3	12	13	...	...	...
William Saunders	1	...	...	1	7	...	...	...
Stephen Saunders	1	...	...	2	4	...	...	...
John Saunders	1	...	...	1	...	...	...	...
Robert Turnbull	3	38	43	19	93	(Vehicle		4
James Thweat	1	8	15	7	26	" not named)		2
Isaac Tucker	1	11	12	10	34	...	...	...
Robert Tucker	1	3	7	5	13	...	...	...
Berryman Tucker	1	2	8	5	9	...	...	...
Joseph Turner	1	4	10	7	23	...	...	...
John Tarpley	1	2	...	4	15	...	...	...
Isaac Tucker	1	3	4	5	6	...	...	...
John Tarpley Senr	1	6	4	4	12	...	...	...
St George Tucker	1	5	6	4	20	...	...	...
Joseph Tucker	1	4	...	4	8	...	...	...
William Thrift	1	...	1	3	...	...	...	...
Drury Thrift	1	...	...	2	3	...	...	...
Richard Turbeville	1	...	...	3	...	...	...	...
James Trotter	1	3	...	4	17	...	...	...
James Vaughan	1	...	...	...	9	...	...	...

Adam Wills Junr	1	1	1	2	...	...	...	...
Robert Watmoreland	1	4	4	4	7	...	...	...
George Wilson	1	2	2	4	8	...	...	...
Robert Wilson	1	2	3	...	...	...	...	...
Jesse Warren	1	2	...	3	9	...	...	...
Isaac Wall	1	3	3	7	11	...	...	...
Adam Wills	1	3	6	3	6	...	...	...
Drury Wills	1	...	...	3	6	...	...	...
Alexander Wills	1	...	...	1	...	...	...	...
Joshua Wynne Senr	1	1	2	1	7	...	...	...
Joshua Wynne, Junr	1	...	...	2	...	...	...	...
Thomas Walker	1	...	...	1	...	...	...	...
Alexander Walker	1	...	...	3	...	...	...	...
David Williams	1	6	2	3	...	...	...	...
Robert Walker	1	26	26	21	63	(Vehicle		4
Randolph Wills	1	...	...	1	2	not named)		
Joshua Wall	1	1	...	2	3	...	...	...
Edward Wyatt	1	11	14	8	13	...		1 chair
Reaves Westmoreland	1	3	3	2	...	...	...	...
Priscilla Walker	..	4	5	3	4	...	...	...
Susanna Wynne	..	1	...	2	4	...	...	...
Thomas Westmoreland	1	10	8	...	...	...	...	...
Robert Wynne	1	2	...	4	3	...	...	...
James Warren	1	5	3	4	21	...	...	...
Peter Wall	1	1	...	2	1	...	...	...
John Wall	1	...	...	...	...	...	...	...
Estate Freeman Walker	..	1	...	2	...	...	...	...
Edward Young	1	4	5	8	27	...	...	...
Reuben Yarmouth	1	...	...	1	1	...	...	...

A true copy teste

July 27th 1782. Jno Nicholas, C. D. C.

849 whites	£ 424	10	—
2679 Blacks above 16			
3067 Blacks under 16			
5746 Blacks	2873	—	—
3130 horses	313	—	—
9178 Cattle	114	14	6
180 wheels	45	—	—
4 licence	20	—	—
2 Billiard Tables	100	—	—
	£3890	4	6

A POLL

for the Election of Burgesses for the County of Elizabeth City, when Coll° John Tabb & Capt William Wager were chosen July 11th 1758

Coll° John Tabb	Capt Wm Wager	Capt Cary Selden
Augustine Moore	John Poole	John Poole
John Parsons	John Loyell	John Loyell
John Buck	John Minson	Starkey Robinson
Thomas Kerby	Starkey Robinson	Robert Brough
John Minson	George Wray	Thomas Butt
Banister Minson	Banister Minson	Charles Pasteur
Janey Latimer	Janey Latimer	David Davis
James Naylor	James Naylor	Wm Armistead
Robert Tucker	Robert Brough	Joseph Selden
William Loyell	Robert Tucker	Henry Batts
Joseph Meredith	Thomas Butt	George Waff
William Read	John Nelson	Richard Bickardick
Thomas Hawkins	Charles Pasteur	James Brown
William Baker	David Davis	John Shepard jun^{r}
William Naylor	William Armistead	Morris Jones
Henry Allen	Joseph Selden	Robert Hundley
William Smelt	Henry Batts	Francis Ballard
Samuel Tompkins	Joseph Meredith	George Thomas
Cary Mitchell	George Waff	Richd Wilsen
John Jones	Richard Bickardick	John Hicks
John Tabb jun^{r}	William Read	Richd Wallis
John Matthews (S)	Thomas Hawkins	William Baylis
John Lowry	James Brown	Joseph Jegitts
Johnson Mallory	William Baker	Edward Ward
Edwd Latimer	John Shepard jun^{r}	Minson Proby
Mallory Ross	William Naylor	Henry Robinson
Thomas Skinner	Morris Jones	Bertram Servant
William Cross	Robert Hundley	William Williams
John Smith	William Smelt	Daniel Ronton
Joseph Banister	Francis Ballard	Thomas Watts jun^{r}
John Armistead	George Thomas	Thomas Dixon
Thomas Watts	Peter Puryear	Charles Cooper
Owen Dailie	Cary Mitchell	Thomas Wooten
John Moore	John Jones	Thomas Smith
Saml Roland	Thomas Skinner	Saml Dubery
John Casey	John Smith	Robert Armistead

King Umphlet
John Kerby
William Ballard
Merritt Moore
John Creek
Carter Tarrant
Joseph Jequitts
Peter Pierce
Tho[s] Skinner jun[r]
Thomas Davis
John Stores
Nicholas Bailey
James Allen
John Herbert
Thomas Latimer
Thomas Baylis jun[r]
William Latimer
Frazey Stores
Sidney Parish
Philip Cooper
George Walker
Anthony Hawkins
Christopher Pierce
William Dumn
John Sheparrd

Joseph Banister
John Armistead
Thomas Watts
Own Dailie
Samuel Roland
John Casey
King Umphlett
Benj[a] Lester
Richard Wilson
John Hicks
William Ballard
Samuel Curle
John Creek
Benj[a] Ham
Carter Tarrant
Rich[d] Wallace
William Baylis
Peter Pierce
Thomas Skinner jun[r]
Thomas Davis
Edward Ward
John Stores
Minson Probey
Henry Robinson
Nicholas Bayley

William Wager

CAP[T] ROSCOW SWEENEY

Augustine Moore
John Parsons
John Buck
Thomas Kerby
Henry Allen
Johnson Mallory
Edward Latimer
William Cross
John Kerby
Meritt Moore
William Wager
James Wallace
John Tabb

ROBERT BROUGH

Samuel Curle
Benj[a] Hamm

GEORGE WYTHE

Benj[a] Lester

ESSEX COUNTY: AN ANNOTATED COPY OF THE RENT ROLL OF 1704 *

By John Bailey Calvert Nicklin

William Abbott.
James Acres (appears also on the Rent Roll of 1715) (See this Magazine, vol. 18, pps. 203-6).
William Acres (died in Richmond Co., 1714).
Edward Adcock (married Elizabeth Smith).
Henry Adcock (d. 1738).
Erasmus Allen (d. 1720; married Dinah Waggoner. 100 acres in 1704 and 350 in 1715).
William Allen. (d. 1739; married Margaret Waggoner). 100 acres on both Rolls.
George Andrews.
William Arvin. 100 acres on both Rolls.
William Ayres (d. 1705; married, license dated April 7, 1694, Anne Smith).
Henry Baker (d. 1743?). He appears on both Rolls.
John Ball (d. 1707). Charged with 150 acres in 1704.
Andrew Barron.
Thomas Bartlett (married Patience Bentley). Charged with 100 acres in 1704 and 50 in 1715.
John Battaile (d. 1706; married Catherine Taliaferro and Elizabeth Smith).
John Baylor (d. 1721; married Lucy Todd O'Brien). Charged with 800 acres in 1704 and 300 in 1715.
Symon Beckham (d. 1716).
William Beesley (d. 1719). Charged with 100 acres in 1704 and 200 in 1715.
Thomas Bell (d. 1748?). Charged with 100 acres in 1704 and 50 in 1715.
John Bendall.
Widow Bendry. (Evidently of William who died 1701).
William Berry of Richmond Co. (Died in King George Co., 1721; married Margaret Doughty).
Harry Beverley (Died in Spotsylvania Co., in 1730; married Elizabeth Smith). On both Rolls.
Mary Billington (d. 1727). (Widow of John Billington who died 1700?).
Widow Bird (Arabella, widow of Randall Bird who died 1703? He married Arabella White).
Robert Bizwell.
Robert Bizwell, Jr. (d. 1761?).
Argol Blackstone (d. 1722).
Widow Booth (Phoebe, widow of Humphrey who died 1702).
Henry Boughan (d. 1736?). He was charged with 100 acres on both Rolls.
James Boughan, Sr. (d. 1712; married Sarah Brown.
James Boughan (Jr.?) (d. 1718). Charged with 150 acres on both Rolls. He married Sarah, daughter of Thomas Edmundson (d. 1715).
James Boulware (d. 1718). Charged with 1000 acres which in 1715 were charged to James, Mark and James Boulware, Jr., as follows: 550, 225 and 225 acres. He married Margery, daughter of William Gray (d. 1673).
John Boulware (d. 1714). He married Susanna, daughter of John Williams (q. v.).
John Bourne (d. 1721).
Arthur Bowers.

*See pp. 545-556, this volume.

Peter Bowman. Charged with 400 acres on both Rolls.
Richard Bradburn.
———— Brakin's Quarter.
John Brazier (d. 1712). Married Elizabeth Holt, who survived him and married William Hudson (q. v.).
Henry Brice (d. 1724; married Susannah Miller) (d. 1725). Charged with 400 acres on both Rolls.
John Bridgate (Bridger?) of England.
Peter Brook (d. 1710).
Robert Brooke (d. 1744?). Married Catherine Booth.
William Brooking's Quarter. He married Susannah Upshaw.
James Brooks.
Robert Brooks.
Burkenham Brown (d. 1735, aged 64; married Elizabeth Maestiche) (sic). Charged with 400 acres in 1704 and 596 in 1715.
Charles Brown (d. 1727; married Susanna Berry).
Daniel Brown, Sr. (d. 1708).
Daniel Brown, Jr. (Died in Orange Co., 1747; married Elizabeth Coleman).
Francis Browne (d. 1709; married Elizabeth, daughter of Mary Allen).
Thomas Brown.
William Brown (d. 1705; married Frances Moss and Elizabeth Allen).
Richard Brush.
Richard Brutnall (d. 1717).
Richard Buckner. Died in Caroline Co., 1733; married Elizabeth Cooke. Charged with 1200 acres in 1704 and 1400 in 1715.
Thomas Buckner.
William Buckner of Gloucester Co.
John Burnett (d. 1717; married Amy Gatewood). Charged with 365 acres in 1704 and 425 in 1715.
Thomas Burnett, Jr. (d. 1749?). He married Jane, admx. of John Powell (d. 1699).
John Butcher (d. 1710).
John Butler (d. 1717).
Henry Byrom (d. 1718). Charged with 100 acres in 1704 and 430 in 1715.
Joseph Callaway.
Hugh Cary (d. 1753?). Charged with 50 acres on both Rolls.
John Catlett (d. 1724; married Elizabeth Taliaferro). Charged with 1800 acres on both Rolls.
Leonard Chamberlain (d. 1709).
Larkin Chew. Died in Spotsylvania Co., 1729; married Hannah Roy (d. 1743).
John Cheyney (d. 1740?). One Cheyney married Rachel, daughter of Erasmus Allen (q. v.).
William Cheyney (d. 1727). Charged with 700 acres in 1704 and 450 in 1715.
Samuel Coates. (Died in Richmond Co., in 1718; married Margaret Watkins).
Symon Cobnall (d. 1705).
Thomas Coggan (d. 1707).
Frederick Coghill (d. 1715). Charged with 250 acres in 1704 (as Cogwell) and with 300 in 1715.
William Cole (d. 1710). Charged with 200 acres on both Rolls.
Robert Coleman (d. 1712; married Anne Spilsby, who survived him and married John Hunter (d. 1721). She died 1717.
William Compton (d. 1751?). Charged with 50 acres on both Rolls.
Nathaniel Conduit (d. 1730).
Edmund Connelly (d. 1738). Charged with 200 acres on both Rolls.

John Cook (d. 1727). Charged with 112 acres in 1704 and 150 in 1715.
Richard Cooper (d. 1736). Charged with 100 acres on both Rolls.
Thomas Cooper (d. 1709).
William Cooper (d. 1730; married Elizabeth, daughter of Mary Billington) (q. v.). Charged with 50 acres in 1704 and 200 in 1715.
John Copeland. Charged with 175 acres in 1704 and 50 in 1715.
Nicholas Copeland (d. 1720).
Gawin Corbin's Quarter. He died in 1744; married Catherine Wormley and Jane Lane. On both Rolls.
Thomas Corbin's Quarter. Charged with 440 acres in 1704 and 4000 in 1715.
Richard Covington (d. 1726; married Anne Young). He was the maker of this Roll.
William Covington (d. 1721). Charged with 400 acres in 1704 and 530 in 1715.
William Cox.
John Crow (d. 1718). Charged with 440 acres in 1704 and 886 in 1715.
Thomas Crow (d. 1708).
John Daingerfield (d. 1720; married Margaret Gaines and Mary Conway, who survived him and married Maj. James Ball (d. 1754).
William Daingerfield (d. 1735). Charged with 270 acres in 1704 and 970 in 1715. (Married Elizabeth Tomlin).
James Daniel (d. 1742?).
Evans Davies. Charged with 150 acres on both Rolls.
Thomas Davis (d. 1718). Charged with 150 acres in 1704 and 250 in 1715.
Richard Day (married Mary Bunbury).
Thomas Dicks (probably Thomas Dixon who died 1711).
Jacob Divilliard.
Daniel Dobbins (d. 1712; married Elizabeth Smith).
John Doughty.
Timothy Driscall (d. 1716).
Andrew Dudding (d. 1713; married Esther Dyke).
William Dunn (d. 1732). Charged with 220 acres in 1704 and 400 in 1715.
Jeffrey Dyer (d. 1716).
William Dyer (d. 1714).
James Edmundson (d. 1734; married Judith Parr). Charged with 500 acres in 1704 and 350 in 1715.
Thomas Edmundson (d. 1715).
Alice Ellett (d. 1720 and widow of John Ellett who died 1700).
Rees Evans (d. 1713).
Thomas Evet (d. 1729). Charged with 100 acres in 1704 and 150 in 1715.
John Farguson (d. 1717; married Anne Stubleson (d. 1735). Charged with 150 acres on both Rolls.
Charles Farrell (d. 1727).
Edward Faulkner (d. 1722). Charged with 530 acres in 1704 and 540 in 1715.
Nicholas Faulconer (d. 1743). Charged with 100 acres on both Rolls.
Benjamin Fisher (d. 1716; married Elizabeth Boughan). Charged with 150 acres in 1704 and 225 in 1715.
Jonathan Fisher.
Isaac Flowers (d. 1723).
William Fossett. Charged with 100 acres on both Rolls.
John Foster (d. 1710?) (but a John Foster appears on both Rolls charged with 300 acres!).
Robert Foster (d. 1715). Charged with 200 acres in 1704 and 350 in 1715.
Thomas Frank (d. 1715).

Nicholas Franklin.
James Fullerton (d. 1714).
Bernard Gaines (Died in Richmond Co., 1749?). He married Martha Taylor and appears on both Rolls.
John Gaines (d. 1722).
William Gannocke (d. 1710).
John Garnett (d. 1714).
Thomas Garnett (d. 1743?). Charged with 1000 acres in 1704 and 150 in 1715.
John Gatewood (d. 1706). He married Amy ——— who survived him and married Joseph Baker (d. 1720). She died 1745.
Jonathan Gibson (Died in King George Co., 1729).
John Glover.
Edward Golding.
John Golding.
William Golding (d. 1747; married Anne Short). Charged with 200 acres on both Rolls.
Richard Goode (d. 1719). Charged with 200 acres on both Rolls.
William Gording (d. 1723). Charged with 100 acres on both Rolls.
Price Gould.
Francis Gouldman (d. 1716; married Martha Tomlin).
Abner Gray (d. 1717). He married Sarah ——— (d. 1733).
George Green (d. 1706; married Elizabeth Clapham, who survived him and married Richard West (d. 1711); she died 1722.
Samuel Green (d. 1709).
Thomas Gregson (d. 1705; married Anne Cooper, who survived him and married James Alderson (d. 1732). She died 1733.
Thomas Griffen (d. 1720).
William Grimmall (sic) (William Greenhill died 1726). Charged with 100 acres on both Rolls.
David Gwyn's Quarter. He married Catherine Fauntleroy and died in Richmond Co., 1705.
John Haile (dead in 1714/5). Charged with 900 acres in 1704 and 700 in 1715. He married Anne ——— who survived him and married Thomas Cox.
Henry Harman (dead in 1715; married Sarah ———).
John Harper.
Thomas Harper (d. 1709).
William Harper (d. 1714).
Andrew Harrison (d. 1718).
James Harrison (d. 1712; married Elizabeth Mott).
Peter Harrood (d. 1709). He married Mary ——— who survived him and married Owen Owens (d. 1749).
Samuel Harwar (d. 1710).
Thomas Harwar (d. 1713).
John Hawkins (d. 1726).
John Hay's Quarter. He died 1709; married Anne Robinson.
Samuel Henshaw (d. 1719).
Leonard Hill (d. 1728). Charged with 300 acres on both Rolls.
Thomas Hilliard (d. 1718). Charged with 100 acres on both Rolls.
Thomas Hinds (d. 1709).
Arthur Hodges.
Richard Holt.
David Hould.
Alexander How's Quarter. He died 1722.
Thomas Howerton. Charged with 175 acres in 1704 and 200 in 1715.

Thomas Hudson (d. 1706). In 1704 he was charged with 50 acres and in 1715 Henry Hudson was charged with 150 acres.
William Hudson (Jr.) (d. 1729; married Elizabeth Brazier). Charged with 100 acres on both Rolls.
Joseph Humphreys (d. 1706).
David Jameson (d. 1711); married Mary ——————, who survived him and married Richard Edwards (d. 1722).
David Jenkins (d. 1706).
John Jenkins (sic) (John Jenkinson died 1712).
Thomas Jewell. Charged with 100 acres in 1704 and 149 in 1715.
Widow Johnson (Christian, widow of Henry who died 1703. She died 1713 and was Christian Bourne).
Richard Johnson. (Died in Spotsylvania Co., 1726. Married Jael Williams (d. 1733). Charged with 50 acres in 1704 and 600 in 1715.
Thomas Johnson.
William Johnson (d. 1729).
John Jones (d. 1706). Charged with 300 acres on both Rolls.
Rice Jones (d. 1728). Charged with 500 acres on both Rolls.
Richard Jones (Jr.) (d. 1735). Charged with 350 acres in 1704 and 340 in 1715.
Walter Jones. Charged with 100 acres on both Rolls.
William Jones (d. 1743?). Charged with 465 acres in 1704 and 415 in 1715.
William Journey (d. 1705).
Robert Key (d. 1726; married Mary Waight). Charged with 209 acres in 1704 and 200 in 1715.
Henry Kirbey.
John Lacy.
James Landrum (d. 1739; married Mary Brown) (d. 1754?).
John Landrum (d. 1707).
Lewis Latane (d. 1733; married Phoebe, daughter of Phoebe Slaughter). Charged with 250 acres on both rolls.
John Law (sic) (John Lawrence died 1721).
Claude Lawson.
Robert Leveritt.
———— Leverson's Quarter.
John Lightfoot, Esq. of New Kent Co. (d. 1707; married Anne Goodrich).
Abraham Little. Charged with 60 acres in 1704 and 50 in 1715.
John Lomax (d. 1729; married Elizabeth Wormley).
Richard Long.
George Loyd (d. 1713; married Johanna Diskin).
David Magcon (sic).
John Maguffey.
John Martin (d. 1716). Charged with 400 acres in 1704 and 216 in 1715.
Benjamin Matthews (d. 1722). Charged with 200 acres on both Rolls.
Richard Mathews (d. 1705; married Elizabeth Spicer).
Robert Mayfield (d. 1714).
John Meader (d. 1721). Charged with 100 acres on both Rolls.
Thomas Meader (d. 1717). Charged with 300 acres in 1704 and 500 in 1715.
Francis Meriwether (d. 1713; married Mary Bathurst, who survived him and married Reubin Welch (d. 1729) whom she also survived and married John Robinson of Spotsylvania Co.
Thomas Meriwether (d. 1708; married Elizabeth Williamson).
John Merritt. Charged with 100 acres in 1704 and 95 in 1715.
Thomas Merritt. (Died in Lancaster Co., 1717?).

John Michael.
Paul Micou (d. 1736; married Margaret, who died 1740, daughter of Margaret Cammock). Charged with 150 acres in 1704 and 575 in 1715.
Lath (sic) (Nath?) Mifflin. ——— Mifflin married Mary, widow of John Dyke, and died before 1710.
Zachary Mifflin.
John Miller (d. 1743).
John Mice (sic) (Mize or Size?).
William Montague (d. 1710).
John Moody (d. 1738). Charged with 150 acres on both Rolls.
John Morgan (d. 1733). Charged with 100 acres in 1704 and 150 in 1715.
John Morris (d. 1720; married Dorcas Sorrell).
John Morse.
Benjamin Moseley (d. 1709).
Edward Moseley (d. 1727). Charged with 550 acres in 1704 and 450 in 1715.
Robert Moseley (d. 1707).
Robert Moss (d. 1714).
John Motley (d. 1736).
Thomas Munday (d. 1719; married Elizabeth Harrison).
Salvator Muscoe (d. 1741; married Mary Hucklescott) (d. 1750). Charged with 100 acres in 1704 and 130 in 1715.
Nathaniel Newbury (sic) (Nathaniel Newbill died 1743).
Henry Newton (d. 1713). Charged with 275 acres in 1704 and 100 in 1715.
Nicholas Newton (Nickles Newton died 1708).
John Nightingale (d. 1705).
Henry Nixson. (Died in Middlesex Co., 1709?).
Widow Noell (of Cornelius who was naturalized in 1686 and died in 1697).
Daniel Noell.
William North (d. 1706).
James Osman (d. 1708).
Edmund Paget (d. 1722).
John Parker (d. 1712; married Martha Tandy).
Samuel Parry (d. 1707).
Widow Payne (of Robert who died 1701 and married Catherine Thompson who died in 1704).
John Payne (d. 1710).
Thomas Peteras (sic) (Thomas Pettit who died 1720?).
John Pettus of King & Queen Co.
John Pickett.
John Piskell (John Pickles who died in Westmoreland Co., 1733?). Charged with 300 acres in 1704 and 250 in 1715 as John Pickles.
John Pitts (d. 1730).
Widow Pley (of Robert who died 1697 and married Elizabeth Parker who died 1719). She was widow of Thomas (d. 1697). Elizabeth Pley was charged with 200 acres in 1715 while the Widow Pley was charged with 800 acres in 1704!
Samuel Poe (d. 1725).
Honor (sic) Powell (Probably Honoria, widow of John Powell who died 1703).
Place Powell (d. 1717).
Thomas Powell.
William Powell. (Died in Richmond Co., 1714?).
John Price (d. 1713).
William Price (d. 1718). Charged with 100 acres on both Rolls.
Roger Pritchard (d. 1721). Charged with 167 acres in 1704 and 100 in 1715.

John Prosser (d. 1706).
Henry Purkins (d. 1736). Henry Purkins, *Jr.*, married Cary Caston and died 1739.
Thomas Ramsey (d. 1745?). Charged with 550 acres in 1704 and 500 in 1715.
Peter Ransom (married Dorothy, daughter of Dorothy Henry). Charged with 300 acres in 1704. *Robert* Ransom was charged with 700 acres in 1715.
Peter Ransom's Quarter.
Henry Rebs (sic) (Henry Reeves who died 1729?).
James Reeves (d. 1707).
Joseph Reeves (d. 1717). Charged with 200 acres on both Rolls.
James Renolds, Sr. (d. 1724). Charged with 500 acres on both Rolls.
James Renolds, (Jr.?) (d. 1731; married Sara Carber). Charged with 500 acres on both Rolls.
Robert Richardson.
John Ridgdall.
Edmond Roberts (d. 1705).
John Roberts (Died in Spotsylvania Co., 1724?). Charged with 50 acres in 1704 and 70 in 1715.
Christopher Robinson's Quarter. (Died in Middlesex Co., 1727; married Judith Wormley Corbin Beverley. (d. 1720).
Edward Rowzee (d. 1720; married Mary Pierce, who survived him and married Dr. Henry Oswald (d. 1726). She died 1728. Charged with 300 acres in 1704 and 400 in 1715.
Ralph Rowzee (d. 1719; married Mary Gaines and Rebecca Tomlin). First marriage conjectural!
John Royston (Died in Spotsylvania Co., 1748?).
Peter Rucker (Died in Orange Co., 1743; married Elizabeth Fielding). Charged with 500 acres in 1704 and 56 in 1715.
Cornelius Sale (d. 1746?). Charged with 73 acres in 1704 and 640 in 1715.
Widow Sallis (of Samuel who died 1703/4; he married Sarah Taliaferro who married Samuel Short later).
John Salmon.
Anthony Samuel (d. 1731). Charged with 300 acres in 1704 and 550 in 1715.
John Sanders (Died in Richmond Co., 1719?). Charged with 300 acres in 1704 and 766 in 1715.
William Scott (d. 1716).
Francis Shackleford (married Frances Gatewood).
Henry Shackleford. Charged with 50 acres in 1704 and 100 in 1715.
Jeremiah Shepherd (d. 1744).
John Shipley (d. 1720). Charged with 200 acres on both Rolls.
Josias Shipp (d. 1706).
Thomas Short (d. 1740; married Katherine ————.). Charged with 150 acres in 1704 and 800 in 1715.
Phoebe Slaughter (widow of William. She died 1710). She was also widow of William Hodgskin (d. 1673).
Charles Smith (d. 1710).
Francis Smith (Died in Spotsylvania Co., 1746?).
John Smith (d. 1744?). He married Elizabeth, daughter of John Cox (d. 1695).
John Smith's Quarter.
John Smith, Esq. of Gloucester Co. (d. 1712; married Anne Alexander).
Jonas Smith.
Thomas Smith (d. 1743?).

William Smith (Died in Richmond Co., 1714? He married Eve Williams who died 1705). Charged with 150 acres in 1704 and 650 in 1715.
William Smith's Quarter.
Thomas Snead (married Phoebe Wilson).
Job Spearman. Charged with 300 acres in 1704 and 470 in 1715.
John Spiers (d. 1744).
Samuel Stallard (d. 1720).
Thomas Staners (sic) (Stanard?).
John Stanton (d. 1718).
Abraham Stapp (d. 1714; married Dorothy Moss).
John Stephens (d. 1724). Charged with 100 acres on both Rolls.
John Stodgell.
Richard Stokes (d. 1711).
Thomas Streshley (d. 1735; married ——— Carber). Charged with 200 acres on both Rolls.
John Strong (d. 1718). Charged with 100 acres on both Rolls.
Peter Sullenger (d. 1706; married Elizabeth Clotworthy).
Charles Taliaferro (d. 1721; married Anne Kemp, who survived him and married Edward Evans (d. 1726). Charged with 300 acres in 1704 and 1820 in 1715.
Francis Taliaferro (d. 1710; married Elizabeth Catlett) (d. 1717).
John Taliaferro (d. 1720; married Sarah Smith). Charged with 2000 acres in 1704 and 1200 in 1715.
Richard Taylor (d. 1742). Charged with 650 acres in 1704 and 350 in 1715.
Samuel Thacker (d. 1713; married Mary Keeling who survived him and married Rev. John Bagge (d. 1726). She also died 1726.
Widow Tharpe (of Thomas who died 1703/4).
John Thomas (d. 1712).
Robert Thomas's Quarter (d. 1714).
William Thomas (Died in Spotsylvania Co., 1726?). Charged with 200 acres in 1704 and 300 in 1715.
Samuel Thompson (Died in Surry Co., 1721; married Mary Marriott who predeceased him).
Francis Thornton (Died in Spotsylvania Co., 1752? He married Mary Taliaferro). Charged with 700 acres in 1704 and 1100 in 1715.
Matthew Tilley.
Thomas Tinsley (d. 1715).
Thomas Todd's Quarter (d. 1720; married Elizabeth ———.). Charged with 550 acres in 1704 and 1100 in 1715.
Widow Tomlin (of Thomas who died 1704. He married Rebecca ———.). (d. 1714).
William Tomlin (d. 1709; married Elizabeth Bathurst who survived him and married William Daingerfield (d. 1735).
Peter Trible (d. 1738).
George Turner.
William Upshaw's Quarter (d. 1720; married Hannah Carber, who died 1763). Charged with 1000 acres in 1704 and 800 in 1715.
Vincent Vass (d. 1727; married Anne Sharp). Charged with 450 acres in 1704 and 250 in 1715.
Bartholomew Vawter (d. 1717). Charged with 400 acres in 1704 and 450 in 1715.
Job Virgett (d. 1713). He married Elizabeth Gibson, extrx. of John Gray (d. 1695).
John Waggener (d. 1716, aged 73; married Rachel ——— who died in 1718 aged 58). He was charged with 400 acres in 1704 and 100 in 1715.

William Wakeland.
Widow Ward (of William who died in Middlesex Co., in 1703?).
George Ward (b. 1651).
John Waters (d. 1711), married Katherine ——— who survived him and married Edward Price.
Thomas Watkins (d. 1707).
William Wead (sic).
Isaac Webb (d. 1729). Charged with 200 acres on both Rolls.
James Webb (d. 1716). Charged with 200 acres in 1704 and 100 in 1715.
John Webb (d. 1713; married Anne Smith).
Robert Webb. Charged with 375 acres in 1704 and 330 in 1715.
Edward Weedon.
Thomas Wheeler (d. 1719. Probably married Elizabeth Gregory).
Widow Whitehorn (Ann, widow of Daniel. She died 1715).
Emanuel Williams (d. 1737). Charged with 100 acres in 1704 and 450 in 1715.
John Williams (d. 1712; married Elizabeth Lawson).
William Williams (d. 1712; married Jael Harrison). Charged with 100 acres on both Rolls.
John Williamson (d. 1744?). Charged with 100 acres in 1704 and 200 in 1715.
Thomas Williamson. Charged with 100 acres on both Rolls.
William Williamson (d. 1743?).
David Wilson.
Richard Wilton (d. 1711). Charged with 150 acres in 1704 and one of same name charged with 120 acres in 1715.
Henry Winslow.
Thomas Winslow (d. 1726; married Anne Parker). Charged with 150 acres in 1704 and 298 in 1715.
Thomas Wood (d. 1709).
Henry Woodnott. Charged with 300 acres in 1704 and 100 in 1715.
Richard Wyatt of King & Queen Co. (married Katherine Long).
Giles Young (b. 1652).
William Young (d. 1718). Charged with 1000 acres in 1704 and 1700 in 1715.

N. B.—I have corrected the spelling of these proper names whenever and wherever possible. Whoever compiled this Rent Roll spelled as he pleased or as a name sounded to him!

QUIT RENT ROLL FOR THE YEAR 1715—ESSEX COUNTY, VIRGINIA

Contributed by JOHN BAILEY CALVERT NICKLIN

Names.	*Acres.*
James Acres	100
John Adcock	50
Erasmus Allen	350
William Allen	100
John Armstrong	100
William Arvin	100
Thomas Ayres	150
Henry Baker	350
Joseph Baker	250
John Ball	1100
Richard Ballard	50
Sarah Barefoot	150
Thomas Bartlett	50
John Baylor	300
James Beckham	70
William Beckham	200
William Beezley	200
William Beezley, Jr.	50
John Bell	50
Robert Bell	100
Thomas Bell	50
George Berry	140
Harry Beverly	3840
Robert Beverly	488
Elias Blackburn	150
Edmund Booker	250
Edmund Booker	100
Henry Boughan	100
Joseph Bowton	320
James Boulware	550
James Boulware, Jr.	225
Mark Boulware	225
Thomas Bourn	300
William Bourn	100
Peter Bowman	400
William Bradburne	100
Richard Brazier	250
Henry Brice	400
William Brisden	50
Richard Brook	75
William Brook	100
Thomas Brooks	75
Abraham Brown	150
Burkenham Brown	596
Henry Brown	300
Lancelot Brown	220
William Brown	150
Thomas Bryant	300
Richard Buckner	1400
William Burch	100
John Burnett	425
Thomas Burnett	200
Richard Bush	242
Henry Byrom	430
Peter Byvelin	300
John Cammack	1050
Richard Carter	150
Hugh Cary	50
Colo. (John) Catlett	1800
John Catlett, Jr.	500
William Cheyney	450
Rawleigh Chinn	500
Richard Cocke, Jr.	700
Frederick Coghill	300
John Coghill	250
William Cole	200
Richard Collier	17
Mathew Collins	700
John Combs	200
William Compton	50
Edmund Connely	200
John Cook	150
Richard Cooper	100
Richard Cooper	100
William Cooper	200
John Copeland	50
Gawin Corbin	900
William Covington	530

Names.	*Acres.*	*Names.*	*Acres.*
William Covington	450	Richard Goode, Jr.	150
Mathew Cox	50	William Gording	100
Thomas Cox	100	Francis Graves	300
John Croft	180	John Graves	50
John Croswell	200	Thomas Graves	200
John Crow	886	Peter Greble	100
William Daingerfield	970	William Grenall	100
William Daniel	300	Elizabeth Gugee	80
Evans Davis	150	John Haile	700
Thomas Davis	250	John Hainey, Jr.	900
John Dickerson	190	Sarah Harmon	75
James Dicks	170	John Hart	118
Thomas Dicks	284	Henry Harway	170
Nathaniel Driscoll	150	Henry Hill	100
William Dunn	400	Leonard Hill	300
John Dyer	170	Richard Hill	350
Benjamin Edmundson	175	Thomas Hilliard	100
James Edmundson	350	Nathaniel Hogg	175
Mary Edmundson	600	James Holloway	100
Robert Elliott	600	John Hoskins	70
Samuel Elliott	310	Joseph Hoskins	70
Henry Emberson	150	Daniel Howell	600
Edward Evans	300	James Howell	250
Thomas Evet	150	Thomas Howerton	200
John Farguson	150	Henry Hudson	150
Nicholas Faulconer	100	William Hudson, Jr.	100
Edward Faulkener	540	John Hunter	75
Benjamin Fisher	225	Thomas Jefferies	100
Ann Fitzhugh	9019	Thomas Jewell	149
William Fossett	100	John Johnes	60
John Foster	300	Richard Johnson	600
Robert Foster	350	William Johnson	450
John Fox	100	John Jones	70
Mathew Frank	150	John Jones	300
Bernard Gaines	450	Rice Jones	500
John Games	150	Richard Jones, Jr.	340
James Garnett	200	Samuel Jones	180
Thomas Garnett	150	Walter Jones	100
Richard Gatewood	90	William Jones	300
Thomas Gatewood	150	William Jones	115
Thomas Gatewood	150	Matthew Kemp	40
Paul Gibbons	50	Patrick Kernall	50
William Golding	200	Robert Key	200
Richard Goode	200	Lewis Latané	250

Names.	*Acres.*	*Names.*	*Acres.*
Edward Lawrence	198	Giles Page	200
Joseph Leman	250	Francis Pagett	200
David Lewis	200	Robert Parker	125
John Linitt	150	Robert Payne	2400
Abraham Little	50	John Pendleton	200
Gabriel Long	100	Henry Perkins	200
John Long	200	Henry Perkins, Jr.	100
Dack Lowere	500	Aaron Perry	30
Arthur Mackdaniell	50	John Pickells	250
John Mackemy	100	William Pickett	300
John Mackemy	100	Godfrey Piles	150
William Mackemy	200	Elizabeth Pley	200
John Madoro	150	Richard Price	150
Benjamin Martin	100	William Price	100
Henry Martin	97	Roger Pritchard	100
John Martin	100	Thomas Ramsey	500
John Martin	116	Robert Ransom	700
James Masters	100	Henry Reeves	850
Benjamin Matthews	200	Joseph Reeves	200
John Meader	100	Cornelius Reynolds	50
John Meader, Jr.	150	James Reynolds, Sr.	500
Thomas Meader	500	James Reynolds, Jr.	500
Richard Meador	150	Thomas Ripley	100
Thomas Meadows	100	John Roberts	70
Major Meriwether	1800	Henry Robinson	400
John Merritt	95	John Row	150
Joseph Merritt	30	Edward Rowzee	400
Paul Micou	575	Peter Rucker	56
John Mills	200	St. Anne's Glebe	140
John Mitchell	160	Thomas St. John	100
John Moody	150	William St. John	375
Robert Moody	100	Cornelius Sale	640
Francis Moore	125	Anthony Samuel	550
John Moore	150	Anthony Samuel, Jr.	100
Thomas Moore	200	James Samuel	100
John Morgan	150	John Sanders	766
John Morgan	100	James Scott	600
Edward Mosely	450	Margaret Scott	600
William Mosely	200	Henry Shackelford	100
Salvator Muscoe	130	Stephen Sharp	2000
James Newball	200	William Sheperd	200
Henry Newton	100	John Shiply	200
Jane Olive	70	Thomas Short	800
Owen Owen	75	Daniel Smith	41

Names.	*Acres.*	*Names.*	*Acres.*
Joseph Smith	750	Nathanial Vicars	200
Nicholas Smith	1000	William Viccary	50
William Smith	50	Herbert Wagoner	200
William Smith	600	John Wagoner	100
William Snither	200	Charles Waller	200
Job Speerman	470	Thomas Waring	150
John Spicer	2500	John Watkins	200
William Stanard	1485	Isaac Webb	200
Godfrey Stanton	280	James Webb	100
George Stapleton	200	James Webb, Jr.	300
John Stephens	100	Idem for Fullerton	300
Thomas Streshley	200	Richard Webb	200
John Strong	100	Robert Webb	330
Charles Taliaferro	1820	Elizabeth Weedon	50
John Taliaferro, Jr.	1200	William West	100
Richard Taylor	350	John Willard	150
William Taylor	50	Martin Willard	70
Edwin and John Thacker	817	Emanuel Williams	450
John and Edwin Thacker	817	Joseph Williams	100
William Tharpe	250	Thomas Williams	100
William Thomas	300	William Williams	100
William Thomas	200	John Williamson	200
Francis Thornton	1100	Thomas Williamson	100
Rowland Thornton	400	Richard Wilton	120
Thomas Todd	1100	Thomas Winslow	298
Joseph Trohard	200	William Winston	450
James Turner	200	John Wood	200
William Upshaw	800	William Woodford	2600
John Vass	490	Henry Woodnott	100
Vincent Vass	250	William Young	1700
Bartholomew Vawter	450		

This list was made and arranged alphabetically from the copy among the Miscellaneous Manuscript Papers in the Archives Division of the Virginia State Library and bears the following notation: "Quitt Rents for the Year 1715 According as they have been paid to the Receiver Gen'll for the pattented Lands in Essex County. April the 17th, 1716. Philip Ludwell. Auditor. Leo: Tarent, Sheriff."

TRUE AND EXACT POLL OF THE ELECTION OF BURGESSES, ESSEX COUNTY, VIRGINIA, NOVEMBER 20, 1741

Contributed by William Montgomery Sweeny

Candidate
Wm Beverley

1 Doctr Alexr Parker Gt
2 Wm Covington
3 Jas Wall
4 Wm Pilkinton
5 Wm Beezley
6 Fredk Coghill
7 Jas Masters
8 Edwd Murray
9 John Willard
10 David Dishman
11 Bernard Noell
12 Wm Ballard
13 Wm Jones
14 Wm Golding
15 Wm Gray
16 John Goode
17 James Evans
18 Wm Tharp
19 Robt Marsh
20 Hugh Cary
21 Jas Boulware
22 Jno Rutherford
23 Danl Noell jr
24 Jno Pitts
25 Jno Boulware
26 Walter Stallard
27 Francis Attwood
28 Saml Brown
29 Jno Clements
30 Danl Noell
31 Jno Boulware jr
32 Phillip Davies
33 Job Spearman
34 Robt Edmondson
35 Jno Farguson
36 Gabriel Jones
37 Cornelius Noell
38 Ben Johnston
39 Saml Piles
40 Jno Chamberlain
41 Jno Spires
42 Willm Hull
43 Jno Bush
44 Saml Brookes
45 Micajah Evans
46 Jas Newble
47 Ludy Piles
48 Jos Patterson
49 Jeremiah Shepard
50 Thos Coghill
51 James Clark
52 Wm Brookes
53 Jonathan Jones
54 Thos Paine
55 Jno Vass
56 Jno Brooke
57 John Hall
58 Peter Mitchell
59 Isaac Mitchell
60 Jos: Leemon
61 Richd Tyler
62 Wm Tribble
63 Nichs Adkinson
64 Jno Mercy
65 Jno Bush jr
66 Jno Mcguffy Sworn
67 Wm Dobson
68 James Medley jr
69 Jos: Monday
70 Saml Hyndshaw
71 Jas Medley
72 Wm Langham
73 Wm Jones
74 Jno Webb
75 Thos Dean
76 Jno Long
77 Richd Johnson
78 Henry Padgett
79 Jno Boughton
80 Nichs Smith jr
81 David Pitts
82 Thos Johnson
83 Saml Johnson
84 Thos Tinsley
85 Jno Conduit
86 Wm Basket
87 Jas Goulding
88 Hugh Williams
89 Jno Webb
90 Hugh Williams jr
91 Andrew Hardey
92 Mark Hamer

93 Wm Ramsey
94 Nathl Pendleton
95 James Jones
96 Thos Burk
97 Wm Mitchell
98 Jas Boughan
99 Jas Johnston
100 Jno Pitts jr
101 Peter Brooke
102 Henry Croutcher
103 Henry Faulconer
104 Thos Britchford
105 Peter Godfrey
106 Edward Rowzie jr
107 Tobias Ingram
108 Cornelius Sale
109 Thos Hastey
110 Wm Brooke
111 Thos Brooke
112 Jno Colquit
113 Edward Davies
114 Thos Waring jr
115 Jno Smith
116 Fra: Brown
117 Stephen Chenault
118 Jno Chick
119 Mungo Roy Gent
120 Banjn Winslow Gent
121 Jno Andrews
122 George Reeves
123 Wm Hawkins
124 Jas Atkins
125 Jno Clark
126 Thos Airs
127 Wm Crow
128 Peter Dickerson
129 Wm Wortham
130 Robt Sp. Coleman
131 Adam Dickie, Clark
132 Thos Price Gent
133 Lunsford Lomax Gent
134 Thos Herd
135 Majr Robt Brookes
136 George Newble
137 Jno Williams jr
138 Jno Davies
139 Fran: Brown jr
140 Jno Coffie
141 Charles Atkinson
142 Mark Boulware
143 Jno Satterwhite
144 Joshua Boughton
145 Jas Bradberry
146 Nathl Newble
147 Wm Hains
148 Daniel Smith
149 Charles Breedlove
150 Garrot Fitzsimons
151 Henry Reeves
152 Wm Smith
153 Abra: St John
154 Wm Chinay
155 Nathll Fogg
156 Edward Bowman
157 Saml Landrum
158 George Coleman
159 Danl Gaines Gent
160 Saml Hipkins
161 Paul Scott
162 Robt Parker
163 Bibby Bush
164 Wm Tyler
165 Ralph Farmer
166 Jno Covington
167 Wm Upshaw
168 Fra: Graves
169 Wm Bastine
170 Henry Brown
171 John Hoskins
172 Wm Gilham
173 Edwd Marlow
174 Danl Dobbins
175 Jno Trible
176 Thos Cooper
177 Elias Newman
178 Wm Thomas jr
179 Henry Motley
180 Jno Herman
181 Wm Short
182 Thos Williamson
183 Jno Baker
184 Thos Williams
185 Danl Warner
186 Richd Brown
187 Thos Moor
188 Jno Williamson
189 Jno Hardee
190 Jno Cox
191 Wm Hamer
192 Jno Garnett
193 Joel Halbert
194 James Turner
195 Samuel Noell
196 Jno Young
197 Richd Covington
198 Wm Fauntleroy Gt
199 Robt Rose Ck.
200 Wm Callicoat
201 Jno Robinson Esqr
202 Anthony Garnett
203 Wm Lowry
204 Thos Howerton

205 Thos Munday
206 George Strang
207 George Turner
208 Wm Halbert
209 John Allen
210 Samuel Davies
211 Thos Dunn
212 Timothy Driskell
213 Saml Coats
214 Jno Harrison
215 Cornelius Noell
216 Jno Hale
217 Ja^{s} Gatewood
218 Ja^{s} Reeves
219 James St John
220 Hugh Wilson
221 Bartho^{w} Clark
222 Ja^{s} Rennolds
223 Jno Livingston j^{r}
224 Rice Jones
225 Jno Barbie
226 Thos Kidd
227 Charles Brown
228 James Munday
229 Benj^{a} Fisher
230 John Boughan
231 Wm Taylor
232 Jo^{s} Burnett
233 Edward Webb
234 Jno Watkins
235 Thos Gatewood
236 Danl Suilavent
237 Hazell Cole
238 Ja^{s} Rennolds j^{r}
239 Wm Waller
240 Jno Croxton
241 Jno Edmondson
242 Robt Price
243 Edwd Vauters
244 Jere: Shepard j^{r}
245 Wm Carroll
246 Jno Burnet
247 Jno Stoaks
248 Gregory Smith
249 Henry Robinson Gen^{t}
250 Benj^{a} Waggner
251 Jos: Reeves
252 Jno Smith j^{r}
253 Jno Phillips
254 Wm Covington j^{r}
255 Richd Covington j^{r}
256 Richd Upshaw
257 Jno Evans
258 Jno Gatewood
259 Nich^{s} Pamplin
260 Wm Dix
261 Henry Harper
262 Thos Evans
263 James Fisher
264 Charles Munday
265 Augustine Baughan
266 Richd Cauthorn
267 Jno Vaughters
268 Anth^{y} Samuel
269 Joseph George
270 Wm Dunn
271 Wm Boulware
272 George Wright
273 Thos Edmondson
274 Jno Hill
275 Simon Miller
276 Wm Picket
277 Jno Evans j^{r}
278 James Webb
279 Thos Barker
280 Jno Corgan
281 Patt: Donohoe

Candidate
Thomas Waring

1 Wm Covington
2 Ja^{s} Wall
3 Thos Meddows
4 Daniel Dalley
5 Jno Farguson
6 Gabriel Jones
7 Ben Johnson
8 Jno Chamberlain
9 Wm Hull
10 John Ball
11 Jer: Shepard
12 Jonathan Jones
13 George Moodey
14 Jos: Monday
15 Wm Jones
16 Henry Padgett
17 John Bourn
18 Wm Meadow
19 Jno Armstrong
20 David Faulconer
21 James Jones
22 Thos Burk
23 James Allen
24 Ja^{s} Boughan
25 Harbert Waggner
26 Ja^{s} Johnston

27 James Samuel
28 Jn° Colquit
29 Edward Davies
30 Thos Waring j^{r}
31 Fra: Brown
32 Thos St John
33 Thos Bell
34 Ja^{s} Bradberry
35 Jn° St John
36 Theo^{s} Favour
37 Garrot Fitzsimons
38 Edward Rowzie
39 Henry Brown
40 Danl Warner
41 Thos Lee
42 Ja^{s} Landrum
43 Thos Moor
44 Jn° Pettis
45 Jn° Hunt
46 Wm Fauntleroy Gen^{t}
47 Isaac Gatewood
48 Jn° Allen
49 Ja^{s} Boughan j^{r}
50 Jn° Brown
51 Richd Jones j^{r}
52 James Gatewood
53 Ja^{s} Reeves
54 Ja^{s} St John
55 Hugh Wilson
56 Samuel Allen
57 Wm Gatewood j^{r}
58 Wm Gatewood
59 Thos Burnet
60 Ja^{s} Munday
61 Robt French
62 Wm Gordon
63 Jn° Hale j^{r}
64 Danl Sullevent
65 Thos Edmondson j^{r}
66 Jos: Reeves j^{r}
67 Wm Catlett Thomas
68 James Noell
69 James Merrit
70 Jn° Burnet
71 Jn° Stoaks
72 Gregory Smith
73 Henry Robinson Gen^{t}
74 Jn° Noell
75 Benjn Waggner
76 Thos Evans
77 Petter Kemp
78 Anth^{y} Samuell
79 Isaac Scandritt Gen^{t}
80 Henry Samuell
81 Jn° Hill
82 William Picket
83 Thos Barker

Candidate
James Garnett

1 Wm Pilkinton
2 Wm Beezley
3 Fred^{k} Coghill
4 Ja^{s} Masters
5 Edwd Murray
6 John Willard
7 David Dishman
8 Bernard Noell
9 Wm Ballard
10 Wm Jones
11 Wm Golding
12 Wm Gray
13 Jn° Goode
14 James Evans
15 Wm Tharp
16 Robt Marsh
17 Hugh Cary
18 Ja^{s} Boulware
19 Jn° Rutherford
20 Danl Noell j^{r}
21 Jn° Pitts
22 Jn° Boulware
23 Walter Stallard
24 Fra: Attwood
25 Thos Meddows
26 Samuel Brown
27 Jn° Clements
28 Daniell Noell
29 Jn° Boulware j^{r}
30 Phillip Davies
31 Job Spearman
32 Robt Edmondson
33 Daniel Dayley
34 Cornelius Noell
35 Jn° Spires
36 Jn° Ball
37 Thos Coghill
38 James Clark
39 Jos: Leemon
40 George Moodey
41 Nich^{s} Adkinson
42 Jn° M^{c} guffey
43 Wm Dobson
44 Saml Hyndshaw
45 Jn° Long
46 David Pitts

47 Jno Bourn
48 Wm Meadow
49 Thos Tinsley
50 John Conduit
51 Wm Basket
52 Jas Goulding
53 Jno Armstrong
54 David Faulconer
55 Wm Ramsey
56 Jas Allen
57 Harbert Waggner
58 Jno Pitts jr
59 Thos Britchford
60 Peter Godfrey
61 Edward Rowzie jr
62 Tobias Ingram
63 Thos Newble
64 Cornelius Sale
65 Jas Samuell
66 Stephen Chenault
67 Jno Chick
68 Mungo Roy Gent
69 Benjn Winslow Gent
70 Richd Gatewood
71 Jno Andrews
72 George Reeves
73 Wm Hawkins
74 James Atkins
75 Jno Clark
76 Thos Airs
77 Wm Crow
78 Thos St John
79 Peter Dickerson
80 Wm Wortham
81 Thos Bell
82 Jno Davies
83 Fra: Brown jr
84 Jno Coffie
85 Charles Atkinson
86 Mark Boulware
87 Jno Satterwhite
88 Danl Smith
89 Theos Favour
90 Edward Rowzie
91 Henry Reeves
92 Nathl Fogg
93 Saml Landrum
94 Danl Gaines Gent
95 Saml Hipkins
96 Richd Bush
97 Robt Parker
98 Ralph Farmer
99 Jno Covington
100 Wm Upshaw
101 Fra: Graves
102 Wm Bastine
103 Wm Gilham
104 Edwd Marlow
105 Elias Newman
106 Wm Thomas jr
107 Henry Motley
108 Jno Herman
109 Jno Baker
110 Thos Lee
111 Jas Landrum
112 Richd Brown
113 Jno Williamson
114 Jno Garnett
115 Joel Halbert
116 Saml Noell
117 Jno Pettis
118 Jno Young
119 Richd Covington
120 Isaac Gatewood
121 Anthy Garnett
122 Thos Munday
123 George Strang
124 Wm Halbert
125 Samuell Davies
126 Thos Dunn
127 Timothy Driskell
128 Jno Harrison
129 Cornelius Noell
130 Jno Brown
131 Jno Haile
132 Richd Jones jr
133 Barthow Clark
134 Samuel Allen
135 Jas Rennolds
136 Jno Livingston jr
137 Wm Gatewood jr
138 Wm Gatewood
139 Thos Burnet
140 Rice Jones
141 Jno Barbie
142 Thos Kidd
143 Charles Brown
144 Benjn Fisher
145 Robt French
146 Jno Baughan
147 Wm Taylor
148 Wm Gordon
149 Jno Hale jr
150 Jos: Burnet
151 Edward Webb
152 Jno Watkins
153 Thos Gatewood
154 Jas Rennolds jr
155 Wm Waller
156 Jno Croxton
157 Thos Edmondson jr
158 Jno Edmondson

159 Jo^{s} Reeves j^{r}
160 Wm Catlett Thomas
161 Robert Price
162 James Noell
163 Edwd Vauters
164 Jer: Shepard j^{r}
165 Wm Carroll
166 James Merret
167 Jno Noell
168 Jos: Reeves
169 Jno Smith j^{r}
170 Richd Upshaw
171 Jno Gatewood
172 Nich^{s} Pamplin
173 Wm Dix
174 Henry Harper
175 Charles Munday
176 Augt Baughan
177 John Vauters
178 Jos: George
179 Isaac Scandrit Gen^{t}
180 Henry Samuell
181 Williamson Young
182 Wm Boulware
183 Geo: Wright
184 Thos Edmondson
185 Simon Miller
186 James Webb
187 Jno Corgan
188 Patt: Donohoe

Candidate
Joshua Fry

1 Saml Piles
2 Jno Bush
3 Saml Brooke
4 Micajah Evans
5 James Newble
6 Ludy Piles
7 Jos: Patterson
8 Wm Brookes
9 Thos Pane
10 Jno Vass
11 Jno Brooke
12 Jno Hall
13 Peter Mitchell
14 Isaac Mitchell
15 Richd Tyler
16 Wm Trible
17 Jno Mercy
18 Jno Bush j^{r}
19 Ja^{s} Medley j^{r}
20 Ja^{s} Medley
21 Wm Langham
22 Jno Webb
23 Thos Dean
24 Richd Johnson
25 Jno Boughton
26 Nich^{s} Smith j^{r}
27 Thos Johnson
28 Samuel Johnson
29 Hugh Williams
30 Jno Webb
31 Hugh Williams j^{r}
32 Andrew Hardey
33 Mark Hamer
34 Nathaniel Pendleton
35 Wm Mitchell
36 Peter Brooke
37 Henry Croutcher
38 Henry Faulconer
39 Thos Newble
40 Thos Hastey
41 Wm Brooke
42 Thos Brooke
43 Jno Smith
44 Richd Gatewood
45 Robt Sp. Coleman
46 Adam Dickie Ck.
47 Ale^{x} Parker Gen^{t}
48 Thos Price Gen^{t}
49 Lunsford Lomax Gen^{t}
50 Robt Brooke Gen^{t}
51 Thos Hord Gen^{t}
52 George Newble
53 Jno Williamson j^{r}
54 Joshua Boughton
55 Jno St John
56 Nathl Newble
57 Wm Hains
58 Charles Breedlove
59 Wm Smith
60 Abra: St John
61 Wm Chiniy
62 Edwd Bowman
63 George Coleman
64 Paul Scott
65 Richd Bush
66 Bibby Bush
67 Wm Tyler
68 Jno Hoskins
69 Danl Dobbins
70 Jno Trible
71 Thos Cooper
72 Thos Williamson
73 Thos Williams
74 Jno Hardee

75 Jno Cox
76 Wm Hamer
77 James Turner
78 Jno Hunt
79 Robt Rose Ck.
80 Wm Collicoat
81 Jno Robinson Esq^{e}
82 William Lowry
83 Thos Howerton
84 George Turner
85 Ja^{s} Boughan
86 Samuel Coats
87 Hazell Cole
88 Jno Phillips
89 Wm Covington j^{r}
90 Richd Covington j^{r}
91 Jno Evans
92 Peter Kemp
93 Ja^{s} Fisher
94 Richd Cauthorn
95 Wm Dunn
96 Williamson Young
97 Jno Evans j^{r}

Candidate
Simon Miller

1 Wm Short

A True and Exact Pole of the Election of Burgesses Taken for the County of Essex At the Courthouse of the s^{d} County the 20th Day of November 1741

P Thos Barker C. E. C.

The Said Thos Barker Made Oath before Me Alexander Parker Gent One of his Majesty's Justices of the peace for the said County that the Above is A true poll taken by him Given Under My Hand 10^{ber} ye 15th 1741

Alexander Parker

Truly Recorded

Teste H. Robinson D. C. Cur.

Essex County Deed Book 1738-1742, p. 310

ELECTION OF COL. GEO. WASHINGTON, 1758.

INSPECTOR GENERAL'S OFFICE,
WASHINGTON. D. C., *September 1, 1898.*

Editor Virginia Historical Magazine, Richmond, Va.

SIR: Among the Washington papers in the State Department are a number of polls of electors in Fairfax and Frederick counties, in elections in which Washington was a candidate for the House of Burgesses, extending from 1758 to 1765. I enclose one of the earliest of these, that for Frederick county, in 1758, which you may publish if you see fit. I think it is interesting. You will observe that each elector voted for two candidates, if he wished. The list I have copied is in Washington's own writing, and was arranged in alphabetical order by him from another list among the papers, which was copied from the poll-books in the order in which the votes were cast. There is also among the papers a list of the polls for an election of Burgesses in Fairfax County, in 1748, in which "Major Washington" and others were candidates. On this is endorsed, in the writing of Jared Sparks, a note that this must have been Lawrence Washington (who was a major at that time), as George was then only sixteen years old.

Very truly,

A. C. QUISENBERRY.

An Alphabetical Poll for Frederick County, Taken the 24th Day of July, 1758.

For Colo. Washington.

Robert Ashby,
Thos. Ashby,
Robert Allan,
John Ashby,
Stephen Ashby, 5
Rev. John Alderson,
John Allan,
John Arnold,
James Burn,
Dennis Bow, 10
Christopher Beiler,
And^{w} Blackburn,
James Ballinger,
Jacob Burner,
Jno. Bombgardner, 15
Sam'l Blackburn,
Thos. Babb,
Chas. Baker,
Sam'l Beam,
Reynold Baldwin, 20
Richd Barber,
John Blair,
Jacob Bowman,
Geo. Bower,
Henry Biber, 25
Martin Black,
Philip Babb,
James Burne,
Wm. Baldwin,
Joseph Burdon, 30
James Blair,
Henry Brinker,
Chas. Barnes,
James Barret,
Wm. Barrett, 35
Jno. Briscoe,
Thos. Babb (son of Phil),
George Bruce,
Henry Bowen,
Thos. Babb, Jr., 40
Peter Babb,
Joseph Babb,
Bryan Bruin,
John Buckley,
Jacob Barrett, 45
Joshua Baker,
Colo. John Carlyle,
Doct^{r} Jas. Craik,
Wm. Cockran,
And^{w} Calvin, 50
Martin Cryler,
Simon Carson,
Chris^{n} Clark,
David Chester,
Jacob Cochener, 55
Thomas Chester,
John Cook,
Henry Cloud,
Nathl Carr,
Mathew Colman, 60
Edward Corder,
Wm. Cromley,
Robt. Cunningham,
Jno. Cromley,
Jos. Calvin, 65
Jacob Cowper,
Thos. Carney,
Wm. Cocks,

Valentine Crawford, jr.,
John Colston, 70
Thos. Cooper,
Jno. Chinoweth,
Wm. Coil,
Jas. Carter, jr.,
Edw. Cartmell, 75
Wm. Carrel,
James Catlet,
Fredk. Conrad,
Nathl Cartmell,
Jos. Combs, 80
Wm. Chambers,
Charles Dick,
John Dyer,
Edward Dodd,
David Dedrick, 85
Thos. Doster,
John Dow,
Patrick Duncan,
Isaac Evans,
Wm. Evans, 90
Jos. Edwards, Jr.,
Wm. Ewings,
Thomas, Lord Fairfax,
Paul Frouman,
Richd. Foley, 95
Abr^{m} Fry,
Jacob Fry,
Joseph Fry,
Benj. Fry,
Henry Funk, 100
Martin Funk,
Joseph Fossett,
Saml. Fry,
Joseph Funk,
Jno. Funkhauser, 105
Richd. Fossett,
Wm. Frost,
Matthias Funk,
Geo. Farrar,
Isaac Foster, 110
Col. Geo. Wm. Fairfax,
John Fossett,
Capt. Jno. Funk,
John Glenn,
David Glass, 115
James Grinnan,
Wm. Glover,
Wm. Gaddis,
Jos. Glass,
Robt. Glass, 120
John Grinnan,
Christ^{r} Grable,
Philip Glass,
Adam Hunter,
Noah Hampton, 125
John Harbinger,
Revd John Hoge,
George Hardin,
Jno. Housman,
Jas. Hoge, jr., 130
Henry Heth,
George Henry,
Nich^{s} Hanshaw,
Thos. Hart,
Robt. Harper, 135
Geo. Huddle,
Murtle Handley,
Jno. Harrom,
John Hope,
Jacob Hite, 140
Colo. John Hite,
Isaac Hite,
Peter Jordan,
Aaron Jenkins,
Daniel Johnston, 145
Robt. Johnston, Gent.,

Stephen Johnston,
Joseph Jones,
John Jones,
Wm. Jolliffe, Jr., 150
Gabriel Jones, Gent.,
George Keller,
James Knight,
Fielding Lewis, Esqr.,
Thos. Lemon, 155
Joseph Lupton,
Wm. Lupton,
Edward Lucas,
Samuel Littler,
James Loyd, 160
And'w Longacre,
Jos. Langdon,
Geo. Mich. Louenger,
Francis Lilburn,
Geo. Lochmiller, 165
Isaac Laren,
Robt. Lemon,
Rev'd Wm. Meldrum,
Wm. McGee,
David Miller, 170
Robt. Marney,
Jos. McDonnell,
David Morgan,
Wm. McMahan,
Richd. McMahan, 175
Jno. Milburn,
Jas. McGill,
Robt. McCoy,
Jacob Morgan,
Laughlen Maddin, 180
Jos. McCormick,
Jno. Maddin,
James McCormick,
John McCormick,
Henry Moore, Gent., 185
Robt. Milburn,
Darby McCarty,
Wm. Monger,
Wm. Miller,
Thos. Mason, 190
Darby Murphey,
Pat. McDaniel,
Lewis Moore,
George Nevil,
Samuel Odle, 195
Isaac Perkins,
Nichs. Princeller,
Mich'l Poker,
Wm. Patterson,
George Paul, 200
Chas. Perkins,
Lawrence Pence,
Wm. Pickering,
Jesse Pugh,
Thos. Postgate, 205
Josiah Pemberton,
Jos. Parrell,
Jno. Parrell,
Peter Perry,
Philip Poker, 210
Thos. Perry,
Azariah Pugh,
Jonathan Perkins,
Wm. Russell,
John Road, 215
Capt. Robt. Rutherford,
Thos. Reece,
Jacob Reece,
Henry Rinker,
George Ross, 220
Patrick Rice,
Edward Rice,
George Rice,
Wm. Reynolds,

Isaac Riddell, 225
Henry Reece,
Wm. Roberts,
Wm. Roberts, jr.,
John Reed,
Ulrich Rubble, 230
Cornelius Ruddell,
Lt. Chas. Smith,
Jno. Smith,
Peter Stephens,
John Snap, 235
John Snap, Jr.,
Dan'l Stover,
Henry Stephens,
Jacob Strickler,
Benj. Strickler, 240
David Snodgrass,
John Snodgrass,
Sam'l Smalsolfer,
Nichs Schrack,
Ulrich Stoner, 245
Robt. Stewart,
Jacob Sowers,
Jon. Seaman,
Jno. Strickly
Jno. Sewell, 250
Jacob Sebert,
Jos. Strickler,
David Shepherd,
John Small,
Thos. Shepherd, 255
Lewis Stephens,
Jacob Stover,
Dennis Springer,
Richd Stephenson,
Edw. Snickers, 260
Law. Snap,
Robt. Stewart,
Dan'l Stephens,
Geo. Shade,
Thos. Speake, 265
Jos. Thompson,
Evan Thomas,
Jno. Thomas,
Sam'l Taylor,
Anth. Turner, 270
Ellis Thomas,
Anth. Turner, Jr.,
Harr^{n} Taylor,
Edw. Thomas,
Alex. Vance, 275
James Vance,
Sam'l Vance,
And^{w} Vance,
John Vanmeter,
Abram Vanmeter, 280
Jno. Vestal,
Jacob Vanmeter,
John Vance,
Henry Vanmeter,
Jno. Fred Vanfagan, 285
Colo. James Wood,
Alex. Woodrow, Gent.,
Peter Woolf,
Isaac White,
Geo. Whitsel, 290
James Wright,
Robt. Wilson,
Geo. Wright,
Jacob Wright,
David Wright, 295
Chr. Wendall,
Aug. Wendall,
James Wilson,
Robt. Wilson, Junr.,
Thos. Wilson, 300
Val. Wendall,
Thos. Waters,

Jos. Wilkinson,
Robt. Worthington,
Ralph Withers, 305
Jno. Wilson,
Jno. Wright.
Wm. White,
John Young, 309

For Colo. Martin.

Robert Ashby,
Thos. Ashby,
Robert Allan,
John Ashby,
Stephen Ashby, 5
Rev. John Alderson,
Jno. Armstrong,
James Burn,
Dennis Bow,
And^{w} Blackburn, 10
Jacob Burner,
Jno. Bombgardner,
Sam'l Blackburn,
Chas. Baker,
Sam'l Beam, 15
Reynold Baldwin,
Rich'd Barber,
John Blair,
Jacob Bowman,
Geo. Bower, 20
Henry Biber,
Martin Black,
James Burne,
Henry Brinker,
Chas. Barnes, 25
Jno. Briscoe,
Bryan Bruin,
John Buckley,
Tobias Burk,
John Bentley, 30
Jno. Burden,
Geo. Bowman,
Samuel Baldwin,
Benj. Blackburn,
Jno. Becket, 35
Jno. Baylis,
Charles Buck,
Colo. John Carlyle,
Doct^{r} Jas. Craik,
Wm. Cockran, 40
Martin Cryler,
Simon Carson,
Chris^{n} Clark,
David Chester,
Jacob Cochener, 45
Thomas Chester,
John Cook,
Henry Cloud,
Nathl. Carr,
Mathew Colman, 50
Jacob Cowper,
Wm. Cocks,
Thos. Cooper,
Edw. Cartmell,
James Catlet, 55
Fredk. Conrad,
Jos. Combs,
Wm. Chambers,
James Carter,
Wm. Chaplin, 60

Thos. Caton,
Thos. Colston,
James Cromley,
Wm. Calmes,
Charles Dick, 65
John Dyer,
David Dedrick,
John Dow,
Patrick Duncan,
Wm. Duckworth, 70
Wm. Evans,
Jos. Edwards, jr.,
Wm. Ewings,
Henry Easton,
Thos. Ellis, 75
Thomas, Lord Fairfax,
Paul Frouman,
Richd. Foley,
Ab^{m} Fry,
Jacob Fry, 80
Joseph Fry,
Benj. Fry,
Henry Funk,
Martin Funk,
Joseph Fossett, 85
Sam'l Fry,
Joseph Funk,
Jno. Funkhauser,
Richd. Fossett,
Matthias Funk, 90
Geo. Farrar,
Col. Geo. Wm. Fairfax,
John Fossett,
Capt. Jno. Funk,
John Fite, 95
Martin Funk,
David Glass,
James Grinnan,
Wm. Glover,
Jos. Glass, 100
John Grinnan,
Christr. Grable,
Philip Glass,
Edw. Griffith,
Jacob Gibson, 105
Adam Hunter,
Noah Hampton,
John Harbinger,
Rev. Jno. Hoge,
George Hardin, 110
Jno. Housman,
George Henry,
Geo. Huddle,
John Hope,
Stephen Hotzenbell, 115
Robt. Halfpenny,
Godfrey Humbert,
Thos. Hampton,
Robert Haines,
Colo. John Hite, 120
James Hoge,
Thomas Helms,
Wm. Helms,
Richd. Highland,
Peter Jordan, 125
Robt. Johnston, Gent.,
Gabriel Jones, Gent.,
George Keller,
James Knight,
Fielding Lewis, Esqr., 130
Thos. Lemon,
And'w Longacre,
Jos. Langdon.,
Geo. Lochmiller,
Isaac Laren, 135
John Lemon,
John Leith,
Nich's Lemon,

Henry Loyd,
Jno. Lindsay, 140
Rev'd Wm. Meldrum,
Robt. Marney,
Jos. McDonnell,
Robt. McCoy,
Jno. Maddin, 145
Jno. McCormick,
Henry Moore, Gent.,
Darby McCarty,
Wm. Miller,
Darby Murphy, 150
Pat. McDaniel,
Lewis Moore,
Rich'd Mercer,
Mayberry Maddin,
Colo. M. Morgan, 155
Rich'd Morgan,
Jacob Miller,
Edw. Mercer, jr.,
George Nevil,
Jno. Nisenanger, 160
Samuel Odle,
Alex'r Ogleby,
Nich's Princeller,
Mich'l Poker,
Lawrence Pence, 165
Thos. Postgate,
Philip Poker,
Thos. Perry,
Jno. Painter,
Robt. Pearis, 170
Thos. Pugh,
Sam'l Pritchard,
Wm. Russell,
John Road,
Capt. Robt. Rutherford 175
Isaac Riddell,
Wm. Roberts,
Wm. Roberts, jr.,
Jos. Roberts,
Edward Rogers, 180
Corn. Ruddell,
Jno. Smith,
Peter Stephens,
John Snap,
John Snap, jr., 185
Dan'l Stover,
Henry Stephens,
Jacob Strickler,
Benj. Strickler,
Sam'l Smalsolfer, 190
Ulrich Stoner,
Jno. Strickley,
Jos. Strickler,
Lewis Stephens,
Jacob Stover, 195
Rich'd Stephenson,
Edw. Snickers,
Law. Snap,
Geo. Shade,
Law. Stephens, 200
Thos. Sharp,
Jere Smith,
Peter Stover,
Wm. Stevenson,
Jno. Scene, 205
Jno. Thomas,
Ellis Thomas,
Harrison Taylor,
Zebulon Tharp,
Simon Taylor, 210
James Vance,
Sam'l Vance,
Andw. Vance,
John Vance,
Jno Fred Vanfagan, 215
David Vance,

Jos. Vance,
Wm. Vance,
Peter Woolf,
Isaac White, 220
Geo. Whitzel,
Robt. Wilson,
Geo. Wright,
Jacob Wright,
David Wright, 225
Chr. Wendall,
Aug. Wendall,
James Wilson,
Robt. Wilson, Junr.,
Thos. Wilson, 230
Val. Wendall,
Thos. Waters,
Ralph Withers,
Jno. Wright,
Wm. Wilson, 235
Robt. Worth,
John Young. 239

For Mr. West.

Jno. Armstrong,
John Arnold,
John Anderson,
Christopher Beiler,
James Ballinger, 5
Thos. Babb,
Philip Babb,
Wm. Baldwin,
Joseph Burdon,
James Blair. 10
James Barrett,
Wm. Barrett,
Thos. Babb,
George Bruce,
Henry Bowen, 15
Thos. Babb, jr.,
Peter Babb,
Joseph Babb,
Jacob Barrett,
Joshua Baker, 20
Tobias Burk,
John Bentley,
Geo. Bowman,
Sam'l Baldwin,
Benj. Blackburn, 25
John Becket,
Charles Buck,
Josiah Ballinger,
Robt. Buckles,
And[w] Calvin, 30
Edward Carder,
Wm. Cromley,
Robt. Cunningham,
Jno. Cromley,
Jos. Calvin, 35
Thos. Carney,
Valentine Crawford, jr.,
John Colston,
Jno. Chinoweth,
Wm. Coil, 40
Jas. Carter, jr.,
Wm. Carrel,
Nathl. Cartmell,
James Carter,
Wm. Chaplin, 45
Thos. Caton,
Thos. Colston,
James Cromley,
Wm. Calmes,
Thos. Cordery, 50

Edward Dodd,
Thos. Doster,
Wm. Duckworth,
Henry Easton,
Thos. Ellis, 55
Wm. Frost,
Isaac Foster,
John Fife,
Martin Funk,
Wm. Gaddis, 60
Robt. Glass,
Edw. Griffith,
Jacob Gibson,
James Hoge, jr.,
Henry Heth, 65
Nichs Hanshaw,
Thos. Hart,
Robt. Harper,
Murtle Handley,
Jno. Harrom, 70
Jacob Hite,
Stephen Hotzenbell,
Godfrey Humbert,
Thos. Hampton,
James Hoge, 75
Thomas Helms,
Wm. Helms,
Rich'd Highland,
George Hampton,
Simeon Hyatt, 80
Jos. Horner,
Jonas Hedge,
Jno. House,
Sam'l Isaacs,
Daniel Johnston, 85
Stephen Johnston,
Joseph Jones,
John Jones,
Wm. Jolliffe, junr.,
John Keywood, 90
Joseph Lupton,
Wm. Lupton,
Sam'l Littler,
James Loyd,
Geo. M. Louenger, 95
Francis Lilburn,
Robt. Lemon,
John Lemon,
John Leith,
Nichs. Lemon, 100
Henry Loyd,
Jno. Lindsay,
James Lindsay,
Thos. London,
Edmond Lindsay, 105
David Morgan,
Wm. McMahan,
Richd. McMahan,
Jno. Milburn,
Jas. McGill, 110
Jacob Morgan,
Laughlen Maddin,
Jos. McCormick,
James McCormick,
Robt. Milburn, 115
Wm. Monger,
Thos. Mason,
Richd. Mercer,
Mayberry Maddin,
Colo. M. Morgan, 120
Richd. Morgan,
Jacob Miller,
Edw. Mercer, jr.,
Jno. Mendenhall,
Morgan Morgan, Jr., 125
Jacob Moon,
Jno. Nisenanger,
Isaac Perkins,

Chas. Perkins,
Wm. Pickering, 130
Sam'l Pearson,
Job Pugh,
Jesse Pugh,
Jos. Pemberton,
Jos. Parrell, 135
Jno. Parrell,
Peter Perry,
Azariah Pugh,
Jon. Perkins,
Robt. Pearis, 140
Thos. Pugh,
Sam'l Pritchard,
George Pemberton,
Thos. Reece,
Jacob Reece, 145
Henry Rinker,
George Ross,
Patrick Rice,
Edward Rice,
George Rice, 150
Wm. Reynolds,
Henry Reece,
John Reed,
Ulrich Rubble,
Jos. Roberts, 155
Edward Rogers,
Lt. Chas. Smith,
Nichs. Schrack,
Robt. Stewart,
Jacob Sowers, 160
Jacob Sebert,
David Shepherd,
John Small,
Thos. Shepherd,
Dennis Springer, 165
Robt. Stewart,
Dan'l Stephens,
Thos. Speake,
Law. Stephens,
Thos. Sharp, 170
Jere Smith,
Peter Stover,
Wm. Stevenson,
Jno. Scene,
John Stroud, 175
Jos. Thompson,
Evan Thomas,
Sam'l Taylor,
Anth. Turner,
Anth. Turner, Junr., 180
Edw. Thomas,
Zebulon Tharp,
Simon Taylor,
Owen Thomas,
Jno. Taylor, 185
Magnus Tate,
Jno. Vestal,
Jacob Vanmeter,
Henry Vanmeter,
David Vance, 190
Jos. Vance,
Wm. Vance,
Colo. James Wood,
Alex. Woodrow, Gent.,
James Wright, 195
Jos. Wilkinson,
Robt. Worthington,
Jno. Wilson,
Wm. White,
Robt. Worth, 200

For Capt. Swearingen.

John Anderson,
John Burden,
Josiah Ballinger,
Robt. Buckles,
Thos. Cordery, 5
Isaac Evans,
John Glenn,
Robt. Halfpenny,
Robt. Haines,
Geo. Hampton, 10
Simeon Hyatt,
Jos. Horner,
Jonas Hedge,
John House,
Sam'l Isaacs, 15
Aaron Jenkins,
John Keywood,
Edward Lucas,
James Lindsay,
Thos. London, 20
Edmond Lindsay,
Wm. McGee,
David Miller,
Jno. Mendenhall,
Morgan Morgan, Jr., 25
Jacob Moon,
Alexr. Ogleby,
Wm. Patterson,
George Paul,
Sam'l Pearson, 30
Jno. Stroud,
Owen Thomas,
Job Pugh,
Jno. Painter,
Geo. Pemberton, 35
David Snodgrass,
John Snodgrass,
Jon: Seaman,
Jno. Sewell,
Jno, Stroud, 40
Owen Thomas,
John Taylor,
Magnus Tate,
Alex. Vance,
Jno. Vanmeter,
Abram Vanmeter,
Wm. Wilson, 47

THE VESTRY BOOK OF KING WILLIAM PARISH, VA., 1707–1750.

(Translated from the French and annotated by Prof. R. H. FIFE, Wesleyan University, and with an introduction by Col. R. L. MAURY, Richmond, Virginia.)

From the original, the property of Miss LELIA WALKER,* Ft. Estill, Ky.

INTRODUCTION.

The Huguenot colony at Manakin Town in Virginia was by far the largest settlement of those famous exiles in America, and as their innumerable descendants now abound not only in Virginia but in almost every State, this publication of its church's vestry book will interest a multitude of readers and supply much genealogical information hitherto vainly sought.

Ere Jamestown was three years old, Frenchmen, presumably Huguenots, were here, and for a hundred years and more these noble Christians continued to cross the Atlantic to our hospitable shore. In 1621 sixty families under Jesse de Forest asked leave to come to Virginia, but were diverted by the Dutch to their colony of Manhattan and founded New York. In 1630 Baron de Sancé seated a colony on the lower James. Thereafter, as persecution increased in France and 'twas known how Huguenots prospered in Virginia and were welcomed there, the movement culminated in the coming of eight hundred for Manakin Town. Many others came, sometimes singly, sometimes a family or two, or a little band of relatives and friends, and located where they would in lower Virginia. In a single year, 1687, the Huguenot Relief Committee in London aided six hundred to Virginia, of whom, doubtless, some responding to the liberal offers of William Fitzhugh, of Bedford, settled on his lands on Occoquon creek, and some in Stafford and Spotsylvania. In 1700 came the largest party yet, bound for Manakin Town under

*This Society extends its thanks to Miss Walker for permission to print the vestry book; to Professor Fife for translating the faded manuscript, and to Col. Maury.

the special auspices of King William and the special favour of Virginia.

To secure such coveted colonists, laws had been made from time to time granting unusual priviledges to all who came. They were admitted to full citizenship immediately upon arrival, with right to worship God as they would, under ministers of their own selection, and later, still further to attract and in response to the King's request, that they should be welcomed and assisted by the colony, it donated for their settlement a tract of 10,000 acres, the best on James river, twenty miles above Richmond, being the deserted village and lands of the Monacan Indians, exempted them from taxation and constituted their settlement King William Parish to be under their exclusive control, with the right to select and have two pastors whom they themselves were to support.

The King was deeply grateful to his Huguenot allies who had contributed so effectively to his success, and wished to establish them, and others, in Virginia. He gave £3,000 and procured from the Protestant Relief Fund the gift of £12,000 for their equipment. The first instalment of them sailed from the Thames in 1700, aboard the *Mary Ann*, with their pastor Claude Phillip de Richbourg, led by the Marquis de la Muce; the second aboard the *Peter* and *Anthony* arrived soon after, with the beloved Benjamin de Joux, of Lyons, ordained by the Bishop of London to be their pastor, and who was the real founder and leader of the whole settlement; the third soon followed, and then the fourth, aboard the *Nassau*, with Louis Latané, pastor. Each brought about two hundred. Passenger lists of all save the third, and partial lists of the inhabitants of Manakin Town at sundry dates, have been published by the Virginia Historical Society.

Most of these and doubtless others who had previously come to Virginia, for there were probably several thousands here by now, made their homes at first upon their grant—fields were cleared, 133 acres alloted to each, the village laid out and building commenced, the church, the parsonage and the schoolhouse first; De Joux chosen pastor and leader, and the little community of about five hundred organized.

After the hardships of the first winter and weary waiting for harvest it prospered from the start. Each year brought substantial additions to numbers comforts and property; farms were enlarged, flocks increased and many soon owned negroes to help cultivate their fertile fields, then and now the best corn lands in Virginia.

Its reputation for piety, thrift and successful industry attracted many others and thus was gathered a population in that region the equal of any in prosperity, intellect, influence and social standing. The church was ever open, there were daily services, and the pastor was a Huguenot as long as there were any in Virginia. The service was that of the English Church, in French, though later, as children grew, and others came to the parish, there was also a sermon in English.

For many years the settlement preserved its individuality; in 1728 there were still many who could speak only French; the church still stands and services are still held, but the village has disappeared, for as the Indians retired the frontier advanced; 'twas no longer dangerous to live apart, and farmers preferred to reside upon their farms. And so with lapse of time as children grew and married with Virginians—there was merger with their neighbors, and the distinctive character as a French settlement gradually waned until now but few of the founder's names are heard in the parish of King William.

But there are many, very many of their descendants whose cherished names will ever be conspicuous in the annals of Virginia, and of the United States, for the sweet influence of those heroes for conscience will never die, and the whole land is fairer, lovelier and better for the pure, noble and faithful lives and character of the Huguenots of Virginia.

Never had such immigrants crossed sea before; never have peaceful foreigners so impressed their many virtures upon their new surroundings.

In character, cultivation and attainments they were the flower of their great party, for they were those who successfully resisted the most direful persecution, literally in mind, body and estate; the most overwhelming defeats and calamities; the most tempting bribes of honors, riches, peace and security at home for themselves, their wives and little children, if they would recant, or so pretend. Refusing, they voluntarily accepted banishment, poverty and distress in strange lands rather than renounce their belief. Louis, with all his power, could not prevail against the ramparts of their faith. Had they been weak they would have gone with the stream as king and noble and so many did, securing peace and prosperity in beloved France, but they were staunch and inflexible, courageous to brave all perils and make all sacrifices, save one, in their determination to worship God according to the dictates of their own conscience, to keep the faith at every cost, and rather than abandon the church of their fathers, to abandon all else. Refined in the fires of affliction seven times repeated, for seven generations, purified through the unfailing laws of heredity, strengthened and developed from generation to generation in mind and faith by the constant exercise and teaching of their religion at great danger and sacrifice, and by their heritage of devotion from faithful parent to dutiful child to resist the allurements and attractions of rewards and favors constantly offered if they would recant, and by poverty and need enured to hardship, industry and danger, as survivors they were the fittest of all their glorious race in every class in France, as their children were, and are, in America.

Nothing more clearly shows their high and noble nature, and their superiority, and great attainments in all that makes man great and woman loved, than the esteem and the successes attained in Virginia. They came in direst poverty generally, for they had forfeited all to save their faith; aliens, exiles, speaking only the tongue of heriditary foes, of foreign habit and foreign ways, from fertile, populated France, to the frontier of Virginia, to a country with whom theirs was at war and constant feud, to a colony most loyal and devoted, almost a close corporation governed by a proud and exclusive colonial aristocracy representative of a few of the English nobility jealous of its privileges and zealously opposing any enlargement of its favoured circle. Yet so impressive were they in their many virtues and attractions that prejudice was soon disarmed, exclusion forgotten, that reason and self-interest both prevailed, and the exiles are taken by the hand, and soon to the heart and become the pastors, teachers, valued friends and esteemed and cherished companions of the best; many became prosperous farmers, merchants and professionals, and ere long gained the same social position in Virginia that had been theirs in France. The children play together and intermarry, and their posterity have ever since been found among the leaders of this land first among the foremost wherever danger, duty, the good of mankind, or patriotism called, on sea or land, in court or senate, in peace or war, at home or abroad, in commerce or in science, brilliant examples for emulation in every community blessed by their presence, and diffusing a beneficial influence wherever they were, giving rich return for the welcome and aid given them in their dire distress.

"Of that highminded race, on all who bear
Their names or lineage may their mantle rest—
That firmness for the truth, that calm content
With simple pleasures, that unswerving trust
In toil, adversity and death which cast
Such healthful leaven 'mid the elements
That peopled this new world."

RICHARD L. MAURY,
Fifth in descent from Abraham Maury of Castel Moron,
and eighth from Jean de la Fontaine of Le Mans, Martyred 1561.

PREFATORY NOTE.

THE REGISTER OF THE HUGUENOT CHURCH AT MANAKIN TOWN ON JAMES RIVER, 1707–1750.

The parish register of the French refugees at Manakin Town is a document of considerable importance both from a historical and a genealogical standpoint. The book is a vellum-bound volume of 14x10 inches in a fair state of preservation, containing 116 pages, covering the parish records from December 20, 1707, to December 28, 1750, and two extra sheets giving the land-holdings of the parish. While the title page is missing and a number of pages have been cut out at the end, the register is almost complete for the period named.

The first French refugees landed in Manakin Town in the summer, probably September, 1700, and the settlement was erected into a separate parish by the Virginia General Assembly December 5, 1700,* the first pastor being Benjamin de Joux.†

---

* Cf. R. A. Brock, *Huguenot Emigration to Virginia*, *Virginia Historical Collections*, V, Richmond, 1886, p. 60.

† *Ibid*, p. x. Pastor de Joux died in 1704.

The old register referred to below was probably begun at that time and was continued until within the year 1707, and is now doubtless irrevocably lost.

The book which follows below in translation contains all transactions of church wardens and vestry as representatives of the parish, including tithe rolls, contracts with clergymen, contracts with guardians of the poor, receipts for money disbursed, etc., as well as memorandums of sermons preached and of the administration of the sacrament.* In later years the book seems to have been occasionally used also to record private contracts between individual parishioners.

Many clergymen ministered to the spiritual needs of the parish during these years;† but only four clerks appear in the record, viz: Etienne Reynaud to 1715, Abraham Sallé to April, 1720, Reynaud again for the year 1720, Jacque Soblet, 1721 to September, 1727, and Jean Chastain from 1727 'till the end of the record. Entries in other handwriting than that of the clerk are infrequent. With the exception of an incomplete memorandum under 1727 and two receipts 1748 and 1749 respectively, the entire record is in French, only such untranslatable terms as *glebe*, *shilling*, etc., being given in English; indeed, towards the end of the record there seems to be a tendency to keep the language of the registry as pure as possible from such intruders, doubtless a reaction against the growing use of English in the settlement. The language is that of the later seventeenth century, and the uncertain orthography is rather to be looked on as characteristic of this period than as a mark of ignorance on the part of individual clerks. As a matter of interest, certain passages are given in the original at the foot of the page on which the translation occurs.

Charles W. Baird,‡ the great Huguenot investigator, supposes that the greater part of the Virginia settlers came from the Swiss canton Vaud, whither they had fled from the persecutions of Louis XIV in Piedmont,|| and that consequently the Waldensian

* After 1727.

† Cf. *Huguenot Emigration*, p. x.

‡ *The Huguenot Emigration to America*, New York, 1885, p. 178.

|| More probably from Haute Savoie and eastern French provinces. I am unable to find names in the following which point to Franco-Italian origin.

element was strongly represented. It is more than likely, however, that all parts of the Grand Monarch's dominions were represented among the fugitives at Manakin Town,* and I find nothing in the following pages which can be definitely construed as dialect or provincial coloring. Only a thorough investigation of the names on the part of a genealogical expert can clear up the matter.

It is in the names that the carelessness of the scribes is most apparent, many a name appearing in half-a-dozen forms; indeed, cases occur where the same individual signs his name in two ways. As a matter of course I have reproduced the original so far as possible; but as not a few names occur neither in Brock nor Baird it is often impossible to say whether an *n* or *u*, an *r* or *t* is meant. In later years not a few English names drift in. Negroes and Indians seem to have received English names from the first.

The extract herewith presented covers the first fifteen pages of the record, which are written in the painstaking clerkly hand of Etienne Reynaud.† In the translation I have tried to reproduce the sense without altogether sacrificing the flavor of the original.

ROBERT H. FIFE.

---

* Of the names mentioned in the register the following occur in *Baird* (cf. Index): Claude Philippe de Richebourg was from Berri, Jacob Ammonet from Loudun in Poitou. Bartholémy Dupuy and A. Michaux from the Champagne, Abraham Sallé from the Isle de Ré off La Rochelle and Jean L'Orange from La Rochelle itself, Anthoine Trabue from Montauban on the Tarn in old Guyenne and Pastor Cairon from Figeac in the same neighborhood, Jacque Billebeau and Panetier from Saintonge, and Imbert from Nismes in the Provence. De la Muce, the Moses of the party, whose name does not occur in this register, belonged to a noble family near Nantes in Brittany. One is struck with the truth of Baird's remark "that probably no more interesting party . . . had crossed the ocean in the half century." (II, 178) In view of the heterogeneous elements one does not wonder at Pastor Philippe's troubles.

† M. Reynaud's familiarity with legal forms would indicate that he had been an *avocat* or *notaire* before his exile.

*Book of the Parish of King William, Containing the Proceedings of the Vestry of said Parish, Commencing December 20, 1707.

The vestry assembled at Monocantown the day and date stated above, Mr. Phillippe, minister, being present.

Ch. wardens: Abraham Soblet, Louis Dutartre. Vestry: Jacob Ammonet, Andre Aubry, Jean Farcy, Jean Fonuielle, Abraham Sallé, Gideon Chambon, Jean Maseres, Timothee Moret, Pierre Massot, Anthoine Trabue.

It was decreed that the levy of the present year be made in accordance with the account given below, amounting to the sum of twenty-nine pounds silver, currency of the country, in such manner as has been arranged by the preceding agreement with the vestry, so that each person pay, following the present division, six shillings and one half-penny, there being ninety-six persons on the list made and delivered to the clerk of the said vestry, who * * * a copy of it to the church wardens.

	£.	s.	p.
—— for Mr. Claude Phillippe, minister, for the present year, from the first of March past to the end of the present December, at thirty pounds per year,	£25	0	0
—— for Mr. Reynaud, clerk, for one year, from the first of January past to the end of the present December, - - -	3	0	0
—— for Mr. Sallé for a register for the vestry and paper, - - -	0	12	0
—— for Mr. Martin for a gallon of wine and transportation, - - -	0	8	0
	——	——	——
	——	——	——
Ninety-six persons at six shillings half-penny each makes - - -	29	0	0

* Lievre de la paroisse du roy guillaume contenant les actes du vestry de lad paroisse commencé le 20e Xbre 1707.

Le vestry assemblé a Monocantown le jour & an que dessus Mr. Phillippe, Ministre, present, etc.

Done and decreed by the vestry the day and date above stated.

E. Reynaud, C. of Vestry.

The vestry assembled the 25 of May, 1708, the minister, Mr. Phillippe, being present.

Ch. Wardens: Abraham Soblet, Louis Dutartre. Vestry: Andre Aubry, Jean Farcy, Jacob Ammonet, Gideon Chambon, Jean Maseres, Pre Massot, Anthoine Trabue, Abra. Salle.

The Srs. Abraham Soblet and Louis Dutartre, church wardens, having tendered their resignations to the vestry, their year having expired, it was enacted that the said resignations be accepted,—the day and date as above.

E. Reynaud, C.

The said Srs. Abraham Soblet and Louis Dutartre, stated in the vestry that they resigned the office of vestry-men, also that Mr. Jean Fonuielle did not wish to continue longer in the said office.

It was enacted, as regards the above, that for the present year the Srs. Anthoine Trabue and Gideon Chambon, fill the office of church wardens. In order to qualify they shall take the required oaths before Mr. Abraham Sallé, justice of the peace. Done the day and date as above.

E. Reynaud, C.

The vestry met the 25 of August, 1708. Present: Ch. Wardens Anthoine Trabue, Gideon Chambon. Vestry: Jacob Ammonet, Andre Aubry, Pierre Massot, Jean Maseres, Abraham Sallé.

It was enacted that the levy for the present year be made in accordance with the account given below, amounting to the sum of nineteen pounds, four shillings and ninepence, which is equivalent to eighty-one (persons) at four shillings and ninepence each, in conformity with the list which was delivered to the church wardens and the clerk of the said vestry.

	£	s.	p.
—— for six months for the ministry of Mr. Phillippe, from the first of January, 1708, to the end of June, at thirty pounds per year, - - - - -	15	0	0
—— for Mr. Reynaud, clerk, for one year,			

	£	s.	d.
commencing with the first of January and ending the last of next December,	3	0	0
—— to Mr. Reynaud for a book of common prayer, - - - - - -	0	5	0
—— to Mr. Reynaud for paper, - -	0	1	0
—— to Mr. Trabue for bread and wine for communion, - - - -	0	8	0
—— to the church wardens for bread and wine for the next communion, of which they shall keep account, - - -	0	10	0
	19	4	9

Done and decreed the day and date as above.

E. REYNAUD, Clerk.

It was decreed that the church wardens make a levy of eight pounds, thirteen shillings sixpence, which are due from several individuals for several articles which have been sold to them, in accordance with the list which has been delivered to them, this to be employed in the building of a church for the said parish. Done and decreed the day and year as above.

E. REYNAUD, Clerk.

The vestry met the 20 of May, 1709. Present: Ch. Wardens: Anthoine Trabue, Gideon Chambon. Vestry: Jacob Ammonet, Andre Aubry, Pierre Massot, Jean Maseres, Abraham Sallé.

It was decreed by the said vestry that Anthoine Maton, Jean Forquerand, David Bernard, and Charles Perrot fill the office of vestry, having been elected by a majority of votes of the said vestry and having taken the oaths required by law.

E. REYNAUD, Clerk.

The vestry met the 3 of October, 1710, Mr. Phillippe, the minister, being present.

Ch. Wardens: Jacob Ammonet, Jean Farcy. Vestry: Abraham Sallé, Anthoine Trabue, Louis Dutartre, Jean Fonuielle, Gideon Chambon, Pierre Massot, Jean Forquerand, André Aubry, Charles Perrot, David Bernard, Anthoine Maton,

*It was decreed, in consequence of the arrangement which it pleased his Excellency Alexander Spotswood, esq., Lieutenant-Governor for Her Majesty in Virginia, to make on the 23d of September past, for the maintenance of the peace between the vestry and the parishioners, that all the differences which have existed up to the present time between the said vestry and the said parishioners shall be entirely obliterated, as well with regard to what has been said as with reference to what has been written, and that no reproaches shall be made on that account. As has been set forth in the said arrangement and in conformity with the same, the said vestry approves and confirms the agreement which the said parishioners have made with Mr. Phillippe, the minister, for the present year, and the bargain made with Anthoine Rapine for the building of a church.†

In addition, it has been provided by the said arrangement that the Srs. Abraham Soblet, Louis Dutartre, and Jean Fonuielle, former vestrymen of the said parish, who were last in the office of vestry, as appears according to the record inserted in the present register, be permitted anew to take the oath in order to be qualified as vestrymen. This the aforesaid Louis Dutartre and Jean Fonuielle did on the above date, in conformity with the law, before Abraham Sallé, Her Majesty's Justice of the Peace, Abraham Soblet having declared that he did not wish to take the said oath, not having the intention of qualifying himself for the said office.

Done and decreed in the vestry the day and date above.

E. REYNAUD, Clerk.

---

* Il a esté arretté en consequance de lacord quil aplus ason Exelence Alexandre Spottswood, esq , Luitenant Gouverneur pour sa Majeste en Virginie le 23e 7bre dernier pour le maintient de la paix entre le vestry & les parroissents que tous les diferents quil y'a eux jusqua ce jour entre ledit vestry et lesdits parroissents seroient entierement abolys tant de parole que par ecrit de part & dautre & quaucunes reproches nen pourront etre fait. Ainssi quil est mentionné dans ledit acord, & conformem. a Icelui led vestry aproue & confirme ce traitté que lesd. parroissiens out fait avec M[r] phillippe ministre pour la pre[te] anné & le marché fait avec anthoine rapine pour le batiment dune Eglize.

† For other papers bearing on this "church row," which seems to have begun more than three years before, and which was referred to the Virginia Council for settlement, cf. Brock, p. 69 ff., and below.

The vestry met on December 30, 1710, Mr. Phillippe, the minister, being present.

Ch. Wardens: Jacob Ammonet, Jean Farcy. (Vestry): Abraham Sallé, Anthoine Trabue, Louis Dutartre, Jean Fonuielle, Gideon Chambon, Pierre Massot, Jean Forquerant, Andre Aubry, Charles Perrot, David Bernard, Anthoine Maton.

List of Expenses of the Parish of King William for the Present Year, 1710.

First:	£	s.	d.
—— For Mr. Phillippe, the minister,	40	0	0
—— for Mr. Reynaud, the clerk,	4	0	0
—— for Anthoine Rapine, for building a church,	20	0	0
—— for the bread and wine for communion, to Mr. Phillippe,	1	0	0
—— to Mr. Phillippe for having gone to ask help of the governor,		15	0
—— to Bon Sergent, for having been to get the nails,		10	0
—— to Pre Faure, for two days work,		3	9
—— to Louis Soblet, for three days work of himself and one day of his horse,		6	7
—— to Etienne Chastain, two and one-half days,		4	6
—— to Daniel Maubain, for having made the *chimneys (?) for the church,		6	0
—— to Jean Farcy, two days,		3	9
—— to Pierre Dutoi, two and one-half days,		4	6
—— to Jean Fonuielle, one day,		1	10½
—— to Isaac Parentau, two days,		3	9
—— to Isaac Lafitte, two days,		3	9
—— to Maton, one day,		1	10½
—— to Louis Dutartre, for hauling with his cart and one day,		13	0
—— to Andre Aubry, for one day,		1	10½
—— to Etienne Reynaud, for one day,		1	10½
—— to Mr. Chatain, for hauling and (one) day,		12	0

*Tyax (tuyaux) ?

	£	s.	d.
—— to Gideon Chambon, for one-half day and one day of his horse, - - -		2	5
—— to Bilbaut for one day, - - -		1	10½
	69	18	4½

Account of that which is due to the parish by individuals named below:

	£	s.	d.
—— Abraham Soblet for the levy of 1709, which he has not paid, - - -		12	6
—— Moise Leurau, for a pair of *paigne.**	1	15	0
—— Jacque Bioret, for a pair of *paigne.**	1	12	0
—— by several individuals, according to the account of sale, - - - - -	8	13	6
	12	13	0
—— to Lucadou, for the sale at one shilling per £ - - - - 12 0			
—— to Mr. Chatain for nails, - 4 6		16	6
	11	66	6

	£	s.	d.
Amount of the list of expenses of the parish enumerated elsewhere, - - -	69	18	4½
Less that which is due, according to the above account, - - - - -	11	16	6
Leaves for the levy of the present year 1710,	58	1	10½

LIST OF TITHABLE PERSONS.

Jean Calvet,	1	Isaac Lafuitte,	1
Charles Perrot,	1	Jean Rousse,	1
Pre. Faure,	1	Jean Dep.,	1
Jean Rapine,	1	Mathien Oset,	1
Jean Soulllé,	1	Etienne Mallet,	1
Jean Joenny,	1	Jacque Bioret,	1
Etienne Chastain,	1	Jean Farcy,	1

*The word is plain but its meaning altogether obscure. *Peigne* or *pagne* are orthographically possibly, but neither can denote anything likely to have been sold on behalf of the parish for the price named.

Pierre Dutoy,	2	Jean Solaigr,	1
Jacque Bilbaut,	1	Isaac Parant[a],	1
Jean Lorange,	1	Francois Dupuy,	1
Jean Panattie,	1	Daniel Maubain,	1
Gideon Chambon,	1	Anthoine Matton,	1
Pierre Chatain,	2	Adam Vigne,	1
Pre. Videt,	1	Andre Aubry,	1
Paul Duuerrat,	1	Louis Soblet,	1
Louis Dutartre,	1	Jacque Soblet,	1
Abra. Soblet,	2	Thomas Briant,	1
Etienne Bocard,	1	Etienne Reynaud,	1
Michel Cantpy,	1	Jean Fonuielle,	1
Francois Clapie,	1	Jean Voyer,	1
Timotée Roux,	1	Jacque Febure,	1
Jean Dupre,	1	Pre. Sabattié,	1
Jacob Ammonet,	1	Bart. Dupuy,	2
Jean le Villain,	1	Anth. Giuandan,	1
David Bernard,	1	Abra. Michaud,	1
Pre. Laune,	1	Thomas Alison,	1
Abra. Salle,	2	Pierre Massot,	1
Jean Forqueran,	1	Moyse Leurau,	1
Jean Martin, } Jean Poel, }	2	Jacob Capon,	1
		Abra. Remy,	1
Anthoine Trabue,	1	M. Bon Sergent,	1
Francois Sasin,	1	Pre. Gourry,	1
Jean Dupon,	1	Jean Lucadou,	1
Pre. Morise,	1		
	38		34

		£	s.	d.
38				
34				
72	tithable persons at 16s. 1½d.=	58	1	
Balance,	- - - - - -	0	0	10½
		58	1	10½

It was decreed and ordered that the fifty-eight pounds one shilling mentioned above be levied by the church wardens of the said parish, and, in default of payment, that execution be taken against those who refuse, in conformity with the law.

Done and decreed the day and date as above.

E. REYNAUD, Clerk.

It was decreed that Abra. Salle, Anthoine Trabue, Jacob Ammonet, Jean Farcy shall conjointly contract with a joiner for whatever shall be necessary for the decoration of the interior of our church, arranging and definitely settling that which they shall agree on.

Done the day and date above. E. REYNAUD, Clerk.

*We, the undersigned minister and clerk of the parish of King William, acknowledge having received from the church wardens of the said parish the payment of forty-five pounds, due us for our services for the year 1710, each for the portion which falls to him, namely forty-one pounds for Mr. Phillippe, minister, and four pounds for Mr. Reynaud, clerk.

In testimony of which we have signed the 3 of March, 1711.

C. PHILIPPE DE RICHEBOURG, Minister.
E. REYNAUD, Clerk.

and also for the preceding year we acknowledge having received from the church wardens of the said year the payment of what was due us for our services.

Done the same day.

C. PHILIPPE DE RICHEBOURG, Minister.
E. REYNAUD, Clerk.

The vestry assembled the 3 of April, 1711, Mr. Phillippe de Richebourg, minister, being present.

Church Wardens: Jacob Ammonet, Jean Farcy. Vestry: Abraham Sallé, Louis Dutartre, Anthoine Trabue, Gideon Chambon, Anthoine Matton, André Aubry, Jean Forquerant, Jean Fonuielle, David Bernard.

It was decreed that Jean Forquerant and Jean Fonuielle fill the office of church wardens in the place of Mr Jacob Ammonet and Jean Farcy for the present year, and take the oaths according to law.

Done the day and date above.

E. REYNAUD, Clerk.

The vestry assembled the 30 of June, 1711, Mr. Cairon, minister, being present.

* In Philippe's hand.

Church Wardens: Jean Fonuielle, Jean Forquerant. Vestry: Abraham Sallé, Jacob Ammonet, Jean Farcy, Louis Dutartre, Gideon Chambon, Anthoine Maton, Andre Aubry, David Bernard, Charles Perrot.

List of tithable persons, in order to pay five months and fifteen days services of Mr. Phillippe:

Jacob Ammonet,	1
Anthoine Trabue,	1
Abraham Remy,	1
Moyse Leurau,	1
Andre Aubry,	1
David Bernard,	1
———	
Abraham Sallé,	
Zefir, negro,	2
———	
Paul Duuerrat,	1
Jean Voyer,	1
Louis Dutartre,	1
Adam Vigne,	1
Pierre Viett,	1
Jean Lucadou,	1
Robert Snougs,	1
Gideon Chambon,	1
Joseph Mollinier,	1
Nicollas Souille,	1
Anthoine Matton,	1
Pierre Dutoy,	1
Jean Faisant,	1
Étienne Chastain,	1
Anthoine Rapine,	1
Mathieu Ange,	1
Isaac Lafuitte,	
Francois Lafuitte,	2
———	
Jean Joany,	
William Bif, Indian,	2
	—
	28

Pierre Chastain,	
Jean Chastain,	2
———	
Etienne Malle,	
Jeny, Indian woman,	2
———	
Jean Panetier,	
William (erased),	
Abraham Soblet,	
Jacque Soblet,	
Abraham Soblet,	3
———	
Louis Soblet,	1
Jean Solaigre,	1
Pierre Delaunay,	1
Jean Calvet,	1
Charle Perault,	1
Jean le Vilain,	1
Thomas Briant,	1
Thomas Dupre,	1
Jean Burck,	1
Jean Moore,	1
Jean Forquerant,	1
Francois Sassin,	1
P[re] Gorry,	1
Jean Dupon,	1
Jean Rosset,	1
Jean Depe,	1
Etienne Bocard,	1
	—
	25

(TO BE CONTINUED.)

THE VESTRY BOOK OF KING WILLIAM PARISH, VA., 1707–1750.

Francois Dupuy,	1
Isaac Lefebur,	1
Francois Dulapied,	1
Pierre Sabatie,	1
Pierre Morissie,	1
Thomas Alison,	1
Mathieu Bon Sergent,	1
Michel Cantpy,	1
Bartholemy Dupuy, Pierre Dupuy,	2
Jean Dupuy,	1
Jean Fonuielle,	1
Jean Lorange, Daniel Maubain,	2
Etienne Reynaud,	1
Anthoine Giuaudant,	1
Abra. Michaux,	1
Jean Martin, Joell, negro, Jean Powell,	3
	20

Jacob Capon,	1
Isaac Parantau,	1
Jacque Bilbaud,	1
Jean Farcy,	1
Jacque Bioret,	1
Pierre Faure,	1
Claude Gorry,	0
Jean Corner,	1
	7

Recapitulation of tithable persons:

	28
	25
	20
	7
Tithables,	80

	£	s	d
—— For 5 months 15 days, from Jan. 1 to June 15, which Mr. Philipe has preached, at £40 per year, - - - -	18	6	8
—— for bread and wine for communion, to Mr. Phillipe, - . - - -		18	0
—— paid by Sr Philipe to Martin for hauling the timber, - - - -	2	0	9
—— paid by Mr. Phillippe to Bilbaud for hauling the timber, - - - -		3	9
—— to balance from last year, - - -			10½
	21	10	1½

By one day paid in excess to Mr. Philipe last year, - - - - - - - -		1	10½
	21	8	2

It was decreed that the twenty-one pounds, eight shillings and two pence mentioned above be levied by the church wardens of the said parish, and that in default of payment execution be taken against those who refuse, in conformity with the law, the said tax amounting for each tithable person to the sum of five shillings four pence and one farthing. Done and decreed the day and date as above.

E. REYNAUD, Clerk.

*I have received from the church wardens of the parish of King William the sum of twenty one pounds eight shillings and two pence, due me by the said parish, as well for five months and one-half of my ministry as for expenses, of which I acknowledge receipt. Done at Monocantown, the 21st of November, 1711.

C. PHILIPPE DE RICHEBOURG.†

‡Copy of the proceedings which were erased by Mr. Phillippe on the old register of the vestry:

The vestry assembled at Monocantown, March 27, 1707. Present,—Church Wardens: Andre Aubry. Vestry: Jacob Amonnet, Abra. Sobler, Francois Ribot, Jean Fonuielle, Jean Farcy, Louis Dutartre, Abra. Sallé.

---

* In Phillippe's hand, as follows:

J'ay recu des Church Wardens de la paroisse du Roy Guillaume la somme de vingt et une pieces huit shilings deux sols qui mestoient deub par la d. paroisse, tant p. cinq mois et demy de mon ministere que pou. frais, dont je les tients quitte fait a monocantown ce 21e 9bre, 1711.

C. PHILIPPE DE RICHEBOURG.

†According to Baird, *Huguenot Emigration*, II, 105, Philippe left Virginia for South Carolina, where he became minister of the French settlement at Santee, dying in 1719. Brock, pp. x and 45, note, supposes incorrectly that his departure took place in 1707.

‡ Cf. above, page 295 and note. (Page 101, this volume.)

It was decreed that in view of the indirect methods and the unusual and irregular conduct displayed at the session by Mr. Philipe, the minister, that Mr. Amonnet, vestryman, signify and protest in the presence of the congregation to the said S[r] Philipe that the arrangement and agreement which he has made with several parishioners is entirely disapproved by the vestry, being made contrary to the laws and customs established in Virginia and without the participation of the vestry, that therefore the vestry will make no order nor lay no tax for its payment. Done and decreed at Monocantown the day and date as above. Signed: Abra. Soblet, Andre Aubry, Jacob Amonnet, Louis Dutartre, Jean Fonuielle, Farcy, Ribot, Abrah. Sallé.

*The vestry assembled April 7, 1707. Present,—Ch. Wardens: Andre Aubry. (Vestry) Jacob Amonnet, Abra. Soblet, Francois Ribot, Jean Fonuielle, Jean Farcy, Louis Dutartre, Abra. Sallé.

Regarding the report which has been made us by Mr. Jacob Amonnet, that Sunday, the 30th ultimo, after the divine service, having wished to proceed to the reading of the declaration which we had made against the bad conduct of Mr. Philipe, Jacque Lacaze and some others, he was interrupted by the said S[r] Philipe, who addressed himself to S[r] Reynaud, clerk of the church and of the said vestry, warning him with much heat that if he would not give over to him the book of christenings he would exclude him from communion, as well as all of those generally who did not go to him to get their tickets or order-number.† He declared publicly that he did not recognize any vestry and

---

* Continuation of the foregoing copy.

† Prandre des jettons ou numero en suitte. It is possible that the reference is to some system devised by the minister for preventing crowding at the chancel rail and to keep out improper persons. It was not unusual among contemporary Lutheran churches in Germany and America to require the parishioners to appear before the minister in the week preceding the communion and undergo a sort of confession. Cf. for an interesting account of the practice, as observed by Pastor Muhlenberg of the Pennsylvania Lutheran church in the first half of the eighteeth century, Jacobs' *History of the Evangelical Lutheran Church in the United States*, New York, 1897, pp. 228 and 232. For suggestion and reference I am indebted to Professor Kuhns, of Wesleyan University.

that the people ought not to recognize it. The above Jacque Lacaze, Michel Michel and several others opposed the reading with an uproar and extraordinary confusion, tending to bring about dangerous trouble. The said Lacaze having demanded of the said Jacob Amonnet by what order he wished to read this paper, and having been told by him that it was by order of the vestry, answered him with rage that he had lied and that this was not true and several other insulting expressions, having likewise refused to keep the peace when Abra Sallé commanded them in the name of Her Majesty, saying that this was neither the place nor the occasion, the said Michel approaching the said Sr Sallé with much rage and in a threatening manner. This was done and transpired in our presence, and we attest thereto, that it may serve at such time and place as shall seem best. Done the day and date above.

Signed: Abra. Sallé, Louis Dutartre, Jacob Amonnet, Jean Farcy, Abra. Soblet, Jean Fonuielle, Ribot, A. Aubry and E. Reynaud, clerk.*

† We the vestry having assembled and having made an inspection of the minutes, which have been heretofore adopted in the old register, have found with surprise that two of the said

* Justice Sallé's account of the affair differs slightly from the foregoing. Cf. Brock, p. 69 ff., quoted from the Calendar of State Papers of Virginia, I, pp. 114–116.

† Etant assemblé en vestry et ayant fait la visitte des actes qui ont esté cy deuant passé sur le vieux registre nous auons trouvé avec surprise que deux desdits actes ont esté biffés par le sieur philipe sans quaucun dudit vestry en ayt, en connoissance le p. du 27 mars 1707 et lautre du 7 avril de la meme annee, Il aeste arrettée veu la hardiesse & limpudance dud. sr. phillippe d Entreprendre de son chef de paraille chose quon en registreroit de nouveau lesdits actes sur la registre dud. vestry ayant pour cet Esfait este dechifrés & transcripts, mot pour mot, pour preuue authentique de sa mauvaise conduitte ayant meme trouué les dernieres pages dud. registre ostés le tout ne pouuant avoit éste fait par led. sr. philipe que par un malice extraord[re] & une entiere deliberation de sa volonté lors quil lesdits registres entre ses mains led. sr. reynaud clerc nous ayant protesté quil lui avoit remy dans le meme etat, et que ledit phillipe lui avoit dit que cetoit lui qui avoit biffé lesdits actes layant declaré lui meme au vestry fait et signé le jour et an pour servir et valoir en temps et lieu comme il appariendra.

records have been erased by the Sieur Philipe, without one of the said vestry having anything to do with it; namely, the first, that of March 27, 1707, and the other, that of April 7 of the same year. It was decreed, in view of the boldness and the impudence of the said S[r] Phillippe in undertaking such a thing of his own motion, that the said minutes be entered anew on the register of the said vestry, having been for that purpose deciphered and transcribed word for word, as an authentic proof of his wicked conduct, it having been even found that the last pages of the said register were taken away. All of this could have been done only by the said S[r] Philipe as an extraordinary act of spite and with perfect deliberation and volition on his part, when he had possession of the said register, the said S[r] Reynaud, the clerk, having protested to us that he had delivered it to him in the same state, and that the said Phillipe had told him that it was he who had erased the said minutes, having himself declared it to the vestry. Done and signed the *day and year above, that it may serve and be of use at such time and place as shall seem best.

†Abra. Sallé,	J. Cairon, min.
Farcy,	Louis Dutartre,
Gideon Chambon,	David Bernard,
Antoine Maton,	J. Fonielle,
Charles Perault,	A. Aubry.

The vestry met to-day, November 21, 1711, Mr. Cairon, the minister, being present. Ch. Warden: Jean Forquerant. Vestry: Abraham Sallé, Jacob Ammonet, Jean Farcy, Louis Dutartre, Andre Aubry, Charles Perault, Gideon Chambon, Anthoine Trabue, Dauid Bernard.

List of expenses of the parish of King William for the last six and one-half months of the present year, 1711, ending the last of December next, viz:

	£	s.	d.
——For six and one-half months' salary to Mr. Cairon, minister, at forty pounds per year - - - - - - -	21	18	8

* The date is nowhere expressly stated; it was, however, November 21, 1711, as may be deduced from the preceding and following entries.

† The signatures are all personal.

—for the entire year to Reynaud, clerk,	4	0	0
—for Jean Voyer, joiner, for work which he has done in the parish church, according to the agreement which was made, - - - - - - -	11	0	0
—to Etienne Mallet for a day's work and hauling for the church, - - -		4	0
—to Jean Caluet for a day do., - -		1	10½
—to Francoi Dupui do., - - -		1	10½
—to Adam Vigne for one day and other work do., - - - - - -		3	10½
—to Jean Voier, two days do., - -		3	9
—to Jean Lorange for one day of himself and of his horse, - - - - -		3	10
—to Jacque Soblet for two days of himself and of his horse, - - -		5	9
—to Jean Panetié one day, - - -		1	10½
—to Pierre Viett one day, - - -		3	0
—to Jean Forquerant for having been to get powder and lead for the parish,		6	0
—to Anthoine Trabue for rent of a chamber for Mr. Cairon, - - -		10	0
—Mathieu Agé, who has not paid for the year 1710, - - - - - -		16	1½
—Robert Snogs, —John Powell, —John Corner, } listed in another parish, who have not paid the 5s. 4½d. of the first 5½ months of the present year,		16	¾
	40	15	10¼

List of tithable persons of the present year 1711, in order to pay the six and one-half months of service and other expenses:

Jacob Amonnet,	1	Thomas Dupre,	1
Anthoine Trabue,	1	Jean Burck,	1
Abraham Remy,	1	Jean Moore,	1
Moyse Leurau,	1	Jean Forquerant,	1
Andre Aubry,	1	Francoise Sassine,	1

Dauid Bernard	I
Abraham Sallé, Zefir, negro,	2
Paul Duuerrat,	I
Jean Voyer,	I
Louis Dutartre,	I
Adam Vigne,	I
Pierre Viett,	I
Jean Lucadou,	I
Gideon Chambon,	I
Joseph Molinier,	I
Nicolas Souillé,	I
Anthoine Matton,	I
Pre Dutoy,	I
Jean Faisant,	I
Etienne Chatain,	I
Anthoine Rapine,	I
Mathieu Agé,	I
Isaac Lafuitte, Francoy Lafuitte,	2
Jean Joanny,	I
Willm Bif, Indian,	I
Pierre Chastain, Jean Chastain,	2
Etienne Mallé, Geny, Indian woman,	2
Jean Panettier,	I
Abra. Soblet, Jacque Soblet, Abra. Soblet,	3
Jean Solaigre,	I
Jean Cauet,	I
Jean le Villain,	I

Pierre Gourry,	I
Jean Dupon,	I
Jean Rosset,	I
Jean Depe,	I
Etienne Bocard,	I
Francois Dupuy,	I
Isaac Lefebure,	I
Francois Dulapied,	I
Pierre Morisee,	I
Pierre Sabattie,	I
Thomas Alison,	I
Mat. Bonsergen,	I
Michel Cantpy,	I
Barth. Dupui, Pierre Dupui,	2
Jean Dupre,	I
Jean Fonuielle,	I
Jean Lorange, Daniel Maubin,	2
Etienne Reynaud,	I
Anthoine Giuaudant,	I
Abraham Michaud,	I
Jean Martin, Joel, negro,	2
Jacob Capon,	I
Isaac Parantau,	I
Jacque Bilbaud,	I
Jean Farcy,	I
Jacque Bioret,	I
Pre Faure,	I
Thomas Eliar,	I
Louis Soblet,	I
Pierre Delaune,	I
Charles Perrault,	I
Thomas Briant,	I
	78

	£	s.
78 persons at 10 s. 6 d. each amounts to the sum of,	40	19

There is due from individuals as follows, namely:

	£	s.	d.
By Isaac Lafuitte, - - - - - -		12	0
By Jean Rosset, - - - - - -	1	1	0
By Thomas Eliar, - - - - - -		5	4¼
	1	18	4¼
By Mr. Cairon, amount in excess in the levy, which he will carry over to next year,		3	1¾
	2	1	6

It was decreed and ordered that the forty pounds, nineteen shillings above be levied by the church wardens of the said parish, amounting to the sum of ten shillings and six pence each, to be employed in the payment of Mr. Cairon, minister, and of the clerk and of other items mentioned in the account elsewhere, in default of which execution shall be taken. At Monocantown the day and year as above.

E. REYNAUD, Clerk.

The vestry assembled to-day, June 23, 1712, Mr. Cairon, the minister, being present. Ch. W.: Jean Forquerant, Jean Fonuielle. Vestry: Jacob Amonnet, Gideon Chambon, Andre Aubry, Anth. Trabue, Charles Perault, Anth. Maton, Jean Farcy, Abra. Salle.

Regarding the report of Mr. Cairon, our minister, and several of the vestry, that Dauid Bernard had declared that he no longer filled the office of vestryman, it was agreed that this be adopted in the present minutes. Done at Monacantown the day and year above.

E. REYNAUD, Clerk.

The vestry assembled this day, September 15, 1712, in the presence of Mr. Cairon, the minister.

Ch. Wardens: Jean Forquerant, Jean Fonuielle. Vestry: Jacob Amonnet, Gideon Chambon, André Aubry, Anth. Trabue, Charles Perault, Anth. Maton, Jean Farcy, Abra. Sallé.

Statement of expenses for the current year 1712:

				£	s.	d.
—To Mr. Cairon for his ministry,	£40	0	0			
—for wine for the communion,	0	1	6			
—for Joseph * Molinier, who has not paid for the last year of his ministry,	0	10	6			
				40	12	0
—to Mr. Reynaud, clerk, for his year of service,				4	0	0
—to Mr. Forquerand, Ch. W., for wine for communion,	0	6	0			
—what he paid to Mr. Philipe for the parish,	0	5	4			
				0	11	4
—to Mr. Salle for what he paid for forwarding letter for the parish,	0	2	6			
—for paper which he has furnished,	0	1	6			
				0	4	0
—to Mr. Dupuy for carrying an order of the governor to Col. † Epes concerning the affairs of the parish,				0	4	0
—to Mad[e] Lorange for a lock,				0	5	0
—for bread for the communion,				0	10	0

* Molinier's name having appeared among the tithables in 1711 and his assessment remaining unpaid, Mr. Cairon is out of pocket that amount until re-imbursed by the credit above. Joseph Molinier and his wife were among the passengers who crossed in the ship *Nasseau* in 1700, cf., Brock, *Huguenot Emigration*, p. 30.

Mr. Dutoit is held responsible for the unpaid balance of Molinier's assessment for 1712, cf. expense-account under 1713. It is probable that Molinier died in 1712 or the following year, his name not re-appearing in these records.

† Probably Colonel Francis Eppes, of City Point, who with Colonel Byrd, Colonel Randolph and other prominent men of the colony, visited and gave good advice to the refugees at Manakin Town in May, 1701. The nearness of the Eppes' family-seat and their kind feeling for the refugees may have led to especially intimate relations between Colonel Eppes and the parish. Cf. Brock, p. 42, note.

—for an express sent to *Ligon on business of the parish, - - - - - - - - 0 10 0

	£	s	d
	46	16	4

LIST OF TITHABLES FOR THE YEAR 1712.

Jean Caluet,	1	Etienne Reynaud,	1
Isaac Lafuitte, / Francoy Lafuitte,	2	Anth. Rapine,	1
		Nicola Souille,	1
Thomas Eliard,	1	Francoy Dupuy,	1
Charles Perrault,	1	Pierre Viette,	1
Etienne Bocard, / Wilm Angloy,	2	Jean Jouanny, / Pre Oliuier,	2
Mathieu Age,	1	Jacque Bioret,	1
Jean Rousset,	1	Jean Farcy,	1
Pierre Faure,	1	Etienne Chatain,	1
	10		10
Pierre Dutoy, / Jean Faisant,	2	Adam Vigne, / Jacob Allard,	2
Jean Solaigre,	1	Guillaume Blanc,	1
Jacque Bilbaud,	1	Jean Forquerant,	1
Isaac Parantaut,	1	Moise Leurau,	1
Jean Panetier,	1	Jean Martin, / Jacque, negro, / Jean, negro,	3
Claude Gourry, / Jacque Etelain,	2		
Gideon Chambon,	1	Ab. Remy,	1
Anth. Maton,	1	Anth. Trabue,	1
Pre Chatain, / Jean Chatain,	2	Math. Bonsergent,	1
		Francoy Sassin,	1
Andre Aubry,	1	John Poiret,	1

* Not otherwise mentioned in the register. The name is noted by Bishop Meade as that of one of the families still living in Virginia which are descended from Huguenot ancestry. Cf. *Old Churches and Families of Virginia*, I, p. 468. This is an error, Ligon or Lygon being an English name. The person referred to may have been Thomas Ligon, surveyor of Henrico county at this time. For this note I am in debted to Mr. W. G. Stanard, of the Virginia Historical Society.

*M[de] Duuerra, his (or her) negro Broed, 1
Louis Soblet, } 2
P[re] Delaune, }
P[re] † Dauid, 1
Ab. Soblet, père, }
Jacque Soblet, fils, } 3
Ab. Soblet, fils, }
Thomas Briant, 1
Jean Fonuielle, } 2
Willm, negro, }
Jean Voyer, 1
Francoy Clapied, 1
Michel Cantpy, 1
Jean Dupre, 1
Isaac le Febure, 1
Jacob Amonnet, } 2
Jacob Amonnet, fils, }
Jacob Capon, 1
Bartelemy Dupuy, } 2
Pierre Dupuy, }
Jean le Villain, 1
Anth. Giuaudant, 1
Dauid Bernard, 1
Abra. Michaud, } 2
Jacob Michaud, }
Thomas Alison, 1
Abra. Salle, } 2
Zefir, negro, }

—

41

P[re] Morises, 1
John Corner, 1

—

15
41
10
10

—

76

—

76 tithables at 12 s. 4 d. each makes the sum of:

£	s.	d.
46	17	4

Amount in excess of the tax, carried over by Mr. Cairon to the next year, ... 1 s.

It was decreed and ordered that the forty-six pounds, seven-

* It is impossible to say whether Paul Duuerrat, whose name appears in preceding tax-lists, or his wife (widow) is meant. Hereafter the name disappears from the register. Neither Baird nor Brock offers any name which can be identified with it.

† It is hardly necessary to call attention to clerk Reynaud's constant use of *u* for internal *v*. Cf. Lefebure, Giuaudant, etc., etc.

teen shillings, four-pence mentioned elsewhere be levied by the church wardens of the said parish, amounting to the sum of twelve shillings, four pence each, to be employed in the payment of Mr. Cairon, the minister, as well as of the clerk, and of the other items mentioned in the account elsewhere. In default of which execution shall be made.

Done at Monocantown the day and date above.

E. REYNAUD, Clerk.

By a plurality of votes of the present vestry the Srs Jean le Villain and Pierre Dutoy were elected vestrymen in the place of the Sr Louis Dutartre, deceased, and Dauid Bernard, who has asked for his discharge; and it was decreed that they take the oaths required by law before the Sr Salle.

Done the day and date above.

E. REYNAUD, Clerk.

The vestry assembled this day, April 7, 1713, Mr. Cairon, the minister, being present.

Ch. Wardens: Jean Forquerant, Jean Fonuielle. Vestry: Jacob Amonnet, Gideon Chambon, Andre Aubry, Charles Perrault, Anthoine Maton, Jean Farcy, Jean le Villain, Pierre Dutoy, Ab. Salle.

It was decreed by the present vestry that the Srs Anthoine Trabue and Jean le Villain fill the office of church wardens in the place of Jean Forquerant and Jean Fonuielle for the present year 1713, and take the oaths in conformity with the law before Mr. Abrahd. Salle, Justice of the Peace for Her Majesty.

Done at Monocantown the day and date above.

E. REYNAUD, Clerk.

We, minister and clerk of the church of Monocantown, certify to having received from the Srs Jean Forquerant and Jean Fonuielle, ch. wardens, in full, all due us for the six and one-half months of the year 1711 and for the whole year 1712, of which we hold quit the said church wardens and all others. In testimony of which we have drawn them the present receipt, the day and date as above.

*J. CAIRON, Min.
E. REYNAUD, Clerk.

---

* Mr. Cairon's signature is personal.

The vestry assembled this, the 15th day of June, 1713, Mr. Cairon, the minister being present.

Ch. W: Anthoine Trabue, Jean le Vilain. Vestry: Jean Forquerant, Jean Fonuielle, Jacob Amonnet, Gideon Chambon, Anthoine Matton, Charles Perrault, Jean Farcy, Pierre Dutoy, Abra Salle.

Whereas, Jean * Inbert having deceased and left to his wife Jeanne Inbert two daughters of tender age, named Jeanne and Anne Inbert, and the said Jeanne Inbert having after the decease of her husband married Jacob Capon and having likewise died, leaving the above-mentioned children orphans, the said Cappon taking no care as to their bringing-up nor giving them any education, it was decreed for the welfare of the said infants by the present vestry, assembled for this purpose, that the Sr Anthoine Trabue and Jean le Villain, provide in accordance with their best judgment some good place for the abovesaid orphans, being for this purpose authorized by the present vestry to make such engagement as shall be necessary and possible for the welfare of the said children in conformity with the law of the land.

Done and decreed the day and date above.

E. REYNAUD, Clerk.

We, the minister and clerk of the parish of King William, certify to having received from the Srs Jean Forquerand and Jean Fonuielle Ch. Wardens of the said parish, in full all due us for the year 1712, in accordance with the tax heretofore made for that purpose, of which we hold quit the said church wardens

---

* The list of refugees settled at Manakin Town, printed among other papers taken from the MSS. in the Bodleian Library at Oxford, contains the names of Imbert and wife as passengers in the first ship, arriving in late summer 1700. Cf. Brock, p. 36. Imbert is not mentioned among the tithables of 1709, so that his death probably occurred before that time. The family fled from Nismes in Languedoc, Andrew Imbert, possibly a brother, swearing obedience to the Pennsylvania colony as early as 1683. Cf. Baird, II, 133. The two orphan girls mentioned above, Suzanne and Jeanne, occur in the list of orphans in the colony for 1714. Cf. Brock, p. 76. The unkind step-father appears in the records of the parish as late as 1729 (Brock, 83), but no further mention of the children occurs.

and all others. In testimony of which we have drawn them the present receipt.

Done at Monocantown the 12 of November, 1713.

*J. Cairon, Min.
E. Reynaud, Clerk.

The vestry assembled this day, November 12, 1713, Monsieur Cairon, the minister, being present.

Ch. W.: Anthoine Trabue, Jean le Villain. Vestry: Jacob Amonnet, Jean Farcy, Jean Fonuielle, Jean Forquerant, Gideon Chambon, Charles Perault, Abraham Salle, Anthoine Maton, Pierre Dutoy, Andre Aubry.

Statement of expenses for the current year 1713:

		£	s.	d.
——To Mr. Cairon for his ministry,	£40 0 0			
——for food to † Blakment, - -	0 10 0			
	———	40	10	0
——for Etienne Reynaud, clerk, - - - -		4	0	0
——to the church wardens for wine for communion,		0	14	0
——for transportation of the wine for communion,		0	5	0
——to Mr. Andre Aubry for having furnished bread for the communion, - - - - -		0	3	0
——to Jean Blakment for having made an addition to the house of Mr. Cairon and for ‡ clapboards which have been sold, due him or Chambre, - - - - - - - -		2	0	0
——to Mr. Michaux for having sent an express to the house of Majord § Bollain for wine for the communion, - - - - - -		0	5	0
——to Mr. Etienne Chatain for a bottle of wine which he brought from Willmsbourg, - -		0	1	10½

* Signed by Cairon personally. It is unclear why this receipt, a duplicate of the one above, should have been thought necessary.

† He was probably boarded by the pastor while building the addition to the latter's house. Cf. following items. Blakement's (Blakeman's) name appears among the tithables of 1713.

‡ du *clabor* qui a este vendu. I can find no other explanation. Cf. the expense account for this year.

§ Bolling.

——to Mr. Maton for repairing the chimney of Mr. Cairon's house and uniting the addition with the chimney, - - - - - - - 0 5 0

——to Mr. Remy for the boarding the child of Perru for two months and eleven days, - 0 18 2

	49	2	½

LIST OF TITHABLES FOR THE CURRENT YEAR 1713.

Jean Dupre,	1	Jacob Amonnet, jeune,	1
Moise Leurau,	1	Francois de Clapied,	1
Thomas Dupre,	1	Michel de Cantpy,	1
Pierre Chatain, Robert, negro,	2	Anth. Maton,	1
		Charles Perrault,	1
Jean Chatain,	1	Abraham Salle,	1
Pierre Dauid,	1	Anth. Trabue,	1
Abraham Soblet,	1	Jean le Villain,	1
Abraham Soblet, jeune,	1	Abrah. *Michaud, Jacob Michaux,	2
Jacque Soblet,	1		
Louis Soblet,	1	Jean Burck,	1
Jean Solaigre,	1	Jean Fonuielle, Bety, negress,	2
Pierre Launay,	1		
Thomas Briant,	1	Lanier Potter,	1
Andre Aubry,	1	Jean Forquerant,	1
Jean Farcy,	1	Dauid Bernard,	1
Gideon Chambon,	1	Abraham Remy,	1
Jacob Amonnet,	1	Barthelemy Dupuy,	1
	—	Thomas Dalison, Jacob Alar,	2
	18		—
			20
			—
Etienne Chatain,	1		39
Pierre Dutoy,	1		18

* A curious instance of Clerk Reynaud's carelessness with regard to proper names. He writes here the names of father and son with different final consonant—in pronunciation of course a mute consonant. For details regarding the Champagnese patriarch Abraham Michaux and his large family cf. Brock, p. 133, note. Baird, II, 109, gives a thrilling account of the escape of his wife Suzanne from Sedan.

Jean Caluet,	1	20
Jacque Bilbau,	1	—
Jean Panetier,	1	77
Jean Blackement,	1	—
Pierre Cairon,	1	
Jean Powell,	1	
Pierre Morrisset,	1	
Mathieu Bonsergent,	1	
Francois Sassin,	1	
Claude Gourry,	1	
Isaac Lafitte, Francois Lafitte,	2	
Jean Jouanny, Pierre Oliuier,	2	
Pierre Gourry,	1	
Jacob Laport,	1	
Isaac Lefebure,	1	
Daniel Maubain, Will Fri, Indian,	2	
John Gorner,	1	
Anthoine Rapine, Willm Thomas, Joseph Bernard,	3	
Anthoine Giuandant,	1	
Jean Voyer,	1	
Isaac Parantaut,	1	
Mathieu Age,	1	
Nicola Sonille,	1	
Pierre Rousset,	1	
Etienne Bocard,	1	
Etienne Reynaud,	1	
Pierre Faure, Jean Faure,	2	
Adam Vigne,	1	
Jean Martin, Jacque, negro, Jean, negro,	3	
	—	
	39	

(TO BE CONTINUED.)

THE VESTRY BOOK OF KING WILLIAM PARISH, VA., 1707–1750.

	£	s.	d.
77 tithables @ 12 s. 9 d. makes, - - -	48	19	6
Balance remaining due, - - - - - -	0	2	6½
	49	2	½

(*Oct. 12, 1714—The 2 shillings 6 pence have been turned over to Mr. Cairon, in as much as he paid Mr. Michaux for carrying a request.)

Due from individuals, as follows:

	£	s.	d.
——By Mr. Perrault, - - - - - -	1	1	0
——by Mr. Chatain for † clapboards, - -	0	16	0
——by Mr. Abra. Soblet, - - - -	0	12	6
——by Mr. Chambon, - - - - - -	0	2	6
——by Martin for his (tithe) *billet* (?) - -	0	4	0
	2	16	0

*This note of the succeeding year, which is written in just opposite the figures above, may be regarded as an attempt to rectify a clerical error of Reynaud's. When the levy is ordered, as may be noticed below, it is ordered for £49. 2 s. ½ d., notwithstanding the fact that the balance of two shillings, six and one-half pence has already been subtracted from the assets of the parish. In order to rectify the account, the surplus of two shillings, six and one-half pence is turned over to Pastor Cairon, probably in payment for moneys advanced by him in connection with Michaux's journey to Major Bolling's for communion wine. Cf. XI, 438. The present account, however, is otherwise hopelessly confused by errors in multiplying and adding. M. Reynaud's book-keeping, just here, is a curious mixture of painful accuracy and gross carelessness. For instance, the £4. 10 s. 9½ d. surplus noted below appears nowhere to the credit of the parish in the following year. It is but natural to suppose, however, that some parishioners always failed of payment of their share of the levy.

† Clabors. See XI, 438, note. (Page 124, this volume.)

——balance due to Voyé, - - - -		10	6
	2	6	6
——for court expenses to Mr. Amonnet, -	0	4	0
Balance, - - - - - - -	2	2	6
——by Mr. Dutoit for Molinier* for the levy of 1712, which he has not paid, - - -	0	2	6
Tho. Elliar, - - 12 s. 4 d. Jacob Capon, - - 9 4 Dauid Bernard, - 3 0 Mathieu Bonsergent, 12 4 Franc. Sassin, - 12 4 } - -	2	9	4
	4	13	4
Amount due above in excess of list, - -	0	2	6½
Balance due the parish, - - - - - - -	4	10	9½

It was decreed by the vestry present that the church (wardens) shall make a levy of forty-nine pounds, two shillings, half-penny for the payment of Mr. Cairon and of the clerk and of the expenses mentioned in the account, and that they shall carry over the four pounds, ten shillings, † ten and one-half pence due as above, to the next year.

Done at Monocantown the day and date as elsewhere.

E. REYNAUD, Clerk.

The vestry assembled this day, March 30, 1714, Mr. Cairon, our minister, present. Church W: Anthoine Trabue, Jean le Villain. Vestry: Jacob Amonnet, Jean Farcy, Jean Forquerant, Jean Fonuielle, Gideon Chambon, Charles Perrault, Anthoine Maton, Pierre Dutoy, Andre Aubry, Abraham Sallé.

It was decreed by the vestry present that Mrs Anthoine Maton and Pierre Dutoy fill the office of church wardens, in place of the Srs Anthoine Trabue and Jean le Villain, for the present year 1714, and take the oath therefor in conformity with the law

---

* Cf. XI, 433, and note. (Page 119, this volume.)

† Should read 9½ d. But see above.

before Mr. Abraham Sallé, Justice of the Peace for Her Majesty. Done at Monocantown the day and date above.

E. REYNAUD, Clerk.

The vestry assembled this day, October 12, 1714. Mr. Cairon, the minister, present.

Ch. W: Pierre Dutoy, Anthoine Maton.

Vestry: Abraham Sallé, Anthoine Trabue, Jean Forquerant, Jean Fonuielle, Gideon Chambon, Jean Farcy, André Aubry.

Statement of expenses for the current year, viz:

	£	s.	d.
—To Mr. Cairon for his ministry, - -	40	0	0
—for the clerk, - - - - - - -	4	0	0
—to Mr. Dutoy for wine for the communion,	0	7	6
—for Mr. Amonnet, two bushels of wheat· for nails, - - - - - - -	0	6	0
—for Mr. Remy, for the orphan which he has at his house, - - - - -	4	13	0
	49	6	6

LIST OF TITHABLE PERSONS FOR THE PRESENT YEAR, 1714.

Jacob Amonnet, Jacob Amonnet, fils,	2	Pierre Chatain, Robert, negro,	2
André Aubry,	1	John Garner,	1
Abra. Sallé, Aigy, negro,	2	Jean Dupre,	1
Morise Leurau, Pierre le Grand,	2	Abra. Soblet, l'ainé Abra. Soblet, le jeune	2
Jean Forquerand,	1	Jacque Soblet,	1
Tomas Dalison,	1	Louis Soblet, Daniel Maubain,	2
Jean le Villain	1	T. Briant,	1
		Jean Voyer,	1
	10		11
Michel Cantepie,	1		
Jean Fonuielle, Bely, negro,	2	Math. Bonsergent,	1
		Franc. Sassin,	1
Jacque Bioret,	1	Jean Chatain,	1

Anthoine Giuaudant,	1
Anthoine Trabue,	1
Abra. Michaud, Jacob Michaud,	2
Anthoine Rapine,	1
Mathieu Agé,	1
Pierre Faure, Jean Faure,	2
Francois Dupuy,	1
Gideon Chambon,	1
Claude Gourry,	1
Pierre Dauid,	1
Pre Delaune,	1
Pre Cairon, Daniel Cairon,	2
Jean Farcy,	1
Etienne Chatain,	1
Jean Jouanny, Joseph Bernard,	2
Pierre Dutoy, Lances Pott,	2
Jacque Billbaud	1
Charles Perrault,	1
Abra. Remy,	1
Jean Martin, Jacque, Jean, negro, Jean, overseer,	4
Anthoine Maton,	1
Jean Fillon,	1
Jean Rosset,	1
Nicolas Souille,	1
Pierre Gorry,	1
Jean Panettie,	1
Jean Caluet,	1
Isaac Lafuitte, Franc. Lafuitte, Tobet Lafuitte,	3
Pierre Olliuier,	1

Jean Solaigre,	1
Franc. Delapied,	1
Jean Powel,	1
Isaac Lefebure,	1
Dauid Bernard,	1
Isaac Parantau,	1
Joseph Caillot, Bob, negro,	2
Etienne Reynaud,	1
Bartelemy Dupuy, Jean Pre Dupuy,	2
Pre Morisset,	1
Jacob Capon,	1
George Smiht,	1
Pre Viet,	1
	18
	45
	11
	10
	84

84 tithables @ 11 s. 9 d. per head amounts to the sum of £49. 7 s.

Etienne Bocard,	1
Adam Vigne,	1
	45

It was decreed by the vestry that the church wardens of the parish make the levy as above, making execution in default of payment in conformity with the tax, as has been ordered by the present vestry.

Done the day and date above.

The vestry assembled this day, Dec. 30, 1715. Mr. Cairon, the minister, present.

Ch. W: Pierre Dutoy, Jean Fonuielle.

Vestry: Jacob Amonnet, Jean Forquerant, Anthoine Trabue, Jean le Villain, Abraham Salle, Anth. Maton.

Statement of expenses for the present year 1715:

		£	s.	d.
—for Mr. Cairon, the minister, for his ministry, - - - - -	£40 0 0			
—less amount which he owes Perault and Bonsergent for moneys received, - - - - -	5 3			
		39	14	9
—for Etienne Reynaud, clerk, - - - -		4	0	0
—for Pierre Dutoy for wine for the communion, -		0	7	6
—due Lavigne Sassin for board of * Pre Perrut for the present year, - - - - - -		5	0	0
		49	2	3

List of Tithables for the Present year 1715.

Jean Powell, Andrew Martin,	2	Jean Fonuielle, Bely, Mary, negro.	3
Abra. Salle, Aigy, negro,	2	George Smith,	1
Etienne Bocard, Pierre Deppe,	2	Jacob Amonnet, Jacob Amonnet, Jr.,	2

* The orphan whose board the parish paid to Abraham Remy in 1714 and 1715.

Etienne Reynaud,	1
Pre Dutoy,	1
Anthoine Trabue,	1
Jean Martin, Jac, Jean, Lametatre,*	4
Anth. Rapine, Samuel Sermord,	2
Matthieu Age,	1
Isaac Lafuitte, Francois Lafuitte, Tobit Lafuitte,	3
Joseph Caillaud, Bob, negro,	2
Abra. Soblet, l'ainé, Abra. Soblet, jeuné,	2
Franc. Dupuy,	1
Jean Jouany,	1
Jean Forquerant,	1
Dan. Guerant, l'aine, Da. Guerant, jeune,	2
Adam Lavigne,	1
	29

Charles Perrault,	1
Etienne Chatain,	1
Jean Fillont,	1
Pre Morisse,	1
Daniel Maubain,	1
Claude Gorry,	1
Jean Pene, Wm. May,	2
Jacque Bioret,	1
To. Briant,	1
Michel Cantepy,	1
Jacque Bilbaud,	1
Jean Panettie,	1
Jean Solaigre, Pre Oliuier,	2
Isaac Lefebure,	1
Jacob Capon,	1
Ant. Giuandant, John Robisson,	2
Andre Aubry,	1
Jean Voyer,	1
	27

Wm. Genin, Wm. Peyter,	2
Pre. Chatain, Rober, negro,	2
Jean Chatain,	1
Lances Pott,	1
Moses Leurau, Pre. Legrand,	2
Jean Farcy,	1

	£	s.	d.
The acc't elsewhere,	49	2	3
Balance due the parish:			
Mr. Trabue, 8s 7d; Mr. Villain, 11 10	1	0	5
Balance,	48	1	10

* Or *Camelatre*. Possibly a common noun; if so, its meaning is altogether obscure. Jean Martin appears in the preceding year as paying for two slaves and an overseer. He seems at this time to have been the wealthiest man in the parish.

Jean Dupre, Gaspard Gorn., John G. Garner,	3
Pre Faure, Jean Faure,	2
Bartel. Dupuy, Jean Dupuy,	2
Nicolas Souille,	1
Jacque Soblet,	1
Pre Cairon, Daniel Cairon,	2
Jean le Villain,	1
Jean Caluet, James Bouxing,	2
Gideon Chambon,	1
Isaac Parantau,	1
Ant. Maton,	1
Franc. de Clapied,	1
Pre Dauid,	1
Louis Soblet,	1
Pre Delaune,	1
Pre Viett,	1
Jacque le Grand, Jean le Grand,	2
James Piquet,	1
	34
	27
	29
Jean Garner,	1
Mathieu Bonsergent,	1
Robin, Indian, Mary Chas, By Mr. Grill.	2
	94

In adddition is due:

Mr. Chastain,	4s od	
Mr. Amonnet,	4 0	0 10 6
Mr. Dutoit,	2 6	
		47 11 4

94 Tithables at ten shillings one and one-half pence.

It was decreed by the vestry that the church wardens make the levy for the above, and that in default of payment they make execution in accordance with the tax above.

Done and decreed by the vestry the day and year as above.

E. Reynaud, Clerk.

Mr. Jean Farcy, vestry-man, after this day resigns voluntarily his office in the said vestry.

* It was decreed by the vestry with the consent and agreement of Mr. Cairon, minister, that in case he fill well and worthily the functions of holy minister throughout the entire parish, by personal conduct, preaching, administration of the sacrament, visiting and consolation of the sick, the † quarterly salary in kind shall be continued to him as heretofore, being paid to him at the end of the harvests; and in case he shall miss any sermons, they shall be deducted from his pay, and if he shall fail to fulfill his duty as above, the said vestry reserves to itself the right at the expiration of the quarter, or in the course of succeeding ones, to proceed as it shall deem best, discontinuing the said salary.

Done the day and year above.

E. Reynaud, Clerk.

‡ (Signed) Cairon, minister; Abra. Salle, J. Amonnet, Forquerant, Jean Levillain, Pierre Dutoy, Thoine Trabue, Antoine Maton, Jean Fonuielle.

---

* The reasons for drawing up a contract with Mr. Cairon can only be conjectured. His death occurred within the following two months, as his will was admitted to probate in the Henrico county court Feb. 17$\frac{16}{18}$. Cf. Brock, p. 74. For an account of his wanderings after leaving his home in Haute Guyenne, cf. Baird II, 145. His skill in managing the heterogeneous elements under his care and the flourishing state of the parish during his pastorate are amply attested by the foregoing pages.

With the passing of Mr. Cairon the parish enters on a new phase of its existence. Deprived of the services of a fellow-countryman as spiritual consoler, whose experiences and sufferings had been identical with their own, they were dependent upon the ministrations of pastors from other parishes. The glebe was rented out, nor does it seem to have been regularly occupied by any pastor during the period covered by this register. Contracts were made for a given number of sermons per year, as the number of tithables seemed to justify. Cf. further for a petition regarding this point Brock, p. 112, and the following pages.

† On lui continuera par *cartier* lapantion dans les danrrees comme cy devant, qui luy seront paye dans *leterme des Recoltes*. The explanation of this rather obscure passage is probably that the contract was made *for the quarter*, the salary being paid at the expiration of the wheat, corn, and tobacco harvests, at a fixed price, cf. the following contract, and that made with Salle, p. 29.

‡ The signatures are personal.

We, the undersigned vestry-men of the parish of King William, have by these presents agreed and do agree to deliver to the afore-mentioned Mathieu Bonsergent, of the said parish, Jean Perru, a *weak child in the care of the said parish, to be nourished and cared for in like manner as his own (children), well and worthily, for the space of five years, in consideration of five pounds st., payable annually at Christmas, the first term beginning Jan. 1, 1716, payment to be made in kind at the price made to Mr. Cairon, the minister; and in case the said child shall die, the said Bonsergent shall receive payment for only that quarter which shall have been entered on. With this the said Bonsergent is satisfied and content, promising to acquit himself well of his duty with regard to the said child and to furnish him in general with all that is necessary for his nourishment and clothing, in default of which the said vestry reserves the right to withdraw it, if he fails to fulfill the conditions set forth above.

Done the 31 of December, 1715.

†ABRA. SALLÉ, for the vestry.

The vestry assembled May 18, 1717.

Present: Ch. W., Anthoine Mathon, Pre Dutoid.

(Vestry): Jacob Amonnet, Abra. Sallé, Jean le Villain, Jean Fonuielle.

It was decreed by the vestry present, upon the representation made by Daniel Guerrand, Daniel Maubain, and Wm. Gening, regarding the orphans, male and female, which they have had in their charge for some time, that the church wardens make contracts with them, following the custom and in conformity with the law.

Done and decreed the day and year as above.

ABRA. SALLÉ, for the vestry.

* Enfande infirme.

†The above entry is neither from the hand of Reynaud nor Sallé, although date and signature are Sallé's. With the disorganization following Mr. Cairon's death the register passed out of Reynaud's hands into that of Abraham Sallé, as justice of the peace. No list of tithables or other entry is found for 1716. The following till 1720 is in Sallé's bold hand.

The vestry assembled March 10, $17\frac{17}{18}$.

Present: Ch. W., P^{re} Dutoit. (Vestry) Anthoine Trabue, Jean Forquerand, Abra Sallé, Jean Fonuielle, Jean Villain.

It was decreed by the vestry present that a levy of a * bushel of wheat per tithable person be made for the year past, in order to create a fund for the payment of † Mr. Finny, minister, of ten pounds per year for four sermons, which he shall preach in the church of our parish, and for the support of such poor as may be there, and for repairs which shall have to be made to the church and the dwelling-house of the minister. To which the vestry has agreed, in accordance with the following list:

List of Tithables Returned in July, 1717:

Jacob Amonnet, Sr., Jacob Amonnet, Jr.,	2	Abra. Soblet,	1
		Peter Soblet,	1
Peter Chastain, David Germain, Robin, negro,	3	Peter Dutoit,	1
		George Smith,	1
		Isaac Parenteau,	1
John Martin, Mary Chas, John and Jack, Mathieu Matton,	5	Michel Cantepie,	1
		John Fonuielle, Bely, and Male,	2
		James Soblet,	1

* The first mention in these records of a levy in kind. In the earlier history of the parish the levy was made at a money rate, diminishing with the growth of the settlement from sixteen shillings in 1710 to ten shillings in 1715. The payments, however, were doubtless made in kind; cf. the foregoing contract with Mr. Cairon. Wheat is taken as the standard here as elsewhere in the record, probably because its price remained more steady from year to year than that of tobacco.

† Rev. Mr. Finney, M. A., of the University of Glasgow; cf. Brock, p. 78, note. He is mentioned in Bishop Meade's *Old Churches and Families of Virginia*, II, 393, ff. as attending and taking part in the proceedings of the church convention held at Williamsburg, April, 1719. He may have performed spiritual offices in the parish as early as 1716; together with the Fontaines, he served the parish from time to time till after August 7, 1724. See below. His will was admitted to probate in the Henrico county court June 5, 1727. Mr. Finney's Scottish birth may explain his ability to preach in French.

Abra. Salle, Sr.,	4
Abra. Salle, Jr.,	
John Cook,	
Aigy,	
John Farcy,	I
John Villain,	I
John Chastain,	I
Isaac Lefebure,	I
Stephen Reynault,	I
Moses Leuereau,	3
John Legrand,	
Peter Legrand,	
	22

John Solaigre,	I
Maingo,	I
James Bilbaud,	I
Nicolas Souille,	I
Peter Dauid, Sen.,	2
Peter Dauid, Jun.,	
Tho. Briant,	I
Anthony Givaudan,	I
Jacob Cappon,	I
Wm. Genin,	I
John Penne,	I
	21

Daniel Guerrand, Sen.,	2
Daniel Guerrand, Jun.,	
John Jones,	2
John Robisson,	
Francis de Clapie,	I
Peter Launay,	I
Peter Viet,	I
Francis Dupuy,	I
Peter Faure,	3
John Faure,	
Anthony Deane,	
John Caluet,	I
Daniel Maibain,	I
Isaac Lafuitte,	3
Francis Lafuitte,	
Tobie Lafuitte,	
Stephen Bocard,	I
Mathieu Age,	I
Anthony Rapinne,	I
Peter Broutte,	I
James Bioret,	I
Stephen Chastain,	I

Joseph Caillaud,	4
Bob, and Franc,	
Dauis Dayly,	
Anthony Trabue,	I
Peter Olliuier,	I
Gaspard Korner,	3
John Gaspard Korner,	
John Dupre,	
John Korner,	I
John Powell,	I
Peter Morisset,	I
Daniel Faure,	I
Barthelemus Dupuy,	3
Peter Dupuy, Sen.,	
Peter Dupuy, Jun.,	
John Forquerand,	I
Adam Vigne,	I
John Daither,	2
Robert Brown, Indian,	
Mathieu Bonsergent,	I
	21

Peter Deppe,	1		22
Anthony Mathon,	1		21
Claude Gorry,	1		25
	25	Tithables,	89

It was decreed by the vestry present that the church wardens of the said parish make the levy as above, in conformity with the tax of a bushel of wheat per tithable, in default of which execution (shall be made).

Done and decreed the day and year as above.

ABRA. SALLÉ, for the vestry.

The vestry assembled Aug. 25, 1718. Present, Ch. W.: Pre. Dutoit. (Vestry) Abra. Salle, Anthoine Trabue, Jacob Amonnet, Jean Forquerand.

The Sieurs Pre Chastain, Isaac Lafuitte, Barthelemy Dupuy, Estienne Chastain, Anthoine Rapinne, Anthoine Givaudan, and Jean Joanie were elected by the votes of the vestry present to fill the vacant places. After the election the Sr. Pre Dutoit tendered his resignation, saying that he hoped to be discharged, which the vestry agreed to, and in his place chose unanimously the Sr. Daniel Faure to be vestry-man, and ordered that all qualify for the said office by taking within the month the oaths required by law before Capt. Tho. Randolph, Justice of the Peace, of which (act) they shall procure a certificate.

Done and decreed the day and date above.

ABRA. SALLÉ, for all.

The vestry having assembled Sept. 30, 1718, present: Jacob Amonnet, Jean Forquerand, Anthoine Rapinne, Abraham Salle, Étienne Chastain, Anthoine Givaudan.

The Srs. Estienne Chastain, Anthoine Givaudan, and Anthoine Rapinne, who were elected vestry-men the 25th of August past, took the oaths of office and signed the test* in conformity with the law.

Done the day and date above.

ABRA. SALLÉ, for all.

The vestry assembled Nov. 25, 1718. Present: Jacob Amonnet, Pre Chastain, Jean Forquerand, Isaac Lafuitte, Anthoine Givaudan, Anthoine Trabue, Estienne Chastain, Anthoine Rapinne, Abra Salle.

It was agreed by the vestry present to grant to Sr. Abra. Salle, vestryman, the sum of six† pounds per year, to commence the first of December prox., in consideration of his performing the duties of clerk or secretary of the present vestry, and of reader in the church of the parish of King William, the said six pounds to be paid yearly in products according to their times of maturity; viz: in wheat‡ at three shillings the bushel, or maize at eighteen pence the bushel, or tobacco according as shall be arranged by the levy which the vestry shall judge proper to be made.

In testimony of which the present vestry have signed the day and date above.

---

* The declaration against transubstantiation, required of all assuming public offices in England and her colonies until in the 19th century. For the text of the oaths of abjuration and allegiance required of the vestrymen in the Virginia parishes in the 18th century, cf. Bishop Meade, II, 41, ff.

† The office of *lecteur* became much more important now that the death of Mr. Cairon had deprived the parish of the service of a regular resident minister; hence the two pounds increase in salary.

‡ Cf. contract with Mr. Cairon above. The price of wheat and maize seems to have fluctuated very little. Bruce, *Economic History of Virginia in the Seventeeth Century*, I, 380, gives the price of wheat, 1666 to 1682, as stationary at four shillings per bushel, shelled maize at two shillings during this period. The price of tobacco shows much more considerable fluctuations. Throughout this register wheat and maize are reckoned on the above basis. It is probable, however, that here as elsewhere in the colony, tobacco was the staple of actual exchange. Cf. Bruce as above, note. Only in the last pages of this register, after 1740, are the levies reckoned in pounds of tobacco.

*(Signed): J. Amonnet, Antoine Rapine, Tohin Trabue, Isaac Lafite, Forquerant, Anthoine his X mark Givaudan, Chastain.

ABRA. SALLÉ, Clerk.

As church wardens of this parish the S[rs] P[re] Chastain and Abraham Salle were elected by a majority of the votes of the vestry present.

Done the day and date as above.

*(Signed): J. Amonnet, Estienne Chastain, Antoine Rapine, Anthoine his X mark Givaudan, Chastain, Tohin Trabue, J. Forquerand, Isaac Lafite.

ABRA. SALLÉ, Clerk.

Dec. 18, 1718. The vestry assembled at Monocantown.

Present: Ch. W., P[re] Chastain, Abra. Salle, Jacob Amonnet, Jean Forquerant, Anthoine Trabue, Anthoine Rapinne.

The S[r] P[re] Chastain took the oaths as vestryman, and conjointly with the Sr Salle took the oaths as church wardens, after which the Sr Salle also took the oaths as church clerk.

Done the day and date above, and signed, J. Amonnet.

ABRA. SALLÉ, Clerk.

The vestry assembled at Monocantown, December 26, 1718.

Present: Ch. W., P[re] Chastain, Abra. Salle.

(Vestry): Jacob Amonnet, Jean Forquerand, Anthoine Trabue, Isaac Lafuitte, Estienne Chastain, Anthoine Rapinne, Anthoine Givaudan.

The Sr Isaac Lafuitte, heretofore chosen vestryman, to-day took the oaths and signed the † test, in accordance with the law.

Robert Jones, having to-day presented a request to the vestry asking that the service be read in ‡ English once every six weeks by the clerk of the said parish, the same was granted by the vestry.

---

* The signatures are personal. Sallé signs for Givaudan.

† Cf. above.

‡ The first concession to the growing English element in the parish, otherwise abundantly attested by the English names among the tithables. Cf. also the petition, Brock, p. 112.

To fill the three vacant places as vestry-men, the Srs Jacques Soblet, Jean Calvet, and Louis Soblet were elected by the vestry present, taking the oaths required by law.

Done the day and date above.

Signed, Chastain. ABRA. SALLÉ, Clerk.

The vestry assembled March 26, 1719.

Present: Pre Chastain, Abra. Salle, Ch. Wardens.

(Vestry): Jacob Amonnet, Estienne Chastain, Anthoine Rapinne.

The Srs Jacques Soblet and Louis Pro Soblet, heretofore named as vestrymen, took to-day the oaths of the vestry and signed the test. Signed, Chastain and Abra. Salle.

ABRA. SALLE, Clerk.

Aug. 26, 1719. Account of what is owing by the parish of King William, viz:

		£.	s.	d.
——to Mr. Finny for the balance of the year 1718, - - - -	£1 12s.			
——to the same for the year 1719, -	10 0			
		11	12	0
——to Mr. Abraham Salle for advance,	0 18 3d.			
——for his year 1719, to the end of November, as clerk, - - -	6 0			
		6	18	3
——to pay Mr. Blans, employed by the parish with respect to the high road, - - - -		1	0	0
		19	10	3
Due the parish by individuals, mentioned in the attached list, for the levy of *1717, and for rent of the glebe in 1719, - - - - - -		10	19	9
1719. Levy of the present year:				
94 tithables mentioned in the list attached, taxed at one and one-half bushels of wheat each, amounting to 141 bushels of wheat @ 3s. per bushel,		21	3	0
		32	2	9

* No list is given for 1718. Probably no levy was necessary in that year.

There will be a surplus of £12. 12s. 6d. to make repairs to the church or for other matters which shall be necessary.

King Wm Parish. The vestry assembled August 26, 1719.

Present: Ch. W., P^re^ Chastain, Abra. Salle.

(Vestry): Jacob Amonnet, Estienne Chastain, Anthoine Rapinne, Anthoine Givaudan, Jacq. Soblet, P^re^ Louis Soblet.

It was decreed by the present vestry that in order to pay the nineteen pounds, ten shillings and three pence mentioned elsewhere, that a levy shall be made of the ten pounds, nineteen shillings, nine pence, all of which is due for the year 1717, and of the rent of the glebe for the past year, as well as of a bushel and one-half of wheat per tithable, in accordance with the list attached, as the levy of the present year. In default of which execution shall be made.

*Signed by Pierre Chastain, Estienne Chastain, Anthoine Giuaudan, P^re^ Louis Soblet, Jacob Amonnet, Anthoine Rapinne, Jacques Soblet.

ABRA. SALLÉ, Clerk.

1719. List of tithables of King William parish for the present year 1719, taxed at one and one-half bushels of wheat each:

	Tithables.	Bushels of Wheat.
Abraham Salle, Sen., Abraham Salle, Jun., Jacob Salle, James Reasider, Wm Gardiner, Bob, Aigy, French, Harry,	9	13½
Bartelemy Dupuy, P^re^ Dupuy, Jean P^re^ Dupuy,	3	4½
P^re^ Morisset,	1	1½
P^re^ Deppe,	1	1½
Estienne Bocard,	1	1½
P^re^ Dutoit,	1	1½
Isaac Lafuitte, Tobie Lafuitte, John, negro,	3	4½

* The signatures are in Sallé's hand.

(TO BE CONTINUED)

THE VESTRY BOOK OF KING WILLIAM PARISH, VA., 1707–1750.

(CONTINUED)

	Tithables.	Bushels of Wheat.
Jean Cook, Tho. Cook,	2	3
John Powell,	1	1½
John Dicker,	1	1½
John Gaspard Korner, Abra. Mathon, Isaac Mathon,	3	4½
Nicolas Souillé,	1	1½
Pre Mallard,	1	1½
Daniel Maibain,	1	1½
Pre Louis Soblet,	1	1½
Abra. Soblet,	1	1½
Jacq. Soblet,	1	1½
Franc. de Clapie,	1	1½
Gideon Chambon,	1	1½
Estienne Chastain,	1	1½
Jean Korner,	1	1½
Jean Dupré,	1	1½
Isaac Parenteau,	1	1½
Tho. Briant,	1	1½
Pre Dauid, le jeune,	1	1½
Mathieu Agé,	1	1½
Estienne Reynaud,	1	1½
Pre Faure, Jean Faure,	2	3
Francois Dupuy,	1	1½
Anthoine Rapinne, Daniel Perault,	2	3
Pre Dauid, l'ainé,	1	1½
Jean Chastain, Jean Bernard,	2	3
Moise Leuereau,	1	1½
Jean Legrand,	1	1½
Pre Legrand,	1	1½
Jean Forquerand,	1	1½
Wm. Gening,	1	1½
Roben Jones, Sen., Roben Jones, Jun.,	2	3

Jean le Villain,	1	1½
Jean Pene, Sen.,	1	1½
Jean Pene, Jun.,	1	1½
Jacob Cappon,	1	1½
Daniel Croom, Tho. Boadtil, Tho. Neall, Jack, Indian,	4	6
Daniel Guerrand, l'ainé,	1	1½
Daniel Guerrand, le jeune,	1	1½
Jean Martin, Daniel Mekerte,* Wm. Mickion, Mary Chas, Jack, Harry,	6	9
Rolland Thomas,	1	1½
Claude Gaury,	1	1½
Richard Powell, Betty, negro,	2	3
Anthoine Giuaudan, Tho. Giuaudan,	2	3
Wm. Hudson,	1	1½
George Smith,	1	1½
Pre Bioret,	1	1½
Adam Vigne,	1	1½
Pre Brousse,	1	1½
	94	141 bushels

The vestry assembled April 20, 1720. Present: Ch. W., Estienne Chastain, Louis Soblet. Vestry, Jacob Amonnet, Pre. Chastain, Anthoine Trabue, Isaac Lafuitte, Anthoine Rapine, Anthoine Givaudant, Pre. Dutoy, Jacque Soblet.

It was decreed that six pounds per year be appropriated for Estienne Reynaud, commencing with the first of February of the present year, in consideration of his filling the office of clerk or secretary of the vestry and of reading the word of God in the church of the parish of King William. The said six pounds

* McCarty (?) He was probably an English servant of Martin's. The number of such servants appearing in the tithing-lists is at times by no means small.

shall be paid from year to year as due; viz., in wheat at three shillings per bushel, or maize at eighteen shillings pence per bushel, or tobacco, according as shall be arranged for by the levy which the vestry shall judge proper to make. In testimony of which the vestry present has signed the day and date above.

Estienne Chastain,*	Pierre Dutoy,
Pierre Louis Soblet,	Thoine Trabue,
Chastain,	his
J. Amonnet,	Anthoine X Givaudant,
Anthoine Rapine,	mark
Isaac Lafite,	Jacque Soblet.

E. REYNAUD, Clerk.

The Srs. Estienne Chastaine and Louis Soblet were elected by the vestry present as Church Wardens of the said parish, and the oaths were taken. Done the day and date above.

Estienne Chastain,*	J. Amonnet,
Pierre Louis Soblet,	Thoine Trabue,
Chastain,	Pierre Dutoy,
Ant. X Givaudant,	Isaac Lafite,
Antoine Rapine,	Jacque Soblet.

E. REYNAUD, Clerk.

The vestry assembled April 20, 1720. Present: Ch. W., Estienne Chastain, Louis Soblet. Vestry: Jacob Amonnet, Pre. Chastain, Ant. Trabue, Isaac Lafitte, Ant. Rapine, Ant. Givaudant, Pr. Dutoy, Jacque Soblet.

It was decreed that the Sr. Louis Soblet have the use of the glebe for the term of two years,† commencing Christmas of the year 1719, and terminating Christmas of the year 1721, in consideration of which the said Louis Soblet binds himself to make

* The signatures are personal.

† Cf. note to the entry of December 30, 1715, above. From this time on the glebe seems to have been regularly rented out for terms of one to two years. Finally, as in other parishes, it passed into private hands, doubtless without legal right. Cf. Meade, *Old Churches and Families*, I, 466.

repairs to the house which is built on the glebe; viz., he binds himself to roof the house, to fit on the two chimneys and in case there are any holes about the house, he is to close them with clap-boards, all at his own cost and expense. In addition he binds himself to make a thousand rails (?) for the corn-field of the said glebe.* Done at Monacanton the day and date as above.

PIERRE LOUIS SOBLET,
E. REYNAUD, Clerk.

The vestry assembled at Monocantown April 20, 1720. Present: Ch. W., Estienne Chastain, Louis Soblet. (Vestry) Jacob Amonnet, Pre. Chastain, Ant. Trabüe, Isaac Lafitte, Ant. Rapine, Anto. Givaudant, Pre. Dutoy, Jacque Soblet.

Mr. Estienne Reynaud was elected by a plurality of the votes of the vestry to fill one of the two vacant places in the vestry. Done the day and date above.

Estienne Chastain,
Pierre Louis Soblet,
Chastain,
Isaac Lafite,
Jacque Soblet.

Antoine Rapine,
Thoino Trabue,
his
Ant. X Givaudant,
mark

E. REYNAUD, Clerk.

The vestry assembled at Monocantown September 3, 1720. Present: Ch. W.: Etienne Chastain, Pre. Louis Soblet. Vestry: Jacob Amonnet, Pre. Chastain, Anthoine Rapine, Anthoine Trabue, Anthoine Givaudant, Jacque Soblet, Pre. Dutoy, Etienne Reynaud.

Expense-account of the Parish of King William:

To Mr. Fontaine, Minister, - - -	10	00	00
Etienne Reynaud, Clerk, - -	6	00	00
	†16	00	00

* De faire mille Relles pr lusage du corn fille. A good example of the absurd mixture of French and English to be found in the register.

† The following items stand just below those given above, but were afterward cancelled:

Due the parish from last year, 1719, • 12 12 6

It was decreed by the vestry present that a levy be made of two bushels of wheat per tithable for the present year, 1720, following the list attached. 87 tithables amounts to 174 bushels of wheat @ 3 shillings per bushel, 26 2 00.

List of Tithables of King William Parish for the Present Year, 1720, Taxed at Two Bushels of Wheat Each.

	Tithables.	Bnshels of Wheat.
Estienne Chastain, Jacque Tilleur,	2	4
Abra. Sallé, Isaac Sallé, Willem Guerdiner, Bob, Aigny, Sarry,	7	14
Barthelemy Dupuy, Pre. Dupuy, Jean Jacque Dupuy,	3	6
Pre. Moriset,	1	2
Pre. Deppe,	1	2
Etienne Bocard, Pre. Caluet,	2	4
Pre Dutoit,	1	2
Tobie Lafitte, Jean, negro,	2	4
Jean Jouanny,	1	2
Pre. Chastain, Willem Cardon, Maria, negro,	3	6
Jacob Amonnet, Sen., Jacob Amonnet, Jun., André Amonnet,	3	6
Anthony Trabue, Laurans Berty,	2	4
John Cook,	1	2
John Powelle,	1	2
John Deiker,	1	2
John Gaspar Karner,	1	2
Nicola Souillé,	1	2
Pierre Mallard,	1	2

To Belou for repairing the church, - - 15 00 00
For nails, hinges and clasp, - - - 6 00 00

Daniel Meibain,	1	2
Pre. Louis Soblet, Jean Lucadou,	2	4
Jacque Soblet, Pre. Sabatié,	2	4
Francois Dulapied,	1	2
Gideon Chambon,	1	2
John Kirner,	1	2
Jean Dupré,	1	2
Isaac Parantau, l'aine, Isaac Parantau, jeu.,	2	4
Thomas Briant,	1	2
Pre. Dauid, le jeune,	1	2
Mathieu Agé,	1	2
Etienne Reynaud,	1	2
Pre. Faure,	1	2
Jean Faure,	1	2
Francois Dupuy,	1	2
Ant. Rapine, Daniel Perrault, Jacob Flournoy,	3	6
Pre. Dauid, l'eine,	1	2
Jean Chastain, Jean Bernard,	2	4
Moise Leurau, Dauid Bernard,	2	4
Jean le Grand,	1	2
Jean le Villain,	1	2
Daniel Cromme, Tho. Niell, Jac Indien,	3	6
Daniel Guerand, l'eine,	1	2
Daniel Guerand, jeu.,	1	2
Jean Martin, Willem M . . ion,* Jac and Sarry,	4	8
Roland Th.,†	1	2
Claude Gourry,	1	2
Ant. Giuaudant, Th. Giuaudant,	2	4
Willem Haidson, Daniel Faure,	2	4
George Smith,	1	2
Pre. Bioret,	1	2

*Mickion. Cf. list for 1719.

†Thomas. Cf. list for 1719.

Adam Vigne,	1	2
Pre. Brousse,	1	2
John Elmerton,	1	2
Pre. Spenssell, John Poulouen,	2	4
John Peine, l'eine,	1	2
John Peine, jeu.,	1	2
Padrik Mollin,	1	2
Tithables,	87	174

The vestry assembled at Monocantown this day, April 18, 1721. Present: Ch. W., Estienne Chastain, Pre. Louis Soblet. (Vestry): Jacob Amonnet, Pre. Chastain, Ant. Rapine, Ant. Giuaudant, Ant. Trabue, Pre. Dutoy, Jacque Soblet, E. Reynaud.

Mr Pierre Chastain rendered his account for amounts received and paid out in the year 1719. He received a quittance covering the said year, 1719. Done at Monocantown the day and date as above.

E. Reynaud, C.

The vestry assembled July 29, 1721. Present: Ch. W.: Pierre Louis Soblet, Estienne Chastain. (Vestry): Entoinne Rapine, Entoinne Trabue, Enthoinne Givaudan, Pierre David, Jaque Soblet.

It was decreed by the vestry present that Jaques Soblet* be granted the sum of five pounds per year, commencing July 29th of the current year, 1721, for filling the office of clerk or secretary of this vestry and for reading the word of God in the church of the parish of King William, the said five pounds to be paid him according as the harvests shall fall; viz., in wheat at three shillings per bushel, or maize at eighteen pence per bushel, or tobacco, as shall be agreed on for the levies which the vestry

*Jacques Soblet's clerkship lasted until 1725, the last entry in his hand being on July 21 of that year. In the matter of clerkly neatness he is not to be compared with Reynaud nor Justice Sallé, and the character of his French shows many marks of degeneration. As regards the spelling of proper names, particularly of English names, he out-trumps all of the other clerks in irregularity and carelessness.

shall judge proper to be made. In testimony of which the ves try present has signed the day and date above.

Pierre Louis Soblet,* Pre. Dauid,
Etienne Chastain, his
Antoine Rapine, Anthony X Giuaudan.
Thoino Trbue, mark
Jaque Soblet,

It was agreed by the vestry present that Dannielle Guerant, the elder, have the use of the glebe for one year, commencing the first of the year 1722, and terminating the corresponding day, in consideration of the said Guerant obliging himself to pay to the church wardens twenty-five bushels of wheat, good and sound. Further the said Guerant binds himself to make enclosure and repairs all about the corn-field of the glebe, and to put it in good condition for planting; and in case it happens that we have a minister, he (Guerant) shall vacate the house in order to provide him a lodging, and shall empty the granary, in order to put away the grain, should the vestry deem it proper. Done and decreed the year and date above.

DANIEL GUERRANT.

No liquor or beverage shall be sold in the house of the glebe under penalty of ten pounds in money current, which the said Guerand binds himself to pay.

JACQUE SOBLET, Clerk.

By † a plurality of votes of the present vestry the Sieur Anthoine Rapine and the Sieur Abraham Sallee were elected to be church wardens of the said parish. Done the day and year above. J. SOBLET, Clerk.

Antoine Rapine,
Abraham Salle.

---

* The signatures are personal.

† Between this and the preceding entry stands the following note, afterwards erased:

"The vestry assembled March 28, 1772. The Sieur Etiene Chastain and Louy Soblet, church wardens, offered their resignations, and the vestry assembled granted their discharge. Voted to interline in the second line. J. SOBLET, Clerk."

Then the following.

The vestry assembled July 30th, 1722. (Present) Ch. W., Anthoine Rapine, Abraham Salle. (Vestry) Pierre Chastain, Jacob Amonet, Estien Chastain, Anthoine Givodan, Pierre Dutoy, Pierre David, Jean Chastain, Louis Soblet, Anthoine Trabue.

The accounts were audited for the fifteen months which Reynaud served the parish church, and there was paid, by Estienne Chastain three pounds, eight shillings, six pence; by Mr. Pierre Chastain one pound, eight shillings, sixpence; by Louis Soblet ten shillings, sixpence; Jean le Grand six shillings, for himself six shillings. There remain due one pound, ten shillings, sixpence.

J. Soblet, Clerk.

The vestry assembled July 30th, 1722. It was decreed that a levy be made of one bushel of wheat and one and one-half bushels of maize per tithable, to be paid to the church warden.

Present: Ch. W.: Anthoine Rapine, Abraham Sallee. (Vestry) Pierre Chastain, Jacob Amonet, Anthoine Givodan, Anthoine Trabue, Pierre Dutoy, Pierre David, Estienne Chastain, Pierre Louis Soblet, Jean Chastain.

Jacques Soblet, Clerk.

The vestry assembled April 16, 1723. Present: Ch. W., Abraham Sallee, Anthoine Rapine. (Vestry) the Sieur Pierre Chastain, Estiene Chastain, Anthoine Trabue, Louis Soblet, Anthoine Givodan, Pierre David, Jaque Soblet.

Paid by Mr. Rapine, - - - -	4	1	4
For the Bible, - - - - -	1	18	6
For the woman who is supported by the church,*	1	3	9
for melon or sugar, - - - -	0	3	0
further, for wine, - - - -	0	3	6
	4	8	9

*A guess. The passage is indecipherable.

April 16, 1723.

By a plurality of votes the Sieur Anthoine Givodan and Jean Chastain were elected church wardens of the parish of King William. Done the day and year above.

J. SOBLET, Clerk.

April 16, 1723.

The Sieur Givodan took the oath of church warden before the Sieur Rapine and the Sieurs Abraham Sallee, Pierre Chastain, Estienne Chastain, Anthoine Trabue, Pierre David, Louis Soblet.

J. SOBLET, Clerk.

Jaque Soblet having tendered his resignation as vestryman, it was accepted by the vestry assembled. Sept. 30, 1723.

J. SOBLET, Clerk.

The vestry assembled Sept. 30, 1723. Present: Ch. W., Mr. Givodan, Jean Chastain. (Vestry) Pierre Chastain, Etienne Chastain, Anthoine Rapine, Anthoine Trabue, Pierre Dutoy, Pierre Louis Soblet, J. Soblet.

It was decreed that in order to pay the ten pounds to Mr. Finis and to Jaque Soblet five pounds, a levy* be made of one bushel of wheat per tithable and one-half bushel of maize per tithable, following the list attached, and in default of payment it was ordered that execution be made. Done the day and year above. Signed by

J. SOBLET, Clerk.

The Sieur Jean Chastain took the oath of church warden the year and day above.

LIST OF TITHABLES OF KING WILLIAM PARISH FOR THE PRESENT YEAR, 1723.

Barthelemy Dupuy, Jean Jaque Dupuy, Sary, negress,	3	William Adson, Dannielle Faure,	2
		Jean Du Pree,	1
Pierre Dupuy,	1	Isaac Parranto, le pere, Isaac Parento, le fils,	2
Pierre Morisset,	1		

* The first levy recorded since 1720. It is probable, however, that levies were regularly made during this period.

Name	Tithables
Pierre Louis Soblet, Jean Lucadou,	2
Pierre David, l'enee,	1
Pierre David, le jeune,	1
Pierre Chastain, William Lanedon, Dik, a negro, Maria and Kate, a negress,	5
Gaelle Below,	1
Jean Chastain,	1
James Tellor, Pierre Lucadou, Coffe, a negro,	3
Jacob Amonet, Andre Amonet,	2
Jean le Villain, Francois, a negro,	2
Jean le Grand,	1
Josue Crisson,	1
Jacob Capon,	1
Jean Bernard,	1
Jean Jouany, Jeane, a negress,	
Danielle Maban,	1
Francois de Clapie,	1
Pierre Dutoy, Anthoine Benin, Jean Pierre Bilboun, Jos. and Peigue, negroes,	5
Pierre Brousse,	1
Pierre Malard,	1
Anthoine Givaudan, Thomas Givaudan,	2
Pierre Bioret,	1
Francois Dupuy,	1
Jaque Soblet, Pierre Sabatied,	2
Claude Gaury,	1
Evard Brayer,	1
William Hense,	1
John Gaspar Korner,	1
Anthoine Rapine, Danielle Perots, Etienne Malet, Sara, a negress,	4

Name	Tithables
Pierre Deppe,	1
Dannielle Guerand, Jun.	1
Gideon Chabon, Manoco, a negro,	2
Pierre Faure,	1
Jean Polloven,	1
Pierre Spenselle,	1
Tobit la Fitte, Jean, a negro,	2
Pierre Calvet,	1
Nicolas Soulie,	1
Pierre Guerand,	1
Jean Levinston,	1
George Smithe,	1
Henry Bally,	2
Estienne Bocard,	1
Robert Jean,	1
Thomas Staford,	1
Abraham Sallee, Isaac Sallee, William Sallee, Bob, negro, Francoisse, negress, Marie, negress, Aygue, negro,	7
Thomas Nille,	1
Jhone Grifit, Jack, Indian,	2
Moyse le Vreaux, David Bernard, Pierre Perru,	3
Jean Martin, Jaque Martin, Frank, a negro, Jeny, a negress,	4
Adam Vigne,	1
Nicolas Rode,	1
Daniel Guerand, pere,	1
Total tithables,	108

Anthoine Trabue, Jacob Trabue, London, a negro, Bety, a negress,	4
Mathieux Agee, Thomas Preouet,	2
Jean Pauel,	1
Jean Diker, Elie Sasin,	2
Etienne Chastain, Francois Farcy, Linbou, a negro, Mulle, a negro,	4

January 29, 1723 | 24.

The Sieur Bartalmis Dupuy this day took the oath as vestryman in the presence of the Sieur Anthoine Givodan and Jean Chastain, church wardens.

J. SOBLET, Clerk.

Jean Chastain,
his
Anthoine X Givodan.
mark

The vestry assembled April 7, 1724, to elect church wardens. By a plurality of votes the Sieur Pierre Dutoy and the Sieur Pierre David, Senior, were elected.

The vestry assembled May 25th. The Sieur Pierre David took the oath as church warden.

J. SOBLET, Clerk.

The vestry assembled June 30, 1724, to elect and name two persons of intelligence with regard to the tobacco planted on the lands of King William parish, viz., the Sieur Pierre David, le jeune,* . . . Danielle Guerant.

Church Warden:
Chastain.†

Pierre David,
Pierre Dutoy,

B. Dupuy,
Antoine Rapine,
Pierre Louis Soblet,
Anthoine X Givodan,
Abraham Salle,
Estienne Chastain,
Jean Chastain.

* One-half line is illegible.

† The signatures are personal.

The vestry assembled July 25, 1724. Estiene Chastain rendered account for the year 1720 of amounts received and paid out. There remains (?) one and one-half pounds with respect to ——. Done at Mennekintown the year and day above.

J. SOBLET, Clerk.

In like manner Louis Soblet has rendered account the same day as above. In testimony thereof,

J. SOBLET, Clerk.

The vestry assembled July 25, 1724, to make the levy for the year 1724: one bushel of wheat and one-half bushel of maize per tithable, to be paid to the church wardens.

Pierre Dutoy,*	Chastain,
Pierre David,	B. Dupuy,
Estienne Chastain,	his
Pierre Louis Soblet,	Thoine X Givodan.
	mark

1724. LIST OF TITHABLES OF THE PARISH OF KING WILLIAM FOR THE YEAR.

Pierre Faure,	2	Jean Jouanis,	2
Jaque Faure,		Jeanne, a black woman,	
Isaac Paranteaux.	2	Pierre David, signor,	3
Isaac Paranteaux,		David le Sueur,	
Francois Dupuy,	1	Daniel Fouguinion,	
Jacob Ammonet,	2	Josuee Creson,	1
Andre Ammonet,		Daniel Guerant, le pere,	1
Estienne Chastain,	3	Robert Jhon,	1
Francois Farcy,		Daniel Ford,	1
Limbo & Mall, black,		Pierre Spensel,	1
Anthoine Rapine,	5	James Houk,	1
Daniel Peraut,		Jean Polvin,	1
Estienne Malet,		Pierre Malard,	1
Nicolas du Cree,		Nicolas Soulie,	1
Sara, a negress,		Daniel Guerand, junior,	2
Pierre Louis Soblet,	2	Pierre Guerand,	
Jean Lucadou,		Pierre Dep,	1

---

* The signatures are personal.

Names	Tithables
Abraham Sallee, Pierre Sallee, Isaac Sallee, Guillaume Sallee, Bob & Francoise, Marie & Lucy,	8
Jhons Levinstain,	1
Jhons Powel,	1
Pierre Moriset,	1
Estienne Bocard, Pierre Bocard,	2
Jean Gaspard Corner,	1
Pierre Bioret,	1
Pierre Chastain, Jack & Maria & Kaet,	4
Pierre du Toy, Jean Pierre Billebeaud, Anthoine Benin, Josephe & Peg, black,	5
Jean Chastain,	1
Mathieu Agee,	1
Anthoine Givaudan, Thomas Givaudan, Jean Bernard,	3
Jean le Grand,	1
Jacob Trabue, black: London & Bety,	2
Jean le Vilain, p., Jean le Vilain, f., black, Franc,	3
Jean du Pree, Pierre Perut,	2
Barthelemy du Puy, Jean Jacque du Puy, a negress, Sara,	3
Jacob Capon,	1
William Hense, Samuel Wardry,	2
Tobit la Fitte, Jack, a negro, Pierre Calvet,	3
Jacque Soblet, Pierre Sabatiee,	2
Elisabhet Croom,* Jack, Indian,	1
Thomas Nille,	1
Thomas Craford,	1
Jhons Broun,	1
Jhons Criffitt, Nicholas Rod,	2
Gorge Scmithe, Hennery Byly, William Lansdon,	3
James Tylors, Coffy, black,	2
Jedeon Chambon, Monk, a black,	2
Pierre David, jun.,	1
Estieene Monford,	1
Sum total,	109

* The names of a number of women appear in the tithe-lists, heading the roster of servants and slaves. Such women, even though owning and directing large estates, were not tithable under the Virginia law, the Assembly expressly exempting all women from the payment of tithes, except slaves or servants over sixteen years of age, who were capable of doing work in the field. Cf. *Hening's Statutes at Large*. On the other hand all men of whatever rank or station over sixteen years of age, were regarded as tithable, only the clergy and members of the Council being exempted.

Pierre du Puy,	1
Evard Breyars,	1
Jean Martin, Jaque Martin, Jean Martin, David Bernard, Robert Jhonson, Franc & Jenny,	7

August 7, 1724.

The vestry assembled. It was agreed with Monsieur Finis,* the minister, that he shall come to give us twelve sermons per year, except in case of illness or of bad weather, for which the vestry agrees to give him one hundred and twenty bushels of wheat, delivered at a convenient landing. In case the wheat be injured, either by freshet or other misfortune, Mr. Finis binds himself to accept maize or tobacco, as the vestry shall find suitable. Monsieur Finis commences his year the 3d of September of the above year. Done at Menekintown.

J. SOBLET, Clerk.

The vestry assembled March 30, 1725. Present: the Sieur Pierre du Toy, Pierre David, Church W.; (Vestry:) Barthelmy Dupuy, Estienne Chastain, Anthoine Rapine, Anthoine Givodan, Jean Chastain, Abraham Sallee.

The Sieur Batheleemy Dupuy and the Sieur Jacob Ammonnet were elected church wardens by a plurality of votes.

J. SOBLET, Clerk.

The vestry assembled July 14 to make the levy for the year 1725, at a bushel and one-half of wheat and a bushel of maize per tithable. Church Wardens: Jacob Amonet, Barthelemy

---

* Mr. Finny's former contract was for four sermons at ten pounds. Cf. *Va. Hist. Mag.*, July, 1904, p. 26, March 10, 1717 | 8. The new agreement at the prevailing price of wheat amounted to one pound, ten shillings per sermon. (**Page 136, this volume.**)

Dupuy. (Vestry): Estienne Chastain, Anthoine Rapine, Pierre du Toy, Jean Chastain, Abraham Sallee.

J. Soblet, Clerk.

List of Tithables of the Parish of King William for the year 1725.

Tobit la Fitt,	1	Francois du Puy,	1
Estienne Bocard, Pierre Bocard,	2	Jhon Polwin,	1
Mathieu Agee,	1	Anthoine Rapine, Pierre Calvet, Daniel Perot, Estiene Malet, Nicolas du Cree,	5
Pierre Ford, Jaque Ford, Daniel Kingdel,	3	Pierre David l, Dauid le Sueur, W. Lansdon, Daniel Fouguinon,	4
Nicolas Souliee,	1	Jaque Soblet, Jaque Brian, Pierre Sabatiee,	3
Daniel Maybain,	1	Pierre Dauid, j.,	1
Pierre Guerand,	1	Gorge Smithe,	1
Robert Jhon,	1	Jean le Grand,	1
Jean Jouanis, Jenny,	2	Jak Lindun,	1
Pierre Bioret,	1	a Croom,	
Estienne Chastain, Michel le June, Francois Farcy, Limbo & Mall,	5	Jean Crifit,. Jhon Dillion,	2
Pierre du Toy, Anthoine Benin, Jean Pierre Bilbo, Josephe & Pygue,	5	Jacob Amonet, Andrew Amonet,	2
Jemes Tylor, James Houk, Cofy, negro,	3	Jean Chastain,	1
Jacob Cappon,	1	Jean le Vilin, p., Jean le Vilin, f., Francois, negro,	3
Isaac Parenteaux, p., Isaac Parenteaux, f.,	2	Anthoine Givodan, Thomas Givodan,	2
Daniel Guerand, p., Daniel Guerand, f.,	2	Pierre Dupuy,	1

(to be continued)

THE VESTRY BOOK OF KING WILLIAM PARISH, VA., 1707–1750.

Pierre Dep,	1
Pierre Malard,	1
Glaud Couris,	1
Jean Kaspar Korner,	1
Pierre Chastain,	
(poire?) Pierre Chastain,	
& Jak & Maria,	6
William Baton,	
Katt,	
Barthelmy Dupuy,	
Jean Jaque Dupuy,	3
Saray, negress,	
Pierre Louy Soblet,	1
Gideon Chambon,	2
Monok, a negro,	
Evard Breyard,	1
Thomas Nille,	2
Jhon Nille,	
Pierre Moriset,	1
Danielle Ford,	1
Jhon du Pree,	2
Pierre Perut,	
Williame Hense,	1
Gille Below,	2
Jean Bernard,	
Hanris Bylys,	1
Abraham Sallee,	
Isaac Sallee,	
Bely Sallee,	
Pierre Sallee,	7
a negro, Bobe, &	
Hygue & Maria,	
Adam Vigne,	2
Estiene Monford,	
Roland Thomas,	1
Jean Martin,	
Jean Lucadou,	3
David Bernard,	
Jhon Levinston,	1
Jacob Trabut,	
a negro, London,	3
Bety,	
Jhon Powele,	1
Sum total,	105

Memorandum of books loaned to Mr. Mordock,* minister of St. Jeames, June 14, 1725: First, one volume of Dr. Tiloson's sermons; further, the Concordance of Cambridge, entire, amounting to seventeen volumes. Further, September 14, 1725, loaned to the same—†

February 2, 1725-8, Monsieur Bartehlemis Dupuy rented the

* Rev. William Murdaugh, rector of St. James-Northam, Goochland county. Mr. Murdaugh, like other ministers of his parish, visited the neighboring French colony from time to time, and performed spiritual offices for the parish of King William. Christenings by Mr. Murdaugh in the years 1726 and 1727 are recorded in Brock, pp. 78 and 80. Cf. further regarding Mr. Murdaugh, Meade, I, 459.

† The rest of the memorandum is not filled in, although a blank space is left for doing so.

glebe for a year, for a barrel and one-half of wheat, payable at the next harvest.

Done at Menikintown the day and year above mentioned.

J. SOBLET, Clerk.

The vestry assembled May 14, 1726. Jean Chastain and Anthonine Givodan rendered account of their administration for the year 1723 in the presence of the church wardens and vestrymen. Ch. W.: Barthelmis Dupuy. (Vestry:) Estienne Chastain, Antoine Rapine, Pierre David s., Jean Chastain, Pierre Louy Soblet, Abraham Sallée.

The vestry assembled this day, July 23, 1726, Jean du Prée and Daniel Guerant took the oath as vestrymen in the presence of the church wardens, Pierre Chastain, Pierre Louy Soblet; (Vestry:) Jacob Amonet, Bartholmy Dupuy, Estien Chastain, Anthoine Rapine, Pierre David, Jean Chastain, Abraham Sallée.

J. SOBLET, Clerk.

The vestry assembled this day, July 23, 1726. It was decreed by the vestry that a levy of one bushel and one-half of wheat per tithable be made for this year.

By the present vestry.

J. SOBLET, Clerk.

The vestry assembled this day, July 23, 1726. Mr. Abraham Sallee and Mr. Anthoine Rapine rendered their account for the year 1722. They owe to the parish one pound, ten shillings and ninepence, which Mr. Abraham Sallé binds himself to pay to Mr. Pierre Chastain or to Mr. Pierre Louys Soblet, church wardens.

Church Wardens: Chastain, Pierre Louis Soblet.*

(Vestry:) Estienne Chastain, Abraham Sallé, Jean Chastain, Daniel Guerant, J. Amonnet, Antoine Rapine, Barthellemy Dupuy, Perre David, Jean du Pree.

J. SOBLET, Clerk.

It was decreed that the church wardens make a levy of ten

* The signatures are personal.

pro cent, according to the rule of the country. Done at Moni-'canthovn the day and date above.

J. SOBLET, Clerk.

The vestry assembled this day, July 23, 1726, to make a levy of a bushel and one-half of wheat per tithable.

Church Wardens: Pierre Chastain, Pierre Louy Soblet.

(Vestry:) Estienne Chastain, Abraham Sallée, Jean Chastain, Danielle Gueran, Jacob Amonet, Antoinne Rapine, Barthelemy Dupuy, Pierre David, Jean Duprée.

1726. LIST OF TITHABLES OF THE PARISH OF KING WILLIAM FOR THE YEAR 1726.

Estienne Chastain, Francois Farcy, Estienne Farcy, Isaac Gouris, Limbaut, Hibou, Malle,	7
Tobit la Fitte,	1
Estienne Bocard, Pierre Bocard,	2
Barbarie du Toy's list:	
Jean Pier Bilbour, Michel Yons, Anthoinne Benin,	3
Jean le Vilin, Jean le Vilin, le jeune, Marie, a negress, Francois, a negro,	4
Jean Martin, p. Jean Martin, f. Jhon Heriss, James Smithe,	4
Jhonne le Vinston,	1
Pierre Deppe,	1
Evard Brayard,	1
Barthelmy Dupuy, Jean Jacque Dupuy, Sara, negress,	3
Pierre Dupuy,	1
Thomas Givaudan, David Bernard,	2
Jacob Capon,	1
James Tylors, Robert Hockiby, Joseph Walkar, Pierre Lucadou, Cofy, negro,	5
Jacque Soblet,	1
Abraham Sallee, Pierre Sallee, Bobo, negro, Agare, negress,	4
Jacob Amonet, Andre Amonet,	2
Isaac Sallee, Guilliaum Sallee,	2
Estienne Monford, William Skyls,	2
Jhon Dekare, Elie Sasin,	2
Jean du Pree, Pierre Perut,	2
Roland Thomas, Jhon Judge,	2
Jhon Powell,	1
Danniel Fourd,	1
Pierre Moriset,	1
Jean le Grand,	1
Pierre Sabatiee, Jean Bernard,	2
Pierre David, le jeune, Jacque Brian,	2

Name	Tithables
Jean Jouanis,	2
Jeanne, a negress,	
Gideon Chambon,	2
Monock, a negro,	
Pierre David,	4
David le Sueur,	
Dannelle Fouguigon	
Pierre Fauset,	
Gorge Smithe,	1
Roger Pratt,	1
Jhon Penne,	2
Joseph Bingley,	
Mathieun Agee,	1
Rogar Nill,	3
Thomas Nill,	
Jhon Nealle,	
Danielle Guerand, p.,	1
Isaac Parenteaux,	1
William Lansdon,	1
Danielle Guerand, f.,	1
Pierre Chastain, p.,	8
Pierre Chastain, f.,	
Jacob Trabue,	
William Botom,	
Jac, negro,	
Maria, negress,	
Katt, negress,	
London, negro,	
Claud Gouris,	3
Robert Blakeley,	
William Hond,	
Pierre Gurand,	3
Nicolas Soulie,	
Jhon Varcup,	
Anthoine Rapine,	4
Danielle Perot,	
Estienne Malet,	
Nicholas du Crie,	
Pierre Faure,	3
Jacque Faure,	
Thomas Lahane,	
Jean Chastain,	1
Pierre Louy Soblet,	1
William Hanse,	2
Nicolas Rod,	
Haris Bylys,	1
Sum total of tithables,	*108

This day, September 21, 1726, Mr. Amonet and Monsieur Dupuy rendered account of their administration for the year

* Just below the tax-list occurs the following note in English, in handwriting apparently contemporaneous with the foregoing and following:

"Att a vestry held for king William parish the —— day of —— for laying the Levy, present ——, ——, Church Wardens, —— —— —— —— ——, gent. of the Vestry.

" To the Rev'd —— for — sermons, ——.

" To James Soblet for one year, ending ——.

" To the support of ——, a poor man ——.

" 108 being the number of tythables of this parish, it is ordered that each tythable do pay —— of wheat and that the Church Wardens do collect & pay the same to the several persons to whom it is levyed."

1725. They are relieved in full. Mr. Amonet remains (due?) fourteen bushels and three pecks.

CHASTAIN.
PIERRE LOUIS SOBLET.

Mr. Chastain and Louy Soblet rendered their account for what they received in the year 1726. Pierre Chastain received fifty-one and one(-half?) bushels of wheat; and paid out therefrom to Mr. Finy, the minister, thirty bushels, to Pierre du Puy one bushel two-thirds,* to Jaque Soblet ten bushels, to Mr. Chastain two-thirds of a bushel, to Jacob Capon thirteen bushels; in all fifty-five and one-half. Done the 2nd of September, 1727.

Louy Soblet received ninety-seven bushels of wheat. Paid to Jaque Soblet twenty-three bushels, to Mr. Martin for Mr. Finy,† the minister, forty-two bushels and one-half, to Mr. Capon ten bushels three pecks, to Mr. Martin six bushels; amounting to the sum of 82 (bushels) one (peck). Done the 2nd of September, 1727.

The Sieur Daniel Guerent and the Sieur Jean du Pree were elected by a plurality of votes as church wardens for the year 1727. Daniel Guerant took the oath of church warden September 2, 1727.

JAQUE SOBLET, Clerk.

This day, September 2, 1727, Mr. Gilles Allaigre was elected vestryman by a plurality of votes, and took the oath the 23d in the usual manner.

J. SOBLET, Clerk.

September 23, 1727. The Sieurs Jan Dupre and Daniel Guerand took the oaths as church wardens in the presence of the vestry here assembled, the year and day as above, viz.: ‡ Jean

---

* *Tierre.* The sum should of course read 55⅓.

† Mr. Finny's death occurred late in the spring of 1727. Cf. Note to entry of March 10, 1717-18 above. In addition to Mr. Murdaugh of St. James-Northam, mentioned above, the Rev. Zachariah Brooke of Hanover county, baptized infants in the parish in 1727. Cf. Brock, p. 79.

‡ Jean Chastain served as clerk from this date until the close of the

du Chastain, Clerk. Gilles Allaigre, Estienne Chastain, Pierre David, Abraham Sallé, vestrymen.

The same day Jean Chastain was elected clerk of this church in the place of Mr. Jaques Soblet; and there were assigned to him five pounds, either in wheat at three shillings per bushel, or maize at eighteen pence per bushel, or in tobacco, according as the vestry shall judge proper to make the levy at ten shillings per hundred.

JEAN DU PREE,
DANIEL GUERRAND,
Church Wardens.

The same day there was levied by the vestry for the expenses of the parish seven pounds of tobacco * and three pecks of wheat per tithable.

JEAN CHASTAIN,
Clerk.

September 4, 1727. After the sermon the vestry agreed to give Mr. Neran† 120 bushels of wheat for twelve sermons, commencing September 4 of the present year.

October 14. Mr. Nern preached a sermon.

December 13. Mr. Nern preached a sermon and administered the communion.

1727 | 8. January 26. Mr. Nern preached a sermon.

February 26. Mr. Nern preached a sermon.

1728. April 1. Mr. Nairn preached a sermon.

April 17. Mr. Nairn preached a sermon and administered the communion.

---

register (1750) His entries are written in a fair, legible hand; but his French bears marks of having been learned in the colony.

* The first sporadic instance of a levy in tobacco. Cf. note to entry for Nov. 25, 1718. Later entries indicate, however, that the assessments were often *paid* in tobacco, though reckoned in wheat and maize.

† The name is spelt variously Nearne, Nern and Niern. Cf. Meade, *Old Churches*, I, 466. He served the parish until his departure for England in 1728. The vestry wrote him a very earnest farewell letter, urging his intercession with the Bishop on behalf of the maintenance of the French settlement as an individual parish. Cf. Brock, p. 112.

May 15. Mr. Nairn preached a sermon.

June 15, 1728. Mr. Nairn preached and administered the communion.

June 15, 1728, the vestry assembled. It was decreed by the vestry present that Edouard Brayr and Jean Nil for the county Danrico and David Leseur and Joseph Bingli for Gaug Land* county be named to take account of the tobacco.

August 10, 1728. The vestry having assembled, the Sieurs David Guerat and Jean Dupre rendered account of their administration as church wardens for the year 1727.

JEAN CHASTAIN.

1728. Daniel Guerand received from Mr. Abraham Salle two barrels of wheat, in part payment of amount due from his administration of the year 1723.

JEAN CHASTAIN.

August 10, 1728. The vestry assembled. The Sieurs Etiene Chastain and the Sieur Gille Allaigre were elected church wardens by a plurality of votes, in the presence of Antoine Rapine, Louis Soblet, Abraham Sale, Jean Dupre, Daniel Guerant, Pierre David, Jean Chastain, Clerk.

The levy for the present year, 1728, consists of a bushel and one-half of wheat, per tithable, payable to the church wardens.

August 10, 1728. The Sieur Gille Alaigre took the oath of church warden in the presence of the vestry.

February 20, 1728 | 9. Jean Jaque Dupuy rented the glebe for a year for a barrel and one-half of wheat, payable at the next harvest.

June 16, 1729. The vestry assembled, viz.: Ch. W., Etiene Chastain, Gille Alaigre. (Vestry:) Bartelemi Dupui, Antoine Rapine, Daniel Guerand, Pierre David, Jean Dupre, Abraham Salle, Jean Chastain.

By a plurality of votes the vestry elected David Lesuar and Joseph Bingli to take account of the tobacco in that (Gooch-

* Henrico and Goochland. The parish lay in Henrico county until, with the cutting-off of Goochland in 1727, a part fell to the latter county. Meade, *Old Churches*, etc., I, 463.

land) parish, and Jacob Trabu and Jaque Marbain for the lower district (?) of the parish of King William.*

On the same day, by a plurality of votes, the Sieur Antoine Rapine and Abraham Sallee were elected church wardens for the present year, 1729.

June 16, 1729. By a majority of the votes of the vestry heretofore named, the Sieur Isac Salle was named as vestryman.

The same day Mr. Jean Chastain, in place of his father, and Mr. Louis Soblet rendered their accounts in full for the year 1726, and were discharged of their administration.

June 21, 1729. The vestry assembled, viz.: Estien Chastain, Antoine Rapine, Abraham Salle, Pierre David, Daniel Guerand, Jean Dupre, Gille Allaigre, Pierre Louys Soblet, Jean Chastain. The Sieur Isac Salle took the oath of vestryman.

JEAN CHASTAIN, Clerk.

The vestry having assembled, the Sieur Estiene Chastain and Gille Allaigre rendered account of their administration for the year 1728, in the presence of Antoine Rapine, Abraham Salle, Pierre Louis Soblett, Pierre David, Daniel Guerand, Jean Dupre, Isac Salle, Estienne Chastain, Gille Allaigre.

JOHN CHASTAIN, Clerk.

The same day as above, the vestry having assembled, a levy was made of two bushels of wheat per tithable for thc year 1729. Antoine Rapine, Estiene Chastain, Gill Allaigre, Daniel Gueran, Jean Dupre, Abraham Salle, Isaac Salle, Pierre David, Pierre Louis Sobblett, Jean Chastain.

The same day as above the Sieur David rendered account of his administration for the year 1729, in the presence of the vestrymen named above.

July 24, 1729. The vestry of the parish of King William having assembled, the Sieur Pierre David was elected by a plurality of votes of those present to count the tobacco of the parish in the place of Joseph Bingli. Estienne Chastain, Gille Allaigre,

* Thus the register. The meaning seems to be that different commissioners were appointed for the sections of the county lying in Henrico and in Goochland county.

Antoine Rapine, Daniel Guerand, Jean Dupre, Isac Salle, Pierre David, Jean Chastain.*

December 27, 1729. The vestry assembled. Present: Bartelemi Dupui, Antoine Rapine, Gile Allaigre, Jean Dupre, Abraham Salle, Isac Salle, Daniel Guerand. The Sieur Allaigree and Mr. Rapine were chosen to present a new request to Mr. the Governor William Gooch. They were promised four shillings per day.†

JEAN CHASTAIN, Clerk.

This day, January 1, 1729-30, the glebe was leased to Edouard Scot for one year. He is to give twenty bushels and one-half of wheat rent for it for the present year. He is not permitted to cut wood from the other side of the swamp for any purpose.

February 26, 1729. The vestry, assembled as below, made an agreement with Monsieur Massom‡ for preaching in our church of the parish of King William at two pounds per sermon, payable in wheat, commencing this day, as above. Present: Gille Allaigre, Bartelemi Dupuy, Antoine Rapine, Pierre David, Abraham Salle, Isac Salle, Estienne Chastain, Jean Chastain.

July 18, 1730. The vestry assembled. Present: Jacob Amo-

---

*A slip of paper pinned beside the foregoing entry contains the following receipt:

"I, Jacob Capon, acknowledge receipt from Mons. Barthelemy Dupuy of 8 bushels for the levy of the parish; further, I acknowledge receipt from Mons. Dupuy of 7 bushels and one-half for rent of the glebe.

Monocanton, Sept. 22, 1729.

JACOB CAPON."

† Immediately below stands the following entry, afterwards cancelled: "The same day it was decreed that one church warden shall be elected each year, and that the second one shall remain a second year in order to finish receiving what remains due from the preceding year."

‡ Rev. David Mossom, who served as rector of the parish of New Kent forty years, Meade I, 386. He was born in London in 1690, and inducted into the New Kent parish in 1727, where a tablet bearing a long Latin epitaph afterwards stood in St. Peter's Church to commemorate his virtues, Meade II, 460. For an account of the effect of Mr. Mossom's preaching on a frivolous hearer, Cf. Meade I, 470.

net, Estiene Chastain, Antoine Rapine, Pierre David, Jean Dupre, Daniel Guerand, Pierre Louis Soblet, Abraham Salle, Isac Salle, Jean Chastain. It was concluded to answer the letter of Monsieur Rival.*

List of Tithables of the Parish of King William for the Year 1729.

Jean Barret	3	Pierre David	5
Daniel Pero't	2	Jaque Sobblet	1
Pierre Bocard	4	David Lesueur	2
Thommas Prouet	1	Gorge Smith	2
Roger Pret	2	Jean Legrand	2
Pierre Bioret	1	Gorge Marchbone	3
Pierre Faure	1	Francoi Dupui	2
Joseph Bingli	1	Jacob Ámonet	3
Nicolas Soulie	2	Jean Chastain	2
Jean Peene	2	Jean Levilain	6
Estiene Malet	1	Thommas Givodan	3
Antoine Benin	3	Isac Salle	3
Antoine Rapine	5	Gilleaume Salle	1
Estiene Chastain	6	Pierre Dupui	1
Gideon Chanbon	3	Jean de Ker	2
Pierre Chastain	5	Abraham Salle	4
Jacob Capon	2	William Hens	1
Claude Gori	1	Jaque Marbain	2
Pierre Dep	3	Jean Martain	3
Daniel Guerand	4	Magdelaine Chastain	2
Pierre Bilbau	2	Jacob Trabut	2
Jaque Tayler	3	Jean Nil	1
Barbari Dutoy	4	Elie Sassin	1
Barthelemi Dupuy	4	Edouard Brayer	1
Pierre Louis Soblet	2	Gille Allaigre	5
		Daniel Faure	3
		Jean Dupre	4
			134

* Not otherwise mentioned in the register.

August 16, 1730. The vestry assembled. Present: Mr. Antoine Rapine, Abraham Salle, Barthelemy Dupuy, Pierre Louis Soblet, Isaac Salle, Giles Allegle, Estienne Chastin, Jean Dupre, and Jean Chastin. It was agreed with Mr. Marye,* minister, to give him twenty shillings per sermon, one to be preached every other Sunday, payable in wheat at three shillings per bushel, or in maize at eighteen pence per bushel, or oats also at eighteen cents per bushel, part to be delivered at his house and part at Warwick. There is due to-day to Mons. Marye, minister, six sermons, ... 6 "0 "0

JEAN CHASTAIN, Clerk.

August 29. The vestry assembled. Present: Messieurs Barthelemi Dupui, Antoine Rapine, Gille Allaigre, Abraham Salle, Isac Sallee, Jean Chastain. The Siers Jean Jaque Dupui and Thomma Givodan were elected vestrymen in the place of Pierre David and Daniel Guerand, deceased.

JEAN CHASTAIN.

August 30, 1730. Monsieur Marye preached a sermon.

September 13. Monsieur Marye preached in English.

September 19. Jean Jaque Dupui and Thommas Givodan took the oath of vestrymen. Present: Barthelemi Dupui, Antoine Rapine, Abraham Salle, Isac Salle, Pierre Louis Soblet, Jean Chastain.

September 19. The levy for the present year, 1730, is one bushel of wheat per tithable, 10 (?) lb. of tobacco and a bushel of maize.

---

* Rev. James Marye, of Rouen in Normandy, who came to the Virginia colony in 1729. His services in King William parish began in the spring of 1730. Cf. Brock, Register of Baptisms in *Huguenot Emigration to Virginia*, p. 84ff.; and the above entry. The contract with Mr. Marye was renewed on June 1, 1734, and the last mention of him in this register occurs under September 20 of the same year. He was transferred to the parish of St. George, in Spotsylvania, October, 1735, where he probably gave George Washington his first religious instruction. Meade, II, 242. For an account of this distinguished ancestor of a distinguished Virginia family, Cf. Brock, p. 183ff.

The vestry, as above, appointed the Srs. Antoine Rapine, Louis Soblet, Isac Salle to make a contract for a church.

The same day Isac Salle took the oath of church warden in the place of Abraham Salle.

September 27. Monsieur Marye preached a sermon.

October 24. The vestry assembled. Present: Barthelemi Dupui, Estiene Chastain, Antoine Rapine, Isac Salle, Abraham Salle, Pierre Louis Soblet. It was agreed with Francoi Jams that he build a church for the sum of twenty-one thousand, six hundred pounds of tobacco, to be paid in three years, he to furnish the hogsheads and the press, the same here at Manikaintown. The church wardens and Louy Soblet and Estienne Chastain were appointed to make a contract with the carpenter next Saturday.

JOHN CHASTAIN.

November 6. Mr. Marye preached a sermon and celebrated the communion.

November 22. Mr. Marye preached a sermon.

December 6. Mr. Marye preached a sermon in English.

December 26. Mr. Marye preached a sermon.

January 2, 1730 | 1. Mr. Marye preached a sermon.

The 16. Mr. Marye preached a sermon and administered the communion.

February 18. Mr. Marye preached in English.

February 25. Mr. Marye preached in French.

28. Mr. Marye preached in French.

March 14, 1730 | 1. Mr. Marye preached in French.

March 28. 1731. Mr. Marye preached in English.

April 11. Mr. Marye preached in French.

The 18. Mr. Marye preached in French.

The 19. Mr. Marye preached in French and administered the communion.

May 9. Mr. Marye preached in English.

The 23. Mr. Marye preached in French.

June 5. Mr. Marye preached in French.

The 20. Mr. Marye preached in French.

July 4. Mr. Marye preached in English.

The 18. Mr. Marye preached in French.

August 1. Mr. Marye preached in French.

The 2. Mr. Marye preached in French and administered the communion.

List of Tithables of the Parish of King William for the Present Year, 1730.

Names	No.
John Barrett James & Judith	3
Nicolas Soulie Jean Mexfegh	2
Antoine Chareron,	1
Jean du Crais	1
Jean Legrand	1
Barthelemi Dupui Sara, negro	2
Pierre Dupui	1
Jean Dupui Dic, negro	2
Thomas Brian	1
Pierre Bocar Antoine Calvet James Scots	3
Estiene Malet	1
Daniel Peraud	1
Pierre Brouse Francoi Alcard	2
Pierre Bondurand Jean Bondurand	2
Matieu Age	1
Mr. Dutoi*	
Jean Loucadou Joseph & Peg, negro	3
Estiene Chastain Estiene Farsi Estiene Calvet Isac Gori Limbo, Dic,† Panpi Mal & Sara	9
Pierre, David, Manone, Dic, Daine,	4
James Balar, Pierre Chastain, Pierre Loucadou, Piter, Maria, Dik, Joseph, Morfeld,	7
Jacob Capon,	1
David Barnard	1
Jean Levilain, Jean Levilain, Antoine Levilain, Piter, Sesar, Marie,	6
Andre Amonet,	1
Jacob Amonet, Charle Amonet,	2
Jean Chastain & Charo, negro,	2
Jean Quantain	1
Edouard Scott, Couper, Pope, Dic, Breeches, Dilso,	6
David Lesueur, Jemes Brian,	2
Thomas Givodan, Beti, negress,	2

*The omission of the number was probably an oversight.

† Pompey. The English names of the negroes in their naïve French form are not the least interesting thing about the quaint old register.

Antoine Rapine, Dic, Sara, Peg, negro,	4
Daniel Guerand, Glode Rouviere, Pierre Guerand, Yama, Franc, Sam, Hanath, Robin, Mal,	9
Francoi Dupui,	1
Jean Pierre Bilbo, Sara, negress,	2
Antoine Benain, Billi, Cofi, Jeni, Duch Couper,	5
Gideon Chanbon, Manac, Beti,	3
Jean Decars, William Nails,	2
Jean Chapman	1
Daniel Faure, a black,	2
Jean Dupre and his blacks,	4
Gille Alaigre and his blacks,	4
Gorge Marchebench & Chester,	2

Jean Pain, Bilippain,* Nat. Battom,	3
James Soblet,	1
Pierre Soblet s., Pierre Soblet, Jean Grifin,	3
Rodrig Ivins	1
Jems Ford	1
Pierre Salle	1
Francoi Farsi	1
Isac Salle, Jean Bernard, Jeni, Betti, negro,	4
Guilaume Salle, Antoine Bernard, Gorg, negro,	3
Pierre Faure,	1
Jean Faure,	1
Pierre Biouret,	1
Pierre Dep Estiene Paratie March Gobrig	3
Nicolas Duerai,	1
Thomas Prouet,	1
Abraham Salle, Bob, Agar,	3
Jean Bottler,	1
William Hans,	1
Jean Marbain, Wil Marbain, Jean Haris,	3
Jaquè Marbain,	1
Jean Nill,	1
Jacob Trabit. London,	2
Antoine Trabit, Beti,	2
Pierre Sabatie,	1
Elie Sasin,	1

For the most part they are easily recognized, Mal, Cofi and Sesar readily resolving themselves into Moll, Coffee and Ceasar. Others, such as Breches, Dilso, Hanri, Gorg, Hanath, Beti, etc., offer no difficulty. Yama, Limbo and Charo are perhaps African inportations; Manac may be the name of an Indian.

* Billy Payne.

Edouard Brayer,	1
Claude Gori,	1
Gorge Smith,	1
Hanri Beli,	1
Rene Chastain & Jack	2
Jacob Copli,	1
Thommas Oblin,	1
Willeam Devis	1
	160

Monsieur Marye preached September 12, after the meeting of the vestry.

The 27th he preached in French.

October 1. Mr. Marye administered the communion.

October 24. Mr. Marye preached in English.

November 7. Mr. Marye preached in French.

December 5. Mr. Marye preached in French.

December 19. Mr. Marye preached in English.

December 25. Mr. Marye preached in French.

December 27. Mr. Marye preached in French.

January 9, 1731 | 2. Mr. Marye preached in French.

January 20. Mr. Marye preached in French.

February 13. Mr. Marye preached in English.

February 27. Mr. Marye preached in French.

March 13. Mr. Marye preached in French.

The 26, 1732. Mr. Marye preached in French.

April 9. Mr. Marye preached in English.

The 10. Mr. Marye preached in French and administered the communion.

The 25. Mr. Marye preached in French.

May 7. Mr. Marye preached in French..

The 25. Mr. Marye preached in French.

June 5. Mr. Marye preached in English.

The 20. Mr. Marye preached in French.

July 2. Mr. Marye preached in French.

The 16. Mr. Marye preached in French.

The 30. Mr. Marye preached in English.

August 12. Mr. Marye preached in French.

Do. 27. Mr. Marye preached in French.*

April 23, 1731. The vestry assembled. Present: Estiene Chastain, Gille Allaigre, Antoine Rapine, Pierre Louis Soblet, Jean Jaque Dupui, Jean Dupre, Jean Chastain. Mr. Barthelemi Dupui tendered his resignation and the vestry accepted it, the day and date above.

This day Jean Jaque Dupuy took the oath of church warden in the presence of the vestry named above, the day and date as above.

July 23, 1731. The Sieurs Andre Amonet and Pierre Faure took the oath of vestrymen for this church. Present: Gile Allaigre, Antoine Rapine, Jean Jaque Dupui, Jean Dupre, Estiene Chastain, Jean Chastain, Clerk.

The present vestry, named above, agreed to pay five pounds in wheat and maize, viz.: the wheat at three shillings per bushel and the maize at a shilling and one-half per bushel, to Jean Okeley, who binds himself to transfer across the river and back all the parishioners of the parish of King William, from morning at the break of day to dusk; namely, men and women on foot and on horseback. Done the day and date above.

JEAN CHASTAIN.

Aagust 19, 1731. The vestry assembled. Present: Antoine Rapine, Jean Jaque Dupui, Estiene Chastain, Pierre Louis Soblet, Jean Dupre, Gille Allaigre, Pierre Faure, Andre Amonet, Guilleaume Salle. Jean Levilain having asked his discharge, the vestry granted it to him.

JEAN CHASTAIN.

This day, as above, Guillieume Salle took the oath of vestryman, in accordance with the law, in the presence of the vestry named above.

JEAN CHASTAIN.

(TO BE CONTINUED)

*The record of Mr. Marye's sermons is continued to the bottom of the page of the register, without regard to the interruption in chronology resulting therefrom.

THE VESTRY BOOK OF KING WILLIAM PARISH, VA., 1707–1750.

This day, September 1, 1731, Jean Levilain[1] took the oath of vestryman in the usual manner in the presence of the vestry named below: Gille Alaigre, Estiene Chastain, Pierre Louys Soblet, Antoine Rapine, Jean Jaque Dupui, André Amonet, Guillaume Sallé, Pierre Faure.

September 1, 1731. The same day Mes. Antoine Rapine (and) Abraham Sallé conjointly rendered their account for the year 1729. There is due to Mr. Rapine fourteen bushels and one-half of wheat.

The same day the accounts of Mr. Rapine and of Isaac Sallé for the year 1730 were examined in full vestry. There is shown to be owing forty-five bushels of wheat and sixty-seven bushels of maize.

JEAN CHASTAIN.

The Sr. Antoine Rapine paid to the carpenter, Francois James, the sum of nine thousand nine hundred and forty-seven pounds of tobacco, in part payment for the church.

Mr. Marye received seventy-four bushels of wheat and eighty-five bushels of maize on the amount due him, which amounts to seventeen pounds, seventeen shillings, threepence. There is (now) due him fifteen pounds, nine shillings, ninepence.

JEAN CHASTAIN.

This day the levy for the parish of King William for the present year, 1731, was made, at forty pounds of tobacco and a bushel of wheat and a bushel of maize per head. Present, the vestry named above.

JEAN CHASTAIN.

This day the Sr. Guillieaume Sallé took the oath of church warden in the presence of the vestry above named.

JEAN CHASTAIN.

---

[1]Not the same one whose resignation was accepted by the vestry on August 19, above. There were two Jean Levilains in the parish, probably father and son, as their names are usually bracketed together in the tax-lists.

January 1, 1731|2. The vestry assembled. Present: Estiene Chastain, Gile Alaigre, Antoine Rapine, Jean Dupré, Jean Jaque Dupui, Guilleaume Sallé, André Amonet, Jean Levilain, Jean Pierre Bonduran and Estiene Malet were appointed to procession[2] the land above the creek of Mr. Joni; Jean Pierre Billiebo, Nicolas Soulié between the two creeks; Jean Bernard, Jacob Trabue the other side of the creek below.

November 22, 1731. Antoine Rapine paid to Mr. Maton forty bushels of wheat for the year 1730 of the balance due him.

JEAN CHASTAIN.

---

[2]The first mention in the register of "processioning" or "perambulating," a method of formally fixing the boundaries of the various land-holders in the parish. By an Act of Assembly of March, 1661-2, it was decreed that "within twelve months after this act, all the inhabitants of every neck and tract of land adjoining shall goe in procession and see that the mark-trees of every mann's land in these precincts be renewed," and that the same course be taken once every four years. *Henings, Statutes at Large,* II, 102. The same act provides "that each county court shall appoint and order the vestries of each parish to divide the parishes into soe many precincts as they shall think necessary for the neighbors to joyne and see each others markes renewed," and fixes the period between Easter and Whitsuntide for the processioning. In an act of October, 1705, the above act was renewed, and the county courts were directed to order the vestries to appoint two intelligent and honest freeholders in each precinct to see such processioning performed. These freeholders were required to make report, which should be duly registered and certified to by the church wardens. The period for processioning was by this act fixed from the last day of September to the last day of March, and the time was to be announced in advance by the committee. Boundaries three times processioned were to count as unalterably fixed. Cf. *Hening,* III, 325. The last-mentioned act went into effect in 1708; but there is no notice of processioning in the present register until the entry above. In the following pages committees are appointed to procession on the following dates: March 29, 1735; August 20, 1739; June 24, 1747. The custom was one of those brought over from England; and it is of interest to note that according to Rapalje and Lawrence, *American and English Law Dictionary,* II, this manner of impressing boundaries still exists in some parts of North Carolina and Tennessee.

LIST OF TITHABLES OF THE PARISH OF KING WILLIAM FOR THE YEAR 1731.

Name	Tithables
Jean Chastain, Charo, black,	2
Jacob Amonet, Charle Amonet,	2
André Amonet,	1
Jean Faure,	1
Jean Bernard, Antoine Bernard,	2
Nicolas Soulié, Jean Ducré,	2
Mathieu Agé,	1
Jean Pierre Bonduran, Jean Bonduran, Pierre Bonduran,	3
Pierre Bioret, Jaque Faure,	2
Pierre Brousse, Francoi Allierd, André Goodin,	3
Thommas Deekens, Roberd Peen, Pierre Martin, Jaque Houk, Jacque Scott, Nicolas Scotelar,	6
Edouard Scott, Jean Quantain, Dilsi, Debora, Thommas, Cooper, Dick, Brichis, Robin,	9
Pierre Louy Soblet, Pierre Soblett, Jo. Grifin, Mark Gotrig,	4
Francoi Dupui,	1
David Bernard,	1
Pierre Sallé,	1
Jacque Brean,	1
Daniel Pero,	1
Estiene Malet, W. Batom, J. Ma. fil.,	3
Estiene Chastain, Estiene Calvet, Estiene Farsi, Linbo, Dick, Panpi, Mal, Sara,	8
Antoine Benin, Joseph Benin, Billi, Cofe, Jini,	5
W. Sallé, Gorge, Gini, Betti,	4
Barbara Dutoi, Jo, Peg, black,	3
Jean Harris, W. Harris,	2
Barthelemi Dupui	1
Pierre Dupui,	1
Jean Jacue Dupui, Dick, black,	2
Pierre Faure,	1
Jean Chapman,	1
Anne David, Manuck, Dick, Dina,	3
David Lesueur,	1

Jean Loucadou,	1	Pierre Guerand,	
Jean Pierre Bilbo, Sara,	2	Glaude Rouviere,	
Jean Peen,		Jame,	
Isaac Gori,	3	Jem,	8
Antoine Calvert,		Robin, Frenc,	
Pierre Bocar,	1	Hand,	
Judith Giuodan, Betti,	2	Mall,	
Jaque Teler		Hanry Belly,	1
Pierre Chastain,		William Story,	1
Jean Mouni,	5	James Holman (tithables)	2
Piter,		Jque Judith,	
Maria,		Jean Dupré, tithables,	4
Jideon Chanbon,		Gille Allaigre, tithables,	5
Monoc,	3	Daniel Faure, tithables,	4
Betti,		Edouerd Brayer,	1
Jaque Soblet,	2	Elie Sasin,	1
Gouard Borgars,		Jacob Trabu,	2
Jean Vilain,		Antoine Trabu,	2
Jean Vilain,		Jean Martin,	2
Antoine Vilain,		Jaque Martin,	2
Piter,	6	Richard Dine,	1
Siser,		Jean Dekey,	1
Marie,		Jean Bottes,	1
Añtoine Rapine,		Magdelaine Sallé, Bob,	2
Dick,		Agar,	
Sara,	4	Thomas Prouet,	2
Kett,		Nicolas Duerai,	
		Thomas Brian,	1

April 22, 1732. The vestry assembled. Present: Estiene Chastain, Antoine Rapine, Jeane Levilain, Gillieaume Sallé, Jean Jaque Dupui, André Amonet, Pierre Louys Soblet. The vestry discharged Glaude Gori from all future charge of the parish of King William.

JEAN CHASTAIN.

The same day Monsieur Rapine rendered his account for the year 1730, and is quit of the same. Done in the presence of the vestry as above.

JEAN CHASTAIN.

July 31, 1732. The vestry assembled. Present: Antoine Rapine, Estiene Chastain, Pierre Faure, P. Louys Soblet, Jean Jaques Dupuy, Guileaume Sallé, André Amonnet. Mr. Estiene Chastain was appointed to go and present to Mr. the

Governor a petition to fix the boundary of our parish of King William. He was promised four shillings per day.

JEAN CHASTAIN, Clerk.

August 28, 1732. The vestry assembled. Present: Jean Jaque Dupui, Guillieaume Sallé, Estiene Chastain, Antoine Rapine, Pierre Gaure, Louys Soblet, André Amonet. The vestry gave full power to Mr. Marye to write to the gentlemen of the Society for the twenty pounds which it had the kindness to give to us in the last letter which we have received, dated November 24, 1729.

The same day the church wardens, Guilieaume Sallé (and) Jean Jaque Dupi, rendered account of the maize. There is due to them two bushels of maize, and they are discharged of the wheat, saving errors in the account.

JEAN CHASTAIN.

September 30, 1732. The vestry assembled. Present: Estiene Chastain, Gile Alaigre, Pierre Faure, Jean Dupré, Pierre Louys Soblet, André Amonet, Guileaume Sallé, Jean Jaque Dupui. The church wardens rendered their account of the tobacco. They still owe six hundred and seventy-seven pounds of tobacco.

JEAN CHASTAIN.

The vestry, as above, made the levy for the present year of a bushel and a half of wheat and a bushel and a half of maize per tithable.

JEAN CHASTAIN.

The Sieurs Pierre Faure and André Amonet took the oath of church warden in the presence of the vestry named above.

JEAN CHASTAIN.

List of Tithables of the Parish of King William for the Year 1732.

Name	Tithables
André Amonet,	1
Charle Amonet,	1
Jean Chastain & Charo,	2
Thommas Dickins, Peter Martain, Willeam Giles, Nicolas Scotte, James Scott, James Houk, Maria,	7
James Bryant,	1
Willeam Sallé, George, Betti, Gini,	4
Edward Scott, Dick, Robin, Cooper, Dilcey, Joni,	6
Thimote Eley,	1
Estiene Malet, Edward Peen, John Mansfield, Dick,	4
James Soblet,	1
Peter Faure,	1
John Faure,	1
Nicolas Dueray,	1
Estiene Chastain, Linbo, Dick, Panpi, Jack, Moll, Sara, Jene,	8
Nicolas Soulié, Sam,	2
Antoine Benin, Will, Cofe, Jene,	4
Peter Dupui,	1
Peter Louys Soblet, Peter Soblet, John Grifin, Luci,	4
John Peter Bilbo, Sara,	2
Gedeon Chanbon, Manac, Bet,	3
John Quantain,	1
James Smith,	1
William Stanford,	1
James Robinson,	1
Rene Chastain, Betti,	2
John Bernard, Antoine Bernard, Nicolas Scott,	3
Moyse Forquera(?), David Bernar,	2
John Watt, Junier Watt,	2
John Harris, Will Harris, Fillis,	3
William Bottum,	1
Antoine Rapine, Dick, Sara, Kat,	4
Antoine Calvet, John Peen,	2
John Dupré,	3
Giles Allaigre,	4
Daniel Faure,	2
John Faure,	2
Isaac Robinson,	1
Edward Bryar,	1
Elie Sasin,	1
Antoine Trabue,	1
Jacob Trabu,	2
John Dakar,	2
John Martain,	2

Names	Tithables	Names	Tithables
Thommas Portur, Peter Loucadou,	2	Jacque Martain,	2
John Loucadou, Joseph, Peg,	3	Richard Dine,	2
John Levilain, Antoine Vilain, Peter, Sisar, Marie,	5		58
Peter David, Dik, Manuel, Daina,	4	Magdelaine Sallé, her tithable Bob,	1
David Lesueur, Joseph Brian,	2	John Villain,	2
Barthelemi Dupui,	1	John Adman,	1
John James Dupui, Dick,	2		
Peter Dep, Panetié, John Pierre Panetié,	3		
	70*		

January 31, 1732|3. The vestry having assembled, it gave full power to Monsieur Allaigre to ask of Major Alwes his opinion regarding the tobacco which we are to pay to the carpenter, viz: whether he shall pay thirty per hundred; and he was directed to pay a guinea for his opinion. Present: André Amonet, Pierre Faure, Gile Alaigre, Antoine Rapine, Pierre Louys Soblet, Jean Jaque Dupui, Guillaume Sallé.

JEAN CHASTAIN.

March 8, 1732|3. The vestry assembled. Present: Pierre Faure, André Amonet, Antoine Rapine, Guilieaume Sallé, Jean Jaque Dupui, Louis Soblet. It was agreed to give Glaude Gori two barrels of wheat and two barrels of maize for cleaning the church, commencing March 11, 1732|33.

March 17, 1732|3. The vestry assembled. Present: Pi-

*Clerk Chastain's figures are wrong. The sum should be 67.

erre Fore, Louis Soblet, Anthoine Rapine, Jean Jaques Dupuy, Jean Dupré, André Amonet, Giles Allegre, Jean Levillain, Guilleaume Sallé, Jean Chastain. Accounts were settled with Capn. Francis James,[3] and there appears due him from the parish for having built the church 5286 pounds of tobacco, in accordance with which, as well as for 650 lbs. due to Capn. Rapine, etc., a levy was made of 40 pounds per tithable, if sufficient,[4] or 52 otherwise.

Antoine Rapine rendered his account of the tobacco for the year 1730. There remains due him 160 lbs. of tobacco.[5]

Jean Levilain asked his discharge. The vestry granted it to him.

JEAN CHASTAIN.

November 23, 1734.[6] Antoine Rapine received the tobacco due him by the parish at the hands of Pierre Faure and An. Amonet.

ANTOINE RAPINE.

The vestry appointed as members David Lesueur and Jean Pierre Bonduran to fill the vacant places.

JEAN CHASTAIN.

June 16, 1733. David Lesueur took the oath as vestryman for the church of the parish of King William, in the pres-

---

[3]The contract made with Captain James is noted above under October 24, 1730. Cf. *Va. Magazine of Hist. and Biog.*, XII, 4, p. 380. In accordance with this contract, the full amount, 21,600 pounds, was to be paid in three years from date. See below under date of June 16, 1733. **(Page 170, this volume.)**

[4]de 40 livres par tithables convenient ou bien 52 autrement.

[5]Il se trouve redevable de 106 lb de tabac. Littré, Sachs, and other lexicographers give *redevable* only in an active sense; but that it is used passively in the above passage, is confirmed by the receipt which follows. Elsewhere in the register it seems to have the same meaning, and is doubtless a provincialism, or perhaps another evidence of the degeneracy of the colonial French current in Manakintown at this time.

[6]This receipt is written in at the bottom of the register, and is not in chronological order. There is a tendency on the part of Clerk Chastain to let the receipt follow immediately on the entry showing the obligation.

ence of the vestry, as follows: Pierre Faure, André Churus Amonet, Estiene Chastain, Antoine Rapine, Pierre Louys Soblet, Guilieaume Sallé, Jean Jaque Dupui, Jean Chastain.

Guillieaume Sallé and Jean Dupuy paid the tobacco which they owed to the parish for their administration of the year 1731.

JEAN CHASTAIN.

The vestry the same day settled accounts with Captain Jamse. In accordance with the account which we made with him, we have paid him twenty thousand, nine hundred and eighty-one pounds of tobacco, and we owe six hundred and nineteen pounds.

JEAN CHASTAIN.

August 11, 1733. The vestry assembled. Present: Pierre Faure, André Amonet, Estiene Chastain, Antoine Rapine, Jean Dupré, Guillieaume Sallé, Jean Jaque Dupuy, Pierre Louis Soblet, David Leseur. Isaac Paranto having asked to be relieved from the charges of the parish, the vestry granted it to him.

The same day Gile Allaigre tendered his resignation. The vestry accepted it.

JEAN CHASTAIN.

August 18, 1733. Pierre Gueran took the oath as vestryman for the church of the parish of King William. Present: Pierre Faure, André Amonet, Estiene Chastain, Antoine Rapine, Guilieaume Sallé, Pierre Louy Soblet, Jean Jaque Dupuy, David Lesueur.

JEAN CHASTAIN.

The same day Pierre Louis Soblet tendered his resignation. The vestry accepted it.

JEAN CHASTAIN.

The same day Pierre Faure and André Amonet rendered account of their administration for the year 1732. They gave their note for the amount due in arrear.

JEAN CHASTAIN.

The same day Estiene Chastain and Jean Chastain were elected church wardens by a plurality of votes.

February 4, 1731 | 2.[7] The vestry agreed with Cp. Franc Jamse to make the flooring for the vestry and shutters for the windows of the church for five pounds, payable in wheat at three shillings per bushel, delivered at Waric, in maize at eighteen pence per bushel, delivered at Mr. Rapine's place.

August 27, 1733. The vestry assembled. Present: Estiene Chastain, Jean Jaque Dupuy, Antoine Rapine, Pierre Faure, Guilleaume Sallé, André Amonet, David Lesueur, Pierre Guerand. We settled accounts with Monsieur Marye, the minister. The parish remains due him six pounds, thirteen shillings, ninepence.

JEAN CHASTAIN.

August 27, 1733. The same day the vestry made a levy of a bushel of wheat per tithable and a bushel of maize, payable to the church wardens.

June 16, 1738. Pierre Faure and André Amonnet have settled their note for the arrearage in their year as church wardens, the year 1732.

JEAN CHASTAIN.

Present:

DAVID LESUEUR,[8]
ESTIENNE MALET, } Church Wardens,
RANE CHASTAIN, }
ANTHONY BENNIN,
GUILLAUME SALLE,
ESTIENNE CHASTAIN,
JEAN PIERRE BILBOU,
PIERRE GUERRANT,
JOHN DUPUY.

[7]This entry, as will be noted, is a supplementary contract with Captain James, and stands here out of its chronological position. Cf. the contract for the building, dated October 30, 1730.

[8]The signatures are personal.

List of Tithables of the Parish of King William for the Year 1733.

Barthelemi Dupuy, 1
Pierre Dupuy, 1
Jean Jaque Dupuy, Dik, 2
Antoine Rapine, Dik, Ket, 3
Nicolas Soulié, Sem, Robin, Mal, 4
Pierre Gueran, Antoine Trabu, 2
Jean Pierre Bilbo, Seri, 2
Pierre Faure, Pierre Bioret, 2
Jaque Soblet, 1
André Amonet, 1
Jaque Faure, 1
Jean Faure, 1
Jean Jaque Florinoirs, his blacks, 3
Jeame Le Vieux, Jeame Franc,[9] ..
Jean Edmen. Henri Colins, 2
David Thomas, 1
Thomas Porter, Jo. Peg, 3
Charle Vernion, 1
Pierre Louy Soblet, Grifin, Lousi, 3
Estiene Farsi, Sem, 2
Jean Pierre Bonduran,
Jean Bonduran, } 3
Pierre Bonduran,
James Holl, 1
Willeam Higgins, 1
John Higgin, 1
Willeam Smith, 1
Estiene Chastain, Limbo, Dik, Panpi, Jac, Mall, Seri, Gini, 8
Thomas Bradli, 1
Pierre Loucadou, 1
Rene Chastain, Jek, Betti, 3
Jean Harris, Willeam Harris. Willeam Bottom, Fillis, 4

Pierre Dep,
Estiene Panetie, } 3
Jean Pierre Panetie,
Jean Peen, William Peen, 2
Thomas Dikeens,
Jamse Houk,
Nicolas, } 4
Scotar,
Jean Martain,
Pierre Martain,
Daniel, } 4
Mall, Agar,
Elie Sasin, 1
Edward Scott,
Joseph Scott,
Tam,
Brichis,
Pop, } 8
Couper,
Dilso,
Teb.
Jean Levilain,
Antoine Levilain,
Sizer, } 5
Marie,
Nanni,
Estiene Cavet, 1
Estiene Calvet, 1
Dik, 3
Pierre Soblet, 1
Nicolas Dueray, 1
Jamse Jons, 1
Jamse Robinson, 1
Guillieaume Sallé,
Jean Chimo,
Gorge, } 5
Betti, Gini,
Jean Bernar, Antoin Bernar, 2
David Bernar, 1
Pierre David, Dik, Manoni,

---

[9]The number of tithables is left blank in the register.

Pierre Sallé, Jaque, black,	2	Dina,	4
Antoine Benin, Joseph Benin, Cofe, Billi, Gini,	5	David Lesueur, Joseph Brian,	2
Gile Allaigre, Chico, Belander,	3	Jaque Brian,	1
Jeane Dupré, Pierre Forqueran, Tobi, Nanni,	4	Jaque Martain, Betti,	2
Jacob Trabu, London,	2	Joseph Tharanton,	1
Edward Bryer,	1	Daniel Peraud, Job,	2
John Wett, Wott,	2	Jean Chastain, Charo,	2
Daniel Faure, Pierre Peru,	2	Gideon Chambon, Monoc, Betti,	3
Jean Faure, Moyse Forqueran,	2	William Stanford,	1
Isaac Robinson,	1		144*
Jean Levilain,	1		
Charle Amonet, Bob,	2	Samuel Weaver,	1
Jean Deker, Jean Chapmen,	2		

June 1, 1734. The vestry assembled. Present: Estiene Chastain, Antoine Rapine, David Lesueur, Pierre Faure, Jean Jaque Dupuy, André Amonet, Guillieaume Sallé, Pierre Gueran, Jean Chastain. An agreement was made with Monsieur Marye[10] to give him twenty shillings per sermon, one of which is to be preached every two weeks, payable in wheat at three shillings per bushel (or) in maize at eighteen pence per bushel, delivered partly at his place and partly at Warwick.

JEAN CHASTAIN.

The vestry in session chose as church wardens David Lesueur and Pierre Gueran, they having taken the usual oath.

JEAN CHASTAIN.

August 3, 1734. The vestry assembled and agreed with Mr. Stephen Woodson to do the ferrying across the river for the Parish of King William one year, commencing to-day. He binds himself to transfer the people on foot, on horseback, (and) laden horses from the break of day to dusk; we bind ourselves to pay him six pounds, half in wheat and half in

*Chastain's system of arithmetic is again unintelligible, as the figures add up 150.

[10]A renewal of the contract of August 16, 1730.

maize, delivered with the church wardens, the wheat at three shillings per bushel, the maize at eighteen pence per bushel. He is to have the maize at the end of next April and the wheat at the end of September of the year 1735. He is to transfer the minister on account of the parish as a part of the contract.[11]

JEAN CHASTAIN.

The same day it was decreed that all of the acts passed with respect to the parish of King William, as well as all of the laws of Virginia, be procured and kept in the vestry.

JEAN CHASTAIN.

September 20, 1734. The vestry assembled. Present: David Lesueur, Pierre Gueran, Estiene Chastain, Antoine Rapine, Guilieaume Sallé, André Amonet, Jean Jaque Dupuy. We settled accounts with Mr. Marye. We remain due him two pounds, nineteen shillings.

JEAN CHASTAIN.

The same day the levy was made for the present year, 1734, of one bushel of wheat and a bushel and one-half of maize per head.

JEAN CHASTAIN.

LIST OF THE PARISH OF KING WILLIAM FOR THE YEAR 1734.

Capt. Antoine Rapine,	5	Thomas Dikens,	3
Samuel Birch,	1	Benjamin Haris,	1
Pierre Dep,	3	Jean Haris,	3
Estiene Chastain,	7	Edward Scott,	7
Barthelemi Dupuy,	1	Jemse Petey,	1
Jean Jaque Dupuy,	2	Pitar Sallé,	2
Pierre Dupuy,	1	John James Florinoir, tithables,	3
Pierre Louys Soblet,	4	Thomas Bradley,	1
Jean Pierre Billiebo,	2	David Thomas,	1
Thomas Porter,	3		

[11]A former contract of July 23, 1731, with Jean Okebey fixes the amount to be paid for ferriage at five pounds, and does not include free transfer for the minister. The free transportation of the minister and his household comes up later as a matter of dispute with Reverend Gavain. Cf. entry below, December 3, 1736.

Isaac Gori, 1
Jean Levilain, signor, 5
Pierre Faure, 1
Jean Faure, 1
Jean Chastain, 2
André Amonet, 1
Anne David, her tithables, 4
Antoine Benain, 4
Joseph Benain, 1
Daniel Perault, 3
David Lesueur, 3
Jaque Brian, 1
Jean Bernard, 1
Rene Chastain, 4
David Bernard, 2
Guillieaume Sallé, 6
Guilleaume Stenford, 1
Pierre Gueran, 3
Gedeon Chambon, 3
Charle Vernion, 1
Nicolas Soulie, 4
Jaque Robinson, 0
John Witt, 3
Samuel Wever, 1
Estiene Malet, 3
Pierre Loucadou, 1
Jean Bonduran, j., 1
Jaque Faure, Pierre Bioret, 2
Jean Pierre Bonduran, 2
Estiene Calvet, 1
Estiene Farsi, 2
John Edmonns, 1
John Hamilton, 0
Jaque Soblet, 1
Joseph Bingley, 1
Jean Morises, 1
Jean Dupré, 4
Edward Bryar, 1
Giles Allaigre, 3
Daniel Faure, 1
Jean Faure, 2
Isaac Robinson, 1
Elie Sassain, 1
Jacob Trabu, 2
Jean Martain, 3
Magdelaine Sallé, 2
Jean Willeamson, 1
Jean Vilain, 1

November 23, 1734. The vestry assembled. Present: David Lesueur, Pierre Guerand, Antoine Rapine, Pierre Faure, Guilieaume Sallé, André Amonet. Antoine Benin took the oath of vestryman.

JEAN CHASTAIN.

March 15, 1734-5. The vestry assembled. Present: David Lesueur, Pierre Gueran, Estiene Chastain, Antoine Rapine, Antoine Benin, Jean Jaque Dupuy, André Amonet, Guilieaume Sallé. Jean Pierre Bilbo took the oath of vestryman for the parish of King William.

JEAN CHASTAIN.

The same day Estiene Chastain and Jean Chastain submitted their account. They owe twenty-seven bushels and one-half of wheat and seventeen bushels of maize for the year 1733.

JEAN CHASTAIN.

March 29, 1735. The glebe was rented by the church wardens, David Lesueur and Pierre Guerant. Louys Soblet rented it until next Christmas for three bushels of wheat, payable to the church wardens.

JEAN CHASTAIN.

The vestry assembled. Present: David Lesueur, Pierre Gueran, Antoine Rapine, Jean Jaque Dupuy, Guillieaume Sallé, André Ammonet, Jean Pierre Bilbo. The vestry appointed Jacob Trabu and Edoward Bryer to procession the ground beyond the creek below, and between the two creeks Thomas Porter and Louys Soblet, and above the creek Jean Harris and Daniel Pero.

JEAN CHASTAIN.

August 9, 1735. The vestry assembled. Present: David Lesueur, Pierre Gueran, Antoine Rapine, Estiene Chastain, Guilieaume Sallé, Jean Jaque Dupuy, Antoine Benin, Jean Pierre Bilbo, Pierre Faure. Antoine Bening and Jean Pierre Bilbo took the oath of church wardens.

JEAN CHASTAIN.

The same day David Lesueur and Pierre Gueran rendered account of their administration for the year 1734. They remain owing twenty-two bushels and one-half of wheat, and twenty-two bushels and one peck of maize, and two pounds and four shillings in money.

JEAN CHASTAIN.

September 20, 1735. The vestry assembled. Present: Antoine Benin, Jean Pierre Bilbo, Antoine Rapine, Guilieaume Sallé, Pierre Gueran, Jean Jaque Dupuy, André Amonet. The levy for the present year, 1735, is one bushel of wheat per tithable.

JEAN CHASTAIN.

List of Tithables of the Parish of King William for the Year 1735.

Name	Tithables
Edward Scott, Edward Miller, Cooper, Dick, Pope, Gloster, Friday, Dilcy, Tob, negro,	9
John Edmond, Bess,	2
Anthoiny, Mathieu Ogé,	2
James Robinson,	0
René Chastain, Jack, Nicl Scottar,	3
William Sallé, John Chimon, John Below, Gorg, Betti, Gini,	6
Gideon Chambon, Monock, Betti, Gorg,	3
Robert Ellis,	1
Louys Soblet, Lousi,	2
Charle Vernion,	1
Jean Levilain, Antoine Levilain, Marie, Nani,	4
Estiene Chastain, Limbo, Dick, Pampi, Jack, Sara, Gini,	7
Andre Amonet,	1
Estiene Panetie, Jean Panetie, Pierre Loucadou	3
Jean Chastain, Charo,	2
Charles Amonet,	1
David Lesueur, Joseph Brian,	1
Jaque Brian,	1
Cp. Holman's Wott, Cain, negro,	2
Barthelemi Dupuy,	1
Jean Dupuy, Dick,	2
Pierre Dupuy,	1
Pierre Faure, Pierre Faure, j.,	2
Jean Faure,	1
Thomas Porter, Joe, Peg,	3
Joseph Benin,	1
Antoine Benin, Billi, Cofe, Jinc, Hanna,	5
Williem Harris,	1
Nicolas Soulie, Robin, Sam, Mol,	4
Pierre Gueran, Antoine Trabu, Gorg, Tom,	4
Antoine Rapine, Dick, Piter, Kate, Jinc,	5
Christopher Charlton,	1
Piter Soblet,	1
David Tommas,	1
Joseph Bingli,	1
Estiene Farsi, Sam	2
Estiene Calvet,	1
Jean Martain, jun., Jack, Filis,	3
Janne Dupre, tithables,	4
Jean Faure, Pierre Peru,	2
Daniel Faure,	1
Jean Moriset,	1

THE VESTRY BOOK OF KING WILLIAM PARISH, VA., 1707–1750.

Antoine Bernard,	1
Pierre Sallé, Jimi,	2
David Bernard,	1
Jean Bernard,	1
Jaque Faure, Pierre Bioret,	2
Jean Bonduran, Pierre Bonduran,	2
John Harris, Patrick, Fillis,	3
Daniel Pero, Stiphin Reno, Joe,	3
John James Florinoir; John Worley, Sesar, Yemma, Suky,	4
Samuel Wever,	1
Jaque Soblet,	1
Jaque Desasi,	1
Jean Pierre Bilbo, Sara,	2
Isaac Gori,	1
Wm. Stanford,	1
Pierre David, Dick, Manue, Dina,	4
Isaac Robinson,	1
Edward Brayer,	1
Thomas Dikins, Henry Bely, Tom, London, Gini, Matt, Maria,	7
Jacob Trabu, London,	2
Thomas Martain, Marque, Betti,	3
Jaque,	1
Elie Sasin,	1
John Williamson,	1
Jean Vilain, j.,	1
Magdelaine Salle's Bob,	1
Pierre Dep.,	1

February 7, 1735-6. The vestry assembled. Present: Antoine Benin, Jean Pierre Billiebo, Estiene Chastain, Pierre Faure, Jean Jaque Dupuy; Guillieaume Sallé, Pierre Gueran, André Amonet, David Lesueur. Received of David Lesueur one pound six shillings in money.

JEAN CHASTAIN.

July 25, 1736. The vestry assembled at the close of the preaching. Present: Antoine Benin, Jean Jaque Bilbo, Estiene Chastain, Antoine Rapine, Pierre Faure, David Lesueur, Guilieaume Sallé, Pierre Gueran, André Amonet. We agreed with Mr. Gavin to preach 26 sermons per year in our church, he binding himself to preach seventeen on Sunday and the rest in the week, at twenty shillings per sermon, payable in wheat at three shillings per bushel or in maize at eighteen pence per bushel, delivered partly below and partly at his place.[12]

JEAN CHASTAIN.

LIST OF TITHABLES OF THE PARISH OF KING WILLIAM FOR THE YEAR 1736.

Willeam Stanford,	1	Antoine Rapine,	7
Thomas Dickens,	10	Jean Jaque Florinoir,	3
Estiene Calvet,	4	Mathieu Ogé,	3
Barthelemi and Pierre Dupuy,	2	Jaque Faure,	1
André Amonnet,	1	Pierre Depp,	3
Jean Levilain, signor,	5	Cp. Jaque Holman,	2
David Leseur, constable[13]		Daniel Pero,	4
Pierre David,	6	Christophe Charlton,	1
Thomas Porter,	4	Jaque Brian,	2
Antoine Benin,	7	Estiene Malet,	4
Jean Porter,	3	Mathieu Jordin,	1
Pierre Bilbo,	2	John Haris,	1
Thomas Bradley,	1	Benjamin Haris,	1
Guilieaume Sallé.	5	Samuel Wever,	1
Edw. Tanner and Edw. Tanner, jun.,	2	Eduard Scott,	7
Jean and Pierre Bonduran	2	Ralph Flipin,	2
Pierre Sallé,	2	Magdelaine Sallé's tithables	1
		Jean Levilain,	1
		Moyse Forqueran,	1

[12]Mr. Marye was transferred to St. George's Parish, Spottsylvania county, in October, 1735, cf. note to entry of August 16, 1730, above, and Rev. Anthony Gavain seems to have entered at once into his labors. Mr. Gavain's first engagement in the parish is, however, brief, as he becomes dissatisfied with the way in which his contract is being fulfilled, and retires in favor of Mr. Brooke in December, 1736. The agreement with him is renewed in 1739, 1740, 1741 and 1743-44, when he appears for the last time in this register.

Mr. Gavain received the Bishop of London's blessing in May, 1735, and departed for the Virginia colony in that year. Cf. a letter from him in Perry's *Papers Relating to the Church in Virginia*, pp. 360-61, dated from St. James' Parish, Goochland, Aug. 5, 1738. Beyond this reference, which I owe to Mr. W. G. Stanard, of the Virginia Historical Society, and the record of one baptism performed by Mr. Gavain in King William Parish in 1739 (Brock, *Hugenot Emigration*, p. 99), I have not been able to find out any facts concerning him.

[13]*conetable*. The present list contains the only mention of such officers in the register.

Antoine Chareron,	1	Jaque Martain,	3
Pierre Louys Soblet,	2	Jacob Trabue,	2
Pierre Soblet,	1	Jean Willeamson,	1
The Widow Soulié's tithables,	3	Elie Sasin,	1
René Chastain,	3	Edward Bryer,	1
Pierre Faure,	2	Isaac Robinson,	1
Antoine Bernar,	1	Jean Moriset,	1
David Thomas,	1	Jean Thomas,	2
Pierre Loucadou,	1	The Widow Dupré,	2
Jean Jaque Dupuy,	2	The Widow Martain,	2
Estiene Farsi,	3	The Widow Dupuy,	1
Estiene Chastain,	6	Daniel Faure,	2
Patrick Gilbliet,	1	Jean Faure,	1
Willeam Ashfield,	1	Wm. Lansdon,	2
Joseph Bingli,	4	Jean Smith,	1
Jean Chastain,	2	Jaque Robinson, constable,	
Gedeon Chambon,	4	Jaque Soblet,	1
		Pierre Gueran,	7

The vestry assembled August 3, 1736. Present: Antoine Benain, Jean Pierre Bilbo, Antoine Rapine, Pierre Faure, wheat and a bushel and a half of maize per tithable.

JEAN CHASTAIN,

The vestry assembled December 3, 1736. Present: Jean Pierre Bilbo, Antoine Rapine, Estiene Chastain, Pierre Faure, David Lesueur, Jean Jaque Dupuy, Pierre Gueran, Antoine Benin. Monr. Gavin having encountered difficulties regarding his payment, he stands by his first agreement. He had not been granted ferriage for his servants nor the glebe.

JEAN CHASTAIN,

This day, June 4, 1737, the vestry agreed with Mr Brook[14] to preach six sermons per year, and we are to pay him two

[14]Rev. Zachariah Brooke, the first minister of St. Paul's Parish, in Hanover county. Cf. Meade, I, 469. He had already found time although in charge of a phenomenally large parish, to perform baptisms in King William Parish in 1727. The contract with him is renewed for twelve sermons per year in 1738; but in the following year Mr. Gavain takes his place. Mr. Brooke likewise performed baptisms in the parish in 1737 and 1738. Cf. the register of baptisms in Brock, *Huguenot Emigation to Virginia.*

pounds per sermon in wheat at three shillings a bushel, in maize at eighteen pence a bushel, delivered at the falls' mill. He commenced on this arrangement to-day.

JEAN CHASTAIN,

September 13, 1737. The vestry assembled. Present: Antoine Benin, Jean Pierre Bilbo, Estiene Chastain, Pierre Faure, Guillieaume Sallé, Jean Jaque Dupui, Pierre Gueran, André Amonnet. The vestry employed Antoine Chareron to carry a letter to Mr. Lapierre, in order to know if he can come, and to bring us the answer to it. The vestry assigned him three pounds, ten shillings, payable, three pounds in wheat and in maize, and ten shillings in money.

JEAN CHASTAIN.

The same day the assessment was made of one bushel of wheat and one bushel of maize per head.

JEAN CHASTAIN.

September 23, 1737. Estiene Malet and René Chastain took the oath of vestrymen for the Parish of King William. Present: Antoine Benain, Jean Pierre Bilbo, David Lesueur, Estiene Chastain, Jean Jaque Dupuy, André Amonnet, Estiene Malet, Guillieaume Sallé, René Chastain, Pierre Gueran.

JEAN CHASTAIN.

The same day Estiene Malet and René Chastain took the oath as church wardens.

JEAN CHASTAIN.

The church wardens are to make a contract with a doctor to cure Isaac Gori, and in case he recovers, he is to repay the parish.

JEAN CHASTAIN.

April 21, 1738. The vestry assembled. Present: Estiene Malet, René Chastain, Estiene Chastain, Pierre Faure, Antoine Benin, Jean Pierre Bilbo, Guilieaume Sallé, David Lesueur, André Amonnet, Pierre Gueran, Jean Jaque Dupuy. It was agreed with Mr. Brook to pay him twenty-six shillings per sermon. He is to preach twelve times per year, commencing to-day. He is to be paid in wheat at three shillings per bushel, delivered at his place, in maize at eighteen pence per bushel, delivered at his place.

JEAN CHASTAIN.

The same day it was decreed by the vestry that Estiene Mallet bind himself to furnish Isaac Gori with food and lodging and bed and washing for a year; and in case of death, he shall be paid in proportion as is agree, viz: six (pounds) per year, payable half in wheat, half in maize, at three shillings for the wheat, the maize at eighteen pence.

JEAN CHASTAIN.

LIST OF TITHABLES OF THE PARISH OF KING WILLIAM FOR THE YEAR 1737.

Jean Chastain,	2	Jaque Faure,	2
André Amonnet,	1	Edward Tanner,	1
Jean Bernard,	1	Joseph Bonduran,	1
René Chastain,	1	Jaque Robinson,	1
Pierre Martain,	6	Thomas Honi,	1
Daniel Perault,	4	Joseph Bingli,	4
Jean Porter,	3	Edward Scott,	9
Estiene Malet,	3	Pierre Soblet,	1
Estiene Farsi,	2	Jean Harris,	4
Jean Levilain, s.,	5	Richard Stones,	1
Thos. Gadsi,	4	Samuel Wever,	1
Jean Trutin,	1	Thomas Porter,	2
Guilieaume Sallé,	7	Edward Sargent,	1
Barthelemi Dupuy,	1	Benjamin, Haris,	1
Pierre Dupuy,	1	Pierre Gueran,	6
Pierre Faure,	3	Cholmen's Wott,	1
Antoine Benin,	7	Jean Jaque Florinoir,	3
Jean Dilion,	1	Christophe Charlton,	1
David Leseuer,	1	Thomas Dikins,	8
Jaque Brian,	2	Charle Amonnet,	1
Estiene Panetie,	1	The Widow Sallé,	1

Jean Panetie,	1	Jean Levilain, j.,	1
Jean Bottler,	5	Richard Dine,	2
Pierre Loucadou,	1	Moise Forqueran,	1
Jean Biblo,	2	The Widow Dupré,	1
Mathieu Ogé,	3	Jaque Martain,	3
Pierre David,	7	Jacob Trabue,	3
The Widow Soulié,	3	Jean Williamson,	1
Thomas Bradli,	1	Elie Sassin,	1
Pierre Sallé,	2	Edward Bryer,	1
Jean Bonduran,	1	Isaac Robinson,	2
Pierre Bonduran,	1	Jean Morisset,	1
Pierre Louis Soblet,	2	Jean Thomas,	2
Antoine Chareron,	1	Charle Pene,	2
David Tomas,	1	The Widow Martain,	2
Estiene Chastain,	6		
Jean Jaque Dupuy,	2		170

July 15, 1738. The vestry assembled. Present: Estiene Malet, René Chastain, Estiene Chastain, Pierre Gueran, Antoine Benin, Jean Pierre Bilbo, Guilieaume Sallé, Jean Jaque Dupuy were elected church wardens, having already taken the oath prescribed by law.

JEAN CHASTAIN.

The same day Estiene Mallet and René Chastain rendered their account of their administration for the year 1737. They gave their note for the amount which they owe.

JEAN CHASTAIN.

The same day Antoine Benin and Jean Pierre Bilbo were discharged of their administration for the years 1735 and 1736. They gave their note for the money.

JEAN CHASTAIN.

The vestry assembled. Present: Guilieaume Sallé, Jan Jaque Dupuy, Estiene Chastain, Pierre Faure, André Amonnet, Jean Pierre Bilbo, Pierre Gueran, David Lesueur, Estiene Malet. The levy for the present year, 1738, amounts to one bushel of wheat and a half-bushel of maize per head.

JEAN CHASTAIN.

June 11, 1739. The vestry assembled. Present: Jean Jaque Dupuy, Guilieaume Sallé, André Amonnet, Jean Pierre Bilbo, Pierre Faure, René Chastain, Jean Levilain, le june, and Jean Bernar took the oath of vestrymen for the Parish of King William.

JEAN CHASTAIN.

LIST OF TITHABLES OF THE PARISH OF KING WILLIAM FOR THE YEAR 1738.

Barthelimi Dupuy,	1	Edward Tanner, jun.,	1
Pierre Dupuy,	1	Anne David,	6
Pierre Gueran,	5	Jaque Soblet,	2
René Chastain,	3	Pierre Louys Soblet,	4
Jean Chastain,	3	Charle Beler,	2
Thomas Godsi,	4	Willeam Banton,	1
Jeame Th. Dilion,	1	Thomas Elsoan,	1
David Thomas,	1	Anne Scott,	7
Jean Pierre Bilbo,	2	Estiene Malet,	2
Thomas Porter,	4	Jean Levilain, sig.,	5
John Porter,	2	Jean Jaque Florinoir,	4
Antoine Benin,	5	Roberd Craghad,	1
Daniel Pero,	4	Samuel Wever,	1
Pierre Martain,	6	Jean Harris,	4
Jean Jaque Dupuy,	2	Estiene Chastain,	6
Pierre Dep,	2	Jean Bottler,	3
Estiene Farsi,	2	Jaque Gase,	1
Matthieu Agé,	3	Cp. Holmen,	1
Richar Dudleey,	1	Binjamen Haris,	2
Joseph Bingly,	3	Thomas Dikins,	1
Jaque Brian,	2	Willeam Ashfild,	1
David Lesueur,	1	Charles Peen,	2
André Amonnet,	1	The Widow Martain,	2
Guilieaume Sallé,	4	Jean Moriset	1
Estiene Panetie,	1	Isaac Robinson,	2
Francoise Soulié,	4	Edward Brayer,	1
Jaque Faure,	2	Elie Sasain,	1
Jean Bonduran,	1	Jonathan,	1

The Widow Bonduran,	3	Jean Willeamson,	1
Thomas Bradli,	1	Jacob Trabu,	3
Jean Bernar,	1	Jaque Hood,	1
Pierre Sallé,	2	Jaque Martain,	4
Rober Davidson,	1	The Widow Dupré,	1
Jaque Robinson,	2	Moyse Forqueran,	1
Pierre Faure,	3	Richard Dine,	2
Jean Carner,	1	Jaque Lester,	1
Pierre Soblet,	1	Jean Levilain,	1
Antoine Trabue,	1	Charle Amonnet,	1
	—	The Widow Sallé,	1
	88	Thomas Richison,	2
		John Thomas,	
			178

April 7, 1739. The vestry assembled. Present: Guillieaume Sallé, Jean Jaque Dupuy, Estiene Chastain, Pierre Faure, Estiene Malet, David Lesueur, Rene Chastain, André Amonnet, Jeane Pierre Bilbo. The vestry gave full power to the church wardens to prosecute Pierre Martain for the money which Mr. Rapine was owing to the parish of King William.

JEAN CHASTAIN.

August 20, 1739. The vestry assembled. Present: Guillieaume Salle, Jean Jaque Dupuy, David Lesueur, Pierre Guerant, André Amonnet, Estiene Malet, Jean Bernar, Jean Jaque Bilbo. The vestry appointed Charle Peen and Edward Bryer to procession the land from the line of Jacob Trabu to the line of Charle Peene; Jacob Trabu and Richard Deen from Jacob Trabu to the creek below; and Pr. Louys Soblet and Thomas Porter from the creek below to the creek above, the old line of the ten thousand acres; and Edward Kamton and Estiene Farsi from the first line along the branch to Mr. Dutoy on both sides; and above the creek Pierre Martain and Jean Harris.

JEAN CHASTAIN.

The same day Jean Bernar and André Amonnet took the oath of church wardens in the accustomed manner.

JEAN CHASTAIN.

The same day Guilieaume Sallé and Jean Jaque Dupuy rendered their account for the year 1738 in the presence of the vestrymen named above. The parish owes them three bushels and one-half of wheat.

JEAN CHASTAIN.

The late Mr. Chastain[15] left by will to the poor of the parish of King Willam five pounds, of which the church wardens, Guilieaume Sallé and Jean Jaque Dupuy, have paid out three pounds, one shilling and sixpence.

JEAN CHASTAIN.

Estiene Malet has received a guinea from Mr. Chastain; from Antoine Benin and from Jean Pierre Bilbo one pound eighteen shillings, which was due the parish; from Jean Papeham, four pounds, six shillings and one penny; and René Chastain has received fourteen shillings from David Lesueur, which was due the parish.

September 1, 1739. The vestry assembled at the close of the preaching. Present: André Amonet, Jean Bernar, Jean Jaque Dupuy, Guilliaume Sallé, Pierre Ffaure, Jean Pierre Bilbos, Estienne Mallet, Pierre Guerrant, Rane Chastain, David Le Sueur, Jean Levilain. We agreed with the Reverend Mr. Gavin to preach in our church seventeen sermons for one year, including four in French. He is to give us one Sunday notice before coming to preach to us; but in case he fail of preaching the day appointed, one sermon shall be subtracted from the seventeen sermons for each time that he shall fail. For which we oblige ourselves to pay to him at the hands of Monsieur André Amonnet two barrels of maize and two bushels

---

15Probably Etienne Chastain, who appears for the last time in the tax-list of 1737. He and his wife were among those who arrived in the colony in the first ship-load of French emigrants, 1701. Cf. Brock, p. 45. His wife died in 1725, aged 52 or 53.

of wheat for each sermon that he shall preach to us, and the said Monsieur Gavin binds himself to preach to us on Sunday from the month of April to the month of September. The maize above is to be paid after Christmas Day.

ANT. GAVIN, Minister.
ANDRE AMONNET,
JEAN BERNARD.

STEPHEN MALLET,[16]
GUILLAUME SALLE,
RANE CHASTAIN,
PIERRE GUERRANT,
PIERRE FAURE,
JOHN DUPUY,
JEAN PIERRE BILBOU,
JEAN LEUILAIN,
DAVID LE SUEUR.

September 8, 1739. The vestry assembled. Present: André Amonnet, Jean Bernar, Estiene Mallet, Guillieaume Salle, Pierre Gueran, Jean Jaque Dupuy, Jean Pierre Bilbo, Jean Levilain. The levy for the present year is one bushel of wheat and one bushel of maize per tithable, and those who shall pay eight pence in silver shall be quit of half a bushel of wheat. The eight pence in money are for the suit at Williamsburg between Thomas Dikins and the parish, and for the moulding.[17]

JEAN CHASTAIN.

The same day it was agreed to give Jean Chastain six pounds, the grain to be accepted as in the first contract.

JEAN CHASTAIN.

November 17, 1739. The vestry assembled. Present: An-

---

[16]The signatures are personal.

[17]pour le prossé de williambourg entre Thomas Dikins et la paroisse et pour le godron. The above translation is simply a guess. *Godron* has a number of uses, signifying, in the main, boss-work or a fluted decoration.

dre Amonnet, Jean Bernar, David Lesueur, Guillieaume Salle, Jean Jacque Dupuy, Estiene Malet, Jean Levilain, Rene Chastain, Pierre Gueran. The vestry received the moulding, which Guileaume Salle bought in order to decorate[18] the church, amounting to twelve shillings in money.

The expenses of Estiene Malet and Rene Chastain, on account of the suit of Dikins, amount to seven pounds and one penny, for which we have made the levy of one bushel of wheat and a bushel of maize, likewise in order to defray the expenses of the parish; and those who shall pay the eight pence in silver shall be quit of a half-bushel of wheat, according to the levy made Sept. 8, 1739.

March 1, 1739 | 40. The vestry assembled. Present: Andre Amonnet, Jean Bernard, Pierre Faure, David Lesueur, Jean Jaque Dupuy, Guillieaume Salle, Pierre Gueran, Jean Pierre Bilbo, Rene Chastain. The vestry gives full power to the church wardens to prosecute Pierre Martain for the tobacco that Mr. Rapine has received from the parish.

JEAN CHASTAIN.

The same day the vestry gave full power to the church warden to prosecute Estiene Panetie for the levy of the parish of King William, for not being listed in our parish above mentioned.

JEAN CHASTAIN.

The same day it was decreed by a plurality of votes to rent the ferry for a year.

JEAN CHASTAIN.

March 8, 1740. The vestry assembled. Present: Andre Amonnet, Jean Bernard, David Lesueur, Guillieaume Salle, Rene Chastain, Estiene Mallet, Pierre Gueran. The church wardens rented the ferry for a year for five pounds and one-half, payable in wheat and maize, viz.: half in wheat and half

[18]le godron . . . pour godroner leglise.

in maize, the wheat at three shillings and the maize at eighteen pence. The grain is to be fetched from the church wardens.

JEAN CHASTAIN.

October 6, 1740. The vestry assembled. Present: Andre Amonnet, Jean Bernar, David Lesueur, Jean Jaque Dupuy, Pierre Gueran, Guillieaume Salle, Jean Pierre Billiebo, Jean Levilain. David Lesueur and Jean Chastain were elected church wardens by a plurality of votees for the present year.

JEAN CHASTAIN.

The same day an agreement was made with the Reverend Mr. Gavain to give him twelve bushels and one-half of maize per sermon and a bushel of wheat, to preach ten times per year, the wheat and the maize to be fetched from the church wardens. Four sermons in French.

ANT. GAVIN.

And he promises to preach Sundays from April 1 to September 1.

ANT. GAVIN,[19]
DAVID LE SUEUR, JEAN CHASTAIN, } Church Wardens.

PIERRE GUERRANT,
JEAN VILEN,
JEAN JAQUE DUPUY,
GUILLAUME SALLE,
ANDRE AMONNET,
JEAN PIERRE BILBOUT.

November 12, 1740. The vestry assembled. Present: David Lesueur, Jean Chastain, Andrew Amonnet, Jean Bernar, Guillieaume Salle, Jean Jaque Dupuy, Rene Chastain, Jean Pierre Bilbo. Andre Amonnet and Jean Bernar rendered their account, and they owe the parish one pound, thirteen shillings, sixpence, and two bushels and a half of maize.

JEAN CHASTAIN.

---

[19]The signatures are personal.

The levy for the present year is a bushel and a half of maize and a half-bushel of wheat per head, in order to defray the expenses of the parish of King William.

JEAN CHASTAIN.

October 19, 1741. The vestry assembled. Present: David Lesueur, Jean Chastain, Andre Amonnet, Rene Chastain, Jean Jaque Dupuy, Jean Pierre Bilbo, Pierre Faure, Guillieaume Salle, Jean Bernar. Pierre Gueran and Jean Villain were elected by a plurality of votes church wardens.

October 23, 1741. The said Sieurs Pierre Gueran and Jean Levilain took the oath and the test according to the usage of the Anglican church. Present: Pierre Gueran, Jean Levilain, David Lesueur, Jean J. Dupuy, Rene Chastain, Pierre Faure, Pierre Bilbo, Jean Bernar, Pierre Faure, Andre Amonnet.

JEAN CHASTAIN.

I have pledged myself to the French vestry to preach 17 sermons, four in French; and if I fail any time, I will make good after my year is finished, so that my year shall be completed when I shall have preached the 17 sermons. October 23, 1741. According to my contract made the past year.

Witnesses: ANT. GAVIN.

JEAN VILEN,[20] } Church Wardens.
PIERRE GUERRANT, }
DAVID LE SUEUR,
JEAN CHASTAIN,
RENE CHASTAIN,
ANDRE AMONNET,
JEAN BERNAR,
JEAN PIERRE BILBO,
PIERRE FAURE,
JEAN J. DUPUY,

The same day David Lesueur and Jean Chastain rendered

[20]The signatures are personal.

their account. They remain owing forty-five bushels of maize and a peck and a half-bushel of wheat, for which we have given our note.

JEAN CHASTAIN.

The levy for the present year is one bushel of maize and a half-bushel of wheat per head.

JEAN CHASTAIN,[21]
JOHN JAMES DUPUY.
PIERRE GUERRANT,
JEAN VILEN,
ANDRE AMONNET,
JEAN BERNAR,
DAVID LE SUEUR,
RANE CHASTAIN,
JEAN PIERRE BILBO,
PIERRE FAURE,

July 10, 1742. The vestry assembled. Present: Pierre Guerrant, Jean Levilain, Jean Jaque Dupuis, Andre Amonnet, Guilliaume Salle, Estienne Mallet, Rane Chastain and David Lesueur. Estienne Mallet and Rane Chastain rendered account for the suit against Thos. Dickins, and they are quit by the payment of nine shillings, ninepence, which is the amount remaining due Monsieur Guilliaume Salle, of which the said Salle acknowledges payment.

JEAN CHASTAIN.

The same day the vestry decreed that Sieur Andre Amonnet sell for money, the tobacco which has been recovered from Pierre Martain, amounting to 520 pounds of tobacco, and that he rendered account for the same to the church wardens.

JEAN CHASTAIN.

PIERRE GUERRANT,[22]
JEAN VILAIN,
ESTIENNE MALLET,

---

[21]The signatures are personal.

[22]The signatures are personal.

JEAN, JACQUES DUPUY,
RANE CHASTAIN,
GUILLAUME SALLE,
ANDRE AMONNET,
DAVID LE SUÈUR,

October 30, 1742. Pierre Faure asked his discharge, and it was granted to him, in the presence of the vestry named below: Pierre Gueran, Jean Levilain, David Lesueur, Estiene Malet, Andre Amonnet, Jean Jaque Dupuy, Jean Bernar, Rene Chastain, Guilieaume Salle, Jean Pierre Bilbo.

JEAN CHASTAIN.

The same day Daniel Pero took the oath of vestryman for the parish of King William in the presence of the vestrymen named above.

JEAN CHASTAIN.

The same day Estiene Mallet and Jean Pierre Bilbo took the oath of church wardens for the present year.

JEAN CHASTAIN.

The same day. The levy for the parish of King William is a bushel of maize and a half-bushel of wheat per tithable. In the presence of the vestrymen named above.

JEAN CHASTAIN.

STEPHEN MALLET, [23]
JEAN PIERR BILBO,
RANE CHASTAIN,
GUILLAUME SALLE,
DAVID LE SUEUR,
ANDRE AMONNET,
JEAN JACQUES DUPUY,
PIERRE GUERRANT,
JEAN VILAIN,
DANIEL PERO.
JEAN J. DUPUY.

---

[23]The signatures are personal.

April 16, 1743. The vestry assembled. Present: Estiene Mallet, Jean Pierre Bilbo, David Lesueur, Andre Amonnet, Jean Jaque Dupui, Guillieaume Salle, Jean Levilain, Rene Chastain. The vestry deputed Estiene Mallet and Guillieaume Salle to go to speak with the Governor in order (to urge him) to maintain the parish.

JEAN CHASTAIN.

September 12, 1743. Jean Jaque Dupuy and Guilleaume Salle were installed as church wardens. Present: Estiene Mallet, Jean Pierre Bilbo, Andre Amonnet, Daniel Pero, Jean Vilain, David Lesueur, Jean Chastain.

The same day Estiene Malet and Jean Pierre Bilbo rendered their account for the year 1742. Estiene Mallet is quit of all and there is owing to Jean Pierre Bilbo 8 shillings.

JEAN CHASTAIN.

The same day, Andre Amonet and Jean Bernar are quit of all.

JEAN CHASTAIN.

January 7, 1743 | 4. The vestry assembled. Present: Guilieaume Salle, Jean Jaque Dupuy, Andre Amonnet, Pierre Gueran, Rene Chastain, David Lesueur, Jean Vilain, Daniel Pero, Jean Pierre Bilbo. The vestry agreed with the Reverend Mr. Gavain to preach twelve sermons for the present year, two of which have been preached, at twenty shillings per sermon; that is, he shall preach twelve sermons from December 17 passed to December 17 next, 1744. And the vestrymen bind themselves to pay him the twenty shillings according as they and Gavin shall agree together, and Gavin binds himself to preach Sundays from April to September.

ANT. GAVIN, Minister,[24]
GUILLAUME SALLE,

[N. B. Though it was expected that the King William vestry book would be concluded in this number of this Magazine; but it has been found impossible to do so. The concluding portion will be printed in January.]

(TO BE CONTINUED)

---

[24]Signatures personal.

THE VESTRY BOOK OF KING WILLIAM PARISH, VA., 1707–1750.

January 21, 1743. The vestry assembled: Present Guilieaume Salle, Jean Jaque Dupuy, Etiene Malet, Andre Amonnet, Jean Pierre Bilbo, David Lesueur, Jean Vilain, Daniel Pero. The vestry made the allotment in tobacco for discharging the expenses of the parish of King William. For the Reverend Monsieur Gavain, twelve pounds in money, amounting to 1997 lbs. of tobacco; for the Clerk, eight months' arrears, 666 lbs., and for a year's salary, 1,000 lbs.; for the sexton, 250 lbs., and for the *coclecte* (*collecte*)[25] 234 lbs. The church wardens shall levy eighteen pounds of tobacco per tithable, the whole amounting to four thousand one hundred and forty-seven pounds.

JEAN JACQUES DUPUY,[26]
GUILLAUME SALLE,
ESTINNE MALLET,
ANDRE AMONNET,
JEAN VILEAIN,
DANIEL PERRO,
DAVID LE SUEUR,

The same day David Lesueur and Jean Chastain settled their note, which they owe to the parish, and they are quit for the year 1740.

GUILLAUME SALLE,[27]
JEAN JAQUE DUPUY,
ESTIENNE MALLET,
ANDRE AMONNET,
JEAN VILAIN,
JEAN PIERRE BILBO,
DANIEL PEREAUD.

The year of the clerk commences Christmas, 1743.

JEAN CHASTAIN.

---

[25]A collection for the poor of the parish is probably meant.

[26]Signatures personal. [27]Signatures personal.

October 1, 1744. The vestry assembled. Present: Jean Jaque Dupuy, Andre Amonnet, David Lesueur, Pierre Gueran, Jean Levilain, Jean Bernar, Jean Pierre Bilbo, Pierre Faure. The vestry appointed Jean Jaque Dupuy and Jean Levilian to go to Wmbourg to bear a petition to the Governor and to the Council to maintain our parish.

JEAN CHASTAIN.

November 17, 1744. The vestry assembled. Present: Jean Jaque Dupuy, Guilieaume Salle, David Lesueur, Jean Levilian, Jean Pierre Bilbo, Daniel Perro, Jacob Trabu, took the oath and the test of vestryman for the parish of King William.

JEAN CHASTAIN.

January 19, 1744|5. Pierre David took the oath of vestryman for the parish of King William, in the presence of the vestry named below: Jean Jaque Dupuy, Guilieaume Salle, David Lesueur, Jean Pierre Bilbo, Jacob Trabu, Pierre Gueran, Jean Villain, Andre Amonnet, Daniel Perro.

JEAN CHASTAIN.

The same day Daniel Perro and Jean Chastain were named Church Wardens by the vestry present for the present year, and took the usual oath.

JEAN CHASTAIN.

The same day the Sieurs Jean Jaque Dupuy and Guilieaume Salle rendered account of their administration for the year, 1744. They are quit of all.

JEAN CHASTAIN.

DANIEL PERO,[38]
JACOB TRABUE,
PETER DAVID,
ANDRE AMONNET,
JEAN PIERRE BILBO,
PIERRE GUERRANT,
JEAN VILEAN,
DAVID LESUEUR.

[38]Signatures personal.

The same day, January 19, 1744|5. The levy for the present year was made. The levy amounts to fifteen pounds of tobacco per head, viz : one thousand pounds for a minister, one thousand for the clerk, two hundred and fifty for the sexton, for the poor, six hundred, for the expenses of the parish, two hundred and fifty, amounting to 3,500.

JEAN CHASTAIN.

Novmber 2, 1745. The vestry assembled. Present: David Lesueur, Andre Amonnet, Guiliaume Salle, Pierre Gueran, Daniel Pero, Pierre David, Jean Pierre Bilbo. The vestrymen took the oath prescribed by the canon law in the usual manner.

The same day Andre Amonnet and Pierre David took the oath of church wardens.

JEAN CHASTAIN.

The same day Daniel Perro and Jean Chastain rendered their account for their administration for the year 1744. They owe two hundred and fifty pounds of tobacco.

JEAN CHASTAIN.

PETER DAVID,[29] } Church Wardens.
ANDRE AMONNET, }
DAVID LE SUEUR,
GUILLAUME SALLE,
PIERRE GUERRANT,
JEAN PIERRE BILBO,
DANIEL PEROT.

November 2, 1745. The vestry having assembled, the assessment was made, amounting to sixteen pounds of tobacco per head. The whole amounts to 3,840.

JEAN CHASTAIN.

ANDRE AMONNET, { Church Wardens.
PETER DAVID. {
GILLAUME SALLE,[30]
JEAN PIERRE BILBO,
DAVID LE SUEUR,
DANIEL PEROT.

---

[29]Signatures personal.

[30]Signatures personal.

April 1, 1746. The vestry assembled according to the custom prescribed by law.[31]

JEAN CHASTAIN.

ANDRE AMONNET,[32] } Church Wardens.
PETER DAVID. }

DAVID LE SUEUR,

JACOB TRABUE,

GUILLAUME SALLE,

PIERRE GUERRANT,

December 1, 1746. The vestry assembled. Present: Andre Amonnet, Pierre David, David Lesueur, Guilaume Salle, Jacob Trabu, Daniel Perro, Jean Pierre Bilbo, Pierre Guerran, Jean Chastain.

The same day Pierre Gueran and David Lesueur were named as church wardens for the present year, 1746, in the presence of the vestrymen above mentioned, and they took the oath prescribed by law.

December 1, 1746. Andre Amonnet and Pierre David rendered their account of their administration for the year 1745, in the presence of the vestrymen named above. They owe eighty-two pounds of tobacco, payable to the church wardens of the present year.

The same day, by order of the vestry named above, the glebe will be let from the creek to the highroad on the river, under such conditions as the church wardens shall find proper.

The same day Andre Amonnet asked his discharge, and it was granted him.

PIERRE GUERRANT,[33] } Church Wardens.
DAVID LE SUEUR, }

DANIEL PEROT,

JEAN PIERRE BILBO,

GUILLAUME SALLE,

JACOB TRABU,

JEAN CHASTAIN.

---

[31]No business seems to have been transacted.

[32]Signatures personal.

[33]Signatures personal.

March 7, 1746|7. The vestry assembled. Present: David Lesueur, Pierre Gueran, Guilieaume Salle, Jean Jaque Dupuy, Jacob Trabu, Daniel Perro, Jean Pierre Bilbo. Isaac Dutoy took the oath of vestryman for the parish of King William.

JEAN CHASTAIN.

The same day it was agreed that the service shall be half in English and half in French.

JEAN CHASTAIN.

March 7, 1746|7. Daniel Pero and Jean Chastain settled their account for two hundred and fifty pounds of tobacco, which they owed on their administration of the year 1745.

JEAN CHASTAIN.

The same day the levy was made for the present year, 1746|7, of sixteen pounds of tobacco per head; viz.:

For the minister	1,000
For the clerk	1,000
For the sexton	150
John Chendler, for the poor girl	150
For Jaque Brian, for burying a poor man	150
For Samuel Wever, for Judith Lahane	50
For Monfor, poor (man)	200
For Mr. Gueret, pauper	300
For a Bible for the church	400
	3,400

JEAN CHASTAIN.

DAVID LE SUEUR,
PIERRE GUERRANT, } Church Wardens.

JEAN PIERRE BILBO,
GUILLAUME SALLE,
JOHN J. DUPUY,
JACOB TRABUE,
DANIEL PERO,
ISAAC DUTOY.

June 24, 1747. The vestry assembled. Present: David Lesueur, Pierre Gueran, Jean Jaque Dupuy, Daniel Perro, Jean Pierre Bilbo, Guilieaume Salle, Isaac Dutoy, Jacob Trabu. The vestry appointed Pierre David and Charle Amonnet to run the lines from the creek below to the county line; and between the two creeks, Benjamin Haris and Isaac Dutoy for the first five thousand acres; and from the creek above to the line above, Wm. Harris and James Holman; from the road of Frenc Jamse to Etiene Malet, Jean Jaque Dupuy and Etiene Malet; and from the creek to the road of Frenc Jamse as far as the branch of Dutoy, and from the branch of Dutoy to the creek below, Jean Panetie and Pierre Depe, and from the creek above to the road of Frenc Jamse up to the branch of Dutoy.[84]

JEAN CHASTAIN.

Pierre David and Charle Amonnet, the first Monday of November;

Benjamin Haris and Isaac Dutoy, the second Monday;

Wm. Haris and Jamse Holman, the third Monday;

Thomas Smith and Jean Bonduran, the fourth Monday;

J. Jamse Dupuy, Steve Malet, the first Monday of December;

Jean Panetie and Pierre Dep, the second Monday.

February 6, 1747|8. The vestry assembled. Present: David Lesueur, Pierre Guerand, Jean Jaque Dupuy, Jean Pierre Bilbo, Isaac Dutoy, Estiene Malet. Abraham Salle took the oath of church warden of the church of the parish of King William, and took the oath of loyalty and signed the test. Jean Jaque Dupuy and Estiene Malet took the oath of loyalty and took the test.

ESTIENE MALET,
JOHN JAMES DUPUY,
ABRAHAM SALLE.

[84]The passage is altogether innocent of punctuation, and consequently far from clear. It is evident that this is another of the "processionings," the last mentioned in the Register.

The same day Jacob Trabu received his discharge, as he is no longer willing to conform to the canon of the Anglican church, and he is no longer vestryman of the parish of King William.[35]

The same day Mr. Jean Harris took the oath of loyalty and took the test. The same day he took the oath as vestryman of the church of the parish of King William and signed the test.

JOHN HARRIS.

The same day Isaac Dutoy and Estiene Malet took the oath of church wardens of the parish of King William for the present year.

JEAN CHASTAIN,
ESTIENNE MALET,
ISAAC DUTOY,

February 13, 1747|8. The vestry assembled. Present: Isaac Dutoy, Pierre Gueran, David Lesueur, Daniel Perro, John Harris, Jean Pierre Bilbo. Samuel Florinoir took the oath of loyalty and signed the test.

SAMUEL FLOURNOY.

The same day Samuel Florinoir took the oath of vestryman of the parish of King William in the presence of the vestry above named.

The vestry made an agreement with Samuel Wever to serve as sexton at two hundred and fifty pounds of tobacco per year, commencing February 13, 1747|8.

The vestry assembled February 24, 1747. Present: Isaac Dutoy, Estiene Mallet, David Lesueur, Pierre Guerand, Guillieaume Salle, Daniel Perro, Samuel Florinoir. The church wardens, David Lesueur and Pierre Gueran, rendered account of their administration for the year 1746. They are quit of all

[35]The only mention of doctrinal defection on the part of a member of the parish, if, indeed, we may assign Trabue's defection to this cause.

that they have received, both as regards what was levied and what was given into their hands during the said year.

JEAN CHASTAIN.
ISAAC DUTOY,
STEPHEN MALLET.
Church Wardens.

The same day the levy was made for the parish of King William. It amounts to twenty-five pounds of tobacco per head, viz.:

For the minister	1,600
For the clerk	1,000
For the sexton	250
For Monfor[86]	300
For Judith Lahon[86]	1,000
For Sarah Chandler,[87] for arrears	500
For Sarah Chandler to the month of October	1,200
For Mary Goin,[86] for one week	100
	5,950
The tithables of Gooch[88]	205
The tithables of Enrico	42
	247

The church wardens have in their hands 718 lbs. of tobacco, carried over from the year 1746.

JEAN CHASTAIN.

DAVID LE SUEUR.
SAMUEL FLOURNOY,
GUILLAUME SALLE,
PIERRE GUERRANT.

STEPHEN MALLET,
ISAAC DUTOY.
Church Wardens.

March 10, 1747. The vestry assembled. Present: Isaac Dutoy, Estiene Mallet, John Harris, David Lesueur, Guilie-

[86]A pauper. cf. entry of March 7, 1746-7.
[87]Probably for maintaining the poor of the parish, or herself a pauper
[88]Goochland, Henrico.

aume Salle, Jean Pierre Bilbo, Pierre Gueran. The vestry assembled to receive the returns of the processioners named below: Isaac Dutoy, Benjamin Harris, Estienne Mallet, Jean Jaque Dupuy, Wm. Harris and James Holeman, Pierre David and Charles Amonnet.

JEAN CHASTAIN.

ISAAC DUTOY,
STEPHEN MALLET.
Church Wardens.

JOHN HARRIS,
DAVID LE SUEUR,
PIERRE GUERRANT,
JEAN PIERRE BILBO,
GUILLIAUME SALLE.

November 10, 1748. Samuel Florinoir and Abraham Salle took the oath of church wardens in the presence of the vestry-men named below: Isaac Dutoy, Estiene Mallet, Pierre Gueran, Daniel Perro.

ABRAM. SALLE,
SAML. FLOURNOY.
Church Wardens.

STEPHEN MALLET,
ISAAC DUTOY,
PETER GUERRANT,
DANIEL PARO,
JOHN CHASTAIN.

The same day the levy was made for the present year, amounting to twenty pounds of tobacco per head, viz.:

For the minister, one thousand, three (?) hundred.

For the clerk, one thousand.

For Benton, one thousand for Sara Chandler.

For Peter Dep, one hundred and sixty pounds.

For the sexton, two hundred and fifty pounds.

For arrears, two hundred and sixteen pounds for Isaac Dutoy.

The number of parishoners amounts to 250.

The same day the above-mentioned Isaac Dutoy and Estiene Mallet rendered their account for their administration for the year 1747, in the presence of the vestrymen.

ABRAM. SALLE,
SAMUEL FLOURNOY.

[39]I promise to pay unto the Church Wardens of King William parish four pounds, two shill, and two pence, current mony, for value recd. of the parish.

Wittnis my hand this 10th day of Dec., 1748.

STEPHEN MALLET.

Pierre Depp has taken Monfor for another year for one hundred and sixty pounds of tobacco, commencing February 24, 1749.

JEAN CHASTAIN.

Isaac Dutoy has made a bargain with Wm. Banton for Sara Chandler at 1,000 lb. of tobacco for a year, commencing November 1, 1748.

JEAN CHASTAIN.

Abraham Salle and Samuel Florinoir put Elizabeth Rober out of the parish November 21.*

JEAN CHASTAIN.

.... [40]The vestry assembled. Present: Abraham

---

[39]The original of the receipt is in English, a proof of the growing disuse of French among the parishoners. Clerk Chastain's French is ragged enough, and Mr. Mallet, although a vestryman and a man of dignity in the parish, no longer ventures to write the tongue of his fathers.

* Some light is thrown on this drastic action of the church wardens by the following entry in the Register of Baptisms in King William Parish; Brock, p. 101:

"The 14th June, 1741, was born Jesse, reputed son of John Harris and of Elizabef Roberd; had for godfather, John Bernar and Jean Chastain; for godmother, Charlote Judith Chastain."

[40]The date is obliterated from the top of the page. Possibly it is December 9, 1749, certainly some time in that year.

Salle, Samuel Florinoir, Estene Malet, Jean Chastain. Joseph Bonduran, Jean Bonduran, Jean Chastain j. took the oath of vestrymen for the parish of King William.

JOHN BONDURANT,
JOSEPH BONDURANT,
JOHN CHASTAIN, JUN.[41]

The same day Joseph Bondurant and Jean Chastain took the oath of church wardens for the present year.

JEAN CHASTAIN.

The same day the church wardens, Samuel Florinoir and Abraham Salle, rendered their account. They owe 281 lbs. of tobacco, for which they have given their note.

JEAN CHASTAIN.

The same day the levy for the present year, 1749, was made. It amounts to 16 lbs. of tobacco per tithable.

JEAN CHASTAIN.

1,600 for the minister.
1,000 for the clerk.
1,000 for Sara Chendler.
300 for Sara Lahene.
150 for Peru.
250 for the sexton.

4,300

February 3, 1749|50. The vestry assembled. Present: Samuel Florinoir, Guillieaume Salle, Estiene Mallet, Isaac Dutoy, David Lesueur, Daniel Perro, Jean Chastain. Jean

[41]The following quaint memorandum is pinned over the foregoing entry:
"Rec'd of the Church Wardens of King William Parish £4 s. 4 for the Church Bible for the Yous of John Harris.
December 9, 1749. Sam'l Flournoy."

Bonduran, Joseph Bonduran, Jean Chastain took the oath of vestrymen for the parish of King William and took the test.

Jean Chastain and Joseph Bonduran took the oath of church wardens for the present year.

JEAN CHASTAIN.

The same day Estiene Mallet settled his note, which was due for four pounds, two shillings, two pence.

The same day the levy for the present year was made of sixteen pounds of tobacco per head, viz.:

For the minister	1,600
For Sara Chandler	1,000
For the clerk	1,000
For the poor	300
For Peru	150
For the sexton	250
	4,300
By *note inspeteur* (?)	140
By the note of the church wardens for the year 1749	281
The number of tithables for the year 1749	266

[42]The proceedings of December 9 are cancelled. The vestry agreed that the service is to be two-thirds in English.

JEAN CHASTAIN.
JOSEPH BONDURANT,
JOHN CHASTAIN.
Church Wardens.

WILLIAM SALLE,
DAVID LE SUEUR,
STEPHEN MALLET,
JOHN BONDURANT,
DANIEL PARO,
ISAAC DUTOY,
SAMUEL FLOURNOY.

[42]The entry referred to is not recorded in this Register. The concession to the everincreasing number of English-speaking parishioners is apparent.

December 28, 1750. This day Captain Porter and Charles Clarck took the oath of vestrymen for the parish of King William in the presence of Joseph Bondurant, Jean Chastain, Isaac Dutoy, David Lesueur, Samuel Flournoir, Jean Bonduran, Daniel Perro.

JEAN CHASTAIN.

The same day Charle Clarck and Jean Bonduran took the oath of church wardens and took the test, in the presence of the vestrymen named above.

JEAN CHASTAIN.

Joseph Bonduran and Jean Chastain rendered their account of their administration for the year 1749. They owe 86 lbs. of tobacco.

The same day the levy was made for the present year. It amounts to twenty-two pounds of tobacco per head, viz.:

For the minister, two thousand, four hundred.
For the clerk, one thousand pounds.
For Sara Chandler, one thousand pounds.
For the sexton, two hundred and fifty pounds.
For Sara Ocquebe, three hundred pounds.
For repairing the church, five hundred and eighty-four.

CHAS. CLERKE,
JOHN BONDURANT.
Church Wardens.

JOHN CHASTAIN,
DAVID LE SUEUR,
SAML. FLOURNOY,
JOS. BONDURANT,
ISAAC DUTOY,
THOS. PORTER,
JEAN CHASTAIN, JUNIOR,
DANIEL PERROW.

Daniel Pero asked his discharge and the vestry granted his request.

JEAN CHASTAIN.

[48]List of land which each holds in the parish of King William and adjacent thereto:

Tobit la Fitt, acres	133
Estiene Bocard	093
Mathieux Agee	220
Pierre Louy Soblet	133
Pierre Faure	107
Estiene Reynaud	133
Charle Perot	133
Antoine Rapine	122
Estiene Malet	123
Danielle Meban, Jacob Capon	046
Tobit la Fitt	075
Nicolas Soullie	133
Pierre Soblet	089
Anthoine Maton	165
Jean Jouanis	840
Madame Timson	168
Pierre David, jun	066
Jean Farcis,	040
Estien Chastain	981
Pierre Dutoy	461
Jean Pierre Bilbo	162
Isaac Parenteaux	044
Jacob Capon	034
Danielle Guerand	059
Glaud Goris	050
Pierre Chastain	65.
Gedeon Chan	...
Pierre Dep	076
Pierre Sabatiee	088

[48]This list is on the last remaining leaf in the book. It bears no date, but its date may be approximately deduced as follows: Anthoine Trabue, whose name appears in the list, died January, 1723-4 (Brock, p. 111), thus affording a *terminus ad quem* for the list. The hand-writing appears to be that of Jacques Soblet, whose clerkship begins in 1722. It is probable therefore that the list belongs to 1722 or the preceding year.

Bartelmis Dupuy	208
Pierre Dupuy	068
Anthoine Givodan	128
Jacob Amonet	274
Pierre David, signor	088
Jean Chastain	090
Abraham Soblet	088
Jean le Vilin	200
Francois Fleurinoy	133
Danielle Croom	052
Jean le Grand	051
Anthoine Trabue	268
Abraham Sallee	477
Jhon Levingston	170
Jean Martin	1200
Jean Pierre Perut	122
Jean Forquerent	170
Moyse Levereaux	117
Adam Vigne	025
Elisabeth Sasine	172
Jean Soulaigre	275
Sum total of land	490

[44]List of the lands which each inhabitant of the parish of King William owned in the year 1727|8:

Pierre Chastain	1063
Gedeon Chanbon	0033
Glaude Gori	0050
Pierre Dep	0076
Daniel Guerand	0059
Joseph Bingley	0047
Tobie Lafite	0208
Jean Pierre Billebo	0044

[44]The list is on a loose sheet torn from the back of the Register. On the establishment of the parish in 1700-1 each family was allowed 133 acres. cf. *Calendar of State Papers of Virginia*, I, 189, quoted by Brock, page 68. In a majority of cases the amount of land held seems to have been reduced or increased by purchase in the decades following.

Estiene Chastain 0909
Barbary Dutoy 0061
Estiene Malet 0125
Jacob Capon 0047
Susane Kerner 0177
Nicolas Soulie 0133
Antoine Rapine 0133
M. Joannis ....(figures erased) 0909
Rager Prat 0133
Pierre Faure 0107
Pierre Champagne 0090
Louis Soblet 0133
Matieu Age 0211
Pierre Bocar 0091
Daniel Pero 0133
Pierre Calvet 0444
Pierre Soblet 0088
Pierre David, s. 0088
Jaque Soblet 0088
Pierre David, j. 0066
Jean Legrand 0050
Jorge Merhbenc 0402
Pierre Sabatie 0088
Jacob Amonet 0270
Jean Chastain 00.0
Jean Levilain 0200
Thomas Givodan 0128
Isaac Salle 0055
Guilaume Salle 0057
M. Timson 0168
M. Tillitt 0582
Antoine Trabu 0186
Jean Pierre Bilbo 0119
M... Alaigre 0180
M. Amonet 0182
Daniel Faure 0296
....d Moriset 0130
Jean Loucadou 0103
Daniel Guerand 0133
Edwd. Bryers 0092
Elie Sasain 0104

(CONCLUDED.)

LAND TAXED IN KING WILLIAM COUNTY IN 1782.

William Smith, Commissioner.

CONTRIBUTED BY IDA J. LEE.

John Allen, 100 acres
Thos. Avera, 140 acres
Wm. Alvey, 195
Wm. B. Browne, 1,000
John Bowles, 42
Geo. Brett, 654
Wm. Brett, 150
Wm. Boswell, 290
Thos. Boxley, 50
Hickerson Bagwell, 46
Carter Braxton, 4,426
Geo. Braxton, 1,547
Stephen Bingham,7 lots (W. P.)
Geo. Brookes est., 777
Eliza Burras, 50
Thos. Blackwell, 502
Eliza Chandler, 70
Wm. Chandler, 450
Eliza Claiborne, 250
Wm. D. Claiborne, 1,572
Herbert Clayborne, 1,000
Wm. Curle, 196
Edward Cary, 331
Anthony Crow, 28
John Parke Custis, est., 4,600
Geo. Crump, 150
John Collins, 190
Jas. Crouch, 175
Thos. Chamberlayne, 512
Richard Claybrook, 20
Ambrose Lipscomb (U. H.), 221
Nunn Lipscomb, 234
Pemberton Lipscomb, 196
Geo. Lipscomb, 428
John P. Lipscomb, 650
Daniel Lipscomb, 240
Keziah Lipscomb, 306
Wm. Langbourne, 2,200
Thos. Littlepage, 468
Wm. Mattox, 100
T. P. Madison, 455
Ambrose Madison, 117
John Madison, 117
Henry Madison, Jr., 117
Thos. Moore, 333
Ann C. Moore, 1,840
Jack Mitchell, 100
Cary Mitchell, 320
John Mitchell, 200
Jas. Mitchell, 225
Jas. Mayton, 150
Wm. Mooring, 782
Samuel Meredith, 494
Jas. Martin, 482
Philip Mallory, 336
John S. Moore, 8
Jane Netherland, 100
Daniel Neaves, 207
Jane Neale, 430
Wm. Neale, 475
Greogory O. Neale, 170

John Camm's est., 426
Samuel Dickens, 70
Robert Davis, Sr., 130
Robert Davis, Jr., 100
Richard Davis, 150
Wm. Dandridge, 1,000
Francis Dandridge, 415
Eliza Dowles, 64
Robt. Drewry, 203
Jas. Dugar, 75
Samuel Edwards, 180
Ambrose Edwards, 656
Thos. Ellett, 409
Wm. Ellett, 300
Jas. Fox, 615
Richard Foster, 75
Christian Foster, 307
Wm. Foster, 173
Wm. Frazer (F.), 1,703
Wm. Frazer, Jr., 1,110
Chas. Fortson, 148
Francis Graves, 460
Geo. Gearton, 59
Benj Grimes, 761
Henry Grimstead, 75
Ambrose Green, 125
Rebecca Goodwin, 800
Sam Garlick's est., 515
(ditto in St. Davids), 457
Wm. Hollings, 55
Jas. Hill, 642½
Wm. Hall, 160
Wm. Hartgrove, 128½
John Hawse, 86
Cary Hunt, 150
Eliza Inge, 113
Wm. Johnson, 315
Mildred Powers, 70
David Pannill, 287
Geo. Peers, 150
Hudson Powell, 312
Bernard Powers, 149
Ann Palmer, 200
John Pemberton, 292
John Pomfrett, 295
John Perrin, 270
Julius Powers, 139
John Quarles, est., 294
Hannah Quarles, 147
Isaac Quarles, 843
Dorothy Quarles, 200
Frances Quarles, 110
John Quarles, Jr., 410
Jas. Quarles, 574
Drewry Ragsdale, 807
Jos. Reynolds, 150
Thos. Robinson, 880
Holt Richeson, 847
Jas. Ruffin, 1,725
Sterling Ruffin, 2,000
Peter Richeson, 400
Jas. Rascow, 2 lots
John Rains, 100
Geo. Slaughter, 133
Wm. Stark, 437
Alice Slaughter, 300
Fendal Sutherland, 1,359
Ann Slaughter, 120
Martin Slaughter, Sr., 400
Thos. K. Slaughter, 480
Martin Slaughter, Jr., 274
Henry Slaughter, 350
Augustine Seaton, 403
Wm. Smith, 300

Sarah Inge, 37
Jas. Johnson, Jr., 456
Jas. Johnson, Sr., 745
Ambrose Jackson, 150
Mary Kinknear, 25
John King, 330
Richard King, 220
Wm. King, 200
Robert King, 942
Thos. King, 250
Bernard Lipscomb, 476
Jas. Lipscomb (Taylor) 196
Josiah Lipscomb, 180
Chas. Lipscomb, 227
Ambrose Lipscomb (Jesee), 500
Ann Lipscomb, 387
Eliza Lipscomb, 600
Ambrose Lipscomb (Lott), 26
Jas. Lipscomb, 240
John Lambeth, 133
Meredith Lambeth, lots
Jane Lipscomb, 100
Benoni Lipscomb, 141
Mary Lipscomb, 60
Mary Shirley, 200
Richard Timberlake, 198
Wm. Towler, 143
Matthew Towler, 35
Wm. Terry, 130
Jas. Terry, 50
John Terry, 130
Chas. Terry, 200
Mary Terry, 60
Wm. Trimmer, 50
John Trimmer, 50
Wm. White, 200
Judith Winfrey, 175
Thos. White, 105
Eliza Watkine, 125
Jas. Willeroy, 224
Isaac Winfrey est., 239
John Willeroy, 298
Frances West, 250
Susanna Ware, 30
Thos. Westley, 60
Thos. Waller, 233
Eliza Waller, 117
Mary Ann White, 108
John Waller, 1,496

KING WILLIAM COUNTY PERSONAL TAX LIST, 1782-1850.

By Ida J. Lee.[1]

Abraham, Jos., 1782-1798.
Abraham, Mordecai, 1782-1792 (est.). Taxed for 2 in 1782, for 3 in 90-91.
Abraham, Solomon, 1782-1793.
Abraham, Solomon, 1798-1805.
Abraham, Jacob, 1787-1792.
Abraham, Jacob, 1819.
Abraham, Susanna, 1794-1826. Taxed for 2 in 1794-1799.
Abraham, Mordecai, 1800-1825.
Abraham, Mordecai, Jr., 1807-1841. (Estate in 1842.)
Abraham, Wm. F., 1828-1833.
Abraham, Jack, 1822-1843.
Abraham, Henry L., 1834-1850.
Abraham, Maria F., 1843-1844.
Abraham, Mordecai, Jr., 1836-1850. Taxed for 2 in 1849-50.
Abraham, Wm., 1800-1802.

Acree, Edward, 1782-1821. (Taxed for 3 from 1804-21.)
Acree, Wm., 1782-1788.
Acree, Joshua, 1810-1825.
Acree, Ambrose, 1827-1850. (Minister.)
Acree, Leonard, 1816-1822.
Acree, Leonard, 1845-1850.
Acree, Wm. J., 1841-1844.

Adams, Thos., 1782-1793.
Adams, Ellyson, 1782-1821. (Taxed for 2 in 1816.)
Adams, Richard, 1782-1821.
Adams, Geo., 1782-1784.
Adams, John Peter, 1787-1824. (Taxed for 2 in 1798-1804.)
Adams, Wm., 1802-1821.
Adams, Jas., 1812.
Adams, Richard, Jr., 1806-1807.
Adams, Wm. W., Jr., 1822.
Adams, Lucy, 1817.
Adams, Sally, 1819-1821.
Adams, John P., Jr., 1805-1810.
Adams, Alexander, 1817.
Adams, Warren, 1833.
Adams, John, 1806-1823.
Adams, Wm., 1837-1850.
Adams, Bev. R., 1828-1850.
Adams, Jack, 1840-1848.

1. Miss Lee has examined all the personal tax books and all the land tax books of King William county from 1782 to 1850, under the letter A. The dates after a name indicate that the name appears on the tax list for each year between the inclusive dates. Thus the name of Joseph Abraham appears on the tax list for 1782, and for every succeeding year through 1798.

Adams, Spotswood, 1840-1850.
Adams, Samuel, 1841-1850.
Adams, Geo., 1837-1850.
Adams, Walker, 1837-1846.
Adams, Miles, 1841-1850.
Adams, Leory, 1848-1850.
Adams, Hamilton, 1848-1850.
Adams, Jefferson, 1847-1848.
Adams, Conway, 1848.

Allen, Thos., 1782-1803. (Taxed for 2 in 1802-03.)
Allen, Wm., 1782-1815. (Taxed for 2 in 1788-89.)
Allen, Wm., Jr., 1790-1806.
Allen, John L., 1782-1795.
Allen, Obadiah, 1799.
Allen, Thos. (S. C.), 1800.
Allen, Andrew, 1800.
Allen, Levina, 1803-1819.
Allen, Elizabeth, 1804-1817. (Taxed for 2 in 1806-11, 3 in 1812, 4 in 1813.)
Allen, Wm., estate (Reuben Dugar), 1818.
Allen, George, 1806-1819.
Allen, Lew, 1812-1816.
Allen, James, 1816-1817.
Allen, Richard, 1817-1818.
Allen, Thos. T., 1817.
Allen, Abner, 1807-1824.
Allen, Richard M., 1822-1829.
Allen, John F., 1830-1843.
Allen, Levina, 1829-1843.
Allen, Jas. W., 1850.
Allen, Geo. W., 1843-1845.
Allen, Lindsey, 1832-1850.
Allen, Waller, 1836-1849.
Allen, Samuel, 1841-1850.
Allen, Judith D., 1843-1844.
Allen, John O. L., 1832-1844.
Allen, Thos., 1837-1850.

Alvey, Wm., 1782-1807. (Taxed for 2 in 1787-1789, 3 from 1790-1807.)
Alvey, Wm., Jr., 1809-1821.
Alvey, John, 1809-1815, estate 1816-1818.
Alvey, Elizabeth, 1810-1815, estate 1816.
Alvey, Milly C., 1819-1842.
Alvey, Eliza and Jane, 1817. (From John Alvey.)

Alexander, Thos., 1799-1800. (Taxed for 2 in 1799.)
Alexander, Edmund, 1787-1791.
Alexander, Jas., 1782-1794.
Alexander, Jas., Jr., 1792-1799.
Alexander, Dixon, 1789-1817.

Alexander, John, 1787-1822. (Taxed for Richeson Leigh in 1787.)

Alexander, Jas. D., 1795-1826. (Taxed for 2 in 1801-05.)

Alexander, Aquilla, 1806-1818.

Alexander, Churchwell, 1809-1819.

Alexander, Robt., 1812-1829, estate 1830-31. (Taxed for 2 in 1816-18, 3 in 1819-21.)

Alexander, Dudley, 1829-1840.

Alexander, Thornton, 1828-1850. (Taxed for 2 in 1849, 3 in 1850.)

Alexander, Wm., 1832-1841, estate 1842.

Alexander, Polly, 1832-1837.

Alexander, Elizabeth (relict of D.), 1841-1849.

Alexander, Robert, 1828-1842.

Alexander, John, Jr., 1807-1850.

Ancarrow, Martin, 1782-1800. (No tithables from 1784-1794, taxed for 2 in 1799-1800.)

Ancarrow, Wm., 1802-1841.

Ancarrow, Mildred, 1802-1811.

Ancarrow, Thos. W., 1806-1850.

Ancarrow, Robt., 1824-1850.

Ancarrow, Wm. P., 1842-1845.

Ancarrow, Martin, 1812-1847. (Taxed for 2 in 1845.) Estate 1848-50.

Ancarrow, Henry B., 1845-1847. Address Richmond.

Arnold, Samuel, 1792-1793.

Arnold, Jos., 1812-1848.

Arnold, Robert, 1837, 1849.

Arnold, Rhoda, 1833-1842.

Arnold, Samuel, 1847-1849.

Arbuthnot, John, 1782-1783.

Arbuthnot, Jane, 1784-1807.

Arbuthnot, John, 1795-1807.

Avera, Thos., 1782-1810.

Avera, Ann, 1811-1817.

Avary, Wm., 1837.

Anderson, Frances, 1806-1807.

Anderson, John, 1782-1805. (Taxed for 2 [Richeson Leigh], 1787-1805.)

Anderson, Wm., 1787-1799.

Anderson, David, 1798-1802.

Anderson, Jos., 1797-1798.

Anderson, Benj. B., 1825.

Anderson, Benj. B., trustee for Juanita West.

Anderson, Jas., 1828-1838.

Allard, Humphrey, 1840-1845.

Allard, Thos., 1816.

Archer, Abraham, 1823-1829.
Allman, Thornton, 1836-1850.
Alvis, Spencer, 1844.
Ames, Jas. W., 1845-1850.
Andrews, Franklin, 1846.
Ainslee, W., 1841-1844.

Apperson, Major, 1844.
Apperson, Jas., 1845.

Armstrong, Wm., 1782-1811. Taxed for 3 in 1784, 2 in 1794-95.
Armstrong, Wm., estate, 1812-1813.
Armstrong, Wm., Jr., 1783-1795.
Armstrong, Jane, 1795-1805.
Armstrong, Eliza, 1806-1828.
Armstrong, Dudley, 1801-1848, estate 1849-50.
Armstrong, John D., 1821-1844.
Armstrong, Wm. B., 1823-1833.
Armstrong, Sally, 1822-1824.
Armstrong, Nancy, 1836-1849, estate 1849-50.
Armstrong, Thos., 1830-1850. Taxed for 2 in 1850.

Armistead, Robt., 1783-1784.
Armistead, Thos., 1796-1801. Taxed for 2 in 1796, 3 in 1797-98, 2 in 1799.
Armistead, Dudley, 1800.
Armistead, Wm., Jr., 1822-1832.
Armistead, Willie Ann, 1833.

Atkins, John, 1782-1790.
Atkins, Reuben, 1798-1850. Taxed for 2 from 1803-1821, 2 in 1845-1847.
Atkins, Benj., 1801.
Atkins, Jas., 1810.
Atkins, Johnson, 1819-1850. (Taxed for 2 in 1849-50.)
Atkins, Absalom W., 1820-1850. Taxed for 2 in 1847-49.
Atkins, Reuben, Jr., 1823.
Atkins, Sally, 1826.
Atkins, Alexander, 1850.
Atkins, Wiley, 1841-1850.
Atkins, Dudley, 1848.

Atkinson, Nathaniel, 1790-1791. (No tithables.)
Atkinson, Major, 1794-1825 (est.). Taxed for 2 in 1810, 2 from 1815-22.
Atkinson, Dudley, 1829-1850. Taxed for 2 in 46-50.
Atkinson, Jas., 1823-1826.
Atkinson, Iverson L., 1843-1850.
Atkinson, Wm., 1846-1848. Taxed for 2 in 1847-48.
Atkinson, James, 1849.

Aylett, Wm., estate, 1784-1791.
Aylett, Philip, 1787-1834.
Aylett, Mary, 1782.

Aylett, Wm., 1799-1807.
Aylett, Philip, Jr., 1823-1848.
Aylett, Elizabeth, 1832-1833.
Aylett, Ann and Rebecca; Philip Aylett, guardian.
Aylett, Judith or Jane P., 1849-1850.
Aylett, Patrick H., 1849-1850.

Free Negroes.

Anderson, Richard, 1809.
Anderson, Amos, 1809.
Anderson, Geo., 1809.
Anderson, Mingo, 1819-1850.
Anderson, Phill.
Anderson, Saney, 1841-1846.
Anderson, Robert, Jr., 1844-1846.
Anderson, Tom and son, 1850.
Anderson, Sam, 1850.
Anderson, Jim, 1850.

Adams, Washington, 1848-1849.
Adams, Gloucester, 1848-1850.
Adams, Thos., 1844-1850.

Abraham, George, 1841-1850.
Abraham, Robert, 1844-1850.

LAND TAX FOR KING WILLIAM COUNTY, 1782-1850.

Abraham, Mordecai, 1783-1793.
Abraham, Susanna, 1794-1827.
Abraham, Mordecai, 1800-1825.
Abraham, Jack M., 1833-1834.
Abraham, Henry L., 1848-1850.
Abraham, Mordecai, Jr., 1837-1850.

Adams, Geo., 1783-1785.
Adams, John P., 1783-1822.
Adams, Thos., 1783-1794.
Adams, Jas., 1812-1815. Lots at West Point.
Adams, Lucy, 1816-1828. Lots at West Point.
Adams, John, 1819-1823.
Adams, Thos., 1823-1849. (Richmond, Va.)
Adams, Ellison E., 1816-1822.
Adams, Ellison E., estate, 1823-1831.
Adams, Beverly R., 1837-1850.
Adams, Ann, 1837-1850.
Adams, Mary, 1837-1841.
Adams, Alexandria, 1817-1829. Lots at West Point.
Adams, Wm., 1787.

Alexander, John, 1787.
Alexander, Jas. D., 1797-1811.

Alexander, Robt., 1810-1830.
Alexander, Robt., estate, 1830-1832.
Alexander, John, 1812-1840.
Alexander, John, estate, 1841-1850.
Alexander, Thornton, 1832-1850.
Alexander, Polly, 1832-1836 (relict of Robt.).
Alexander, Polly, estate, 1837.
Alexander, Polly, Jr., 1832-1833.
Alexander, Dudley, 1832-1840.
Alexander, Dudley, estate, 1841.
Alexander, Eliza, 1841.
Alexander, Robt., 1832-1842, from Dudley A., by division.
Alexander, Wm., 1832-1841.
Alexander, Jas. D., 1824-1826.
Alexander, Jas. D., estate, 1827-1850.

Alvey, Wm., 1782-1813.
Alvey, Wm., 1817-1821.
Alvey, John, 1809-1815.
Alvey, John, estate, 1816-1819 (relict).
Alvey, Elizabeth, 1809-1816.
Alvey, Eliza, Ann and Jane, 1814-1816 (Ann deceased, 1816).
Alvey, Eliza and Jane, 1817-1819.
Alvey, Jane and Eliza Johnston, 1820.
Alvey, Jane and Chas. L. Johnston, 1822.
Alvey, Milly C., 1819-1845.
Alvey, Mary Ann C., 1819-1834.
Alvey, Richard T., 1819-1850.
Alvey, John, 1819-1829.
Alvey, Elizabeth T., 1819-1830.
Alvey, Va., 1819-1830.

Allen, John Langley, 1782-1795.
Allen, Thos., 1783-1803.
Allen, Wm., 1801-1816.
Allen, Wm., estate, 1818-1830.
Allen, Wm. C., 1831-1850.
Allen, Eliza, 1804-1828.
Allen, Richard M., 1822-1829.
Allen, Richard M., estate, 1830.
Allen, Levina, 1803-1820.
Allen, Abner, 1819-1821.
Allen, Abner, 1833.
Allen, John, 1839-1850.
Allen, Lindsey, 1840-1846.

Ancarrow, Wm., 1805-1835.
Ancarrow, Wm., estate, 1836-1839.
Ancarrow, Martin, 1820-1849.
Ancarrow, Martin, estate, 1850.
Ancarrow, Thos. W., 1821-1833.
Ancarrow, Robt., 1821-1832.
Ancarrow, Henry B., 1845.

Allman, Thornton, 1842-1850.

Anderson, John, 1783-1805.
Anderson, Frances, 1806-1807.
Anderson, Geo., 1809-1831.
Anderson, Geo., estate, 1832-1850.
Anderson, Amos, 1809-1826.
Anderson, Amos, estate, 1827.
Anderson, Richard, 1809-1832.
Anderson, Richard, estate, 1832-1850.
Anderson, Jas., 1821-1850.
Anderson, Thomas, 1821-1826.
Anderson, Thomas, estate, 1827-1850.
Anderson, Sawney, 1821-1850.
Anderson, Phill, 1821-1850.
Anderson, Daniel, 1821-1822.
Anderson, Daniel, estate, 1823.
Anderson, Richard, Jr., 1821-1842.
Anderson, Richard, Jr., estate, 1843-1850.
Anderson, Daniel, 1826-1850.
Anderson, Richard, 1842-1848.
Anderson, Richard, estate, 1849-1850.

Armistead, Wm., 1815-1826.
Armistead, Willie Ann, 1833-1837.
Armistead, Wm., Jr., 1826.
Armistead, Wm., estate, 1829-1832.

Acree, Leonard, 1838-1850.
Acree, Ambrose, 1840-1850.
Acree, Edward L., 1848-1850 (King and Queen).

Atkins, Reuben, 1798-1850.
Atkins, Johnson, 1826-1850.
Atkins, Absalom W., 1826-1850.
Atkins, Sally, 1847-1850.
Atkins, Wiley, 1850.

Atkinson, Major, 1794-1824.
Atkinson, Major, estate, 1825-1826.
Atkinson, Maria F., 1826-1838 (infant).
Atkinson, Mary A. F., 1826-1838 (infant).
Atkinson, Dudley, 1814-1850.
Atkinson, Iverson L., 1843-1850.
Armstrong, Wm., 1783-1796.
Armstrong, Jane, 1797-1812.
Armstrong, Wm., estate, 1813-1816 (relict).
Armstrong, Eliza, 1813-1830.
Armstrong, Sally, 1817-1841.
Armstrong, Lucinda, 1817-1820.
Armstrong, Wm. B., 1817-1838.
Armstrong, John D., 1817-1830.
Armstrong, Thos., 1830-1850.

Armstrong, Wm. Rufus, 1849-1850.
Armstrong, Ann, 1831-1849.

Avera, Thos., 1782-1811.

Aylett, Mary, 1783-1784.
Aylett, Philip, 1788-1832.
Aylett, Ann and Rebecca, 1798-1801. (Philip Aylett, guardian.)
Aylett, Philip, Jr., 1816-1835.
Aylett, Wm., 1799-1807.
Aylett, Martha and R. P., 1849-1850.
Aylett, Elizabeth, 1832-1842.
Aylett, Philip, 1833-1848.
Estate of Wm. Aylett, 1785-1797.
Estate of Philip Aylett, 1832-1833.
Estate of Philip Aylett, 1849-1850.

ALTERATIONS IN LAND TAX.

1783. Thos. Allen of Alice Slaughter, by survey.
1785. Wm. Alvey of Wm. Frazer, by deed.
John Anderson of Robt. Cowne, by deed.
Mordecai Abrahams of Wm. Gwathmey, by deed.
Wm. Allen of Chas. Forson, rent.
Mordecai Abraham of Joshua Toler, by deed.
Callohill Minnis of Wm. Aylett's estate, by marriage, formerly set to Augustine Peay.
1786. Wm. Adams of Thos. Adams, gift.
1788. Thos. Avera of John Perrin, deed.
Philip Aylett, heir of Wm. Aylett.
1789. Mordecai Abraham of Wm. Gwathmey, deed.
John P. Adams of Wm. Adams, by deed.
1791. Philip Aylett of Wm. Aylett's estate.
1799. License granted Thos. Armistead to retail.
1802. Merchant's license to John Appleton.
1809. George, Richard and Amos Anderson, freed by John Anderson.
1815. Armistead, Wm., from Philip Clayborne's estate by will and marriage, in right of wife.
1816. Lucy Adams from Jas. Adams.
Eliza, Ann and Jane Alvey from Eliza Alvey, deceased.
1818. Sally and Lucinda Armstrong from Wm. Armstrong's estate, by division.
1819. John, Virginia, Eliza, Richard T., Mary Ann C. and Milley Alvey, from John Alvey's estate, by division.
1821. Sawney, Phill and Daniel Anderson from Amos Anderson's estate, by division.
1822. Richard M. Allen from Reuben B. Lipscomb's estate, by division.
1823. Thomas Adams from John P. Adams, by deed.
1826. 35 acres from Reuben Atkins to Absalom and Johnson Atkins, by deed.
1827. Maria F. and Mary A. F. Atkinson, infants, from Major

Atkinson's estate.
Reuben Atkins from Reuben Atkins' estate, balance charged to Geo. B. Pollard, except 27½ acres to Sarah White and children.

1831. Ann Armstrong from Eliza Armstrong, by will.

1832. Polly Alexander, Polly Alexander, Jr., Robert Alexander, Wm. Alexander, Thornton Alexander and Dudley Alexander from Robt. Alexander. by division.

1832. Elizabeth Aylett from Philip Aylett, by will.

1833. Jack M. Abraham from Wm. Sizer's estate, by division.

1833. Abner Allen from Thos. A. Lipscomb's estate, by division.

1837. Ann Adams from Polly Winn, by will.

1841. Eliza Alexander from Dudley Alexander, by division.

1850. Thos. Armstrong from Ann Armstrong, by will.

TITHABLES OF LANCASTER COUNTY, VA., 1654, WITH NOTES.

During the Seventeenth Century (with the exception of the years 1645–1648), all the revenues of the Colony of Virginia and of the separate counties, were raised by a poll tax. Every person subject to this tax was called a "tithable." About the middle of the century these tithables embraced all freemen above the age of sixteen, all male (white) servants, imported, of whatever age, and all imported negroes, male or female, all Indian servants, male or female, above the age of sixteen. No provision appears to have been made by the law at this time for negroes born in the Colony. They were doubtless few in number, and were taxed as imported slaves.

In each county a levy was annually laid and apportioned among the various public creditors. The amount of the levy and the names of the persons to whom payments are to be made are duly set forth in the records of the counties, universally; but while the numbers of tithables is always given, there is only one instance, so far as the writer is aware, in which the names of the heads of familys taxed, are given. This was in the county of Lancaster, and the practice continued for a number of years. The first levy was dated October 25, 1653, but as this appears to have been incomplete, the one of the next year, dated Feb. 6, 1654, is given. Lancaster then included all the territory on both sides of the Rappahannock river from its mouth, as far west as the settlements extended. The numbers given are, of course, the tithables for which each person was accountable. The numbers in parenthesis refer to notes.

Levy 1654.

Mr. John Catlet (1) to collect these: Mr. Loyd 2 (2), Mr. Lewcas 4 (3), Wm. Veale 3 (4), Mr. Hankins 3 (5), Mr. Catlet 5, Rich. Lawson 6 (6).

Mr. Andrew Gilson (7) to collect these: Ra. Warrener 3, Robert Moss 4, Robt. Tomlin 4 (8), Mr. Gilson 4, Jno. Gellett 4, Cle. Thrush 6, John Mills 1, Robert Armstrong 3, Robert Younge 2, Wm. Jnoson 1.

Mr. James Bagnall (9), to collect these: John Cobbe 1, John Bebey 1 (10), Thos. Paine 6 (11), himselfe [*i. e.*, Jas. Bagnall] 4, Rog. Faris 3 (12), Cyp'ian Bishop 2, Henry Dedman 2, John Gregory 3 (13), Robt. Bryan 1 (14), Thos. Griffith 1, Mr. Loes 3 (15), Mr. Jackman 2, Mr. Jones 4 (16).

Mr. Richard Perrott (17) to collect these: himselfe 5, Wm. Thompson 3, Fra. Browne 3, Oliver Segar 2 (18), Fra. Cole 5 (19), Abr. Weekes 3 (20), Mr. Burnham 12 (21), John Wealch 5, Mr. Boswell 4 (22), Mr. Willis 3 (23), Mr. Obart 2 (24), Thos. Kid 3.

Mr. John Cox (25) to collect these: Mr. Moone 7 (26), Sir Henry Chicheley 24 (27), Capt. Wm. Brocas, Esq., 12 (28), Wm. Leech 12 (29), Mr. Kemp 5 (30), La. Lunsford 12 (31), Mr. Cox 4, Mr. Tignall 7, Ja. Bonner 3 (32), Wm. Lewcas 2.

Mr. Thomas Bourne to collect these: himselfe 5, Dennis Coniers 2 (33), George Keble 3 (34), Mr. Rigby 4, Row. Hadaway 2, Thos. Stamper 2 (35), John Needles 2 (36), John Bell 1.

Captain Henry Fleete (37) to collect these: himselfe 11, Elias Blake 3, John Prout 2, Teague Floyne 1, Toby Horton 3, Edey Benison 4.

Major John Carter (38) to collect these: himselfe 12, Mr. Row. Lawson 3 (39), Wm. Harper 3, Wm. Clapham, Jr., 7, Mr. Thos. Carter 4 (40), Hen. Rye 2, John Baylor 3 (41).

Mr. Thomas Brice (42) to collect these: himselfe 9, Thos. Hardinge 1, Capt. Hacke 2 (43), Thos. Powell 2 (44), Walter Dickinson 6, Mr. Edwards 4 (45), Thos. Hopkins 4 (46), Thos. Roots 1 (47), Dominie 4, Widow Grimes 4 (48), Edward Dudley 1 (49), John Merriman 2 (50), Wm. Neesham 6, Mr. Hankes, Mr. Beach 3, John Paine 7 (51).

Mr. Wm. Clapham, Sr. (52) to collect these: himselfe 5, John Meredith 5 (53), Mr. Conaway 4 (54), John Nichols 1.

Mr. David Fox (55) to collect these: himselfe 16, Mr. Sharpe 14, John Philips 3, Mr. Powell 7, Mr. Travers 7 (56), Thomas Williams 2.

Mr. Toby Smith (57) to collect these: himselfe 5, John Edgecombe 2, Thos. Staines 6, Capt. Fauntleroy 7 (58), Mr. Griffin 5 (59).

Mr. James Williamson (60) to collect these: Mr. Lambert 5, Jen. Hall 2, Thos. Robinson 2, Fra. Gower 3 (61), Mr. Wm'son 7, Thos. Meade 3, Mr. Bradshaw 6 (62).

Mr. George Taylor (63) to collect these: Wm. Ireland 3, himselfe 3, Mr. Weir 5 (64), Ex per Rixham 2, Sil. Thatcher 3 (65), Thos. Whitlock 5, Joh. Ayres 3.

NOTES.

(1). Col. John Catlett, long a man of prominence in Rappahannock county. For notices of him and his descendants see this Magazine, III, 35, 61–66;* and Hayden's Virginia Genealogies, 244, 280. A manuscript pedigree of the family is in possession of the writer. President Madison was a descendant.

(2). "Mr. Loyd," was doubtless Col. Wm. Lloyd long a prominent man in the Northern Neck. On April 17, 1667, with John Biddle, he patented 4,750 acres in Westmoreland on Nominy river; on April 18, 1668, he patented 2,467 acres on Rappahannock creek (now in Rd. county), and on the same day an adjoining tract of 300 acres. He had other grants. In 1686, Lt.-Col. Wm. Lloyd was a justice of Rappahannock and Lieutenant-Colonel of militia. He married, 1st, Mary, widow of Moore Fauntleroy (there is a deed dated June, 1666, which shows this). He married 2nd, Elizabeth, widow of John Hull. (Her daughter, Elizabeth Hull, married Col John Carter, Jr., of "Corotoman.") In a deed dated Jan. 10, 1690, and recorded in Lancaster, Elizabeth, wife of Wm. Lloyd, gent., states that she was one of the overseers of Col. Jno. Carter's will, and grandmother of his daughter Elizabeth. Col. Wm. Lloyd had, it is believed, two sons, John and Thomas. John Lloyd was a justice of Richmond county 1692, and was in 1693, recommended by the Governor as one of "the gentlemen of estate and stand-

***For pp. 61-66 see *Virginia Land Records: From The Virginia Magazine of History and Biography, the William and Mary College Quarterly, and Tyler's Quarterly* (Baltimore: Genealogical Publishing Co., Inc., 1982), pp. 558-563.**

ing," suitable for appointment to the Council; married about 1693, Elizabeth, only child of Col. John Carter, Jr., and returned to England about 1700. There is on record in Richmond county, a power of attorney from John Lloyd, of the city of Chester, Eng., to his "worthy kinsman, Griffin Fauntleroy, gent.," which states that he owned several considerable plantations in Virginia, which had been entrusted to his brother Thos. Lloyd, lately deceased. Another deed speaks of lands he inherited from his brother Thomas. Thomas Lloyd was a justice of Richmond county. His inventory, dated 1699, shows a very large estate.

(3) "Mr. Lewcas." Thomas Lucas, member of the House of Burgesses from Rappahannock, March, 1657–8. For notice of him see this Magazine III, 36, 61,* 112.

(5). "Mr. Hawkins." Thomas Hawkins, Sr., afterwards of Rappahannock county. See this Magazine I, 60; III, 36, 61–66.

(6). Richard Lawson, brother of Epaphroditus Lawson, and Rowland Lawson, of Lancaster county, died between 1656 and 1662, leaving a widow, Elizabeth. See this Magazine IV, 203.*

(7). Andrew Gilson was J. P. for Lancaster in 1655, and on the formation of Rappahannock, was appointed, December 11, 1656, one of the first justices of that county. He afterwards lived in Stafford, and as Major Andrew Gilson, was a justice of that county in 1680.

(8). Robert Tomlin died in Rappahannock county in 1688; his will was dated March 7, 1683, and proved October 9, 1688; legatees: sons Robert and William, cousin George Tomlin, wife Rebecca, daughters Rebecca, Hannah and Martha, brother Captain George Taylor, cousin Martha Taylor, sister Mrs. Martha Taylor. He patented land on the south side of the Rappahannock river in 1653. His son Wm. Tomlin lived in Essex, and was J. P. for that county in 1704, &c. He married Anne, widow of George Hazlewood, and daughter of Richard Robinson, both of Middlesex. Robinson arms as shown on documents at Middlesex C. H., were the same as those of Bishop Robinson. There is a deed recorded in Richmond county, and dated Dec. 1, 1697, from Wm. Tomlin and Anne his wife, conveying the

*For pp. 61-66 and 203 see *Virginia Land Records: From The Virginia Magazine of History and Biography, the William and Mary College Quarterly, and Tyler's Quarterly* (Baltimore: Genealogical Publishing Co., Inc., 1982), pp. 558-563 and 612.

plantation, 700 acres in Richmond county, where James Williamson formerly lived, and which was granted to said Williamson on May 22, 1650. Robert Tomlin, the other son of Robert the elder, married Hester or Esther, daughter of Col. John Walker, of the Council, and died in 1689. On July 3, 1689, Mrs. Easter Tomlin was granted administration on the estate of Mr. Robert Tomlin, deceased. On Oct. 8, 1690, she made a deed for 300 acres of land in Sittenbourne parish, part of a tract of of 2,000 acres, which had belonged to her father, Col. John Walker, decd. The Virginia Tomlins are probably desended from Robert and Esther (Walker) Tomlin, as the name Walker has been a favorite in thc family.

(9). James Bagnall was J. P. for Lancaster, Jan. 1, 1652, and on Dec. 11, 1656, on the formation of Rappahannock, was appointed a justice and of the quorum in that county.

(10). The name Beby or Biby appears in the register of Christ Church parish, Middlesex.

(11). There is recorded in Lancaster a deed, dated Apl. 10, 1654, from Thos. Paine and Penelope his wife, conveying 300 acres on the north side of the river. There were several persons named Paine or Payne, resident at an early date in Lancaster.

(12). Probably ancestor of the family of Farish, afterwards resident in Essex and Spotsylvania.

(13). John Gregory was doubtless the person of the name who afterwards lived in Rappahannock county. John Gregory of Rappahannock, made a deed dated April 16, 1666, to his son-in-law, Thos. Edmondson. Robt. Bishop, of Rappahannock, by will dated April 21st, 1676, left all his estate to John Gregory, Jr. John Gregory, the elder, who was a vestryman of Sittenbourne parish, 1665, had two sons, John and Richard, and a daughter Mary, who married in 1682, James Taylor, the immigrant ancestor of President Taylor. There was a grant in April, 1687, to James Taylor, for land left by Mr. Robt. Bishop, to John Gregory, and by him to his sister Mary, "now the wife" of the said Taylor. There is on record a deed from John Gregory and Elizabeth his wife, of Rappahannock, dated Feb. 26, 1673-4. The will of John Gregory was dated Dec. 18, 1671, and proved in Rappahannock, Sept. 4, 1678; legatees, his sisters

Mary and Elizabeth, brother Richard, Executor. The will of Richard Gregory of Essex, was dated Feb. 17, and proved May 10, 1700; legatees: sons Richard and John, sons-in-law (probably step-sons), Thos. and Wm. Bowin, daughter Elizabeth, and wife Katherine; speaks of his land in King and Queen county. Either this Richard or his son of the same name, was J. P. for King and Queen, 1693, 1699, 1702. Of course after 1700, the justice must have been the son. It is stated (*Richmond Standard*), that Richard Gregory had a son Roger, who was father of Roger Gregory, whose son Richard, married a sister of Col. Francis West, and had, with other issue, a daughter Martha Ward Gregory, who married General John Pegram, and died Dec. 31, 1836. There is a deed from Roger Gregory, Gent., of Stratton Major parish, King and Queen, and Mildred his wife, May 17, 1726, to Augustine Washington. The seal attached is described as "a bloodhound on scent, standing on what may be a wreath." Mrs. Mildred Gregory was a daughter of Lawrence Washington, and by her marriage with Roger Gregory had three daughters: Frances who married, in 1736, Francis Thornton; Mildred who married in 1740, John Thornton, and Elizabeth who married in 1742, Henry Willis, all of Spotsylvania county.

A Roger Gregory was a justice of Mecklenburg in 1784, and sheriff in 1799–1801. Richard Gregory was sheriff of King William county, 1742. Roger Gregory was member of the House of Delegates, 1786. Richard Gregory, J. P. for King William in 1732. "Died Jan. 21, 1840, aged 73, Wm. Gregory, Sr., of 'Elsing Green,' King William Co., a justice for 50 years, and member of the House of delegates for 13, beginning in 1798–9; descended from ancestors of more than ordinary celebrity in England, and maternally from John West, Governor of Virginia; left many children." (*Newspaper Obituary*). T. W. S. Gregory, member of the House of Delegates from King William, 1827 and 1828. Judge Roger Gregory, of "Elsing Green," present professor of Law at Richmond College, has been county judge and member of the House of Delegates.

(14). The distinguished genealogist, Mr. Lyon G. Tyler, believes, as a result of his researches in the county records, that William Jennings Bryan, the late Presidential candidate, is descended from a family resident in the Northern Neck.

(15). Richard Loes was J. P. for Lancaster, 1652–56, and on Dec. 11, 1656, was appointed a justice, and captain of militia in the new county of Rappahannock. His will dated April 2nd, and proved in Rappahannock, July 7, 1675, makes bequests to his son-in-law (step-son ?) James Taskett, of all his estate in Maryland, and fifty hogsheads of tobacco, the testator had recently shipped out of Maryland, to Walter Tucker, merchant; also gives him half his stocks of horses, cattle, &c., two slaves, a gun, &c., and all the pewter that was his deceased mother's, to son-in-law Mr. Henry Williamson, all of his lands on Rappahannock, and the rest of his personal estate.

(16). While it is difficult to speak with certainty of a "Mr. Jones," it is probable that this was Rice Jones, who in January, 1652, received from Lancaster court, a certificate that he was entitled to 200 acres of land. In the same year he made a deed for land, and on June 2, 1653, sold two patents of 320 and 88 acres, on the north side of the Rappahannock. He married Jane, daughter of Nicholas Cocke, of Middlesex county, who by his will dated October 22, 1687, made bequests to his son, Maurice Cocke, daughter, Jane Jones, and grandsons, Rice and Nicholas Jones. There is on record in Middlesex, a petition, dated July 5, 1686, from Mrs. Jane Jones, widow of Mr. Rice Jones. The will of Maurice Cocke, of Middlesex, dated May 15, 1696, makes bequests to his nephews, John, Rice, and Nicholas Jones, sons of Rice Jones, deceased. An order of Middlesex Court, dated May 19, 1698, directed that the guardians of the children of Rice Jones, deceased, should have a portion of the estate of Mr. Maurice Cocke, deceased. There is a deed in Middlesex, 1704, from Rice Jones, of Middlesex, gent., grandson and heir of Nicholas Cocke, and a deed in Middlesex, May 4, 1706, from Rice Jones, of South Farnham parish, Essex. The will of William Jones of Middlesex, dated April, 1747, proved April, 1748, names his sons Rice and Thomas, and daughter Susanna Jones, and makes his brothers Rice and John executors.

In October, 1765, the General Assembly passed an act reciting that Rice Jones, the elder, was in his lifetime seized of a valuable tract of land lying in the parish of South Farnham, county of Essex, containing about 800 acres, and another tract in Middlesex, and by his will, dated November 23, 1676, did, among other things, devise his land in Essex to his son, John Jones, and that in Middlesex to his son, Rice Jones; and after the death of testator and of his son, John (without issue), Rice Jones became seized of both tracts, and died, leaving issue: John Jones, his eldest son and heir, who died, leaving three sons, Rice, John and William, which Rice and John had since died without issue, and the said William was dead, leaving Rice Jones, his eldest son and heir, who is now seized in fee tail of said lands, and asks that the entail be docked.

(17). "Mr. Richard Perrott." There is in Lancaster a deed dated January 12, 1655, from Richard Perrott, conveying 300 acres of land lying up the creek, at the head of the land where the said Perrott lives. On December 13, 1656, the General Assembly appointed him one of the justices of Lancaster, and on December 15, 1657, was chosen vestryman and sidesman of Lancaster parish. On January 5, 1657, he was appointed sheriff of Lancaster, and in 1670, of Middlesex. It appears that he had formerly lived in York county, for in the records of that county, in 1647, is an order that Richard Perrott shall appraise the estate of Captain Robert Morrison, being in York; and on Aug. 24, 1648, is a deed from Richard Perrott, and Sarah his wife, to her children, Thomas, Joane, and Sarah, by her former husband, Nicholas Dale. There is recorded in Lancaster, a deed, dated March 15, 1668–9, from Nicholas Spencer to Richard Perrott, conveying 1,900 acres on Pianketank river, called Mottram's Mount. Richard Perrot, Sr., who, besides the offices named above, was presiding justice of Middlesex, died November 11, 1686. His will was dated December 20, and proved February 7, 1686, in Middlesex; legatees: wife Margaret, son Richard, grandson Henry, eldest son of Richard, and friend Ralph Wormeley, Esq. The will of Mrs. Margaret Perrott (2d wife), was dated October 21, 1687; legatees: godson Henry Perrott, daughter Margaret Price, godson Philip Warwick, goddaughter Margaret Prior, daughter Mrs. Sarah Perrott, friend Mrs. Mary Goodlow, goddaughter Mrs. Winifred Griffin (to whom she gives her diamond ring), friend Mrs. Elizabeth Wilkes, brother

Mr. Anthony Haywood (of Boston, Mass.), sister Mrs. Catharine Hide, nephew Mr. Thomas Hide; Thomas Drawne to have her wedding ring, and Thomas Blott her other plain rings. Ralph Wormeley, Esq., Dr. Walter Whittaker, Mr. Christopher Robinson, and Mr. Francis Weeks, overseers of the will. "Richard Perrott" patented 450 acres on south side Rappahannock river, March 13, 1649. "Richard Perrott, gent.," patented on August 21, 1666, 1,100 acres on the south side of Rappahannock; head rights: Richard Perrott, Richard his son, &c. Richard and Sarah Perrott had issue: 2. *Richard*[2]; 3. "Henry Perrott; second son of Richard Perrot, of Rappahannock River, in Virginia, Esq." entered Gray's Inn, November 14, 1674 (*Foster*). He was the first American known to have enteredthis Inn.

2. RICHARD[2] PERROTT "the son of Mr. Richard Perrott, deceased, was born the 24th of ffebruary, 1657, Being the first Man child that was gott and borne in Rappahannock river, of English parents." (*Christ Church Register*. This entry was made a number of years subsequent to his birth.)

"Mr. Richard Perrott, Jr.," was a justice of Middlesex, 1673. There is mention in the Lancaster records, in September, 1659, that Richard Perrott, Jr., was half-brother of Thomas Dale. He married November 11, 1672, Sarah (born in Gloucester co., August 16, 1657), widow of Wm. Halfhide, and daughter of Thomas Curtis and Averella his wife. Issue: 4. Henry,[3] born January 25, 1675. (*Parish Register*). There is in Middlesex, a deed dated January 16, 1706, from Richard Perrott (grandson of Richard Perrott, dec'd), to Mrs. Penelope Perrott, widow of Henry Perrott, of Middlesex, dec'd, conveying to her for life, in full of dower, all the plantation said H. P. lived on, except half the apple trees in the orchard. Inventory of Capt. Henry Perrott, Middlesex, January 6, 1706, Penelope Perrott, ex'tx. He died without issue (*Hening*). 5. Frank,[3] born August 28, 1677; 6. Sarah,[3] born September 21, 1679. On May 20, 1697, Henry Perrott, in consideration of the love he bore to his sister Sarah, the intended wife of Paul Thilman, conveyed to them, that plantation called Perrott's Quarter, and 300 acres adjoining. 7 *Richard*; 9. Amanda,[3] born August 3, 1683; 10. Robert,[3] born October 25, 1685. The inventory of Robert Perrott, of Middlesex (including a parcel of books), was dated December 3, 1793; 11. Curtis,[3] born August 19, 1688. The bond of Curtis P., as administrator of Curtis P., was dated September 2, 1740, in penalty of £100. Robert Brown in his will, March, 1741, makes bequests to Charles and Frances, children of Curtis P., dec'd. Division of estate of Curtis P., dec'd, October 5, 1742, between the widow Ann, the sons, Curtis, Charles, and Daniel, and the daughters, Ann, Agatha, and Frances; Clara, wife of Wm. Marks, and Averella, wife of Wm. Long.

7. RICHARD PERROTT,[3] had a son, Henry,[4] whose only daughter and heiress, Mary,[5] married Robert Chew, of Spotsylvania. In 1753, the entail on "Perrott's Neck," in Middlesex, which had descended to her from the first Richard, was docked.

Seals of the Perrotts at Middlesex C. H., bear three pears.

(18). Olliver Segar died in 1659. His will dated Jan., 1658, and proved in Lancaster, March, 1659, names his oldest son, Olliver, son Randolph, wife Ellinor, and daughter Elizabeth. Friends, Nicholas Cocke, and Richard Lee, executors. Deed, October 30, 1663, from Ellinor Owen, to her children, Olliver and Randolph Segar, and Ellinor Owen. Mrs. Segar married secondly, Humphrey Owen, who was dead in 1663. She married a third time, Humphrey Jones.

The inventory of the son Oliver, on record in Middlesex, was dated, November 13, 1699, apparently without issue. Randolph Segar (who is mentioned in 1661, as son of Oliver Segar, deceased), married, in or before 1693, the administratrix (doubtless the widow), of Captain Oswald Cary. She married thirdly, Rev. Samuel Gray, minister of Christ Church, Middlesex. He appears to have married first, Mary, daughter of Humphrey Jones (of course daughter of another wife than Ellinor), who in his will, dated October, 1684, named his grandchildren, Winifred, Catharine, and Oliver Segar, and daughter, Marie Segar.

The will of "Randle Segar," of Middlesex, was dated Dec., 1693, and proved in 1694; legatees: wife Ann, son Oliver, daughters, Winifred and Catharine Segar, sons, John and William; and "my father Jones." He owned in Middlesex, a plantation called, "Jamaica," and others. In February, 1685–6, Mrs. Mary Segar was the executrix of Humphrey Jones.

The Inventory of "Mr. Randolph Segar," was recorded in

Middlesex, and dated, February 3, 1700. Oliver Segar (son of Randolph), gave bond as sheriff of Middlesex, June, 1711. Oliver Segar was justice of Middlesex in 1732.

The will of John Segar was dated, October, 1729, and proved in Middlesex, January, 1740; legatees: Jane Segar Nicholas, whole estate; his brother Oliver and Wm. Segar, and Josiah, son of Oliver Segar, executors. The inventory of Capt. Oliver Segar was recorded in Middlesex, July, 1741. The following marriage bonds are on file in Middlesex: Catharine Segar and George Fearn, September 4, 1753, Randolph Segar, security; Joseph Eggleston and Judith Segar, December 11, 1753; Wm. Moulson and Mary, daughter of Oliver Segar, July 26, 1745; John Segar and Priscilla Hackney, December 17, 1764.

(19). Francis Cole was a vestryman of Lancaster parish, December 15, 1657. His will was dated and proved in Lancaster, 1657, or 1658 (the record is defaced), and his legatees were his wife, and daughters, Frances and Mary. There is in Lancaster, a deed, dated November 30, 1659, from Mr. George Marsh, who married Alice, widow of Frances Cole, and Mr. John Edwards, who married Francis Cole, one of the daughters.

(20). Abraham Weekes was chosen a vestryman of Lancaster parish, 1657, was a justice of Lancaster, 1666, and of Middlesex. There is a deed recorded in Middlesex, and dated June 30, 1688, from Abraham Weekes, of the county of Middlesex, gent., and Millicent his wife, conveying to Mr. Henry Williamson, of Rappahannock county, and Catharine his wife (daughter of the said Weekes), part of a tract of land, the remainder of which had been conveyed to Francis Weekes, son of said Abraham Weekes. Mr. Abraham Weekes was a justice of Middlesex, 1676. The will of Abraham Weekes was dated, January, 1691–2, and proved March, 1691–2; legatees: son Francis, daughter Mary, daughter Letty Lidford, neice Katharine Collins, daughter Elizabeth Wheeling, son-in-law John Jones. Mr. Mathew Lidford, Mr. Francis Weekes, and Mr. Henry Williamson, executors. There is recorded in Middlesex, a power of attorney, dated January 3, 1703, from Mildred, widow of Abraham Weekes, to her son Henry Goodloe, authorizing him to acknowledge a deed to her son-in-law Wm. Montague, and Lettice his wife. Francis

Weekes, gave bond as sheriff of Middlesex, May 10, 1697, and as Francis Weekes, gent., was a justice of that county in 1700, and 1702. There is on record in Lancaster, a deed dated, May 31, 1687, and recorded April 8, 1702, from Francis Weekes, of Middlesex, gent., and Elizabeth his wife, conveying to Andrew Jackson, 350 acres in Lancaster, called Fairweather, lately purchased from Mr. Rawleigh Travers.

There is a deed in Lancaster, 1713, from Hobbs Weekes, of Middlesex, planter, son of Frances Weekes; and a deed in Middlesex, dated July 25, 1738, from Thomas Hobbs Weekes, of the town and county of Southampton, England, Esq., eldest son and heir of Hobbs Weekes, who was the surviving son (and only one who had issue), of Francis Weekes, who was the only son of Abraham Weekes, of Middlesex, Va., gent., conveying to Richard Corbin, of Virginia, Esq., 450 acres in Middlesex, called Weekes' creek, or plantation, first granted to the aforesaid Abraham Weekes.

W. G. S.

[NOTES TO BE CONTINUED.]

NOTES.

(21) "Mr. Burnham." See this Magazine, I, 33, 37, 91,* 256–58.

(22) "Mr. Boswell." Edward Boswell was vestryman and "sidesman" of Lancaster Parish in 1657. Edward Boswell, of "Lancaster Co., on Rappahannock River, planter," by deed dated December 3, 1658, took John Vause, of the same county, into partnership for twelve years in said Boswell's plantation, stock, servants, &c.; each party was to be allowed to dispose of his own proper estate in England as he might think fit; John Vause was to pay (out of his own estate), so long as said Boswell should abide in England, the sum of £15 sterling annually, towards his maintenance; and agreed that if the said Boswell and wife should not go to England in that year, or hereafter, before the expiration of the twelve years, they should return to Virginia, they should have liberty to abide on said plantation with Vause.

(23) "Mr. Willis." Thomas Wyllys was a "sidesman" of Lancaster Parish 1657. There is recorded in Lancaster a deed dated October 1, 1667, from Thomas Wyllys, of Lancaster, and Mary, his "now wife," to Abraham Weekes. There is in Middlesex (formerly a part of Lancaster) a marriage contract dated February 6, 1670, between Mary Willis, widow, and Matthew Bentley, shoemaker, making provision in favor of her children, Richard, John and Eleanor Willis. This Mary Willis was doubtless the widow of Thomas Willis Her second husband, Matthew Bentley, was one of the leaders of the adherents of Nathaniel Bacon in Middlesex and vicinity. At Middlesex Court February, 1677, Matthew Bentley was summoned to answer the charge that during the late rebellion, when in command of forty or fifty men-in-arms at Major Lewis' plantation, in New Kent county, he killed three hogs and four sheep, used a great deal

***For p. 91 see *Virginia Land Records: From The Virginia Magazine of History and Biography, the William and Mary College Quarterly, and Tyler's Quarterly* (Baltimore: Genealogical Publishing Co., Inc., 1982), p. 454.**

of corn, and took meal for the whole rebel army at Major Pate's. In this case Bentley took an appeal to the General Court. On July 23d, Colonel Christopher Wormeley, of Middlesex, sued Matthew Bentley and others for trespass and for taking from him in October, 1676, twelve beeves, forty sheep, twelve bushels of salt, &c., &c. He obtained judgment for £435. In Middlesex, March, 1677, Mr. William Gordon and Mr. Alexander Smith became securities for the good behavior of Matthew Bentley. The will of Matthew Bentley, dated January, 1685–6, was proved in Middlesex February, 1685–6. He left Mary Allden a young mare; Robert Allden "a cloth serge suit I now have and my great cloth coat;" John Willis his broadcloth suit with gold buttons on it; son, Richard Willis, executor, and to have the remainder of his estate. Matthew Bentley died January 8, 1685, and Mrs. Mary Bentley September 27, 1684. It appears from the register of Christ Church Parish, Middlesex, that Thomas and Mary Willis had the following children: (1) Mary, christened February 23, 1660; (2) Thomas, born September 8, 1660; (3) Ellianor, born April 18, 1655; (4) Richard, born August 29, 1656; (5) John, born November 24, 1658. [This is the order in which they appear in the register.] "Mr. John Willis" qualified as executor of Anthony Barlow, June, 1685. An entry in the Middlesex records, December, 1687, speaks of John and Richard Willis as brothers. John Willis died May 4, 1688 (*Christ Church Register*). His will, dated April, 1688, and proved in Middlesex in July, included bequests to Elinor, John and Mary Allden, John Barlow, and brother, Richard Willis. Eleanor, daughter of Thomas Willis, probably married, first, Robert Alden (births of children of Robert and Eleanor Alden are noted in the register, 1683–85), and, secondly, —— Kemp. There is in Middlesex a deed dated October 5, 1717, from Eleanor Kemp, of Essex, widow, to her daughters, Mary Nalle and Catherine Terbetts, and to person named Allden. She speaks of the land where her brother, Richard Willis, lived and died, and conveys a considerable amount of land in Essex and Middlesex. Richard Willis, the brother of John and Eleanor, was appointed a justice of Middlesex April, 1698. He appears to have married several times. There is in Lancaster a deed dated April, 1683, from Richard Willis, of Middlesex, with consent of his wife, Dorothy; in it he mentions his "father-in-law," John Gibson. And in Middlesex a deed from Richard Willis and Ann, his wife, reciting that the said Willis, "now of Lancaster," married Ann, widow of Michael Griggs, of Lancaster. There is also a deed in Lancaster, July, 1691, from Richard Willis, gent., of Lancaster, and his wife, Ann, late widow of Michael Griggs, gent. His third wife was Betty, daughter of Thomas Landon, of Middlesex. The latter, in his will, dated November 9, 1700, names his son-in-law, Captain Richard Willis, and his wife, Betty. Richard Willis died in 1700, leaving a large estate. His inventory, dated February 4, 1700, and recorded in Middlesex ("Inventory of Richard Willis, gent., deceased"), included goods at the store valued at £1,475.6; a well furnished dwelling, and at the quarter 84 head of cattle, 6 horses, &c., amounting in all, total value of personal estate, £1,778.14.11. In addition, there were debts due the estate from persons in Virginia, New England, Dublin, Whitehaven, &c., &c., to the amount of 38,983 pounds tobacco, or £2,930.14. On February 3, 1700, Betty gave bond in the sum of £20,000 [?] sterling as executrix of her deceased husband, Richard Willis, with Sir William Skipwith and Gawin Corbin as securities. There is recorded in Lancaster a deed dated April 9, 1701, between Robert Carter, of Lancaster, &c., and Betty, widow of Richard Willis, in view of a marriage about to take place between them. On January 30, 1701–2, is an entry in the Middlesex records which states that Robert Carter had married the widow and executrix of Richard Willis.

(24) "Mr. Obart." Bertram or Bartram Obert or Hobert (the names are variously spelled in the records) was a foreigner, probably a Dutchman, who settled in Lancaster. Arthur Dunn, in his will, dated in Lancaster November 16, 1655, makes bequests to his friend, Bartram Hobert, and to Chichester Hobert, son of the said Bartram. The will of Bartram Obert was dated November 30th and proved in Lancaster June 25, 1659; legatees: sons, Bartram and Chichester, daughters, Lettice and Agatha, and wife, Anne. The daughter, Agatha, married Christopher Robinson, of "Hewick," Middlesex, the first of that family in Virginia. The records speak of Bertram Obert as an alien.

Elizabeth, a daughter not named in the will, married James Curtis (*Middlesex Records*).

(25) "Mr. John Cox." John Cox was a justice of Lancaster 1653–55. The will of John Cox, of Rappahannock county, was dated November 9, 1669, and proved February 10, 1695; legatees: Henry, son of Michael White, a tract of land; John and Elizabeth White, children of same; legacies to other friends; appoints nephew, Henry, son of brother, William Cox, "now present in Virginia," sole executor, and leaves him and his other nephews and nieces residuary legatees. John Cox had a grant of 600 acres in Lancaster in 1650, and later ones for 1,150 acres and 1,000 acres "on the south side of the Rappahannock."

(26) "Mr. Moone." Lancaster Court in 1654 granted a certificate to Abraham Moone for land due him for the importation of his wife, Anne, John Brewster, William Attaway, &c. December 12, 1655, Abraham Moone made a deed in Lancaster, selling his dwelling house, plantation and servants to Thomas Hawks, but reserving for himself and wife house room and one servant. He died soon after. The inventory of the personal estate of Abraham Moone, deceased, was recorded in Lancaster February 20, 1655; appraised at 18,152 pounds tobacco. John Curtis was his administrator. There is recorded in Middlesex a deed dated June 7, 1710, from John Curtis, of Great Wicomico Parish, Northumberland, as only surviving brother and next of kin to Elizabeth Hazlewood, deceased, daughter and heiress of Abraham Moone, deceased. And another deed in Middlesex, November 8, 1684, from Richard Robinson and Ann, his wife, to John Curtis, of Northumberland, son of the said Ann. Also a deed recorded November, 1684, in Middlesex, from Richard Robinson and Ann, his wife, to their children, Richard and Anne Robinson, with reversion (in case of failure of issue) to John Curtis, of Northumberland (son of the said Mrs. Ann Robinson), and failing his issue, to Ann, daughter of Christopher and Agatha Robinson, conveying property obtained from Abraham Moone, the former husband of Mrs. Ann Robinson. Elizabeth Hazlewood (referred to above) appears to have been the wife of John Hazlewood, described in 1674 as of Middlesex, merchant, and in 1683 as of the parish of White Chapel, London. There is recorded in Middlesex copy of a bill of exchange, August 4,

1692, on "Madam Elizabeth Hazlewood, at her house in Chamber Street, Goodman's Fields, London." She died without issue.

(27) Sir Henry Chichley. See this Magazine, I, 115, 422, 453; II, 408; III, 39.*

(28) Captain William Brocas. See this Magazine, I, 421, 422.

(29) William Leech lived in Lancaster on the north side of the Rappahannock in 1657, and was appointed a justice of that county in 1659. It appears from a deed in Middlesex, dated 1686, that he died without issue, and left his property to his wife's grandchildren, William Tignor, Jr., son of William Tignor, of Wickomico, and William Poole, Jr., son of William Poole, of Middlesex.

(30) "Mr. Kemp." See this Magazine, I, 420, 421; II, 174; III, 40, &c.

(31) "Lady Lunsford." See this Magazine, I, 115, 421.

(32) James Bonner. In Lancaster, November 11, 1663, administration on the estate of James Bonner, deceased, was granted to Matthew Kemp, his next of kin. Bonner had married Elizabeth, daughter of Matthew Kemp, Esq., of the Council, and apparently died without issue.

(33) Dennis Coniers may have been the ancestor of the family whose descent is given by Mr. Hayden (*Virginia Genealogies*) in an excursus, pages 288, &c.

(34) George Keble. See this Magazine, II, 412.*

(35) Thomas Stamper. The name Stamper appears fifty-eight times in the register of Christ Church Parish, Middlesex, which has been published by the Virginia Society of Colonial Dames.

(36) John Needles. The name appears in the Christ Church Register.

(37) Captain Henry Fleete. See this Magazine, II, 71–76.** To this may be added, from Nicholl's Topographer and Genealogist, which prints an account prepared in 1620. Mary, daughter of Robert Atwaters or Waters, Esq., of Royston, Essex, married Robert Honywood, of Henewood, Kent. She was born in 1527 and married in February, 1543, her husband dying in 1576; but she lived to see 367 descendants. Her por-

---

***For pp. 408 and 412 see *Genealogies of Virginia Families: From The Virginia Magazine of History and Biography* (Baltimore: Genealogical Publishing Co., Inc., 1981), Vol. I, pp. 70 and 74.**

****See *Virginia Land Records: From The Virginia Magazine of History and Biography, the William and Mary College Quarterly, and Tyler's Quarterly* (Baltimore: Genealogical Publishing Co., Inc., 1982), pp. 504-509.**

trait was formerly ("and may be now") at Coleshill, Berkshire, the seat of the Earl of Rodnor. Lady Mildmay had another portrait, and at Mark's Hall, Essex, was still another. Her daughter, Katherine, married, first, William Fleete, who died between 1584 and 1586. William and Katherine Fleete had issue: I. Robert; II. William, married Deborah Scott; III. Priscilla, married John Seaman, Doctor of Laws; IV. Mary, married George Stroode, of Dorsetshire; V. Katherine, married John Parkhurst, gent.; VI. Mary; VII. Ann; VIII. John; IX. Thomas; X. Margaret, married Francis Tooke, of Goddington, Kent; XI. Joice, married John Roberts, of Hertford. William and Deborah Fleete had issue: I. Charles; II. George; III. Thomas; IV. Katherine; V. Elizabeth; VI. William; VII. Henry [who came to Virginia]; VIII. Brian; IX. Francis; X. Daughter; XI. Edward; XII. Elizabeth. Francis and Margaret (Fleete) Tooke had issue: John, Richard, Anthony, Nicholas, Mary and Francis. Mrs. Katherine (Honeywood) Fleete married, secondly, William Henmarsh, and had a daughter, Jane, who married Richard Willis, of Cambridgeshire, and had issue: Thomas, Richard, William and Elizabeth. (Thomas Willis, of Lancaster county, Va., the same county in which Henry Fleet lived, may have been the Thomas just named.) Colonel (afterwards Sir) Philip Honeywood, who came to Virginia in 1649 on the downfall of the Royal cause, was a nephew of Mrs. Katherine Fleet.

(38) John Carter. See this Magazine, II, 235-38; IV, 364-5. To these notes may be added that Major John Carter was present as a justice of Lancaster August 6, 1657, and that in 1653 he was resident in Lancaster. Lancaster, February 6, 1655, mention in the records of the estate of Captain Brocas, deceased, and that Major John Carter had married his widow. On October 27, 1658, November 30, 1659, and November 15, 1660, Colonel John Carter's wages as burgess for Lancaster were paid out of the county levy.

(39) "Row. Lawson." See this Magazine, IV, 201-3, 313-4.*

(40) "Mr. Thomas Carter." There is recorded in Lancaster a deed dated January 14, 1656, from Thomas Carter, of Lancaster, planter, conveying land. Captain Thomas Carter was a justice of Lancaster, 1663, &c. There is on record in Lancas-

---

See** ***Virginia Land Records: From The Virginia Magazine of History and Biography, the William and Mary College Quarterly, and Tyler's Quarterly **(Baltimore: Genealogical Publishing Co., Inc., 1982), pp. 610-614.**

ter, dated December 6, 1674, from Edward Dale of Lancaster, gent., and Diana, his wife, "in consideration of a marriage already had," between Thomas Carter and Katherine, daughter of the said Dale; and Dale, in his will, dated August 4, 1694, names his grandsons, Peter, Edward and Joseph Carter, and his granddaughters, Elizabeth and Katherine Carter. The will of Thomas Carter, Sr., was dated August 16th, and proved in Lancaster November 14, 1700. His legatees were his sons, Edward, John, James and Henry ("now in England"), and wife, Katherine; mentions "my son-in-law's grandfather-in-law, Edward Dale." [Edward Dale, as the grandfather of Thomas Carter's daughter, would be grandfather-in-law to her husband.] "If the said Wm. George [?] shall not be accountable for it, he shall have noe part of my estate; but only one shilling in full of his wife's portion;" son, Thomas Carter, executor. (As no provision is made for Thomas Carter by the will, it is probable that the sons named in Dale's will, Peter and Joseph, were alive, and had also been given their share in the estate.) Thomas Carter was a justice of Lancaster 1706, Henry Carter in 1728, and Joseph Carter in 1729. The will of Peter Carter was proved in Lancaster October 11, 1721. There is of record in Lancaster a deed dated May 23, 1749, from John Carter and Mary, his wife, of Stafford county, conveying to James Gordon, of Lancaster, five acres on the Corotoman River, Lancaster, part of a tract which Henry Carter, by his will, dated 1732, left to his son, Gany Carter, who dying intestate, his eldest brother, the said John Carter, succeeded. Also a deed in Lancaster, April, 1778, from Rawleigh Carter, of Amelia county, conveying to Edward Carter, of Lancaster, eighty acres in that county. It is believed that the records of Lancaster contain much more information in regard to this family. So far as the records show, Thomas Carter and Colonel John Carter, of Corotoman, were not related.

(41) John Baylor. If this was the ancestor of the well known Virginia family of the name, he must have returned to England, for the family account (which seems to be based on documentary evidence) states that John Baylor, the earliest of the name, who has been home, came to Virginia in extreme old age, with his son, John, who was born in 1650. It is expected that a genealogy of the Baylor family will be published in this Magazine.

(42) "Mr. Thomas Brice." Thomas Brice was justice of Lancaster, 1652; in August of that year the court sat at his house. The will of Thomas Bries, of Rappahannock, in Virginia, gent., was dated April 24th, and proved May 19, 1657. He gave his wife his whole estate in Virginia and England. On May 19th, Lancaster Court made an order in regard to the estate in favor of Martha, widow of Major Thomas Bries, and on the same day was recorded a marriage contract between her and William White. There is mention in the Lancaster records, December, 1657, of Mr. William White, clerk, and his wife, Martha. The will of William White was dated January 25th, and proved February 12, 1678, in Lancaster. His legatees were his sons, John, William and Edward, daughter, Deborah, and daughter-in-law [step-daughter ?], Mary Alford. In a deed in Lancaster, dated March 3, 1660, it is stated that the land given Martha, widow of William White, clerk, by her former husband, Thomas Brice, was given by the said Martha (who died during her widowhood) to the son and daughter of said White, and by order of the Governor and Council, this land was ordered to be sold to Jeffreys and Colclough; and notice thereof being given to Mr. John Jeffreys and Mr. Thomas Colclough and to Mr. Jeremiah White and Mr. George Hewit, guardians of the said White children, it was sold to Lieutenant-Colonel Edward Carter, of Nansemond county, for £330 sterling. An entry in the General Court records states that the quantity of land given by Mrs. Martha White was 1,650 acres, and that it was sold to Colonel Carter in 1665. There was recorded in York in 1658 the will of Martha, widow of Rev. William White, of York Parish. Her legatees were her (or his) children, Jeremiah and Mary, who were then living in London, and Rev. Jeremiah White was one of their guardians. Therefore, the William White, an abstract of whose will has been given, could not have been the Rev. William White.

(43) "Capt. Hacke." Dr. George Hacke married Anna, sister of Augustine Herman, the founder of Bohemia Manor, in Delaware (she was a native of Amsterdam, Holland), and came to Virginia, settling first in Northampton county, where he received a grant of 400 acres of land July 1, 1653. On March 28th of that year, "Doc[r] George Hacke, Practicon[r] in Physicke,

a high German (both by parents and birth), born in ye Citty of Collyne [Cologne], under the Palatinate," was naturalized. According to a deposition in 1661, he was then aged thirty-eight. He had a grant of land in Northumberland in 1652. In 1663 he and his wife and children were naturalized in Maryland. In 1666 the Maryland Assembly passed an act natura izing Anna Hacke, born at Amsterdam, and her sons, George and Peter, born at Accomacke, in Virginia, but who had removed to Maryland. On March 22, 1666, Ann, George Nicholas and Peter Hacke, the widow and sons of Dr. George Hacke, deceased, received a regrant of 1,000 acres in Northampton county, Va., which he had patented, but which at his death had escheated, as he was an alien. No doubt Dr. Hack was the "Captain Hacke" who was in Lancaster in 1654. He had issue: I. George Nicholas; II. Peter. The destruction of many of the records of Northumberland county renders it difficult to compile an account of the family. George Nicholas Hacke married Ann Wright, then a minor, daughter of Mr. Richard Wright, who, with Nicholas Spencer, Esq., had patented 1,100 acres on the Potomac river, September 25, 1661, which by survivorship came to Spencer, who, by deed, September 6, 1665, gave it to his niece, Ann Wright. Hacke got a regrant in 1690 (*Northern Neck Land Books*). Nothing appears in the extant records of Northumberland in regard to George N. Hacke or his descendants. He probably lived in another county. His brother, Peter Hack, was appointed ranger-general of the Northern Neck in 1690. In 1699, as Captain Peter Hack, he was a justice of Northumberland, and in 1700 was one of the executors of Captain Spencer Mottram. His pay as a member of the House of Burgesses for Northumberland is included in the county levy December 3, 1706. At this time or a little later, he became a colonel of the Northumberland militia. His wife is spoken of in the records as "Madame Mary Hacke," but her surname does not appear. She was dead before 1706. On January 17, 1727, Peter Hack, of Northumberland, conveyed to his son, John Hack, the land he had bought from Colonel St. Leger Codd. Colonel Hack had also a daughter, Ann, born 1697, died August 28, 1747, "greatly lamented, being a gentlewoman of amiable character" (*Gordon Bible*, quoted by Hayden), who married Colonel Edwin Conway, of Lancaster county, and a son, whose name does not appear. The will of John Hack (who married Elizabeth Kirk—marriage bond in Lancaster, dated February 13, 1718–9) was dated November 2, 1742, and proved in Northumberland May 15, 1747. His legatees were wife, Elizabeth, nephew, Peter Spencer Hack, nephew, Tunstall Hack; gives certain land, after the death of his wife, to George Nicholas Severn Waters; legacy to George Waters. There is recorded in Northumberland a deed dated May 22, 1749, from Peter Spencer Hack, of Somerset county, Md., leasing land in Northumberland. Also deed, July 3, 1753, from Peter Spencer Hack, of Northumberland; and another, January 13, 1755, from Peter Spencer Hack and Mary Anne, his wife, of Northumberland, to their daughters, Mary and Elizabeth Hack. The will of Tunstall Hack (who was probably the Tunstall Hack, of Maryland, whose marriage bond, dated April 22, 1746, to Hannah, daughter of Colonel Edwin Conway, is on file in Lancaster) was dated August 29th, and proved September 12, 1757. His legatees were Ann, daughter of Colonel James Gordon, of Lancaster; ———, son of Captain George Conway, of Lancaster; brother Spencer Hack's children; Sarah Conway McAdden, daughter of Joseph McAdden; Dr. Joseph McAdden; brother Spencer Hack's son, Peter John Tunstall Hack; directs that a tombstone be put over him (the testator), and that the burying-place of the family of Hacks be inclosed with a brick wall. Gives his wife and son, John Tunstall Hack, his whole estate, including his lands in Northumberland and the Eastern Shore.

(44) Thomas Powell. "Mr. Thomas Powell" was a justice of Lancaster 1659–69. On October 2, 1664, he made a deed on account of the love and affection he bore "Mrs. Jane Catesby, whom I intend suddenly to marry," giving her as a jointure £200 sterling and one-third of the land on the north side of Rappahannock, where he lived, containing 500 acres. There is also a deed dated October 15, 1665, from Thomas Powell, of Lancaster, and his wife, Jane, to their son, Thomas. The will of Thomas Powell, dated January 19th and proved March, 1669, is on file at Lancaster court-house. He leaves his son, Rawley (or Rowley) Powell, his whole estate; son, Thomas Powell, and cousin, John Gibson, executors. The will of Rawley Powell, of

Lancaster, was dated October 9th, and proved March 9, 1686; legatees: father-in-law John Kerly, sister Ann Dacres, brother Thomas Kerly, Nathaniel Norton, and goddaughter Ann Mason. Colonel William Loyd, of North Farnham Parish, Rappahannock county, obtained a regrant in 1690 of 300 acres in Lancaster, formerly belonging to Mr. Thomas Powell, and by the will of Rawley Powell, his son, bequeathed to Mrs. Ann Dacres alias Tomlin for her life, and then to the said Loyd.

(45) "Mr. Edwards." Lancaster Court, in May, 1657, granted John Edwards a land certificate for the importation of his children, John and Mary Edwards. Thomas Rootes, of Lancaster, "chirurgeon," in his will, January 25, 1660, makes a bequest to his godson, Thomas, son of John Edwards, "chirurgeon." In November, 1664, there was a suit in Lancaster by Mrs. Bathseea Pee *vs.* her brother-in-law, Mr. John Edwards. A deed from John Edwards, chirurgeon, dated December 7, 1658, is recorded in Lancaster. The original will of John Edwards is on file in Lancaster; he requests William Ball to take his estate in charge, make sale of the land, servants, negroes and other personal property, and also his share in the ship, Susan, and make returns to the testator's friend, Mr. Spencer Pigott, in Duke's Place, London; his estate is to be equally divided between his wife and those children whom he left behind in England; Spencer Pigott executor; dated February 3d, and proved in Lancaster March, 1667. The seal bears arms: *a fesse indented, between three martlets;* Crest: *on an esquire's helmet* (what is probably) *a horse rampant.* The seal is somewhat defaced.

John Edwards, the surgeon, appears to have once lived on the Eastern Shore. There is on record in Northampton the petition of John Edwards, dated March 1, 1652, in which he states that he is the son of Mrs. Katherine Hunlocke, and is authorized by her to call to account Mr. John Edwards, chirurgeon, administrator of Stephen Taylor, deceased. The petition states that he is a stranger in the country, his residence being on the Bay [perhaps in Lancaster], and his sole business in Northampton being concerning the estate of Mr. Stephen Taylor, who married his sister. The court ordered that John Edwards, chirurgeon, make his appearance at the next court, and if the sheriff could not arrest him it should be sufficient to leave the notice at his house.

Copies of several letters were recorded in Northampton as evidence in this case. On August 1, 1649, Katherine Hunlocke wrote from London to her "Dearest Daughter" [Mrs. Taylor], in Northampton; mentions daughter's husband—"I understand your brother is well beloved in ye Countrye." In another letter to "Daughter Margaret," she states that she sends her servants, wearing apparel, &c.—"I heare your husband is an honest man and gave a great price for you." [Mrs. Taylor had evidently been an indentured servant.] Again, in September, 1652, from London to her "Lovinge Sonne," tells him that his brother, John, and sister Stockdell and her husband are well, but his father-in-law [step-father?] died about sixteen weeks before. "You will be out of your time next Spring;" refers to "your master" and "your sister's estate." There is no one else of his kindred in Virginia to inherit it but himself; she had sent his sister goods to the value of £100, and also sent a servant to release him; she was at present in London on business; his sister (another) still lived on Bishopgate Street, London.

[Notes to be concluded in next number.]

NOTES.

(46) Thos. Hopkins. There is recorded in the books of old Rappahannock Co., a deed dated Nov. 2d, 1686, from Christopher Wormeley, Esq., to Malachy Peale, of Stafford Co.; for land granted to Thos. Hopkins in 1654; escheated and granted to Thos. Hopkins Hone, Gent.; by him made over to Justinian Aylmer, and by Aylmer given to his wife Frances, who, when the deed was made was the wife of Christopher Wormeley. He was a justice of Northumberland, 1655. A record in Northumberland, June 19, 1672, states that Mr. John Cossens had married the relict of Mr. Thos. Hopkins.

(47) Thos. Roots. There is a power of attorney, dated May 5, 1654, and recorded in Lancaster, from Nicholas Haile, of York Co., planter, to his friend Thos. Roots, of Va., surgeon; and another of same date, from same, to Thos. Roots, of Lancaster Co., surgeon. A marriage contract, dated Oct. 14, 1653, and recorded in Lancaster between Thos. Rootes, chirurgeon, and Francis Attawell, daughter of Margaret Grymes, widow. The will of Thos. Roots was dated Jan. 25, and proved in Lancaster, March 14, 1660; legatees: to Mr. Thos. Marshall, a man servant, &c.; to godson, Thos. Roten [Raughton, or Wraughter], a maid servant, &c.; to "my sister Roten;"—Samuel Tucker—to Elizabeth Robinson, two cows for the use of her two children, Elizabeth and Robert Dudley; to sister Anne White; to godson, Thomas Edwards, son of John Edwards, chirurgeon.

(48) "Widow Grimes." There is recorded in Lancaster a release deed, dated Nov., 1653, from Cuthbert Potter, attorney of Capt. Daniel Huse, to Margaret, widow of Edward Grymes. There is also in Lancaster a marriage contract, dated March 16, 1652, and recorded Feb 10, 1653, between Samuel Gooch and Mary, daughter of Thos. Attawell, dec'd, and his wife Margaret, who had afterwards been the wife of Edward Grymes, deceased. The will of Edward Grymes, of Lancaster, was dated Aug. 1, 1653, and proved Feb. 10, 1653 [4?]; legatees: wife Margaret,

daughter-in-law Frances Attawell; Wm. Wraten, Anne White and Mary Gooch. Lancaster court was held at "the house of the widow Grymes," Oct., 1655. The will of Margaret Grymes, of Lancaster, widow, was dated Feb'y 18, 1658, and proved March 30, 1659, "long afflicted and visited under the hand of the Almighty;" legatees: "son Wm. Raughton;" Thomas, son of Wm. Raughton, daughter Ann White, son-in-law Wm. White; Will White, the younger, daughter Frances Rootes, "son Wroughton." There is recorded in Northumberland, Feb., 1655, the deposition of a Richard Grymes, aged 34 years.

(49) Edw'd Dudley. Rev. Thos. Sax, of Lancaster, in his will dated April, 1654, makes bequests to Richard, second son of Edward Dudley. Edw'd Dudley was witness to a deed in York county in 1651. It is probable that he was the father of Wm. Dudley, of Middlesex, and Richard Dudley, of Gloucester, from whom most of the name in Virginia and the West appear to descend.

(50) John Merriman. There is recorded in Lancaster, a deed dated Nov. 10, 1680, from Wm. Merriman, of Lancaster, planter, eldest son of John Merriman of the same county, dec'd; Charles M. of same, wheelwright, youngest son of said John M., and Edward Carter of same, planter, and Audrie his wife, late the widow of said John M.; conveying to Lt.-Col. Jno. Carter, gent., and Captain David Fox, of same, gent., for the use of the county, to establish a town, 50 acres, part of a patent dated Nov. 14, 1649, to said John M., deceased. Others of the name in the county were Wm. Merryman, chosen a churchwarden for the parish on the north side of the river, April 1st, 1657; Richard Merriman, of Lancaster, gent., who in behalf of Mr. Thos. Kelland, and Mr. Anthony Haywood, "residing in the town of Boston, in New England," made a deed, dated May 11, 1681, and recorded in Middlesex, to Mr. Richard Perrott, of the county of Middlesex, Va. His wife Susanna joins in a deed in 1665. The will of Rich'd Merriman was proved in Lancaster, June 10, 1696; legatees: son and daughter William and Susanna Payne, grandsons Wm. Payne, Jr., and Richard Payne. A John Merryman was a magistrate of Anne Arundel county, Maryland, in 1650.

(51) John Payne. There appear to have been several families named Payne or Paine, who settled in the Northern Neck in the

latter half of the 17th century. A deed from John Payne, Sr., to his son Richard, was dated Nov. 9, 1656, and proved in Lancaster. A deed from Henry Thacker, Middlesex, dates April 7, 1690, recites that John Paine, Sr., late of Rappahannock co., gave a certain tract of land to his daughter Anne Paine (wife of his son Jno. P., Jr.), for her life, and then to her child, whose birth was expected. This child was named Elizabeth, and was wife of said Thacker. A record in Lancaster, September 28, 1659, states that Richard Robinson was the nearest kinsman of Mr. John Payne, deceased. There is recorded in Lancaster, a deposition dated Jan. 6, 1659, from John Paine, aged 44 years; his wife was named Margaret. This Paine lived in Lancaster in 1654. Robert Payne and Elizabeth his wife, lived in Rappahannock county, in 1670. The will of Richard Paine (evidently a son of Wm. and Susanna P., named in the will of Wm. Merryman, above), was dated April 4, 1709, and proved Lancaster, August 9, 1709; legatees: brothers Wm., John and George Paine, mother Susanna Lardner, sisters Susannah, Margaret and Katherine Paine; brother Wm. Paine executor. The will of Wm. Payne (the brother), dated August 27, and proved, Lancaster, September 14, 1726; legatees: wife Judith, son Merryman Payne, son Wm., daughter Susanna Payne, daughter-in-law Katherine, wife of Mr. Mark Bannerman; brothers John and George Payne, brother Robert Mitchell; mother Susanna Lardner; sisters. Apparently there was a different family of the name in Westmoreland. The will of John Paine, Cople parish, Westmoreland, dated October 9, 1668, proved Westmoreland, 1668 or 69; legatees: sons John and James; daughter Elizabeth; wife Milicent. Will of Wm. Paine, dated January 31, 1697–8, proved Westmoreland, February 23, 1697–8, legatees: wife; sons Wm. and Edward; eldest daughter Anne, by a former marriage; daughters Betty and Mary. For additional information in regard to Payne, see Hayden's *Va. Genealogies.*

(52) Mr. William Clapham, Sr. His son, William Clapham, Jr., was elected church warden for the north side of Lancaster Parish, April 1, 1652.

(53) John Meredith was a shipwright in Lancaster county.

(54) "Mr. Conway." Edwin Conway, for an account of whose family see Hayden's "*Virginia Genealogies.*" The following additions are from the county records: Deed of gift from

Lady Agatha Chicheley of a brown calf called Thacker, to Eltonhead, daughter of Edwin Conway, dated May 7. and recorded in Lancaster August 6, 1653. Edwin Conway's receipt to Mrs. Eleanor Bidos for one heifer, given "by the appointm't of my sister ffenwicke in ye time of her widowhood to my daughter Eltonhead, as a gift from her Aunt ffenwicke," dated 15th May, 1653, recorded August 10, 1653; witnesses Sir Henry Chicheley and Cuthbert Potter. Letter from Edwin Conway, June 10, 1654, "from my house at the head of Corotoman," to Mr. Toby Smith. States that Elias Edmonds, by will, left him (Conway) overseer of his children, and that John Meredith had opposed his holding the position on pretence that he was a Papist, and ought not to have the bringing up of children, "which God knows was not my intent, but some honest, careful man should bring them up," and not diminish the estate, "which I am sure is a good Virginia estate." Edwin Conway could hardly have been a Catholic, as he had before been clerk of Accomac. Deed, Lancaster, May 7, 1653, from Lady Agatha Chicheley, "for the consideration of ye love and affection I have unto my neece, ye daughter of Edwin Conway," gives to said Eltonhead one cow, with reversion to Martha Conway, sister of Eltonhead. On August 10, 1653, there were recorded in Lancaster for Mr. Edwin Conway the cattle marks of Edwin Conway, Edwin Conway, Jr., and Eltonhead Conway.

(55) Mr. David Fox.

(56) Mr. Travers.

(57) Toby Smith. Moore Fauntleroy made an assignment, dated October 24, 1651, and recorded in Lancaster, to his brother-in-law, Toby Smith, gent., and his heirs by his marriage with Phœbe his wife. Mr. Toby Smith was a justice of Lancaster 1652, 1653. There was recorded in Lancaster in 1653 a deed of gift, dated September 29, 1647, from Toby Smith, of "Nansemum," to his children, Toby and Phœbe, in consideration of the love he bears to Moore Fauntleroy, "of Roye's rest, his brother-in-law, in ye Nansemum, aforesaid, gent." In a deed, Mrs. Phœbe Smith calls Moore Fauntleroy "brother." Toby Smith patented land in Lancaster May 7, 1655. When Rappahannock was formed he was appointed by the General Assembly

of Virginia, December 11, 1656, one of the justices (and of the quorum), and colonel of militia in the new county. His daughter Phœbe married (1) William Hodskin, who died 1673; (2) William Slaughter. Phœbe Slaughter, daughter of the last marriage, married (1) William Peachey; (2) Rev. Lewis Latané. Colonel Toby Smith also left a son, Henry. In a deed, recorded in Lancaster and dated 1653, Mrs. Phœbe Smith acknowledged that certain cattle, deeded to her by her husband, were in exchange for land on Mulberry Island, made over to feoffees for her and her children, with her own and her brother Moore Fauntleroy's consent. Toby Smith, Burgess, Warwick River, March, 1642–3; for Nansemond, October, 1649.

(58) Capt. Fauntleroy. An account of the Fauntleroy family, not complete however, was printed in "Wallace's Weekly," now altogether out of print.

(59) "Mr. Griffin," was probably Thomas Griffin, who had grants of land as early as 1651. For an account of his descendants, who resided in Richmond county, York, Williamsburg, &c., and included Judge Cyrus Griffin, last President of the Continental Congress, see *Virginia Historical Magazine*, I, 254, &c. There is on record in Lancaster a deed dated Sept. 22, 1653, from Moore Fauntleroy to Leroy Griffin, son of Thos. Griffin, of Lancaster Co., conveying 300 acres of land.

(60) James Williamson was a justice of Lancaster from Jan., 1652. On Dec. 8, 1656, is a statement in the records of Lancaster that Mr. James Williamson, late of that county, died intestate, and administration was granted, in behalf of the orphans, to Mr. Wm. Underwood, who was uncle to said orphans, on the mother's side. (See *Virginia Historical Magazine*, III, 66.)* James Williamson appears to have left only daughters—see Hayden's "*Virginia Genealogies;*" but Richard Williamson lived in Middlesex, 1697; Andrew Williamson died in Middlesex, 1682 (where will was proved), leaving sons Augustine and Andrew; Thos. Williamson and Mary, his wife, late Mary Dudley, widow, lived in Middlesex in 1695. Mr. Henry Williamson and his wife Catherine, daughter of Abraham Weekes, lived in Middlesex, 1688, &c.

(61) A note on the Gower family will appear in a later Magazine.

---

*See ***Virginia Land Records: From The Virginia Magazine of History and Biography, the William and Mary College Quarterly, and Tyler's Quarterly*** **(Baltimore: Genealogical Publishing Co., Inc., 1982), p. 563.**

(62) Mr. Bradshaw. The will of John Bradshawe, was dated July 12, 1655, and proved in Lancaster, March 23, 1656, desired to be buried between his two daughters, in his brother's orchard; gives wife Temperence 345 acres; Wm. Hill 60 acres; if wife died without issue, the land left her to go to the first child of his brother Robert, "and soe to go from generation to generation to the name of the Bradshawes, springing from their Loynes & never to be sold or mortgaged." His brother to have his books. Legacies to Winifred and Thomas Griffin, children of "my countryman" Thomas Griffin ["countryman" in the sense here used, generally meant a person from the same county, so it is probable that Robert Bradshaw and Thomas Griffin came from the same county in England—Cheshire perhaps.] Brother Robt. Bradshawe and neighbor Anthony Linton, executors. The will of Robert Bradshaw was proved in Northumberland, probably about 1660; but the record book is so mutiliated that only the names of his wife Anne and daughter Anne can be made out. There is a deed in Northumberland, Dec. 7, 1707, from Wm. Lambert and Anne his wife for certain land granted to Robert Bradshaw in 1651, and by him left to his daughter, the said Ann.

(63) George Taylor was a justice of Lancaster from January, 1, 1652. Captain Rich'd Taylor was a justice of Lancaster, 1674–80. Robert Taylor a vestryman of Lancaster parish, 1657. Administrator on the estate of Capt. Richard Taylor, deceased, of Lancaster, was granted to his widow Mary on April 11, 1683. This George Taylor was probably the Captain George Taylor who was a justice of Richmond county at its foundation in 1692, and Burgess 1699, 1701 (when styled Col. Geo. Taylor).

(64) Mr. Weir. There is recorded in Richmond county a deed dated July 7, 1697, from Elizabeth Gardner, widow, of St. Mary's county, Maryland, daughter and heiress of John Weire, late of Rappahannock county, Va., deceased, conveying 2,502 acres in Richmond county, which was granted to Jno. Weire, June 6, 1666. In 1666 Major Jno. Weire had three grants of land, aggregating 6,570 acres. He was Burgess for Rappahannock, March, 1658–9.

W. G. Stanard.

(concluded.)

TITHEABLES, LANCASTER COUNTY VIRGINIA, COURT OF DECEMBER 1696, COURT ORDER BOOK 1696 TO 1702 PAGE 7.

Contributed by A. A. WAYNE

Mr. Thomas Sampson	5	Samuell Parr	7
John Flower	1	John Payne	3
Thomas Prefitt	1	John Lowry	3
William Mitchell	3	Richard Ball	3
Wm' Rogers	1	Mrs. Margret Ball	4
James Stanton	2	Mary Merriman	1
James Dagon	1	Nich. George, Sen.r	1
Francis Frissell	2	Mr. Wm! Ball	8
Mr. George Heale	12	John Roach	1
John Cooke	1	Wm! Abbey	1
Cordear Davis	1	Rich.d Abbey	1
Wm! West	1	John Buckston	1
Richard North	1	John Bush	1
Mr. Thilman	4	Tho. Stafford	1
John Browne	1	Henry Stoneham, Sen.r	3
Thomas Smith	1	Marmaduke Sanders	1
Joseph Hollard	1	Tho. Cotton	1
John Reeves	3	Mathew Brookes	1
Abraham Taylor	2	Oloa Christian	1
Thomas Chetwood	4	Thomas Taylor	1
John Harris	2	Mr. Tho. Chatwyne	4
William Wormells	1	John Mare	1
Ambrose Barefoot	1	John Luckham	1
Noah Rogers	2	Wm. Dawson	1
William Newsum	1	John Coates	1
Francis Towers	1	Giles Robinson, Sen.r	4
Joseph Harrison	3	John Leatham	1
James Wood	2	Mr. Hugh Ladner	3

Jno. Mott, Sen.r	3	Wm. Lewys	1
Job. Hill	1	Blazen Vanaver	1
Rich.d Wood	2	Jno. Serjant	1
Rich.d Alderson	3	Mr. Wm. Mann	7
Randolph Miller	3	Jno. Farmer	1
Rob.t Pollard	2	Jon. Barles	1
Darbe Dunaway	1	Jno. Stritchley	1
Ricee Thomas	1	Capt. Nusum	6
Wm. Cornelius	1	Rich.d Flint	3
Edw.d Tomlyn	1	At. Mrs. Price's	1
George Finch	1	Josias Draper	2
Wm. Goodridge	2	Robert Mitchell	1
Stephen Tomlyn	8	Jno. Wells, Jun.r	1
Mr. Jackson	5	Tho. Wells	1
Wm. Wood	1	Tho. Everet	1
Wm. Lax	1	Jno. Flowers	1
Timothy Stamps	2	Rich.d Davis	1
Edward Cox	1	Oswald Whaley	3
Mr. Wm. Rogers	2	Tho. Davis	3
Nath l Carpenter	1	James Phillips	6
Henery Pullen	1	Mr. Tho. Marlyn	8
Rich.d Loyd	1	Tho. Lee	3
Jno. Pitman	1	Capt. David Fox	21
Nath. Clark	1	Jno. Gibson	3
Wm. Stott	2	Wm. King	1
James Stott	1	Mr. Wm. Lawrence	1
Jno. Tayntor	1	Tho. Blanch	1
Joseph Clayton	2	Nich. George, Sen.r	1
Brian Stott, Jun.r	2	Wm. George	1
Jno. Ball	3	Elmore George	1
Nich. Hoskins	1	Robt. Hopkins	1
Capt. Jos. Ball	15	Jno. Pinchard	2
Wm. Lawrence	1	Jno. Boateman	1
Jno. Sharpe	2	Henery Boateman	1
Daniell Armes	3	David Mazey	1
Wm. Richardson	1	Peter Butler	5
Wm. Paine	3	Mr. Tho. Carter	5
Mr. John Bertrand	4	Jno. Flowers	1
James Paull	3	At Jno. Semans	1
James Camell	3	Jno. Wright, pl.e	1
Tho. Harwood	1	Step. Chilton	5
Wm. Bings	2	Benj. Dogget	1
Tho. Barker, Sen.r	6	Jno. Mullis	3
Mr. Edw.d Carter	2	Tho. Buckley	2

Tho. Chilton	3
Wm. Heard	3
George Harwood	5
Wm. Simons	1
Sam.ll Wright*	3
Jno. Moore	1
Tho. Barton	2
Capt. Rich.d Willis	7
Mr. Row. Lawson, Sen.r & Jr.	8
Mr. Mott. Wright	18
Jno. Bruce	1
Tobias Pursell	4
Jno. Hart	1
Mich. Dymer	6
Jno. Emberson	1
Tho, Prison	1
Clem.t Shevile	1
Tho. Baker	4
Jno. Davis	2
Percevell Simson	1
Edw.d Richardson	1
James Storey	2
Robert Scholfield	4
Hugh Brent	3
George Flowers	4
Jno. Adams	2
Robert Horton	1
Tho. Price	1
Benj. Wale	1
Jno. Wale	1
Maj.r Wm. Taylor	7
Wm. Shorcraft	1
Nich. Wren	2
Wm. Short	1
Wm. Janeway	1
Jno. Bradley, Sen.r	2
Jno. Dabbs	1
Mr. Jackson	7
Jno. Smallwood	1
Tho. Yerby	1
Robt. Denham	1
Fortunat.s Sidnor	1
Wm. Brush	1
Jno. Leather	1
Rich.d Harrold	1
Tho. Ball	1
Tho. Grigg	1
Francis Hadway	1
Wm. Wren	1
Jno. Chilton	3
Maj.r Ro. Bristow	18
Edw.d Gibson	10
Jerome Paskyt	3
Jno. Hutchins	2
Tho. Thompson	1
Robt. Bennett	2
Peter Kilgore	2
Rich.d Stephens	2
Jno. Lehore	1
Nath. Hedgeman, Sen.r	2
Capt. Alex Swan	9
Jno. Bryan	1
Jno. Bond	1
Wm. Nash, Sen.r	2
Abraham Loe	1
Jno. Davis	1
Jno. England	1
Jno. Wright	2
Wm. Edmonds	3
Tho. Harding	1
David Dickey	1
Wm. Morgan	1
George Horne	1
Wm. Garton	3
Christ.r Kirck	1
Capt. Lister	9
Mr. Robt. Carter	61
Mrs. Eliz. Pinchard	14
Jno. Sibley	1
at Michaell Cartridge	3
Charles Kelly	2
Tho. Winslow	1
Nich. Lissum	1
Wm. Hartland	2
The Widd. Carroll	1
Roger Kelley	1
Wm. Waller	2
Uriah Angell	5

Edw.d Walder	2	Rich.d Porter	2
Jno. Crouch	3	Roger Willis	2
Charles Sallard	2	Jno Kelley	2
Tho. Cox	1		—
James Haynes Smith	3	Total	669
Mr. Henr. Fleet	4		

TITHABLES IN LANCASTER CO., 1716.

Att a Court held for Lancaster County, the 14th day of November Anno Dom: 1716.

Present

Capt Henry ffleett	Mr Thomas Carter
Mr John Turberville	Richard Chichester Esqr Justices
Major William Ball,	Capt. George Heale
Mr Thomas Lee	

The County of Lancaster being indebted the sum of six thousand pounds of tobacco do order that a levy of five pounds and three quarters of a pound of tobacco by the poll be collected by Capt Richard Ball Sheriff of this County off and from every tithable person in this County and that he pay the same to the severall Creditors hereafter named, viz

To the Hon^r^ble Robert Carter Esq. for keeping the ferry	1400
To Mrs. Barbara Tayloe	1000
To Wm Dare att^r^ny for the King	1000
To Mrs Martha Howard for water, candles, and cleaning the Court House	800
To the Sheriff for extraordinary service	500
To Mr John Turberville for Coroners Enquiry	133

To Mr Thomas Lee for one levy last year	36
To ditto for one in Anno 1714	31
To the Sheriff for 3 days attendance in each parish 200 ℔ day	1200
	6100

Pr Contra Cr.

By 1065 Tithables at 5¾ ℔ poll is	6100

Christ Church List of Tithables

Mr. Rowland Lawson's List

Robert Scholfield 1
John Hutchins 3
Cap: Hen ffleet 8
Jno Smallwood 2
Mr Tho Lee 8
Charles Kelly 3
Wm Moore 2
John Sage 2
Christop^r Kirk Jr 4
Thos Kirk 2
Tho Hubert 2
Lilia King 3
Elias Edmunds 6
Tho Carter 2
Robt Carter Esq. 126
Wm Nash 4
Tho Mason
At. Edw. Angell 1
Tho Percivall 3
William Lawrence 2
Jos. Gregory 2
Henry Shelton 4
Wm Oliver 3
Robt Kirk 1
Mch^l George 3
M^r. Pasquet 1

Mr John Grayson's List

John Johnson 3
Geo ffluven 5
Mr Hugh Brent, deced 6
Jno Wolfe 1
Jno Hudnall 2
Jno Grayson 3
Wm. Dymer 5
Patrick Conelly 3
Robt Horton 1
Jno Ackershaw 1
Hugh Brent 3
Rand McDough 1
Jno Claker 6
Ro^t Bristow, Esq. 15
Tho Yerby 6
Toby Horton 1

Grills Ackerman 2
Dennis Conner 1
Uriah Gorton 1
Jn° Gibson 3
Rob[t] Dennis 1
Tim Mahoan 2
Edw[d] Jackson 2

Totall of this List is 74.

Totall of Tithables in Christ Church Parish is 569.

Saint Maryes White Chappell Parish

List of Tithables.

Capt Richard Ball's List

Charles Ewell 7
Hen Stoneham 1
Wm Dodson 3
Jn° Alderton 3
Theoph Morgan 1
George ffinch 2
John Moll 5
Darby Dunaway 1
Dan[ll] Bryan 1
John Crosted 1
Wm Pittman 3
Jno Reeves 2
Wm Dodson 3
John Wilkinson 3
Wm Bertrand 6
Tho Carpenter 4
Edw[d] Jones 1
Peter Revier 1
Geo. Downton 2
Wm ffrizell 2
Wm Robertson 2
Wm Delaney 1
Darby Callahan 1
Jno Callahan 1
James Stott 2
Wm Bell 2
Hen ffleet jr. 4
Jn° Cox 2
Jn° Stanno 1
Chas. Christy jr 1
Charles Kelly Jr 1
George Home 1
Edw[d] Mager 3
Wm Brush 2
Tho Davis 2
Tho Nutall 2
Alt. Butler 1
Wm. Martin 5
Isaac Currell 5
Jn° Killgore 1
M[r] Jn° Turbervile 10
Rowland Cornelius 1
Dan[ll] M[c]Rey 2
Gawin More 1
James Plummer 2
Jn° Hewes 2
Jn° Hart 2
Murto Wood 1
Jn° Bell Clerk 4
Walter Heard 5

Wm Wood 2
Wm Norris 2
Charles Taylor 2
William ffleet 2
Henry Head 3
Symon Hickerson 2
John Nicholls 2
Henry Lawson 7
Rod Gibson 6
Jon Cox on y[e] hills 1
John Swan 9
Wm Norton 1
Tho Heanaugc 1
George Henry 1
Thomas Thompson 2
Hugh Kelly 1
Rob[t] Angell 1
Walter Heard 5

Doc[tr] Attkins Quarter 3
Epaph: Lawson 7
Patrick Mahone 1
Edw[d] Gibson 11
ffort: Sydnor 2
Nic[s] Martin 2
Francis Hattaway 3
John Hawkins jun[r] 1
M[rs] Mary Harwood 5
James Garton 1
Wm Brent 3
Rowld Lawson 8
Walter James 2
Tho Purcell 4
Ri. Chichester Esq 5
Wm Thompson 1
Leonard Knight 1

Totall of this List 201.

Mr Tho Carters List

Jn[o] Pinkard 4
Henry Carter 3
Sam[ll] Davis 1
Eliz George 2
Rich[d] Wallace 1
Rich[d] Porter 2
Hen Boatman 5
Wm, Doggett 2
Ralph Briggs 2
Frank Wright 1
D[r] Rawson 2
Jn[o] Lewis 1
Jn[o] Taylor 1
ffrancis Edward 3
Jos. Tayloe 6
Tho Pinton 2

Rich[d] Doggett 2
Edw[d] Carter 2
Jn[o] Mullis 2
Thomas White 1
Jno Davis 1
Rich[d] Stevens 10
Edw[d] Mekin 1
Jn[o] Wright 1
James Cene 1
James Burn 1
Gabriel Thatcher 1
Walter Pasquet 1
Benj: Doggett sen[r] 4
Jn[o] Kirk 2
Tho Chatwin 2
Rich[d] Cotton 1

Elenor George sen 3
Benja George 2
Stephen Chilton 3
Edwin Conway 13
Murto Noland 1
Richard Curtis 1
Benj. Doggell junr 2
Wm. Meredith 2
Mchll Tarkleson 1
Dumasery Pasquet 1
Jno ffindley
Jno Boatman 2
Eliz Parquet 6
Christophr Kirk 4
Peter Wood 2

James Mitchell 1
Natt Carpenter 1
Coll Corbin 19
Wm Chilton 1
ffran ffrizell 4
Tho Sherer 1
Giles Robertson 2
Robert Miller 1
Jnoo Sampson 2
David fflint 1
Pet Ja Bailey 1
Edwd Talbord 1
Richd Wooding 2
Richd Ball 12

Totall of this List is 114.

Capt George Heales List of Tithables

John Roach 2
Hugh Perry 1
Abra. Dale 2
Ed Tomlin 2
Bryan Puller 2
Jno Miller 3
Tho Thornton 2
Wm Jacobs 1
Jno Morris 1
Patrick Marks 1
John Pollard 3
Hen: Newby 2
Wm Samon 1
Bricum Phillips 2
Angus Alexandr 2
Jno Bailey 2
Richd Welch 2
Samll Bromley 1

Nicho Butler 2
James Whaley 4
John Heale 6
Jos Brosier 3
Peter Miller 2
Jno Voss 2
Wm Philips 2
Wm Clarkson 2
Richd Davis 2
Att Coll Carter's Quarter 6
Michll Gill 1
Widdow Rogers 5
Wm Matthews 2
William Miller 2
Roger McCarrell 1
Laz. Conway 6
George Lovett 1
Rawl: Chinn 12

David Jones 4
John Davis 2
James Ball 11
Jos. Ball 14
William Heale 3
Oswald Whaley 2
Wm Coates 2
Jno Taylor 3
James Robertson 1
Richd Cooper 1
Jno Stott 1
Wm Mitchell 2
Tho Wherton 2
John Doggin 1
Arch Robinson 2
Jos: Neale 6
Wm Rogers 4
James Strachan 2
John Brown 1
Wm ffox 25
Bryan Stott 1
Robt Mitchell 2
Jno Willcox 3
Jno Steward 1
John Jones 1
Madm ffox 23
Wm More 1
George Heale 8

Totall of this List is 228.

Majr William Balls List of Tithables

Richd fflint 4
Mrs Catlett 4
Noah Rogers 2
Tho: Lyne 2
Robert Neesome 1
Wm Ladner 4
John Grice 1
George Chewning 3
Wm Hewitt 1
Att Wido Chilton 1
John Pynes 4
Walter Armes 3
Josiah Mussell 1
James Bryan 1
Peter Carter 3
Raw Downman 4
Danll Burn 1
Geo. Light 2
Pat McCarry 1
Wm Chilton 1
Richd Price 1
Edwd Harris 2
Widd. Davenport 2
Wm Cornelius 2
Thomas Sharpe 2
Tho Cluttwood 1
Wm Dare 4
Arthur Clark 1
Wm Lewis 1
Darby Bryan 1
Jno Cornelius 1
Mino. Brady 1
Att Rob: Hopkins 1
Wm Payne 9
John Marshall 3
Mathias Rose 1
Tho: Harwood 1
Danll Gaines 1

James Campbell junr 2	Hen: Johnson 1
Tho: Merryman 4	Wm Wallis 1
Jno Holland 1	Tho Marshall 2
Jno ffarmer 1	R. Chichester 7
James Quick 1	George Wale 5
Owen Kelly 2	Jos. Carter 1
Cha. Mills 1	Jno Lowry 4
Jno Barber 1	Jno Brown 2
Hen Towles 3	John Holder 1
James Campbell 3	Tho: Ward 1
Charles Pasquet 1	Thos New's Quarter 5
Wm fford 1	Pat Smith 1
Christo Stevens 1	Wm Ball 22

Totall of this List is 154.

Totall of Tithables in St. Mary's White Chapel Parish is 496.

LUNENBURG COUNTY

Tithable list taken by William Caldwell in 1749. Contributed by W. S. Morton

Name	Tithables	Negroes
Abney, Dennet	1	
Abney, Dennet, Sr.	0	
Abney, George	1	
Abney, Abraham	1	
Alday, Perrin, (overseer)	1	2 negroes
Adams, Richard	1	
Adkins, Thomas	1	
Austin, Richard	1	
Austin, John	1	
Ayres, Aaron	1	
Anderson, James	2	2 negroes
Anderson, Wm.		
Bedford, Stephen	0	
Stunt, William (overseer)	1	2 negroes
Bouldin, Thomas	1	2 negroes
Bouldin, Christopher	1	
Baldwin, John	1	
Brumfield, William	1	
Brumfield, William		
Brumfield, James, Sr.	2	
Breedlove, James	1	
Bays, Joseph	1	
Brook, Charles	1	
Bynum, John		
Bynum, John, Junr.	2	
Major Booker's		
Watkins, Thomas, (overseer)		
Simmons, Jonathan	3	3 negroes
Cobb, Robert		
Cobb, Ambross	2	1 negro
Cobbs, John's		
Williams, James (overseer)	2	2 negroes
Cunningham, Thomas	1	
Cunningham, John	1	
Cunningham, William	1	
Cunningham, Andrew	1	
Chaney, Charles	1	
Childrey, Jeremiah	1	
Childrey, Robert	1	
Cartwright, John	1	
Canke, [?] George March	1	
Caldwell, William	1	1 negro
Caldwell, William	1	
Caldwell, John	1	
Caldwell, David	1	1 negro
Caldwell, James		
Caldwell, James, Jr.	2	
Cole, Major John, Dec.		
East, William (overseer)	1	10 negroes
Collins, Joseph	1	
Collins, James	1	
Crighton, Hugh	1	
Campbell, Archibald	1	
Denney, John	1	
Duvall, Samuel	1	
Dudgeon, Wm.	1	
Dudgeon, Richard		
Burn, Mitchell	2	
Davie, Samuel	1	
Daniel, James	1	
Dennis, Nathaniel	1	
Dickson, Josiah	1	
Dougherty, Thomas		
Siser, John		
Siser, William	3	
Duggens, Thomas	1	
Davis, Richard	1	
Dabbs, Ann	0	
Webb, James, (overseer)	1	5 negroes
Ewing, Chas.	1	
Ewing, Robert	1	
Emmanuel, David	1	
Easten, James	1	1 negro
Edwards, Thomas		
Edwards, Thomas, Junr.	2	
Edwards, William	1	
Evans, George		
Evans, John	2	
East, William's	0	1 negro
Echols, Joseph		
Echols, Isaac	2	
East, John	1	
East, John	1	
Frank, Nehemiah	1	
Forth, Daniel	1	
Fuqua, William		
Fuqua, John	2	7 negroes
Foregarty, Thomas	1	
Foster, George		
Foster, George, Junior	2	1 negro
Feris, Thomas	1	

Feris, Thomas	1	
Feris, Joseph	1	
Feris, William		
Feris, Charles	2	
Feris, James	1	
Franklin, Lewis		
Franklin, Edward	2	
Franklin, Edward		
Franklin, Thomas		
Wood, Thomas	3	2 negroes
Franklin, James	1	1 negro
Frances, James	1	
Grymes, Frances	1	
Griffeth, John	1	
Galloway, John	1	
Guin, David	1	3 negroes
Gwin, John	1	2 negroes
Gray, Edmund	0	
Guillingdon, John	1	
Hodge, James		
Hodge, Milcom	2	
Hodges, Thomas	1	
Hucheson, Robert	1	
Heath, William	1	
Higgins, John	1	1 negro
Harris, Charles	1	
Hill, Richard	1	
Hancock, Thomas		
Hancock, John	2	
Henson, Matthew	1	
Henry, Hugh	1	
Hickey, John	1	
Hudson, Joshua	1	
Harris, William	1	
Hays, John	1	
Hunt, Joseph	1	1 negro
Ironmonger, Joseph	1	
Ireland, George	1	
Isbell, Henry	1	
Harwood, George		
Berry, Richard	2	
Howard, Henry	1	
Hall, Moses	1	
Hus (Hughes) Richard	1	
Hall, Thomas	1	
Johnston, Samuel	1	
Jones, Robert		
Jones, William		
Jones, Thomas		
Jones, Samuel	4	6 negroes
Jones, Godfrey		
Russel, John	2	3 negroes
Jones, Philip		
Williams, John	2	2 negroes
Jones, Richard	1	
Jones, Richard	1	

Jonas, Joseph	1	
Jones, Richard	1	
Kennon, Richard	0	
Thorton, Thomas (overseer)	1	1 negro
Kennady, Andrew		
Lee, Widow		
Lee, John	1	
Logan, James	1	
Logan, John		
Hanna, George	1	
Logan, David	1	
Lovel, George	1	
Little, James	1	
Lanier, Joseph	1	
Lain, Dutton	1	
Light, John	1	
Lawson, Bartley	1	
Lawson, Jonas	1	
Lawson, John		
Lawson, William		
Lawson, John, Junr.	3	
Lain, John	1	
Moore, Samuel	1	
Moore, John	1	
Moore, George	1	
Mathew, William	1	
Maddox, William	1	
Morton, Joseph, Sen.	1	5 negroes
Martin, ———, sen.		
Martin, Samuel		
Martin, Robert	3	
Mayes, William	1	2 negroes
Mayes, Joseph	1	2 negroes
Mayo, Maddox		
Reibs, Daniel	2	3 negroes
Mullens, John	1	
Mount, John	1	
Middleton, John		
Middleton, Ainsworth	2	
Man, Francis		
Mann, Page	2	
McDavid, George	1	
McConnal, Alexander	1	
McMurday, James	1	
McNeese, James	1	
McDavid, John	1	
McLauchlin, James	1	
McHene, James	1	
McDuel, Michael	1	
Payne, William, Junior	1	
Osborn, Reps	1	
Orr, John		

Name		
Orr, John, Junior		
Orr, James	3	
Payne, William	1	
Perrin, Joseph		
Perrin, William		
Perrin, Samuel	3	
Pratt, John	1	
Pruet, Michael	1	
Parsons, Richard	1	
Payne, William, Sr.	1	
Pickens, Israel		
Pickens, William	2	
Pendleton, George	1	
Parson, Christopher	1	
Pruet, Henry	1	
Randolph, Richard		
Worthy, Thomas (overseer)	1	4 negroes
Maxcey, Radford (overseer)	1	4 negroes
Randolph, Col. Wm.		
Harris, Thomas (overseer)	1	4 negroes
Rutherford, Griffith	1	
Russell, John	1	
Russell, William	1	
Reese, William	1	
Roddgers, Wm. of Fallen Riv.	1	
Randolph, Col. Wm.		
Thomas, Wm. (overseer)	1	2 negroes
Rodgers, William	1	
Rodgers, Thomas	1	
Rutherford, James		
Rutherford, Wm.	2	
Roy, William	1	
Ruffin, Capt.		
Stott, Thomas (overseer)	1	4 negroes
Reed, John	1	
Roy, Reubin	1	1 negro
Rice, Thomas	1	
Stevens, William	1	
Sullivan, Owen	1	
Sullivan, John		
Sullivan, James	2	
Sullivan, Charles	1	
Sullivan, John		
Sullivan, James	2	
Stunt, James		
Stunt, Charles		
Stunt, James	3	3 negroes
Smithen, Robert		
Smithen, Edward	2	
Spragen, Wm. (overseer for Demit Abney	1	2 negroes
Smith, Luke	1	2 negroes
Semkins, John	1	2 negroes
Sanders, John	1	
Simon, Harry (Indian)	1	
Smith, Gideon	1	
Stuart, James		
Cassaday, Wm.	2	
Shipley, Robert	1	
Spencer, Thomas		
Easter, Ambross (overseer)	1	1 negro
Stalle, William	1	1 negro
Smith, John	1	
Stuart, John		
Marrow, Daniel	2	
Smith, Daniel	1	
Savory, John	1	
Stuart, John's (Indian)	1	
Smith, Thomas	1	
Servis, Thomas	1	
Stover, Jacob	1	
Stuart, John (mulatto)	1	
Self, John (overseer for Edmund Gray)	1	6 negroes
Stunt, John	1	
Thomas, Evans		
Thomas, Thomas	1	
Treadway, Richard (overseer) for John Cole	1	3 negroes
Taylor, William	1	
Talbot, Charles	1	1 negro
Tanner, Joseph	1	
Treadway, Richard	0	
Ussury, Wm.	1	
Vernon, John	1	
Vaughan, Abraham	1	
Vernon, Jonathan	1	
Vernon, Thomas		
Vernon, Isaac		
Vernon, James	3	
Vernon, James, Jun.	1	
Watkins, James	1	
Waller, John	1	
White, James	1	
Womack, Richard	1	3 negroes
Word, Thomas	1	
Weatherford, John	1	
Ward, Thomas	1	
Wachup, James	1	
Weakley, Robert	1	

Wood, Robert	1	Webb, Merry	1	
Walton, John	1	Williams, Joseph	1	
Williams, Daniel	1	Weakley, Wm.		
Wooten, John	1	Weakley, James	2	
Williams, John	1	Ward, Seth	1	1 negro
Ward, Richard	1	Young, John	1	
Waters, John	1	Young, Philip	1	

The above is one of seven lists of tithes taken for that section of Virginia which was Lunenburg County in 1749, and is usually known as Southside Virginia. The following counties were subsequently formed from this section: Bedford, Halifax, Mecklenburg, Charlotte, Campbell, Pittsylvania, Patrick, Henry. Copied and arranged by W. S. Morton, Farmville, Va.

List of Tithables in Northampton County, Virginia, August, 1666.

(From the Records in the Clerk's Office.)

Communicated by T. B. Robertson, Eastville, Va.

A list of Tythables in North'ton county, Anno Dom., 1666, delivered in att a court held for the s'd county the 28th of August, 1666.

Thomas Dunton,
Isaac Russell,
Robt. Dunworth,
Wm. Smith,
John Dike,
Daniel Jill.—6

Jeasse Harman,
Tho. Owen.—2

Benjamin Cowdree,
Josias Cowdree,
Cornelius Harman.—3

John Kendall,
Owen Edmond,
Geo. South,
John Farrier,
John Tomblings,
Henry Newton,
Owen Hall.—7

Peter Lang,
Cornelius George.—2

James Sanders,
Perse Davis,
John Dalby.—3

Arthur Armitradings,
Isaac Jacob,
Thomas Needy,
John Dawson,
Francis Broukes,
Sliven Avis,
Morgan Pouldin,
Wm. Stevens,
Henry Reade,
Derick Derickson.—10

John Dalby, Sen.,
John Dalby, Jun.,
John Seawell,
Hen. Bowans,
Richard Costinge.—5

John Cole,
John Field,
Robt. Twilly,
Wm. Rabishaw.—4

Thomas Bagley.—1

Will Gatehill,
John Evans.—2

Nicholas Hudson.—1

Henry Hall.—1

Lieft. Isaack Foxcoroft,
Philip, } Irishmen,
Patrick, }
Thomas Lucas,
4 negros.—8

Richard Nottingham,
Wm. Ewin.—2

Thomas Ast.—1

Att the Widow Gunter's:
Richard Wildgoose,
Tony—A Frenchman.—2

Simon Foscus, Sen.,
" " Jun.,
Thomas "
Mathew Patrick.—4

Walter Mills.—1

John Winborough, sen.,
" " jun.,
Frank " —3

Capt. Wm. Spencer,
Wm. Whittington,
Robt. Wiggin,
Wm. Scriven,
Jacob Hill,
Patrick Strelby,
Thomas Powell,
2 negros.—9

Mr. Wm. Westerhouse.—1

Lawrence Schyn,
Adryan Westerhouse,
John Richards,
Armstrong Foster.—4

Mr. Tho. Evens,

John Faris,
Clause—A Dutch
boy.—2

Edward Joyne.—1

Wm. Gaskin,
Robt. "
" Butler,
Nath'l Starkey,
Nat—A negro.—5

Thomas Bulluck.—1

Sampson Robins,
Rich'd Ridge.—2

Amos Garris.—1

John Walter,
Jeremiah Walter.—2

Will Morris.—1

Jas. Davis, sen.,
" " jun.,
Thomas Davis,
Steven Lang,
Abraham Bownamy.—5

Capt. Will Joanes,
John Lukes,
John Bulluck,
Harman Johnson.—4

John Lyons,
Thos. Collins.—2

John Mapp,
Peter Watson.—2

Wm. Marshiall,
Will Jipshott.—2

Wm. Hickman,

Mr. Haggaman.—2

Att Wilcox. Lambet Groton.—1

John Stockley,
John Bowin,
Thomas E. Smith.—3

Robt. Foster,
John "
Phillipp Jacob,
Martin Saks.—4

Wm. Foster,
1 Servant.—2

Walter Price,
John Clarke.—2

Edw. Stevens,
John Wilson.—2

Jacob Bishopp,
Rich'd Bibbins.—2

John Plumb.—1

Thos. Church,
Sam'l Church.—2

Thomas Parker,
John Hornby.—2

Joseph "
Thomas Rice.—3

Mr. Thos. Rideinge,
Mr. Argall Yardley,
Sam'l England,
Will Vaughanghom,
Hen. Matthew,
Griffin Morgan,
Tho. Rock,
Catalina—A negro.—8

Abraham Vansoult.—1

Nicholas Granger,
Thomas Wilson,
John Robins.—3

Cannlus Pence.—1

John Abbott.—1

Phillipp Mongon } negros.—2
Mary "

Geo. West.—1

Rich'd Ast,
Miles Growk,
Robt. Warbeton.—3

Christopher Turner.—1

(TO BE CONCLUDED)

List of Tithables in Northampton County, Virginia, August, 1666.

(From the Records in the Clerk's Office.)

COMMUNICATED BY F. B. ROBERTSON, EASTVILLE, VA.

Duncan Macknabb.—1.

John Basy.—1.

Robt. Harrison,
Robt. Hopkins.—2.

Abraham Sheppard.—1.

Edw. Cable.—1.

Will. Lawrence,
Thos. Berisford.—2.

Rich'd Duparke—
Att Wibly's.—1.

Will. Kennitt.—1.

Thos. Dimmer,
Tho. Nabe.—2.

Rich'd Patrick,
John Denby.—2.

Richard Jester.—1.

Coll. John Stringer,
John Tatum,

Joseph Godwin,
Ceasar " —2.

Abraham Heath.—1.

Capt. John Savage,
John Amis,
Edw. Ashby,
Robt. Tygar,
Tempsy Betha,
Sidney Field.—6.

Francis Pettitt,
Justman " —2.

Christopher Stanley.—1.

Joseph Parkes,
Wm. Gilsty,
Wm. Smart,
Tho. Claydon.—4.

Nath. Wilkins,
Rich. Cox,
George—Negro man.—3.

John Daniel,
James Bowden,
Wm. Edmonds,

Robt. Chew,
David Grim,
Richd. Curtisse,
Tho. Oxford.—6.

John Dorman,
Roger Kirkman.—2.

Att Miss Robins':
John Margetts,
Richd. Robins, Jun.,
John Symonds,
John Wooters,
John Archer—Negro,
Tony—Negro.—7.

Robt. Blacks,
John Jackson.—2.

Mr. John Robins,
Tho. Parnell,
John King—negro,
3 negros.—6.

Walter Mathews,
Andrew Smaw,
Wm. Savage.—3.

Wm. Lyne,
Wm. Padgett.—2.

John Webb,
John Glassell,
Hen. Lartin,
Cornelius Areale,
Nan, negro woman.—5.

Francis Jane, negro.—1.

Black Jack—Negro.—4.

Richard Hanby.—1

Thomas Harminson,
Daniel Call,
Geo. Jenkins,
John Marainge,
Wm. Sharpe,
John Wills—at mill.
Nan—negro woman.—7.

Att M. Vosses':
Thos. Loffing,
Nan—negro woman.—2.

John Francisco, } negros
Arisbian, his wife, } —.2

Lieft. Coll. Wm. Kendall,
Daniel Baker,
Geo. Mortimer,
John Abraham,
John Parsons,
John Harris,
Jeter Morgan,
Morgan Thomas,
Geo. Massy,
Walter Mannington,
Mingo—negro,
Charles, "
Aron Franson, } Sea-
Mathew Williams, } men-14

Mr. John Michaell,
Ed. Lockitt,
Peter Fountaine,
John Aleworth,
Rowland Williams,

Manuel Drigg—negro.—1.

Willis Saunders,
Daniel Keeth.—2.

Maj. Wm. Andrews,
John Andrews,
John Pirce.—2.

Geo. Isdell.—1.

Nicholas Howell,
Dexmon Hardlins,
Richard Williams.—3.

Will. Smith,
Tho. Hennige.—2.

John Wilkins,
John Floyd.—2.

John Waterson,
Jacob Glassfield,
John Wiltshire,
John More.—4.

Will Starlinge,
Tho. Turnell,
Hen. Morgan,
John Willett.—4.

Will Paule.—1.

Tho. Blacklock.—1.

Dennis Omalegon.—1.

Harman Johnson,
John Mathies.—2.

William Gray,
Anthony Joanes,
Antony, Banelo, Frank, Dennisse, Ann, } Negros.—12.

Wm. Hamon, Jane Hamon, } Negros. —2.

Wm. Millinge,
Robt. Jilkin,
Arthur Bowzer,
Peter Vickar,
Isaak Venan,
John Wyer.—6.

Joseph Warren.—1.

Jerom Griffith.—1.

Tho. Shepperd.—1.

Provice Nelson,
Daniel Paine.—2.

Bartholomew Cosier,
Francis Roberts.—2.

Wm. Geldinge,
Luke Geldinge,
Charles Geldinge.—3.

Left. Coll. Wm. Waters,
Peter Bastianson,
Lawrence Jacobson,
Tho. Reade,
Edw. Joanes,

James Walker,
Hen. Williams,
Richd. Jacklock.—3.

Mr. Tho. Hunt,
John Follicome,
John Darnell,
Wm. Shore.—4.

John Bagwell.—1.

Thos. Bagwell.—1.

Capt. John Custis,
John Robinson,
Michael Stone,
Tho. Joanes,
Chas. Weissell,
Hen. Foreman,
Daniel Swindell,
Benjamin Perry,
George Lilly,
John Warppell,
5 negroes.—15.

Robt. Hayes.—1.

Tenge Odeere.—1.

Matthew Trippin.—1.

Jeremia Robinson,
Robt. Smith,
Judith—negro—3.

John Adolph,
Wm. Cord,
Jonas Dixon,
Jacob Chilton,
Geo. Treherne,
Ed. Evans, als. Hopkins,
Sam Handee,
William—negro,
Bill— " —10.

Richard Whitmarsh,
Wm. Waltum,
Robt. Holliday,
Sam. Ames,
Tho. Davis.—5.

Mr. Francis Piggott,
Peter, John, Thomas, Jane, } Negros.—5.

King Tony—negro.—1.

Bastian Cane—negro.—1.

Thomas Bell,
Tho. Coleman.—2.

Ellis Ap Hugh.—1.

Thomas Swendel.—1.

Bossaur—negro—1.

Mr. Thomas Harmar.—1.

Stephen Costin,
Benoni Ward.—2.

Thomas Clay.—1.

Derman Fox.—4.

Tho. Scott,
John Watts.—2.

Thomas Moore,
John Owen,
John Moore,
Thos. Somersett,
James Bookett.—5.

Wm. Harper,
Rich'd Quinch.—2.

Geo. Freshwater,
Dic.—negro.—2.

John Knight.—1.

Thos. Poynter,
John Hankins,
Tho. Dregue—negro,
Rich'd Richardson,
Mary Richardson, his wife,
Derman Olandum,
Francis Driggue, } Negros
James, } —8.

Neale Mackmillins,
John Jewett.—2.

Att the Widow Hall's:
Hen. Michael.—1.

Wm. Ennis —1.

John Stevens.—1.

Geo. Willis.—1.

Thos. Hogg,
Abraham Collins.—2.

Att Mathew Gittinge's, Constable:
Walter Carter,
Howell James,
John Fothery.—3.

Francis Harper.—1.

Geo. Frizzell.—1.

Darman Lassland.—1.

Alex. Mills,
Rich'd Core.—2.

George Smith,
Wm. Lewis.—2.

John Allen,
Edw. Allen.—2.

Edw. Ennis.—1.

James Weatherly.—1.

Wm. Baker.—1.

Hen. Marshmant.—1.

424

[The numbers below the names show the number of tithables on each plantation. According to races, the tithables stood 372 white and 52 negroes. Estimating the tithables at one-third of the total population would make Northampton's population in August, 1666, 1,116 white, and 156 negroes—total, 1,272. This was about three years after Accomack county was cut off from Northampton.]

F. B. ROBERTSON.

Eastville, Va.

POLL OF VOTE OF NORTHAMPTON COUNTY, VIRGINIA

For President of the United States, 1789

To the Editors of William and Mary Quarterly:

Below will be found a copy of the record in the clerk's office of Northampton County, showing the individual vote for presidential elector under the first election held in the United States. Henry Guy was the elector who was expected to vote for General Washington. The other two votes were purely personal compliments, as is shown by the fact that Henry Guy voted for another than himself on the occasion.

Thomas B. Robertson.

Poll of Election for an Elector to choose a president held for Northampton Co. on Wednesday the 7th of Jany, 1789.

Votes for Henry Guy

William Harmanson
Geo Brickhouse Jr
Wm. Roberts, Jr
John Brickouse Sr
Joab Bell
John Rogers
Smith Snead
Edw. Robins
Harrison Thomas
David Stott
William Bell
Joshua Westcot
Richard Smith
Matthew Harmanson
Daniel Fitchett
Thos Nottingham
Henry Giddings
Henry Harmanson
Nathaniel Wilkins
Jacob Abdeel
Josias Willis
Isaac Smith
Levin Matthews
Thomas Hunt
Zarobabel Core
Wm Wilkins Sen.
Bowdoin Kendall
John Gluson Sen.
John Evans
Richard Dunton Jr.
John Guy
William Carpenter
John Respass
William Trower
John Savage
Griffin Stith
Littleton Savage
Hancock Jacob
John Joynes
Littleton Eyre
John Satchell
James Sanford
Henry Wilkins
John Williams
Daniel Luke
Auben Westerhouse
William Dalby
Hillary Warren
John Parsons
Robt. C. Jacob
Elijah Baker
John L Fulwill
William Bloxom
Coventon Simpkins
John Carpenter Senr.
William Satchell Senr.
John Kendall Jr.
Johnathan Elligood
John S. Harmanson
George Powell
Littlton Major
Nathaniel Powell
William Scott
John Haggoman
James Parkerson
John Darby
Coventon Stott
Johnathan Stott
Thomas Kendall

Smith Major	Teakle Jacob	Robt. Rodgers
William Fischer	Robinson Johnson	John Wilkins Jr.
Saml S. McCroskey	John Tompkins	Peter Warren
William Jervise	Hillary Stringer	John Carpenter Jr.
John Upshur Sr.	Kendall Addison	Robt. Nottingham
Custis Kendall	Rowland Dowty	Stuart Holt
John Stratton Jr.	Moses Griffith	Littleton Upshur
Thos Darby Sr.	John Brickhouse Jr.	Ellyson Armistead
Joshua Fitchett	Chas Carpenter	Robt. Wilkins
Daniel Scott	Michael Matthews	Nathaniel Tyson
William Dixon	John Stratton Sen.	Arthur Downing Senr.
John Core	John Kendall Sen.	Dickey Dunton
Amos Underhill	Thos Upshur Sr.	Joshua Turner
Robt. Haggoman	Matthew Guy	Seth Powell
Wm. Harrison	Geo. Brickhouse, Sr.	William Simkins Senr.
Henry Abdel	John Dixon	Thomas James

In all 117 for H. Guy.

VOTES FOR LITTLETON EYRE
John Robins

VOTES FOR JOHN ROBINS
Henry Guy

HILLARY STRINGER,
Clerk.

The above poll was sworn to before me by Hillary Stringer. Given under my hand this 8th day of Jany 1789.

JOHN DARBY.

Teste Wm Stith
C. N. C.

NOTE

John Stratton, Jr., represented the district in Congress about 1800. Richard Dunton, Jr., was a surveyor for many years. Griffin Stith had been clerk of the court for fifty-nine years, resigning the office about that time. Littleton Savage became clerk of the court afterwards. Littleton Eyre was a conspicuous citizen, as was John Satchell. Teakle Jacob lived in Savages Neck, as did John Savage. Hillary Stringer had held office of sherif, and his family for many years before him had had office. John L. Fulwell helped organize the old Northampton Masonic lodge, oldest on the "Shore." William and John Kendall were the representatives of that prominent family at that time and had held many posts of honor, and so with many of the others named.

The vote was taken at the court house in Eastville, so it was comparatively small for the population of the county at the time.

ORANGE COUNTY TITHE LISTS

Orange County was created by act of assembly August 1734 from the westernmost portion of Spotsylvania County. This act was directed to take effect on January 1, 1734/5 and the boundaries of the new county of Orange were defined as "all that territory of land adjoining to, and above the said line [i. e. the line as established by act of May, 1730, dividing St. George's Parish, Spotsylvania into two parishes to be known as St. George's and St. Mark's; St. Mark's being *above* the said line, or to the west thereof. Henning IV., 305] bounden southerly, by the line of Hanover county, northerly, by the grant to the Lord Fairfax, and westerly, by the utmost limits of Virginia." (Hening IV., 450). Orange County when first created included the now counties of Augusta, Frederick, Culpeper, Madison, Greene, Shenandoah, Rockbridge, Rockingham in Virginia, a great proportion of the territory of the present State of West Virginia, and the whole of the present State of Kentucky.

The tithe lists given below are four for the years 1734, 1738 (two) and 1739 respectively, while four of the lists are not dated. For a full account of Orange County see *A History of Orange County, Virginia, from Its Formation in 1734 (O. S.) to the End of Reconstruction in 1870 . . . By W. W. Scott . . . Richmond, Va. Everett Waddey Co., 1907.*

* * * 1734 * * * *[1]

John Christopher	9	John Ferrell	2
Willm Dann[?]	3	John Walker	1
John Hawkins	13	George [M?]offett	2
Alex^{d} Waygh [Waugh?]	6	Soloman[?] Ryon	1
Samll George	6	William Christopher	2
Vollontine Morgin	6	[Nico?]laus Christopher	2
Willm Clark	3	Old Adam	1
Beniamin Horn	1	Thos Whurtun [Wharton?]	3
Cap^{tt} Spenser	13	Charles Watt**	3
John Smith	3	Willm Chronoker	4
Nathan Turner	3	James Thortun [Thornton?]	1
James Whitun	2	John Wells	1
William Minor	2	John Dozer	5
John Bramham	9	Thos Night	1
William Mortun	14	A^{tt} Co^{ll} Willesquarter	4
William Smith	4	Willm Davis	2

[1] This list is very much faded and many names are scarcely legible.

Jonathan Ferrell 5
Willm Hokins [Hawkins?] 1
John [H?]orin 1
John Edwards 1
George Whotun [Wharton?] 3
Beniamin Porter *
Willm Buccom[?][2] *
James Stuner[?] 1
Simon Buccom[?] 1
George Anderson, Senir, 4
John Under Wood 3
George Anderson Junr[?] 1
Samll * * * 2
John Manewell 5
Richd Sims 1
John Dotwood[?] 1
Theofelus Edings 2
Thos Rocefurd[?] 2
Thos Russell 1
Henry Jonsun[?] 2
H[?] John Curtis 1
Steven Raccom[2] 1
Thos Fore[?] 12
Edward Price *

Allenastbon[?] Newman 4
Briant Sisson 3
Willm S. * * * 1
Robt *urvil[?] 11
Thos Sims 2
Thos Rolloy[?], Senior, 4
Jhn Ingrom 4
John Marks 4
Samll[?] Graves 4
Richd Pennun[?] 4
John Pottoy[?] 3
Thos Pottoy[?] 1
Arebun[?] Moor 3
Frans * * * 2
John Fisha [Fisher?] 2
* * * * [undecipherable] 5
Robt Rusell 2
Thos Shambles 2
Willm Conew [Connor?] 2
Luke Thorntun 2
John Ranfiel[?] 1
Thos Michael 1
George Wells 2

A List of Delinquents for the Year 1738

Jacob Stover 3 { added by order of Court & in Mr Russel's List

John Tilly 1 who was Constable
Jacob Cassel 1 in Mr Russel's List & added
David Finley 1 ran away
David Evans 1 ran away
Jas Hamilton 1 ran away
Jas Keatton 1 no effects
Buckner Allison 1 not found
Robt Adams 1 no distress
John Bledso 1 a mistake
Thos Baskill 1 not found

Thos Bryen 1 no distress
Jas Barry 1 not found
Wm Coxes, 1 not found
Wm Clark, 1 a mistake
Joseph Fenn 1 ran away
Edwd Ferral 1 ran away
John Ferral 1 no distress
John Fox, 1 ran away
John Gon 1 not found
Wm Harrison 3 I know not the man

[2] The first letter of this name may be B, and hence Baccom, a corruption of the present Beckham.

Wm Hawkins, 1 dead no effects
Timothy Johnson 3 ran away
Richd Jenkins 1 no effects
John Lenderwood 2 I know not the man
Turles Lewis 1 not found
Wm Layfe, 1 not found
Thos Mitchell, 1 not found
Wm Mathews 1 not found
[Co]rnelius McClarey 1 ran away
Brot over 37
John Noel 1 ran away
Chas Oaks 1 ran away
John Palley 2 not found
Wm Rush 1 dead no effects
Jas Stevens 1 no effects
Robt Skelton 1 not found
Antho Thornton 4 a mistake
Mark Worrell 1 not found
Geo: Crow 1 not found
John Roberts 1 no effects
Edward Watts 1 ran away
Thos Wooton 1 ran away
Wm Collins 1 ran away
Thos Little 1 ran away

55

Orange County to Henry Downs Dr

To a Called Court on Richd Cross als Breden	140
To 55 Levies @ 22 h ℔ Tithe	1237½
	1377½
To a Called Court on Rebecca Shaw	140
	1517½

A List of the Delinquents Over Shenandore, for ye year 1738.

George Hill run away
Willm Fuller run away
Frances Ward run away
Fras Fleat Crust run away
William Co run away
Phillip Kenny run away
John Haywood run away
Samll Haywood run away
Joseph Haywood run away
Ellick Sender run away
John Warbinton run away
Andrew Van [?] cannot be found
James Renfroe hath no estate
Stephen Renfroe hath no estate
John Sheldon run away
John Turner Run away
Robart Turner no estate
John Jones Run away
Joseph King Run away
John Setterfield Run away
William Arnol Run away
* * * Arnoll Run away
Constables Refuseth to pay
Hutzin [Hudson?] Gilder
James Hill
Richard Morgan
Robert Warth

Per Thos Postgate, D. Sher.

The List of tithes wherein I am Constable for the year 1739.
Mr Richard Thomas Sixteen tithes
Thomas Red at Barbers [Barbour's?] Courter six tithes
Mr Battaile Courter[1] seven tithes
Cap Rucker four tithes
Ambros Powel at Materson's [Madison's?] home house seven tithes
Samuel Drak three tithes
George Burd one tithe
Zachary Gibbs three tithes
James Coleman six tithes
William Bell three tithes
Joseph Motten [Morton?] six tithes
Edward Walker two tithes
Hezekiah Rhods two tithes
William Rhods one tithe
William Croswait three tithes
George Anderson three tithes
Edward Tandsley[?] three tithes
James Thusten[?] one tithe
Samuel Backer [or Baker, or possibly Rucker] one tithe
John Barnitt four tithes
Earey[?] Taylor three tithes
Robard Bohanaugh at Balors [Baylor's?] Courter seventeen tithes
John Gof three tithes
Richard Cemp [Camp, Kemp?] at Cap Hills Quarter five tithes
Thomas Jones seven tithes
Mr Zachary Talor [Taylor] ten tithes
John Davice [Davis?] two tithes
Cap Scott's Corter nine tithes
John Hathon[?] at Docter Gorden Courter three tithes
James Choward at Beale Courter six tithes
Mr Materson [Madison?] black leavel six tithes
George Eastham Curnal Grimes [Colonel Grymes?] Courter eighteen tithes

---

[1] The word spelled throughout this list *Courter* is a corruption of Quarter.

Richard Durrut [Durrett?] at mines Courter six tithes
John Botts at madom tods [Madam Todd's?] Courter nine tithes
John Lukess at madom tods [Madam Todd's?] Courter ten tithes
James mcColady[?] at Curnal Williss Courter [Colonel Willis?] eight tithes
John McCoy at Thomas Edmondson courter five tithes
Thomas Gresona[?] at Beniamin Waislow [Winslow?] Courter seven tithes
Richard Winslow three tithes
Robert Deadin two tithes
Mark Thorton at James Taylor Courter seven tithes
William Clark at talerfers [Taliaferro?] Courter seven tithes
Cornal [Colonel?] Chew eight tithes

In all the List of Tithes comes to 251 by me

Elijah Daniel, constable.

A List of Tithables in the precinct of James Pickett, Constable.

Name	Tithes	Name	Tithes
Thomas Rucker	3	Walter Vaughan	1
John Howard	1	John Rogers	3
Wm Crawford	2	Walter Lenord	3
Benja Coward	3	Thos Brown	2
Richd Maulden	3	John Shelton	1
Thos Morgan	2	Wm Loggins	1
Benja Thomson	1	Jonathan Gibson's Quarter	4
Major LeVaune[?]	3	Martin Trapp	1
Thos Jackson	6	John Bush [or Rush?]	2
Thoss Coleman	1	John Forrester	3
Fras Pickett	1	Wm Williamson	1
Michael Gary	2	John Farrow	1
Isaac Tinsley	1	Moses Battley's Quarter	5
Henry Ware	3	Leonard Phillips	2
Wm Rucker	1	Patrick Walsh	3
Wm Pierce	2	John McDaniel	2
Peter Rucker	6	David Phillips	2
John Gath	3	John Zachary	2
Thos Stanton	1	Wm Phillips	5
Thos Zachary	1	Robert Morgan	1
David Zachary	2	Benja Cave	5
Ann Stogdill's Quarter	2	Blan Ballard's Quarter	2
Wm Offil	1	John Grymes Esqr Quarter	15
Jonas Archer	2	John Stone	1
Jas Stevens	1	Michael Holt	3

David Ford	1
Anthony Head	3
John Haresnipe	1
Geo Bruce	2
Abraham Bledsoe	3
Abraham Bledsoe, Junr	1
Thos Downer	1
Isaac Smith	1
Wm Terril's Quarter	2
Mark Stowers	1
Saml Taliaferro	1
Guy Meek	1
	143

Henry Downs Quarter	2
Michael Pearson	1
Wm Stone	2
Geo Simmons	2
John Simpson	3
Thos Jones	3
Joshua Yarbrough	2
Mark Wormell	1
Richd Yarbrough	2
Henry Sparks	1
Richd Holcomb	3
Lau: Crees	2
Cortney Browel	1
George Lun [Long?]	1
John Hoymen	1
John Carpenter	2
Mathias Castler	1
Michael Cook	1
Henry Snider	1
Robt Tenner [Tanner?]	2
Geo: Tenner [Tanner?]	1
Lodowick Fisher	1
Geor Jeter	1
Phillip Roote's Quarter	15
Henry Moceoy[?]	1
Anthony Strother's Quarter	5
John Killy [Kelly?]	1

Adam Carr [Garr]	3
Wm Carpenter	4
Richs Yager	5
Thos Watts	4
Edwd Watts	2
Thos Edmondson	1
Geo Thompson	1
John Phillips	3
Wm Henderson	3
Thos Coker	1
John Eddins	1
Daywall Cristler	1
Adam Yager	1
Mathew Smith	2
Henry Crowder	1
Christley Browel	1
John Hansborgow	1
Michael Smith	3
Daywat Cristler	1
Michael Keiffer	1
Geo. Moyers	2
John Rowse	2
Thos Wayland	1
Mark Finks	2
Henry Haws	5
John Blueford	2
John Wisdom	3
Wm Jackson	2
Wm Eddins	4
John Scott's Quarter	3
Elias Smith	1
James Barbour	8
David Bruce	1
Wm White	1
Thos Bledso	1
Robt Cave	2
Wm Rice	1
Chas Blunt	1
151	
143 In all 294	151

A List of the Tithables in my Precinct [Henry Rice, Constable]

Henry Isbell	2
Wm Cuddin	2
James Haley	1
Edward Haley	3
Wm Cox Junr	1
Geo Cox	2
Obediah Howerton	1
Wm Cox	5
Daniel Singleton	1
at Colo Willis Mine Run Qr	4
Capt Wm Bledsoe	2
Isaac Bledsoe	2
Wm Thompson	1
George Brasbone on Ye Mine Run	6
Capt George Harden	5
at Madm Fleets Quarter	7
at Richd Bradley's	2
John Evens	1
Saml Smith	6
Backnel Alverson	1
Geo: Steward	1
Jeremiah Dear	1
John Collins	1
at Nathaniel Clayborns	4
Wm Wood	2
Capt Wm Beals' Quarter	..
Joseph Thornell	..
Stephen Gubbon	..
James Coleman	..
Thomas Jones	..
Thos Hill	..
Charles Curtis	3
Richd Bridge	..
John Cook	3
Moses Harris	1
Jos[?] Woolfolk	6
	177

Brot up	177
John Henderson	1
Wm Mathews	1
John Brock	1
Thos [Duerson?]	2
Colo Auge Moore	4
Lazs Tilly	1
Thos Burghs	1
Jos: Shears	1
Saml Brock	2
Roger Bell	1
Thos Cook	2
John Biving	4
John Goldson	3
David Cave	3
Daniel Cook	1
Malachi Chiles	3
Abraham Mayfield	2
James Stephens	4
Richd Lamb[?]	1
John Stephens	1
Larkin Chew	5
John Thomas	2
Daniel White	3
Wm Prat[?]	1
Wm Taylor	7
George Smith	3
Charles Stephens	4
Jostophonice Smith	1
James Elliot	5
David Griffen	1
Wm Jones	1
John Griffen	1
John Clayton	7
Wm Stephens	1
John Hiott	1
Andrew Harrison	5
Henry Rice	3
Total	197

₰ Me Henry Rice Constable

A List of Tithables in the precinct of Tho[s] Callaway Constable

Geo: Braxton's Quarter	8	James Stodgill	1
Robt Brooks's Quarter	6	Tho[s] Buttery	1
Sarah Brooks's Quarter	5	Honorius Powell	2
Madam Stanard's Quarter	6	John Hunt	1
James Lindsey	3	Tho[s] Wood	1
M[r] Lawson's Quarter	5	Trueman Fry	1
Mrs. Rippon's Quarter	2	William Bunch	2
W[m] Callaway	1	David Rock	1
Jeffry Crowley	2	W[m] Herren	1
Joseph Keatton	1	Joseph Phillips	1
James Keatton	1	James Ireland	1
James Meredith	1	James Dier[?]	1
John May	1	Henry Findell [or Tindell?]	1
Geo: Douglass	1	James Tiley	1
John Goodall	2		
Fra[s] Williams	2	in all	66
John Ennis	1		
W[m] Smith	1	per me Thos. Callaw[ay]	
James M[c]Kenny	1	Constable.	

John Mickell This List of Tithables in his Precinct.

At M[r] Frys Quarter	10	Christopher Moyers	1
John Smith	1	Peter Deaver	1
Alexander M[c]fearson	1	Mithaell Wilhite	2
Joshua Yarbrough	2	George Woods	3
Zacharias Sparks	1	Pals Plunkabeamer	2
John Layton	2	Nicholas Plancabecner	2
John Toles [Towles?]	2	George Shively	1
Thomas Waker [Walker?]	3	Conrat Slater[?]	1
Spentor Bobo	1	Jacob Broill	1
Henry Fields	3	Zacharia Fleshman	2
Francis Mickell	1	Peter Fleshman	2
Mathew Stanton	1	Richard Birdine[?]	2
W[m] Duett	2	John Wilhide	1
John White	1	Michaell Claur	2
John Duett	1	Martin Dattuck[?]	1
James Morgan	1	Michaell Oneall	1
Tobias Wilhite	1	George Paylor	1
John Stolts	1	W[m] Martin	3
Frederick Bumgarner	1	Zachary Martin	4

Nicholas Coplin	1
Nicholas Coplin	3
David Onell	1
John Kyner	3
Christopher Onell	2
Thomas Fargison	1
John Thomas	1
Henry Sluter	1
John Zimmerman	1
John Dotson	1
John Sutton	1
Robert Hutchison	2
Joseph Bloodwoth	3
Thomas Canely	1
John Fiell	2
Christian Clemon	1
Jacob Manspoill	1
Totall	100

FIRST LIST OF TITHABLES OF PITTSYLVANIA COUNTY, YEAR 1767.

(Contributed by Mrs. N. E. Clement, Chatham, Va.)

A List of Tithables and Lands Taken by George Jefferson (1) in Pittsylvania County and Cambden Parish for the year 1767.

	tithe	land
Levy Shockley	1	
Francis Kirby	1	100
Elisha Estis	1	260
Jacob Hubbard	1	100
Josiah Kerbey	1	
William Young	1	270
John Kirby & Jesse Kirby	2	135
Daniel Collins	1	
Geo. Peak & Wm. Peak	2	100
Charles Lucas & John Lucas	2	50
David Kirby	1	100
James Shockley	1	400
John Kirby Jr	1	100
John Peak (Pr. Edward County)		185
Wm. Mullins & Wm. Mullins Jr	2	100
Robt Neilly	1	178
George Jefferson (Mecklenburg), John Davis, overseer, & negroes, to-wit: Sam, Chance, Pompey, Phillis, Patt & Lacy	7	8000
William Terrell Mills & Thomas Hudson, Joseph Toler, John McLin Handy, Sam & Israel, negroes	7	

(1.) George Jefferson was one of the Commission of Peace & Dedimurs appointed for Pittsylvania's first Court, held Friday 26th, June, 1767. Appointed Captain of Militia in 1768.

Elizabeth Irwin (Bedford). John Carter, Ov'sr & negroes Tom, Dick, Sam Estes, Lucy & Iris	7	130
Jeremiah Salesbury & negro Lacbey	2	
John Smith & Henry Hains	2	
William Justice	1	100
John Lucas		100
William Neilley	1	170
Isham Hodges	1	150
John Hodges	1	
Robert Hodges	1	
Robert Frazier	1	
William Dillingham	1	97
Fredrick Rives & negro Phillis	2	2500
William Stegal	1	
John Glass & Stephen Thompson	2	
Thomas Ramsey		200
Fulker Fulkerson		119
Total	56	13644

A List of Tithes &c taken by John Donelson (2) 1767.

Francis Bucknall	1	
William Holder	1	
Robert Martin	1	
Charles Rigney	1	
Thomas Greenwoods List, Peter Brooks, Ov'sr, negroes Duk, Sam, Matt & Judith	5	260
Hall Hudson & negro woman	2	650

(TO BE CONTINUED)

(2.) John Donelson one of the earliest settlers in this section, was appointed surveyor of Pittsylvania in 1767, which office he held till 1779, when "John Wimbish, Abram Shelton, and Wm. Todd are appointed to view and inspect the Records of John Donelson, Gent, late Surveyor of their County, and report to the Court the condition thereof." Nov. Court 1779. Nov. 1767 John Donelson took oath of Vestryman of Camden Parish—Member of House of Burgesses for Pittsylvania County in 1769-70-71-72-73-74. Wed 25, Sept. 1775, John Doneldon Esq. was appointed County Lieutenant. Served as Colonel in the Cherokee Expedition. In 1779 he emigrated to Tennessee. See V. Hist. Mag, Vol. 8, Page 13—His daughter Rachel became the wife of President Andrew Jackson.

TITHABLES OF PITTSYLVANIA COUNTY, 1767.

(Contributed by Mrs. N. E. Clement, Chatham, Va.)

Name		
Ralph Shelton	1	
John East	1	190
Arthur Kesee	1	
Joseph Hale	1	100
Chas. Faris	1	100
David Barber		
John Barber		
Thomas Darr	1	100
Thom. Mustein	1	400
John Walrope	1	
Jas. Walrope	1	
Richard Hamock	1	
Thomas Bennett	1	76
Stephen Bennett	1	
Richard Bennett	1	94
John Bobbitt	1	
William Bobbit & Jas. Bobbit	2	90
Eliz[th] Bobbit & negro Joe	1	
Wm. Bennet & Chas. Good	1	410
Joseph Farris	1	200
John Boyer	1	
John Boyer, Jr.	1	
James Farris & James Farris, Jr.	2	200
John Donelson, Thos. Henry, negroes Peter, Caneer, Tobe, Hannah & Sall	6	611
Bryan Ward Nowling	1	
Jas. Logan & negro Phillis	1	300

Crispen Shelton, Shenon Sheltor, negroes, Tom, Lucy & Primus	5	814
Thomas Chandler (Dinwiddie)		400
Joseph Cunningham (Charlotte)		100
Gabriel Shelton (30), Abraham Payne, negroes Zachery & Vilet	4	304
Lewis Shelton, negro Patt	2	441
John Chandler	1	
Isaac Sibbly	1	
John Justice (shoemaker)	1	
William Williams	1	
James Leak	1	300
Joseph Leak	1	100
Robt. Leak	1	
Abraham Caldwell, negroes Tom & Phillis	3	300
The estate of W. Lightfoot, Dec[d], John Henry, Ov'sr, negroes Peter, Chasl, Sam, Lawrence, Will, Lutis, Moll, Ester, Ross & Sarah	11	4320
Uriah Cammeron	1	
Edmond Hodges	1	
Henry Blank	1	
Abraham Shelton, Egmond J. Williams	2	300
Lames Milum	1	
Richard Prewet*	1	
Henry Prewit & Joseph Prewit	2	250
John Payne, John Payne Jr., & Greenwood Payne	3	200
Thomas Farris & Michael Farris	2	400

(30.) Gabriel Shelton, son of Christopher Shelton and brother of Abraham Shelton, all three of whom were members of the Committee of Safety. All three were Vestrymen of the Parish and Captains of Militia. Gabriel Shelton commanded a Company of Pitts. Militia at battle of Guilford Courthouse. "At a meeting held for Cambden Parish at the house of Mr. Joseph Roberts, April 1, 1785, Haynes Morgan and Abraham Shelton, Gent., is appointed to attend the Convention to be held in the City of Richmond the eighteenth day of May next.

Signed

Haynes Morgan, Ch. W.
Vincent Shelton, C. O. C. P.

(TO BE CONTINUED)

TITHABLES OF PITTSYLVANIA COUNTY, 1767.

(Contributed by Mrs. N. E. Clement, Chatham, Va.)

Elijah Farris	1	
Richard Keezee & John Keezee	2	130
Joseph Bags & negro Silfox	2	350
Tully Choice & negro Sarah	2	1570
William Hall	1	200
Robt. Large	1	200
John King, Malachi King, negro Phillis	3	278
William King	1	
Benjamine Lawless	1	200
John Sargent	1	
Moses Swinney	1	
John Swinney	1	
Josiah Maples	1	
Reuben Payne	1	150

A List of Tithables for Pittsylvania County taken by John Wilson, (3) Gent., in year 1767.

		acres
John Stone & son John	2	85

(3.) John Wilson was appointed a Justice of Peace for Pittsylvania in 1767. In 1779 took the oath of Vestryman of Camden Parish. In 1775 was appointed Major of the Militia of the County, and when Col. John Donelson resigned his Commission as County Lieutenant in 1777, John Wilson was appointed in his stead. Gen. "Light Horse Harry Lee" says in his memoirs that "General Stevens conducted his Militia to Pittsylvania Court House for the purpose of laying up their arms and hearing that General Green and his Army were likely to be crippled before he crossed the Dan, Stevens, instead of going home, returned to camp, taking with him some of the Militia of Pittsylvania, collected by the exertion of the County Lieutenant, determined to share the fate of Green and his Army."

George Lumpkin, son Robert & son George, John Lewis, negroes Jack & Betty	6	150
Absolom Bostick, negro Pato	2	77
Nathan Bostick	1	90
Thomas Garner, negroes Harry, Lillis, Cate & Peg	5	
William Shelton	1	80
John MacMillion	1	
William Munkers	1	
Richard Andin	1	
Daniel Sallahan	1	
John Yates & son John, negroes Bob. & Cate	4	358
Charles Little	1	
Barsheba Beverly (Mulato)	1	
Moses Ridle (Indian)	1	
William Ridle	1	
John Wynne	1	
Robt Worsham	1	
John Ferrol	1	
David Lay	1	150
Robert Macconoway	1	
John Simmons	1	
Zachariah Scags	1	
Henry Stone and Son William, Mason Combs, negro Sarah	4	150
Henry Greens Land	3	323
John Owen & Sons William & John, negro Sam	4	208
George Holms Gwin, negroes Lill, Lucy, Fillis & Gwin	5	
Dexrous Musick	1	
William Nelson	1	
James Sartain	1	
Peter Grimsted	1	
John Owen(Cain Cr)	1	
Small Wood Owen	1	
Timothy Stamps, John Stamps & Thomas Stamps	3	

Benjamine Thrasher & negro Luck	2	
Wm. W. Hodges	1	240
Goram Brown	1	
William Wotson		
William Rice		
Isiah Watkins & Edward Lester (Miller)	2	250
Peter Perkins and James, son, negroes Lownon & Hannah	4	550
John Wilson, negroes, viz: Roger, Will, Charles, Isaac, Betty, Lin & Doll	8	2009
Isaac Sartain	1	
Richard Adams	1	
Valentine Hatcher & negroes Matt, Beck and Charles	4	120
David Stephins	1	

A list of Tithes taken by Theop'l Lacy (4) 10th of June 1767.

John Madding, John Madding, Jr. & William Ingram	3	316
Peter Terry	1	
Thomas Woters, negro Lucy	2	200
John Hall	1	
Robt. Worters & Wm. Worters	2	400
Richard Colyer	1	
Christopher Sneed	1	
Thom. Cole	1	
James Connor	1	
Wm. Lynch		
Bob. Terrys List of Tithes himself and son Jo^s Terry	2	300

Robt Terry's List.

Rob. Terry, negroes Sammy, Jack, Harry, Gregory, Abram, Jenney, Abby & Phillis	11	300

(4.) Theophilus Lacy, one of the Justices appointed for Pittsylvania 1767. Also appointed Vestryman for Camden Parish in 1767. When the town of Peytonsburg was established in 1759, while Pittsylvania was still a part of Halifax County, Theophilus Lacy was one of the trustees appointed for the town. Peytonsburg was one of the 9 Posts established in 1781 in Virginia, for collecting supplies for the use of the Southern Continental Army. Sheriff of Pittsylvania in 1773.

Daniel Coleman (Cumberland)	1	300
The Rev[d] Alexander Gordon's (5) List, Thom Riddle, overseer, Davis & Harry	3	
Capt John Quarles List, Jopph Ferguson, overseer, negr crozier Eljah King	3	
Capt. Jo[s] Terry's List, Jo[s] Terry Jun, negroes Savoey, Abraham, Cupid, Betsey & Sarah	7	1580
Thos. Straton	1	
David Terry's List, negroes Cate, Matthew, Dourkkin & Sal of Champ Terry	5	465
John Fitzgerald	1	
Thos. Dodson's List, negroes Peter, Adam, Joseph, Dinah, Sall, Winny, Lucy, & Nora	9	
John Creel	1	
Lazarus Dodson	1	
John Piggs (6) List, negroes Harry, Bob., Sam, Sary, Beck	6	886
Griff Dickenson, Jun'r	1	
Rich. Murphy & Bob. Scott	2	200
Geo. Dodson	1	
James Thompson & Jno. Terry	2	
Jas. Roberts (7) Jim & negro Isbell	2	200
Ambrose Haley & Ben. Haley	2	278

(5.) The Rev. Alexander Gordon, in 1769, was engaged by the Vestry of Pittsylvania to fill its appointment, for 16,000 lb. Tobacco, which he did, till the Rev. James Stephenson was engaged in 1770. From Hening 8, Page 610, we find the Rev. Alexander Gordon, rector of Antrim Parish, Halifax County, petitioning for the same salary that other ministers receive.

(6.) John Pigg was member of the first Vestry appointed for Pittsylvania. In the Parish Levy for 1771, we find "To John Pigg for boarding Rev. Lewis Gwilham for one year, 3200 lbs. Tobacco." 1768 John Pigg was appointed Captain of Militia of Pittsylvania County. He was the son of Paul Pigg.

(7.) James Roberts, jun'r, was one of the first Commissioners of Peace for Pittsylvania County. He was also one of the trustees for Peytonsburg town, when established in 1759. It was "Jas. Roberts, the younger," who laid off 100 acres of land, adjouning the Court-house, into streets and lots for the town. In 1769, James Roberts gives 50 more acres for the establishment of another town, "where the Courthouse of the said County now stands" "to be known by the name of Chatham. (Pittsylvania was now a separate County, but Patrick & Henry were yet within the boundaries, & the Court house was then in the Western part of the County, at what is now called the little village of Callands).

Richard Persons for his son John	1	1186
James Panley	1	
Tho[s] Fee	1	35
Isaac Jones	1	
Masses Poor	1	
Tho[s] Townsend	1	
Joseph Austin	1	600
Jacob Chaney, Jas. Chaney & Ezekiel Chaney	3	
Wm. Astin & John Astin	2	545
Wm. Compton	1	344
Andrew Pokson	1	
Thom. Hill	1	
John Pedler	1	
Wm. Davin & Son Ja[s] Davin	2	
John Bulard	1	
Nich Baker	1	
Theop. Lacey's List Mark, Hardin Overseer, negroes Dove, Abraham, Rachell and Bess	6	1100

List of Tithables taken by Thomas Dilliard, (8) Jr., in June 1767.

Joshua Ahston, Edm[d] Turner, negro Lucy	3	250
John Ahston		300
John Bolinger	1	
Thomas Boulding	0	Land
Benjamin Clement, (9) James Clement (negroes) Yourk, Robert & Tamor	5	529
Benjamin Clement Jr	1	

(8.) Thomas Dilliard, jun, was one of the first Commissioners of Peace for Pittsylvania in 1767. Also one of the first Vestrymen for Camden Parish. Also appointed Lieut-Col. of Pittsylvania Militia in 1767. In 1776 he commanded a company of Minute Men from Pittsylvania, which marched to Gwinn's Island and assisted in driving off Lord Dunmore (from David Irby's Declaration). In 1778 he commanded a Company of Pittsylvania Men on the Illinois Expedition. Marched to Boonesboro, Ky. (Pittsylvania Pensions).

(9.) Benjamine Clement was one of the earliest settlers of Pittsylvania County. In 1741 he patents land on both sides of Sycamore Creek, on South side of Staunton River. Here he built his home. At Court held for Fairfax County September 1752, Benjamine Clement is recommended for one of the Justices of the Peace. At Court held for Fairfax County Aug. 1755, Benj. Clement is appointed Captain of the Rangers. His will is probated in Pittsylvania C. H. in 1780.

Isaac Clement (10)	1	266
Benjamin Cadle	1	100
Adam Clement	0	200
William Collins & negro Dick	2	
John Chisom (Chisom)	1	200
James Chisom	1	150
Wm. Check, Joseph Luck, overseer (negroes) Peter & Jane	3	400
Francis Caloway	0	013
Thomas Dilliard Sn	3	650
Thomas Dillard, Sn, negro Will & Sarah	3	650
Thomas Dillard Jr., Wm. Gregory, negroes Hinory & Race	4	370
James Doss & John Dicker	2	370
Richard Deakens	1	400
Zacheriah Doss & John Doss	2	
Jacob Farris	1	320
Jonadab George	1	
Edward Hubbard	1	550
John Harness	1	
Thomas Henderson	1	
Edmond Hodges	1	100
Jonathan Jones	1	367
James Jones		
Edmond King (negro) Juday	2	150
Francis Luck (negro) Isom	2	730
James Lyle	0	420
Benjamine Lankford (11) (negro) Moll	2	632

(10.) Isaac Clement & Adam Clement were executors for their father, Benjamin Clement's estate. Adam Clement lived in Campbell County and was one of the original Trustees of the Town of Lynchburg when established 1786 (Howe's Virginia). Isaac Clement commanded a Company of Pittsylvania Militia under General Stephens in the Southern Campaign, first under Gates and then General Green. Also member of Committee of Safety for Pittsylvania in 1775.

(11.) Benjamine Lankford was the first Sheriff of Pitts County. Also a member of her first Commission of Peace. He was chosen a member of the Co. Committee of Safety of 1775. Also Captain of the Militia when County was put in state of defense in 1775. Member of House of Burgess for 1774 & 1775, and of the Conventions of March & December 1775 & 1776. Was clerk of the Vestry for Camden Parish for many years.

Richard Morton	0	800
Wm. Owen, Thomas Owen	2	
John Smith (12) (negroes) Dick, Daniel, Jack, Cyrus, Breachey, Vall, Chloe, Kate, Lucy, Edy, Delsey	12	700

(12.) John Smith owned a plantation in Pittsylvania which he called "the Pockett," for it lies in a rounding bend of Staunton River. He died in 1776 and was buried on his plantation, and I have an old trunk filled with his letters & business papers, from which I have learned that in 1749-50 he was serving as Sub-Sheriff of Albemarle under Col. Peter Jefferson. Among his papers are many fat rolls of Sheriff tickets, signed by Col. Jefferson. In 1760 we find him the Surveyor of Goochland County. In 1750 he purchased the Pockett Plantation from Col. Peter Jefferson, and his Account Books show that he kept an overseer and several negroes there & raised tobacco, they also show that he moved up to his Pockett Plantation in October 1762. "Oct. 1762. Riding chear bought of Capt. Thom. Starke £16. to John Hammond............£5. By going to Goochland after my cattle, 11 Days gone." The memorandum Booke shows that he built a new Dwelling in 1765. "To Stephen Woods for building Dwelling House £45.00. To Stephen Lownes for building two chimneys to New House £6.10. Also for building chimney to old house £2.0.0." John Smith raised much tobacco which he rolled & waggoned to Rocky Ridge, Chesterfield, where Mr. Alexander Stewart, a merchant seemed to look after the tobacco. Many letters from Mr. Stewart reveal much concerning the customs of the times. There were tailors and dress-makers at Rocky Ridge, & Mr. Stewart looked after these matters for John Smith. In May '66, Stewart writes, "your clothes I have at last got out of the Taylor's Shop, have sent them by this opportunity. They are packed up in a light cask where I hope they will not get wet. As to any news of the Stamp Act we have not received any certain account of its being repealed, but by the last accounts from home it was the opinion of everybody there that it would be repealed in a few days after the last ship came away, have sent you the last Newspaper wherein you'll find the acco't brought by her." Accompanying this letter was the men'd of articles sent back by the wagons in which we find

1 pr. Wm. Kid Gloves.......................................£0.1.9
1 pr. Wm. Thread Stockings.......................................0.2.4
4 yds White Sattin Ribbon.......................................2.6
1 pr. Men Shoes.......................................3.2
1 pr. Men's brown thread Hose.......................................3.2
2 Ivory Combes.......................................1.10
4 yds. Irish Linnen.......................................4.4
6 yds. Holland.......................................14.3
and etc. In Sept. '66, he writes that he should have sent the Gown and Stays but Mrs. Young had not done them. Letters received from Dr. James Hopkins, of Albemarle, reveal the fact that John Smith's health is very poor, and in 1769 he goes to "the Warm Springs" in Augusta. Dr. Hopkins recommends "the Sovereign Remedy of Riding" for a Consumption, showing in that early day fresh air was recognized as a great healer of bad lungs. However he died in 1776, & his will is probated in Pitts. C. H. He left following children: Ralph Smith, Sam'l Smith, John Smith, Bowker Smith, Elizabeth, wife of Sam'l Calland, and Anna B, wife of William Calloway.

John Owen	1	600
John Pemberton, Constable	0	260
Byrd Prewet	1	360
Jessy Pattey & Chas. Pattey	2	
Phileman Payne	1	100
Benjamin Potter	1	200
John Short	1	400
To. Micajah Terrell, George Hearden, overseer (negroes) Toby, Daniel, Leason, Sarah, Diner	6	
George Thomas	0	216
John Vaughn	0	390
Mathew Vance	1	
George Wilcox	1	340
Geo. Wilcox Jr. negro Philis	2	
Col. Richard Whitton for Land		5716
Thomas Robertson	1	200
George Evans (negro) Cate	2	
John Ward (13) for John Lynch	0	585
Christopher Gorman & Son Wm	2	
Richard Farthing	1	
George Parsons	1	100
Joseph Parsons	1	100
Jesse Ahston (negro) Casar & Nann	3	

A List of Tithables taken by Robert Chandler for 1767.

Elisha Walling (14) & negro Jake in all	2
Francis Kinton	1
John Blevins (son of Daniel)	1
Benj. Hubbard	1

(13.) John Ward married the 2nd time Mrs. Sarah Lynch, widow of Major Charles Lynch, of whom John Lynch was the son. Thus Major John Ward was step-father of John Lynch.

(14.) Elisha Walling (Walden). In 1767 Elisha Walden was elected Captain of a Company of Militia for Pittsylvania County. Major John Redd in his "Reminiscences" (see Va. Mag. of Hist. Vol. 7, 249) that Walden lived in Pittsylvania County on Smith's River, and that he had been a long hunter for many years. "Walden always returned home with his horses heavily ladened with skins and furs."

Richard White	1	
Thomas Hubbard	1	
James Sams	1	
Geo. Daniel	1	
William Rice	1	570
William Sams	2	
James Wilson and Moses his son	2	70
Merry Webb, Jr	1	
Henry Bates, Isaac Bates, Henry Bates, Jr., Mathew Steed & negro Samson	5	
Jas. Blevins, Jr	1	
John Ray	1	40
Abnon Harber	1	296
John Bolling	1	100
John Bowman	1	
John Blevins, Sr	1	
Geo. Rowland, negros Samson, Winey, Hannah Mimsey, Luck	6	
John McGuffey	1	
Wm. Dugger	1	
Jas. Guinn	1	
Shockley F. Simmons	1	
Martin Webb	1	
Chas. Burns	1	
Alex. Burns	1	
Thomas Baby	1	
Pyerce Guinn	1	
Sam'l Hall	1	162
Arch. Boling	1	
Sam'l Burns	1	
Merry Webb Sen., Bartley O'Neal, negroes Robert, Brinter, Judy, Jeanx, Jas. Webb the son of Merry	7	150
Dillion Blevins	1	
Benj. Bullington	1	
Jno. Acoff	1	
Thomas Wilson	1	70

A List of Tithes taken by John Wimbish, (29) Gent., for the year 1767.

Robert Adams (15)	1	100
Mrs Sarah Piggs (16) Tithes, Richard Pigg, Phillis, Jim, Lucas, Dorcas & Peter	6	500
James Pigg	1	200
Henry McDaniel	1	700
Jeremiah Worsham	1	
Joseph Gorman	1	
ThomasHardy		200
Jonathan Jenings	1	
Thomas Hardy, Jr., & Jno. Bailey	2	200
Richard Thurman	1	250
Nathaniel Christian	1	200
Adam Clement		200

(15.) Robert Adams was the son of Robert and Mourning Adams of Louisa County. He married Penelope Lynch, daughter of Major Charles Lynch and his wife Sarah Clark, daughter of Col. Christopher Clark of Louisa County. "His home was on Staunton River in Northern part of Pittsylvania County. In 1776, Robert Adams served as Lieutenant in expedition to guard the Lead Mines on New River. In 1787, he commanded a company of Militia, under Col. Chas. Lynch, his brother-in-Law. (From Pension Papers of John West.)

(16.) Mrs Sarah Pigg was the widow of Paul Pigg who came to Pittsylvania from Amelia County in 1756. His will is the first to be recorded in Pittsylvania County, bearing date 1766.

(To be continued)

TITHABLES OF PITTSYLVANIA COUNTY, 1767.

(Contributed by Mrs. N. E. Clement, Chatham, Va.)

	Tithes	Land
Capt. John Wards (17) Tithes	17	
John Cleveland, Thos. Hardy, Peter Lee, Harry, Jack, Abram, Bess, Tom, Ben, Nant, Jack, Dick, Matt, Tom, John, Thomas & Nant	17	
John Nichols	1	100
Samuel Smith, Jack, Tom, Will, Hannah, & Bess,	6	150
Edward Polley, Jr.,	1	
John Adams, John Adams, Jr.,	2	894
Allan Adams,	1	200
Charles Beasley,	1	
William Pigg,	1	200

(17.) John Ward came to Pittsylvania from Albemarle about 1763. (Book of Surveys, Pittsylvania Records). He built his home on the north side of Staunton River, now Campbell, which he called the "Mansion," for its elegance in those pioneer days. It is standing to-day, a quaint old homestead, with its corner fire places and cabinets either side the mantel. There are three stories and the third story was the ball room, covering the entire house, and here the daughters of the house were married. John Ward married 1st Anne Chiles, daughter of Henry Chiles of Amelia (Va. Mag. Hist. Vol. 20), by this marriage there was issue:

1. William Ward, married Mildred Adams, daughter of Robert Adams and Penelope Lynch.
2. Agatha Ward, married Col. John Calloway.
3. Anne Ward, married Christopher Lynch, son of Major Chas. Lynch and Sarah Clark Lynch.
4. Thomas Ward married Mildred Walden.
5. Jeremiah Ward moved to Texas.
6. John Ward, settled "Sulphur Springs" home.
7. Henry Ward, born Ap. 5, 1751, died Ap. 12, 1823 (taken from tomb at the "Mansion.") Married Martha Barbour.

John Ward married secondly Mrs Sarah Clark Lynch, widow of Major Charles Lynch, Dec. 17, 1766 (Bedford County Records).

During the Revolutionary War, John Ward was appointed Major of the Bedford Militia. His will is recorded in Campbell County, 1817.

A List of Tithables Taken by John Hanley (18), Gent for year 1767.

	Tithes	Land
William Hinton,	2	
John Panill,	1	
John Condaman,	1	
Wm. Huntsman,	1	
James Lyon,	4	200
John Bollin,	1	
Wm. Bollin,	1	
Wm. Stevens,	3	
James Anderson,	1	
Daniel Wells,	2	
Joshua Bewclett,	2	
Jac. McPais (?)	1	
Abraham Brend,	1	
William Brend,	1	
Beni Sanders,	1	
John Hall,	1	
Nathan Bewclett,	3	
Daniel Con,	1	
John McGown,	4	
Bedford Jinkins,	1	
Eliphes Shalton,	2	
George Cowton,	4	
———— Shelton	2	
George Carrail, (?)	1	
John Williams,	1	
Ralph Shelton, Sen.,	4	200
John Hanby,	4	

A List of Tythables Taken July 17, 1767 by Peter Copland (19) Gent

John Kendricks,	1
James Roberts,	1

(18.) John Hanbey was one of the first Justices of the Peace for Pittsylvania County, and lived in that portion which later was known as Patrick County. In 1775, was appointed Captain of the Militia.

(19.) Peter Copland, one of the first Justices of Peace for Pittsylvania, and lived in that portion of the county which later became Henry.

	Tithes.	Land
Dauzwell Rogers,	1	
Thom. Nunn,	3	
Rich White,	1	
John Rowland, John Palfery, Jack & Pegg,	4	
Capt. William Blevins, Dawl & Peter,	3	
Daniel Newman Jun,	1	
Dennis Bryan,	1	
Thomas Wright,	1	
John Rice,	1	
Neel Roberts,	1	
James Wallen,	1	
Charles Scaggs	1	
Edw[d] Callaham,	1	
D'o. Baker,	1	
Harry Dillen,	1	
Wm. Young,	1	
Wm. Baily Jun,	1	
Rich. Baker,	1	
Little William Blevins,	1	
Frederick D. O. Daniel,	1	
William Bailey, Sen[r],	1	
Wm. Ashart,	1	
David Shadwell & Bob,	2	150
John Handy,	1	
Jacob Cooger & son Henry,	2	
James Filley,	1	
Wm. Reed,	1	
David Hailey,	1	
Robt McVatta	1	
Wm. McVatta	1	
John Barker	1	
Jeremiah Claimck, Jun	1	
John Newman	1	
Kave Bailey	1	
Thomas Cooper, Sen	1	
Wm. Reeding	1	
Thomas Shanam & David Cazey	2	

	Tithes	Land
Jessey Bound & Pompey	2	
Enguim Nunn	1	
Joseph Nunn & Nan	2	
Thomas Gazaway	1	
Joseph Wallen	1	
Elisha Wallen Sen[r]	1	
Thomas Cooper, Jr., Terence Daniel, negroes George & Winney	4	300
William Bass	1	
Elisha Harbour	1	150
Elijah Harbour & negro Hannah	2	310
Fosyth Bradberry	1	
James Merrydeth	1	
Barclay Merrydeth	1	
William Merrydeth, Constable	1	
Thomas Webb	1	
John Wells	1	
William Thomas, John Davis, Benj Davis & Charles Mitchell	4	
Waters Dunn, Waters Dunn, Jr., Rich[d] Dunn, Rich[d] Bradberry, negroes Tom, Moll & Lilly	7	
Peter Copland; Rich[d] Copland, Dan'l Mc-Bride & negro Hannah	4	
Ambrose Jones, negroes Dinah & Judy	3	
Thomas Cooper, jr	1	
Philip Ryan	1	
John Talbot	1	765
James Calk	1	
John Cox, Sr., John Cox, Jr., Neg[o] Lucy	3	
Nemian Prater, Nemiah Prater	2	
Charles Semple	1	
Matthew Small	1	
	99	

The above List of Tithables taken by me.

Peter Copeland.

	Tithes	Land
A List of Tithables & Land taken by.........................Gordon, Pittyslvania County, 1767.		
John Wimbsih, James Mitchell, negro Cyrus, Orange, Sall, Pegg, in all	6	627
John Martin, Joseph Cox	2	
William Candler, Arestripes Baghan, negro Chester	3	
William Stanley, John Stanley, Wm. Stanley, Jr.	3	
William Pain	1	
Thomas Stone	1	
John Stone, jun^r	1	
James Stone	1	100
Thomas Justice	1	
Israel Justice	1	300
Simeon Justice	1	
Samuel Gordon	Torn	
Archibald Gordon (20), negros Dick, Kildare, Lucy, Sarah	5	(torn)
John Hickey (21)		(torn)

A List of Tithables taken by Hamon Critz (22), Gent., for the year 1767.

Thomas Walling	1	125

(20.) Archibald Gordon, one of the first Justices of the Peace. Was appointed Lieutenant of the Militia in 1767. In 1774 was made Col. of of the County. Elected Sheriff in 1771. "He was Scotch by birth, and lived and died without marrying" (Va. Mag. Hist. Vol. 7).

(21.) John Hicky, very probably the Mr. Hikki mentioned in the Moravian Diary, 1753. (Va. Mag. Hist. Vol. XIII). When passing through what is now Henry County, they say, "Mr. Hikki who lives half a mile from here and keeps a store (which is nearest house at which we can buy salt), came to us and showed himself very friendly. We had a miserable road to his house. Here we bought some provisions." In the earliest records of the county we find mention of "Hicky's old road." It traverses the county from Staunton River on the north straight to the Court house, and then turns due west into Henry County, and this same road is to-day called Hicky's road.

(22.) Hamon Critz, one of the first Justices of the County. He lived in that part of the county later known as Patrick. At a meeting of the Vestry of Camden Parish at Pittsylvania Courthouse, July 22, 1769, "a chappel of ease" was ordered to be built near Captain Haman Crites of a size 20 by 24 feet, Round loggs for the body, a clapboard Roof and Benches, & etc."

	Tithes	Land
William Hays	2	
Cillis Ratlift	1	
Arch'l Hughes	1	
Geo. Allan		
Henry France		
David Gowing	3	272
Nicholas Langford	2	
James Fee	1	
Geo. Poor	2	
Rob[t] Crump, Jun[r]		
Rob[t] Crump, Sen[r]		
Frederick Fulkerson		
Alex[r] Deputy		
Adam Loving (23)	2	
William Loving	1	
Joseph Cameron	1	400
John Pluk	3	
Zacheriah Cook	1	
Thos. Harbour	4	790
David Witt	1	
Paletiah Shelton	1	144
Geo. Gibson	1	
John Wildrich Bender		402
John Parr	2	400
William Denson	1	
William Tirpin	1	
Geo. Gray	1	
William Harrald	1	
John Jinings	1	
Peter Rentfro	2	
John Koger	1	
John France	3	
John Camron	1	

(23.) Adam Loving is mentioned in the Moravian Diaries, 1753. They were passing through what is now Henry County and write "we drove four miles further and ate dinner at Adam Loving's plantation. They were very friendly to us. The man showed us the ford across the first branch of Mayo River." (Va. Mag. Hist. Vol. 13.)

	Tithes	Land
David Lyler	1	
Miles Jinings	2	185
Lambath Dodson	1	
Phillip Buzzard	1	
Thom. Murry	1	
Solomon Smith	1	
John Spain	1	
John Gooch	1	
James Pritchard	2	
Haman Critz	2	200

A List of Tithables taken for Pittsylvania in 1767 by John Dix (24).

John Armstrong Annica	2	210
Thomas Ayers	1	
Daniel Ayers	1	
Moses Ayers	1	
John Bynum	1	200
Arthur Bynum	1	
Lawrence Barker	1	
William Barker	1	
Edward Burges	1	
John Bynam Jr.	1	
Moses Cornelius	1	
Thomas Colley	1	
William Cornelius	1	
William Colley	1	
John Chipman, Constable	1	
James Collie	1	
Thomas Dudley	1	
Henry Dixon, Jas. Durough, Jas. Borough	3	
John Dix, Ephraim Dismunkes, James Evalto, Will, Joe, Minkes, Ben, Lett, Old Janney & Janney and 1 chair, deduct 2 tithes being ferrymen	10	307

(24.) John Dix, established a ferry across Dan River in 1766, which was used constantly in Southern Campaign of Revolution (see Pitts Records). Was one of the first Justices of the County. Appointed Captain of the Militia in 1775.

	Tithes	Land
William Durrett, Peter	2	
Edward Floyde		180
Lewis Green, William Green	2	100
John Hamilton		400
Samuel Harris (25), Bob. Honeyball, York, Pompey, Janney, Sally, Lucy	8	757
James Hogan, William Hogan	2	100
John Hensley	1	
Thomas Pistole	1	
Samuel Pruett	1	590
Hugh Mahone	1	165
John McClane	1	
Thomas Merriwether, William Meriwether, Jason Bowcock, Paul, Frank, Southsea Betty, Nann, Hannah, Nann, Nedd, Sue, Judy, Creshea, Joe, Paul, Jacob, Cate, Peter & Judy	20	545
William McDaniel, Tom, Dick, Daniel, Lovoney, Milley, Liddy & Janney	9	960
Daniel Ober	1	
William Owen	1	100
John Roberts, Jas. Roberts & Jas. Roberts, Jr.	3	383
Gabriel Richards	1	200
David Ross		640
Geo. Southerland	2	175
John Southerland	1	
Jacob Stillwell	1	
Philip Southerland	1	

(25.) Samuel Harris was a pioneer Baptist Minister of Virginia. He was also an early settler of this county, having many surveys made Ap. 2, 1748. An old book entitled "Pioneer Baptist Preachers of Virginia" says of him that "he was born 1724, in Hanover County. When young he moved to the County of Pittsylvania. As he advanced in age he became a favorite of the people. He was appointed church warden, sheriff, a justice of the peace, burgess for the county, Colonel of the Militia, Captain of Mayo Fort, and Commissary for the Fort and Army. On one of his visits to the fort in his official character he called at the home of William and Joseph Murphy, dressed in his uniform * * * * Was converted and was baptized in 1758 by the Reverend Daniel Marshall During the war when it was extremely difficult to procure salt, kept two wagons running to Petersburg to bring up salt for his neighbors."

	Tithes	Land
John Stamps	1	
Timothy Stamps	1	
James Terry		3065
William Travis	1	
William Thomas, Arthur & Janny	3	1005
William Tredwell	1	
William Wynne, Prince, Peter, Nedd, Cale & Judy	6	400
Thomas Wynne & Lucy	2	165
Robert Wright	1	
William Wynne, jr., Saunders Southerland & Prince	3	500
John Worsham & Sirus	2	
Joshua Worsham, Will, Frank, Abram, Lucy, Judy & Pegg	7	300
Robert Wynne	1	
Thomas Wynne, jr.	1	400
John Wheler	1	

Signed John Dix.

List of Tithables taken by Peter Perkins (26) for the year 1767.

	White	Blacks	Acres	Wheels
George Chadwell Land			125 ac	
Dutton Lain tith, Land	1		83 ac	
David Terrill Land			275	
Edward Sweeton (?) tithe	1			
John Morton tithe, land	1		450	
James Burnett tithe	1			

(26.) Peter Perkins was the son of Constant Perkins and owned a large plantation "Oak Hill," in southern part of the county, on Dan River. He took an active part in the life of the county, being one of the first Justices of the Peace. Was a Vestryman, member of the County Committee of Safety. & in 1775, appointed Captain of the Militia. Commanded a Pittsylvania Company of Minute Men in Cherokee Expedition of 1776. By the close of the Revolution, had been promoted to Colonel and commanded a regiment in battle of Guilford (Pittsylvania Pension Papers). In the spring of 1781, a Continental Hospital was established at his home for three months, as the Book of Claims, for Pittsylvania shows.

	White	Black	Acres	Wheels
Davie Fields tithe	1			
George Russell Land			180	
George Young, 1 negro woman, 1 Land	1	1	520	
Christopher Bowlin, son William	2			
Joseph Bowlin, 1 tithe	1			
James Bowlin, 1 tithe	1			
Ephram McGoff	1			
George Thompson	1			
Richard Churchwell, tithe	1			
John Rich tithe	1			
..................Conoway, 1 tithe	1			
Archibald Thompson	1			
Rodden Thompson	1			
Randolph Gipson, tithe, negro Bomber. Land	1	1	100	
Thomas Calaway, sons Charles and Richard's land	3		100	
John Court & soninlaw Jas. Coursey Peterson	2			
John Frederick Richel, 1 tithe Land	1		190	
William Rice Sadler	1			
Patrick Stiel, 1 tithe	1			
Thomas Smith, son Thomas, Land	2		400	
Edward Smith, negro Will, Land	1	1	150	
John Fulton, 1 tithe Land	1		300	
John Smith, negro Dinah Land	1	1	355	
Henry Lansford, negro Judy, Land	1	1	377	
Ralph Elkins Jun	1			
Richard Elkins, 1 tithe	1			
Nathaniel Elkins, son Jessey	2			
John Rukey, son James	2			
Thom. Gresham	1			
Christopher Bowling Jun	1			
John Gresham son of Phil Gresham	1			
Edward Perogog, tithe	1			
James Elkin on leather wood	1			
Samuel Shields, Land	1		130	

	White	Black	Acres	Wheels
John Gresham son of Thom Gresham	1			
Jesse Elkins, 1 tithe	1			
John Cox	1			
John Givins	1			
William Shields	1			
George Button	1			
Henry Burnett	1			
Thom. Cunningham Jun	1			
James Shields, 1 tithe, Land	1		210	
James Strong	1			
Benjamine Croley, negro Peter, Land	1	1	48	
Thomas Strong	1			
Charles Cloke, tithe	1			
Benjamine Croly, 1 tithe land	1		210	
John Strong, Joseph Martin	2		100	
Jeremiah Walker, negro	1	1		
Joseph Cunningham 1 tithe land	1		370	
Joseph Morton, 1 tithe, negro Dinah Land	1	1	400	
Abraham Passley 1 tithe	1			
Martain Dunkin	1			
John Scags	1			
James Edwards 1 tithe land	1		90	
Thom. Bullock	1			
Richard Bullock	1			
John Lankford 1 tithe Land	1		360	
Joseph Cotton	1			
James Presnall son James, negro Jane	2	1		
George Hide 1 tithe	1			
Owen Wait	1			
Joel Certain 1 tithe	1			
Shadrack Turner sons John & Josiah	3		256	
Thomas Watson, 1 tithe land	1		100	
John Watson Jun, Land	1		220	
James Gravely Jun'r	1			
John Watson, sen tithe & Land	1		104	
John Warring	1			

	Whites	Blacks	Acres	Wheels
Thom. Gravely	1			
James Garner 1 tithe	1			
Thomas Garner 1 tithe	1			
Thomas Horgeth tithes	1	2		
John Morton tithes Negroes dogery & seftis	1	2		
Arthur Fuller	1			
Daniel Hankins negroes frank, Nan & patt and Land	1	3	1780	
Nicholas Perkins 1 tithe negro moll	1	1		
Joseph Harris	1			
David Harris	1			
John Harris Constable				
Benjamine Neal Constable				
John Roach 1 tithe	1			
John Oaks	1			
John Rice	1			
Henry Dunlop	1			
John Gwin	1			
John Sams	1			
William Bean & son Wm. Land	2		1083	
John Harchman son Thomas Land	2		100	
Constant Perkins negro Jacob	1	1		
John Chadwell negro Farmer & Tiller, Land	1	2	748	
Zacheriah McCubbins	1			
John Been Jun	1			
John Jones, 1 tithe Land	1		200	
John Join Land			525	
Wm. Edwards son Thom. Land	2		293	
Robt Perriman	1			
Thomas Billings	1			
William Murphy	1			
Thom. Edwards, negro Andrew Land	1	1	91	
William McCubbin	1			
Henry Rice Land	1		200	
Nathan Carter	1			

A List of Land & Tithes taken by Hugh Innes (27) for Pittsylvania County Anno. Dom. 1767.

	Tithes	Land
Samuel Collins	1	
Rowland Judd & Nathaniel Judd	2	
James Keith	1	
Charles Atkinman	1	
Morris Atkinson	1	
Abner Cochrum	1	
John Law John Law jr. negroes Jeany & Keat	4	400
Henry Atkinson jr	1	
Thomas Hall	1	
William Hall & Lansford Hall	2	
Jesse Hall	1	
William Hall jr	1	
William Hill	1	400
Isom Hall	1	200
Thomas Dunkin Jr	1	
Thomas Jones	1	536
Thomas Anderson & James Anderson	2	130
William Griffith	1	
Joseph Clements, Gabriel Clements & Vardiman Clements	3	
Francis Easom & Wm Hungett, John Hungett & Chas. Hungett	4	135
Christopher Shot & Christopher Shot Jr	2	
Benjamine Barten	1	
John Ferguson & negro Dinah	2	130
John Savory Jr	1	
William Bramby	1	
Samuel Walker & negro Judd	2	
William Davis	1	
Joseph Bird	1	400
Reuben Kieff	1	
Robert Hill, Swinfield Hill & Thomas Hill	3	250

(27.) Hugh Innes was a Justice of Peace, Vestryman & member of County Committee of Safety. He, with John Donelson, represented Pittsylvania in Convention of August 1774.

TITHABLES OF PITTSYLVANIA COUNTY, 1767.

(Contributed by Mrs. N. E. Clement, Chatham, Va.)

	Tithes	Land
Swinfield Hill		150
Austin Shot	1	
Thomas Shoat	1	
John Vanbibber	1	400
Henson McDonal	1	
Francis McGuier	1	
John McGuier	1	
Thomas Carter	1	
John McGuier Jr.	1	
Merry McGuier	1	
Paul Henson	1	
John Henson	1	
William Henson	1	
James Standeford	1	
William Murphy	1	113
Miller Dogget	1	
Richard Hough	1	
Joshua Barton	1	107
David Barton	1	
Isaac Barton	1	
William Ferguson	1	
Thomas Miller & William Sumers	2	
Francis Bird	1	240
Andrew Ferguson	1	
Joseph Rentfro		280
Robert Jones, Thomas Jones & Henry Jones	3	520
John Jones	1	400

Robert Jones Jr.	1	220
Philip Smith	1	150
William Cook	1	610
John Fushon	1	225
James Rentfro jr.	1	
James Rentfro Sen, Joseph Rentfro & Peter Rentfro	3	600
Veath Dilingham & negro Jeany	2	100
Peter Vanbibber, jr.	1	200
Isaac Vanbibber	1	
Mack Foster Sen	1	
Richard Pearis's tithes are, William Lowry, negroes: Jack, Harry, Jeany, Hannah & Silviah	6	
Anthony Litle	1	170
Christopher Lackenair	1	
John Meadly	1	200
John Dilingham	1	
James Lamb	1	
William Webb	1	
John Ramsey	1	230
Joshua Weaver & Isaac Weaver	2	
Holden McGee	1	
Edward Richards	1	140
William Dilingham & Joshua Dilingham	2	93
Amos Richardson & negro Moll	2	150
Benj. Jenkins	1	300
Robert Tormet	1	
John Hall	1	200
Francis Farley	1	
Wm. Heard, George Heard & Wm. Beans	3	400
Thomas Bird	1	
Richard Shoat	1	
Jeremiah Muray	1	526
John Stevenson	1	
John Callaway, negroes Flemen, Asher, Nan & Nell	5	500
Abraham Motley & negro Peter	2	

Stephen Heard & Jesse Heard	2	460
Hugh Innes, James Parberry, negroes Juba, Keat & Peat	5	1245
John Heard	1	165
Stephen Heard jr	1	247
Lewes Jenkins & negro Jack	2	1250
John Justice Constable		100
William Henson	1	
William Witcher (28) & negro Sawney	2	100
William Keeny	1	190
James Wade	1	
Daniel McKenzie	1	
William Atkinson & Owen Atkinson	2	200
John Good jr	1	600
Joseph Deal	1	
Richard Shockley	1	50
Daniel Witcher	1	191
David Dalton & Benj. Dalton	2	650
Samuel Paterson	1	1687
John Witcher	1	190
Robt Dalton, John Dalton & Robt Dalton jr	3	30
John Dalton		45
Richard Walding, John Walding & negroes Jed, Jeffry, Greace, Phoebe & Lucy	7	500
Richard Adkinson	1	50
William Lawson	1	76
William Hodges & Thomas Neville	2	
John Hensley	1	
David Polly		150
James Dalton	1	65
Henry Atkinson	1	
Jacob Seartin	1	
James Stewart & James Stewart jr	2	
Arch Graham & negro Robin	2	750

(28.) William Witcher took the oath of Vestryman 1768. Was member of County Committee of Safety. Appointed Captain of Militia in 1775. Commanded a Company of Militia in Indian Expedition of 1776. When the Regiment under Col. Christian pushed on into Tenn., a force of 200 men were left under the command of Capt. Witcher to guard Fort Patrick Henry. (Pittsylvania Pension Papers).

George Philige, Thom. Lawrence, John Blackesley, negroes Tobias, Robin, Tom, Madey, Betty	8	
John Hunsman	1	
Richard Remington	1	
John Heard	1	
William Beams	1	
William Graham		298
Nicholas Alley	1	635
John Willis	1	
Benjamine Griffith	1	130
Jonathan Davis	1	
Jacob Adkinson	1	
Edward Wade & negro Pegg	2	200
David Wade	1	326
William Tyrie	1	
Jacob Stober	1	
Jeremiah Stober	1	
William Hodges	1	
Sherwood Adkins	1	
Thomas Potter	1	400
John Simons	1	150
Bragan Prunty & Robt Prunty	2	
Benj Dunkin		
John Anderson	1	
Richard Perryman & negro Billiak	2	
John Midleton	1	
Nathaniel Evans		315
Hezekiah Pigg	1	
Adam Stilts	1	

Signed

Hugh Innes.

(29.) John Wimbish, a justice of peace & vestryman for Pittsylvania County. There is an order Calendar of State Papers that "the enemy (British) having returned from Dan River, Mr. Wm. McCaw is appointed to that station, and to keep his principal post at Wimbish's stores at Peytonsburg."

A LIST OF TITHABLES BETWEEN BUSH AND BUFFALO RIVERS.

Taken by Thomas Scott, June, 1755.

Contributed by W. S. Morton

Jacob Williamson.... 0
William Nassary..... 6
and 5 Slaves.

William Simmons
and 1 slave......... 2

John Gaulding, Sr.,
John Gaulding, Jr... 2
and 2 negroes....... 4

Hugh Nixon......... 1

James Thackson
and 3 Slaves......... 4

William Price
and 3 slaves......... 4

Joseph Shelton
William Shelton...... 2

John Harrison....... 1

Richard Childers.... 1

John Biggers
and 1 slave......... 2

Richard Morton
and 1 slave......... 2

John Morton
and 3 slaves......... 4

James Brown........ 1

James Durham...... 1

Pugh Price, Sr.,
Pugh Price, Jr.,
and 7 slaves......... 9

David Flournoy
Thomas Ward
and 4 slaves......... 6

Mathew Flournoy
James Archdeacon
Thomas Flournoy
and 2 Slaves........ 5

Silcock Cannon...... 1

Guy Smith
Francis Slead
and 3 slaves......... 5

John Popham....... 1

Alexander Kean
John King.......... 2

John Morton........ 1

Thomas Scott, Jr.
and 6 slaves......... 7

James Carter........ 0

James Hopkins
and 2 slaves......... 3

Hugh Challes
and 3 slaves......... 4

Robert Hastie
John Graham....... 2

Benjamin Atkins
John Moor
and 1 slave......... 3

James Atwood....... 0

John Atwood
and 3 slaves......... 3

John Cox
Abraham Baker
and 2 slaves......... 4

William Satterwhite.. 1

Richard Attwood.... 0
and 1 slave.......... 1

George Davis
John Davis......... 2

Adam Cahoon....... 1

John Bibbs.......... 0
and 3 slaves......... 3

William Williams
Edward Brafford.... 2

John Thompson..... 1

Peter Davis
Thomas Green
and 4 slaves......... 6

John Foster
and 1 slave......... 2

Alexander Womack.. 1

Michael McDearment
Bryant McDearment. 2

Charles Hudson

and 3 slaves......... 4

John Richie......... 1

Archibald McIlroy... 1

James Mcleroy
Hugh Mcleroy....... 2

John Mcleroy....... 1

Thomas Watkins.... 0

John With
and 3 slaves......... 4

Richard Washburn
James Washburn.... 2

Peter LeGrand
Phill Lightfoot
and negroes......... 5

Richard Woodson
and 8 slaves......... 9

Nathaniel Venable... 1

Thomas Baldwin
John Baldwin
Caleb Baldwin
and 3 slaves......... 6

James Archdeacon
Edmund Archdeacon
and 1 slave......... 3

John Watson
and 6 slaves......... 7

John Martin
Daniel Ayres
and 8 slaves.........10

Edward Mackgehee.. 0

James Davenport
and 3 slaves......... 4

William Brown
John Brown
and 1 slave......... 3

Theoderick Carter
William Carter
and 3 slaves......... 5

Col. Charles Anderson
John Philips
and 7 slaves......... 9

John Acuff.......... 1

(Total)............191
346
330

(Grand total.......867
For the year 1755.

W. S. Morton (Researcher).

Farmville, Va. March 17th, 1934.

1755. A LIST OF TITHABLES, FROM BUFFALO TO THE COUNTY LINE.

John LeNeve (5).... 6

James McKeme..... 1

John Caldwell (Fort Creek
and Thomas Caldwell 2

William Boyd and
George Caldwell..... 2

Thomas Caldwell (1). 2

John McClelend and
Abraham McClel'd... 2

Nathaniel Harris (2). 3

Charles Harris....... 1

Francis Reed........ 1

William Aston....... 1

Peter Downey....... 1

Andrew Rostrick.... 1

Jeremiah Penick (2).. 4
and Edward Penick.. 2

Watson Bromfield... 1

Charles Miller....... 1

Daniel Newman
John & James Newman.......... 3

Mark Chamber...... 1

Hugh Richey........ 1

Charles Richie....... 1

Robert Hanna (planter).......... 1

Robert Elliot (1).... 2

Charles Gilliam (3)... 4

Joshua Gilliam...... 1

John Hardy......... 1

John Simmons....... 1

James Parkes (1).... 2

James Mitchell...... 1

William Melwee..... 1

William Martin...... 1

Patrick Galispie &
Crisley Strog........ 2

Thomas Stone and
William Stone and
Andrew Flower (3)... 6

Thomas Armstrong.. 1

Bryan Henry........ 1

Robert Read........ 1

Edward Johnson..... 1

Robert Hanna, Sr., and
Robert Hanna, Jr.... 2

Robert Galispie (3).. 4

Samuel Baker (3).... 4

John May (constable) 1

Williams Burks...... 1

John Burks......... 1

Abraham Vanable &
James Vanable &
John Fulton (9).....12

Douglas Puckett &
Peter Pucket........ 2

John Davis and
William Rice........ 2

James Ewing &
Joshua Ewing....... 2

Joseph Littlejohn (1). 2

Joseph Cunningham.. 1

John Richey........ 1

Arthur Cheatham.... 1

William Watson &
James Watson &
Douglas Watson..... 3

William Gatty....... 1

Sam'l Southerland (2) 3

Isaac Robinson, Jr... 1

Alexander Robinson.. 1

Thomas Baldwin.... 1

Manus McBride..... 1

Robert Martin...... 1

John Porter......... 1

Robert Black........ 1

John Cunningham... 1

Hugh Porter........ 1

Andrew Dunn....... 1

Edward Shillideay... 1

George Shillideay.... 1

Samuel Smith....... 1

Charles Venable &
William Newman (4). 6

1755.
Col. Randolph's list (27)

Richard Welden &
Nathaniel Barksdale—
Ov'ers..............29

Col. Richard Randolph's list (4)
and William Neal—
overseer............ 5

Daniel McKee....... 1

Patrick Shields and
Samuel Shields...... 2

James and John Reed 2

Thomas Bryan...... 1

Mr. McKee's list (4). 4

James Browning (1).. 2

Joseph Jeffres....... 1

Samuel Ewing &
Alexander Ewing (2). 4

George Ewing (1).... 2

John Dunn.......... 1

James Ewing........ 1

James
Cunningham (1)... 1

William Browning... 1

Patrick Napier...... 1

Elkanah Jennings.... 1

James Lax (1)....... 2

Andrew Porter...... 1

Robert Williamson (2) 3

Christopher Hill &
Thomas Roberson (1) 3

William & John Hill.. 2

Capt. List, and
John Anderson (5)... 6

James McMachen... 1

George Ewing (1).... 2

John Chambers (2)... 3

William Thurman (1) 2

Edward Nix &
George Nix (2)...... 4

Edmund Franklin.... 1

James Kelly......... 1

Silvanus Maxey..... 1

Peter Fore.......... 1

Thomas Gibs........ 1

John Kenison....... 1

Jacob Gibson........ 1

Chales Beasley...... 1

Richard Bennett &
James Bennett...... 2

Benjamin Angel..... 1

John May.......... 1

Valentine Gibson.... 1

Henry Dikes........ 1

Benjamin Witt &
Charles Witt &
Lewil Witt........ 3

Douglass Baker &
Robert Baker (3).... 5

James Walker and
Thomas Beard and
Moses Matthews (5). 8

Charles Simmons &
James Simmons..... 2

Manaseth McFeele &
Patrick............. 2

Jacob Stanley....... 1

John Pheps......... 1

Joseph Ashurst...... 1

Joel Watkins (3)..... 4

William Baldwin (1). 2

George Moore and
Charles Moore...... 2

Andrew McAdow.... 1

Peter Coffee and
William Coffee and
Peter Coffee, Jr..... 3

Joseph Hatfield...... 1

John Black......... 1

John McDaniel...... 1

William Ewing and
Thomas Ewing and
William Ewing...... 3

Robert Jennings..... 1

Obediah Woodson's
list

Benjamin Jenkins
(ov'ees and 4 slaves.. 5

Edward Grisam (1).. 2

Robert Grisam...... 1

John Green......... 1

George Cook........ 1

Samuel Mathews and
William Mathews.... 2

Robert Peak and
Samuel Peal (2)..... 4

Allexander Hamilton. 1

William Hall........ 1

Martha Baker's list

William Simmons (4). 5

John Garrington (2).. 3

Alexander Hamelton
Andrew Hamelton &
Robert Hamelton.... 3

John Morrow &
James Morrow...... 2

John Cock's list

John Butler and
John Cock (2)....... 4

Benjamin Phillips.... 1

Moses Phillips....... 1

Robert Bird &
Williamson Bird &
Phillemon Bird (4)... 7

William Campbell (2) 3

John Morrison (1)... 2

James Senton....... 1

Philip McTagert..... 1

John Lightfoot...... 1

James Donald....... 1

Thomas Fulton...... 1

Reubim Stanley..... 1

John Caldwell &
David Caldwell &
George Caldwell..... 3

John Caldwell, Jr.... 1

Samuel Wallace (2).. 3

Thomas Armstrong.. 1

John Limens........ 1

Signed—SAMUEL EWING. (328)

SLAVE OWNERS IN PRINCESS ANNE CO.

Probably in no State was property, before 1861, more equally distributed than in Virginia. Such enormous disparity as existed between the rich and poor of the Northern cities was unknown. Only here and there was seen a man who rose much in wealth above the average of his neighbors. The real poor class was smaller in proportion to the population "than anywhere in the universe."(1) The old servant and convict class had long before left the State spreading North and West.(2) It is easy enough to take the veriest vagabond in the present Virginia counties and trace him through the county records to respectable ancestors. "Poor white trash" was a term originating with the poor negroes, who sought to bolster up their own wretchedness by bragging of the quality of their masters. But no class was more independent, or oftentimes had better pretension to aristocratic descent, than the poor white men. Nor did any person demand, or receive, from their more fortunate neighbors, a distincter recogni-

(1) So stated by Smythe (by .no means a friendly writer) in his "Travels," as early as 1773.

(2) Spotswood, in his "Letters," speaks of the servants, when freed, congregating on the frontiers of the Colony. In 1751, the Pennsylvania papers complained of the runaways from Virginia and Maryland (Extracts cited in the "Virginia Gazette", 1751). After Bacon's rebellion, fugitives from Virginia walked the streets of Boston (Neill's Virginia Carolorum).

tion of their equality before nature and the law.[1] And no wonder, for they bore the same names and were "cousins" in a near or remote degree.[2]

The following list, prepared by Mr. Edward W. James, goes to show the fallacy of the opinion entertained in some quarters that Virginia was divided into two classes—the very rich and the very poor.

Names of Princess Anne County slave owners, who, during the year 1810, *owned ten or more slaves:*

Name	Slaves	Name	Slaves
Henry Bonney	10	Thos. B. W. Corprew	13
John R. Baley	11	Jonathan Corprew	23
James Braithwaite	10	Durant Corprew	19
Gaskins Brock	10	Henry Cornick, Sr	11
Mary Buskey	10	Jennet Dyson	10
Wm. Bishop	15	Wm. Ellegood	12
Wm. Benthall	14	Moses Fentress	11
Caleb Bonsh	45	Jonathan Fentress	11
Wm. Boush, Sr	20	Martha Gornto	10
Willis Butt	24	Geo. S. Gaskins	12
John P. Biddle	18	Joseph Grey	12
John Biddle	17	Simon Hancock	23
John Cornick	21	Erasmus Haynes	16
Lemuel Cornick	17	Thurmer Hoggard	20
Wm. B. Cornick	32	Josiah W. Hunter	13
Thomas Calvert	16	Jonathan Hopkins	20
Wm. M. Christian	16	John Haywood	12
Ezekiel Cox	14	John Haynes, Jr	17
Thomas Cornick	21	Elizabeth Hunter	14
Henry Cornick, Jr	14	James Haynes	24
Adam Cornick	21	Keziah Hopkins	15
Elizabeth Cornick	12	John Haynes, Sr	17
Endymn Cornick	17	Wm. Holt	17

(1) The editor has seen letters of Henry D. Bird (grandfather of Prof. Hugh S. Bird, of this College), a native of Pennsylvania, who came to Virginia in 1832 as civil engineer for the Petersburg & Weldon Railroad. He writes of the spirit prevailing in Virginia as "Democracy run mad," and of the haughtiness and independence of the poor people. This was to be expected, as Virginians idolized the levelling teachings of Jefferson, and his name was a shibboleth of faith. Dinwiddie and Spotswood, in their published letters, fully admitted, years before, the free spirit of the Virginians.

(2) Take any of the old Virginia names, and it is represented in the directories of Norfolk or Richmond by persons of all varieties of fortune.

Name	No.	Name	No.
Jonathan Hunter	11	Wm. Newsum	13
Wm. Hartagan	10	John Nimmo	14
Thomas Henley, Jr	11	Nathaniel Nicholas	11
James Henley	10	George Norris	10
Wm. James, Sr	10	Frederick Old	11
Edward James, son of Wm. James	10	Thomas L. B. Powell	32
Joshua James	25	Nath'l Payntar	13
Edward James (1)	17	Kiteley Philips	19
Rebecca Jones	12	Edward Seymore	17
John T. Keeling	16	Josiah W. Slack	21
Thos. Keeling, Jr	16	Henry Sparrow	14
Wm. T. Keeling	17	Simon Stone	32
Elizabeth Keeling	25	Johnson Stone	37
Molly Keeling	15	Thomas Stone	12
Jacob Keeling	29	Charles Sayer	10
Wm. Kays	13	Wm. Truss	18
Richard H. L. Lawson	18	Jacob Valentine	20
John S. Lovett	12	Wm. C. Veale	14
Francis M. Land	20	James B. Vaughan	14
Ree Land	19	Wm. Walke	16
Peter Land	14	Edward Wilson	14
Hillary Land	31	Arthur S. Woodhouse	22
John Lovett, Sr	20	Anthony Walke, Jr	14
Molly Land	10	Wm. D. Woodhouse	24
Wm. Matthias, Sr	10	Dennis Whitehurst	11
Jesse Morris	11	Jon[a] Woodhouse	11
Dr. James McAlpine	20	James Warden	11
Tully Moseley	12	Anthony Walke, son of A. Walke	18
Mary Moore, Jr	17	John Woodhouse, Sr	15
Henry Mackie	12	Anthony Walke, Sr	65
Edward H. Moseley	24	Henry Wells	15
Isaac Murray	26	Edmund Winder	13
Amy Moseley	12	Elizabeth Weeks	19
David S. Murray	17	John Woodard	24
John Mackie	18	Daniel Whitehurst	13
Christopher Moseley	15	Ann Williamson	14

(1) Edward James was the son of John James, deceased.

Slave Owners in Princess Anne County, Virginia

[In my January number a list of slave-holders in Princess Anne County having more than ten slaves was published. The following list comprises all having under ten slaves. It will be seen that in this county the large majority of the heads of families owned slaves. This by no means represented all the families interested in slave property. Many persons preferred to hire slaves, and, besides the hirers of slaves, there were many persons who, while not owning slaves, were dependent upon that species of property, such as overseers, store-keepers, physicians etc. These last had a more substantial interest in the slaves than the nominal slave-owners. On the whole, slaves were better distributed than horses in East Virginia. The class of low whites was small. However illiterate, they were never dependent on their wealthier neighbors. Beverley, Jones, Smyth, and other early writers, say that poverty, the parent of servility, was almost unknown in Virginia.—EDITOR]

Slave Owners in Princess Anne Co., Va. during the year 1810, who owned less than 10 slaves.

COMMUNICATED BY EDWARD W. JAMES.

Robert Alls	1	Wm Brewer	3
Elizabeth Ackiss	2	Wm Butt	2
Thomas Atwood	3	Travy Burrows	2
Robert Adderson	2	Edward Brown of Smith	1
Aaron, F. B. (1)	4	John Buskey	7
Frederick Ansell	3	Robert Benthall	7
Edward Atwood	4	Charles Burgess	2
Edward Allen	6	Charles Barnes	3
Francis Ackiss Jr.	1	Jeremiah Butt	1
James Absloin	1	Anthony Butt	2
Wm Ashby	5	John Bonney of John	2
John Ansell	9	John Barnes	1
Wm Axtead	1	Samuel Brown	9
John Atwood	6	Thomas Brown	1
Francis Ackiss, Sr.	8	Maxa Bolt	1
Jonathan Ackiss, Sr.	1	Willoughby Bolt	1
Thomas Ackiss	3	John Bolt	3
Wm Bishop, Jr.	8	Josiah Bell	4
Moses Bonney	6	Elizabeth Brown.	2
Lanfair Burgess	1	Boush Butt	4
Wm Boush, Jr.	2	Reuben Brown	2
Edward Brown of Ewd.(2)	6	Kedar Brown	3
David Butt	5	David Busten	1
Moses Brock	3	Anthony Brown	2
John Brown of Hezakiah	6	Francis Barnes	2
Mary Barwell	1	George Butt	5
Anthony Burrows	3	Diana Bonney	1
Wm Burrows	1	Richard Bonney	2
Amos Benson	1	Sarah Brock	3
Cornelius Buskey	2	Anna Bonney	4
Elizabeth Batten	4	Charles Brock	6
James Bonney	4	Jonathan Bonney	7
Harrison Banks	8	Tully Barnes, Sr.	5
George Bashan	1	George Booth	8
John Bivin	5	Noah Brock	2
Joseph Benthall	2	Cornelius Brock	2
Thaddeus Bowman	8	John Bright	2
John Banks	3	John Bonney of Jon.[a]	4

Name	No.	Name	No.
Edward Brown of Moses	2	Ansell Cox	2
Thomas Bonney	3	Joseph Corprew	1
Wm Banks	1	Wm Cannon	1
Jno Banks, Jr.	4	Avarilla Capps	4
Henry Brock	3	Molly Cox	2
Sarah Carraway	3	Morris Capps [5]	1
Margaret Calvert	7	Rodney Capps W^d W^m	3
Josiah Cook	1	Joel Capps	1
Thomas Corprew, W. N.[8]	3	Sally Corbell	2
Jesse Capps	4	Lydia Capps	3
Lydia Capps	4	Lancaster Capps	1
Hilliary Capps	2	James Dyer	1
Wm Campbell	2	Henry Davis	3
Joshua Cone	2	David Dunbar	2
Hilliary Cone	2	Wm Doudge	2
David Cooper	7	William Davis	1
Jno Cox of Geo	2	Richard Davis	4
Frances Capps	1	Tully Doudge of Joab	1
Jeremiah Cane	1	Mary Drewry	9
Henry Cavender	1	David Dawley	4
John Cannon	2	Wm. Dudley	1
Frances Capps	4	Robert Dudley	3
John Cox	7	Wilioughby Dyer	5
Elizabeth Cannon	1	Lewis Drayton	1
Sol° Capps of John	1	Samuel Drayton	1
Mary Cavender	2	Edward Diggs	2
John Cumberfoot	1	Horatio Davis	4
Henry Capps	1	Lewis Dey	8
Leek Creekman	1	Sol° Duncan, F. B.	1
Martin Cummins	4	Wm. Davis	7
Lemuel Curlin	2	Caleb Dawley Sr.	3
Elizabeth Corprew	5	Nathan Doudge	4
John Cannon of Pungo [4]	1	Jn° Etheridge	1
Maryan Capps	2	Henry Edmonds	1
Jacamine Cason	2	Wm Edmunds	1
Mary Capps	3	James Etheridge	3
John Capps	1	John Ewell	6
Hillary Capps	2	Mary Etheridge	2
Charles Capps	1	Ezekiel Ewell	3
Anna Capps	2	James Ewell	3
John Craft	3	Moses Eaton	1

Robert Etheridge	1	Franky Griffin	2
Mary Frizle	5	Wm Holmes	4
Emanuel Fentress	4	Wm Hutchins	1
Nath^{n} Flanagan	1	Jacob Hunter	8
Joshua Fentress, Sr.	3	Wm Hudgin	1
Jn$_{o}$ Fentress of Geo.	2	George T. Hall	7
Edward Fentress	2	Elizabeth Haynes	9
Major Fentress	2	John Hunter	8
Aby Fentress	1	Thomas Hunter	6
Thomas Fuller F. B.	2	Wm Hardason	2
Jn$_{o}$ Fentress of Jno.	3	Joshua Holmes	5
Malachi Fentress	5	James Heath	1
Lemuel Fentress	1	Jesse Hill	4
Joshua Fentress	5	Jeremiah Hosier	1
Jno Fentress of Joshua	8	Blandana Hunter	8
Jno Frizle	5	Thos Henley of Cor^{y}	1
Isriel Fisher	1	Ja^{s} Humphries	8
Moses Fentress of Jno.	9	Thos Humphries	5
Peter Fentress	2	John Henley	4
Jeremiah Fentress	1	Charles Henley	2
China Gibbs F. B.	1	Chas Hartley	1
John Gornto	4	Ja^{s} Harrison	7
James Grimstead	3	Thos Harrison	1
James Gaskins	7	Edward James, Sr	1
Charles Griggs	2	John Johnston	7
Reuben Gornto	8	Keziah Jobson	1
John Garrison	2	Henry James	1
Edmund Garrison	3	Jesse Ives	7
Joseph Grant	1	Thos Old Ives	6
George Guy	9	Thos James[6]	9
Matthias Griffin	4	Bartlett Ives	3
John Griffin	1	Betty James	6
Wm Godfrey	3	Wm James Jr	5
Joel Gammon	4	Jno James Jr	1
Matthew Godfrey	3	Elizabeth James	3
Joel Gisbon	2	Thos Keeling, Sr	3
Arthur Gornto	1	Isaac Keeling	2
Wm Gornto	2	Wm Keeling	4
Thomas Grimstead	3	Henry Keeling	1
Wm Green	9	Jno Keeling	1
Kiziah Garriot	1	Peggy Keeling	7

John Kilgore 4
Henry Parsons Keeling 1
Isaac Land 3
Wm Lufman 2
James Land 9
Reuben Lovett, Sr 8
Batson Land of Hora 1
Jno Lovett, Jr. 4
Simon Land 9
Reuben Lovett, Jr. 4
John Lester 7
Jas Lewis 5
Lancaster Lovett 4
Caleb Land 7
Tully Land 7
Robert Land 2
Lovey Lane 1
John Le Tellier 2
Elizabeth Land 1
Letitia Land 1
Molly Lovett 7
Randolph Lovett 2
Adam Lovett 6
Langley Land 9
Enoch Land 1
Wm Land 5
David Land 5
Joshua Land 2
Henry Lewis 3
John Lewis 5
Adam Lovett Jr, 1
Reuben Land 2
Richard Land 2
Joshua Lawrence 3
Henry Lemount 6
Geo Lewis F. B. 1
Anthony Lawson 7
Evan Legget 2
James Legget 1
Jno Livingston 1
Batson Land 3

Robert J. Legget 1
Simon Murden 2
Kedar Moore 8
David Matthias 5
Elizabeth Matthias 6
Doctor Jas Mosely 3
Hillary Moore 1
Lydia Moore 4
Peter Malbon 4
Malachi Murden 6
Isaac Matthias 4
David Malbon 3
John Munden 4
Wm MClelan 2
Henry K. Manning 2
James Marno 1
Jno Moore, B. S.[7] 9
John Mills 6
Rose Martin 1
Nathaniel Mears 4
Elizabeth Mackie 8
Jas Mills 1
Jno Morrisett 6
Philip Malbon 1
Tully Moses 2
Wm McCoy 7
Elizabeth Moore 1
Malachi Moore 8
Cason MClalin 2
Malachi Murden, B. W.[8] 7
Caleb Moore 5
Wm Moseley 1
Jas MClalen of Joab 2
Jas Murden 2
Daniel Murden 4
Henry Murden 3
Henry Moore 2
Jas Moore, D. N.[9] 4
Enoch Moore 2
Moses MClalen, Sr 6
Moses MClalen, Jr 2

John MClalen	1	Laban Pettet	2
Thos MClalen	1	Horatio Parsons	5
Jas Moore of Cason	6	Jeremiah Plummer	2
Wm Moore of Cason	4	Charles Paydon	9
Jas Malbon	2	Colo Jas .Robinson	1
Francis Malbon	4	John Rose	1
John Malbon	1	Wm Raney	4
Abselom Malbon	6	Peggy Robinson	1
John Moore	1	Thomas Robinson	3
William Murphey	8	John Reade	9
Nathan Munden	4	Wm Randolph	1
Joel Morse	2	Lovey Reade	2
David Morse	6	Elizabeth Roberts	1
Joel Morris	1	Jas Robinson of A.	5
David Morris	2	Charles Robinson	3
Jno MClalen, N. C. (10)	1	Mary Raney	4
Molly F. Blk.	1	James Raney	2
James Norris	1	John Smith, Carpenter	3
Wm Norris	4	Chas Smith, K. V. (11)	3
Sowell Norris	7	Bartlet Shipp	5
Wm J. Nimmo	7	Jno Smith Jr.	1
Wm T. Nimmo	7	Henry Styron	3
Nancy, F. Blk.	1	Daingerfield Stark	3
Harris Nelms	3	Jno S. Salusbury	1
Jane Otterson	1	Daniel Sharley	6
Covington Otley	3	Andrew Smith	2
Elizabeth Oliver	4	Molly Scott	2
Nathan Oakum	5	Jas Scaff	3
Joseph Otterson	5	Jas Stephans	4
Cornelius Ostean	6	Hillary Snail	7
Wm Pebworth	2	Jonathan Smith	1
John Petty	7	Isaac Sherwood	5
Francis Petty	7	Isaac Scott	5
Lemuel Peade	4	Jas Stone	7
Sarah Pebworth	2	Miles Smilt	1
Mary Petty	2	Wm Shepherd B. B. (12)	1
Edward Petty	8	Wm Sovey Sr.	3
Jn L. Pebworth	1	Wm Sovey Jr.	1
Matthew Pallett	9	Joy Sovey	1
John Pallett	5	Philip Sovey	1
Wm J. Pebworth	6	Jno Simmons B. W.	1
Tully Philips	9	Malachi Styron	4

Henry Simmons	1	Christ Williamson	2
Peggy Shipp	4	Batson Whitehurst T. (18)	5
Reuben Shipp	8	Wm West Sr.	7
Jno Smith of Diff	2	Thomas Wormsley	4
Ja^s^ Smith of Diff	1	Moses Williamson B. Side	1
Jno Simmons	1	Mary Warren	5
John Shipp	3	James Watson	5
John Simmons, Pungo	8	John Ward	1
Isaac Smith	5	Moses Wilber	4
Wm Seneca	1	Thomas Wilkins	5
Jesse Seneca	3	Moses Whitehurst	3
Eustice Stripes	4	John Whitehurst	4
Charles Smith	1	Josiah Williamson	1
Henry Trower, Sr.	5	Reuben Wiles	1
George Throp	5	John Widgen	5
Aaron Timberlake	1	Isaac Widgen	4
Henry Turner	3	Francis Wilkinson	3
Fanny Vashon F. B.	2	Thos. R. Walker	6
Geo. Valentine F. B.	2	Mary Williams	1
Wm Vangover	1	Wm Wilkins, Sr.	5
Caleb Vangover	7	John Wilkins	2
Robert Waterson	1	Christopher Whitehurst	3
Jno Whitehurst	2	Ja^s^ Williamson	2
Moses Williamson, Sr.	2	George Whitehurst	1
Thos Wright	3	Henry Williamson	2
Chas M. Woodhouse	8	Wm Williams	3
Jno Williamson	2	Joseph Williamson	8
Wm Williamson	1	Robert Williamson	1
Charles Wray	1	Caleb Williamson, Sr.	6
Jon^a^ Woodhouse Jr.	4	Nancy Whitehurst	9
Joshua Whitehurst	9	Corprew Wilkins	8
Caleb Whitehurst	5	Josiah Woodard	4
Oden Whitehurst	3	Lemuel Williamson	4
Joshua Williamson	3	Horatio Woodhouse	1
Jno Whitehurst of Sim^n^	2	Nathaniel West	2
Abraham C. Willaroy	4	James Wickens	7
Ja^s^ Whitehead	1	Jimima Wallace	1
Major Whitehurst	2	John Wickins	5
Willoughby Whitehurst	5	Henry Woodard	7
Hillary Whitehurst	1	George Woodard	2
Henry Whitehurst	2	Wm Williams B. W.	4
Caleb Ward	3	Jesse Woodard	1

Willoughby West	2	John Wickard	1
Thomas West	7	Ja^{s} Woodhouse of Ja^{s}.	1
Joshua Wright, of Jeve	2	Frances Woodhouse	7
Thos Woodhouse	4	Mary Ward	7
Wm Wright	5	Henry Woodhouse of Ja^{s}.	2
Mary Whitehurst	1	Mary Watterman	1
Wm B. Wilkins	3	Malachi Williamson	5
Frances Whitehurst	3	Hillary Whitehurst	2
Philip Wichard	1	Francis Williamson	1
Jno Whitehurst of Jno.	3	Wm Williamson	3
Sarah Whitehurst w^{d} Ja^{s}	5	Lodawick Williamson	5
Richd Whitehurst of Ja^{s}	1	Wm Williams K. I. [15]	7
Nath^{n} Whitehurst	1	Mary Ward	1
Tully Whitehurst A. B. [14]	3	Francis Wright	1
Ja^{s} Whitehurst of Ja^{s}.	1		

In addition to the slaves whose owners names have been given there were on the plantations of

Bramble and Colley	10	Jno Nivison	30
Wm Boush	5	Susan Smith	2
Wm Cuthburt	5	Jno Stone	11
Geo Finch	4	Arthur Taylor	9
Jno Hopkins	3	Littleton W. Tazewell	23
Hermans	2	Jas B. Warren	6
Geo McIntosh	16	Swepson Whitehead	4

The report shows that there were in the County 2681 white males, 2624 white females, 267 free Negroes, and 3926 slaves, that 646 heads of families owned slaves and that 421 did not.

---

1. F. B. and F. Blk. means free black
2. Edward Brown, son of Edward Brown
3. West Neck 4. One of the three districts into which Princess Anne county is divided, formerly one of eight precincts of Lynnhaven Parish. As it took its name from an estate bearing this name, there was a Pungo within a Pungo, and as this led to frequent and amusing mistakes, the inhabitants were, by those ignorant of the fact, erroneously accused of being ashamed of the name of their precinct.

5. Widow of Wm. Capps; 6. Thomas W. James; 7. Bay Side; 8. Black Water; 9. Dam Neck; 10. Nanny's Creek; 11. Kempesville; 12. Back Bay; 13. Tabernacle; 14. Ashby's Bridge; 15. Knott's Island.

16. This article should be read in connection with that in the January Quarterly. (Pages 335-337, this volume.)

17. The names of slave owners are taken from a census report labelled "A Copy of the 3d Census To remain at the Clerk's Office for the inspection of all concerned———Wm. Bishop Asst. to The Marshall of the Virginia district;" and the report is signed: "The above be correct as fair as I know—of the inhabitants of Princess Anne County. Given under my hand this 15th day Decer. 1810

18) W Bishop Asst."

18. Wm Bishop was married to Miss Anne Carmichael by the Reverend Anthony Walke on the 29th of December, 1789. He was a vestryman of Lynnhaven Parish, Princess Anne County, from July 10th, 1806 to April 9th, 1814, being Church-Warden from March 11th, 1810 to April 9th, 1814. His will was made February 10th, 1814, proved April 4th, 1815. He left a widow Anne, and daughter Eliza, and appointed his brother James Bishop executor. He left a plantation of 111 acres of land. His appraisement was made April 12th, 1815. Among other things mentioned were 12 Negroes, 5 horses, 30 head of cattle, 22 sheep, 11 lambs, 28 hogs and 9 shoats, riding-chair and harness, one clock $50, suit bed curtains $15, black walnut bedstead $15, one backgammon box, coffee pot, tea pot, lot table china, mahogany desk and its contents, lot of books $3, one buffet glass, doors $15, mahogany sideboard $15, glass and china on side board $5 and a small table with books thereon.

RICHMOND COUNTY ELECTION POLL, 1771.

A Poll taken for House of Burgesses, Colo. Francis L. Lee, Richmond County, Va., Nov. 21st, 1771. (Copied by W. B. Cridlin.) Voters' Names (Order Book No. 17—pp. 251 to 254.)

Thomas B. Griffin
The Rev[d] T. W. Giberne
George Garland
Charles Carter, Esq.
David Thornton
John Prosser
William Barber (sworn)
Jesse Bryant
William Warner
William Peachey
John Hammond
Landon Carter, Esq.
Hon[ble] Robert Carter
Thomas Hammond
Isaac Alloway
William Jones
David Dawson
William Webster
Henry Harford
James Webb
Richard Glascock
Henry Sisson, Jr.
William Thrift, Jr.
Leroy Peachey
Nathaniel Harrison
Dr. Nicholas Flood
John Belfield
John Brag
Jesse Thornton
Robert Headley
William Brown
Richard Neal
Thomas Belfield
Thomas Bartlett
John Eidson
Elias Wilson
Rawleigh Downman (L)
William Mitchell
William Gupton
Younger Kelsick
Lindsay Opie
Daniel Lawson
Standlay Gower, Jr.
Vincent Garland
George Sisson
John Bayn
William Kirkham
George Weathers
William Fauntleroy
Robert Hammack
John Smith
Griffin Fauntleroy, North[d]
Thomas Omohundro
William Garland
Simon Churchill (objected)
Stewart Redman
Thomas Scott (objected)
William Morton
George Wroe
William Lamberth
Henry Sisson
Job Thrift

Richard Mitchell
William Northern
William Yeatman
Thomas Dozier
Thomas Smith
Andrew Morgan
George Newman
William Sanders
John Marks
Thomas Harford
Reuben Jordan
John Morris (objected)
Joseph Wilson
Henry Asberry (objected)
John Redman
Richard Parker
Hondle John Tayloe
Christopher Lawson
John Yeatman
John Wright
John Sydnor
Rodham Neal
Benjamin Verbidge
John Mullin (refused to swear)
William Packett
William Fitzhugh
John Heath
Moor Brae
Peter Evans
Moore Fauntleroy
John Gordon
Henry Sutton
Edward Pridham
Samuel Colston
Robert Tomlin
Zachariah White
John Corrie
Richard Shackelford
Charles Hammond
Joseph Simmonds
James Deacons
John Turberville
John Clark
Peter Duff
William Brockenbrough
Robert Jordan
John Thrift
William Miskell
Richard McGinnis (objected)
William Hendren
John Yerbey
Samuel Stowers
John Jones
Thomas Beale
George Yerby
John T. Hamilton
John Harford
Samuel Hipkins
Williamson Ball
Henry Dunkin
John Purcell
William Thrift, Senr.
John Demeritt
Robert Ferguson
Standley Gower, Senr.
Roger Beckwith
James Kelley
Newman B. Barnes
William Baker
William Creedson (objected)
Abernezer Balderson (objected)
Joshua Singleton
Raleigh Colston
Joshua Weston (objected)
William P. Wadman (objected)
William Smith (objected)
David Barrick (objected)
Moore Brockenbrough
Samuel Williams
Benjamin Branham
William Smith
William Smith
Francis Randall
John Hartley
Griffin Garland
Matthew Kelley
John Crab (objected)
Robert P. Downman
Pemberton Clayton, Senr.
Robert Clark (Northd)

William Bruce, Jr.	Thomas Smith (Farnham)
Griffin Fauntleroy	Samuel Guy
William Clark	Capt. William Beale
Christopher Collins	John Lawson (objected)
William Bruce, Senr.	Thomas Dabyns
Vincent Jackson	Robert W. Carter
William Robins	Archibald Ritchie
Thomas Wright	Thomas iggett
Morton Wilson	William Rigmadin

Copy Teste—Samuel Williams, S. S. R. C.

Poll for Mr. Robert W. Carter, pps. 249-251, is with few exceptions identical to above.

Poll of Mr. Hudson Muse, pp. 254-256, is quite different, containing names of John Pope, Jr., John Pope, Senr., Leroy Pope, William Lightfoot, Roger Beckwith, Daniel Muse, and many others.

Slave Owners "Spotsylvania" County, 1783.

(Communicated by Edward W. James.)

William Allan, Esqr	35	Joseph Oril Brock	10
Benjamin Allsup	13	Mordica Buckner	41
John Atkinson	4	Thomas Bartlet	8
James Allan	7	Elizabeth Battaley	3
John Anderson	1	Henry Brock	7
William Ashley	5	Harry Bartlet	12
Alexander Adkins	3	Charles Burrage	1
Thomas Allan	5	Edw'd Brasfield	6
John Apperson	17	Jno. Buckner Est	29
Paul Apperson	1	Francis Buckner	13
John Arnold	3	Thomas Burbridge	12
George Arnold	5	William Bridges	1
Thomas Ashman	1	George Bran	1
George Atkinson	11	William Blaydes	22
William Alexander	7	William Brown	9
John Allcock	6	Thomas Tredg Brown	5
David Anderson	1	Major S. K. Bradford	3
David Allen	1	John Benson	3
Thomas Allan Paine	4	John Bengey	1
Anthony Arnold	5	Margret Baggett	3

Charles Beasley	2
John Bowie	11
Thomas Blanton	3
George Blakey	5
Mary Bell	2
Colo. Joseph Brock	31
Richard Bullard	4
Joseph Brock, Jr	4
Mary Burbridge	6
Daniel Brannan	11
Tavernon Branham	2
Benjamin Ballard	3
Thos. Branham	1
Edm'd Bryant	5
Joseph Bullock	1
Joseph Bledsoe	10
Richard Brooke	47
Lawrence Brooke	5
Edm'd Bryant, Jr	1
John Bullock	1
Susa. Bartlet	8
Richard Collins	4
John Clayton	16
William Clayton	13
Thomas Clayton	5
Robert Collins	2
Elizabeth Clayton	8
Rice Conner	11
Colo. Jonathan Clarke	15
Henry Chandler	4
Richard Coleman, Jr	18
Robert Spe. Coleman	10
Robert Coleman	17
John Coates	9
William Cason	5
Susanna Cason	3
Thomas Coleman	19
Richard Coleman	16
John Cary	1
James Crawford	5
Spilsbe Coleman	16
John Carter	6
Christopher Crawford	1
Thomas Colson	33
Capt. Jno. Carter, Jr	9
John Brownlow	2
Thomas Brown	1
Ephraim Beasley	7
William Carter	10
Stapleton Crutchfield	33
Elizabeth Carter	5
Capt. Jno. Carter, Sen'r	31
Rice Curtes	8
Jonathan Carpenter	1
John Chew, Jun'r	8
Haws Coleman	4
Jno. Chiles	8
Clayton Coleman	18
William Coates	1
Nice Coleman	14
Capt. John Chew	28
Kesia Cayle	1
Joseph Collins	5
Ann Cunningham	6
Thomas Carr	4
Thomas Crutcher	14
Benjamin Davis	2
Mary Davis	3
Edmund Dare	3
Richard Dickerson	13
John Day	10
Ambrose Dudley	10
Wm. (Bals) Daingerfield	61
Edward Darnaby	4
William Darnaby, Sen'r	10
Mrs. Mary Daingerfield	71
William Darnaby	6
Peter Dudley	7
James Dudley	1
Thomas Duerson	19
Thomas Dillard	5
William Duerson	8
William Davenport	14
Robert Darrett	3
Elisha Dismukes	5
Richard Dillard	10
James Drake	3
Benjamin Dawson	3
William Dawson	7
Joseph Duerson	11

Benjamin Chapman..........	1	Benjamin Day..............	2
Wm. Cammock Est	18	John Davenport............	6
George Cammock..........	9	William Duvall.............	5
John Cammock	2	William Duvall, Jr..........	1
Mary Chew	9	Henry Duerson.............	10
Joseph Chew	3	Elisha Dickinson............	11
Robert Bev'y Chew	3	Ann Estes	8
Henry Cammock	1	Hezekiah Ellis..............	8
Francis Cammock..........	3	Thomas Estes..............	2
Gawin Corbin	35	Tilley Emerson.............	1
Mark Carrill	1	James Edwards............	33
Edward Collins...........	7	Richard Estes	4
Walter Chiles	12	John Estes................	2
Richard Coleman..........	7	Samuel Estes	4
Edward Coleman..........	2	John Edwards	10
Elijah Carter.............	1	Uriah Edwards.............	3
Charles Cosby............	12	William Ferguson	8
David Chivis.............	4	Abraham Fergusson	4
Caleb Coleman...........	15	William Forson............	2
Christopher Daniel........	5	Samuel Falconer...........	2

(TO BE CONTINUED.)

Slave Owners Spotsylvania County, 1783.

Francis Cammock,	3	Elisha Dismukes,	5
Gawin Corbin,	35	Richard Dillard,	10
Mark Carrill,	1	James Drake,	3
Edward Collins,	7	Benjamin Dawson,	3
Walter Chiles,	12	William Dawson,	7
Richard Coleman,	7	Joseph Duerson,	11
Edward Coleman,	2	Benjamin Day,	2
Elijah Carter,	1	John Davenport,	6
Charles Cosby,	12	William Duvall,	5
David Chivis,	4	William Duvall, Jr.,	1
Caleb Coleman,	15	Henry Duerson,	10
Christopher Daniel,	5	Elisha Dickinson,	11
Benjamin Davis,	2	Ann Estes,	8
Mary Davis,	3	Hezekiah Ellis,	8
Edmund Dare,	3	William Davenport,	
Richard Dickerson,	13	Robert Darrett,	
John Day,	10	Thomas Estes,	2

Ambrose Dudley,	10	Tilley Emerson,	1
Wm. (Bals) Daingerfield,	61	James Edwards,	33
Edward Darnaby,	4	Richard Estes,	4
William Darnaby, Senr,	10	John Estes,	2
Mrs. Mary Daingerfield,	71	Samuel Estes,	4
William Darnaby,	6	John Edwards,	10
Peter Dudley,	7	Uriah Edwards,	3
James Dudley,	1	William Ferguson,	8
Thomas Duerson,		Abraham Ferguson,	4
Thomas Dillard,		William Forson,	2
William Duerson,		Samuel Falconer,	2
Robert Frank,	3	Nathan Hawkins,	11
Thomas Fox, Jr.,	2	David Head,	4
William Fox,	6	Henry Head, Jr.,	9
Elizabeth Foster,	1	Nicholas Hawkins,	1
William Ficklin,	6	Spence Alexa Head,	13
Doctr George French,	5	Joseph Hewell,	4
Jno Farneyhough,	1	Nicho Hawkins, Senr,	1
Robert Forsythe,	10	Joseph Hoomes,	3
Edmund Foster,	8	Henry Head,	5
David Galloway, Jun'r,	15	John Hawkins,	4
John Green,	1	Jarvis Haydon,	8
John Graves,	12	Capt. John Herndon,	11
James C. Goodwin,	13	Jessee Haydon,	6
Henry Glass,	3	Harman Haner,	3
Richard Garner,	2	Benjn Holladay, Jr.,	3
Muscoe Garnet,	11	James Holladay,	1
Henry Gatewood, Jr.,	2	Lewis Holladay,	18
William Golson,	1	Robert Hart,	25
Robert Goodloe,	23	Robert Hill,	17
George Goodloe,	4	Joseph Holladay, Senr,	15
Harry Goodloe,	10	Benjamin Holladay,	15
John Graves,	14	Thomas Henderson,	7
Thomas Goodloe,	6	William Harvey,	9
Henry Gatewood, Senr,	9	James Hackley,	4
William Grayson,	1	John Hudia,	6
Thomas Gardner,	1	Godlove Hiskill,	4
David Galloway, Senr,	9	Jno Hall (mercht),	1
William Hutcherson,	3	Richardson Hensley,	2

John Hutcherson,	2
Charles Hutcherson,	2
William Huvell,	2
Edward Herndon,	36
Reuben Hudson,	1
Joseph Herndon,	29
John Hart,	2
Joseph Hawkins,	11
James Jarvis,	1
James Julian,	7
William Jackson,	3
William Jenkins,	1
Stephen Johnson,	30
Phoebe Julian,	5
Thomas Jinnings,	2
William Jones,	39
Gracey Jones,	3
Aquilla Johnson,	25
Aquilla Johnson, Jr.,	8
Henry Johnson,	13
William Jackson,	49
Gipson Jenkins,	1
John Jinkins,	9
Thomas Jones,	1
Sarah & Francis Jerdone,	35
Alex[e] Kennady,	2
Richard Lowry,	16
Henry Lewis,	4
Joel Lewis,	9
Zachariah Lewis,	39
Jno. Zach'y Lewis,	20
Zachariah Lucas,	2
Cap. John Legg,	5
Capt. Thomas Minor,	13
James Mason,	2
Peter Mason, Jr.,	1
John Mason,	13
Moses Morris,	1
James Marye, est.,	15
Martha Hensley,	4
James Hutcherson,	3
Mildred Holladay,	8
George Hensley,	2
Sarah Hensley,	1
Philip Lipscomb,	12
Benjamin Leavell,	9
William Lewis,	4
James Lewis,	15
Daniel Lindsey,	23
Samuel Luck,	8
Walter Lewis,	24
George Lewis,	14
Edward Ludwick,	1
James Over Lewis,	10
Gilman Lane.	2
Thomas Livingston,	1
Thomas Lipscomb,	13
James Livingston,	2
Henry Lane,	7
John Martin,	4
William Mills,	10
John Mastin,	1
Winefred McAlaster,	2
Barnet Mitchell,	6
Clement Montague,	11
John Mitcham,	8
Thomas Megee, Jr.,	12
Elizabeth Mitcham,	2
Capt. Thomas Minor, Jr.,	25
Benjamin McWilliams,	4
Elizabeth M'Calley,	6
William Maxley,	8
David [illegible]lliam,	7
Joseph Pulliam,	4
Benjamin Perry,	2
Samuel Partlow,	6
Doct'r Thomas Powell,	16
Thomas Pollard,	15

John M'Whert,	1	Henry Pendleton,	12
John M'Quilty,	1	Charles Proctor,	2
Elizabeth Marye,	4	Thomas Proctor,	2
Abraham Maury,	3	Capt. Nicholas Payne,	16
Doct'r Charles Mortimer,	8	Joel Parish,	11
William M'Williams,	6	Henry Pendleton, Jr.,	1
William Massey,	2	Robert Payne,	1
Cornelius M'Coy,	5	Barnet Payne,	2
Frances Merewither,	40	Micajah Poole,	7
John Merewether,	8	James Parish,	4
Zachariah Merewither,	13	Mary Penn,	2
Thomas Montague,	6	Thomas Pritchett,	9
John Mitchell,	1	Larkin Perry,	1
James Mitcham,	3	William Pemberton,	8
Joseph Nelson,	11	Charles Pemberton,	6
John Nelson,	5	John Pruet,	1
Lodowick Oneal,	13	Winslow Parker,	6
James Owen,	7	William Parker,	22
Francis Purvis,	12	William Proctor,	1
William Porter,	6	Thomas Powe,	2
James Purvis,	15	William Plunkett,	3
Mann Page, Esqr.,	159	William Quarles,	33
Major William Robinson	7	James Somerwell	16
Benjamin Robinson	1	Daniel Starke	3
William Robinson	8	George Shepherd	6
Benjamin Robinson	2	George Stubblefield	42
William Richards	2	Alex[d] Spotswood	60
William Robinson	7	Mary Sheaths	2
John Rodgers	12	Ashman Sorrell	1
Mich[l] Robinson Jr.	7	Nathaniel Sanders	5
James Rowlings	15	William Stanard	34
John Rowlings Jr.	6	John Spindle	1
Benjamin Reynolds	4	William Spindle	4
Ann Roy	14	Larkin Stanard	23
Lucy Rogers	10	Oswald Smith	8
George Ridings	13	Joseph Sams	2
John Robinson	4	David Sandidge	18
Joseph Robinson	1	Harry Stubblefield	12
Elizabeth Redd	7	Beverly Stubblefield	14

John Robinson Sen'r	4
James Redd	18
Samuel Roddy	3
John Richards	1
Jno. Fred Robinson	2
Mich' Robinson sen'r.	24
William Smock	3
Norct Slaven	1
Edward Simpson	6
William Smith	2
James Slaytor	1
Jessee Slaven	1
Mary Sullivan	3
John Shirley	7
John Shirley Jr.	3
Thomas Shirley	1
Abram Simons	4
John Scott	6
Reuben Straughan	4
John Schooler Jr.	1
Robert Smith	9
Thomas Strachan	17
William Scott	6
Peter Stubblefield	18
Samuel Sale	11
Peter Stevens	1
Capt. Oliver Towles	35
William Taylor	2
George Taylor	1
William P. Thurston	27
Margaret Tureman	4
John Tankersley	15
John Thornton	3
Ignatious Tureman	5
Elizabeth Towles	22
William Trigg	9
Mary Thornton	26
Richard Todd	2
William Thompson	13
William Smith	27
John Steward	8
William Smither	5
Benjamin Steward	2
John Stadler	7
John Shelton	16
G. W. Spooner	2
Francis Simpson	6
John Schooler	4
Wharton Schooler	3
Ambrose Smith	11
Sarah Steward	1
James Smith	6
Mrs. Frances Thornton	12
Henry True	7
Thomas True	1
Thomas Terry	6
Obadiah Terry	1
Walker Taliaferro, Est.	24
John Taliaferro	15
James Tutt	20
John Taliaferro	23
Francis Taliaferro	8
Robert Thomas	3
Mary Vass	3
Rice Vass	3
Vincent Vass	2
William Vigar	1
John Vest	4
Thomas Wright	1
Colo Beverley Winslow	18
Thomas Waller	3
Harry Woodford	8
John K. W. Waller	2
Jno. Wiglesworth Sen[r]	14
Ditto & Jos. Tox	13
Benoni Williams	1
Ignatious West	4
James Williams	2

William Tittet	1	Pomfret Waller	10
Francis Thornton	18	Benj[a] Waller	22
Jno. Br. Waller,	12	Long Wharton,	6
Thomas Waller,	17	William Wright,	6
William E. Waller,	5	Betty White,	5
Joseph Woolfolk,	3	Basil White,	10
Jeremiah Wilson,	4	Dennis Wright,	2
John Wilson,	10	Joseph Willoughby,	2
John Woolfolk,	6	Lewis Willis,	37
John Washington,	19	George Weedon,	13
Leonard Waller,	7	James Weir,	8
James Wiglesworth, S[r],	14	Jacob Whitler,	4
John Wiglesworth, J[r],	1	John Wallace,	1
James Wiglesworth, J[r],	5	William Wiatt,	5
John Webber,	6	Tully Whitehurst,	1
John Wood,	4	Charles Yates,	37
Ann Waller,	27	Leonard Young, J[r],	5
Capt. John White,	8	Michael Yates, J[r],	2
John Wright,	14	Leonard Young,	7

A True Copy,

Teste JN[o] CHEW, JR., D. C.

p. JN[o] WALLER, Cl.

The names of the slave owners are taken from the records in the Auditor's Office, Richmond. The clerk in summing up the list said there were in the county.

*704 whites (free males) at 10s,	£352.
4581 Blacks,	2290.10
2380 Horses, 2s,	238.
10 Stallions, 3d,	12.14
7676 Cattle,	95.19
134 Carriage Wheels, 6s,	40.
14 Licenses (Ordinary), £5,	70.
Amt. of tax,	3.099.7

*There were in Spotsylvania county in 1790, 5,171 whites, 5,933 blacks, and 148 denominated others. This note, for which I am indebted to the kindness of Mr. Robert Lee Traylor, is from "Typo-

The report shows that

78	persons	owned	1	slave	each,	78
54	"	"	2	"	"	108
44	"	"	3	"	"	132
41	"	"	4	"	"	164
30	"	"	5	"	"	150
32	"	"	6	"	"	192
23	"	"	7	"	"	161
27	"	"	8	"	"	216
16	"	"	9	"	"	144
18	"	"	10	"	"	180
15	"	"	11	"	"	165
13	"	"	12	"	"	156
16	"	"	13	"	"	208
10	"	"	14	"	"	140
12	"	"	15	"	"	180
8	"	"	16	"	"	128
5	"	"	17	"	"	85
9	"	"	18	"	"	162
3	"	"	19	"	"	57
2	"	"	20	"	"	40
5	"	"	22	"	"	110
4	"	"	23	"	"	92
3	"	"	24	"	"	72
3	"	"	25	"	"	75
1	"	"	26	"	"	26
3	"	"	27	"	"	81
1	"	"	28	"	"	28
2	"	"	29	"	"	58
1	"	"	30	"	"	30
2	"	"	31	"	"	62
4	"	"	33	"	"	132
1	"	"	34	"	"	34
4	"	"	35	"	"	140

---

graphical Analysis of Virginia for the years 1790–1," "compiled by Wm. Tatham, and printed by Thomas Nicholson," and "reprinted by Mr. J. W. Randolph in 1853," and "bound up with the revised edition of Jefferson's Notes on Virginia."—E. W. J.

1	"	"	36	"	"	36
3	"	"	37	"	"	111
2	"	"	39	"	"	78
1	"	"	40	"	"	40
1	"	"	41	"	"	41
1	"	"	42	"	"	42
1	"	"	47	"	"	47
1	"	"	49	"	"	49
1	"	"	60	"	"	60
1	"	"	61	"	"	61
1	"	"	71	"	"	71
1	"	"	159	"	"	159
505 Owners.						4581 Slaves.

CENSUS OF TITHABLES IN SURRY COUNTY IN THE YEAR 1668.

Until after the Revolution, taxes were chiefly imposed in Virginia according to the number of the tithables in each county. The tithables consisted of all male natives of the country and imported free persons above sixteen; and all male white servants, and all female white servants who worked in the ground, and all male and female negro and Indian servants, whether above or under sixteen. The population was generally estimated as four times the tithables. Hence the population of Surry, judging from the whole number of tithables (434), was about 1,736 persons in 1668. Taxes of this kind were not as unjust in principle then

as now, for the wealth of a man was for the most part measured by the number of his family and dependents. The following is a census of tithables for Surry county during the year 1668. According to this it seems that the number of small planters must have been very large. Even Mr. Arthur Allen had but eleven in his family. There was no one else who had over eight, except Mr. Thomas Binns, who had ten. All at Mr. Warren's, except a negro, appear to have been free persons working at his house as independent tithables.* There must have been at this time very few negroes in Surry county.

Commission of the Peace, December 20, 1668.

Lt. Coll George Jordan, Capt. Lawrence Baker, Mr. Arthur Allen, Mr. Thos Warren, Capt. John Grove, Majr William Mariott, Capt. Wm Cockersham,† Capt Wm Brown, Mr Tho Binns, Mr Charles Barham, Mr Randall Holt, Mr Thomas Flood.

THE LIST OF LAWNES CREEK TYTHABLES IN ANNO 1668.

Imprs Capt Law: Baker, ..08
Robt Laine, ...01
Wm. Hare, ...02
Richd Harris, ...05
Geor' Corke, ...01
Wm Chambrs, ...03
Michaiel Upchurch, ...01
Mr Wm Butler, ...02
Mr Peter Greene, ...03
James Redicke, ...03
Richd Brigs, ...04
John Beasley, ...03
John Warrin, ...02
Capt Pitman, ...04
John Clarke, ...02
Partrick Bartley, ...02
John Browne, ...01
Richd Smith, ...02
John Bineham, ...01
Mathew Swann, ...01
Xpor Holliman, ...01
Tho. lillicrop, ...02
Robert Gyles, ...01
John Gregory, ...01
Samuel Cornewall, ...04
Tho. Clay, ...01
John Blast, ...02
Peleg Dunston, ...02
Arthur Long, ...02
John Hunicut, ...01
Mr. Charles Barham, ...04
Tho. Clary, ...02
Walter Bartley, ...04
Wm. Tooke, ...03
Timothy Earwell, ...02

——

118

——

Hen. Bradrton, ...01
Capt Wm Cockersham, ...04
Majr Wm Caufield, ...03
Tho. Smith, ...02
Wm Pper, ...02
Mr Robt Caufield, ...02

---

* I infer this from the fact that the names of the persons at his house are given.

† Capt. William Cockersham died in 1669, leaving two sons, William and Thomas.

Richard Jarratt, ...04
Richd Skinner, ...04
Harmon Hill, ...01
Richd Drew, ...03
Mr Arthur Allen, ...11
Robt Reynolds, ...02
Austin Hunicut, ...03
Tho. Taylor, ...02
Obedia Pit, ...02
Roger Delke, ...01
Francis Reynolds, ...02
Tho. Joanes, ...02
Amara Dolores, ...01
Mr Ran Holt, ...02
Mr John Goring, ...03
James Murrey, ...01
Nicholas Craford, ...01
Edward Napkin, ...01
Phillop Oberry, ...01
Wm Clarke, ...01
Wm Judson, ...01
Henry Clarke, ...02
Henry Gord, ...02
Margrit Cornish, ...02
Wm. Seward, ...02
David Williams, ...04
John Kindred, ...02
W^{m}Hancocke, ...02
John Philleps, ...01
Geo. Watkin, ...04
Roger Rawlings, ...03
Tho. Laine, ...02
John Hode, ...02
Henry Lathrie, ...01
James Kilpatrick, ...02
Tho. Jarrell, ...01
Wm Owlis, ...06
Capt Grove, ...08
Mr Bushell, ...04
Alberte Albatson, ...01
Martin Johnson, ...01
Edward Warren, ...03
Geo. Petters, ...01
Edward Tanner, ...01
Joseph Rogers, ...03

88

Teste,

WM. COCKERSHAM.

A list of ye Tythables in South Warke p'ish Anno 1668 ffrom Coll. Jordans upwards as they have been given to him & he Informed June ye 10 1668.

Mr John Barker, ...06
Wm Shorte, ...02
Tho. Stephens, ...01
Wm. Heath, ...02
Tho. Greene, ...01
Mr Tho. Busby, ...03
Tho. Bentley, ...01
Jerremy Ellis, ...01
Henry ffrancis, ...03
Richard Rogers, ...02
Geo. Midleton, ...01
Ralph Rachell, ...01
Mr Tho. Clarke saith 2, his neighbors saith, ...03
Marmaduke Beckwith, ...01
Mathew Rolfe, ...01
John Rawlinger, ...01
Mr Barkers Plantation, ...01
Mr Ben Harrison, ...05
Mr Hen Brigs, ...02

John King, ...01
John Legrand, ...01
Wm. Scarbrough, ...01
Rob[t] Dennis, ...01
Rob[t] House, ...02
M[r] W[m] Simmons, ...06
Rob[rt] Carthrage, ...04
W[m] Newit and Orchard, ..02
John Rogers & Atkins, ...02
W[m] Carpenter, ...02
M[r] W[m] Rookings, ...03
ffran. Howgood, ...01
M[r] W[m] Norwood, ...02
Joh: Kippin, ...02
Tho. Hux, ...02
Maurice Burchen, ...01
Rob[t] Burges, ...01
Taken by Mr. George Jordan.

M[r] Nath Kn[t] wth Dick and Dankes, ...03
M[r]John Cary, ...04
M[r] Arthur Jordan, ...04
Cap[t] Tho. ffload, ...04
L[t] Coll. Jordan, ...03
John Emerson, ...01
Michaell Mischanny, ...01
Hezekiah Bunell saith 1, his Neighb[rs], ...02
Ralph Creed, ...02
M[r] Nicholas Meriwether, ..06

102

Edw[d] Ellis & M[r] Moulson, to p'ish Levy, ...02

A List of Tythables taken by me subscribed y[e] 10th June 1668.

Coll. Tho. Swann himselfe Mr John Salloway & 3 sarvants,...05
Rich[d] Case, ...01
Tho. Gray, ...01
ffrancis Gray, ...01
W[m] Spring, ...01
Tho. Chews & Tho Wicks, ...02
John Bird & his Mann, ...01
W[m] Rose & Edw[d] Hale, ...02
Cap[t] W[m] Browne, ...05
Tho. Forsteraft & Kite, ...02
John Morning W[m] Batt, ...02
Sam[l] Magget, ...01
Tho. Sowersby, ...01
John Collyer, ...01
Fran. Sorsby, Pace & sarv[t], ...03
Henry Foreman, ...01
Wm Foreman, ...01
M[r] Barth Owen, Edward Joanes, ...02
Tho. Andrews, ...01
Xopher Lewis Rog[r] W[m]s, 2 Sarvts, ...04

Rog^r Potter, ...01
Joh. Harlow, Edw. March, Wm Hux & Wm Mills, ...04

William Browne. 43

A List of Tythables taken ye 11th June 1668.

John Brady & three men, ...04
Antho. Spilltimber & 2 Men, ...03
Tho. Ironmonger, ...01
Maj^r Wm Marriott & 4 sarv^ts, ...05
Luke Mizell & Mate, ...02
Christo. Vaughan's Sonn, ...01
Ellis Vantse, ...01
Capt Corker, ...05
Daniel Regan, ...01

Wm Marriott. 23

A List of ye Tythables from ye Colledge to Smiths forte taken ye 10th of June 1668 by Mr Tho. Warren:

Timothy Walker, John Whitson & one negro, ...03
Mr Binns, ...10
Cornelius Cardenpaine, ...01
Andrew Robinson, ...03
Richard Joanes, ...01
Mr Thompson, ...02
Sam. Place, Antho. Evens, ...02
Mr Robert Spencer, Harebottle W^ms, francis davis, Wm Winter, Tho. Sand^rs, Jonas Bennet, ...06
Mr Mathias Marriott Tho. Causby, Joh. Booth & 1 negro, ...04
Mr Pitway, Law. Peach, Edw Ramsey, Jarratt Greene, Walt, .05
Tho. Hurle Joh. Shipp Tho Gibson & 1 negro, ...04
Geo. Foster & Tho. Williams, ...02
Tho. North, ...01
John Clemens, ...01
Edmond Howell, ...01
James Furbush, ...01
Mr Tho. Warren Wm Warren, Wm Hill, vinsent Suttleworth, Hen. Applewhait, James Nibley, Wm Howell, Robert Ewens, 1 Negro, ...09
John Skinner, ...01

57

Slave Owners,* Westmoreland County, Va., 1782.

COMMUNICATED BY EDWARD WILSON JAMES.

[A transcript from the original in the office of the Auditor of Public Accounts of the State of Virginia. S. indicates slaves and W. wheels of vehicles.]

	S.	W.		S.	W.
John Ashton, .	5		George Briscoe, .	5	
Richard Atwell, .	13		Eleanor Bayne, .	12	
Mary Atwell, .	12		James Bulger, .	6	
William Anderson,	1		Daniel Bennett, .	1	
John Bowcock, .	2		John Bailey, .	1	
Warner Bashaw, .	4		William Bailey. .	2	
John Butler, .	6		John Ballentine, .	25	2
Christopher Butler,	4		James Bailey, .	4	
Beckwith Butler, .	45		Daniel Bailey, .	1	
Dorcas Butler, .	9		William Benson, .	1	
Thomas Bowcock,	4		Peter Brickey, .	12	
William Berryman,	27		Thomas Beale, .	13	
Newton Berryman,	3		George Brinnon, .	3	

*There were in Westmoreland county in 1790–91, 3,183 white people, 4,425 blacks, and 114 called all others. The foregoing note is from a Topographical Analysis of the Commonwealth of Virginia, printed August 2nd, 1792, by William Tatham and reprinted in 1853 in the Richmond edition of Jefferson's Notes on Virginia, kindly contributed by Robert Lee Traylor, Esquire. In 1880, the county contained 8,846 inhabitants; in 1890, 8,383; in 1900, 9,243. The names of the slave owners are taken from lists by Joseph Fox, Daniel M'Carty, John Rochester, and Richard Buckner, Gent., justices who were appointed by the court to receive them, by Jas. Bland, D. W. C., for R. Bernard, C. W. C., July 30th, 1782.

	S.	W.		S.	W.
John Bacchus, .	1		Elizabeth Brinnon,	2	
John Berkley, .	12		John Brinnon, .	5	
William Brown, .	11		Thomas Butler, Sen'r,	1	
John Butler, Jun'r,	4		William Barecroft,	7	
William Bussel, .	4		William Butler, .	1	
Margaret Bristol, .	2		Vincent Brann, .	1	
Margaret Ball, .	13		Samuel Bailey, .	16	
James Bankhead, .	19	2	Henry Barnett, .	4	
William Bankhead,	31		Nathaniel Butler, .	1	
William Boulware,	4		Edmund Bulger, .	1	
Elizabeth Bayne, .	2		Hannah Brinnon, .	3	
John Bayne . .	2		Thomas Blundell, Jr.,	7	
James Bland, .	1		Absalon Blundell,	3	
Austin Brockenborough, Est.,			. . . . .	33	
Daniel Briscoe, .	6		Reuben Briscoe, .	4	
John Brown, . .	4		William Brown, .	13	
Richard Buckner,	23	2	William Blundell, .	1	
Thomas Chancellor,	7		Spencer Carter, .	3	
Richard Dozeir, Sen.,	4		Jeremiah Cloxon, .	1	
Joseph Dozeir, .	4		Archibald Campbell,	8	
Richard Dozer, younger, .			. . . . .	1	
John Campbell, .	6		William Dozer, .	6	
Mordicai Cooke, .	17		James Dozer, .	2	
Andrew Crawford,	10	2	Wm. Robinson Dozer,	4	
John Carter, .	19		Christoph'r Edrington,	12	
Robert Carter, The Honble, Esqr,			. . . . .	278	6
William Edwards,	20		Daniel Fitzhugh,	27	
Fleet Cox, . .	57	2	Joseph Fox, . .	16	2
Hannah Corbin, .	28		John Ferguson, Est.,	4	
Charles Carter, .	20		Philip Rich'd Fendal,	51	4
John Crabb, .	13		Tho. Fisher, Est.,	20	
John Critcher, .	23		William Green, .	1	
Christopher Collins,	12		William Gray, .	2	
Jane Crabb, .	10		Thomas Green, .	1	
William Cecil, .	4		Leroy Griffin, Est.,	28	
Rodham Crawley,	1		Mary Griggs, .	10	
Charnock Courtney,	1		Lee Griggs, . .	5	
George Carey, .	1		George Gill, .	7	

	S.	W.
David Crenshaw, .	5	
William Coward, .	1	
Thomas Caverder,	5	
James Cowles, .	2	
Thomas Chandler,	4	
Benedict Crabb, .	6	
Thomas Cowles, .	7	
Presly Crawford, .	1	
Thomas Chilton, Est.,	15	
George Caverder, .	5	
Isabella Chilton, .	10	
John Dishman, .	9	
William Dishman, .	4	
Charles Deane, Jr.,	16	
Charles Deane, Sen.,	8	
William Drake, .	6	
John Douglas, .	4	
John Dickie, . .	6	
Rose Drake, . .	6	
Peter Davis, . .	3	
James Dunbar, .	2	
John Davis, . .	2	
Elizabeth Davis, .	4	
Elias Davis, . .	3	
William Dolman, .	3	
Rich'd Dozier, Jun.,	2	
Francis Jackson, .	6	
Catharine Jett, .	20	
Thomas Jett, .	53	4
William Jett, .	10	
Samuel Jackson, .	4	
Charles Jones, .	3	
Jonathan Jackson, .	4	
William Jeffries, .	3	
Richard Jackson, .	21	
Catsby Jones, .	20	
Thomas King, .	2	
William King, .	1	
Rosanna Garner, .	2	
Jeremiah Garner, .	1	
Nathaniel Garner,	1	
William Gilbert, .	2	
Edward Gill, .	1	
George Garner, .	31	2
George Gordon, .	7	
George Hemage, .	1	
George Hales, .	7	
Richard Hipkins,	38	4
Mary Hilton, .	3	
Anne Hungerford,	20	
Molly Hodge, .	31	
William Holland, .	2	
Thomas Hungerford,	12	2
William Harrison,	7	
Agness Harrison, .	3	
John Hutchins, .	6	
Elenor Habron, .	1	
George Hull, .	1	
Benjamin Hackney,	16	
John Howell, .	2	
William Hutt, .	17	
John Hutt, . .	7	
William Hazlerigg,	2	
Caty Hall, . .	16	2
Richard Hall, .	3	
James Monroe, .	3	
Joseph Mann, .	1	
James Muse, Jun.,	8	
Thomas Muse, .	6	
John Monroe, Jun.,	38	4
Elliot Monroe, .	19	
Jemima Monroe, .	9	
John Monroe, .	8	
William Monroe, .	5	
Jn° Monroe (son of George), . .	4	

	S.	W.
Harrison Lovel, .	2	
Elizabeth Lovell, .	1	
Samuel Love, .	5	
Phil. Ludwell, Lee Es.,	61	
Ashton Lamkin, .	5	
Richard Lee, . .	82	
Geo. Fairfax Lee, .	43	2
Richard Lowe, .	8	
Joseph Lacey, .	1	
Peter Lamkin, .	5	
George Lewis, .	6	
Joseph Lane, .	33	
James Lamkin, .	1	
R'd Lee, of Maryland,	25	
Rich'd Henry Lee,	43	6
John Lawson, .	23	
Jane Muse, . .	23	
William Middleton,	26	2
Daniel Morgan, .	18	
Magdalen M'Clanaham,	7	
William M'Clanaham,	3	
Mary Mors, .	6	
William Middleton,	2	
John Middleton, .	6	
Thomas Middleton,	1	
William Morton, .	2	
Thomas Moore, .	2	
Vincent Moore, .	5	
Thomas Muse, .	7	
Garland Moore, .	4	
Mary M'Guire, .	1	
Samson Marmaduke,	1	
John M'Guire, .	4	
Benedict Middleton,	18	
Peter Mullins. .	7	
Elizabeth M'farlane,	4	
John Marmaduke, .	6	
Dan'l Marmaduke,	2	
Benjamin Monroe,	11	
Jacob Martin, .	19	
David Monroe, .	9	
Nicholas Muse, .	12	
Samuel Muse, .	4	
Charles Monie, .	8	
William Monroe, Jr.,	2	
Pattey Massey, .	2	
Elizabeth Massey,	5	
Richard Moxley, .	14	2
Richard Muse, .	10	
John Mazaret, .	7	
Edward Muse, .	10	
Jeremiah Muse, .	1	
Rodham Moxley, .	8	
John Moxley, .	2	
Anne Muse, .	2	
John Muse, .	5	
Sanford Muse, .	2	
Daniel M'Carty, .	112	4
James Muse, .	20	
John Minor, . .	5	
George M'Kenny,	2	
Nanny M'Kenny,	1	
Vincent Marmaduke,	4	
John Moxley, .	9	
Catey Moxley, .	4	
William Marmaduke,	5	
John M'Clanaham,	6	
Garrard M'Kenny,	11	
George Memory, .	1	
Robert Moxley, .	1	
Mary Nelson, .	23	
William Nelson, .	20	
John Neale, . .	8	2
Richard Neale, .	7	
Rodham Neale, Est.,	4	
Presly Neale, .	7	

	S.	W.
Augustine Moxley, .	10	
Daniel M'Kenny, .	5	
William Muse, .	1	
John Price, Jun., .	5	
William Payton, .	3	
John Price, . .	5	
William Payne, .	26	
Thomas Peed, .	1	
George Payne, .	24	
Lawrence Pope, .	6	
Matthew Partridge, Est,	8	
Demsy Porter, .	4	
John Pilsbury, .	2	
Elizabeth Pratt, .	1	
William Porter, .	8	
Edward Porter, .	4	
Joseph Peirce, .	21	
Daniel Porter, .	1	
Sarah Peirce, . .	18	
Joseph Peirce, Jun.,	5	
Jacob Pumroy, .	1	
Richard Parker, .	26	4
Nicholas Quisenbury,	5	
James Quisenbury,	7	
William Quisenbury,	1	
George Rudolph, .	5	2
William Robinson,	93	4
Benjamin Rogers, .	5	
John Redman, .	2	
George Robinson, .	9	
Henry Roe, Est., .	9	
William Roe, .	5	
Elizabeth Rainey, .	3	
Thomas Rouand, .	31	
Elizabeth Rust, .	11	2
Thomas Shadrick, .	1	
Elizabeth Smith, .	73	4
Alexander Spark, .	49	

	S.	W.
Willoughby Newton,	4	
John Newton, Est.,	12	
John Norwood, .	2	
Tarpley Nash, .	2	
John Nash, . .	6	
Presley Neale, .	3	
John Omohundro,	2	
Thomas Omohundro,	4	
Anthony Payton, .	20	
William Price, .	2	
Ursulla Peirce, .	7	
John Rust, . .	7	
William Rue, .	7	
Vincent Rust, .	7	
Samuel Rust, .	9	
Rebecca Rust, .	17	2
George Rust, .	17	2
James Rust, . .	7	
John Robinson, .	4	
Benjamin Rust, .	6	
Solomon Robinson,	8	
James Robinson, .	5	
Jemima Redman, .	6	
John Rue, . .	2	
Anne Redman, .	4	
Youel Rust, . .	1	
Stuart Redman, .	4	
John Rochester, .	13	
Soloman Redman,	33	
Thomas Randal, .	4	
Benjamin Rust, .	5	
Tho. Redman Robinson, ...	1	
Andrew Read, .	30	
William Smith, .	25	
Benjamin Steward,	7	
John Simms, .	1	
Thomas Streshly, .	36	2

Name	S.	W.
Mary Smith,	77	4
George Steptoe,	45	2
The Revd Thos. Smith,	42	6
John South,	3	
James Sorrell,	16	
John Simpson,	18	2
Samuel Smith,	7	
Thomas Sorrell,	6	2
Stephen Selp, Jun.,	7	
Elizabeth Smith,	1	
Thomas Scott, Est.,	3	
Stephen Selp, Sen.,	2	
George Shoats,	1	
Peter Smith,	1	
Moses Selp,	2	
Reuben Sanford,	1	
John Skinker,	10	
Jeremiah Spurling,	1	
Mary Settles,	14	
Thomas Sutton,	1	
Hannah Sturman,	14	2
James Sutton,	1	
Charles Scott,	1	
Edward Sanford,	17	
William Storke,	11	
Thomas Spence,	8	
Charles Sanford,	5	
William Sanford,	6	
Augustine Sanford,	3	
John Weedon,	3	
George Weedon,	7	
Mildred Weedon,	2	
Jno Augustn Washington,	56	4
George Wilkerson,	2	
Benjamin Weaver,	5	
James Wigley,	1	
Richard Wroe,	1	
Thomas Steel,	1	
Lewis Smith,	1	
Robert Steel,	4	
Franklin Simms,	2	
Geo. Stone, Est.,	4	
Benjamin Strother,	7	2
Willoughby Sanford,	6	
Josiah Sutton,	1	
Youel Sanford,	3	
Robt. Sanford, Est.,	4	
Thomas Sanford,	7	
Thomas Stone,	7	
Uriah Sandy,	11	
Patrick Sanford,	2	
James Triplett,	4	
William Thomson,	2	
Margaret Thomson,	2	
James Taite,	4	
John Tarcil,	9	
John Tinsley,	1	
Alexander Thorn,	5	
Wm. Triplett,	14	2
Job Thomas,	2	
Thomas Turner,	76	6
Stephen Turnbull,	4	
John Turberville,	95	6
George Turberville,	26	6
Elizabeth Tebbs,	2	
W. Carr Tidwell, Es.,	16	
Daniel Tebbs, Est.,	16	
Thomas Thomson,	40	
Anne Barbara Tidwell,	6	
Sarah Vigor,	6	
Benjamin Weeks,	36	
Sukey Washington,	22	2
Rachel Williams,	2	
Samuel Wood,	6	
William White,	2	

	S.	W.		S.	W.
John Washington,	28	6	John Ward, . .	3	
The Revd Francis Wilson, . .	1		Moore Wilson, .	2	
			Thomas Wright, .	12	
Wm. Augustine Washington, .	69	4	John Weaver, .	2	
			Thomas Yeatman,	9	
Presly Wright, ,	10		John Yeatman, .	8	

There were in Westmoreland county, in 1782, 410 slave owners, who owned 4,536 slaves, a fraction more than eleven slaves to each owner. There were also in the county 1,889 horses and 9,886 cattle, and 136 wheels for riding carriages.

66	owned	1	each,	66	50	owned	2	each,	100
24	"	3	"	72	43	"	4	"	172
29	"	5	"	145	27	"	6	"	162
29	"	7	"	203	11	"	8	"	88
10	"	9	"	90	10	"	10	"	100
6	"	11	"	66	10	"	12	"	120
6	"	13	"	78	4	"	14	"	56
1	"	15		15	8	"	16	"	128
5	"	17	"	85	4	"	18	"	72
4	"	19	"	76	9	"	20	"	180
2	"	21	"	42	1	"	22		22
5	"	23	"	115	1	"	24		24
3	"	25	"	75	4	"	26	"	104
2	"	27	"	54	3	"	28	"	84
1	"	30		30	4	"	31	"	124
3	"	33	"	99	2	"	36	"	72
2	"	38	"	76	1	"	40		40
1	"	42		42	2	"	43	"	86
2	"	45	"	90	1	"	49		49
1	"	51		51	1	"	53		53
1	"	56		56	1	"	57		57
1	"	61		61	1	"	69		69
1	"	73		73	1	"	76		76
1	"	77		77	1	"	82		82
1	"	93		93	1	"	95		95
1	"	112		112	1	"	278		278
		410							4,536

A List of Taxable Articles in the City of Williamsburg Taken by Robert Nicolson for the Year 1783 Under the Revenue Act

Owners' Names	*Free Males Above 21 Years*	*Tithable Slaves*	*Slaves Under 16 Years Old*	*Horses*	*Cattle*	*Wheels*	*Ordy. Licenses*
Anderson, James, Nat, Tom, Peter, Fanny, Agga, Dicy Priscilla, Betty Charles, Philis	1	6	4	7	2	2	..
Andrews, Robert, Lemon, Charles, Sarah, Betty, Hannah, Anthony	1	5	1	1	2	..	..
Anderson, Robert (Taylor) Lucy	1	1	..	1	2	..	..
Alison, Francis	1	..	..	1	2	..	..
Abell, Samuel, Betty	1	1	..	1	1	..	..
Anderson, Robert, Jack, Nell, Lucy, Kitt, Sall, Patt, Nan, Adam, Miller, Harry, Lucy, London	1	6	6	2	7	4	..
Bland, William, Milly, Judy, Lewis, Kitty, Edy	1	2	3	1	1	2	..
Bryant, Rachel, Pompey, Hannah, Anny	..	2	1	2	4	2	..
Bucktrout, Benjamin	1	..	..	..	..	..	..
Bentley, Thomas, Abraham, Sam, Charles, Bridget, Kitty	1	4	1	5	..	..	..
Blair, John, Will Evans, Peter, Jerry, Priscilla, Rachel, Grace, Joanna, Clara, Eliza, Barbara, Nanny, Amy, Daniel, Clem, Lydia, Nelly, Sally	1	12	5	5	2	4	..
Burwell, John's Betty Evans	..	1	..	..	..	..	..
Barrom, William, Amy, Esther, Jack, Billy	1	1	3	..	..	..	..
Baxter, Reuben	1	..	..	1	..	..	..
Barraud, Doctr Phil, Billy	1	1	..	2	..	..	..

Williamsburg—List of Taxable Articles—*Continued*

Owners' Names	*Free Males Above 21 Years*	*Tithable Slaves*	*Slaves Under 16 Years Old*	*Horses*	*Cattle*	*Wheels*	*Ordy. Licenses*
Bond, Robert, Grace	1	1	..	..	..	..	..
Brien, Mórto, Phillis, Nan, Lettice, Aberdeen	1	1	3	2	1	..	..
Bingley, Matthew, Dilsey, May, James	1	1	2	1	3	..	..
Baker, Frances's Milly	..	..	1	..	..	..	..
Cole, Jesse	1	..	..	1	..	..	..
Craig, Mary's Lydia, Alice, Sarah, Jemmy, Patty	..	3	2	..	1	..	..
Carter, Doct. James, George, Jack-Beaver, Mary, Nanny, Phillis Letty	1	4	2	3	7	4	..
Crump, Richard, Agga, Harry, Christiana, Lucky-Smith, Rose	1	1	4	2	2	..	..
Carter, John (Merch.t), John Carter, Betty, Tom, Sarah, Patty, Milly	2	1	4	..	3	..	..
Carter, Doct. William, Tom, Sam, Agga, Billy, Judith, John, Ned	1	3	4	1	3	..	..
Couch, Samuel, Daniel, Jem, Sarah, Macklin, Pate	1	3	2	5	1	..	..
Cocke, James, Clem, Lucy, Sally, Lucinda, Betty, Daniel, Johnny	1	3	4	..	2	..	..
Craig, James, Stepney, Kate, Nan, Kitt, Billy	1	3	2	3	3	..	..
Crawley, Samuel, Phillis, Luckey, Jenny, James, Bob	1	2	3	2	2	..	..
Crump John, Dinah, Sylvia, Nancy, Jenny	1	2	3	..	2	..	..
Coke, Sarah, Phil, Billy, Sylvia	..	3	..	..	3	..	..
Coke, John, Milly, Phillis	1	1	1	..	1	..	..
Craig, Thomas, Lewis, Nanny, Nancy, Sally	1	3	1	..	1	..	..
Carter, John (Sadler) Beck, Beck	1	1	1	2	1	..	..
Carter, William (Taylor) Sall	1	1	..	..	..	..	..

Williamsburg—List of Taxable Articles—*Continued*

Owners' Names	*Free Males Above 21 Years*	*Tithable Slaves*	*Slaves Under 16 Years Old*	*Horses*	*Cattle*	*Wheels*	*Ordy. Licenses*
Campbell, Christiana's Shopshire, Nanny, Betty, Agga, Sucky, Fanny, Nancy, Billy, Louisa, Billy, Jack-Toaft, Jack-London, Anthy	..	4	9	..	4	..	..
Charlton, Edward, Ben, Jenny	1	2	..	..	1	..	..
Cary, Wilson Miles's Jonathan	..	1	..	..	..	..	..
Coke, Robey, Sylvia, Will	1	..	2	3	..	..	..
Digges, Dudley, Joseph, Henry, Harry, Jemmy, Lott, Phillis, Jemmy, Joyce, Alice, Lucy, Ophelia, Jenny, Norborne, Fayette	1	10	4	3	1	2	..
Dixon, John's Henry Dixon, Dinah, Peg, Jemima, Sam	1	2	2	..	..	..	..
(Ms. defective) Nell, Jack	1	1	1	1	1	..	..
Dean, Elizabeth's George	..	..	1	..	1	..	..
Davis, James, Sue	1	1	..	..	..	..	..
Dudley, Edward, Jack, Polly, Fanny	1	2	1	3	2	2	..
Davis, Augustine, Moll, Will	1	1	1	1	1	..	..
Dickson, Charlotte's Sall, Daniel & an Infant	..	1	2	..	1	..	..
Drewitz, John, John Oder, Will, Ben, Lettice & Lettice	2	3	1	3	1	4	..
Draper, John, Molly	1	1	..	6	4	..	..
Dickson, Beverley, Jury, Nelly, Grace, Sarah, Tom, Moses	1	3	3	2	..	..	..
Drummond, John's Sylvia, Milly, Will, James, Miles and an Infant	..	2	4	..	..	..	..
Fitzgerald, James	1	..	..	..	..	..	..
Finnie, William, Will, Finnie, Grace, Sall, Edy, George	1	4	2	2	2	4	..
Farquharson, John, Peter, Nanny, Clara	1	2	1	2	5	..	..

Williamsburg—List of Taxable Articles—*Continued*

Owners' Names	*Free Males Above 21 Years*	*Tithable Slaves*	*Slaves Under 16 Years Old*	*Horses*	*Cattle*	*Wheels*	*Ordy. Licenses*
Galt, Doct. John, Sam, Harry, Jenny, Rachel, Betty, Lewis, Suckty, Polly, Jack, Billy	1	5	5	3	5	2	..
Geddy, William, Charlotte, Peg, Joe, Jemmy	1	3	1	3	2	..	..
Greenhow, John, Robt., Will, Wona, Fanny, Lydia, Mary, Mordecai, Marcus, Rachel, Dick, Kitty, Siller, Abell, Kate, Jonathan, Edmund, Sarah	2	4	12	2	12	..	..
Galt, James, Jacob, Violet, Violet, Grace, Sally, Patrick, Dublin, Primus, John	1	5	4	..	2	..	..
Graham, Robert	1	..	..	..	..	..	..
Griffin, Doct. Corbin, James, Daniel, George, Doll, Barry, Hannah, Mene, Daniel, Mary, Mary, Sall, Lucy	1	7	5	3	1	6	..
Harwood, Humphrey, Jerry, Nat, Moses, Grace, Cosar, Betty, Daniel	1	5	2	5	..	2	..
Hatton, Matthew, Jupiter	1	1	..	..	..	..	..
Honey, James, John Miller, Jas. Johnson, Ben, Gabriel, Peter, Kate, Cloe, Dinah	3	6	..	3	3	..	..
Hunter, Margaret, Agga, Jenny, Sall, Will, Chavers, Milly	..	2	3	..	1	..	..
Hornsby, Joseph, John, Molly, Lucy, Nanny, Rachel, James, Dicy, Ally, Ariana, Edmund	1	5	5	4	2	4	..
Hallam, Sarah, James, Nancy	..	2	..	..	..	..	..
Hornsby, William, Cosar, Emanuel, Priscilla, Sylvia, Peter, Harry, Cutchena	1	4	3	1	5	..	..

Williamsburg—List of Taxable Articles—*Continued*

Owners' Names	*Free Males Above 21 Years*	*Tithable Slaves*	*Slaves Under 16 Years Old*	*Horses*	*Cattle*	*Wheels*	*Ordy. Licenses*
Holmes, Basil	1	..	..	..	..	..	..
Hutchinson, Joseph	1	..	..	..	..	..	..
Hubard, Frances, Mortor	..	..	..	..	..	..	..
Hubard, David, Pompey, Scipio, Dick, Charles, Bellina, Dorothy, Patty, Esther, Priscilla, Will, Bob, Nancy	1	10	3	4	3	..	..
Holt, William, Norris, Charles, Jack, Jeffrey, Doll, Peg, Molly, Molly, Mary, Nelly, Alice, Pip, Sarah, Patty, Alice, Dinah, Hannibal, Billy, Jack, Harry, Fanny, Theoditia, Johnny	1	13	10	1	5	2	..
Iaran, Francis, London	1	1	..	1	..	..	..
Innis, James, John, Richard, Violet, Priscilla, Susanna, Fanny, Richard, Julius Rosanna	1	6	3	4	3	..	..
Lewis, William, Charles, Mingo, Phillis, Sall, Jemmy, Lender, Amy, Dick, Emanuel	2	3	5	3	..	..	..
Low, David, Cosar, Charles	1	1	1	1	..	2	..
Lenox, Walter	1	..	..	..	1	..	..
Lafong, George	1	..	..	..	1	..	..
Lewis, John, Lena, Alice, Betty, Daniel, Edmund, Nancy	1	3	3	1	2	2	..
McClurg, Doc^{r}. James, Milford, Bett, Grace, Tom, Jack	1	3	2	2	2	..	..
Moyer, Peter, Christopher Moyer, Matt, Betty, Lucy, Fanny, Patty	2	2	3	4	..	..	..

Williamsburg—List of Taxable Articles—*Continued*

Owners' Names	*Free Males Above 21 Years*	*Tithable Slaves*	*Slaves Under 16 Years Old*	*Horses*	*Cattle*	*Wheels*	*Ordy. Licenses*
Massenburg, Alexander, Sarah, Rachel, George	1	1	2	1	2	..	..
Marr, Andrew	1	..	..	..	..	..	..
McCarty, Michael	1	..	..	1	2	..	..
McCarty, Daniel	1	..	..	..	1	..	..
Morton, David, Jack, Molly, Molly, Billy, Betty, Betty	1	3	3	1	2	..	..
Moody, Josias, Lucy, James, Letty, Harry	1	1	3	1	..	..	..
Moir, James, Sarah, Lucy	1	1	1	1	2	..	..
Maupin, Gabriel, Murreah, Beck, Matt, Sall, Tiller, Neaton, Charles, Cosar, Judy, Mary, Cloe, Billy, Sam, James, Isham, Fanny, Tiller, Nancy, Ariana	1	8	11	5	1	..	..
Martin, Robert's Doll, Jenny, Harry	..	2	1	..	2	2	..
Many, Peter	1	..	..	..	2	..	..
Madison, James, Flora, Nanny, Jenny, James, Sall, Edy, Peyton, Sam, John	1	3	6	1	2	2	..
Moody, Philip, Milly, Lucy	1	2	..	..	2	..	..
Moody, Hugh	1	..	..	..	..	..	..
Mooyer, Peter junr	1	..	..	..	..	..	..
Nicolson, William, Pompey, Hannah, Tom, Warner	1	2	2	5	2	2	..
Nicolson, Robert, Peter, Davy, Clemena, Phillis, Molly, Jemmy, Billy, Bob, Charles, George, Sylvia, John	1	5	7	2	2	2	..
Nicolson, Docr. Robert	1	..	..	2	..	2	..
Nicholson, Henry, Peter, Sarah, Sylvia, Rachel, Nancy	1	4	1	..	1	..	..
Nelson, General Thomas, Bob, Cooper, George, Pompey, George Dean	..	6	..	..	..	..	..

Williamsburg—List of Taxable Articles—*Continued*

Owners' Names	*Free Males Above 21 Years*	*Tithable Slaves*	*Slaves Under 16 Years Old*	*Horses*	*Cattle*	*Wheels*	*Ordy. Licenses*
Orr. Katharine, Joe, Sall, Sarah, Jack, Hugh, Molly	..	3	3	..	1	..	..
Pearson, Maggy, Matt Pearson, Will, Betty, Kate, Sarah, Harry, Milly, Nancy, an Infant	1	4	4	1	1	..	..
Pitt, William, Richard Towns, Sam, Jenny, Amy	2	2	1	1	2	2	..
Ferry, Hartwell	1	..	..	2	..	..	..
Plite, Harman, Stephen	1	..	1	..	..	..	..
Prentis, Joseph, Alexander, Effy, Leah, Hannah, Rachel, George, Betsy, Nancy, Judy, Ariana, an Infant	1	5	6	2	2	..	..
Prentis, Robert, Joshua, James	1	2	..	5	..	8	..
Pasteur, Blovet, Sally	1	1	..	..	1	..	..
Pope, Doc[r]. Matthew, Kent	1	1	..	2	..	..	..
Pierce, William, Will	1	1	..	..	..	..	..
Reid, George, Tom, Patty, Charity, Dinah, Nell, Dick, Ned, Beverly, Billy, Betty, Lucy, Milly, Lucy, Daphne	1	5	9	3	3	..	..
Russell William, Natt, Kate, Amy, Sall, John	1	3	2	3	2	2	..
Roadman, John, Julius, Frank, Betty, Sylvia, Molly, Isabella, Poll, Nan, Clara	1	3	6	3	3	2	..
Readvill, Mrs. Lewis, Crowmell, Davis, Celia, Judy, Arrabella, Peg, Tristran, (Ms. defective), Celia, Arisana, Betty, Lucy	..	7	8	1	1	4	..

Williamsburg—List of Taxable Articles—*Continued*

Owners' Names	*Free Males Above 21 Years*	*Tithable Slaves*	*Slaves Under 16 Years Old*	*Horses*	*Cattle*	*Wheels*	*Ordy. Licenses*
Rowsay, William, Will, Cosar, Sarah, Charlotte, Phil, Lucy, Dick	1	3	4	4	5	2	..
Ross, Donald	1	..	..	..	..	..	..
Robertson, Patrick, Judith, Rachel	1	1	1	3	1	..	..
Russell, William, London	1	1	..	2	..	..	..
Segueyra, Doctr. John, Cain, Sally	1	2	..	2	..	4	..
Saunders, John, Jack, Jack, Lucy, Lucy, Phillis, Effy, Clara, Sarah, Billy, Letty & an Infant	1	6	5	2	..	..	..
Shiphard, John, Hannah, Andrew, Ben, Bristol, Clara, Nan, Joseph	1	2	5	2	2	..	..
Singleton, Capt. Anthony, Roger, Judith, Kate, Hannah, Nanny, Lewis, Lucinda, Polly, Hercules	..	4	5	..	1	..	..
Scouvement, Nicholas, Cottel	1	..	1	..	..	..	..
Southall, James, Sam Trower, Will, (Ms. defective), Jemmy, Davy, Betty, Fanny, Kate, Venus, Ciller, Dinah, Luke, Nan, Sarah, Milly, Phobe, Mary, Betty, Peg, Jenny	2	10	9	7	2	6	1
Selby, Sarah's Hannah	..	1	..	..	..	..	..
Taliaferro, Charles, Gaby, Cosar, Sam, Jack, Jim, Natt, George, Godfrey, King, Judith, Sarah, Fanny, Amy	1	11	2	5	4	..	..
Taylor, James, Charlotte	1	..	1	..	..	..	..
Vobe, Jane, William Duncan, Sam, Lawrence, Gowen, Mary, Lucy, Travis, David, Miller	2	5	1	3	2	..	1

Williamsburg—List of Taxable Articles—*Continued*

Owners' Names	*Free Males Above 21 Years*	*Tithable Slaves*	*Slaves Under 16 Years Old*	*Horses*	*Cattle*	*Wheels*	*Ordy. Licenses*
Urie, William	1	..	..	..	..	..	..
Waller, Benjamin, Bob, Billy, Godfrey, Nanny, Betty, Sall, Eliza, Billy, Lewis, Davy, Rachel, Polly, Fanny	1	7	6	3	3	2	..
Wray, James, Matt, Will, Patty, Molly, Ariana	1	4	1	1	2	..	..
Wood, James, Aberdeen	1	1	..	..	..	..	..
Wythe, George, William Nelson, Ben, Charles, Lydia, Hannah, Secordia, Betty, Jemmy, Fanny & her four Children, Little-Betty, Paul	2	7	7	2	..	6	..
Young, James	1	..	..	..	..	..	..

Williamsburg—CERTIFICATE TAX

Count	Item	Rate	£	s.	d.
126	Whites	at 10/	£ 63.	...	...
350	Blacks	10/	175.	...	...
201	Horses	2/	20.	2.	...
194	Cattle	3d.	2.	8.	6.
98	Wheels	5/	24.	10.	...
2	Licenses		8.	...	...
			293.	...	6.

Count	Item	Rate	£	s.	d.
126	Whites	at 10/	£ 63.	...	...
642	Blacks	10/	321.	...	...
201	Horses	2/	20.	2.	...
194	Cattle	3d.	2.	8.	6.
98	Wheels	5/	29.	8.	...
2	Licenses		10.	...	...
			445.	18.	6.

Correct copy of the original list in the Virginia State Library.

June 26, 1914.

H. R. McIlwaine, *Librarian.*

TITHABLES IN YORK-HAMPTON PARISH, YORK COUNTY, VA.

In his "Single and Distinct View," published in 1763, John Camm, rector of York-Hampton Parish, York County, gave a list of all in his parish as had tithables. Taxes in colonial times were laid according to the tithables. What were the tithables? The act of 1705 states "they were all male persons of the age of sixteen years and upwards, and all negro, mulatto and Indian women of the age of sixteen years and upwards, not being free."

Noticeable is the use by Mr. Camm of the term "Mr." In the preceding century the term was sparingly used, as a term of much respect. But Mr. Camm's usage shows that in the eighteenth century it was applied generally to every one not a servant.

By this list it appears that there were 184 taxpayers in York-Hampton Parish and 1109 tithables.

The object of Mr. Camm in this pamphlet was to show that the richer the man the more he was benefitted by the Two Penny Act.

Every one has heard of Patrick Henry's opposition to this act, and of his speech at Hanover Court House in 1763. In this famous speech he declared that "the King of England, by taking upon himself to disallow the act of the Governor and Assembly, had forfeited all rights of obedience heretofore due from his subjects in Virginia." Such language as this has never been heard before on this continent.

And here it may be stated that Henry's part in the controversy has often been misunderstood. His speech in 1763 has been taken as the beginning of Virginia's protest against the prerogative, whereas the first Two Penny Act, disregarding the accepted Constitution, was eight years earlier, and in the interim the field was occupied by Richard Bland and Landon Carter. These gentlemen had engaged in a wordy controversy with John Camm, the representative of the clergy, who complained of the act, in the course of which they had used language almost as inflammatory as Henry's. Col. Carter, in his pamphlet printed in Williamsburg in December, 1759, declared that "there were exceptions in all cases," and that "justice to the people" and "charity to the poor" made this Tobacco Act an exception, if indeed it was unconstitutional.

Col. Bland, bolder still, in his pamphlet, published in 1760, took the ground of the *salus populi suprema est lex,* and argued that necessity made its own law, and that in certain cases "even royal instructions may be deviated from with impunity."

Nor was Henry's action an advocacy of the poor against the rich, as has been frequently said, as the latter shared best under the Two Penny Act. As a matter of fact, Henry only continued the fight of the two aristocrats, Bland and Carter. He fought the battle of the whole colony, it is true, but of the ruling powers more than of any other element.

	Tithables.	
Col. Carter Burwell, Three Estates.	61	
Col. Edward Digges, Two Estates.	56	
Hon. William Nelson.	38	
Mr. James Burwell.	34	
Mr. John Wormeley	34	
Hon. T. Nelson.	22	235

Mrs. Lightfoot, Two Estates.	38	
Mr. John Godwin,* Senior.	19	
Mr. Thomas Reynolds.	18	
Mr. John Godwin*	17	
Mrs. Frances Nelson.	16	
Mrs. Agnes Smith.	15	
Mr. Robert Smith.	15	
Peyton Randolph, Esq.	15	
Mr. William Allin.	14	
Richard Ambler, Esq.	14	
Mr. Arthur Dickenson.	14	
Mr. Hudson Allin.	14	
Mr. John Norton.	13	
Mr. Robert Ballard.	11	
Mr. Aaron Philips.	11	
Mr. John Chapman.	11	
Mrs. Jemima Barham.	11	
Mrs. Elizabeth Godwin.*	10	
Mr. John Wynne.	10	
Mr. James Mitchell.	10	
Mr. Laurence Smith.	10	
Mr. Nathaniel Buck.	10	T.
Mr. John Tenham.	10	326
Col. Charles Carter, Mem. Assembly.	9	
Mr. William Moss, Junior.	9	
Mr. James Mills.	9	
Mr. Elliston Armistead, Estate.	9	
Mr. John Gibbons.	9	
Mr. Thomas Gibbons.	9	
Mr. Charles Hansford, Junior.	9	
Mr. Everard Dowsing.	8	
Mr. William Powell.	8	
Mrs. Ann Chapman.	8	
Mr. Benjamin Moss, Senior.	8	
Mr. John Lester, Senior.	8	
Mr. David Morse.	8	
Mrs. Mary Moss.	7	
Mrs. Elizabeth Moss.	7	
Mr. Philip Dedman.	7	
Mr. Thomas Pescod.	7	
Col. Dudley Digges, Mem. Assembly.	7	
Mr. Griffin Stith.	7	

*This should have been Goodwin, not "Godwin."

Mr. Joseph Mountfort.	7	
Mr. John Wagstaff.	7	
Mr. Edward Potter's, Estate.	7	
Mr. William Moody.	7	
Mrs. Martha Bryan.	7	
Mr. John Hunter.	6	
Mr. Edward Cross.	6	
Mr. George Riddell.	6	
Mr. Edmund Tabb.	6	
Mr. Thomas Archer.	6	
Mr. William Moss.	6	
Mr. James Moss.	6	
Mr. Robert Godwin*	6	
Mr. Augustine Moore.	5	
Mr. Robert Shield.	5	
Mr. William Stevenson.	5	
Mr. John Baptist.	5	
Mr. Armistead Lightfoot.	5	
Mr. John Chisman, Junior.	5	
Mr. Charles Mills.	5	
Mr. William Adduston Rogers.	5	
Mr. John Burcher.	5	
Mr. John Harvey.	5	
Mr. Philip Burt.	5	
Mr. Young Moreland.	5	
Mr. Basil Wagstaff.	5	
Mrs. Mary Lewis.	5	
Mrs. Martha Wade.	5	
Mr. Thomas Wade.	5	T.
Mr. William Baker.	5	321
Mr. Seymour Powell.	4	
Mr. David Jameson.	4	
Mr. Nicholas Dickson.	4	
Mr. Patrick Mathews.	4	
Mr. Edward Baptist.	4	
Mr. Thomas Gibbs.	4	
Mr. Edward Wright.	4	
Mr. Thomas Wootton.	4	
Mr. John Burcher.	4	
Mr. Anthony Robinson.	4	
Mr. Richard Hobday.	4	

Mr. James Cosby.	4
Mr. John Coman.	4
Mr. Henry Chisman.	4
Mr. Whitehead Lester.	4
Mr. James Matt Ince.	4
Mr. Edmund Glanvill.	3
Mr. William Harris.	3
Mr. Christopher Cortes.	3
Mr. Thomas Gibbs.	3
Mrs. Anne Gibbons	3
Mrs. Mary Moody.	3
Mrs. Martha Satterwhite	3
Mr. Kemp Charles.	3
Mr. John Wootton.	3
Mr. Alexander Maitland.	3
Mr. William Evans.	3
Mr. John Roberts.	3
Mr. Robert Booth Armistead	3
Mr. Matt. Burt.	3
Mr. Samuel Hill.	3
Mr. Charles Hansford, Senior	3
Mr. Benjamin Barham.	3
Mr. John Hyde.	3
Mrs. Mary Patton.	3
Mrs. Frances Lester.	3
Mrs. Elizabeth Barham.	3
Mrs. Mary Cocket.	3
Mrs. Mary Potter.	3
Mr. John Hack.	2
Mr. William Brodie.	2
Mr. Joseph Nisbett	2
Mr. Peter Mace,	2
Mr. Benjamin Moss, Junior.	2
Mr. Samuel Jones.	2
Mr. John McClary.	2
Mrs. Martha Goosley.	2
Mrs. Elizabeth Buckler.	2
Mrs. Elizabeth Irwin.	2
Mrs. Catherine Hansford.	2
Mrs. Bethia Morris.	2
Mrs. Anne Cosby.	2
Mr. William Cary.	2
Mr. John Hay.	2
Mr. Dudley Wright.	2
Mr. Thomas Trotter.	2

Mr. Richard Singleton.	2
Mr. Ambrose Burfort.	2
Mr. Francis Peters.	2
Mr. Dickeson Yeatman.	2
Mr. John Dunford.	2
Mr. George Booth.	2
Mr. John Lester, Junior.	2
Mr. Edward Hansford, Junior.	2
Mr. Robert Martin.	2
Mr. Sacheverel Sclater.	2
Mr. Joseph Freeman.	1
Mr. John Freeman.	1
Mrs. Ann Orton	1
Mrs. Amy Archer.	1
Mrs. Elizabeth Allin.	1
Mrs. Mary Tuomar.	1
Mrs. Martha Pepper.	1
Mrs. Anne Dunford.	1
Mrs. Sarah Bruce.	1
Mrs. Sarah Cosby.	1
Mrs. Mildred Moreland.	1
Mr. Haldenby Dixon.	1
Mr. George Wilson.	1
Mr. William Holt.	1
Mr. Allen Jones.	1
Mr. Thomas White.	1
Mr. John Pearson.	1
Mr. Hillsman Thomas.	1
Mr. John Bower.	1
Mr. Thomas Burroughs.	1
Mr. Will. Mitchell.	1
Mr. John Davis.	1
Mr. Richard Limehouse, Junior.	1
Mr. Richard Coventon.	1
Mr. Charles Freeman.	1
Mr. Will Stroud.	1
Mr. Joseph Stroud, Junior.	1
Mr. Will. Gill.	1
Mr. James Martin.	1
Mr. Joseph Wootton.	1
Mr. Charles Yeatman.	1
Mr. Anthony Roberts.	1
Mr. Hansford Hill.	1
Mr. Robert Harrison.	1
Mr. Thomas Mansfield.	1

Mr. Savage Hooker.	1	
Mr. Edward Mansfield.	1	
Mr. John Mansfield, Jr.	1	
Mr. Edward Parish.	1	
Hon. Robert Burwell's Rachel.	1	227

OLD PAPERS.

Contributed by W. S. Morton.

Mr. George Walker's Poll taken March 22nd. 1754, for House of Burgesses.

James Moore	Jeames Rutledge	Edawrd Selire?
Rich'd. Perryman	Henry Lester	Jacob McGehee
John Witter	Jeames Gravilet	Wm. Searcy
Daniel Brown	Abra. Brown	Godfrey Piles
John Pennix	George Moore	Philemon Holcomb
Thomas Haskins	Michael McDearman	Thomas Crawford (18)

Mr. Jofeph Norton's poll taken March 22nd, 1754, for House of Burgesses.

Phillip Good	Hugh Nickson	John Roberts
Thos. Osborne	John Smith	Wm. Brown
James Center	Henry Baker	George Cook
Manew Mackfeele	Richard Beasley	Wm. Hall
Watson Brumfield	John Chiles	Richard Morton (15)

Mr. John Nash's Sr. Poll taken March 22nd. 1754, for House of Burgesses.

Henry Ligon	Andrew Rosbroke	John Stanton
Riel Bowman	Jas. McQuin	Patrick Gallispie
John Biger	Alexander Ewing	Edawrd Selbye
William Austin	John Watson	David Mckey
James Rutledge	Pugh Price	Jonathan Cheatham
Daniel Brown	James Reed	John Coldwell, Jr.
Isaac Robinson	Jacob McGehee	John Penick
William Ligon	Samuel Ewing	John Fulton
Mich'l. McDearman	Sam'l Sunderland	Richard Perryman
Thos. Osborne	Cuthbert Hudson	William Boyd
James Ewing	James Wimbish	Chas. Hudson
David Flournoy	Thomas Turpin	Chas. Simmons
Duglas Baker	John Whitworth	Robert Reed
William Brown	Henry Johnston	Simcock Cannon
Charles Richie	Jeremiah Penick	Alexander Keen
Hugh Richie	Daniel Davidson	David Hudson
Abraham Womack	James Thackston	Thos. Shelton
James Daniel	Edward Brathwaithe	John Smith
Abram Baker	Abraham Venable, Jr.	Phiemon Holcombe
George Ewing	George Forrest	William Ewing
John Owen	Thomas Certain	Joseph Rice
Peter Davis	Arthur Neal	John Martin
Andrew McAdow	James Mitchell	Philip McTaggartt
James Muckleroy	John Roberts	Thos. Reynolds
Thos. Morton	David Coldwell	Alex'r. Cunningham
Jas. Archdeacon	James Cunningham	John Morrison

John Ritchie
Joel Watkins
Robert Hannah (P)
William Davidson
Samuel Baker
Gideon Johnston
William Atkins
Samuel Cobbs
William King
Robert Jennings
Benja. Haskins
James Browning
John Coldwell
Edawrd Gressum
James Fears
Wm. Crockett
Edward Shelladay
John Gaulding
Henry Baker
Richard Teen?
George Moor
Richard Morton
James Celle
Theodorick Carter
James Moor
Robert Black
Wm. Sadler
James Flowers

Andrew Porter
William Hill
Peter Downey
Henry Lester
Ja' C. Walker
William Baldwin
Robert Peak
George Walker
John Richie
Andrew Dunn
John Morton
Sam'l Matthis
Daniel Dejarnett
Elias Dejarnett
Mathew Rice
Henry Childs
Hugh Challis
Robert Baker
John Coldwell
Lawrance Morrain
Richard Rutledge
George Brown
Herry Lewis
Robert Elliott
Robert Atkins
John Smyth
Robert Gillispie
John Cunningham

William Brown
James Black
William Browning
Thos. Crawford
Thos. Clark
Alexander Womack
William Owen
Manus Mcbride
Alex'r. Frazier
John May
Peter Coffee
John Simmons
John Crockett
George Stewart
Richard Woodson
Thos. Haskins
Robert Hannah (Smith)
Joseph Shelton
James Atwood
Edward Johnstone
Stephen Collins
Richard Swepston
George Davies
Sam'l. Handcock, Jr.
John Cook
William Campbell
John Morrow
Mat. Harris (161)

Copy Test. John Nash, Jr. Sher. April 9th. 1754. Sworn to before me
David Flournoy.

Col. George Walker's Poll this 8th. day of December 1755.

Benjamin Haskins
John Smith
Mathis Flournoy
Isaac Roberson
John Watkins
Thomas Certain
Berry Lewis
Alex'r. Fraser
John Penix
Wm. King
Benjamin Atkins
James Moor

Wm. Owen
Daniel Brown
John Young
James Fears
Wm. Sadler
David Flournoy
Alex. Erskin
Phillip Holcomb
James Hamlett
John Stanton
Thomas Haskins
Ambrose Davis

Jonathan Cheatham
Jacob McGehee
Robert Atkins
Royal Bowman
John Roberts
Thomas Chandler
Wm. Womack
Joel Ward
James Rutledge
George Steward
Dunkin Blue
Henry Lester

Alexander Womack	John Whitworth	Zac. Leigh
William Hill	Hugh Challes	Godfrey Piles
George Brown	Thomas Crawford	Richard Perriman
Will. Searsy	George Moor (Ordinary)	Elias Dejarnett

By Ben Ward.

A copy—John Nash, Jr. Sh'ff.
15th. May, 1756. Sworn before me,

DAVID FLOURNOY.

Col. Charles Anderson's Poll this 8th. day of December, 1755.

Duglass Puckett	Jacob Williamson	William Watson
Nat. Harriss	James Fears	Edward Johnson
John May	James McKune	John Bibb
Gideon Johnson	Manus McBride	Thomas Bauldwen
Joshua Gilliam	John Fulton	Henry Liggon
George Moore	James Read	John Smith
Andrew McAdoe	Patrick Shield	Thomas Tirpin
Chales Riche	Robert Read	Thomas Morton, Sr.
George Davis	George Ewing	John Caldwell
Sherod Massie	Robert Black	Matthew Rice
Hew Riche	John Morrow	Robert Baker
James Mchleroy	William Smith	Alex. Cane
Daniel McFarling	Sam Cunningham	Chas. Hudson
Even Leigh	William Ligon, Jr.	William Hudson
Andrew Dunn	Robert Golaspie	James Cunningham
Will Boyd	Robert Elot	Archebald Mchleroy
James McMahan	William Crockett	Sam Goode
Robert Hanna	Thomas Bauldwin	William Hall
John Cunningham	Davis McKee	Peter Davis
James Kelly	John Richie	Richard Childres
Edward Shelleday	Thomas Ewing	Thomas Clark
William Aston	John Porter	Nicholas Hudson
Peter Downe	William Pauldwin	George Every
Phillip Tiger	Richard Rutledge	Stephens Collins
John Caldwell	Sam Southerland	Duglass Baker
William Caldwell	Sam Baker	Dan Lluelling
Samuel Ewing	John Biggers	Edmund Archdeacon
Thomas Bryan	James Thaxton	Edward Salby
James Browen	Dan Daviss	Pugh Price
Patrick Golaspy	Dan Neuman	Jeremiah Penix
Adam Calhoon	Obediah Woodson	Thomas Carter
George Ewing	James Sinton	John Watson
Alex. Hambleton	William Brownen	Richard Morton

Hugh Nixon	Watson Brumfield	Thomas Morton, Jr.
Robert Peak	Sam Arbuckle	Sam Matthews
Abram Baker	James Wimbish	Godfrey Poyles
Will Atkins	Will Rice	John Martin
Thomas Caldwell	John Gauling	Sam Wallace
Thomas Ozborn	Thomas Scott	John Morton

A Copy—John Nash, Shf.
10th. May, 1756. Sworn before me,

David Flournoy.

APPENDIX

VIRGINIA QUIT RENT ROLLS, 1704

During the colonial period all land owners in Virginia paid to the King an annual "quit rent" of one shilling for every fifty acres. The list of the land owners and the amount each owned was prepared by the sheriffs of the various counties and delivered to the Receiver-General, who collected the quit rents and transmitted the lists, with his accounts, to the English government.

It is singular that, as lists must have been sent annually, only one, that of 1704, has been discovered. The Library of Congress had a copy made of the original in the British Public Record Office, and that used here is from a photostat copy of the one in the Library of Congress.

It is not certain that all of the persons named in these lists owned the lands in fee simple. There are some indications that persons renting or leasing lands may have been charged with the payment of the quit rents. For instance one of the Cary family of Warwick County died after 1704, bequeathing a certain tract of land. It does not appear on this roll in his name, but does appear in the names of two of his sons.

Either the grantees of many large tracts of land bought to sell in smaller tracts (and this did often occur) or, else persons not holding by an absolute fee simple title were charged with the quit rents on the land they occupied. A study of one of the county rolls in connection with the county records, wills, deeds, etc., would be of interest.

It can be readily seen that this quit rent roll is of considerable interest and value. Unfortunately it does not include the counties between the Rappahannock and Potomac to their headwaters. These counties were Lancaster, Northumberland, Westmoreland, Richmond and Stafford. The quit rents for this section—the Northern Neck—were paid to the proprietors, the Culpeper and Fairfax families successively.

The amount derived from quit rents gradually increased. In 1684 it was £574 and in 1751, £16,433. This revenue was usually donated by the Crown for the uses of the colony.

For notices of the subject see P. S. Flippin's "Royal Government in Virginia," 233-235; P. A. Bruce's "Economic History of Virginia in the Seventeenth Century," 556-563, and references given by them.

At this time Henrico included the present Henrico and Chesterfield and westward, on both sides of the James River as far as the settlements extended. The Huguenots, just coming to Manakin Town, are not included.

[Endorsed] Virginia

Copy of the Rent Rolls of the Sev^{ll} Countys in Virg^{a} for the year 1704 referred to in Col. Nicholsons Lres of the 25 July last.

Recd 8 October

Read

705

M. 61 Entred C. fol 365

A True and Perfect Rent Roll of all the Lands held of her Maj^{tie} in Henrico County, Aprill 1705

A

	ACRES
Andrews, Thomas	396
Ascoutch, [Ascough] Mary	633

Archer, Jno.	335
Adkins, Jno.	125
Archer, Geo.	1738
Aldy, John	162
Akins, James, Senr	200
Asbrook, Peter Senr	200
Akins, James, Junr	218
Allen, Kidd	99
	4106

B

Byrd, [Wm] Esqr	19500
Bolling, Robt.	500
Bolling, John	831
Bevill, John	495
Branch, X.^{to} [Christopher]	646
Blackman, W^{m}	175
Bridgwater, Sam^{ll}	280
Bowman, John, Junr	300
Bowman, Edwd	300
Branch, Benj^{a}	550
Brown, Martha	893
Bullington, Benj^{a}	100
Bowman, Len.	65
Bullington	144
Bevell, Essex	200
Baugh, John	448
Baugh, James	458
Burton, Isaac	100
Bottom, John	100
Bayley, Ab'^{r}	542
Brooks, Jane, belonging to Wm Walker, New Kent	550
Braseal, Henry	200
Brazeal, Henry Junr	300
Burton, Robt	1350
Burgony, John	100
Branch, James	555

Burrows, Wm Wm Blackwell, New Kent	63
Branch, Thomas	540
Bailey, Thomas	251
Branch, Matthew	947
Burton, W^{m}	294
Bullington, Robt	100
Broadnax, Jno. J C C [James City Co.]	725
Beverley, Robt.	988
	33590

C.

Cheatham, Tho.	300
Cox, Batt.	100
Cox, John	150
Cox, George	200
Chamberlaine, Maj^{r} Tho.	1000
Childers, Ab^{r}, Senr	368
Cannon, John	108
Cox, W^{m}	300
Childers, Ab^{r} Junr	100
Clark, W^{m}	333
Clark, John	300
Cox, Rich^{d}	300
Cardwell, Tho.	350
Croydall, Roger	200
Cock, W^{m}	1535
Cock, Richd Senr	2180
Childers, Philip Senr	50
Childers, Philip	300
Childers, Tho.	300
Carter, Theo.	75
Cock, Capt. Thomas	2976½
Couzins, Charles	362
Clerk, Alenson	604
Cock, James	1506
Curd, Edwd	600

Cock, Rich[d]	C C C [Charles City Co.]	476
Cock, John		98
		15171½

D.

Dison, Nicholas	150
Dodson, W[m]	100
Douglas, Charles	63
	313

E.

Edw[d], Tho.	676
Entroughty, [Enroughty] Derby	200
Ealam, Robt.	400
Ellis, John	217
East, Tho. Sen[r]	475
East, Tho.	554
East, Edw[d]	150
Epes, Capt. Fra.	2145
Evans, Charles	225
Ealam, Martin	130
Epes, Isham, Epes, Fra. Jun[r] each 444½ Acres	889
	6061

F.

Field, Peter Majo[r]	2185
Farrar, Capt. W[m]	700
Farrar, Tho.	1444
Farrar, Jno.	600
Fowler, Godfrey	250
Ferguson, Robt.	230
Ferris, W[m]	50
Franklin, James Sen[r]	250
Franklin, James Jun[r]	786
Ferris, Rich[d] Sen[r]	550
Farmer, Henry	100
Forrest, James	138

Cock, Rich[d] C C C [Charles City Co.]	476
Cock, John	98
	15171½

D.

Dison, Nicholas	150
Dodson, W[m]	100
Douglas, Charles	63
	313

E.

Edw[d], Tho.	676
Entroughty, [Enroughty] Derby	200
Ealam, Robt.	400
Ellis, John	217
East, Tho. Sen[r]	475
East, Tho.	554
East, Edw[d]	150
Epes, Capt. Fra.	2145
Evans, Charles	225
Ealam, Martin	130
Epes, Isham, Epes, Fra. Jun[r] each 444½ Acres	889
	6061

F.

Field, Peter Majo[r]	2185
Farrar, Capt. W[m]	700
Farrar, Tho.	1444
Farrar, Jno.	600
Fowler, Godfrey	250
Ferguson, Robt.	230
Ferris, W[m]	50
Franklin, James Sen[r]	250
Franklin, James Jun[r]	786
Ferris, Rich[d] Sen[r]	550
Farmer, Henry	100
Forrest, James	138

Hatcher, Wm Junr	50
Hobson, Wm	150
Hatcher, Wm Senr	298
Hatcher, Henry	650
Hancock, Robert	860
Harris, Mary	94
Hall, Edwd	184
Herbert, Mrs.	1360
Hudson, Robt.	281
	9242

J.

Jones, Hugh	934
Jefferson, Thomas	492
Jones, Philip	1153
Jorden, Henry	100
Jamson, John	225
Jackson, Ralph	250
	3154

K.

Kennon, Elizb	1900
Knibb, Samll	209
Knibb, Soloman	833
Kendall, Richd	400
	3342

L.

Liptroll, Edwd	150
Lewis, Wm	350
Lester, Darius	100
Ladd, Wm	70
Ligon, Elizb Widdo	
Ligon, Mary Wido	1341
Laforce, Ren [or Rene.]	100
Lockett, James	50
Lownd, Henry	516
Lockett, Benja	104

Ligon, Rich[d]	1028
Ligon, Hugh	150
	3959

M.

Mann, Robt.	100
Matthews, Edw[d]	330
Mosely, Edw[d]	150
Mosely, Arthur	450
	1030

N.

Nunnally, Rich[d]	70

O.

Osbourn, Tho.	288
Owen, Tho.	68
	356

P.

Perkinson, John	622
Perrin, Ann	500
Pleasants, John	9669
Parker, W[m]	100
Parkins, Nich[o] Sen[r]	500
Pledge, Jno.	100
Powell, Rob[t]	150
Peice, John	130
Pleasant, [Pleasants] Jos.	1709
Porter, W[m]	305
Peirce, W[m]	175
Peirce, Francis	312
Paine, Thomas	300
Portlock, Eliz[t]	1000
Pew, Henry	350
Pattrane, Fra.	778
Pride, W[m] Sen[r]	1280
Polland, Thomas Sen[r]	130
Perkinson, Seth	50

Puckitt, W^m^	192
Puckitt, Tho.	300
Pattison, Joseph	500
Porter, John	100
Polland, Tho jun^r^	235
Polland, Henry	235
Puckitt, John	215
	19937

R.

Robertson, Geo.	1445
Ragsdale, Godfrey	450
Rawlett, [Rowlett] Peter	164
Russell, Charles	200
Rowlett, W^m^	200
Rowen, Fra.	148
Robertson, John	415
Rouch, Rachell	300
Robertson, Thomas	200
Russell, John	93
Royall, Joseph	783
Redford, John	775
Randolph, Coll. Wm. including 1185 Acres in Swamp	9465
	14648

S.

Steward, J^no^ Junr	902
Scott, Walter	550
Soane, Capt. Wm.	3841
Stanley, Edwd	300
Scruggs, Charles	400
Sewell, W^m^	59
Smith, Humphrey	40
Sharp, Robert	500
Stovoll, Barth^o^	100
Sherrin, Widd^o^	75
Steward, Daniell	270

Smith, Obadiah C C C [Chas. City Co.]	200
Stowers, Wid°	200
Sarragin, Stephen	120
	7557

T.

Tancocks Orphans	1230
Trent, Henry	224
Turpin, Thomas	491
Turpin, Philip	444
Turpin, Tho.	100
Turner, Henry	200
Taylor, Tho.	475
Tanner, Edw[d]	217
Traylor, Edw[d]	100
Totty, Tho.	260
Traylor, M[rs]	730
	4471

V.

Voden, [Vaden] Henry	100

W.

Woodson, John	4060
W[ms], Robt.	300
Woodson, Robt. Jun[r]	1157
Ward, Rich[d]	300
Watson, John Sen[r]	1603
Walthall, W[m]	500
Walthall, Henry	832
Whitby, W[m]	215
Watkins, Henry Sen[r]	100
Webb, John	100
Watkins, Tho.	200
Woodson, Rich[d]	180
Woodson, Wid°	650
Williamson, Tho.	1077

Webb, Giles	7260
Wood, Tho.	50
Watkins, Wm	120
Watkins, Jos.	120
Watkins, Edwd	120
Ward, Seth	700
Wood, Moses	100
Wilkinson, Jos.	75½
Wilkinson, John	130
Worsham, John	1104
Womack, Abr	560
Willson, John Senr	1686
Willson, John Junr	100
Walthall, Richd	500
Wortham, [Worsham] Geo.	400
Wortham, [Worsham?] Charles	90
Womack, Wm	100

W	24489½
V	100
T	4471
S	7557
R	14648
P	19937
O	356
N	70
M	1030
L	3959
K	3342
J	3154
H	9242
G	5571
F	9024
E	6061
D	313
C	15171½

B	33590
A	4106
Totall	165814
Out of which must be deducted these sev[ll] quantities of Land following	
viz: Tancockes Orphans Land	1230
Allens Orphans Land	99
	1329
An Acct. of Land y[t] hath been concealed	
John Steward Jun[r]	2
Tho Jefferson	15
Tho Turpin	10
Hen Gee	10
Steph Sarrzen	10
M[r] Lownd	1
James Atkin Sen[r]	32
Matt Branch	10
James Franklin	360
James Hill	50
Rosemond Hill	33
John Bullington	44
Benj[a] Lockett	4
John Russell	23
Charles Douglas	13
Coll Randolph Carles [Curles] Swamp Land	1049
	1669

The Q[t] Rent being 162719 Acres

VIRGINIA QUIT RENT ROLLS, 1704

Prince George County.

[Prince George at this time included, in addition to the present county, the territory now comprised in the counties of Dinwiddie, Amelia, Prince Edward and Nottoway. It is singular that this roll does not appear to include Brandon. The 4600 acres, belonging to "the merchants in London", could not have included all of Coggins Point and Martins Brandon. Nathaniel Harrison bought them from the English owners and when he made his will in 1726, it was stated that the former contained 1973 acres and the latter about 7000.]

A Rent Roll of all the Lands held in the County of Prince George for the year 1704:

A

	ACRES
Tho. Anderson	450
Wm Aldridge	160
Mr. Charles Anderson	505
Richd Adkinson	200
Tho. Adams	250
Matt. Anderson	349
Henry Ally	390
Wm. Anderson	235
Jno. Anderson	228
Henry Anderson	250
Robt. Abnernathy	100
Jno. Avery	100
	3217

B

Rich[d] Bland	1000
Rob[t] Burchett	375
Arthur Biggins	200
James Benford	461
Jno. Barloe	050
Charles Bartholomew	600
Philip Burlowe	350
Nich[o] Brewer	100
Jno. Bishop Sen[r]	100
Jn[o] Bishop Jun[r]	100
Isaac Baites [Bates]	360
Tho Busby Capt.	300
Tho Busby	200
W[m] Batt	750
Coll Byrd Esq[r]	100
Edw[d] Birchett	886
Col. [Robert] Bolling	3402
Edm[d] Browder	100
Matus Brittler	510
Jn[o] Butler	1385
Andrew Beck	300
Henry Batt	790
W[m] Butler	283
Tho Blitchodin	284
	12986

C

Tho Curiton	150
Hen. Chammins	300
Capt. Clements	1920
W[m] Claunton	100
Rob[t] Catte	100
Bartho Crowder	75
Tho Clay	70
Jno Coleman	200
Geo. Crook	489

Francis Coleman	150
Jno Clay	350
Wm Coleman Junr	100
Geo. Crooker	30
James Cocke	750
Robt Carlill	100
Jno Clerk	83
Richd Claunton	100
Stephen Cock for Jones' Orph.	2405
	7622

D

Tho Daniell	150
Roger Drayton	270
Joseph Daniell	50
Jo^{n} Doby	500
Geo Dowing	100
Wm Davis	100
Jno Duglas	300
Richd Durding	500
Christ^{o} Davis	50
Tho Dunkin	136
	2156

E

Robt Ellis	50
Jno Epes Senr	530
Wm Epes Senr	750
Jno Epes	300
Wm Epes	633½
Edwd Epes	500
Littlebury Epes	833½
Benj^{a} Evans	700
Tho Edw^{ds}	250
Dan Epes	200
Jno. Evans	800
Jno Ellis Junr	400

Jn° Ellis Senr	400
Mary Evans	400
Peter Evans	270
Capt. Fra Epes	226
	7243

F

Jn° Freeman	300
Wm Frost	50
Jn° Fountaine	350
Robt Fellows	418
Eliz^b Flood	100
Benj Foster	923
Jn° ffield	100
	2241

G

Jno Green	125
Richd Gord	100
David Goodgame	479
James Greithian	363
Mag^r Goodrick	900
Tho Goodwin	150
Hubert Gibeon	250
Richd Griffith	335
James Griffin	100
Charles Gee	484
Charles Gillam	200
Hugh Goelightly	500
Lewis Green	149
Wm Grigg	200
John Gillam	1000
John Goelightly	100
	5435

H

Coll. [Edward] Hill	1000
Dan^ll Hickdon	280

Rob[t] Harthorn	243
Jn[o] Hamlin	1484½
Coll Harrison Esq[r]	150
Ralph Hill	175
W[m] Harrison	1930
W[m] Heath	320
Edw[d] Holloway	100
Rob[t] Hobbs	100
Jn[o] Hobbs Sen[r]	250
Edw[d] Holloway Sen[r]	620
Jn[o] Hobbs	100
James Harrison	200
Gilbert Haye	200
Rich[d] Hudson	75
Gabriell Harrison	150
Rob[t] Hix	1000
Joseph Holycross	84
Charles Howell	125
Sam Harwell	125
Isaac Hall	450
Jn[o] Howell	183
Tho Howell	25
Mrs. Herbert	3925
Jn[o] Hixs	216
Rich[d] Hamlin	240
Tho Harrison	1077
Eliz[b] Hamlin	250
W[m] Hulme	100
Jeffry Hawkes	125
Adam Heath	300
Jno Hill	160
Jno Hardiman	872
Instance Hall	614
	17366

J

Wm Jones Junr	230
Wm Jones Senr	600
Henry Jones	200
Robert Jones	241
Edmd Irby	800
Nich. Jarrett	700
James Jackson	80
Adam Ivie	200
Tho Jackson	60
James Jones Senr	1100
Henry Ivye	450
Peter Jones	621
Richd Jones	600
Ralph Jackson	110
Joshua Irby	200
John Jones	350
	6542

K

Richd Kirkland	300
John King	50
Henry King	650
Arthur Kavanah	60
Eusobius King	100
	1160

L

John Livesley	300
Samll Lewey	100
Jno Lumbrey	400
Jno Leeneir [Lanier]	700
Mrs. Low	70
Sam Lewey for Nether'ld's [Netherland's] Orph	498
Tho Lewis Senr.	200
Hugh Liegh	762

ffrancis Leadbeatter	100
Jn° Leadbeatter	400
Wm Low	1584
	5114

M

Wm Maddox	190
Robt Munford	339
James Minge, Senr	500
Matt Marks	1500
Sam^ll^ Moody	328
Francis Mallory	200
Dan^ll^ Mallone	100
Jn° Mayes	365
Richd More	472
Henry Mitchell, Senr	100
Jn° Mitchell	170
Wm Mayes	763
Edwd Murrell	100
Tho Mitchell Junr	100
Peter Mitchell	305
Henry Mitchell Junr	200
ffrancis Maberry	347
James Matthews	100
Jn° Martin	200
	6839

N

Richd Newman	120
Walter Nunnaley	299
	419

O

Nich° Overburry	809
Jn° Owen	25
	834

P

Geo. Pasmore	330
Francis Poythres Sen[r]	1283
Joseph Pattison	200
Geo. Pace	246
Nathan[ll] Phillips	150
Jn[o] Price	50
W[m] Peoples	150
Eliz[b] Peoples	235
Joseph Perry	275
Rich[d] Pigeon	524
[bs]/Thomas Potts	200
Joseph Pritchett	50
Jn[o] Patterson	373
Geo. Pace	1000
Ephram Pakham	300
Tho Poythres	616
David Peoples	60
Grace Perry	100
Jn[o] Poythres Jun[r]	916
Jn[o] Petterson	428
M[r] Micajah Perry	600
	9203

R

Jn[o] Roberts	316
Nath. Robinson	100
Roger Reace Jun[r]	100
Henry Read	75
Roger Reace Sen[r]	100
W[m] Reanes	250
Frances Raye	300
Jn[o] Reeks	50
W[m] Rachell	100
Timothy Reading Sen[r]	460
Jn[o] Riners	200

Edw[d] Richardson	300
Coll. [William] Randolph	226
	2677

S

Matthew Smart	100
W[m] Standback	150
Tho Symmons	566
James Salmon	477
W[m] Savage	150
W[m] Sandborne	——
Jn[o] Scott	300
Martin Shieffield	150
James Smith	67
John Stroud	60
Rich[d] Scoking	100
W[m] Sexton	50
James Seveaker	710
Chichester Sturdivant	214
Daniell Sturdivant	850
Rich[d] Smith	550
Jn[o] Spaine	118
Matthew Sturdivant	150
Capt. Stith	470½
	8272½

T

Maj[r] Henry Tooker for ye Merch[ts] in London	4600
Geo. Tilliman	446
Jn[o] Tilliman	530
W[m] Tomlinson	400
Adam Tapley	377
Capt. John Taylor	1700
Mich. Taburd	150
Maj[r] Tooker	181
Rob[t] Tooker	400

Rob[t] Tester	170
Joseph Tooker	200
W[m] Temple	100
Jn[o] Thornhill	350
Jn[o] Taylor	100
Nath: Tatham jun[r] [Tatum]	200
Sam[ll] Tatham Sen[r]	100
Sam[ll] Tatham jun[r]	195
Henry Talley	639
Rich[d] Turberfield	140
Francis Tucker	100
Nath[l] Tatham Senr.	501
Jn[o] Thrower	250
James Taylor	306
Tho Thrower	150
Sanders Tapley	300
Tho Tapley	300
James Thweat Sen[r]	715
James Thweat Jun[r]	100
Eliz[b] Tucker	212
Tho Taylor	400
Edw[d] Thrower	150
	14462

V

Jn[o] Vaughan	169
Sam[ll] Vaughan	169
Nath Urvein	150
Dan[ll] Vaughan	169
James Vaughan	169
Rich[d] Vaughan	309
W[m] Vaughan	309
Tho: Vinson	550
Nich[o] Vaughan	169
	2163

W

Jno Woodlife Senr	644
Wm Wallis	200
Jno Witchett	250
Capt. Jos. Wynn	860
Jno Woodlife Junr	750
Jno Winningham Jun	200
Richd Wallpooll	625
Jno Womack	550
Capt. Tho Wynn	400
Jno Wall	233
Tho Winingham	100
Eliz^{b} Woodlife	844
Richd Worthern	1600
Richd Winkles	450
Capt. Nich^{o} Wyatt	700
Antho. Wyatt	250
Valentine Williamson	250
Hurldy Wick	600
Wm Wilkins	900
Francis Wilkins	150
Robt. Winkfield [Wingfield]	107
Jarvis Winkfield	100
Henry Wall	275
Jno Wilkins	150
James Williams	1436
Geo. Williams	210
Jno White	150
Edwd Winingham	100
Sam^{ll} Woodward	600
	13684

Y

Dorrell Young	383
John Young	200
	583

A	3217
B	12986
C	7622
D	2156
E	7243
F	2241
G	5435
H	17366½
J	6542
K	1160
L	5114
M	6839
N	419
O	834
P	9203
R	2677
S	8272
T	14462
V	2163
W	13684
Y	583
Totall	127218½

Orphans Lands which is refused paying Quit Rents for viz[t]

	Acres
Mr. Jn[o] Banister orphans p Steph: Cock	1970
Capt. Henry Bates [Batte's] orph p their Mother Mrs. Mary Bates	1200
Capt. Hen: Randolph orph[s] p Capt. Giles Webb	129
Morris ffalliham orph[s] p Robt. Rivers	200
Crockson Land formerly who it belongs to now I cannot find	750
	4249

Deduct the new discovered Land 10000

accounted for 117218½ acres at 24[ls] tob[o] p 100 is 28132[ls] tobacco at 5[s] p C[t] is

	£	s	d
	£70	6	6
Sallary 10 p C[t] 2813	7	0	10½
	63	5	7½

p W[m] Epes Sherriff

VIRGINIA QUIT RENT ROLLS, 1704

Rent Rolls of all the Lands held p her Maj'tie In Surry County Anno Domini *1704*

[Surry then included, in addition to the present county, the territory composed in the present Sussex and part of Brunswick, with the usual undefined extension westward.]

A

	Acres
Allen, Arthur, Maj^{r}	6780
Andrews, Bartho	375
Avery, Jno	150
Atkins, Tho	80
Averett, Jno	120
Atkinson, Rich^{d}	100
Andrews, Tho	190
Andrews, Robt	130
Andrews, David	225
	8150

B

Baker, Henry, Coll.	850
Bruton, James	500
Bennett, James	200
Bland, Sarah	1455
Browne, Jno	600
Benbridge, Geo.	200
Bighton, Rich^{d}	590
Bell, Jno	180
Berham [Barham], Robt	650
Blake, Wm.	200
Browne, Edwd	200

Bincham, Jn°	100
Benett, Rich[d]	200
Baker, Sarah	50
Briggs, Sarah	300
Barter, Joell	100
Briggs, Sam[ll]	300
Blico, Christ°	50
Brigs, Charles	331
Brigs, Henry	100
Bentley, ———	180
Blackburn, Wm.	150
Blunt, Thos	1355
Bookey, Edw[d]	180
Browne, Wm. Coll.	2510
Browne, Wm. Capt.	398
Bineham, James	157
Bullock, Mary	100
Barker, John	1160
Bagley, Peter	100
Barker, Jery	420
Bunell, Hezichiah	150
Bougher, Phill	100
Baile, Jn°	250
Bagley, Edw[d]	350
	14716

C

Chapman, Benjamin	500
Cocker, Wm.	100
Cocker, Jn°	900
Crafort, Robert	1000
Crafort, Carter	100
Chambers, Wm.	50
Clark, Jno.	100
Cook, Eliz[b]	200
Carriell, Tho	100
Clements, Jn°	387
Clarke, Jno.	100

Cook, Eliz[b]	200
Carriell, Thomas	100
Cleamants, Jn[o]	387
Clark, Robert	400
Checett, James	50
Cotten, Walter	257
Cotten, Tho	257
Collier, Jn[o]	350
Collier, Joseph	40
Cock, Wm.	630
Cock, Walter	875
Cooper, James	100
Cleaments, ffran	600
Collier, Tho	550
Candenscaine, Obedience	200
	7746

D

Dicks, James	400
Davis, Arthur	460
Drew, Tho	800
Drew, Edw[d]	600
Delk, Roger	790
Davis, Arthur	50
Dean, Rich[d]	100
Davis, Nath	157
	3357

E

Edward [Edwards], Wm. Mr.	2755
Evans, Antho.	100
Edw[d] John	470
Ellitt, Wm.	250
Edm[d] [Edmunds], Howell	300
Ellis, James	180
Edmund [Edmunds], Wm[s]	100
Ellis, Edward	30
Ellis, James	170

Ezell, Geo.	150
Ellis, Jere	50
Evans, Abrah	150
	4705

F

Flake, Rob[t]	200
Foster, Anne	200
Ford, Geo	100
Flood, Walter	820
Flood, Tho	150
Ford, Elias	200
Flemin, Lawrence	360
Foster, Christo	500
Foster, Wm	100
Ferisby, Benj[a]	170
	2800

G

Gray, Wm. Capt.	1750
Gray, Wm Jun[r]	1050
Grimes, Hustis	100
Gwalney [Gwaltney] Wm.	400
Gray, Jno	200
Gwalney [Gwaltney], Wm.	225
Goodman, Wm.	200
Gillham, Hinche	658
Griffin, John	200
Gully, Rich[d]	50
Gray, Wm.	100
Green, Edw[d]	200
Green, Rich[d]	260
	5393

H

Harrison, Benj. Coll.	2750
Harrison, Nath. Capt.	2177
Hunt, Wm.	4042

Holt, Eliz[b]	1450
Holt, Tho Capt.	538
Holt, John	150
Holt, Wm.	630
Harris, Wm.	150
Hart, Henry	725
Humfort, Hugh	150
Hancock, Colin	60
Hart, Robert	600
Humphrey, Evan	70
Hollyman, Mary	290
Harde, Tho	900
Hill, Robt.	200
Holloman, Rich[d]	480
Hargrove, Bryan	100
Humfoot, Wm.	50
Hill, Syon	300
Holloman, Tho.	450
Heath, Adam	200
Harrison, Dan[ll]	70
Ham, Rich[d]	75
Heart, Tho.	750
Hyerd, Tho.	50
Hunt, Wm.	696
Horne, Rich[d]	100
Hollingworth, Henry	60
Howell, Wm.	50
	18413

J

Jackman, Jos. John Mr.	2980
Jones, James	1000
Jarrell, Tho.	115
Jarrett [or Jarrell], Charles	615
Judkins, Sam[ll]	100
Judkins, Wm.	100
Jurdan, Geo.	620
Jarrett, Fardo	630

Johnson, Wm.	360
John, John	350
Jurdan, Rich[d]	350
	7220
Kigan, Mary	200
Killingworth, Wm.	60
Knott, Wm.	300
	560

L

Ludwell, Phill Coll	1100
Lancaster, Robt	100
Lacey, Mary	100
Lang, Mary	77
Lamb, Tho	200
Lane, Tho Jun[r]	200
Laughter, Jn[o]	300
La Neere [Le Neve?], Geo.	300
Lasley, Patrick	520
Lucas, Wm.	315
	3212

M

Matthew, Edw[d]	50
Morriell, Geo	250
Moorland, Edw[d]	225
Mason, Eliz[b]	300
Mallory, Francis	147
Merrett, Matt	60
Middleton, Tho	100
Moss, Wm	100
Moreing, John	695
Mierick [Merrick], Owen	250
	2177

N

Newson [Newsom], Wm.	225
Newson [Newsom], Robt	250
Newitt, Wm.	330
Norwood, Rich[d]	80
Nicholl, Geo.	150
Nichols, Robt	230
Nolway, Barefoot	150
Norwood, Geo	330
	1745

P

Park, Mary	100
Pittman, Tho Jun[r]	100
Phillips, John	270
Price, Jn[o]	340
Pettoway, Eliz[b]	650
Pulystone, Jn[o]	1400
Parker, Rich[d]	269
Phelps, Humphrey	100
Pully, Wm	300
Proctor, Joshua	660
Persons, John	830
Phillips, Wm	300
Pettfort, Jn[o]	200
Pettfort, Wm	50
	5569

R

Randolph, Wm, Coll.	1655
Ruffin, Eliz[b]	3001
Reynolds, Rob[t]	150
Richardson, Joseph	300
Reynolds, Eliz[b]	150
Reazon, Frances	200
Reads, Wm	150
Rollings, Gregory	106

Read, Wm	450
Rose, Rich[d]	100
Rachell [Rochelle], Geo.	70
Rowling, Jn[o]	476
Rohings, Wm	596
Roger, Wm	450
	7854

S

Seat, Joseph	295
Sims, Geo	200
Sesoms, Nich[o]	800
Savage, Charles	358
Stringfellow, Rich[d]	75
Suger, Jn[o]	250
Sewards, Anne	300
Sharp, Tho	70
Sewins, Thomas	400
Steward, John	200
Smith, Rich[d]	200
Savage, Mary	263
Smith, Tho	700
Swann, Wm	1800
Shrowsbury, Joseph	260
Shrowsbury, Francis	820
Savage, Henry	200
Short, Wm	200
Scarboro, Edw[d]	150
Scagin, Jn[o]	100
Summons, Jn[o]	1300
Shrowsbury, Tho	566
Stockly, Rich[d]	100
Smith, Tho	380
	10237

T

Thompson, Sam[ll]	3104
Tooker, Henry Maj[r]	700

Taylor, Etheldred	538
Thorp, Joseph	250
Tyons [or Tyous], Tho	400
Taylor, Rich[d]	77
	5069

V

Vincent, Mary	187

W

Wright, Thomas	100
William, Charles	100
Wall, Joseph	150
Williams, Wm.	300
Ward, Tho	100
Ward, Joseph Jun[r]	150
Warren, Allen	300
Warren, Thomas	1040
Watkins, Rich[d]	1345
Williams, Roger	150
Webb, Robert	340
Wattkins, John	1160
Warren, Robert	150
Welch, Henry	100
Warrick, John	80
Wilkinson, Matthew	200
Wiggins, Tho	300
Waple, Jno	300
Witherington, Nich[o]	100
Will, Roger	78
White, Charles	136
	6679

Y

Young, John	300

A	8150
B	14716

C	7746
D	3357
E	4705
F	2800
G	5393
H	18413
J	7220
K	560
L	3212
M	2177
N	1745
P	5569
R	7854
S	10237
T	5069
V	187
W	6679
Y	300
	116089
New Land allowed p ord^r	3841
	112248

Aprill 19th 1705

Errors Excepted p Jos John Jackman
Sher/

Persons denying paym^t or Lands held in this County (Viz) Capt Tho Holt as belonging to Mr. Tho Bennees[?] Orph^n	950
Mrs. Mary White	200
	1150

Lands held by persons living out of the County

Capt. John Taylor	850
Mrs. Sarah Low	500
Mr. Jno Hamlin	100

Capt. Tho Harrison	530
Bartho Clements	1150
	3130

Bartho Clement one tract of land he living in England the Quantity unknown

Jno Davis one tract Living in Isle of Wight

Geo. & River Jorden one Tract & denys to pay Q[t] Rents for it & no persons living thereon, there is one Bray Living in Warwick has a small tract Land.

(To be continued)

VIRGINIA QUIT RENT ROLLS, 1704

A LIST OF HER MAJ^tys QT. RENTS IN THE ISLE OF WIGHTE COUNTY IN THE YEAR 1704.

Jno. Atkins	200
James Atkinson	400
Wm. Exam	1440
Wm. Brown	150
Frances Exam	200
Richd Bennett	70
James Briggs	100
Ph. Bratley	200
Abr. Drawler	200
Jno. Branch	45
Francis Branch	50
Edwd Brantley	175
Jno Brantley	364
Edwd Boykin	1100
Geo. Barloe	80
Jno. George	200
Tho. Carter	700
Reubin Cooke	250
Jno. Clarke	850
Tho. Cook	300
Wm. Clark	600
Edwd Champion	600
Jno Dowles	150
Peter Deberry	100
Thomas Davis	100
Jno Davis	250
Peter Hayes	600
Christ^o Hollyman [Holeman]	400
Richd Hardy	700

Tho. Holyman	150
Jn° Harris	365
Silvester Hill	925
Roger Hodge	300
Arthur Jones	900
Edw[d] Jones	250
Rich[d] Jones	250
Jn° Johnson	890
Roger Ingram	300
Matt Jorden	1950
Tho. Newman	360
Geo. Readick [Riddick]	790
Francis Lee	100
Ph. Pardoe	100
Jno. Parsons	155
Geo. Moore	400
Jn° Mangam	100
Robt. Mongo	400
Henry Martin	200
Jn° Murray	650
Francis Rayner	80
Jn° Rich[d]son	150
James Sampson	12000
Jn° Stevenson	150
Tho. Sherrer	200
Jn° Sherrer	200
Wm. Thomas	250
Tho. Tooke	1228
Tho. Throp	350
Baleaby [Barneby?] Terrell	100
Peter Vasser	230
Jn° Williams	600
Geo. Williamson	2735
Fra. Williamson	2035
Tho. Wood	50
James Lupo	45
Eliz[b] Reynolds	100
Jn° Sojourner	240
Rob[t] Hoge	60
Andrew Woodley	770
Arthur Allen	1800

Henry Baker	750
Rubin Prockter	250
Tho. Howell	100
Nath. Whitby	170
Jane Atkins	600
Jn° Mongo	100
Natt Ridley	200
Jn° Bell	200
Wm. West	250
Charles Goodrich	80
Jn° Britt	350
Jn° Barnes	200
Henry Goldham	1000
Jn° Waltham	450
Charles Edwards	405
Wm. Exam	150
Maj^{r} Lewis Burwell	7000
Henry Applewaite	1500
Tho. Pitt	300
Jn° Pitt	3400
Mary Benn	675
Robt. Clark	450
Antho. Holliday	860
Wm. Westrak	450
Eliz^{b} Gardner	100
Jn° Gardner	246
Jn° Turner	950
Anth° Foulgham	100
Anne Williams	150
Edwd Harris	240
Jn° Cotten	200
Tho. Joyner	1400
Jn° Lawrence	400
Tho. Mandre	200
Wm. Mayo	300
John Garland	100
James Bryan	1200

Wm. Keate	200
Jn° Browne	100
Francis Sanders	100
Jn° Rogers	200
Hodges Council	420
Hardy Council	900
Jn° Council	760
Tho. Reeves	600
Wm. Crumpler	580
Bridgman Joyner	1100
Eliz[b] Swan	600
Tho. Jones	700
Arthur Whitehead	250
Tho. Allen	150
Jerimiah Exum	300
Nich° Casey	550
Jn° Giles	1150
Alex[d] Camoll	200
Jn° Rutter	300
Godfry Hunt	600
Wm. Trygell	100
Benj[a] Jorden	150
Tho. Jorden	207
Jno. King	300
Wm. Wilkinson	200
Tho. Groce	160
Wm. West	50
Jn° Penny	300
Robt Richards	100
Tho. Northworthy	600
Fra. Parker	210
Widd° Long	104
Trustram Northyorthy [Norsworthy]	1000
Geo. Green	250
Jn° Druer	100
Phil Pierce	500
Wm. Best	100
Humphry Marshall	600
Tho. Breever	200
Wm. Smith	2100

Saml[l] & Wm. Bridger	12900
Wm. Williams	100
Richd Ratcliffe	380
Joshua Jordan	150
Danll Sandbourne	180
Nicho Foulgham	780
Mary Marshall	200
Joseph Godwin	250
Joseph Bridger	580
Henry Pitt	700
James Baron	300
Arthur Smith	3607
Robt. Brock	400
Wm. Godwin	400
Hugh Bracey	1000
Henry Turner	350
Tho. Wootten	963
Richd Reynolds, Senr	853
Richd Reynolds	746
Jno Parnell	400
Benja Deall	467
Theo. Joyner	595
Jno Jordan	100
Henry Wiggs	506
Wm. Body	1375
Arthur Purcell	750
Jno Porteus	100
Wm. West	690
Simon Everett	1100
Walter Waters	150
John Jordan	150
John Nevill	433
Robt Colman	1500
Wm. Green	150
Mary Cobb	150
Robert Edwds	150
Anne Jones	100
Abraham Jones	100
John Jones	200
Richd Lewis	100

Henry Dullard [Dillard] ?	100
Tho. Williams	100
James Mercer	100
Pooll Hall	350
Jno. Howell	100
Tho. Lovett	100
Geo. Anderson	150
Daniell Notteboy	100
Henry Wilkinson	350
Jno. Watkins	200
Tho. English	100
Tho. Page	203
Francis Davis	100
Rich[d] Braswell	100
Robt. Johnson	2450
Jn[o] Minshea	300
Wm. Pryan	200
Wm. Dawes	400
Nich[o] Tyner	300
Isaac Ricks	700
Robt. Scott	300
Jn[o] Roberts	950
Wm. Duck	180
Robt. Lawrence	400
Jn[o] Denson	200
Rob[t] Sneely	600
Francis Bridle	250
Roger Failton	237
Tho. Bullock	100
Wm. Murfry	600
Tho. Powell	100
Widd[o] Glyn	390
Jn[o] Pope	250
Tho. Gayle	200
Wm. Powell	200
Rich[d] Hutchins	300
Hen Boseman	100
Henry Pope	557
John W[ms]	971

Hen. Sanders	700
Jn° Selloway	900
Jn° Bardin	100
Phill Rayford	650
Phil Pearse	500
Jn° Terseley	150
Geo. Northworthy [Norsworthy]	1176
Robt Rich^ds^	450
Tho Bevan	100
Wm Hunter	150
Madison Street	150
Tho Wheatley	400
Richd Wilkinson	150
James Bragg	500
Jn° Porteus	300
Tho. Harris	350
Edwd Harris	100
Nich° Askew	80
Ambrose Hadley	100
Widd° Powell	480
Tho. Jones	100
Tho. Underwood	100
Robt King	300
Tho. Giles	880
Lewis Smelly	550
Wm Smelly	280
Godfry Hunt	600
Edmund Godwin	400
W^m^ W^ms^	1000
John Wilson	1200
John Bryan	200
John Askew	100
Sam^ll^ Bridger	200
Roger Nevill	200
Coll. Godwin	600
Jacob Durden [Darden?]	500
	138533

Wm Bridger

VIRGINIA QUIT RENT ROLLS, 1704

A Compleat List of the Rent Roll of the Land in Nansemond County In Anno 1704.

	Acres
John Murdaugh	300
Jn° Duke	113
Tho. Duke Junr	930
Edwd Roberts	250
Paul Pender	240
Tho. Duke	400
James Fowler	440
Robt. Baker	50
Isaac Sketto	100
Edwd Sketto	200
Anth° Gunnus	50
Francis Sketto	100
Wm Parker	100
Francis Parker	170
Tho Parker	300
Jn° Small	100
Moses Hall	95
Edwd Beamond	550
Richd Parker	514
Capt. James Jossey	550
Wm. Sanders	200
Jn° Sanders	165
Tho Mansfield	60
Wm. Woodley	350
Andrew Bourne	200
Gilbert Owen	120
Wm. Sanders Junr	165
Capt. John Speir	500

Capt. James Reddick [Riddick]	943
James Griffin	500
Nich° Stallings	965
John Stallings	250
Rich[d] Stallings	165
Elias Stallings Jun[r]	250
Joseph Baker	740
Wm. Jones	500
Rob[t] Roundtree	245
John Roundtree	475
Geo. Spivey	200
James Spivey	600
James Knight	300
Jn° Gorden	330
Edw[d] Arnold	80
James Mulleny	500
Tho Docton	200
Wm. Britt	400
Nath. Newby	850
Elias Stalling	470
Robt. Lassiter	850
Patrick Wood	200
Wm. Thompson	133
Jonathan Kitterell	300
Adam Rabey	586
Jno. Powell	758
John Reddick [Riddick]	300
Henry Copeland	150
Thomas Davis	250
Jno Smith	100
Tho. Harrald	652
Rich[d] Baker	40
Sam[ll] Smith	230
Wm. Hood	200
Tho. Roundtree	350
Henry Hill	175
Jn° Larkhum	500
Wm. Vann	100

Joseph Cooper	267
John Harris	600
Francis Copeland	513
Eliz[b] Price	150
Wm. Hill	150
Tho. Spivey	200
Jn[o] Campbell	400
Jn[o] Morley	100
Jos. Rogers	15
Jn[o] Cole	814
Tho. Harrald	100
Christ[o] Garvin Jun[r]	20
Daniell Horton	200
Wm. Bruin	300
Peter Eason	400
Anne Pugh	2300
Benj[a] Blanchard	130
Tho. Norfleet	500
John Odum	50
Tho. Gough	150
Hugh Gough	150
Epapap Boyne	100
Henry Baker	375
Christo. Gwin	1010
James Speirs	200
Epaphra Benton	250
Wm. Eason	180
Andrew Brown	25
Wm. Horne	100
Robt. Reddick [Riddick]	200
Henry Hackley	210
Tho. Roberts	30
Abr. Reddick [Riddick]	400
Jn[o] Parker	240
Rich[d] Barefield	900
John Benton	660
Jn[o] Pipkin	100
Jos. Brady	250

Christ° Dudley	200
Tho. Norris	100
Tho. Wiggins	100
Patrick Lawley	50
Robt. Warren	100
Richd Odium	50
Tho. Davis	340
Tho. Barefeild	100
John Eason	150
Jeremiah Arlin	250
Jn° Perry	870
Jn° Drury	87
Joseph Booth	987
Cresham Cofield	350
Richd Sumner	600
Edwd Norfleet	200
Jn° Norfleet	600
Edwd Moore	250
Tho. Moore	200
James Lawrey	40
James Daughtie	400
John Wallis	150
Richd Sanders Junr	100
Wm. Byrd	300
James Howard	700
John Brinkley	430
Robt. Horning	80
Wm. Speirs	200
Sarah Exum	150
Jn° Larrence	175
Nich° Perry	200
Sampson Merridith	400
Coll. Tho. Milner	1484
Joseph Merridith	250
Thomas Kinder	160
Henry King	300
Joseph Hine	150
Wm. King	140

Julian King	700
Mich. King	80
Capt. Tho. Godwin Jun[r]	697
Henry Lawrence	200
Jn[o] King	1000
Rich[d] Hine	200
Capt. Fra. Milner	479
Benj[a] Nevill	475
Elib[b] Nearlor	80
Wm. Keene	200
Jn[o] Symmons	678
Hen. Johnson	150
Jn[o] Darden	500
Wm. Everett	150
Wm. Pope	890
Joseph Worrell	270
Tho. Jernegan Jun[r]	135
Rich[d] Lawrence	200
Jonathan Robinson	400
Robt. Yates	150
Tho. Odium	20
John Barefield	300
John Raules	600
Thomas Boyt	400
Tho. Vaughan	200
Jn[o] Parker	300
Rich[d] Green	200
Elisha Ballard	300
Sam[ll] Watson	200
Francis Spight	400
Joseph Ballard	200
John Oxley	100
Benj[a] Rogers	600
Robt. Rogers	300
Hen. Jerregan	200
Jn[o] Stansell	500
Henry Jenkins	400
Capt. Wm. Hunter	800

Jn° Moore	200
Richd Moore	250
Edwd Homes	300
Fra. Cambridge	100
Wm. Ward	200
Jn° Rice	140
Wm. Battaill [Battle]	800
Wm. Spite	500
Abr. Oadham	520
Jacob Oadham	20
Jn° Lee	100
Wm. Macklenny	200
Robt Coleman	1400
Jn° Bryan	200
Wm. Daughtrie	100
Jn° Copeland	600
Jn° Butler	200
James Butler	75
Tho. Roads	75
Wm. Collins	1220
Jn° Hodgpath	700
Jn° Holland	700
Robt Carr	200
Wm. Waters	600
Robt Lawrence	400
Wm. Bryon	350
Lewis Bryon	400
James Lawrence	100
Wm. Gatlin	100
Joseph Gutchins	250
Geo. Lawrence	400
Lewis Daughtree	100
Tho. Rogers	50
Jn° Rogers	200
Henry Core	50
Edwd Cobb	100
Richard Taylor	300
Robt. Breever [Brewer?]	200

Wm. Osburne	200
Tho. Biswell	400
Jn[o] Gatlin	200
Rich[d] Folk	100
Thomas Parker	100
Peter Parker	140
Wm. Parker	140
Rich[d] Hine, Jun[r]	200
Stephen Archer	200
Charles Roades	800
Henry Roades	100
James Collings	300
Henry Holland	400
Wm. Kerle	325
Joseph Holland	100
Jn[o] Thomas Jun[r]	100
Jn[o] Thomas	275
Tho. Mason	350
Edw[d] Mason	150
Jn[o] Sanders	150
Mich Brinkley	200
James Moore	400
Henry Blumpton	1500
Jn[o] Symmons	100
Jeremiah Edmunds	70
John Gay	200
Phillip Aylsberry	100
James Copeland	390
Jn[o] Brothers	460
Rich[d] Creech	200
Rich[d] Bond	90
Tho. Handcock	30
James Knott	1050
Wm. Edwards	150
Robert Elkes	175
Edw[d] Price	140
Jane Belson	100
Wm. Staples	210

Robt. Mountgomery	150
John Moore	100
Capt. Edm[d] Godwin	800
Thomas Wakefield	150
Godfry Hunt	360
Henry Wilkinson	250
Nich[o] Dixon	200
Geo. Keeley	650
Rich[d] Taylor	300
Anne Coefield	300
Joseph Hollyday	1000
Mr. Jn[o] Braisseur	400
Tho. Best	160
Alex[dr] Campbell	500
Capt. Charles Drury	570
Tho. Drury	75
Luke Shea	650
John Babb	500
Abraham Edwards	400
Rich[d] Sanders	500
Antho. Wallis	80
Dan[ll] Sullivan	100
Joseph Ellis	290
Nich[o]. Hunter	190
Rich[d] Webb	200
John Hare	190
Christ[o] Norfleet	400
Jn[o] Heslop	148
Francis Benton	200
Capt. Wm. Sumner	275
Eliz[b] Syrte	100
Anne Hare	600
Jn[o] Porter	450
Edw[d] Welsh	100
Jn[o] Winbourne	400
Paul Pender	200
Mich. Cowling	100
John Cowling	100

Rowland Gwyn	75
Andrew Ross	150
Jn° Ballard	400
Benj[a] Montgomery	910
Tho. Corbell	200
Jn° Yates	400
Jn° White	150
Geo. White	50
Jn° Bond	150
Wm. Hay	100
Henry Bowen	600
Wm. Sevill	85
Jn° Hambledon	200
Robt. Jordan	850
James Howard	25
Ruth Coefield	110
Jn° Chilcott	100
Jn° Rutter	80
Tho. Rutter	75
Wm. Rutter	75
Capt. Barnaby Kerney	460
Tho. Cutchins	150
Robt. Lawrence	130
Sam[ll] Cahoone	240
Jn° Iles	220
Tho. Sawyer	180
Wm. Outland	400
Coll. Geo. Northworthy [Norsworthy]	650
Coll. Tho. Godwin	810
Caleb Taylor	200
Tho. Carwell	320
Rich[d] Bradley	250
Jn° Corbin	300
Wm. Sykes	150
Maj[r] Tho. Jorden	700
Rich[d] Lovegrove	150
Tho. Davies	144
Sam[ll] Farmer	160

Henry Bradley	500
Jn[o] Clarke	25
Margarett Jorden	200
Wm. Elkes	100
Humphrey Mires	150
James Ward	100
Widd[o] Hudnell	45
Wm. Grandberry	300
Izraell Shepherd	200
Benj[a] Small	100
Anne Granberry	75
Charles Roberts	50
Rich[d] Sclator	300
Rob[t] Murrow	320
Eliz[b] Peters	334
Tho. Jones	200
Eliz[b] Butler	200
Coll. Sam[ll] Bridger	500
Jn[o] Larrance	100
Tho. Jarnegan	165
Tho. Jarnegan, Jun[r]	600
Wm. Drury	80
Wm. Butler	120
Henry Jenkins	860
Edw[d] Bathurst	250
Tho. Houffler	200
Edw[d] Streater	200
Wm. Duffield	50
Charles Tho Jun[r]	50
Jn[o] Blessington	150
Ursula Goodwin	100
Tho. Atwell	440
Wm. Peale	180
John Lambkin	50
James Murphree	160
Rob[t] Peale	275
John Peters	368
James Peters	340

John Wakefield	50
Richd Wynne	890
James Lockhart	800
John Keeton	2000
	19322
	16826
	15567
	17000
	16010
	13548
	18751
	17024
John Murrow	200
	117224
Added to make up equll the last year list wch may be supposed to be held p p persons that have not made oath.	13850
	131074

Persons living out of the County and other y[t] will not pay or give acct. viz[t]

Capt. Thomas Lovett
Capt. Jn[o] Wright
Fra. Parker, Jun[r]
Tho. Martin
Jn[o] Wright
Wm. Lapiter [Lassiter]
Jn[o] Lapiter [Lassiter]
Capt. Luke Haffield
Mrs. Eliz[b] Swann

Errors Excepted p me

Henry Jenkins

(To be continued)

VIRGINIA QUIT RENT ROLLS, 1704

An Alphabetical List of the Quit Rents of Norfolk County, 1704.

A	Acres
Ashley, Dennis	150
Avis, Widd°	50
Adam, Wm.	100
Alexander, John	300
B	
Barington, Wm.	100
Barties, Robt.	150
Bull [Butt?], Robt. Sen.	1050
Blanch, Wm.	100
Bond, Wm.	200
Brown, Widd°	270
Bruce, Abr.	1010
Brown, Wm.	100
Bowers, Jn°	166
Bolton, Wm.	212
Bryon, Roger	200
Bayley, Walter	290
Bruce, Jn°	300
Bishop, Wm.	100
Bull [Butt?] Henry	1500
Bucken, Wm.	410
Babington, Thos.	150
Balington, Jn°	150
Balington, Rich[d]	50
Burges, Geo.	200

Burges, Robt.	535
Butt, Rich[d]	1840
Brown, Edw[d]	300
Bigg, Tho.	100
Balingtine, Alexander	300
Balingtine, Geo.	510
Bull [Butt?] Tho.	2200
Bramble, Henry	100
Blake, Arthur	200
Bolton, Rich[d]	700
Branton, Jno.	330
Bacheldon, Joseph	300
Bush, Sam[ll] Maj[r]	1628
Balingtine, W[m]	60
Bowles, Henry	330

C

Cartwright, Peter	1050
Cooper, W[m]	150
Cooper, Jno.	150
Cramore, Geo.	100
Carling, Walter	50
Carling, Joseph	200
Curch [Church], Rich[d]	1050
Churey, Widd[o]	600
Cuthrell, Going	470
Chekmore, Edw[d]	800
Cartwright, Widd[o]	800
Corprew, Jno.	650
Corprew, Tho.	650
Crekmore, Jn[o]	750
Caswell, Widd[o]	350
Colley, Jn[o]	100
Cottell, Tho.	200
Corden, Tho.	390
Conner, Lewis	2200

Carney Rich[d]	100
Carney, Jno.	100
Collins, Wm.	100
Crekmore, Edw[d]	690
Charleton, Jn[o]	50
Cutrell, Tho.	150
Chapman, Rich[d]	50
Churey, Tho.	100
Churey, Jn[o]	150

D

Dixon, Jn[o]	300
Davis, Wm. Sen[r]	250
Davis, Wm.	158
Dresdall, Robt.	318
Davis, Tho.	332
Doonall, Wm.	100
Davis, Edw[d]	300
Dalley, Henry	1524
Dalley, Wm.	156
Davis, Tho.	340
Denby, Edw[d]	100
Daniell, Hugh	100

E

Etherdge, Tho., Cooper	75
Etherdge, Tho. B. R.	50
Etherdge, Tho. Sen[r]	34
Etherdge, Tho. Jun[r]	33
Etherdge, Edw[d]	66
Etherdge, Wm.	250
Etherdge, Wm Jun[r]	80
Etherdge, Marmaduke	525
Edmonds, John	50
Ellis, Wm.	200

Etherdge, Edwd, Cooper	200
Estwood, Thomas	170
Estwood, John	75
Etherdge, Edwd Senr	33
Edw^{ds}, John	250
Etherdge, Charles	75
Evans, Abigall	100
Furgeson, Tho.	100
Freeman, Jno	190
Foreman, Alexand^{r}	750
Foster, Henry	1000
Ferbey [Ferebee?] Jno	500
Fulsken [Fulcher?] Jno	1396

G

Godfry, Waren	350
Godfry, John	1470
Godfry, Matthew	450
Grefen, Jno	200
Garen, Dan^{ll}	50
Guy, Jno	110
Gwin, W^{m}	350
Gilligan, Ferdinando	182
Gilligan, John	200
Grimes, James	0150
Grimes, John	050
Guy, James	100
Herbert, Thomas	150
Hayes, Wm.	200
Harris, John	110
Holyday, Jno	440
Hodges, Joseph	50
Hoges [Hodges?], Tho.	407
Hoges [Hodges?] John	526
Hollowell, Jno Senr	524
Hollygood, Tho.	100
Hollowell, Jno.	200

Holsted, Henry	633
Hollowell, Joseph	1280
Holsted, John	350
Hues, Edwd	1404
Hullett, Jno	300
Hodges, Roger	109
Hodges, Tho.	50
Hodges, Rich^{d}	375
Harvey, Rich^{d}	265
Handberry, ———	300
Hollowell, Elener	1550
Herbert, Jno	400
Hargrave, Benj^{a}	250
Hartwell, Rich^{d}	150
Henland, Jno	800
Ivy, Geo.	496
Jackson, Symon	720
Ives, Tim^{o}	400
Ives, Tim^{o} Junr	100
Ives, John	434
Johnston, John	275
Johnston, Mercey	275
Jolef, Tho.	200
Joyce, Jno	200
Jolef, Jno Junr	300
Jennings, Henry	100
Jolef, Jno Senr	840
Kaine, Rich^{d}	50
Langley, W^{m}	1487
Langley, Tho.	878
Loveney, James	100
Luelling, Edwd	315
Luelling, Rich^{d}	200

Lovell, Widd°	740
Low, Henry	191
Lane, Robt.	460
Ludgall, Matthew	250
Levinia, John	510
Lenton, Wm.	150
Mercer, Tho.	600
Manning, Tho.	97
Maning, Nich°	260
Mones, Joseph	73
Matthias, Matthew	100
Miller, Wm.	1090
Miller, Jn°	200
Miller, Widd°	100
Murden, Widd°	2000
Miller, Tho.	1050
Maund, W^{m}	200
Maning, Jn° Senr	300
Miller, Joseph	882
Mocoy, Dennis Senr & Junr	160
Mohan, James	100
Mufrey, Alex^{dr}	800
Maning, Jn° Junr	100
Moseley, Widd°	300
Miller, Widd° Senr	200
Mason, Tho.	125
Mason, Lemuell	400
Mason, Tho.	653
Mason, Geo.	300
Mockey, Adam	400
Newton, Geo.	1119
Nicholson, Jn°	160
Nash, Tho.	50
Nicholson, Henry	320
Nash, Rich^{d}	100

Nicholson, Wm.	300
Norcote, Tho.	273
Outlow, Edw[d]	208
Owens, Wm.	650
Odyan, Wm.	200
Pearce, Wm.	100
Peters, Widd[o]	698
Portlock, ———	360
Porter, Sam[ll]	100
Prescot, Moses	1200
Philpot, Rich[d]	200
Powell, Rich[d]	100
Powell, Lemuell	246
Powell, Wm.	624
Perkins, Wm.	50
Patison, Robt.	350
Roberts, Jos.	100
Robert, Sam[ll]	800
Rose, Robt.	385
Rose, Jn[o]	60
Randall, Giles	150
Richardson, Tho.	379
Spring, Robt.	98
Spevey, Matt.	600
Smith, John	127
Scott, Tho.	400
Smith, Rich[d]	600
Smith, John	200
Silvester, Rich[d]	1280
Smith, John Senr.	1200
Sickes [Sykes], Walt[r] Senr.	550
Sickes [Sykes], Jn[o]	200
Sugg, George	408

Sugg, W^m	200
Sayer, Francis	600
Smith, Humphrey	100
Standbro, Jno	40
Standley, Rich^d	200
Sharples, Henry	100
Sugg, Joseph	300
Symons, Thomas	166
Symon, James	200
Sparrow, M^t	350
Tuker [Tucker] W^m	100
Thornton, Francis	200
Thurston, Matthew	100
Theobald, James	140
Thellaball, Widd^o	600
Tuker [Tucker] Rich^d	100
Tuker [Tucker] Tho.	280
Taylor, Jno	100
Taylor, Rich^d	75
Tully, Jno	165
Tarte, Elezar Senr	300
Taylor, Andrew	222
Tuker [Tucker], Jno	400
Tart, Alice	300
Tarte, Elezar Junr	595
Taylor, W^m	265
Trigoney, Henry	200
Velle, Morriss	335
Walice, Tho.	150
Weston, Edwd	100
Willoughby, Tho. Coll.	3200
Wishart, John	150
Woodly, Robt.	350
Williams, John	125

Wilder, Mich.	200
Watkins, Tho.	190
Williamson, Jno	750
Whedon, Jno Jr.	100
Willoughby, Tho. Capt.	660
Whedon, Wm.	200
West, John	500
Watson, Robt.	80
Wallis, Richd	250
Wallis, Jno	135
Wallis, Wm	450
Whithurst, Richd	150
Whithurst, Wm	150
Wilkins, Wm	200
Williams, John	200
Whedbey, Geo.	200
Worden, James	400
Wilson, James junr	200
Wilson, Lemuell	300
Wilson, James Coll.	2800
Woodward, Henry	280
Whedon, Jno Junr	320
White, Patrick	500
Willis, John	470
Wildey, Dorothy	25
Ward, Jno	320
Wākfield, Tho.	40
Wilden, Nath.	100
Wooding, Tho.	170
Wood, Edwd	100
Watford, Joseph	97
Wate, John	400
Wright, Wm	574
Wright, James	216
Wadborn, Mich.	500
Wins, Jane	400
Webb, Mary	100

Worminton, John	200
Wilden, Francis	100
Widdick, Henrey	343
	113684
New Discovered Land	1615
	112069
An Acct of the Land belonging to Such persons out of the County and also others out of the Country	
Coll. Cary	
Tully Robinson	
James Daves	
Robt Berrey	95
Jn° Bennett	33
Coll Nasareth [Norsworthy]	400
Cornelius Tullery	150

James Wilson
Sherriff

(To be continued)

VIRGINIA QUIT RENT ROLLS, 1704

PRINCESS ANNE COUNTY RENT ROLL, 1704.

John Carraway	180
Tho More	100
Henry Chapman	250
Geo. Poole	1085
James Whitehurst	600
Tho Morris	63
Tho Joy [Ivy?]	600
Thomas Scott	100
Geo Smith	250
Tho Hife	200
Rich[d] Smith	200
Tho Hattersley	90
Tho Jolley	150
Mich Ventress [Fentress?]	450
Capt. Blomer [Plummer] Bray	270
James McCoy	200
Francis Bond	264
Edw[d] Wood	50
Jn[o] Morrah	200
Alex[r] Morrah	200
Ruth Woodhouse	450
Horatia Woodhouse	525
Joseph White	330
Jo[n] Basnett	250
Owen Wilbe (Wills)	100
Mr. W[m] Corneck	1974
Jn[o] Oakham	390
David Scott	600

Jn° Keeling	2000
Adam Keeling	500
Humphry Smith	50
Jn° Aclise [Ackiss?]	130
Capt. Will. Crawford	2650
Rich[d] Williamson	450
Edw[d] Tranter	180
Jn° Sherland	800
Rob[t] Rany	70
Edw[d] Old	450
Coll Lemuel Mason	650
Mr. Francis Emperor	400
James Kemp	681
Bartho Williamson	400
Symon Hancock, Jun[r]	200
Geo Batten	150
Matthfl Brinson	250
Mr. Edw[d] Mosely Sen[r]	1000
Wm. Martin	200
James Joslin	100
Alex[d] Lilburn	500
James William	100
Mr. Henry Spratt	1736
Symon Hancock Senr.	300
Tho Walk	298
Jn° Kemp	340
Randolph Lovett	100
Edw[d] Davis	200
Jn° Sammons	150
Eliz[b] Edw[ds]	50
Mr. Benja. Burrough	800
Jn° Muncreef	140
Matt. Pallett	600
Mrs. Thurston [Thruston]	290
Lancaster Lovett	1850
Robt. Cartwright	260
Jn° Cartwright	100
Nath: Macklahan [Macklanahan]	100

Adam Thorowgood	700
Henry Walstone	800
Edwd Land	400
Tho Hall	400
Wm. Catherill	150
Doct^{r} Browne	600
John Richardson	1000
Robt Richmond	1000
Tho Benson	225
Lewis Pervine	800
Edwd Attwood	400
Wm. Moore	414
Mr. Henry Woodhouse	3000
Tully Emperor	300
Jno Godfrey	170
Wm. Dyer	700
Edwd Cooper	200
Wm. Ship	300
Jno Buck	250
Peter Malbourn	280
Benja. Robt^{s}	100
Capt. Jno Gibbs	3100
Sarah Sandford	1200
Henry Harrison	300
James Lemon	1500
Wm. Wallsworth	100
W. M. Capps	1500
Jacob Taylor	80
Steph: Pace	50
Adam Hayes	1360
Wm. Chichester	400
Robt Dearemore	514
Capt. Francis Morse	1300
Patrick Anguish	150
Tho. Brock	400
Wm: Brock	100
Jno Sullivant	200
Fran. Sheene	300

Jn° Acksted	400
Charles Hendley	100
Duke Hill	70
Job Brooks	150
Jn° Brooks	100
Tho Turton	110
Peter Crosby	250
Jn° Pisburn	314
James Sherwood	200
Edwd Cannon	550
Richd Capps	100
John Doley	640
Matthew Mathias	80
Mr James Peters	889
John Owens	190
Josias Morris	900
Tho. Mason	140
Wm. Wishart	200
Jn° Russell	300
Stephen Sall	250
Timothy Dennis	100
Geo. Walker	425
Wm. Ashby	100
Charles Griffin	216
Symon Franklin	100
Alice Thrower	125
James Wishart	225
Richd Draught	500
Doct^r Wm. Hunter	80
Mr. Joⁿ Sanders	203
Wm. Grinto	650
Henry Fitchgerreld	200
Coll Anth° Lawson	3100
Capt. Jn° Thorowgood	940
Robt. Thorowgood	940
Henry Suthern	640
John Wharton	850
Joseph Doller	150

Jn° Biggs	600
Francis Jones	100
Tho Lurrey	100
Tho Walker	820
Steph. Swaine	450
Edwd Mulsin	100
Geo. Bullock	300
Jn° Leggett	400
Mark Tully	300
Wm. Walstone	400
Mark Powell	550
Elizb Nicholls	500
Hugh Hoskins	50
Wm. Burrough	50
Wm. Warren	100
Capt. Hugh Campble	800
Geo. Warrinton	400
James Tully	400
Wm. Lovett	1300
Wm. Grant	150
Tho. More	100
Richd Whitehurst	350
Capt. Tho. Cocke	800
John Connis	175
Tho Griffin	200
Tho Spratt	600
Jn° Russell	150
James Heath	550
David Duncon	100
Daniell Lane	350
George Fowler	600
Jn° Booth	350
Gills Collier	500
Jacob Johnson	1700
Alexr Willis	150
Richd Bonny	2000
Mr. James Doage	784
Antho. Barnes	200

Jn° Macklalin	100
Tho Etherington	108
Jn° James	328
Wm. Woodhouse	300
John Mayho	160
Joseph Perry	35
Tho Perry	650
Mr. Argoll Thorowgood	1000
Capt. Wm. Moseley	600
Jn° Moseley	325
Wm. Smith	180
Wm. Symmons	400
Adam Forguson	120
Benj[a] Commins	200
Jn° Elkes	500
Patrick White	1250
Rich[d] Jones	200
Evan Jones	600
Mich Jones	200
Rich[d] Wicker	300
Henry Snaill	250
M[r] Sam[ll] Bush [Boush]	550
M[r] Tully Robinson	500
Jn° Briberry	50
W[m] Moseley	50
Capt. Christ° MerChant	400
Rich[d] Cox	50
Matt Godfrey	150
Thomas Tully	600
Hector Denby	600
Tho Keeling	700
Wm. More	100
Tho Cason	550
Sarah Jackson	600
Jacob More	200
Totall	98728

Henry Spratt

(To be continued)

VIRGINIA QUIT RENT ROLLS, 1704

ELIZABETH CITY COUNTY

A True & Perfect Rent Roll of the Lands in Elizabeth City County for the year 1704:

Coll. Wm. Wilson	1024
Mr. Wm. Smelt	150
Mr. Pasquo Curle	300
Mr. Nicholas Curle	950
Coll. Dudley Diggs	216
Sam[ll] Pearce	100
Mary Jenings	250
Mark Powell	184
Wm. Davis	42
Jno. Skinner	50
Tho. Baines	50
Wm. Latham	90
Tho. Tucker	60
Matthew Smell	100
Charles Cooley	200
Jno. Chandler	150
Wm. Umplese	25
Charles Tucker	240
Tho. Allin	227
Wm. Williams p ye School	600
Wm. Williams p himself	260
Mrs. Bridgett Jenkins	100
Christ[o] Davis	25
Wm. Spicer	60
Tho. Hawkins	270
Jno. Bowles	360
Jno. Theodam	100

Barth° Wethersby	300
Jos. White	200
Capt. Henry Royall	750
Robt. Bright Senr.	100
Tho. Naylor	100
Geo. Cooper Senr.	100
Tho. Needham	100
Chas. Cooper	100
Wm. Dunn	100
Charles Jenings	225
Sam[ll] Davill	100
Paltey Davill	100
Francis Rogers	200
Tho. Babb p Selden	300
Richard Horsley	90
Sarah Nagleer	230
Henry Dunn	50
Peter Pearce	50
Moses Davis	150
Mich :Breltnen	100
Henry Robinson	200
Christ° Copeland	340
Tho. Faulkner	50
Mr. James Wallace	1300
Mr. Bertram Servant	418
Robt. Taylor	50
Joseph Harris	50
Wm. Robinson	50
Wm. Boswell	220
Wm. Winter	70
John Lowry p Selden	110
Edw[d] Roe	100
Henry James	100
Richard Roatton	50
Tho. Poole	1200
John Wheat Land	66
Geo. Bell	80
Widd° Ballis	350

Geo. Walker	325
Mr. Robt. Beverley	777
Jno. House	157
Jno. Bushnell Junr.	150
Roger Masnibred	50
John Shepherd	210
Wm. Winsor	150
Edw[d] Lattimore	190
James Baker	225
Tho. Tucker	60
Jno. Cotten	50
Mark Johnson	400
Maj[r] Wm. Armistead	460
Coll. Anth[o] Armistead	2140
Daniell Preeday	50
Matthew Watts	454
Bryan Penny	50
Giles Dupra	150
Jno. Bayley	415
Mary Simmons	200
Jno. Parish	50
Anth[o] Griggs	50
Abr. Parish	100
Mark Parish	200
Benj[a] Smith	650
Tho. Nobling p Archer	212
Wm. Mallory	200
Widd[o] Croashell	100
Charles Powers	400
Robt. Charwill p Jno. Young	440
Sam[ll] Fingall	333
Francis Savoy	50
Mr. Edw[d] Mihills	600
Jane Nichols	50
John Francis	25
James Priest	50
Simon Hollier	200
Mr. Tho. Gebb	630
Mr. Rven[d] Booker [pro Rev. Jas. Bowker]	526

Mr. Wm. Lowry	526
Mr. Meory or Mrs. Dunn	500
Wm. Haslyitt	100
Capt. Augustine More	285
John More	250
John Passones [Parsons?]	780
Rebecka Morgan	50
Tho. Roberts	250
Mr. John Turner	50
Henry Lais	50
Capt. Henry Jenkins	300
Mr. Francis Ballard p Selden	460
Totall	29560

Henry Royall Sherriff

WARWICK COUNTY

A True and Perfect Rent Roll of all the Lands that is held in Warwick County 1704:

Maj[r] Will. Cary	300
Mr. Nedler plantacon	80
Robt. Hubbert	101
Wm. Harwood	625
Rich[d] Glanvills Orphans	165
Wm. Hubbert	200
Henry Gibbs	315
Wm. Hewitt	150
James Hill	135
John Golden	50
Tho. Harwood	575
Jno. Harwood	705
Capt. Tho. Charles	100
Hump Harwood	400
Matthew Wood	300
Edw[d] Joyner	60
Coll. Dudley Diggs	4626
Eliz[b] Lucas	800

John Hillard	74
Edw[d] Loftes	60
Wm. Rowles Orphans	150
Sam[ll] Hatton	225
Isaac Goodwin	225
Geo. Robinson	70
Seymor Powell	250
John Dawson	300
Wades Orphans	100
Henry Dawson	200
John Bowyer	100
Joseph Cooper	200
Robt. Robt[s]	60
Geo. Burton	330
Capt. Mills Wells	425
Roger Daniell Orphans	196
Jno. Hansell	100
Emanuell Wells	325
Eliz[b] Wells Widd[o]	155
Widd[o] Lewelling	100
Wm. Wells	615
Elias Wells	50
Widd[o] Pierce	155
Tho. Haynes	850
John Scarsbrook	850
Francis Jones	150
Matthew Jones	750
Jno. Read	875
Mr. Brewer Land	1350
Mr. Henry Cary	670
Langhorne Orphans	602
Coll. Coles Orphans	1350
Peter Jones	150
Sam[ll] Crew Orphans	150
Sam[ll] Symons	173
Mrs. Eliz[b] Whitaker	600
Capt. Miles Cary	600
John Cannon	75
John Linton	75

Rich[d] Gough	60
Coll. Miles Cary	1960
Mr. John Mallnote	61
Rowland Wm[s]	170
Robt. Chapell	150
James Chapell	100
Edward Powers	200
James White	40
Peter Sawers Orphans	95
Wm. Cotton	143
James Cotton	70
John Croley	100
Stephen Burgess	128
Widd[o] Yorgen	60
Geo. Jackson	193
Sarah Ranshaw	125
Rich[d] Wootton	243
Sam[ll] Hoggard	120
James Floyd	100
Fr: Rice Orphans	200
Mr. Nath Hoggard	270
Widd[o] Chapell	321
Tho Ascow	50
Garrett Ridley	300
Sam[ll] Ranshaw	238
Charles Strukey	86
Jos. Naylor	100
Jos. Russell	150
Charles Allen	295
Mr. Newberry	100
John Turner	100
Wm. Smith	150
Eliz[b] Holt	150
James Browne	150
Henry Royall	246
Edw[d] River	375
Tho. Blackistone	75
Mark Noble	215

James Reynolds	75
John Holmes	200
Sam[ll] Duberry	200
Edw[d] Powers	200
Jn[o] Hatton Orphans	93
Wm. Towland	25
Tho Merey	3655
Wm. Bracey	150
Cope Doyley	500
Nath Edw[ds]	100
Sam[ll] Groves	490
Croucher Orphans	50
Henry Whitaker	60
Woodman Land	200
Wm. Cook	29
Jno. Tignall	392
Tho. Mountfort	890
Joseph Montfort	558
James Priest	50
Abr: Cowley	80
Wm. Jones	70
Edward Davis	200
The County Land	150
Denbigh Psh Gleab	130
Mulberry Island Gleab	50
Tho Hansford	75
Mr. Roscoes Orphans	1195
	37685
Tho: Hansford never before pd.	75
	37610

Persons out of the County

Jn[o] Trevillian	248)	
Holman Orphans	200)	448

Robert Hubberd Sherriff

(To be continued)

VIRGINIA QUIT RENT ROLLS, 1704

A Rent Roll of all the Land in York County, 1704.

	Acres
Wm. Jackson	200
Matt Pierce	100
Jno Latin	150
Robt. Cobb	100
Francis Sharp	100
Geo: Baskervyle	350
Richd Gilford	100
Jos: Frith	50
Wm. Jones	70
Nath Crawley	384
Tho Crips	750
Wm. Davis	200
Lewis Barnoe	80
Arthur Lun	50
Jno Bates	669
Jno Serginton	150
Wm. Taylor	100
Richd Page	150
Wm. Jorden	580
Jno Lynes	150
Alex. Baneyman	50
Wm. Cobb	50
Mary Whaley	550
Henry Tyler	180
Richd Kendall	150
Wm. Hansford	300
Nicho Sebrell	150
David Stoner	50

Ralph Hubbard	50
Wm. Harrison	50
Jn° Wyth	100
Tho. Hill	930
Tho. Vines	200
Morgan Baptist	100
Phil Deadman	75
Bazill Wagstaff	127
Wm. Allen	117
Robt. Read	750
Jos. Mountford	307
Roger Boult	100
Edw[d] Fuller	70
Tho Jefferson	100
Henry Duke	25
Jn° Hansford	100
Robt. Peters	160
Jn° Morland	100
Wm. Lee	350
Rich[d] Burt	200
John Eaton	170
Rob: Starke	250
Robt. Harrison	200
Jn° Morris	125
James Bates	117
Eliz[b] Jones	94
Edwd. Young	100
Robt. Green	200
Tho: Fear	100
Edward Thomas	223
John Loyall	100
Stephen Pond	200
Wm. Wise	850
Cornelius Shoehorn	100
Joseph White	750
Daniell Park, Esq.	2750
Tho Fear Jun[r]	130
Orlando Jones	450

Ambrose Cobbs	163
Henry Dyer	50
Wm. Davis	100
Wm. Buckner	302½
Tho Barber	600
Eliz[b] Tindall	60
Dudley Diggs	1350
Wm. Hewitt	150
Mary Collier	433
Charles Collier	684
Tho Hansford	75
Geo Browne	150
Wm. Gibbs	50
Wm. Pekithman	650
Jno Smith	150
Baldwin Matthews	1300
Jn[o] Daniell	200
Seamor Powell	130
Jn[o] Lewis Esq[r]	300
Wm. Timson	1000
Jn[o] Page	490
Jos. Benjafield	80
Tho Stear	60
Stephen Fouace	565
Edw[d] Jenings Esq.	850
Eliz[b] Archer	370
Wm. Coman	50
Eliz[b] Hansford	100
Sam[ll] Hill	25
Jn[o] Anderson	50
Tho Buck	350
Lewis Burwell	2100
Robt. Crawley	400
Robt. Hyde	200
Robt. Harrison	250
Jeffrey Overstreet	50
Tho Overstreet	50
John Myhill	52

Mary Roberts	25
Jenj[a] Stogsdall	50
Tho Wade	375
Jos: Walker	615
Jn° Sanders	100
Mongo Inglis	400
Tho Holyday	100
Jn° Williams	100
Autho: Sebrell	50
Robt. Jones	100
James Causebee	200
Rich[d] Booker	200
James Morris	100
Henry Adkinson	82
Robt. Jackson	150
Anthony Robinson	183
Hannah Lamb	50
James Calthorp	900
Tho Boulmer	265
Peter Pasque	12
Jn° Chapman	70
Jn° Pond	112
Sarah Tomkins	250
Robt. Kirby	200
Tho Kirby	270
Edw[d] Curtis	200
Jn° forgison	200
Wm. Row	902
Jn° Hunt	550
Wm. Taverner	100
Armiger Wade	424
Rich[d] Dixon	450
Edw[d] Jennings, Esq[r]	1650
Jn° Persons	300
Tho Nutting	375
Peter Manson	150
Rich[d] Slaughter	275
James Persons	350

Tho Roberts	450
Jn° Toomer	335
Dan[ll] Taylor	225
Robt. Hayes	220
Henry Andros	274
Jn° Wells	750
Robt Curtis	250
Tho Cheesman Sen[r]	1800
Jos Poter	25
Hen: Heywood	1300
David Holyday	600
John Northern	130
Jn° Doswell	367
Isaac Powell	100
Symon Staice	200
Jn° Drewett	200
Rob[t] Topladie	100
Jn° Potter	93
Lewis Vernum	150
James Slaughter	250
Tho: Burnham	50
Jn° Doswell Jun[r]	100
Rob[t] Shields	400
Wm. Wilson	50
Owen Davis	247
Tho Walker	100
Rich[d] Nixon	150
Henry Clerk	100
Elias Love	25
Wm. Howard	100
Jn° Sanderver	100
Jn° Cox	50
Tho Gibbins	100
Tho Hind	100
Tho Cheesman Jun[r]	600
Wm. Browne	200
Jn° Rogers	650
Jn° Moss	150

Jn[o] Lawson	100
Nich[o] Phillips	150
Wm. Sheldon	750
Jn[o] Wayman	100
Tho Edwards	150
Lawrence Smith	1700
James Paulmer	150
Wm. Gurrow	150
Peter Goodman	400
Rob[t] Snead	50
Edw[d] Cawley	150
Wm. Gorden	150
Jn[o] Hilsman	75
Jn[o] Wright	100
Jn[o] Gibons	50
Eliz[b] Goodwin	1200
Sam[ll] Cooper	150
Jno Fips	150
Tho Wooton	150
Edw[d] Moss	759
Rebecha Watkins	100
Wm. Whitaker	1800
Hampton Parish	200
Bruton Parish Gleabe	300
Rob[t] Ivy he living in James City County & no Tenn[t] on ye Land	100
	61132½
added to make up the old Roll	168
	61300½

Wm. Barbar S. Y. C.

(To be continued)

VIRGINIA QUIT RENT ROLLS, 1704

The Rent Roll of the Land in James City County, 1704

A

	Acres
Adkinson, Tho	50
Adkinson, Henry	250
Armestone, Joshua	50
Adams, Anne	150
Argo, James	200
Abbitt, Francis	100
Aperson, W[m]	80
Allen, Rich'd	540

B

Baker, Jn[o]	100
Bentley, Jn[o]	125
Best, Edw[d]	75
Burwell, Lewis	1350
Beckett, Tho	60
Bray, James	3500
Bryon, Jn[o]	100
Bingley, James	100
Benham, Jn[o]	50
Brown, James	250
Bower, W[m]	50
Broadnax, W[m]	1683
Bayley, Wm.	100
Black, Geo.	200
Bush, Jn[o]	800

Ballard, Tho	100
Bray, David	5758
Burton, Ralph	200
Blankett, Henry	100
Brand, Rich[d]	125
Breeding, Jn[o]	100
Bruer, Shackfield	350
Blackley, W[m]	142
Barratt, W[m]	305
Barron, Tho	100
Blankes, Henry	650
Bagby, Tho	180
Barnes, Francis	200
Brackitt, Tho	150
Brown, W[m]	1070
Buxton, Sam[ll]	300
Bimms, Christ[o]	300
Ballard, W[m]	300
Boman	90
Benge, Robt	60
	19123

C

Center, Jn[o]	100
Clerk, Wm	1100
Charles, Phill	200
Capell, Tho	200
Cearley, W[m]	450
Clerk, Robt.	300
Clerk, Sarah	200
Cole, Rich[d]	80
Cooper, Tho	60
Cook, Rich[d]	75
Cosby, Charles	250
Crawley, Robt.	460
Cryer, Geo.	100
Cobbs, Ambrose	350

Cock, Jonathan	250
Cowles, Thomas	675
	4850

D

Dorman, Jn°	100
Drummond, W^m^	150
Deane, Jn°	150
Duckitt, Abraham	290
Danzee, Jn° Jacob Coignan	4111
Deane, Tho	80
Deane, W^m^	100
Drummond, Jn°	200
Deane, Tho	150
Duke, Tho	750
Davey, Francis	778
Doby, Jn°	300
Duke, Henry, Junr	1000
Davis, Geo	50
Duke, Henry, Esqr.	2986

E

Elerby, Eliz^b^	600
Edmunds, Eliz^b^	175
Eggleston, Joseph	550
Eglestone, Benj^a^	1375
	2700

F

Fearecloth, Tho	277
Farthing, W^m^	50
Frayser, Jn°	250
Fox, W^m^	50
Fonace, Stephen	150
Fish, Jn°	100
Freeman, Geo	197

Farrbush, W[m]	400
Flanders, Francis	350
	1824

G

Goodrich, Benj[a]	1650
Gwin, Jn[o]	100
Garey, Tho	60
Guilsby, Tho	300
Graves, Joseph	250
Goss, Charles	171
Goodall, Jn[o]	400
Geddes	476
Gill, Jn[o]	100
Green, Tho	050
Gregory, Nich.	50
Green, Wm.	100
Genings, Phill	400
Gibson, Gibey	150
Goodman, John	275
Grice, Aristotle	700
Greene, Tho	500
	5882

H

Hudson, W[m]	50
Herd, Zeph	100
Hadley, Dyonitia	100
Hall, Jno.	50
Harvey, Geo.	1425
Howard, Jn[o]	25
Hughes, Geo.	250
Hanfield, Mich.	50
Hudson, Geo.	100
Hudson, Leonard	170
Hood, John	250
Harris, W[m]	140

Hamner, Nich°	500
Henley, Leonard	360
Hooker, Edw[d]	1067
Higgins, Jn°	75
Henley, Jn°	100
Holiday, Tho	250
Hitchcock, John	100
Holeman, James	150
Hubert, Matt	1834
Hendcock, Robt	300
Haley, James	310
Hook, Mich.	260
Hill, Tho.	310
Hatfield, Rich[d]	100
Hilliard, Jerimiah	225
Hilliard, John	200
Hopkins, John	120
Hunt, Wm.	1300
Hix, John	115
Harrison, Wm.	150
Hawkins, John	200
Hix, Joseph	100
Harrison, Benj[a] Jr	100
	10936

J

Inch, Jno.	30
Inglis, Mongo	1300
Jones, Fred	300
Jenings, Edw[d] [Edmund] Esqr.	200
Jaquelin, Edw[d]	400
Jeffrys, Tho	60
Jackson, Eliz[b]	200
Jackson, Rich[d]	150
Jeffrys, Matt	100
Johnson, Antho	100
Jones, Wm.	50

Johnson, John	260
Jones, Wm.	115
Jordan, John	1000
	4265

K

Knewstup	150

L

Lawrence, Rich[d]	250
Ludwell, Phil, Esqr.	6626
Lattoon, John	75
Lund, Thomas	100
Lillingtone, Benj[a]	100
Lidie, Robt.	500
Loftin, Corneles	200
Lightfoot, Phil	1650
Lightfoot, John, Esq[r]	250
Love, Jn[o]	100
Loftin, Corneles, Jun[r]	200
Livey, Wm.	55
	10106

M

Mookins, Roger	160
Macklin, Wm.	300
Marston, Wm.	150
Morris, Edw[d], Jun[r]	100
Manningaren	150
Marston, Tho.	1000
Martin, Rich[d]	150
Maples, Tho.	300
Mattlow, Jn[o]	170
Morris, James	800
Morris, David	170
Myers, Wm. Jun[r]	100
Mountfort,Tho	600
Morris, John	195

Marble [Marrable?] Geo.	135
Mallard, Poynes	100
Morryman, James	300
Morecock, Tho	700
Meekinge, Tho	175
Marraw, Dennis	30
Major, John	100
Major, John	100
	5885

N

Norrell [Norvell] Hugh	328
Nicholson, Jn[o]	144
Nicholls, Henry	100
Nailer, Wm.	300
O'Mooney, Mary	126
	998

P

Prince, George	50
Page, John	1700
Page, Mary	900
Pigot, Benj[a]	90
Pall, Wm.	450
Parker, Tho.	1650
Peper, Stephen	100
Phillips, Jn[o]	300
Pattison, Alex	100
Perkins, Charles	320
Philips, Edw[d]	100
Philips, Wm.	300
Pearman, Wm.	270
Pearman, Jn[o]	200
Pendexter [Poindexter], Tho.	550
Parish, Tho	100
Pattisson, Tho	200

Parke, Dan[ll] Esq[r]	1800
Pattison, Catherine	150
	9330

R

Rhods, Randall	50
Ryder, Mary	50
Rhodes, Francis	100
Rovell, Jn[o]	50
Revis, Wm.	150
Russell, Sam[ll]	350
	1050

S

Stafford, Mary	210
Sanders, Jn[o]	50
Sewell, Jn[o]	75
Sprattley, Jn[o]	350
Smith, Clerist[o]	450
Short, Jn[o]	90
Smallpage, Robt.	190
Santo, Robt.	100
Smith, Jn[o]	114
Slade, Wm.	80
Soane, Henry	750
Sykes, Burnard	1012
Selvey, Jacob	50
Sharp, Jn[o]	800
Shaley, Jn[o]	150
Simes, Wm.	650
Sorrell, Mary	500
Sherman, Eliz[b].	500
	6121

T

Tinsley Edw[d]	100
Tinsley, Rich[d]	100

Tomson, James	100
Thackson, John	289
Tyery, Wm.	1590
Thurson, John	500
Thomas, Wm.	150
Tyler, Henry	730
Tullett, John	625
Thomas, Hanah	100
Thomson, Henry	150
Tevine, Tho	100
Thomas, Jn[o]	250
	4784

V

Vaughan, Henry	1900
Udall, Matthew	50
Verney, Wm.	50
Vaiding, Isaac	300
	2300

W

Weathers, Tho.	130
Wood, Rich[d]	130
Whitaker, Wm.	320
Waid, Tho.	100
Weldon, Sarah	100
Whaley, Mary	200
Winter, Tim[o]	250
Wilkins, Sam[ll]	170
Wright, Sam[ll]	100
Winter, Wm.	100
Williams, Matt	75
Walker, Alex	500
Williamson, John	120
Walker, David	150
Walker, Alex. Jun[r]	2025
Warberton, Tho.	190

Weldey, Geo	317
Wragg, Tho	500
Wooten, Jn°	150
Willson, Jn°	140
Wilkins, Tho	600
Wood, Edw[d]	300
Wood, Tho	200
Walker, David	100
Ward, Robt.	800
Wright, Mary	175
Woodward, Lanslett	650
Woodward, John	650
Woodward, Geo.	350
Woodward, Sam[ll]	350
Waid, Henry	150
Waid, Edw[d]	150
	10662

Y

Young, Robt.	350
Young, Thomas	350
	700

A	1420
B	19123
C	4850
D	11695
E	2700
F	1824
G	5882
H	10936
J	4264
K	150
L	10106
M	5885
N O	998

P	9330
R	1050
S	6121
T	4784
V	2300
W	10662
Y	700
	114780

Benj[a] Shottwater of York County	300
Tho Sorrell	300
Mary Nesham at the Blackwater	168
	768

Henry Soane jun[r]. Sher.

The Totall of the Acres in James City County	114780	
Discovered of this for wch the Sherriff is to be allowed the Q[t] R[t] according to his Ex[cy] ord[s] in Councill	6000	
Remaine	108780	
108780 acres at 24[l] tob[o] p 100 is	26107[l]	Tobo.
Whereof p[d] in Aronoco at 6[s] p ct	4000 is	12–0–0
In sweet scented at 3[s] 4[d] p ct	22107	92–2–3
	26107	104–2–3

VIRGINIA QUIT RENT ROLLS, 1704

NEW KENT COUNTY RENT ROLL

A Rent Roll of the Lands held of her Majtie in the Parish of St. Peters & St. Pauls, Anno 1704.

	Acres
Alford, John	240
Allen, Rich'd	550
Alex. [Alexander] Abraham	100
Allen, Robt	100
Austin	245
Austin, James	700
Amoss, Fran	100
Ashcroft, Tho.	180
Aldridge, Jno	250
Atkinson, Jno	300
Anthony, Mark	190
Anderson, Jno	100
Anderson, Robt.	900
Arise, Margt	200
Austin, Richd	50
Anderson, Robt	700
Anderson, David	300
Anderson, Richd	200
Allen Reynold	205
Allvis, George	325
Aron, Josiah	200
Amos, Nicho	50
Allen, Daniell	250
Allen, Samll	150

	Acres
Anderson, John	100
Ashley, Charles	100
	6785

B

Bourn, Wm.	140
Bray, Sarah	790
Bradbury, Geo.	100
Brothers, Jn[o]	200
Bayley, Jno.	80
Beck, Wm. Mr.	200
Butts, Alice	150
Burnell [Burwell?] Mary, Mrs.	2750
Bassett, Wm.	550
Ball, David	200
Baughan, Jn[o] Jun[r]	300
Bassett, Tho.	350
Blackburn, Rowland	700
Baker, Christ[o]	100
Bear, Peter	100
Brooks, Rich[d]	85
Burnell, Edw[d]	200
Brown, Jn[o]	100
Bullock, Rich[d]	450
Blackwell, James, Jun[r]	200
Brooks, Rob[t]	45
Bulkley, Benj[a]	200
Blackwell, James	950
Baughan, Jn[o]	100
Baughan, Joseph	100
Bostock, Jn[o]	100
Bostock, Wm.	80
Bumpass [Bumpas] Rob[t]	100
Burwell, Lewis	200
Bryan, Charles	100
Bullock, Edw[d]	450

	Acres
Blalock, Jn[o]	492
Baker, Jn[o]	130
Bearne, Henry	50
Burly, Jn[o]	225
Bow, Henry	200
Bradley, Tho.	255
Barker, Chas.	100
Bugg, Sam[ll]	60
Bassett, Wm., Esqr.	1250
Beck, Wm.	433
Beare, Joseph	150
Barrett, Christ[o]	60
Baughtwright [Boatwright], Jn[o]	250
Bad, Sam[ll]	150
Banks, Andrew	50
Baker, Rich[d]	80
Bowles, John	500
Buncle, John	100
Burnett, John	150
Barnhowes, Rich[d]	1600
Barbar, Tho.	500
Burkett, Tho.	41
Bates, Edw[d]	50
Breeding [Breeden], John	300
Brewer, Mary	100
Bassett, Wm. Esqr.	4100
Bradingham, Rob[t]	150
Baxter, James	90
	21786

C

Cotrell, Rich[d]	200
Clarkson, David	200
Crump, Stephen	60
Crump, Wm.	330
Clopton, Wm.	454

	Acres
Chandler, Rob[t]	160
Crump, Rich[d]	60
Cambo, Rich[d]	80
Crawford, David, Jun[r]	400
Crawford, David, Sen[r]	300
Chambers, Edw[d]	235
Clerk, Edw[d]	282
Collett, Tho.	100
Clerk, Christ[o]	300
Cocker, Wm.	1000
Case, Hugh	100
Carley, Rich[d]	80
Chiles, Henry	700
Cook, Abraham	200
Crump, Eliz[h]	80
Colum, Rich[d]	130
Crump, James	150
Crump, Robt.	150
Clough, Capt. [George?]	80
Chandler, Wm.	300
Chandler, Frances	150
Cordey, Tho.	150
Curnell, Andrew	330
Croome, Joell	600
Crutchfield, Peter	400
Chesley, Wm.	500
Crutchfield, Jun[r]	400
Carlton, Wm.	140
Chambers, George	100
Cox, Wm.	350
	9251

D

Dolerd, Wm.	50
Dennett, John	350
Durham, James	100
Dumas, Jeremiah	250

	Acres
Depriest, Robt.	350
Dodd, John	300
Daboney [Dabney], James	320
Davis, Eliazar	375
Duke, Henry, Esqr.	325
Dibdall, Jn[o]	800
Darnell, Rachell	100
Duke, Henry, Esqr.	170
Davis, John	80
Davenport, Mea[t]	125
Daniell, John	100
	3845

E

Eperson, John	120
Elmore, Tho.	300
Elmore, Tho., Jun[r]	100
Ellison [Ellyson], Garratt [Gerrard] Rob[t]	520
England, Wm.	490
Elderkin, John	300
Elmore, Peter	100
English, [Ingles] Mungo	500
Ellis, Wm.	100
	2530

F

Finch, Edw[d]	300
Foster, Joseph	800
Forgeson, Wm.	507
Fleming, Charles	920
Francis, Tho.	150
Freeman, Wm.	200
Fenton, Widdo	270
Feare, Edw[d]	200
Fisher, Wm.	100
	3447

G

	Acres
Goodger, Jn[o]	200
Green, Edw[d]	200
Gibson, Tho.	370
Garrat, James	375
Gorton, Jn[o]	250
Glass, Tho.	150
Graham, Tho.	250
Gleam, Jn[o]	300
Giles, Jn[o]	120
Gentry, Nich[o]	250
Garland, Edw[d]	2600
Glass, Anne	150
Granchaw [Crenshaw], Tho.	480
Greenfield, Fran.	80
Gillmott, Jn[o]	160
Gawen, Phillip	50
Gillmott, Rich[d]	150
Glassbrook [Glazebrook] Rob[t]	400
Gadberry, Tho.	200
Gill, Nich[o]	222
Gosling, Wm.	460
Goodring, Alexander	100
Gills, John	100
Grindge, Rich[d]	225
	7442

H

Herlock, John	320
Hilton, Jn[o]	300
Hughes, Jn[o]	180
Huberd, Jn[o]	827
Howle, Jn[o]	150
Howle, Jn[o] Jun[r]	100
Hughs, Rob[t]	966
Harris, Edm[d]	100
Harris, Tho.	100

	Acres
Hawes, Haughton	850
Harris, John	146
Hill Jn[o]	250
Hester, Fra	300
Horsley, Rowland	250
Horman, Rob[t]	300
Hughes, Rees	400
Hill, Sam[ll]	300
Holled, Sam[ll]	100
Harrelston [Harrelson], Paul	360
Hatfield, Wm.	218
Harris, Wm.	125
Harris, Benj[a]	100
Horkeey, John	800
Hairy, John	280
Haiselwood, Jn[o]	200
Haiselwood, Tho.	50
Hockiday, Wm.	300
Holdcroft, Henry	95
Hogg, Mary	140
Harmon, Wm.	350
Hogg, Jn[o], Jun[r]	260
Harris, Wm.	100
Hopkins, Wm.	200
Howes, Job	300
Hight, John	100
Hankins, Charles	340
Harris, Wm.	150
Harris, Rob[t]	75
Handey, Wm.	150
Hogg, Wm.	200
Haselwood, Rich[d]	100
Harlow, Tho.	230
Hutton, Geo.	150
	11312

J

	Acres
Jackson, Tho.	500
Izard, Fran	1233
Jarratt, Rob[t]	1600
Johnson, Mich[ll]	40
Jones, John	100
Johnson, Wm.	265
Jones, Jane	200
Johnson, John	100
Johnson, Edw[d]	150
Jenings, Robt.	100
Jones, Fredrick	500
Jones, John	100
Jeeves, Tho.	100
Jones, Francis	200
Jones, John	100
Jones, Evan	500
	5838

K

King, Eliz[b]	300
Kembro [Kimborough?], Jn[o]	540
Kembro, Jno, Junr	150
Keeling, Geo.	1500
	2490

L

Lightfoot, John, Esqd.	3600
Littlepage, Rich[d]	2160
Lesplah, Peter	100
Lestrange, Tho.	200
Liddall, Geo. Coll.	100
Lawson, Rich[d]	200
Levermore, Phill	1000
Lewis, John, Esqr.	2600
Lawson, John	050

	Acres
Lewis, John	375
Lovell, Geo.	920
Lovell, Charles	250
Leak, Wm.	280
Logwood, Tho.	100
Lacey, Wm.	500
Lacey, Tho.	100
Lacey, Emanuell	180
Luke, Jn[o]	150
Lochester, Robt.	80
Lewis, Tho.	115
Lee, Edw[d]	120
Lochester, Edw[d]	80
Law, James	100
Laton, Reuben	100
Linsey, Joseph	1150
Linsey, Wm.	50
Lane, Tho.	100
	14760

M

Mellington, Wm. Jun[r]	450
Mitchell, Stephen, Jun[r]	75
Millington, Wm.	200
Moss, Sam[ll]	200
Mitchell, Tho.	300
Meanley, Wm.	100
Minis, Tho.	200
Mitchell, Stephen	200
Moor, Pelham	125
Martin, Tho.	100
Martin, Martin	150
Morris, Rob[t]	245
Moss, Tho.	430
Morgan, Edw[d]	50
Moon, Stephen	70
Major, Wm.	456

	Acres
Murroho, Jn°	100
Moor, Jn°	250
Masey [Massie], Tho.	300
Martin, John	400
Masey [Massie] Peter	100
Madox, John	300
Martin, Wm.	230
Martin, James	100
Moss, James	720
Moor, Tho.	65
McKing, Alexander	170
McKoy, Jn°	300
Merridith, Geo.	400
Melton, Rich[d]	290
Morreigh, John	100
Merfield, John	210
Mills, Nich°	300
Mask, Jn°	411
Medlock, John	350
Moor, Edw[d]	65
McKgehe, Wm.	131½
Merriweather, Nich°	3327
Mage, Peter	450
Mitchell, Wm.	512
Marr, Geo.	100
Moor, Anne	75
Matray, Tho.	382
Merideth, James	270
Mohan [Mohun] Warwick	850
Mattlow, James	150
Morgan, Matthew	210
Morris, John	450
Markham, Tho.	100
Moxon, Wm.	100
Mackeny, Eliz[b]	250
Meacon [Macon], Gideon	270
	16149½

N

	Acres
Nucholl, James	300
Neaves, James	150
Nonia, Rich[d]	100
Norris, Wm.	100
	650

O

Osling, John	150
Otey, John	290
Oudton, Matt.	190
	630

P

Page, John, Jun[r]	400
Pendexter [Poindexter], Geo.	1490
Pattison [Patteson], David	300
Park, Jn[o], Jun[r]	300
Park, John	200
Pease, John	100
Philip, Geo.	100
Penix, Edw[d]	200
Plantine, Peter	240
Pendexter [Poindexter], Tho.	1000
Pyraul, James	150
Pullam [Pulliam], Wm.	575
Purdy, Nich[o]	200
Page, Mary Mad[m]	3450
Perkins, John	120
Paite [Pate] Jerim[iah]	220
Pasley, Robt.	300
Perkins, Wm.	305
Pait [Pate], John	1500
Petever, Tho.	100
Pittlader, Wm.	147
Pickley, Tho.	281

	Acres
Pittlader, Tho.	295
Petty, Stephen	200
Porter, John	100
Petty, John	2190
Park, Coll [Daniel]	7000
Purly, John	100
	21573

R

Raglin [Ragland], Evan	300
Raglin [Ragland], Evan jun^{r}	100
Raglin, [Ragland], Tho.	100
Ross, Wm.	150
Richardson, Henry	300
Raymond, James	80
Reynold, Tho.	355
Reyley, Jno.	100
Reynolds, Jonah	50
Rhoads [Rodes], Charles	175
Reynolds, Sam^{ll}	820
Rice, Tho.	300
Redwood, John	1078
Rule, Widdo.	50
Richardson, Richard	890
Russell, John	550
Richardson, John	1450
Richard, Eman	1250
Round Tree [Roundtree], Wm.	100
Randolph, Widd^{o}	100
	8298

S

Styles, John	200
Smith, Nath^{ll}	82
Sanders, Wm.	40
Spear, Robt.	450
Sanders, James	60

	Acres
Scott, John	300
Scrugg, Rich[d]	100
Strange, Alexander	450
Smith, Wm.	110
Scrugg, Jn[o]	50
Snead, Tho.	200
Sunter, Stephen	478
Symons, Josiah	100
Sanders, John	130
Stephens, Wm.	100
Stanley, Tho.	150
Sandidge, Jn[o]	100
Sprattlin, Andrew	654
Snead, John	75
Smith, James	80
Sexton, Wm.	80
Sims, John	1000
Smith, Roger	300
Sherriff, Henry	100
Salmon, Thomas	50
Sanders, Tho.	25
Symons, George	125
Stamp, Ralph	625
Stanup [Stanhope], Capt. [John]	1024
Stanup [Stanhope], Rich[d]	325
Shears, Paul	200
Stepping, Tho.	350
Slater, James	700
	9813

T

Tony, Alexander	170
Tovis, Edm[d]	100
Turner, Henry	250
Turn'[r], Wm.	250
Turner, Geo.	400

	Acres
Thorp, Tho.	200
Thurmond [Thurman] Rich[d]	131½
Tucker, Tho.	700
Turner, James	50
Thompson, James	100
Tully, Wm.	200
Turner, Geo. Jun[r]	200
Tate, James	160
Town, Eliz[b]	100
Thomasse's Orphans	500
Tinsley, Cornelius	220
Tyler	100
Tinsley, Tho.	150
Terrell, Wm.	400
Taylor, Tho.	25
Tinsley, Jn[o]	130
Tapp, Jn[o]	110
Tyrrey, James	150
Tyrrey, Alexand[r]	210
Thompson, Capt. [Roger?]	2600
Tyrey [Tyree?], Thom.	190
Taylor, Joseph	150
Taylor, Lemuell	212
Taylor, Thomas	350
Twitty, Thomas	200
	8708½

V

Upsherd, Jo[n]	60
Vaughan, Wm.	300
Vice, Amer.	50
Venables [Venable], Abr:	100
Venables [Venable], John	200
Vaughan, John	250
Vaughan, Vincent	410
	1370

W

	Acres
Wintby, Jacob	250
Winfry, Charles	100
Waddill, Jn°	40
Walker, Wm.	650
Walton, Edw[d]	150
Wilson, John	200
Waddill, Wm.	375
Warring, Peter	88
Wingfield, Tho.	150
Weaver, Sam	100
Wyatt, Alice	1300
West, Nath.	6370
Webb, Mary	200
Wilmore, Jn°	100
Webster, Joseph	80
West, Giles	200
Wharton, Tho.	270
Willis, Fran.	134
Waddy, Sam[ll]	150
Willford, Charles	100
Waid [Wade], James	150
White, Jn°	320
Wood, Henry	100
Woody, Symon	50
Woody, John	100
Winstone, Antho.	310
Winstone, Isaac	850
Woody, James	130
Winstone, Sarah	275
Watson, Theophilus	325
Woodson, John	600
Walton, Edw[d]	450
Wood, Walter	100
Watkins, Wm.	50
Wilkes, Joseph	250

	Acres
Williams, Clerk	300
Willis, Stephen	500
Williams, Tho.	100
Worrin, Robt.	300
Woodall, James	200
Walker, Capt.	400
Wilson, James	60
Wheeler, John	75
Williams, Wm.	100
White, John	190
	17292

Y

Yeoman, John	50
Yeoell, Judith	150
	200
Quit Rents yt hath not been pd. this year viz[t]	
Richardson, Matt.	200
Wm. Wheeler	150
Coll. Parkes	300
	650
Lands that the Persons lives out of the County viz[t]	
Coll. Lemuell [Lionel] Batthurst	800
Robb Valkes [Vaulx?]	500
The Heirs of Bray	500
	1800

A	6785	E	2530
B	21786	F	3447
C	9291	G	7442
D	3845	H	11312

J	5838	R	8298
K	2490	S	9813
L	14760	T	8708½
M	16149½	V	1370
N	650	W	17292
O	630	Y	200
P	21573		
			173870

James Mosse, Sherriff

(To be continued)

VIRGINIA QUIT RENT ROLLS, 1704

A full & Perfect Rent Roll of All the Land held of her Maj[tie] in Charles City County this Present year 1704 by Patets &c.

A

	ACRES
Aliat, John	100

B

Bradley, Joseph	200
Baxter, John	250
Bishop, Robt.	200
Bedingfield, Theo	110
Botman, Harmon	100
Burton, Henry	100
Burwell, Lewis	8000
Brooks, Robt.	150
Blanks, Richard, Sen[r]	250
Blanks, Richard Jun[r]	125
Blanks, Tho.	125
Bradford, Rich[d]	1397
Brown, Marmaduke	100
Bray, David	230
	11337

C

Cole, Robt.	80
Codell, Rich[d]	100
Clark, Edw[d]	962¼
Clark, Daniell	250
Clark, Joseph	230
Christian, Tho	1273
Cock, Edw[d]	350

	ACRES
Cock, Rich[d]	975
	3258

D

Davis, Thomas	200
Davis, Richard	118
	318

E

Edwards, John	287½
Epes, Littlebury	400
Epes, John	500
Ele, Sam[ll]	682
Evans, John	800
	2669½

F

Floyd, Geo.	243
Fowler, Rich[d]	150
Flowers, Sam[ll]	200
	593

G

Gunn, James	250
Grosse, Edw[d]	0100
	350

H

Hamlin, John	143½
Hill, Edw[d]	2100
Haynes, Nich[o]	125
Harrison, Benj.	6350
Harwood, John	100
Howood, James	200
Hattle, Shard	112
Harwood, Joseph	659
Harwood, Sam[ll]	350

	ACRES
Harwood, Robt.	312½
Hunt, Wm.	3130
Hunt, John	1500
Harmon, Eliz[b]	479
Hyde, Wm.	120
Hamlin, Stephen	80
Hamlin, Tho	254
	16015

J

Irby, Wm.	103
Javox, James	100
Jordin, Edw[d]	100
Justis, Justinian	200
	503

L

Lowlin, Dan[ll]	600
Lawrence, James	100
	700

M

Manders, James	100
Minge, James	1086
Mountford, Jeffry	100
Marvell, Tho.	1238
Moodie, Sam[ll]	82
Muschamp, John	80
	2686

N

New, Edw[d]	100
New, Robt.	300
	400

O

Owen, Wm.	100
Owen, David	100
	200

P

	ACRES
Parker, Tho.	1667
Parish, Wm.	100
Parish, Charles	100
Parker, James	160
Parish, Edw[d]	100
Parish, John	100
	2227

R

Roach, Jn[o] sen[r]	630
Renthall, Joseph	270
Russell, Sam[ll]	253
Roper, John	220
Royall, Joseph	262
	1635

S

Smith, Obediah	100
Sampson, Widd[o]	211
Stith, Drewry	1240
Stith, John	1395
Stockes [Stokes], John	476
Stockes [Stokes], Silvanus sen[r]	250
Stockes [Stokes], Silvanus jun[r]	550
Speares, Geo	225
	4447

T

Tanner, Tho.	2000
Tarendine, John	150
Turner, Edw[d]	195
Trotman, Anne	120
	2465

V

Vernon, Walter	240

W

	ACRES
Wyatt, Widd°	800
Woodam, Tho.	100
Waren, John	54
	954

A	100
B	11337
C	3258
D	318
E	2669½
F	593
G	350
H	16015
J	503
L	700
M	2686
N	400
O	200
P	2227
R	1635
S	4447
T	2465
V	240
W	954
	52059½

An Acct of what Land y[t] I cannot gett the Quitt Rents the persons living out of the County.

Joseph Parish at Kiquotan	100
Rich[d] Smith, James City Cty.	350
Dan[ll] Hayley	200
Wm. Lagg, Henrico Cty.	100
	750

Tho Parker, Sherrif

VIRGINIA QUIT RENT ROLLS, 1704

The Rent Roll of King William County.

	ACRES
Armsby, John	200
Alvey, Robt.	400
Andrew, Wm.	100
Abbott, Robt.	100
Arnold, Anthony	100
Arnold, Benj^{a}	1000
Alcock, John	190
Adams, James	400
Anderson, Wm. Capt.	150
Burwell, Maj^{r}	4700
Bunch, Paul	150
Baker, John	250
Burgis, Edwd	150
Buttris, Robt.	400
Bibb, Benj^{a}	100
Browne, Joseph	270
Bell, Edwd	580
Burch, Henry	200
Burrel, Suprian [Cyprian?]	350
Baker, Tho.	100
Bobo, Eliz^{b}	200
Bird, Wm. Maj^{r} q^{r} [quarter]	1200
Burrus, John	60
Butler, Thomas	150
Burrus, Thomas	60
Bassett, Coll. q^{r}	1550
Bray, James q^{r}	1400
Browne, Abraham	250
Brightwell, Eliz^{b}	300
Bickley, Joseph	150

	ACRES
Claibourne, Wm. Coll.	3000
Claibourne, Tho. Capt.	1000
Claibourne, John	50
Coakes, Robert	100
Cradock, Sam[ll]	600
Cockram, Wm.	200
Cockram, Joseph	600
Celar, John	100
Chadwick, Wm.	150
Sachern, John	180
Carr, Thomas	500
Chiles, Henry q[r]	700
Cranshaw, [Crenshaw?], Thomas	150
Clark, Margarett	100
Coates, Wm.	50
Douglas, Wm.	200
Davis, Lewis	200
Davis, Wm.	200
Downer, John	300
Downes, Elias	300
	23850
Davenport, Davis	200
Dorrell, [Darrell] Sampson q[r]	5000
Davenport, Martin	100
Davis, Robert	200
Dickason, Wm.	100
Dickason, Thomas	100
Dillon, Henry	150
Dabney, James	200
Dabney, George	290
Dabney, Benj[a]	200
Davis, John	200
Elly, Rich[d]	100
Egny, Eliz[b]	100
Elliott, Thomas	480
Edward, James	350

	ACRES
Elliott, James	1700
Fox, John Capt.	600
Fox, Henry	2000
Finton, Francis	100
Fuller, Anthony	150
Foord, John Jun[r]	300
Foord, Wm.	800
Fullalove, Thomas	100
Fleming, Charles q[r]	1700
Graves, John q[r]	100
Garratt, [Garrett], Thomas	200
Geeres, Thomas	100
Green, John	100
Gravatt, Henry	150
Goodin, Maj[r] q[r]	200
Glover, Wm.	100
Harriott, George	200
Hollins, John	200
Higgason, John	350
Holderbee, Wm.	100
Holliday, Wm.	100
Hayfield, Wm.	100
Hampton, John	50
Huckstep, Edw[d]	150
Hurt, Wm. Jun[r]	90
Hurt, Wm. Sen[r]	250
Hurt, John	500
Hendrick, Hans	700
Handcock, Thomas	200
Hayden, John	150
Hobday, Edw[d]	150
Hill, Thomas	150
Hutchinson, Wm.	600
Hill, Francis	300
Hill, Gabriell	250
	20,760

	ACRES
Hill, Edw[d] Coll q[r]	3000
Hayle, Joseph	200
Johns, Jane	240
Johnson, Wm.	300
Johnson, Coll q[r]	600
Johns, Wm.	100
Isabell, Wm.	150
James, Jonathan	300
Inge, Vincent	100
Jones, Frederick q[r]	2850
Jenings, Coll. q[r]	4000
King, Robert, q[r]	300
Kettlerise, Symon	200
Lee, John	20
Lypscomb, Ambrose	600
Lasy, [Lacy], Wm.	100
Lypscomb, Wm.	300
Littlepage, Rich[d] Capt. q[r]	2600
Lypscomb, John	200
Mallory, Thomas	150
Mallory, Roger	100
Miles, Daniell	350
McGehee, Thomas	250
Marr, John	200
Morris, Wm.	440
Maybank, Wm.	100
McDonnell, John	150
Maddison, Henry	650
Merriweather, Nich[o] q[r]	600
Mullens, Matthew	150
Maddison, John q[r]	300
Norment, Joseph	800
Norment, Sam[ll]	100
Noyce, Wm.	650
Napier, Robert	100
Owens, Hugh	300

	ACRES
Oustin, John	350
Oakes, John	350
Oliver, John	140
Palmer, Martin	1200
Peek, John	100
Pynes, Nathaniell	1400
Pee, Thomas	400
Purlevant, Arthur	100
Powers, David	200
Pollard, Wm. q[r]	500
Pemberton, Geo.	180
	26520
Page, John, qr.	1000
Pickrell, Gabriel	100
Parks, [Parke's] Coll. qr.	4500
Quarles, John	100
Reynolds, Wm.	100
Robert, Maurice	200
Randall, John	100
Ray, James	100
Rhodes, Nicholas	150
Sandlon, Nicholas	700
Strutton, Thomas	150
Streett, Wm.	350
Shilling, George	300
Satterwhite, Charles	150
Slaughter, Geo.	100
Slaughter, Martin	130
Stark, John	500
Sanders, Joshua	100
See, Mathew	200
Sellers, Jacob	350
Spruse, Jeremy	150
Smith, Edw[d]	150
Spencer, Thomas	600

	ACRES
Slaughter, John	90
Smith, Christ° q[r]	800
Slaughter, Henry	100
Toms, Wm.	150
Towler, Matthew	150
Terry, Thomas	300
Terry, Stephen	330
Tomason, Thomas	150
Terry, James	400
Troncer, John	100
Vickery, Henry	450
West, Jn° Coll	1800
Winfree, Henry	300
West, Tho. Capt.	1000
Whitworth, John	200
Whitlock, John	200
Willeroy, Abraham	550
Williams, Phillip	100
Williams, Griffith	240
Wood, Thomas	300
Whitehead, John	100
Woolsey, Jacob	130
Williams, John	150
Williams, Sam[ll]	600
	18970
Wright, Thomas	150
Whitbee, Robert	800
West, Nathan[ll], Capt.	2000
Waller, John Maj.	800
Willis, Wm.	250
Wheeles, Joseph	130
Wormley, Madame, q[r]	3000
Winston, William	170
Whitehead, Phillip	3000
Yancey, Charles	100

	ACRES
Yarborough, John	150
Yarborough, Richard	300
	10850
	23850
	20760
	26520
	18970
	100950

Wm. Standard [Stanard], M. S. [Middlesex]	1000
James Wood, K. Q. [King and Queen]	500
Zachary Lewis, K. Q.	450
Peter Kemp, G. C. [Gloucester Co.]	600
Wm. Beck, N. K. [New Kent]	1600
Tho. Hickman, K. Q.	550
Benj[a] Clement, G. C.	600
David Bray, J: C: C: [James City Co.]	1000
Job House, N. K.	2000
Harry Beverley, M. S.	600
Chillian White, G. C.	300

(To be continued)

VIRGINIA QUIT RENT ROLLS, 1704

King and Queen County

A True Account of the Lands in King & Queen County as it was taken by Robt. Bird, Sheriff, in the year 1704.

A

	ACRES
Alford, John	200
Austin, Dan[ll]	80
Asque, John	320
Adams, John	200
Arnold, Edw[d]	150
Allen, Thomas	100
Adkinson, John	250
Austin, Thomas	100
Adamson, David	100
Anderson, Rich'd	650
Allcock, Dorothy	150
	2300

B

Baker, Wm.	350
Beverley, Robt. q[r]	3000
Bennett, Alexander	200
Breeding, George [Breeden]	200
Bennett, Wm.	150
Bowles, Rob[t]	100
Bennett, Sawyer	150
Baylor, John	3000
Bell, Roger	150
Burford, Wm.	150

	ACRES
Bray, John	230
Blake, Wm.	290
Boisseau, James Quart[r]	900
Blake, Wm. Jun[r]	210
Brown, Lancelet	385
Burch, Jn[o]	100
Burch, Wm.	100
Brown, Tho: Blakes Land	300
Bridgforth, James	355
Bagley, Robt.	550
Banks, Wm.	1079
Bullock, John	200
Bird, Wm.	572
Broach [Brock?], Jn[o]	1200
Braxton, Geo.	2825
Blanchet, John	125
Bowker, Ralph	330
Bine, Edm[d]	111
Barber, James	750
Burgess, Wm.	100
Bond, Jn[o]	100
Breemer, John	1100
Bland, Henry	150
Breemer, John Jun[r]	200
Bowden, Tho:	150
Barton, Andrew	150
Barlow, Henry	200
Baskett, John	150
Batterton, Tho.	100
Baker, James	322
Bell, Robt.	150
Bocus, Reynold	150
Bourne, George	200
Bird, Robt.	1324
	22535

C

	ACRES
Cane, Jn°	300
Chessum, Alexandr	150
Cook, Benjamin	200
Cook, Thomas Junr	50
Cook, Thomas Senr	100
Cook, John	50
Clayton, John	400
Chapman, Mary	200
Clayton, Jeremy	325
Crane, Wm	120
Camp, Thomas	250
Carleton, Christ°	200
Carleton, Jn°	300
Carter, Tim°	350
Coleman, Tho.	300
Coleman, Daniell	470
Clayton, Susannah Widd°	700
Collier, Robt	100
Crane, Wm	300
Crane, Tho	320
Chapman, John	200
Caughlane, James	100
Cotton, Catherine	50
Collier, Charles	450
Collier, John	400
Collins, Wm	350
Cammell, Alexander	200
Chin, Hugh	100
Conner, Tim°	1410
Collin, James Yard qr	300
Corbin, Gowin [Gawin]	2000
Crisp, Tobias	100
Carters qrts	300
Carlton, Tho	200

	ACRES
Carlton, Anne	300
Clough, George q^{r}	390
	12235
Clerk and Cordell both in Gloucester	1000

D

Widd^{o} Durrat	200
Day Alexand^{r} Maj^{r} Beverley q^{r}	300
Doe, Wm.	300
Dilliard [Dillard], Nich^{o}	150
Dilliard, Edwd	150
Dimmock, Tho	150
Dismukes, W^{m}	200
Duett, Charles	900
Didlake, James	200
Durham, John	100
Dunkley, John	380
Duson, Tho	448
Davis, Nath^{ll}	300
Deshazo, Peter	450
Davis, Jno	90
Davis, Edwd	100
Dillard, Thomas	170
Dewis, Rich^{d}	250
Dillard, Geo.	325
Duglas, James	275
Dayley, Owen	180
	5618

E

Eachols, John	220
Ellis, John	400
Eastham, George	300
Ewbank, W^{m}	350
Eastham, Edwd jun^{r}	800
Edw^{ds}, John	100

	ACRES
Eastham, Edw[d]	100
Eastes, Abraham	200
Eyes, Cornelius	100
Emory, Ralph	100
Ellis, Timothy	350
	3020

F

Forsigh, Thomas	150
Farguson, James	300
Flipp, John	80
Farish, Rob[t]	1400
Fielding, Henry	1000
Farmer, John	50
Fothergill, Rich[d]	675
Forteon, Charles	400
Forgett, Charles	150
Fothergill, Rob[t]	150
	4355
Farmer, John not paid for	200
Fox, Margarett not paid for	100

G

Gadberry, Edw[d]	100
Griffin, Edw[d]	100
George, Rich[d]	100
Griffin, David	100
Graves, Rob[t]	150
Graves, Jn[o]	150
Gardner, Ringing	200
Gray, Joseph	200
Gilby, John	300
Gray, Sam[ll]	40
Gresham, Jn[o]	200
Gresham, Edw[d]	175
Good, John	200

	ACRES
Gresham, George	150
Garrett, Danll	200
Gamble, Tho: L. Majors Land	450
Gresham, Tho	225
Graves, Jn°	150
Guttery, Jn°	230
Gregory, Frances Widd°	700
Gough, Alice Widd°	800
Griggs, Francis	250
Garrett, John	330
Garrett, Humphrey	200
Gibson, Widd°	200
Garrett, Rob[t]	200
	6100

H

Hand, Thomas	150
Hayle, John q[r]	685
Honey, James	200
Holloway, W[m]	100
Hernden [Herndon], James	100
Hoomes, George	725
Hodges, Thomas	250
Hayle, Joseph	250
Hayes, John	100
Haynes, W[m]	494
Holcomb, W[m] Brayfords Land	700
Henderson, John Thackers Land	200
Hodgeon, Widd°	200
Henderson, Widd°	300
Henderson, W[m]	162
Housburrough [Hansborough?] Morris Harts Land	200
Hesterley, John	100
Hill, John	200
Horedon, W[m]	70
Harris, W[m]	250

	ACRES
Hart, Tho.	200
Hockley, Robt	100
Howard, Peter	300
Hardgrove, W^m	100
Herring, Arthur	50
Hickman, Thomas	700
Hunt, W^m	312
Hobs, W^m	250
Hicks, Rich^d	250
Howden, W^m	100
Howerton, Thomas	300
	8098
Holt, Joseph lives in Maryland	321
Haywood, Tho: in Glocester	600

J

Jones, Tho.	150
Jones, Robt.	200
Jeffreys, Rich^d	337
Jones, Robt. Junr	130
Johnson, James	200
Jones, W^m	900
	1917

K

King, John	150
Kallander, Tim^o	100
Kink, Anne	275
King, Edwd	200
Knowles, Dorothy q^r	150
King, Robt.	100
Kenneff, Darby	160
King, Daniell	200
	1335

L

	ACRES
Loveing, John	100
Lyon, Peter	250
Leigh, John	6200
Lumpkin, Robt.	400
Lee, W[m]	230
Lobb, W[m]	100
Lœoft, Rich[d]	320
Lewis, Zachary	350
Lumpkin, Jacob	950
Lewis, David	120
Lewis, John Esq[r]	10100
Lewis, Edw[d]	1400
Lemon, Eliz[b]	100
Lynes [Lyne?], Rebecca	405
Levingstone, John	600
Levingstone, Sam[ll]	100
Lawrence, Matthew	210
Letto, Arthur	475
Langford, John	150
Levingstone, Jn[o] Sowels Land	750
	23310
Leftwitch, Thomas in Essex	75

M

May, John	300
Mulick, George	100
Major, Jn[o]	250
Martin, John	300
Moore, Austines q[r]	200
May, Tho	300
Moore, Sam[ll]	100
Maddeson, Jn[o]	500
Morris, W[m]	130
Martin, Eliz[b]	400
Mackay, Sarah	177

	ACRES
May, John, Piggs Land	200
Major, Francis	700
Mansfield, Thomas	60
Morris, Henry	100
Major, John	400
Mels, Nich^{o}	200
Marcartee [McCarty?], Daniell	200
Morris, W^{m}	300
Mead, W^{m}	100
Matthews, Edwd	160
Martin, Cordelia Widd^{o}	200
	3377

N

Nelson, Henry	440
Neal, John	50
Nason, Joshua	200
Norman, W^{m}	300
Norris, James	100
	1090

O

Owen, Ralph	120
Ogilvie, W^{m}	300
Orrill, Lawrence	290
Orrill, W^{m}	500
Osbourn, Michaell	90
Overstreet, James q^{tr}	180
Ditto at home	50
	1530

P

Powell, Robt.	500
Prewitt, W^{m}	200
Paine, Bernard	130
Pomea, Francis	100
Philip, Charles	250

	ACRES
Pettitt, Thomas	548
Pollard, Robt.	500
Pollard, Wm.	100
Phinkett, Eliz[b]	500
Pemberton, Tho	115
Pickles, Tho	93
Potters, Francis Widd[o] Neals Land	100
Parks, James	200
Purchase, Geo. q[r]	580
Page, Jn[o]	100
Pritchett, David	225
Pigg, Henry	61
Page, John Jun[r]	300
Pigg, Edw[d]	250
Phelps, Tho	400
Pendleton, Philip	300
Pendleto [Pendleton], Henry	700
Pann, John	200
Payton's quar[tr]	500
Pigg, John	100
Pamplin, Robt.	150
Pryor, Christ[r]	175
Paulin, Eliz[b]	175
	7552
Pate, John in Gloucester	1000

Q

Quarles, James	300
Quarles, Dyley, Zacha. Lewis's Land	300
	600

R

Richard, Robt.	300
Rings Quarter	1000
Robinson, Daniel	100
Roger, Giles	475

	ACRES
Rice, Michaell	200
Richeson, Tho	460
Richeson, Elias	180
Read, Eliz[b]	550
Russell, Alexand[r] Wyatts Land	400
Robinson, Robt.	980
Rowe, John	100
Richards, W[m]	400
Richards, John	914
Richards, Oliver	250
Riddle, Tho. Reads Land	700
Roy, Rich[d]	1000
Ryley, Elias	200
Rollings, Peter	150
	8359
John the son of Robt. Robinson holdw'ch no body pays for	750

S

Sebrill, John	130
Stone, Mary	100
Smiths in Bristoll q[r]	2800
Stone, Jn[o]	295
Stubblefield, Geo. q[r]	400
Scandland, Denis	1470
Swinson, Rich[d]	170
Smith, Christ[o]	200
Smith, John, Cooper	273
Smith, Alexander	275
Seamour, W[m]	268
Sones, Tho	150
Shepard, Isaac	100
Southerland, W[m]	800
Shoot, Tho	100
Shepheard, Joseph	100
Shea, Patrick	200

	ACRES
Southerland, Dan[ll]	200
Smith, Nich[o] q[r]	700
Sanders, Nath[ll]	200
Smith, Jn[o] Sawyer	80
Shuckelford [Shackelford], Roger	250
Skelton [Shelton?], John	100
Snell, John	150
Simpio, Charles	100
Sawvey, John	113
Stringer, Mary T.	175
Spencer, Tho	300
Sykes, Stephen	50
Smith, Francis	100
Smith, Rich[d]	150
Sparks, John	200
Surly, Tho	100
Stapleton, Tho	200
Story, John	3000
Spencer, Katherine	600
	14599
Skippath [Skipwith], Sir W[m] is not paid for	700
Stark, Tho of London w'ch is not paid for	920
Stubblefield, Geo. in Glocest[r]	400
Smith, Austin in Glocester	4000
	800

T

Turner, Richard	200
Todd, Thomas quart[r]	2300
Taylor, James	4000
Toy, Thomas	175
Taylor, Dan[ll]	70
Thomas, Rowland	610
Tunstall, Tho	550

	ACRES
Todd, Rich[d]	1050
Towley, John	200
Trice, James	350
Tureman, Ignatius	100
Turner, Thomas	267
Thacker, C. C.	1000
	10872

U

Vaughan, Cornelius	500
Vize, Nath[ll]	100
Uttley, John	200

W

Wood, James	800
Wilkinson, John	100
Wright, Tho	300
Watkins, Wm	137
Wiltshire, Joseph	60
Watkins, Edw[d]	98
Watkins, Philip	203
White, Thomas	200
Walker, John	6000
Wilson, Benj. Wyats Land	420
Wyat, Rich[d]	1843
Walton, Thomas	200
Wyat, John	530
Withby, Thomas	50
Williams, Thomas	200
Watts, Tho.	235
Ward, Sam[ll]	160
Watkins, Benj.	60
Watkins, Tho: jun[r]	125
Williams, Eliz[b]	900
Waldin, Sam[ll]	275
Ware, Edw[d]	735
William, John	125

	ACRES
Ware, Valentine	487
Willbourn, Tho.	250
Wildbore, Wm	100
Ware, Nicho	718
White, Jerimiah	200
Whorein, John	200
Wise, Richd quartr	209
Walker, John Johnsons Land	1000
	16920

Wadlington [Waklington], Paul not paid for being	150

Y

York, Matthew	100

A	2300
B	22535
C	12235
D	5618
E	3020
F	4355
G	6100
H	8098
J	1917
K	1335
L	23310
M	5377
N	1090
O	1530
P	7552
Q	600
R	8359
S	14599
T	10872
U	800

	ACRES
W	16920
Y	100
	158522
Lands returned not pd for	
C	1000
F	300
H	920
L	75
P	1000
R	750
S	6020
W	150
	10215

(To be continued)

VIRGINIA QUIT RENT ROLLS, 1704

Gloucester Rent Roll

A Rent Roll in Petso [Petsworth] Parish.

	ACRES
Capt. David Alexander	1050
James Amis	250
Wm. Armistead	430
John Acre	100
Ralph Baker	150
Martha Brooken [Brooking?]	600
Thomas Buckner	850
Sam[ll] Bernard	550
Wm. Barnard [Bernard]	810
Rich[d] Bailey	600
Mary Booker	100
Thomas Cook	350
Wm. Crymes	400
Jno. Cobson	100
Robt. Carter	1102
Wm. Collone	400
Hannah Camell	100
Benja. Clements	400
Jno. Clarke	100
Wm. Cook	135
Jno. Coleman	200
Jno. Day	400
Jerim Darnell	150
Jn[o] Darnell	60
James Dudley	780

	ACRES
Richd Dudley	400
Thomas Dudley	200
Thomas Dixon	300
Jno Drument	80
Samll Fowler	150
Wm. Fleming	600
Wido Forginson	150
Wm. Fockner	180
Jno Grymes	1400
Susannah Grinley	200
Darcas Green	400
Jno Grout	300
Jno Harper	100
Wm. Howard	300
Richd Hubard	100
Wm. Hansford	500
Jno Hanes	150
Alexander How	120
Richd Hill	70
Robt Hall	100
Richd Hull	250
Samll Hawes	200
Stephen Johnson	150
Wm Jones for Northington	530
Glebe Land	127
Jno Kingson	400
Cap. Edward Lewis	1000
Richd Lee Esqr	1140
Nicho Lewis orphen	350
Wm. Milner	900
Richd Miner	250
Edwd Musgrove	100
	21364
Hayes an Orphan	60
Elizb Mastin	360
Jno Mackwilliams	50

	ACRES
Robt. Nettles	300
Wm. Norman	150
Isaac Oliver	100
Dorothy Oliver	130
Jn° Pritchett	850
Jn° Pate	1100
Richd Price	600
Mad^m Porteus	500
Mad^m Page	550
Robt. Porteus	892
Guy Parish	100
Wm. Roane	500
James Reynolds	200
George Robinson	300
John Royston	570
Thomas Read	2000
Wm. Richards in Pamunkey	150
Jn° Shackelford	280
Edward Symons	500
Nich° Smith	280
John Stubs	300
Thomas Simpson	280
John Smith	1300
Augustin Smith	200
Augustin Smith, Junr	500
Wm. Stanbridge	159
Wm. Thornton Senr	525
Wm. Thornton Junr	800
Wm. Thurston	200
Wm. Upshaw	490
Francis Wisdom	150
Thomas West	112
Thomas Whiting	450
George Williams	100
Conquest Wyatt	2200
Seth Wickins	50
Walter Waters	200

	ACRES
Jane Wortham	60
Robt. Yard	450
Robt. Hall	250
Wm. Whittmore Desarted	150
Wm. Parsons Orphan	100
Edw[d] Stephens	70
John Kelly Orphan	150
	19768
	21364
	41132

Tho Neale

Gloucester Rent Roll

A Rent Roll in Kingston Parish.

Rose Curtis	400
Robt. Peyton	680
Rich[d] Perrott	35
Henry Preston	1500
Sarah Green	200
Robt. Cully	200
Thomas Hayes	140
Andrew Bell	128
Humphrey Toy	1100
Anne Aldred	350
Dunkin Bahannah [Bohannon?]	113½
Rich[d] Hunley	50
Capt. Gayle	164
Math Gayle, Jun[r]	250
James Hundley	100
John Hundley	130
Philip Hundley	660
Tho Cray	200

	ACRES
Hen. Knight	240
John Williams	50
Rich[d] Beard	380
Timothy Hundley	300
Thomas Bedford	50
Jn[o] Floyd	250
John Bohannah	113½
Capt. Armistead	3675
Christopher Dixon	300
Robt. Bristow Esq[r]	900
Edw[d] Gowing	100
Tho. Ryland	272
John Nevill	100
Lawrence Parrott	340
Wm. Brooks	720
Joseph Bohannah	148
Wm. Hampton	348
Widd[o] Green	150
Capt. Dudley	650
Capt. Knowles	575
Capt. Tho: Todd	775
Wm. Beard	100
Wm. Tompkins	100
Henry Bolton	50
Wm. Eliott	1060
Humphrey Tompkins	100
Daniel Hunter	200
Thomas Peyton	684
Rich[d] Dudley	350
James Ransom jun[r]	310
Tho Peters	30
Robt. Elliott	1247
Mich: Parriott	100
Jn[o] Meachen Jun[r]	600
Caleb Linsey	140
Alexander Ofield	23
Mark Thomas	300

	ACRES
Jn° Garnet	250
Wm. Plumer	510
Wm. Brumley	750
Wm. Credle	50
Charles Jones	225
Robt. Sadler	50
Edwd Sadler	20
Geo. Roberts	170
	24256
Richd Longest	600
Tho Fliping	300
Charles Watters	100
Wm. Gundry	200
Thomas Kemp	200
Tho Allaman	842
Coll Kemp	200
Ralph Shipley	430
George Turner	50
Coll James Ransom	1400
Thomas Putman	300
Richd Marchant	180
Widd° Sinoh	300
Christopher Rispus	200
Benj. Read	550
Walter Keble	550
Joseph Brooks	500
Capt. Gevin	1100
Lindseys Land	390
Thomas Garwood	77
John Callis	1000
Tho Miggs	100
Richd Glascock	500
Jn° Lylley	584
Geo. Billups	1200
Robt. Singleton	650
James Foster	225

	ACRES
John Andrews	50
Thomas Rice	34
John Martin	200
Capt. Smith	550
Capt. Sterling	1100
John Diggs	1200
Wm. Howlett	300
Jn° Miller	100
Andrew Ripley	40
Francis Jarvis	400
Wm. Armistead	300
John Banister	650
Tho: Plumer	400
Isaac Plumer	200
James Taylor	50
Edw[d] Borum	360
Widd° Davis	300
Sam: Singleton	300
Wm. Morgan, Sen[r]	50
Wm. Morgan, jun[r]	200
John Bacon	825
Henry Singleton	600
John Edwards	534
Patrick Berry	250
Anne Forrest	500
	22281
	24256
	46537

Ambrose Dudley
1705

(To be continued)

VIRGINIA QUIT RENT ROLLS, 1704

Gloucester Rent Roll

A Rent Role in Ware Parish.

	ACRES
Thomas Poole	600
Anne Croxson	300
Thomas Purnell	163
Nicholas Pamplin	210
Simon Stublefield	200
Jno. Price	600
Sam[ll] Dawson	350
Sam[ll] Vadrey	400
Nathan. Burwell	600
John Dawson	780
Tho: Bacop	200
Robt. Frances	400
Walter Greswell	50
Tho Read	400
James Shackelford	035
Robt. Freeman	135
Jno. Marinex	100
Isaac Valine	100
Tho: Haywood	70
Hugh Marinex	50
Leonard Ambrose	200
Philip Grady	200
Capt. Wm. Debnam	1250
James Burton	100
Jno. Spinks	300
Wm. Hurst	200
Sarah More	67

	ACRES
John Ray	100
Robt. Pryor	300
Christ° Greenaway	270
Capt. Throgmorton	500
James Clark	250
Philip Cooper	200
Jno. Kindrick	100
Sam[ll] Simons	120
Wm. Radford	200
John Robins	900
Alice Bates	200
Jno. Easter	350
James Davison	100
Robt. Morrin	200
Anne Bray	100
Grace Easter	200
Sampson Darrell	300
Capt. Francis Willis	3000
Thomas Powell	460
Wm. Holland	300
Capt. Cook	1500
Giles Cook	140
Wm. Jones	120
Tho Colles	100
Philip Smith	700
Tho: Cheesman	650
Geo: More	40
James Morris	250
	16710
Abraham Iverson Senr.	1000
Robert Bristow Esqr.	2050
Anthony Gregory	700
Rich[d] Bailey	800
Wm. Foulcher	100
Widd° Jeffes	216
Rich[d] Dudley Junr.	300

	ACRES
John Buckner	900
Thomas Todd	884
John & Peter Waterfield	143
Henry Whiting	800
Mad[m] Whiting	950
Jn. Goodson	150
Wm. Morris	350
Mary Lassells	200
Peter Ransone	220
Charles Waters	200
Dorothy Kertch	220
Dorothy Boswell	1600
Rich[d] Cretendon [Crittenden]	280
Eliz[b] Anniers	250
Eliz[b] Snelling	250
Joseph Boswell	230
John Bullard	100
Anthony Elliot	100
Wm. Armistead	100
Peter Kemp	650
Maj[r] Peter Beverley	800
Ditto P Tillids Lands	150
Dudley Jolley	100
Robt. Couch	100
	14893
	16710
	31603

Gloucester Rent Roll

A Rent Roll in Abbington Parish.

Mr. Guy Smith	30
James Cary	50

	ACRES
Wm. Sawyer	150
Edw[d] Cary	100
Robt. Barlow	62
Tho: Cleaver Sworne	200
Edw[r] Stevens	80
Henry Stevens	60
Chillion White	100
Jeremiah Holt	350
of Ditto for ye Widd[o] Babb	150
Robt. Yarbborrow	100
Robt. Starkey	100
Henry Seaton	170
Hugh Howard	200
Capt. Booker	1000
Jno. Stoakes	300
Jno. Dobson	400
Wm. Dobson	950
Edm[d] Dobson	350
Hugh Allen	1250
George Jackson	117
Jno. Teagle	30
Widd[o] Jones	45
Mary Thomas	100
Thomas Seawell	200
Benj. Lane	50
Valentine Lane	80
Jeffry Garves	33
Thomas Coleman	250
Johanna Austin	40
Maj[r] Burwell	3300
Jno. Satterwight	50
Jeremiah Holt Junr.	150
Charles Stevens	75
Rich[d] Roberts for wife	300
Jno. Sadler	125
James Steavens	100
Susannah Stubbs	300

	ACRES
Rich[d] Foster	150
Henry Mitchell	50
Nathan[ll] Russell	550
Eliz[b] Richardson	500
Wm. Camp	175
James Row	300
John Butler	100
John Smith Esqr.	2000
Ditto for Robt. Bryon	400
Capt. Blackbourne	550
Peter Richeson	250
Benj. Clements	500
Thomas Graves	70
Robt. Page	175
Joseph More	150
	17417
Richard Dixon	200
Eliz[b] Turner	150
Owen Grathmee [Gwathmey]	250
Rich[d] Woodfolk	125
Jn. Waters	50
Wm. Hilliard	80
Rich[d] Heywood	100
Mary Hemingway	150
Wm. Kemp	75
Robt. Francis	104
Joshua Broadbent	200
Joseph Coleman	200
Grustam Clent	100
Philip Grady	150
Jno. Hall	15
Tho: Walker	300
Jno. Mixon	400
Tho: Sanders	450
Wm. Smith for Kittson	50
John Banister	2750

		ACRES
Mad[m] Mary Page		3000
Jno. Lewis Esqr.		2000
		11009
		17417
		28426
	Ware	31603
	Petso	41132
	Kinston	46537
		147698

(To be continued)

VIRGINIA QUIT RENT ROLLS, 1704

A Perfect Role of the Land in Middlesex County
Anno Dom. 1704

	ACRES
Richard Atwood	100
Richard Allen	150
Tho Blewford	100
Mr. Blaiss	300
John Bristow	140
Robt. Blackley	100
Coll. Corbin	2260
Coll. Carter	1150
John Cheedle	50
Wm. Carter	170
Widd[o] Chaney	800
Nath. Cranke	50
Tho. Dyatt	200
John Dowie	75
Wm. Daniell	150
Robt. Daniell	225
Henry Freeman	200
John Goodrick	50
Geo. Goodloe	50
Geo. Guest	50
Rich[d] Gabriell	30
Wm. Finley	50
Wm. Gardner	100
Robt. George	180
David George	150

	ACRES
Widd° Hazellwood	200
John Hoare	100
Rich[d] Reynolds	50
Jno. Southerne	100
Rich[d] Shurly	200
Tho. Stapleton	200
Wm. Southworth	50
Wm. Jones	300
Evan Jones	50
Esqr. Wormeley Estate	5200
Wm. Churchill	1950
Jacob Briston	100
Jno. Pace	200
John Logie	300
John Price	519
Henry Perrott	1100
Rich[d] Kemp	1100
Tho. Kidd	250
Francis Weeks	225
Widd° Weekes	225
Henry Webb	100
Tho. Wood	70
Robt. Williamson	200
Tho. Lee	100
Edm[d] Mickleburrough	200
Valentine Mayo	100
	20069
Wm. Montague	500
Garrett Minor	225
Marvill Mosseley	225
Joseph Mitcham	75
Minie Minor	225
Humphrey Jones	150
Jno. North	200
Henry Tugill	200

	ACRES
Henry Thacker	1875
Thomas Fozeley	500
Charles Moderas	100
Wm. Mullins	150
John Smith	700
James Smith	400
Harry Beverley	1000
George Wortham	400
Capt. Grimes	900
Sarah Mickleburrough	1000
Christ° Robinson	4000
John Vilson	100
James Daniell	150
James Curtis	300
Tho Cranke	54
Phil Calvert	200
John Hipkins	100
Richd Daniell	210
Geo. Blake	100
Edwd Blade	100
Pat Mammon	100
Alexander Murray	250
Poplar Smith	550
Oliver Seager	380
Edwd. Gobbee	90
Henry Barnes	200
John Davis	100
Paul Thilman	300
Hugh Watts	80
Edwd Clark	300
Charles Williams	100
Edwin Thacker Estate	2500
Thomas Dudly	200
Thomas Malkham	200
Richd Paffitt	200
Tho. Stiff	100

	ACRES
Peter Bromell	100
Tho. Blakey	100
John Robinson	1350
Roger Jones	100
John Nicholls	200
George Berwick	100
Widd° Hurford	50
	21189
Widd° Hackney	300
Wm. Kilbee	600
Ezekiah Rhodes	300
John Handiford	100
John Miller	200
Wm. Scarborow	200
Wm. Herne	75
Robt. Dudley	300
Widd° Mason	100
Peter Chilton	100
Francis Dobson	150
James Dudley	200
Capt. Berkley	750
Wm. Sutton	150
Sr. Wm. Skipwith	350
Coll. Kemp	900
Wm. Barbee	150
Wm. Wallis	300
Adam Curtis	200
Capt. Wm. Armistead	2325
	7750
	22069
	21189
	49008

(To be continued)

VIRGINIA QUIT RENT ROLLS, 1704

A True and Perfect Rent Roll of all the Lands held in Essex County this present year 1704.

	ACRES
Abbott, Wm.	150
Andrews, Geo.	200
Adcock, Edwd.	230
Adcock, Henry	250
Acres, James	100
Arving, Wm.	100
Allen, Erasmus	100
Allen, Wm.	100
Ayres, Wm.	200
Acres, Wm.	200
	1630

Boulwar, James	800
Bendall, John	135
Butler, John	125
Bowers, Arthur	600
Boulwar, James	200
Beesley, Wm.	100
Barron, Andrew	50
Bartlett, Tho.	100
Brown, Buskinhan [Buckingham]	400
Beeswell, Robt.	100
Beeswell, Robt., Junr.	150
Brown, Wm.	420
Brown, Charles	1000
Buckner, Rich'd.	1200

	ACRES
Buckner, Tho.	2000
Brice, Henry	400
Bourn, Jno.	100
Beverley, Harry	1000
Battail, John	1100
Boulwar, John	50
Booth, Widdo.	800
Butler, Jno.	100
Butcher, Jno.	150
Bendrey, Widdo.	700
Bird, Widdo.	100
Beckham, Symon	100
Brutnall, Rich'd.	100
Brook, Robt.	400
Ball, Jno.	150
Brooks, James	100
Billington, Mary	200
Brooks, Peter	275
Bowman, Peter	400
Brooks, Robt.	150
Brasur, Jno.	300
Brush, Rich'd.	250
Baker, Henry	350
Bradburn, Rich'd.	100
Brown, Francis	150
Brown, Danll., Junr.	150
Byron, Henry	100
Burnett, Tho., junr.	1000
Baughan, James, Senr.	600
Baughan, James	150
Baughan, Henry	100
Brown, Danll., Senr.	450
Brown, Tho.	50
Blackeston, Argail [Argall]	200
Burnett, John	365
Burnett, Tho., Junr.	130
Bailer [Baylor], Jno.	800

	ACRES
Brukins, Qtr.	250
Bell, Thomas	100
	19980
Condute, Nathn.	20
Cary, Hugh	50
Connoly, Edw.	200
Cogwell, Frederick	250
Copland, Nicho.	300
Cattlett, Jno.	1800
Coventon [Covington], Rich'd.	1000
Cook, John	112
Chew, Larkin	300
Crow, Tho.	300
Covington, Wm.	400
Cheney, John	200
Cole, Wm.	200
Cheney, Wm.	700
Corbin, Tho., qr.	440
Cockin, Tho.	120
Coates, Samll.	300
Cooper, Rich'd.	100
Cooper, Tho.	100
Copland, Jno.	175
Crow, Jno.	440
Chew, Larkin	550
Cooper, Wm.	50
Compton, Wm.	50
Cox, Wm.	500
Callaway, Jos.	87
Coleman, Robt.	450
Cobnall, Symon	100
Chamberlain, Leond.	350
	9764

	ACRES
Daniell, James	100
Devillard, Jacob	80
David, Tho.	150
Dudding, Andrew	230
Davis, Evans	150
Dobbins, Danll.	550
Dressell, Timo.	175
Daughty, John	200
Dyer, Wm.	100
Daingerfield, Jno.	270
Daingerfield, Wm.	270
Dunn, Wm.	220
Dyer, Jeffrey	100
Day, Rich'd.	100
Dicks, Thomas	500
	12959

Evans, Rice	200
Edmondson, James	500
Elliott, Alice	75
Evitt, Tho.	100
Edmondson, Tho.	700
Flowers, Isaac	250
Faulkner, Nicho.	100
Farrell, Charles	50
Franklin, Nicho.	130
Foster, Robt.	200
Foster, Jno.	200
Fisher, Jonathan	250
Fisher, Benj.	150
Frank, Tho.	175
Fullerton, James	400
Fossett, Wm.	100
Farguson, Jno.	150
Faulkner, Edw.	530
	17219

	ACRES
Green, George	300
Gray, Abner	350
Goulding, Wm.	200
Gannock, Wm.	2100
Gaines, Barnard [Bernard]	450
Griffin, Tho.	200
Gibson, Jonathan	700
Grigson, Tho.	300
Gouldman, Francis	300
Goulding, John	200
Goulding, Edwd.	380
Good, Rich'd.	200
Garnett, John	150
Glover, John	100
Hawkins, John	1066
Hinshaw, Samll.	200
Hutson, Tho:	100
Harrison, James	400
Harrison, Andrew	300
Hilliard, Thomas	100
Harper, Wm.	240
Harman, Henry	75
Hoult, Rich'd.	100
Humphrie, Joe	100
Hail [Hale?], Jno.	900
Harper, John	748
Harper, Tho.	350
Hould, David	100
Hudson, Wm.	100
Hinds, Thomas	100
Howerton, Thomas	175
Hodges, Arth.	100
Hows, Qurt.	300
Harwood, Peter	125
Harway [Harwar], Tho.	1000
Hudson, Tho.	50

	ACRES
Hudson, Wm.	300
Hill, Leond.	300
Harwar, Samll.	300
Jamison, David	250
Jones, Wm.	165
Jenkins, David	50
Jewell, Tho.	100
Johnson, Widdo.	300
Jones, Walter	100
Johnson, Rich'd.	50
Johnson, Wm.	650
Jones, John	300
Jones, Rich'd.	350
Jenkins, John	93
Jones, Wm.	300
Journey, Wm.	243
Johnson, Thomas	500
Jones, Rice	500
Key, Robt.	209
Kerby, Henry	60
	17779
Landrum, John	300
Landrum, James	100
Long, Rich'd.	300
Lomax, John	2000
Loyd, George	800
Lawson, Claudy	100
Little, Abraham	60
Lacy, John	100
Law, John	300
Lattaine [Latane], Lewis	250
Leveritt, Robt.	100

	ACRES
Micou, Paul	150
Martin, John	400
Morgan, John	100
Miller, John	150
Medor, Tho.	300
Moseley, Benj.	1100
Mottley, John	100
Morris, John	200
Moss, Robt.	180
Merritt, Tho.	124
Merritt, John	100
Munday, Tho.	500
Mogson, David	400
Mill, Jno.	200
Mosseley, Robt.	100
Mayfield, Robt.	100
Matthews, Rich'd.	250
Mosseley, Edw.	550
Merriweather, Francis	3200
Moore, Fran.	175
Michaell, Jno.	200
Merriweather, Tho.	2100
Mefflin, Zack	400
Medor, John	100
Merse, John	400
Matthews, Benj.	200
Mountegue [Montague], Wm.	850
Newbury, Nathl.	200
Nixon, Henry	500
North, Wm.	900
Newton, Nich.	100
Nightingall, John	200
Osman, John	300
Presser [Prosser], John	450
Poe, Samll.	800

	ACRES
Pley, Widdo.	800
Parker, Jno.	250
Pitts, Jno.	200
Piskell, Jno.	300
Pain, Jno.	135
Price, Wm.	100
Peteras, Tho.	200
Powell, Honor	72
Powell, Wm.	72
Powell, Place	72
Powell, Tho.	72
	28832
Payne, Widdow	1000
Perkins, Henry	300
Prichett, Roger	167
Paggett, Edmd.	700
Price, John	1100
Pickett, John	800
Perry, Samll.	225
Price, Wm.	100
Quarter Xpher Robinson	2200
Quarter Tho: Corbin	4000
Quart. Robt. Thomas	200
Quart. John Hay	1000
Quart. Wm. Smith	3000
Quart. Gawen Corbin	2000
Quart. Peter Ranson	300
Quart. David Gwin	950
Quart. Wm. Upshaw	1000
Quart. Leversons	600
Quart. Tho. Todd	550
Ridgdall, John	300
Ramsey, Tho.	550

	ACRES
Rowze, Ralph	610
Rucker, Peter	500
Rowze, Edwd.	300
Royster, John	1000
Roberts, Edwd.	300
Rebs, Henry	400
Reeves, Joseph	200
Reeves, James	200
Roberts, John	50
Richardson, Robt.	200
Reynolds, James Senr.	500
Reynolds, James	500
Ranson, Peter	1200
Strange, Jno.	100
Stepp, Abrm.	390
Samll. Anthy.	300
Sail [Sale], Cornelius	73
Salmon, John	60
Spiors, Jno.	160
Smith, Wm.	150
Stokes, Rich'd.	500
Smith, Charles	3000
Sullenger, Peter	400
Sales [Sale], Widdo.	1150
Shipley, Jno.	200
Spearman, Job	300
Smith, Francis	500
Stallard, Samll.	100
Ship, Jos.	350
Short, Tho.	150
Scott, Wm.	1100
Stogell, Jno.	100
Stephens, Jno.	100
Slaughter, Phebe	352
Smith, Jno.	75
Smith, Jonas	100

	ACRES
Sanders, John	300
Stanton, Jno.	95
	31427
Shepherd, Jeremiah	300
Smith, Tho.	50
Shackelford, Francis	300
Strashley, Tho.	200
Staners, Tho.	500
Snead, Tho.	950
Shackelford, Henry	50
Thorp, Widdo	400
Tinsley, Tho.	111
Thackett, Samll.	110
Tomlin, Widdo.	400
Taliaferro, Francis	1300
Thornton, Fran.	700
Tomlin, Wm.	1600
Thomas, John	100
Taliaferro, Charles	300
Thomas, Wm.	200
Taliaferro, John	2000
Turner, George	200
Tomlin, Wm.	950
Trible, Peter	100
Taylor, Rich'd.	650
Tilley, Matthew	200
Vanters [Vauter], Bartho	400
Virget, Job	50
Vincent, Vaus	450
Wakeland, Wm.	100
Wood, Tho.	50
Winslow, Tho.	150

	ACRES
Winslow, Henry	100
Williams, John	450
Williams, Wm.	100
Wilson, David	50
Wilton, Rich'd.	150
Wheeden, Edwd.	50
Ward, Widdo	200
Whitehorn, Widdo	260
Wms. Emanuell	100
Watkins, Thomas	400
Waters, John	150
Webb, James	200
Webb, John	200
Wead, Wm.	200
Wood, Tho.	300
Williamson, Tho.	100
Williamson, Wm.	100
Williamson, John	100
Webb, Robert	375
Webb, Isaac	200
Woodnatt, Henry	300
Wagener, John	400
Ward, George	350
Wheeler, Tho.	250
Young, Wm.	1000
Young, Giles	100
	18996
Muscoe, Salvator	100
Moody, John	150
Maguffe, John	100
Brookins [Brooking's], Quart.	250
Smith, Jno. Quart.	1000
Newton, Henry	100
Newton, Henry	175

	ACRES
Nowell, Dall	400
Newell, Widdo	300
Garrett, Tho.	1000
Gould, Price	200
Green, Samll.	97
Gouldman, Fran.	300
Gawdin, Wm.	100
Grimmall, Wm.	100
Gaitwood, John	400
Games, John	475
Samll. Thompson	1000
	6247
	19980
	17219
	17779
	28832
	31427
	18996
The Totall is	140580

Lands held in the above said County the Rents not paid and held by the Severall Gentlemen as followeth, viz: John Smith Esqr. of Gloucester County received 800
Wm. Buckner of Gloucester by information 1500
Jno.Lightfoot Esqr. New Kent County 900
Jno. Bridgegate in Engd. 700
Rich'd. Wyatt & John Pettus of King & Queen Cty. 800
Wm. Berry of Richmond County 400
Richard Covington.

(To be continued)

VIRGINIA QUIT RENT ROLLS, 1704

Accomac Rent Roll

A

	ACRES
Alexander Richards	150
Arthur Upshot [Upshur]	2020
Antho: West	700
Ann Simkins	1000
Arthur Donas	100
Arnoll Harrison	630
Alex. Harrison	400
Alex. Bagwell	413
Anne Chase	200
Arthur fframe	500
Alexdr. West	550
Abraham Lambedson	100
Alex. Benstone	270
Anne Blake, Widdo.	120
Anne Bruce	180
Mr. Arcado Wilburn	1854
	9187

B

Burnell Niblett	100
Majr. Bennie[?] Scarbrough	521
	621

C

Cornelius Hermon	321
Christo. Stokly	200
Charles Scarbrough	1000
Charles Leatherbury	1100
Charles Bally	959½
Charles Pywell	150
Chauchhil Darby	125
Charles Evill [Ewell]	550
Charles Champison	270
Christo. Hodey	500
Cornelius Lofton	166
Charles Stockley	170
Charles Taylor	580
Catherine Gland	217
	6312½

D

Dorman Derby	225
Danell Derby, senr.	300
Dorothy Littlehouse	250
David Watson	200
Delight Shield	300
Daniel Derby Jr.	125
Daniel Harwood	100
Denis More	200
Daniel Gore	3976
	5676

E

Coll. Edmund Scarbrough	2000
Edwd. Hitchins	170
Edwd. Turner	750

Edwd. Killam [Kellam]	720
Edmd. Allen	200
Edwd. Bagwell for Col. Wm. Custis	200
Edmd. Jones	800
Elizb. Tinley	200
Edwd. Taylor	300
Edmd. Tatham	200
Edmd. Bally	800
Edm. Ayres	1000
Edwd. Miles	413
Elizb. Mellchop	210
Edmd. Bell	101
Edwd. More	500
Edwd. Gunter	600
Edwd. Brotherton	600
Elias Blake	430
Edwd. Robins	782
Edwd. Bally	300
Elias Taylor	1500
Elizb. Wharton	200
Mrs. Elizb. Scarbrough	4205
	17181

F

Mr. Francis Mackenny [Mackemie]	5109
Francis Robts	200
Francis Wainhouse	700
Francis Crofton	200
Francis Young	100
Tinley Mack Wm. [McWilliam]	100
Francis Ayres	300
Francis Jester	200
Francis Benstone	400
Francis Wharton	600
	7909

G

Geo: Anthony	100
Geo: Hastup	300
Coll. Geo Nicho. Hack	2700
Capt. Geo: Parker	2609
Gercis Bagally	700
Garrart Hutchins	170
Geo Parker, Sea Side	1200
Griffin Savage	650
Geo Middleton Senr.	588
Geo Trent	400
Geo Pounce	400
Geo Middleton, Junr.	150
Geo Johnson	200
Capt. Geo Hope	900
	11067

H

Henry Armtrading	175
Henry Chance	445
Henry Selman	180
Henry Ubankes [Eubank]	400
Henry Lurton	363
Henry Stokes	208
Henry Custis	774
Henry Bagwell	412
Henry Read	350
Henry Ayres	250
Hill Drummond	483
Henry Toules [Towles]	300
Henry Hickman	135
Henry Gibbons	250
Henry Truett	240
	4965

J

John Tounson	200
Joseph Stockley	664
Jno. Read	200
Jno Blake	310
Joseph Ames	375
Joseph Clark	200
Jno. Fisher	200
James Gray	900
Jno. Huffington	240
Jn. Legatt	300
James Lary	100
James Longoe	200
Jno. Merrey	350
Jno. Milbey	500
Jno. Pratt	50
Jno. Revell	1450
Jno. Road	110
Jno. Rowles	650
Jno. Savage, Senr.	350
Jno. Charles	480
Jno. Willis, Senr.	430
Jno. Willis, Junr.	350
James Fairfax	900
Joseph Milby	830
John West, Junr.	500
Jno. Jenkins	400
Jonathan James	150
John Rodgers	100
Jno. Collins	100
Jno. Sincocke	125
Jno Metcalfe	
Isaac Metcalfe	600
and Saml. Metcalfe	
Joseph Touser	200

Jno. Stanton	200
Jno. Bally	1000
	13715
Jno. Melson	180
Jno. Bernes, Senr.	657
Jno. Littletone	200
John Nock	300
Jno. Kelly	100
Jacob Morris	200
Jno. Morris	640
Jono. Aylworth	200
James Davis	1000
Jno. Parkes	200
Jno. Evans	200
Jno. Hues	100
Jno. Blocksom	700
Jno. Abbott	1170
Jno. Arew	234
Jno. Grey	116
Jno. Baker	400
Jno. Wharton	150
James Taylor	100
Jno. Glading	207
Jno. Loft Land	167
James Smith	756
Majr. Jno. Robins	2700
Jno. Collins for Asban	1666
James Walker	525
Jno. Whetton	90
Jno. Marshall	1666
Jono. Owen	230
Jacob Wagaman	150
Capt. John Broadhurst	1100
Jno. Dyer	200
Mr. John Watts	2450
Jno. Booth	300

John Bradford	364
Ingold Cobb	150
Jno. Griffin	150
Jno. Mitchell	400
John Parker	970
James Alexander	1250
Jno. Burock	200
James Sterfarar	50
Jno. Perry	217
Jno. Drummond	1550
Jno. Carter on Fox Island	203
Jno. Warington	100
Jno. Bagwell	465
Jno. Wise, Senr.	800
Jno. Wise, Junr.	400
Jno. Dix	500
Isaac Dix	500
Jno. Hickman	454
Jno. Onians	200
Coll. Jno. Custis Esqr.	5950
John Coslin	50
	46692

M

Michaell Recetts	300
Mrs. Mattilda West	3600
Marke Evell [Ewell]	250
Mary Wright	200
	4350

N

Nicholas Mellchops	285
Nathaniell Williams	64
Nathaniell Rattcliff	300
	649

(To be continued)

Accomac County, Cont'd

O

Owen Collonell	500
Overton Mack Williams	200
Obedience Pettman	115
	815

P

Peter Major	113
Philip Parker	150
Peter Rogers	167
Perry Leatherbury	1750
Peter Turlington	79
Peter Ease	250
Philip Fisher	433
Peter Chawell	250
	3192

R

Robt. Bell	650
Richd. Bally Senr.	2100
Richd. Bally Junr.	180
Richd. Garrison	468
Roules Major	157
Rowland Savage Senr.	950
Robt. Taylor	95
Richd. Rodgers	450
Richd. Killam [Kellam]	1900
Robt. Wattson	425
Richd. Jones	500

Robt. Hutchinson	934
Reynold Badger	150
Robt. West	400
Richd. Cuttler	450
Robt. Cole	125
Richd. Drummond	600
Robt. Stocomb	300
Robt. Norton	1050
Richd. Grindall	350
Roger Hickman	135
Robt. Lewis	200
Rodger Abbott	450
Richard Hill	350
Ralph Justice	1050
Richd. Hinman	1800
Robt. Davis	384
Ragnall Ayres	300
Roger Miles	200
Richd. Bundike	773
Richd. Kittson	1300
Robt. Bally	100
Richd. Starlin	150
Richd. Flowers	200
Richd. Price	100
Robt. Pitts	2300
Robt. Adkins	200
Rebeckha Benstone	270
Richd. Hillayres	300
	22816

S

Samuell Benstone	300
Sarah Beach	300
Sillvanus Cole	250
Syman Sosque	325
South. Littleton['s] widdo.	2870
Stephen Woltham	244

Steph. Warrington	400
Symon Mitchell	300
Stephen Drummond	300
Selby Harrison	50
Sollomon Evell [Ewell]	125
Samll. Young	50
Sarah Royley	150
Sebastian Dellistations, Senr.	500
Sebastian Dellistations, Junr.	400
Skinner Wollope	2485
Samll. Sandford	3250
Sebastian Silverthorn	150
Symon Smith	200
Sarah Coe	900
Samll. Taylor	1232
Sarah Evins	150
Sebastian Croper [Cropper]	600
Samll. Jester	200

T

Tho Burton	600
Tho Bud	500
Tho Bowles	300
Tho Clark	100
Tho Middleton	350
Tho Stringer	600
Tho Haule	500
Tho Taylor	100
Tho Toches	300
Tho Bagwell	465
Madm. Tabitha Hill	3600
Tho Rose	7
Tho Webb	50
Tho Savage	450
Tho Jones	100
Tho Scott	100
Tho Reyley	225
Tho Ternall	150

Tho Simpson	520
Tho Coper	711
Tho Miles	202
Thomas Bonwell	300
Tho Bell, Senr.	100
Tho Bell, Junr.	100
Tho Touson, Kiquotan	800
Tho Stockley	363
Tho Jester	100
Tho Smith	300
Thomas Crippen	648
Tho Wilkinson	50
Tho Jenkinson	374
Tho Moore	166
Tho Allen	700
Tho Smith, Savannah*	200
Tho Perry	232
Tho Tonnson	400
Tho Smith, Gingateague	693
Liuet. Coll. Robinson	600
	155956

* This was the name of a part of Accomac county.

W

Wm. Robins	200
Wm. Patterson	200
Wm. Bevins	400
Wm. Matthews	400
Wm. Shepherd	200
Wm. Whett	400
Winfred Woodland	333
Wm. Andrews	300
Wm. Custis	1500
Wm. Darby	83
Wm. Fletcher	200
Wm. Killam	450
Wm. Lingoe	300

Wm. Major	130
Wm. Meeres	150
Wm. Nock, Senr.	800
Wm. Savage	150
Wm. Waite	110
Wm. Sill	200
Wm. Waite Junr.	600
Wm. Bradford	3500
Wm. Rogers	200
Wm. Wise	400
Wm. Finney	800
Wm. Consalvins	100
Wm. Phillips	200
Wm. Parker	362
Wm. Cole	375
Wm. Merill	150
Wm. Johnson	150
Wm. Lewis	150
Walter Hages	130
Wm. Chance	450
Wm. Milby	250
Wm. Nicholson	600
Wm. Burton	500
Wm. Willet	842
Wm. Hudson	270
Wm. Lewis	300
Wm. Young	144
Wm. Leichfield	154
Wm. Bunting	150
Wm. Nock, Junr.	400
Wm. Lucas	300
Mary Mellichop	498
Wm. Daniell	200
Wm. Silverthorn	160
Wm. Garman	475
Wm. White	600
Wm. Broadwater	500

Wm. Taylor	100
Wm. Williamson	600
Wm. Brittingham	538
Wm. Benstone Junr.	270
Wm. Dickson for Mr. Littleton	1050
Wm. Waite Senr.	225
Wm. Taylor	1400
	24599

A	9187
B	621
C	6312½
D	5676
E	17181
F	7090
G	11067
H	4965
J	46692
K	4350
N	645
O	815
P	3192
R	22816
S	15731
T	15956
W	24599
	196899½

Added to this Rent Roll the following lands of wch. the Qt. Rents may possibly be recovered tho the Owners live out of the County viz:

Jonas Jackson	500
Robt. Andrews	500
Joseph Morris	200

Robt. Meres	200
Hillary Stringer	950
Tho Fisher	133
Francis Lailor, Northampton	100
Obedience John, Northampton	300
Henry Smith at ye Southerd	1000
Grattiance Michell, North	200
Matt Tyson, Southerd	300
Teagle Woltham, Maryld.	200
Peter Waltham, New Engld.	200
Jno. Waltham, Maryld.	200
	11707

Jno. Wise Sherifff

Jno. Fisher	133
Timo. Coe	4100
David Hogard	130
	6846

An Acct. of what land in Accomack County the Owners where of are not dwellers—

Tho. Preson of Northampton	200
Geo Corbin of Northampton	150
Joshua Fichott of Northampton	200
Alexdr. Mercy, Maryld.	200
Tho Dent	500
Mr. Wm. Kendalls Orphans of Northampton County	2850
Mr. Hançock Lee, Dividing Creeks	4050
Richd. Watters in Maryld.	1057

VIRGINIA QUIT RENT ROLLS, 1704

The Rent Roll of Northampton County for the Year of our Lord 1704

A	ACRES
Andrews Robt.	300
Andrews Andrew	100
Addison John	350
Abdell Tho.	125
Abdell Jno.	200
Abdell Wm.	125
Alligood John	300
Angell James	100
Alligood Henry	100

B	
Bullock Geo.	100
Berer Geo.	150
Brown Tho.	1862
Benthall Joseph Senr.	793
Benthll Joseph Junr.	150
Branson ffrancis	100
Bateson	200
Billot Jno.	400
Bell Geo.	400
Billott Wm.	100
Brewer Jno.	50
Blackson [Blackston] Jno.	100
Brooks Jeane	100
Beadwin Jno.	200
Benthall Danll.	258

	ACRES
Baker John	400
Brickhouse Geo.	2100

C

Cob Samll.	130
Coape Wm.	200
Custis Jno Coll.	3400
Collier Bartho	150
Carpenter Charles	240
Cox Jno	500
Church Samll	143
Cleg Jno Henr.	204
Cleg Henry	204
Carvy Richd.	100
Cowdry Josiah	167
Cormech Mich.	100
Clerk Jno	100
Corban [Corbin?] Geo	250
Clerk Geo	823
Caple Nath	100
Callinett Jno	100
Crew John	300
Costin ffrancis	275
Custis Majr. John	3250
Custis Hancock	50
Chick Tho	100

D

Dowing Jno	70
Dewy Geo	300
Dewy Jacob	100
Delby Margery	450
Dowty Rowland	150
Dunton John	170
Denton Tho	400
Downman John	100

	ACRES
Dullock John	100
Dunton Tho Senr.	120
Dunton Tho Junr.	120
Dunton Wm.	420
Dunton Benj.	220
Duparks Tho	90
Davis Jno	850
Dunton Joseph	120
Dixon Michaell	460

E

Eshon Jno	600
Evans John	200
Edmunds David	500
Evans Tho	300
Esdoll Geo	100
Eyres [Eyre] Tho	1133
Eyres Nich	325
Eyres Capt. John	774
Eyres Anne Wido.	733
Esdoll Edwd.	100

F

Fisher John	637½
Francisco Danl	150
Fisher Tho	637½
Foster Robt	150
Fabin Paul	60
Frost Tho	100
Frank Jno	500
Floyd Charles	378
Freshwater Geo	200
Frizell Geo	140
Freshwater Wm.	200
Fitchett Joshua	100
Floyd Berry & Matthew	535

G

	ACRES
Gogni David	150
Gill Robt	200
Gascoyne Robt	125
Gascoyne Wm	525
Greene Jno Senr.	2200
Giddens Tho	227
Grice Peter	200
Godwin Devorix	600
Goffogan Tho	100
Gullding Charles	200
Griffith Jerimiah	345
Griffith Benja.	200

H

Hill ffrancis	100
Henderson John	250
Haggaman Isaac	750
Harmanson Jno	1600
Harmanson Henry	1250
Hanby Charles	25
Hanby Richd.	75
Hanby Danll.	50
Hanby John	150
Harmonson Capt. Wm.	308
Harmonson Geo	1586
Harmonson Tho	400
Hawkins Jno Senr.	66
Hawkins Jno Junr.	66
Hawkins Gideon	66
Hunt Groton	485
Hunt John	440
Hunt Tho	290
Hall ffrancis Widdo.	340

I

Isaacs John Junr.	100

J	ACRES
Johnson John senr	250
Johnson John junr	100
Johnson Jacob	350
Joynes Majr.	150
James Joan Widdo.	250
Johnson Obedience Capt.	400
Johnson Tho Junr.	75
Johnson Tho Senr.	400
Jackson Jonah & John	625
Joynes Edmd.	200
Joynes Edwd.	200
Johnson Jeptha Senr	50
Jacob Phillip Senr.	350
Johnson Obedience & Peptha Senr.	250
Johnson Edmd.	400
Johnson Jeptha Junr.	200
Jacob Richd.	200
Jacob Abraham	50

K

Kendall Wm.	2410
Knight John	100

L

Lawrence John	120
Lailler Luke	100
Lucas Tho	100
Lewis Robt	100
Littleton, Susannah, Widdo.	4050
Luke John	400

M

Marshall Geo	250
Marshall Jno	250
Maddox Tho	1500
Michaell Yeardley	400

	ACRES
Matthews John	275
Major John	390
Map John	50
Moore Matthew	175
Mackmellion Tho	300
More Gilbert	225
Morraine John	119½
More Jno	545
More Eliner	175

N

Nicholson William	600
Nottingham Wm.	150
Nottingham Joseph	150
Nottingham Richd.	350
Nottingham Benj.	300
Nelson John	100

O

Only Clement	200
Odear John	100

P

Parramore Tho	400
Preson Tho	600
Powell :rances Widdo	1225
Palmer Saml.	1562
Pyke Henry	150
Powell John	636½
Pettett Tho	300
Pettett Justian	200
Pettett John	275
Powell Samll	200
Paine Daniell	150
Piggott Ralph	1368

R	ACRES
Read Thomas	150
Roscow Arthur	100
Ronan Wm.	150
Roberts Jno	200
Richards Lettis	150
Robins Jno. Majr.	1180
Robins Littleton	1000
Rabishaw Wm	55
Roberts Obedience	260
Robinson Benjamin	250

S	
Savage Tho	450
Shephard Jno	200
Smith Abrah	300
Smith Jno	200
Smith Joseph	250
Smith Samll.	150
Smith Tho	400
Seudy Antho	120
Sott Widdo [not clear]	750
Smith Richd Minor	300
Scot Geo	100
Smith Richd.	99
Scot Jno	100
Scot Henry	800
Scot David	300
Smith Peter	450
Sanders Richd.	100
Smaw John	800
Shepherd Tho	140
Sanders Eustice	100
Sanderson John	636
Savidge John	410
Stringer Hillary	1250
Savidge [Savage] Capt. Tho	1600

	ACRES
Savidge Elkington	750
Scot Wm. Senr.	153
Straton Benja.	745
Smith Geo	133
Stockley Jno Senr.	370
Shepheard Widdo.	830
Seamore John	200

T

Tilney John	350
Tryfort Barth.	147
Teague Simeon	100
Turner Richd.	50
Teague Tho	200
Tankard Wm.	450
Tanner Paul	148

W

Webb Henry	100
Wills Thorne	300
White John	400
Wilson Tho	250
Westerhouse Adryan Senr.	200
Walker John	300
Ward Tho	120
Walter John	400
Waterfield Wm.	200
Warren John	525
Warren Argoll	350
Widgeon Robt.	100
Wilkins Jno	150
Webb Edwd.	200
Wilcock John	200
Warren James	50
Waterson Wm.	855
Warren Robt.	190

	ACRES
Water [Waters] Lieut. Coll. Wm.	700
Webb Charles	133¼
Willett Wm.	2650
Waterson Richd.	150
Wilkins Argoll	150
Walter Elizab. Widdo.	100
Warren Joseph	50
Totall Acres	99671

INDEX

ADDENDA

CPSIA information can be obtained
at www.ICGtesting.com
Printed in the USA
BVHW032142100822
644332BV00013B/312

9 780806 310435